7/15/13
#60.00

As Certain as Death

As Certain as Death

A Fifty-State Survey of State and Local Tax Laws

Susan Pace Hamill

Professor of Law,
University of Alabama School of Law

CAROLINA ACADEMIC PRESS

Durham, North Carolina

Copyright © 2007
Susan Pace Hamill
All Rights Reserved

Library of Congress Cataloging-in-Publication Data
Hamill, Susan Pace.
  As certain as death : a fifty state survey of state and local tax
laws / by Susan Pace Hamill.
       p. cm.
  Includes bibliographical references and index.
  ISBN-13: 978-1-59460-325-9 (alk. paper)
  ISBN-10: 1-59460-325-1 (alk. paper)
  1. Taxation--Law and legislation--United States--States. 2.
Local taxation--Law and legislation--United States. 3. Revenue--
United States--States. 4. Education--United States--States--
Finance. I. Title.

  KF6750.Z95H36 2008
  343.7304'3--dc22   2007036580

Carolina Academic Press
700 Kent Street
Durham, NC 27701
Telephone (919) 489-7486
Fax (919) 493-5668
www.cap-press.com

Printed in the United States of America

With sincere appreciation I dedicate this book to my sixty-five research assistants who have toiled in the trenches over the past fourteen years, conducting the empirical research needed to fully discover the truth revealed by my scholarship.—SPH

Contents

Foreword and Methodology

This book surveys the state and local tax laws in each of the fifty states. For each state, the information in this survey includes a discussion of the distribution of the tax burden among taxpayers enjoying different levels of income and wealth, a picture of the state's tax and other revenue sources and K–12 public school funding, as well as other characteristics, including population, race, religious, family income and poverty statistics and information describing the state's geographic location and major industries. For each state, this book presents a "helicopter" view—a view much more detailed than the one-page summary of each state's tax and revenue picture in the impressive and indispensable February 2003 issue of GOVERNING MAGAZINE but far less detailed than what one finds in treatises and CCH material. No other source has the perspective of this "helicopter" view, which I created in order to take my scholarship morally evaluating tax policy to the next level. In addition to furthering my goals, the information in this survey is very valuable to the goals of a wide variety of others. How this book helps others is best understood in the context of the story inspiring the project, a thorough description of the material the book covers for each state, and a brief explanation of how I plan to use the survey for the next phase of my work.

This book got started with my article, *An Argument for Tax Reform Based on Judeo-Christian Ethics*, published in the fall 2002 issue of the ALABAMA LAW REVIEW (and later reprinted in paperback under the title THE LEAST OF THESE: FAIR TAXES AND THE MORAL DUTY OF CHRISTIANS). This article of over one hundred pages attacks Alabama's state and local tax policy as immoral under the principles of Judeo-Christian ethics and challenges Alabama's Christian population of over 90 percent, especially the political and religious leaders, to meet their moral obligations and to work toward reforming the system. Using extensive data compiled in thirty pages of empirical tables, the article documents how Alabama's income, sales and property tax structures oppress poor and lower-income Alabamians in the form of extremely regressive tax burdens and inadequate education funding in most areas. The article also identifies Alabama's property taxes, which are the lowest in the nation, as the principal feature driving both injustices and reveals the largest timber farms as the class of property proportionally contributing the least (less than 2 percent) of property tax revenues despite covering 71 percent of the land and accounting for a substantial part of the state's economy. This study of Alabama's state and local tax laws and K–12 funding descends far lower than a "helicopter" view, reaching "foot soldier" range. Although the detailed empirical picture, much of which other studies corroborate, greatly helps proponents of tax reform in Alabama, the real power of this work lies in the moral analysis. Rather than relying on arguments of economic development or liberal theories of justice, the biblical exegesis and hermeneutics developing the moral principles conclusively condemning Alabama's state and local tax laws on faith-based grounds use the finest conservative evangelical biblical commentaries highly regarded by the professors at the Beeson Divinity School of Samford University, a conservative evangelical seminary where I spent my sabbatical and wrote this article as my master's thesis.

The reaction to this article was far more intense than anyone had expected. Before the article was even published, a newspaper article in the MOBILE REGISTER in August 2002 set off a firestorm of interest across Alabama. Within days, hundreds of requests for a copy flooded into my office, prompting us to post the latest draft on the Internet. Several major newspapers in Alabama carried editorials expressing hope that maybe a biblically based moral command would spark the tax reform others had been trying to achieve for over twenty-five years. The issue of faith-inspired tax reform came up during the gubernatorial race in late 2002. Both candidates agreed that Alabama's tax laws were immoral. The winner, Governor Bob Riley, a Republican and a Southern Baptist deeply committed to his faith, later proposed a major tax reform plan that would have materially addressed Alabama's tax injustice. By the close of 2002, interest had started to seep outside Alabama's borders, at first slowly and largely confined to other southeastern states with abysmal tax structures and a deeply religious population, such as Tennessee. In 2003, a front-page article in the WALL STREET JOURNAL propelled the story into the national spotlight. In addition, the NEW YORK TIMES named my article on its list of best ideas. By then, I was receiving numerous inquiries how the moral principles of Judeo-Christian ethics would apply to states outside the Southeast and to federal tax policy, given that President Bush's first-term tax cuts, largely benefiting the wealthiest Americans, were being thrashed out in Congress. After being interviewed for a June 2003 article in the LONDON TIMES, *Alabama Puts Bush Tax Cuts to Biblical Test*, I realized that I needed to do substantially more work developing a theological framework that could be applied to any tax policy outside Alabama, including federal tax policy.

After first clarifying my ideas in a 2004 symposium sponsored by the University of St. Thomas Law School in Minneapolis and later published in their law journal, I published *An Evaluation of Federal Tax Policy Based on Judeo-Christian Ethics* in the VIRGINIA TAX REVIEW in 2006. In addition to documenting that nearly 80 percent of Americans claim to adhere to either Christianity or Judaism and establishing that using faith-based moral principles as a guide for tax policy does not raise concerns of separation of church and state, this article argues that "the common ground of conservative Evangelical, mainline Protestant, Catholic and Jewish standards of justice require that all persons, especially those with less wealth and power, be free from oppression and enjoy a reasonable opportunity to reach their potential." In addition to establishing that only adequate tax revenues can fund "a reasonable opportunity," which "covers a broad category of areas regarding basic human dignity, including access to minimum subsistence, decent health care and housing, as well as education and job training," the article argues that these faith-based standards of justice require the tax burden to be allocated in moderately progressive fashion. Finally, the article explains why President Bush's first-term tax cuts raise very troubling moral issues and reveals that the real values driving the Bush administration's tax policy are based on objectivist ethics, a form of atheism that worships the individual.

While I was working on my federal tax policy article, I was also doing more and more speaking engagements outside Alabama. Since 2002, I have spoken at least once in twenty-five states, and my work evaluating tax policy on faith-based grounds continues to generate widespread interest across many states. At its General Conference in 2004, the United Methodist Church adopted a resolution urging all United Methodist Conferences nationwide to study the state and local tax laws in their jurisdiction and spearhead tax reform efforts if those laws fail to meet the moral principles of Judeo-Christian ethics.

Especially when asked to speak outside the Southeast, I often felt very ill equipped to respond to the practical concerns of my audience. It always wanted to know how its state compared with other states under the moral principles of Judeo-Christian ethics. Even if my audience was quite sure that its state and local tax structure had significant moral issues, it still wanted to know what needed to be done to improve the situation, as well as some examples of "good states." I always traveled with an increasingly dog-eared copy of the one-page summary for each state in GOVERNING MAGAZINE and did the best I could. Over time, I developed a strong hunch that the state and local tax structures of most of the states either contained a level of injustice comparable to Alabama's or were headed in Alabama's direction.

In 2005, the Reverend Bruce Davidson, the director of Governmental Ministry in New Jersey of the Evangelical Lutheran Church in America convinced me to make a presentation to a group of Lutheran leaders. Because New Jersey's state and local tax structure looked passable from a distance, I did not believe they needed my work. During my visit, I discovered how wrong I was. After speaking to many people, I discovered that New Jersey's state and local tax laws indeed have serious moral issues, and the Lutherans assured me that the church would use my work to push for reform. I then realized I had, at best, a limited grasp of the justice issues hidden beneath the surface of the state and local tax structures in most of the states. This experience convinced me to start a research project that would provide a much more detailed picture of each state than the one-page summary in GOVERNING MAGAZINE. At the same time, I knew that I could not realistically accomplish for the other forty-nine states a thorough "foot soldier" study along the lines of my article morally condemning Alabama's state and local tax structure.

Over the summer of 2005, I made preliminary plans to launch a massive project creating what I would later describe as a "helicopter" view of the states—a view much more detailed than the one-page summary and much less detailed than the treatises—with a goal of including information that would allow me to evaluate the state under the moral requirements of reasonable opportunity and moderate progressivity. During the 2005–2006 academic year, I and nine research assistants—Trey Hill, the team leader; Nancy Busey; Joe Chambers; Mike Chaudhuri; Chris Kuffner; Jimmy Long; Justin Parsons; Ira Taylor; and Jeff Wells—prepared the first draft. Meeting once a week in the faculty lounge (the group was much too large to fit in my office), we brainstormed about categories, trying to decide what information to include and how to present it in categories that fostered comparison among the states. During that year, I became interested in studying the trends among the states and realized that we had built a foundation but not the house and that therefore the project needed another year. This first group of research assistants worked very hard building that foundation out of my preliminary plans. The finished book would not have been possible without their efforts.

During the summer of 2006, I studied the draft that came from the first research team's substantial efforts and planned to finish the project during the 2006–2007 academic year with a second team of research assistants. Dan Filler, a former colleague, reviewed the draft and suggested that I publish the fifty-state survey as a book. Dan convinced me that numerous others, many of whom would have goals differing substantially from my own, would find the information in the survey interesting and useful. I am very grateful to Dan for helping me see the market from a broader perspective than my own research interests and for being such a supportive colleague during his time at the University of Alabama. Paul Pruitt, the acquisitions librarian of the University library, connected me with Keith Sipe, the publisher of Carolina Academic Press.

In the fall of 2006, a second team of research assistants—Adam Brimer, Richard Calhoun, Joe Kerr, Angela Lenski, Bobby Riccio, Kristen Schwedler and Matt Taylor—began their work. In addition to our weekly team meetings (which by now had been moved into my more spacious new office, containing a roundtable, plenty of chairs, power strips for laptops, coffee for everyone, and a candy bowl), we discussed the revision of the draft as part of the materials I used in the course State and Local Tax, which I taught for the first time in fall 2006. Inspired by the discussions in the course, Aaron Shapiro joined the team in the spring of 2007. Throughout a number of brainstorming sessions, building on the work done during the previous year, we came up with substantially revised categories, some with several subcategories, of broad topics to be addressed for each state. Over the course of the year, the project grew in such intensity and magnitude that I began to refer to it as "Project Jupiter" to curious colleagues asking me about the steady stream of large numbers of students routinely gathering in my office.

Bobby Riccio served as team leader over the entire year and was assisted by Kristen Schwedler. Bobby, Kristen, and I worked with Creighton Miller, the best research librarian I have ever had the privilege of working with, and developed detailed instructions and guidelines for everyone to follow. Creighton's seemingly limitless knowledge of research materials and his keen sense of what I needed in order to accomplish my research goals continues to amaze me. In addition to drafting the instructions for the team to follow, Bobby Riccio reviewed one half of the states other team members had been assigned, covered two states by himself and served as a role model for the entire team in this process. Kristen Schwedler reviewed the other half of the states other team members had been assigned and covered three states herself. Although Bobby Riccio and Kristen Schwedler served as the primary leaders of the team, other team members also assumed leadership roles as we pushed the book toward completion. Adam Brimer did the final style review and editing; Matt Taylor came up with the idea and instructions for the lottery section and led efforts—with significant help from Richard Calhoun (who had accepted, without complaining, a Saturday morning overnight package the week before exams)—to perform a final review of the property tax sections; Joe Kerr coordinated the team's efforts and filled gaps in the book by compiling a comprehensive list of other sources for each state; finally, Sunday Vanderver, who will serve on the 2007–2008 research assistant team, volunteered to check for correctness the Bluebook formatting of the approximately 6,000 footnotes in this manuscript of over 500 pages. This book could not have been accomplished without the hard work and creative efforts of this research team. I continue to be shocked with awe and wonder at the high level at which my students are able to perform when they are given the chance and encouragement to do so.

In order to facilitate the moral evaluation of each state individually as well as foster the discovery and comparison of the trends across the fifty states, the research team fit carefully selected information into five categories, most of which are further divided into sections. The first category, GENERAL INFORMATION, has two sections. The section, *Basic Profile — Geography, Population and Industry*, provides the basic facts for each state, including geographical location, size (as measured in both square miles and population), and major industries. This section also details the racial composition and religious affiliations of each state's population. In order to paint this big picture of the state's characteristics, the research team consulted a number of sources, including the U.S. Census Bureau and the U.S. Department of Agriculture, as well as the Web site and statistics maintained or produced by the state itself. The team selected the American Religious Identification Survey as the best source for the religious affiliations of each state's population. In 2001, the Graduate Center of the City University of New York conducted this survey as a follow up to their original one in 1990. It is the most extensive survey of religious identification in the last fifty years.

The second section, *Family Income and Poverty Indicators*, addresses the state's per capita gross product and family income statistics as well poverty indicators from a number of perspectives, including that of race. The research team used statistics and reports generated by federal agencies, including the U.S. Census Bureau, the U.S. Department of Commerce, and the U.S. Department of Education, as well as compilations produced by Morgan Quitno Press in STATE RANKINGS 2006. In order to determine whether (and if so, to what degree) the state's African American population is disproportionately affected by poverty, the team used U.S. census data to compare the percentage of the population made up of African Americans with the percentage of those in poverty made up of African Americans.

In the second category, PUBLIC ELEMENTARY-SECONDARY SCHOOL SYSTEM, three sections address each state's public education. The first section, *Overall Spending and Performance*, lays out (1) the amount of money each state spent on its K–12 students during the 2003–2004 academic year; (2) the origin of that money and the level of academic proficiency the students achieved at the fourth and eighth grade levels (the only grade levels where the reports provided performance statistics); and (3) the average teacher salary and the pupil/teacher ratio. The research team used the annual Public Education Finances Report of the U.S. Census Bureau as well as information periodically compiled by the National Center for Education Statistics, a division of the U.S. Department of Education. Although this section does not attempt to evaluate the adequacy of each state's K–12 education funding (because the research team placed the funding and performance statistics side by side, in a manner that fosters comparison among the states), a general and rudimentary sense of adequacy can be determined — at least at the extremes.

The second section, *Equity Issues*, identifies funding gaps between high-poverty school districts and other school districts and compares the performance of students receiving free or reduced-price lunches (a recognized poverty indicator) with the performance of other students. For a number of reasons, the research team used an extensive study by the Education Trust, an independent nonprofit organization dedicated to closing the achievement gap between poor and more affluent students. First, for purposes of comparison, this study identifies the amount of money allocated to the school districts with the highest and lowest poverty levels as well as to the school districts with the highest and lowest numbers of minorities rather than simply determining the funding shortfall or surplus of a particular school district as compared with the state's funding median. Second, this study adjusts for the differences in purchasing power across school districts on the basis of the formula used by the National Center for Education Statistics. Third, on the basis of the formula used by the American Institutes of Research, this study takes into consideration the additional funds needed for special education programs in school districts with disproportionate numbers of students with disabilities. Finally, this study recognizes that it costs 40 percent more to educate a child in poverty (for example, if a state provides general funding at $10,000 per pupil, equity demands $14,000 per low-income pupil), and in so recognizing, the study uses a conservative 40 percent adjustment, which reflects the federal Title I formula to determine whether state funding policies are fair to low-income students, rather than a higher figure assumed by some other studies. Using the National Access Network Web site and Internet and legal databases such as Westlaw and LexisNexis, the research team also determined whether the state was (or currently is) involved in any litigation challenging public education funding.

The third section, *Availability of Publicly Funded Prekindergarten Programs*, determines whether the state offers publicly funded prekindergarten programs and the percentage of the state's three- and four-year-old population actually receiving publicly funded prekindergarten education, including those from federal Head Start programs. The research team used a study by the National Association Institute for Early Education Research, which was established at the Rutgers University Graduate School of Education through grants from a number of trusts and foundations.

The third category, WHERE DOES THE STATE GET ITS REVENUE, first provides a big picture of revenue sources from state and local taxes, federal funding, and all other sources and then discusses *Tax Revenue*, *Federal Funding*, and *Lottery Revenues* in more detail in three separate sections. For the fiscal year ending in 2004, the *Tax Revenue* section provides the total amount collected, the amount per capita collected, the rank of amounts collected as compared with those of other states and indicates the percentage of tax revenue coming from individual income taxes, property taxes, general and selective sales taxes, and corporate income and other taxes. In order to gauge the degree to which particular states rely more heavily on federal funding when compared with that of other states, the *Federal Funding* section provides the percentage of the state's total revenue that comes from federal funding and indicates the dollar amount of federal funding received as compared with the dollar amount of federal taxes paid. The section also ranks the state as compared with other states. Because of the increasing prevalence of state lotteries over the past twenty years and claims made that this revenue source can supplement tax revenues, especially for funding of education, the *Lottery Revenues* section provides basic information about the state's lottery, including its stated purpose, how its revenues are allocated, and recent financial information indicating how much of the state's lottery revenues have actually been transferred to the state coffers. This section does not attempt to determine whether the state's lottery provides effective and meaningful alternative revenue sources. For the initial overview, as well as the more detailed statistics of the state's tax revenue and federal funding, the research team used statistics from the U.S. Census Bureau (although some of these statistics were subsequently compiled and translated by The Tax Foundation). The team consulted Web sites and reports generated by the particular state to present basic information about the state's lottery.

The fourth category (by far, the largest and most complex), LEGAL STRUCTURES OF MAJOR TAX SOURCES, has four sections, covering the *Income Tax*, the *Property Tax*, *General and Selective Sales*, and *Corporate Income and Other*. In order to define the tax base, the applicable rates, major exemptions, and other important details for all these sections, the research team used the relevant state statutory provisions (which are up-to-date as of this book's publication date); explanations and summaries by Commerce Clearing House (CCH), which were very helpful in sorting through the voluminous statutory material; U.S. Census Bureau data, some which was compiled by Morgan Quitno Press in STATE RANKINGS 2006: and individual state reports and Web sites.

The first section, the *Income Tax*, shows that most states use federal adjusted gross or taxable income as a starting point and make numerous adjustments to that amount before arriving at taxable income for state purposes. *See also* JEROME R. HELLERSTEIN & WALTER HELLERSTEIN, STATE AND LOCAL TAXATION: CASES AND MATERIALS 929 (8th ed. 2005) (noting "the overwhelming majority of states with broad-based income taxes employ federal adjusted gross income or federal taxable income as the computational starting point for determining state taxable income."). The research team concluded that cataloging all of these adjustments, or even just a few of them, was beyond the scope of this text. In order to obtain the most realistic estimate of the amount of income exempt from the income tax for a family of four (husband and wife and two dependent children), the team used a report by the Center on Budget and Policy Priorities entitled "Impact of State Income Taxes on Low-Income Families in 2006," which in addition to adding up the standard deduction and statutory exemptions (or their equivalents), accounts for other tax benefits, such as earned income credits and other general tax credits. This section also outlines the number of tax brackets and the corresponding tax rates based on the state's tax laws in effect for 2006. Finally, using only the standard deduction and four personal exemptions (or their equivalent), this section estimates at what point the income tax rate flattens out by estimating the level of income where the highest income tax rate kicks in.

The second section, the *Property Tax*, fleshes out the contours of each state's property tax regime in reasonable detail, but it does not attempt to identify all of the numerous intricacies and nuances contained in those states with very complicated property tax structures. The overview first indicates whether the state taxes property at both the state and local levels or whether property taxes are only imposed locally. Then, for the fiscal year 2003–2004, it discloses how much money the state's property taxes raised at each level and the state's rank when compared with other states in property tax revenues collected per capita. Using the definition of the real property tax base for each state, this section sets out the state's classifications of property for purposes of determining the percentage of the property's value included in the base and also discloses the valuation methods the state uses to appraise property, how often appraisal is required, and whether the particular state values certain classifications of property differently, especially focusing on whether agricultural and timber properties enjoy some form of discounted valuation through current use formulas. For states with complicated property tax structures, this section does not attempt to detail every type of special property within a group that enjoys an exception from the general classification or valuation rules.

The *Property Tax* section identifies the tax rate on real property, imposed at the state level, provides the range of millage rates imposed locally within the state, and indicates whether state statutory or constitutional provisions restrict the rates or the dollar amount of property tax that can be collected. This range of millage rates is accurate as of this book's publication date, but in many cases, it will change in the future. This section also indicates whether each state taxes personal or intangible property and if so, it provides a big picture of the types of properties taxed as well as the rates. Most states that impose property taxes on personal or intangible property contain numerous exceptions and special rules that substantially narrow the scope of the tax. This section does not attempt to detail these numerous exceptions and special rules. Finally, this section documents the most important exemptions from property taxes in each state, but it does not attempt to detail every exemption or class of property or taxpayers entitled to an exemption on the basis of a membership in a special class. In addition to a state's statutes, U.S. census data, and other general sources, the research team consulted other sources specifically addressing property taxes, including the CCH Multistate Property Tax Guide and the ABA Property Tax Deskbook.

The third section, *General and Selective Sales*, starts with the state's general sales tax structure, first indicating whether the state falls in the majority group that taxes only the sale of tangible personal property or whether the state also taxes the sale of services or intangible property. This section then shows the degree to which the state relies on sales tax revenues by calculating the percentage of the state's total tax revenues coming from sales taxes. In addition to documenting the sales tax rate imposed by each state and whether localities within the state have the power to impose sales taxes (and any limits placed on this power), this section indicates the highest and lowest combined state and local sales tax rate found within each state. This section also identifies the major exemptions—especially whether the state exempts food purchased at the grocery store and medicine—but it does not attempt to cover every special exemption from general sales taxes. This section also does not attempt to distinguish how the individual states resolve the vast and complex legal issues that arise when administering the general sales taxes—for example, drawing lines establishing the scope of the sale for resale and business-purchases exemptions as well as defining whether a particular sale involves taxable tangible personal property or exempt services or intangible property. *See* HELLERSTEIN, *supra* at 696–702 (discussing interpretations by different states).

In addition to the general sources used for all four sections of this category, the research team consulted the CCH Multistate Sales Tax Guide. For each state's selective sales taxes designated by the U.S. Census Bureau (i.e., those for motor fuel, alcoholic beverages, tobacco products, and public utilities), this section calculates the percentage each contributes to the state's total tax revenues and identifies how much each selective sales tax provides per capita as well as the state's per capita ranking when compared with that of other states.

The fourth section, *Corporate Income and Other*, first calculates the percentage of the state's total tax revenues coming from corporate and other taxes and then provides a basic overview of the base and tax rates of the corporate income tax. This section also indicates whether or not subchapter S corporations and unincorporated business organizations such as limited liability companies and limited liability partnerships are subject to the state's corporate income tax. Finally, this section briefly discusses "other taxes" — such as gift and estate taxes, corporate stock or franchise taxes, and any other significant taxes imposed by the state — but not covered elsewhere.

The fifth and final category, BURDEN ANALYSIS, first explores the overall distribution of the tax burden across different income groups in each state and then examines separately each state's distributional burden of the income, property, and sales and excise taxes. The research team relied on the extensive study sponsored by the Institute on Taxation & Economic Policy (ITEP) entitled WHO PAYS? A DISTRIBUTIONAL ANALYSIS OF THE TAX SYSTEMS IN ALL 50 STATES. The team chose this source because it contains a large sampling and a wide range of sources backing up its information and therefore appears to be the most reliable and complete state-by-state analysis of individual tax burdens.

The end of the book contains a list of other sources recently published. The sources primarily involve the work of academics and tax professionals focusing on state and local tax law and policy. In addition to several prominent sources addressing state and local taxes from a general perspective, this list features in-depth, state-specific tax studies and also provides an overview of those who are researching and reporting on tax issues in each state. The research team used the University of Alabama Libraries Database and OCLC WorldCat (a worldwide card catalog) for books and pamphlets, LexisNexis and Westlaw for tax and law review journal articles, and Google for Internet-based tax publications. The team identified the sources by searching for title, subject, and author fields that contained such keywords as the state's name and various permutations of the following terms: "tax," "excise," "income," "sales," "property," "corporate," "ad valorem," "school funding," and "equity."

During the 2007–2008 academic year, I will be leading another team of research assistants in a in-depth study and analysis of the information contained in this book. Focusing on each state, we will estimate how far away it is from complying with the Judeo-Christian moral principles requiring both adequate revenues that meet the reasonable opportunity threshold and a moderately progressive allocation of the tax burden. We will also diagnose the broad areas of each state's tax policy that need the most reform. In addition, we will look closely for trends across the states, asking which states are similar in their tax policies and why. We will look for patterns based on common characteristics such as similar regions, racial diversity, the prevalence of poverty among the population, and primarily urban versus rural culture. We hope to discover unexpected patterns that shed light on how the country as a whole can move toward having truly adequate and fair tax policy.

I sincerely hope that other scholars and organizations interested in justice issues—especially faith-based organizations—will use this information to help achieve fair state and local tax policy in their state. Well-documented information revealing the state and local tax picture in order to identify the causes of the injustice, combined with moral analysis demanding reform, is powerful indeed. In May 2003, Alabama's Governor Bob Riley put forth an enormous tax reform proposal that would have materially improved the fairness and adequacy of its state and local tax structure. Although his proposal was defeated at the polls, largely because special interests fought the proposal with lies and distortions that scared the voters who would have benefited the most into voting against the plan, Governor Riley has pushed forward, nipping at the margins of Alabama's injustice by raising the threshold for the income tax for a family of four from the disgusting level of $4,600 to $12,500—an improvement that still has a long way to go. Over coffee one afternoon, when I was complaining of Alabama's glacially slow progress, Dan Filler reminded me that because of this very modest improvement in the income tax structure, perhaps thousands of low-income families would have some extra money which, although it would seem like pocket change to us, would provide them with meat on the table more often. I will never stop fighting for more just tax policy in my state, and I hope that the information contained in this book and in my forthcoming work morally evaluating the individual states and the trends among them will help others in states all over America to go and do likewise.

Although addressing justice issues is perhaps the most compelling use of this book, the information in this fifty-state survey will be of great interest to a variety of individuals and organizations with other goals and agendas. Professors teaching courses such as State and Local Tax as well as courses focusing on business and multijurisdictional issues, especially at an advanced level, will want to consider using this book in addition to a standard textbook. Any person or organization interested in public education from any perspective will find the easy comparison of the states in the public school funding category very useful. Law firms, accounting firms, and real estate and other investment firms—in fact, any businesses that cross state lines—will find the comparisons across the states in this survey invaluable. Internationally based businesses and all other internationally based organizations interested in the individual American states will appreciate the "helicopter" view of this book. Scholars interested in population, racial, religious, poverty, and geographical trends for any reason will find the information in this survey helpful.

In addition to my research assistants, Creighton Miller, Dan Filler, Paul Pruitt, and Bruce Davidson, there are a number of others I need to thank. First, I gratefully acknowledge the financial support of the University of Alabama Law School Foundation, the Edward Brett Fund and the William H. Sadler Fund. As I was working on the book, I benefited from the ideas contributed by my tax colleagues Norman Stein and Jim Bryce (who also kindly agreed to share the State and Local Tax course with me in order to further this book); from Al Brophy, my colleague who serves as Director of Faculty Scholarship; and from Bruce Ely, Alabama's most prominent expert in state and local tax. Walter Hellerstein and John Swain were very helpful as I prepared to teach State and Local Tax for the first time last fall. My secretary Donna Warnack, our reference librarian Penny Gibson, and Terry Davis and his staff of in-house computer experts are unsung heroes who helped me extensively over the course of researching and writing this book. Finally, given my reference to this book as "Project Jupiter," it is fitting to use astronaut John Glenn's words (as quoted in Tom Wolfe's *The Right Stuff*)—"I don't think any of us could really go on with something like this … if we didn't have pretty good backing at home"—to thank the most important people who make everything I do possible: my loving husband Brad, my children William and Nancy Lee, my father and stepmother, my brother and sister and in-laws, and especially Aunt Bernardis, probably the only person on the planet who has read everything I have written, including footnotes.

Susan Pace Hamill
University of Alabama School of Law
Tuscaloosa, Alabama
September, 2007

As Certain as Death

Alabama

General Information

Basic Profile – Geography, Population, and Industry

Admitted to the Union in 1819, Alabama is known as the "Heart of Dixie."[1] It is located in the southern United States and is part of the central time zone. It is bordered by Georgia on the east; Florida and the Gulf of Mexico on the south; Mississippi on the west; and Tennessee on the north. Montgomery is the state's capital.

Alabama ranks 30th in total area (52,419 square miles)[2] and 23rd in population (approximately 4.5 million residents).[3] Its population is approximately 71.4% white and 26.4% black.[4] The state is 13% Catholic; 71% Protestant; and 1% Jewish; 15% claim a religion outside the Judeo-Christian tradition or none at all.[5] Approximately 71% of Alabama's population reside in urban areas.[6] Major industries are timber and agriculture, and its primary exports are poultry, cotton, and peanuts.[7]

Family Income and Poverty Indicators

In 2004, Alabama's per capita gross product was $30,901, which ranked among the ten lowest states in the country and below the national average of $39,725.[8] During this

---

1. State Rankings 2006, vi, 1 (Kathleen O'Leary Morgan & Scott Morgan eds., Morgan Quitno Press 2006).

2. *Id.* at 225.

3. *Id.* at 429.

4. Alabama Quick Facts from the U.S. Census Bureau, http://quickfacts.census.gov/qfd/states/01000.html (last visited Feb. 21, 2007). The remaining population is made up of 0.8% Asian persons; 0.5% American Indian and/or Alaska Native persons; and 0.9% persons reporting two or more races. *Id.* Additionally, 2.3% of Alabama's total population identify themselves as persons of Hispanic or Latino origin. *Id.* (noting that because Hispanics may be of any race, they are included within the other applicable race categories).

5. Barry A. Kosmin, Egon Mayer & Ariela Keysar, American Religious Identification Survey 2001, at 40, *available at* http://www.gc.cuny.edu/faculty/research_studies/aris.pdf.

6. USDA Economic Research Service, Alabama Fact Sheet, http://www.ers.usda.gov/StateFacts/AL.htm (last visited January 29, 2007).

7. *Id.*

8. State Rankings 2006, *supra* note 1, at 89.

same period, although the median household income in Alabama was $38,111,[9] 15.5% of its population lived in poverty, which was above the national average of 12.4% and ranked among the top ten states nationally.[10] More specifically, poverty affected 23.2% of Alabama's children,[11] 11.9% of its senior citizens,[12] and 13.1% of its families.[13] Of its female-headed households with children, 46.2% lived in poverty,[14] and 50.5% of the state's public elementary and secondary school students were eligible for free or reduced-price meals.[15] Of those living in poverty, approximately 50% were black, which represented 30% of Alabama's black population and 8% of its total population.[16] In an attempt to combat this poverty, Alabama spent approximately $4.1 billion on public welfare programs in 2002,[17] which made up 16.9% of its total government expenditures.[18]

Alabama's Public Elementary-Secondary School System

Overall Spending and Performance

For the 2003–2004 school year, Alabama spent $6,553 per pupil in its public elementary-secondary school system, which was substantially below the national average of $8,182.[19] Of this amount, 11.7% was provided by the federal government, 55.5% was provided by the state government, and 32.8% was provided by the local governments,[20] with property taxes making up 13.8% of the total funding.[21] Out of these funds, Alabama paid its elementary and secondary school teachers an estimated average annual salary of $38,863 during the 2004–2005 school year,[22] and in 2003, it pro-

---

9. *Id.* at 96.

10. *Id.* at 495.

11. *Id.* at 497.

12. *Id.* at 496.

13. *Id.* at 498.

14. *Id.* at 499.

15. *Id.* at 532.

16. *See* Fact Sheet, American FactFinder, http://factfinder.census.gov/home/saff/ main.html ?_lang=en (select "Alabama" under "Get a Fact Sheet for your community") (last visited Feb. 21, 2007). Note that these numbers are based on the 2000 census because more recent numbers were not available.

17. *Id.* at 500.

18. *Id.* at 502.

19. Governments Division, U.S. Census Bureau, Public Education Finances 2004, at 8 tbl.8 (2006), *available at* http://www2.census.gov/govs/school/04f33pub.pdf.

20. *See id.* at 5 tbl.5.

21. *See id.* at 4 tbl.4.

22. Thomas D. Snyder et al., National Center for Education Statistics, Digest of Education Statistics 2005, at 116 tbl.77 (2006), *available at* http://nces.ed.gov/pubsearch/pubsinfo.asp?pubid=2006030.

vided a student/teacher ratio of 12.6, which was better than the national average of 15.9.[23]

In academic performance, Alabama's fourth and eighth grade students scored lower than the national average in mathematics,[24] reading,[25] science,[26] and writing.[27]

Equity Issues

In 2004, revenues spent per student in Alabama's highest poverty districts were determined to be $323 less than the revenues spent in its lowest poverty districts.[28] When adjustments were made for the additional costs of educating students growing up in poverty, however, the funding gap grew to $656.[29] Similarly, Alabama spent $241 less per student in its highest minority districts, and this amount grew to $437 when adjustments for low-income students were made.[30]

Fourth graders eligible for free or reduced-price school lunches had test scores that were 10% lower in mathematics,[31] 12% lower in reading,[32] and 14% lower in writing[33] than those of students who were not eligible. The results were similar for eighth graders eligible for free or reduced-price lunches; their test scores were 10% lower in mathematics,[34] 10% lower in reading,[35] and 15% lower in writing[36] than those of students who were not eligible.

---

23. *Id.* at 98 tbl.65.

24. NATIONAL CENTER FOR EDUCATION STATISTICS, U.S. DEPARTMENT OF EDUCATION, THE NATION'S REPORT CARD: MATHEMATICS 2005, at 14 fig.11, 16 fig.12 (2005), *available at* http://nces.ed.gov/nationsreportcard/pdf/main2005/2006453.pdf [hereinafter MATHEMATICS 2005].

25. NATIONAL CENTER FOR EDUCATION STATISTICS, U.S. DEPARTMENT OF EDUCATION, THE NATION'S REPORT CARD: READING 2005, at 14 fig.11, 16 fig.12 (2005), *available at* http://nces.ed.gov/nationsreportcard/pdf/main2005/2006451.pdf [hereinafter READING 2005].

26. NATIONAL CENTER FOR EDUCATION STATISTICS, U.S. DEPARTMENT OF EDUCATION, THE NATION'S REPORT CARD: SCIENCE 2005, at 16 fig.12, 28 fig.22 (2006), *available at* http://nces.ed.gov/nationsreportcard//pdf/main2005/2006466.pdf [hereinafter SCIENCE 2005].

27. HILARY R. PERSKY ET AL., NATIONAL CENTER FOR EDUCATION STATISTICS, U.S. DEPARTMENT OF EDUCATION, THE NATION'S REPORT CARD: WRITING 2002, at 23 tbl.2.2, 24 tbl.2.3 (2003), *available at* http://nces.ed.gov/nationsreportcard/pdf/main2002/2003529.pdf [hereinafter WRITING 2002].

28. THE EDUCATION TRUST, FUNDING GAPS 2006, at 7 tbl.3 (2006), *available at* http://www2.edtrust.org/NR/rdonlyres/CDEF9403-5A75-437E-93FF-EBF1174181FB/0/Funding Gap2006.pdf.

29. *Id.*

30. *Id.* at 7 tbl.4.

31. MATHEMATICS 2005, *supra* note 24, at 20 tbl.5.

32. READING 2005, *supra* note 25, at 20 tbl.5.

33. WRITING 2002, *supra* note 27, at 75 tbl.3.24.

34. MATHEMATICS 2005, *supra* note 24, at 21 tbl.6.

35. READING 2005, *supra* note 25, at 21 tbl.6.

36. WRITING 2002, *supra* note 27, at 76 tbl.3.25.

Education finance has been the subject of ongoing litigation in Alabama since the mid-1990s. In 1995, the Alabama Coalition for Equality (ACE) filed a lawsuit on behalf of parents, students, and school systems against the state of Alabama. In the action, ACE challenged the constitutionality of the public school system and alleged that the state had failed to provide equitable and adequate educational opportunities to all schoolchildren regardless of the wealth of the communities in which the schoolchildren reside, as required by the state constitution. As a result, various state officers were ordered to implement a fairer education system that provided equal opportunities to all students.[37] More recently, Alabama courts have refused to rule on education finance issues. In 2002, the Alabama Supreme Court dismissed a case challenging the school funding system on grounds that the state constitution forbade the courts from making decisions that are traditionally made by the legislature.[38]

Availability of Publicly Funded Prekindergarten Programs

The Alabama Prekindergarten Program serves students four years of age and is operated by educational institutions across the state, including public and private schools, head start centers, universities, and private child care institutions.[39] Although Alabama is making efforts to expand the Prekindergarten Program, its current enrollment stands at just 1,026,[40] which represents only 1% of Alabama's 118,187 three- and four-year-old children.[41] The federally funded Head Start program enrolls an additional 14,894 children,[42] which represents 13% of Alabama's three- and four-year-old children.[43]

Where Does Alabama Get Its Revenue?

At the end of fiscal year 2004, Alabama had total revenues of approximately $32 billion. Of these revenues, 33% were raised from state and local taxes and 21% were received from the federal government. The remaining 46% were derived from utilities, liquor stores, insurance trusts, and other sources.[44]

---

37. Pinto v. Ala. Coalition for Equality, 662 So. 2d 894 (Ala. 1995).

38. *Ex Parte James,* 836 So. 2d 813 (Ala. 2002).

39. W. STEVEN BARNETT ET AL., NATIONAL INSTITUTE FOR EARLY EDUCATION RESEARCH, THE STATE OF PRESCHOOL 2006, at 40 (2006), *available at* http://nieer.org/yearbook/pdf/yearbook.pdf.

40. *Id.* at 41.

41. *See id.* at 232.

42. *Id.* at 41.

43. *See id.* at 232.

44. U.S. Census Bureau, State and Local Government Finances - 2003–04, http://www.census.gov/govs/www/estimate04.html (last visited January 31, 2007) [hereinafter Government Finances].

Tax Revenue

During fiscal year 2004, Alabama collected $10.5 billion in state and local tax revenue.[45] As a result, Alabama residents paid approximately $2,328 per capita in state taxes, an amount which ranked 50th nationally.[46] The different types of tax sources were approximately apportioned as follows:

Individual income taxes	22.3%
Property taxes	15.8%
General and selective sales taxes	49.5%
Corporate income and other taxes	12.4%
	100.0%[47]

Federal Funding

During fiscal year 2004, 21% of Alabama's total revenues came from the federal government.[48] For every dollar of federal taxes paid, Alabama received $1.71 in federal funding, a amount which ranked 6th nationally and was far above the average of $1.17.[49]

Lottery Revenue

Alabama does not operate a state lottery.

Legal Structures of Major Tax Sources

Income

Alabama employs a broad-based income tax that uses adjusted gross income for federal income tax purposes as a starting point for determining the state's taxable income.[50] However, numerous adjustments may be available to various individuals in calculating this amount.[51] The Alabama constitution only empowers the legislature to raise revenue from income taxes for state purposes, thereby indirectly forbidding local gov-

---

45. *Id.*
46. *Id.*
47. *Id.*
48. *Id.*
49. *See* The Tax Foundation, Federal Spending Received Per Dollar of Taxes Paid by State, 2004, http://www.taxfoundation.org/files/ftsbs-20060316.pdf (last visited February 22, 2007).
50. ALA. CODE § 40-18-1.1(b)
51. *Id.* § 40-18-14.2

ernments from imposing income taxes to raise revenues for local purposes.[52] During fiscal year 2004, Alabama collected individual income tax of $496 per capita, an amount ranking 37th nationally.[53]

For many years, Alabama had the lowest threshold of income exempt from tax in the country, exempting only the first $4,600 of income for a typical family of four (i.e., married taxpayers who file jointly and have two dependent children),[54] an amount disgracefully below the national poverty line of $20,615.[55] Alabama's income tax structure contains three tax brackets and imposes a minimum rate of 2% and a maximum marginal rate of 5%.[56] When statutory exemptions and the standard deduction are taken into account, the maximum marginal rate applies to every dollar of income exceeding $13,300.[57] Starting in 2007, Alabama raised its standard deduc-

---

52. ALA. CONST. OF 1901, art XXII, amend. 25.

53. STATE RANKINGS 2006, *supra* note 1, at 321 citing U.S. Bureau of the Census, Governments Division "2004 State Government Tax Collections," *available at* http://www.census.gov/govs/www/statetax04.html.

54. JASON A. LEVITIS, CENTER ON BUDGET AND POLICY PRIORITIES, THE IMPACT OF STATE INCOME TAXES ON LOW-INCOME FAMILIES IN 2006, at 12 (2007). In 2006, Alabama taxpayers who were married and filing jointly could claim a standard deduction of $4,000 or 20% of the total income, whichever was less. ALA. CODE § 40-18-15(b)(1). Married taxpayers filing jointly were also entitled to a personal exemption of $3,000 (both spouses combined) and dependent exemptions of $300 each. ALA. CODE § 40-18-19(a)(9). Note, however, that the threshold calculation of $4,600 is greater than the sum of these deductions and exemptions because it includes additional tax benefits available to low-income families such as the earned-income tax credit. *See* LEVITIS *supra*. $4,600 is actually rounded up from $4,562.50. That figure is derived from the following calculations. Prior to 2007, married taxpayers who filed jointly and had two dependents were allowed the following exemptions:

Personal Exemption: $3,000

Dependent Exemptions: 2 × $300 = $600

Standard Deduction: 20% of income

Taxable income is exactly zero at $4,500 AGI. Therefore, any AGI greater than $4,500 yields taxable income. At a 2% tax rate, however, the tax liability on that income is under $1 until taxable income reaches $50, which corresponds to an AGI of $4,562.50.

If X is AGI,

$X - 3000 - 600 - .2(X) = 50$

$X = \$4,562.50$

55. U.S. Census Bureau, Preliminary Estimates of Weighted Average Poverty Thresholds for 2005, http://www.census.gov/hhes/www/poverty/threshld/05prelim.html (last visited Oct. 16, 2006).

56. ALA. CODE § 40-18-5. Alabama's middle tax bracket is 4%. *Id.* The Alabama constitution caps the maximum rate at 5%. ALA. CONST. of 1901, amend. 25 (1932). In order to adjust the maximum rate, the state legislature must first introduce a bill that passes both the House and Senate by a three-fifths vote; then, if the bill is enacted into law, it must be ratified by the majority of voters participating in a statewide election. ALA. CONST. of 1901, art. XVIII, §§ 284 and 285.

57. The standard deduction and exemptions of $4,000 and $3,300, respectively, plus the threshold for taxable income for the highest tax bracket of $6,000 equals $13,300. *Id.*

tion[58] and dependent exemption amounts.[59] Taking into account the increased standard deduction and exemptions, a typical family of four is not required to pay tax until their income exceeds $12,600, an amount still well below the national poverty line of $20,615.[60] Moreover, Governor Bob Riley continues his effort to further raise the tax exempt amount to $15,600, supporting a bill[61] which would again raise exemptions to meet this increased threshold.[62]

Property

Overview

Alabama has a typical property tax scheme that taxes the value of real property, personal property, and mixed property at both the state and local levels.[63] During fiscal year 2004, the revenue Alabama collected attributable to property taxes totaled approximately $221 million at the state level and $1.4 billion at the local

---

58. For tax years beginning after 2006, the standard deduction for married taxpayers filing jointly with an AGI of $20,000 or less is $7,500. The deduction is reduced by $175 for each $500 of AGI in excess of $20,000, but it is not less than $4,000. For married taxpayers filing separately with an AGI of $10,000 or less, the standard deduction is $3,750, but it is reduced by $88 for each $250 of AGI in excess of $10,000; however, it is not less than $2,000. ALA. CODE § 40-18-15(b)(2). The increase in the standard deduction and exemption amounts does not require a constitutional amendment because although the Alabama constitution sets forth a minimum level of required exemptions, thereby requiring an amendment to lower exemptions, it does not explicitly address increasing exemptions; therefore, no amendment is required. ALA. CONST. of 1901, amend. 25 (1932).

59. For tax years beginning after 2006, the exemption for each dependent allowed to taxpayers with adjusted gross income equal to or less than $20,000 is $1,000. For taxpayers with adjusted gross income in excess of $20,000 and equal to or less than $100,000, the exemption amount is $500 for each dependent. ALA. CODE § 40-18-19(a)(9).

60. JASON A. LEVITIS, CENTER ON BUDGET AND POLICY PRIORITIES, THE IMPACT OF STATE INCOME TAXES ON LOW-INCOME FAMILIES IN 2006: ALABAMA (2007), *available at* http://www.cbpp.org/states/3-27-07sfp-fact-al.pdf.

The $12,600 figure is derived from the following calculation. For tax years beginning after 2006, married taxpayers who file jointly and have two dependents are allowed the following exemptions:

Personal Exemption: $3,000

Dependent Exemption: 2 × $1,000 = $2,000

Standard Deduction: $7,500

Total: $12,500

An AGI of $12,500 yields zero taxable income, and any amount higher technically results in a positive taxable income. However, at a 2% tax rate, the tax remains under $1 until taxable income reaches $50. This corresponds to an AGI of $12,550, which rounds up to $12,600.

61. H.B. 277, 2007 Leg., Reg. Sess. (Al. 2007).

62. Kim Chandler, *Riley Urges Tax Cut, Boost for Education*, BIRMINGHAM NEWS, March 7, 2007, at A1.

63. ALA. CODE § 40-11-1.

level.[64] As a result, Alabama residents paid approximately $367 per capita in state and local property taxes, an amount ranking 50th nationally.[65]

Defining the Real Property Tax Base

Alabama classifies property into four classes based on its use. Class I property consists of property used in the business of a utility. Class III includes agricultural/forest property, historic buildings and sites, and residential property. Class IV includes passenger automobiles and motor trucks. Class II property is broadly defined as all taxable property not otherwise classified, including all commercial property.[66] The tax base for real property is a percentage of its assessed value, which varies according to its class. In other words, after valuation, Class I is assessed at 30% of its appraised value, Class II at 20%, Class III at 10%, and Class IV at 15%.[67] Alabama generally uses the "fair and reasonable market value" as the basis for assessment of property;[68] however, the state constitution requires the legislature to provide an alternate valuation structure for timber acres and agricultural property based on their "current use," resulting in a deep valuation discount which is often well below their fair market value.[69] The Alabama Department of Revenue, which supervises the appraisal process, recommends that property be reappraised at least every three years.[70]

Real Property Tax Rates

Alabama's property tax rate at the state level is limited by the 1901 Alabama constitution to 6.5 mills per year on the assessed value of taxable property in the state.[71] This translates to $0.65 on each $100 of assessed value per year. In addition to the state's property tax, localities have their own property tax rates. The state constitution also limits the property tax rate at the county and municipal levels to 7.5 mills and 5 mills, respectively.[72] The aggregate property tax rate for Alabama counties, when taking into account state, local, municipal, and county-wide school district property taxes, ranges from 28 mills to 69.5 mills.[73]

---

64. Government Finances, *supra* note 44.

65. *Id.*

66. ALA. CONST. of 1901, amend. 373(a) and (b) (1978).

67. *Id.*

68. ALA. CONST. of 1901, art. XI, § 217.

69. ALA. CONST of 1901, amend. 373(j) (1978).

70. CCH-EXP, PROP-TAX-GUIDE AL ¶ 20-665, Reappraisals.

71. ALA. CONST. of 1901, art. XI, § 214.

72. *Id.* §§ 215, 216. Although the property tax rate limitation for municipalities imposed by section 216 is generally 5 mills, several municipalities are individually identified and given specific millage limitations and specific directives for spending property tax revenues, which do not apply to municipalities not identified. These rates range from an additional 5 mills to an additional 15 mills. *Id.*

73. CCH-EXP, AL-TAXRPTR ¶ 20-405, Rates of Tax.

Personal and Intangible Property

For tax purposes in Alabama, property is categorized as either real or personal. Personal property is further classified as either tangible or intangible. Tangible personal property held for personal use is generally tax exempt.[74] However, intangible personal property, unless specifically exempt, is subject to state property tax.[75] Of the numerous types of intangible personal property exempt from the property tax, the most significant categories include federal and municipal bonds and government obligations,[76] money on deposit,[77] mortgages (if they have been recorded and the privilege tax has been paid), Alabama UCC security agreements and security interests,[78] and shares of stock in domestic and foreign corporations.[79]

Exemptions

Alabama grants property tax exemptions to certain types of property as well as certain types of property holders. Banks and financial institutions, district electrical corporations, charitable organizations, and disabled homeowners are examples of property holders generally exempt from tax.[80] Agricultural products grown in Alabama, homesteads, and property in transit are examples of types of property exempt from tax.[81] The homestead exemption applies to $4,000 of the assessed value of a dwelling and up to 160 acres of land adjacent to it.[82]

General and Selective Sales

General Sales

Alabama imposes a general retail sales-and-use tax, which makes up approximately 30.5% of its total tax revenue.[83] A tax equal to 4% of gross receipts is imposed on persons, firms, and corporations engaged in the retail sales of tangible personal property or in operating places of entertainment or amusement.[84] Businesses that provide services other than entertainment and amusement are not subject to the sales-and-use tax.[85] The general rate of sales-and-use tax is 4% of the gross proceeds of the sale or

---

74. CCH-EXP, AL-TAXRPTR ¶ 20-295, Tangible Property.
75. ALA. CODE § 40-11-1(b)(16).
76. *Id.* § 40-9-1(1).
77. *Id.* §§ 40-9-1(1) & 40-1-1(7).
78. *Id.* § 40-9-1(1).
79. *Id.* § 40-9-32.
80. CCH-EXP, AL-TAXRPTR ¶ 20-510, List of Exemptions.
81. *Id.*
82. ALA. CODE § 40-9-19. Taxpayers over 65 years of age or those permanently disabled, deaf, or blind are completely exempt from property tax on their primary dwelling. *Id.*
83. Government Finances, *supra* note 44.
84. ALA. CODE § 43-23-2.
85. CCH-EXP, AL-TAXRPTR ¶ 60-230, Amusement, Entertainment, and Dues.

rental of personal property and 4% of the proceeds from entertainment and amuse-ment provided.[86] Localities are authorized to impose their own sales-and-use taxes without limit.[87] Local sales-and-use tax rates range from 1% to 6%, and there are typ-ically different rates for automotive vehicles, machinery, and farm equipment.[88] Ex-emptions from Alabama's sales-and-use taxes include prescription drugs (over-the-counter drugs are not exempt),[89] food stamp purchases (food bought from a grocery store is generally not exempt),[90] durable medical equipment,[91] and utilities.[92]

Selective Sales

Selective sales taxes make up approximately 19% of Alabama's total revenue.[93] The sales tax on motor fuel accounts for approximately 5.5% of the state's total revenue.[94] During fiscal year 2004, Alabama residents paid $118 per capita in motor fuel sales taxes, an amount which ranked 33rd in the nation and was just above the national per capita of $115.[95]

Sales taxes on alcoholic beverages make up 1.6% of Alabama's tax revenue. During fiscal year 2004, Alabama residents paid $30.32 per capita in state alcoholic beverage sales taxes, an amount which was the 7th highest in the country and nearly twice the national average of $15.74.[96]

The sales tax on tobacco products comprised 1% of Alabama's tax revenue during fiscal year 2004.[97] Alabama residents paid $20.61 per capita in state tobacco sales taxes, an amount which ranked 41st nationally.[98]

The remainder of Alabama's selective sales taxes makes up 10.9% of the total state tax revenue.[99] Of this amount, 6.1% represents taxes on public utilities and the other 4.8% represents taxes on specific commodities, businesses, or services not reported above (e.g., on contractors, lodging, lubricating oil, fuels other than motor fuel, motor vehicles, meals, soft drinks, margarine, etc.).[100]

---

86. ALA. CODE §§ 40-23-2, 40-12-222.

87. *Id.* § 11-3-11.2.

88. CCH-EXP, AL-TAXRPTR ¶ 61-735, Local Rates.

89. ALA. CODE § 40-9-27.

90. *Id* § 40-23-4.2.

91. *Id.* § 40-9-30.

92. *Id.* § 40-21-50.

93. Government Finances, *supra* note 44.

94. Government Finances, *supra* note 44.

95. STATE RANKINGS 2006, *supra* note 1, at 327.

96. *Id.* at 335.

97. U.S. Census Bureau, *supra* note 4.

98. STATE RANKINGS 2006, *supra* note 1, at 332.

99. Government Finances, *supra* note 44.

100. *See* GOVERNMENTS DIVISION, U.S. CENSUS BUREAU, GOVERNMENT FINANCE AND EM-PLOYMENT CLASSIFICATION MANUAL, at ch.7 (2000), *available at* http://ftp2.census.gov/govs/class/classfull.pdf [hereinafter CLASSIFICATION MANUAL].

Corporate Income and Other

Corporate Income

Alabama's corporate income tax makes up 2.8% of its total tax revenue.[101] This broad-based tax is imposed at a flat rate of 6.5% on a corporation's taxable income,[102] although some corporate taxpayers can elect to pay tax on the basis of their gross receipts.[103] In general, S corporations, limited partnerships, and limited liability partnerships, as well as limited liability companies (assuming they are treated as partnerships for federal tax purposes) are exempt from Alabama income tax just as they are exempt from federal income tax.[104]

Other

During fiscal year 2004, the collection of all other taxes not previously mentioned accounted for 9.6% of Alabama's total tax revenue.[105] Of this amount, approximately $29.5 million was generated by the estate and gift tax.[106] The "other taxes" category is also made up of motor vehicle license taxes, documentary and stock transfer taxes, severance taxes, and all other taxes not listed separately or provided for in other categories, such as taxes on land based on a specified rate per acre (rather than on assessed value).[107]

Burden Analysis

The overall state and local tax burden on taxpayers in Alabama is extremely regressive; indeed, the state has one of the ten most regressive tax systems in the nation.[108] In Alabama, taxpayers in the lowest quintile—those with incomes of less than $13,000—bear a tax burden equal to 10.6% of their income, while taxpayers in the top

---

101. Government Finances, *supra* note 44.

102. ALA. CONST. of 1901, amend. 662 (2001). The corporate income tax is capped at 6.5%. *Id.* The computation of taxable income begins with computing federal taxable income and subsequently modifying it to account for differences between Alabama and federal tax laws. If the corporation also does business in other states, the modified amount is apportioned to determine what portion is taxable by Alabama. ALA. CODE § 40-18-31.

103. ALA. CODE § 40-18-23. This option generally applies to corporations doing business in states other than Alabama and whose only in-state activities consist of sales whose dollar volume does not exceed $100,000. In addition, the company must not own or rent property in Alabama. These companies can elect to pay tax at a rate of .25% of their in-state sales. *Id.*

104. ALA. CODE § 40-18-160(a).

105. Government Finances, *supra* note 44.

106. *Id.*

107. *See* CLASSIFICATION MANUAL, *supra* note 100, at ch.7.

108. *See* ROBERT S. MCINTYRE ET AL., WHO PAYS? A DISTRIBUTIONAL ANALYSIS OF THE TAX SYSTEMS IN ALL 50 STATES 3 (2d ed. 2003), *available at* http://www.itepnet.org/wp2000/text.pdf.

1%—those with incomes that exceed $229,000—bear a tax burden of just 4.9% of their income.[109] It is also worth noting that, although Alabama obviously has no control over federal tax policy, federal itemized deductions for state and local personal income and property taxes nonetheless further reduce the burden on taxpayers in the top 1% to 3.8%.[110] Furthermore, between 1989 and 2002, the tax burden on the bottom quintile rose by approximately 1%, while the burden on the top 1% actually fell by 0.2%.[111]

In terms of the income tax, the burden across income groups in Alabama is almost flat, with taxpayers in the lowest quintile bearing a tax burden of 1.9% and those in the top 1% bearing a tax burden of 2.9%.[112] In contrast, however, the sales and excise taxes imposed by Alabama are very regressive, with taxpayers in the lowest quintile bearing a tax burden of 7.3% and those in the top 1% bearing a tax burden of just 1.1%.[113] Property taxes in Alabama are also regressive, with taxpayers in the lowest quintile bearing a tax burden of 1.4% and those in the top quintile bearing an average tax burden of 1.0%.[114]

---

109. *Id.* Taxpayers in the second quintile bear a 10.5% total tax burden on incomes between $13,000 and $21,000; those in the third quintile bear a 9.8% tax burden on incomes between $21,000 and $36,000; those in the fourth quintile bear a 8.4% tax burden on incomes between $36,000 and $58,000; those in the 80th–95th percentiles bear a 7.3% tax burden on incomes between $58,000 and $108,000; finally, those in the 96th–99th percentiles bear a 6.1% tax burden on incomes between $108,000 and $229,000. *Id.*

110. *Id.* Taxpayers in the lowest and second lowest quintiles did not receive any benefit from these federal offsets, while those in the third quintile were able to reduce their individual tax burdens by 0.1%, those in the fourth quintile by 0.3%, those in the 80th–95th percentiles by 0.6%, and those in the 96th–99th percentiles by 1.0%. *Id.*

111. *Id.* at 17.

112. *See id.* at 16. Taxpayers in the second quintile bear a 2.7% income tax burden; those in the third quintile bear a 2.9% burden; those in the fourth quintile bear a 2.9% burden; those in the 80th–95th percentiles bear a 2.9% burden; finally, those in the 96th–99th percentiles bear a 2.8% burden. *Id.* Note, however, that these percentages include both individual and corporate income tax burdens; that within the 96th–99th percentiles, corporate income taxes represent 0.1% of the income tax burden; and that in the top 1%, corporate income taxes represent 0.2% of the income tax burden. *Id.*

113. *See id.* Taxpayers in the second quintile bear a 6.6% sales-and-excise tax burden; those in the third quintile bear a 5.7% burden; those in the fourth quintile bear a 4.5% burden; those in the 80th–95th percentiles bear a 3.4% burden; finally, those in the 96th–99th percentiles bear a 2.1% burden. *Id.*

114. *Id.* Taxpayers in the second quintile bear a 1.2% property tax burden; those in the third quintile bear a 1.2% burden; those in the fourth quintile bear a 1% burden; those in the 80th–95th percentiles bear a 1% burden; those in the 96th–99th percentiles bear a 1.2% burden; finally, those in the top 1% bear a 0.9% burden. *Id.*

Alaska

General Information

Basic Profile – Geography, Population, and Industry

Alaska achieved statehood in 1959. Nicknamed "the last frontier," Alaska is separated from Washington, the closest state, by roughly 500 miles of Canadian territory. Juneau is the state capital. Most of Alaska is located in the Alaska time zone, which is four hours behind eastern standard time; a small portion is located in the Hawaiian-Aleutian time zone.

Alaska ranks 47th in population (approximately 663,661 residents[1]) but first in total land and water area (663,267 square miles[2]). Alaska's population is approximately 70.5% white, 3.7% black, and 16.0% American Indian and Alaska Native.[3] The state is approximately 9% Catholic, 18% Protestant, less than 1% Jewish, and 72% Other.[4] Roughly 66% of Alaska's residents live in urban areas.[5] The state's top industries include oil and gas, manufacturing, mining, tourism, services, fishing, forestry, and agriculture.[6]

---

1. STATE RANKINGS 2006, vi, 429 (Kathleen O'Leary Morgan & Scott Morgan eds., Morgan Quitno Press 2006).

2. *Id.* at 225.

3. Alaska Quick Facts from the U.S. Census Bureau, http://quickfacts.census.gov/qfd/states/02000.html (last visited Jan. 31, 2007). The remaining population is made up of 4.6% Asian persons; 0.6% Native Hawaiian and other Pacific Islanders; and 4.7% persons reporting two or more races. *Id.* Additionally, 5.1% of Alaska's total population identify themselves as persons of Hispanic or Latino origin. *Id.* (noting that because Hispanics and Latinos may be of any race, they are also included within the other applicable race categories). *See id.*

4. DALE E. JONES ET AL., ASSOCIATION OF STATISTICIANS OF AMERICAN RELIGIOUS BODIES, RELIGIOUS CONGREGATIONS & MEMBERSHIP: 2000, *available at* http://www.thearda.com/mapsReports/reports/state/02_2000.asp (last visited Mar. 26, 2007). Note that Alaska and Hawaii were not included in the religious identification survey that is cited in the other chapters of this book. *See* BARRY A. KOSMIN, EGON MAYER & ARIELA KEYSAR, AMERICAN RELIGIOUS IDENTIFICATION SURVEY 2001, at 42, *available at* http://www.gc.cuny.edu/faculty/research_studies/aris.pdf.

5. *See* USDA Economic Research Service, Alaska Fact Sheet, http://www.ers.usda.gov/StateFacts/AK.htm (last visited Sept. 17, 2006).

6. ALASKA DEPARTMENT OF COMMUNITY AND ECONOMIC DEVELOPMENT, ALASKA ECONOMIC PERFORMANCE REPORT 2003, at 2 (2004), *available at* http://www.commerce.state.ak.us/dca/pub/AEPR2003.pdf (last visited Apr. 1, 2006).

Family Income and Poverty Indicators

In 2004, Alaska's per capita gross product was $51,726, which ranked 3rd nationally and was well above the national average of $39,725.[7] During this same period, the median household income in Alaska was $54,627,[8] and 9.2% of Alaska's population was living in poverty, which was substantially below the national average of 12.4% and ranked among the bottom ten states.[9] More specifically, poverty affected 10.4% of Alaska's children,[10] 3.4% of its senior citizens,[11] and 5.5% of its families.[12] Of its female-headed households with children, 20.4% of them lived in poverty,[13] and 27.3% of the state's public elementary and secondary school students were eligible for free or reduced-price meals.[14] Of those living in poverty, approximately 3.7% were black, which represented 9.8% of Alaska's black population and 0.3% of its total population.[15] Alaska spent approximately $1 billion on public welfare programs in 2002,[16] which made up 12.3% of its total government expenditures.[17]

Alaska's Public Elementary-Secondary School System

Overall Spending and Performance

For the 2003–2004 school year, Alaska spent $10,114 per pupil in its public elementary-secondary school system, which was substantially above the national average of $8,182.[18] Of this amount, 19.4% was provided by the federal government, 54.9% was provided by the state government, and 25.7% was provided by the local governments,[19] with property taxes making up a significant part of the total funding.[20] Out

---

7. STATE RANKINGS 2006, *supra* note 1, at 89.

8. *Id.* at 96.

9. *Id.* at 495.

10. *Id.* at 497.

11. *Id.* at 496.

12. *Id.* at 498.

13. *Id.* at 499.

14. *Id.* at 532.

15. *See* Fact Sheet, American FactFinder, http://factfinder.census.gov/home/saff/main.html?_lang=en (select "Alaska" under "Get a Fact Sheet for your community") (last visited Feb. 16, 2007). Note that these numbers are based on the 2000 census because more recent numbers were not available.

16. *Id.* at 500.

17. *Id.* at 502.

18. GOVERNMENTS DIVISION, U.S. CENSUS BUREAU, PUBLIC EDUCATION FINANCES 2004, at 8 tbl.8 (2006), *available at* http://www2.census.gov/govs/school/04f33pub.pdf.

19. *See id.* at 5 tbl.5.

20. Although none of the total funding has been specifically designated as provided by property taxes, 20.9% of the total funding comes from "Parent Government Contributions." *See id.* at 4 tbl.4., which is defined as "tax receipts and other amounts appropriated by a parent government and transferred to its dependent school system." *Id.* at app. A-1. This amount, how-

of these funds, Alaska paid its elementary and secondary school teachers an estimated average annual salary of $52,424 during the 2004–2005 school year,[21] but in 2003, it provided a student/teacher ratio of 17.2, which was worse than the national average of 15.9.[22]

In academic performance, Alaska's fourth grade students scored lower than the national average in mathematics[23] and reading,[24] while Alaska's eighth graders scored lower than the national average in reading[25] but higher than the national average in mathematics.[26] Alaska's test scores for science[27] and writing[28] were unavailable.

Equity Issues

In 2004, the funding per student in Alaska's highest poverty districts actually exceeded that in its lowest poverty districts by $2,474,[29] although when adjustments were made for the additional costs of educating students growing up in poverty, that excess narrowed to $2,054.[30] Similarly, Alaska spent $4,955 more per student in its highest minority districts, although this amount fell to $4,435 when adjustments were made for low-income students.[31]

Fourth graders eligible for free or reduced-price school lunches had test scores that were 8% lower in mathematics[32] and 13% lower in reading[33] than those of students who were not eligible. The results were somewhat better for eighth graders eligible for

---

ever, "[e]xcludes intergovernmental revenue, current charges, and miscellaneous general revenue." *Id.*

21. THOMAS D. SNYDER ET AL., NATIONAL CENTER FOR EDUCATION STATISTICS, DIGEST OF EDUCATION STATISTICS 2005, at 116 tbl.77 (2006), *available at* http://nces.ed.gov/pubsearch/pubsinfo.asp?pubid=2006030.

22. *Id.* at 98 tbl.65.

23. NATIONAL CENTER FOR EDUCATION STATISTICS, U.S. DEPARTMENT OF EDUCATION, THE NATION'S REPORT CARD: MATHEMATICS 2005, at 14 fig.11 (2005), *available at* http://nces.ed.gov/nationsreportcard/pdf/main2005/2006453.pdf [hereinafter MATHEMATICS 2005].

24. NATIONAL CENTER FOR EDUCATION STATISTICS, U.S. DEPARTMENT OF EDUCATION, THE NATION'S REPORT CARD: READING 2005, at 14 fig.11 (2005), *available at* http://nces.ed.gov/nationsreportcard/pdf/main2005/2006451.pdf [hereinafter READING 2005].

25. READING 2005, *supra* note 24, at 16 fig.12.

26. MATHEMATICS 2005, *supra* note 23, at 16 fig.12.

27. *See* NATIONAL CENTER FOR EDUCATION STATISTICS, U.S. DEPARTMENT OF EDUCATION, THE NATION'S REPORT CARD: SCIENCE 2005, at 16 fig.12 (2006), *available at* http://nces.ed.gov/nationsreportcard//pdf/main2005/2006466.pdf.

28. *See* HILARY R. PERSKY ET AL., NATIONAL CENTER FOR EDUCATION STATISTICS, U.S. DEPARTMENT OF EDUCATION, THE NATION'S REPORT CARD: WRITING 2002, at 23 tbl.2.2 (2003), *available at* http://nces.ed.gov/nationsreportcard/pdf/main2002/2003529.pdf.

29. THE EDUCATION TRUST, FUNDING GAPS 2006, at 7 tbl.3 (2006), *available at* http://www2.edtrust.org/NR/rdonlyres/CDEF9403-5A75-437E-93FF-EBF1174181FB/0/FundingGap2006.pdf.

30. *Id.*

31. *Id.* at 7 tbl.4.

32. MATHEMATICS 2005, *supra* note 23, at 20 tbl.5.

33. READING 2005, *supra* note 24, at 20 tbl.5.

free or reduced-price lunches; their test scores were 8% lower in mathematics[34] and 10% lower in reading[35] than those for students who were not eligible.

In *Kasayulie v. State*, a case decided in 1999 that involved a challenge to the equity and adequacy of the state's system of funding school facilities, an Alaskan superior court held that the system was arbitrary, unconstitutional, and racially discriminatory.[36] The state subsequently allocated significant funds for the construction of rural schools, but the dual system of facilities financing that the *Kasayulie* court held to be unconstitutional still exists.[37] A case in which the plaintiffs challenge the adequacy of Alaska's overall education finance system, *Moore v. State*, is currently being litigated.[38]

Availability of Publicly Funded Prekindergarten Programs

Alaska does not provide any publicly funded prekindergarten programs, but the state does supplement the federal Head Start program.[39] In 2005–2006, approximately 525 three- and four-year-olds were served through state-funded Head Start slots,[40] which represented 3% of Alaska's 20,064 three- and four-year-old children.[41] The federally funded Head Start program enrolled an additional 2,300 children,[42] a number which represented 11% of Alaska's three- and four-year-old children.[43]

Where Does Alaska Get Its Revenue?

At the end of fiscal year 2004, Alaska had total revenues of approximately $11.0 billion. Of this amount, 22% was derived from state and local tax revenues and 22% was received from the federal government.[44] The remaining 56% came from other sources, including insurance trust revenue and revenue from government-owned utilities and other commercial or auxiliary enterprises.[45]

---

34. MATHEMATICS 2005, *supra* note 23, at 21 tbl.6.

35. READING 2005, *supra* note 24, at 21 tbl.6.

36. National Access Network, State by State, Alaska, http://www.schoolfunding.info/states/ak/lit_ak.php3 (last visited Mar. 19, 2007)

37. *Id.*

38. *Id.*

39. W. STEVEN BARNETT ET AL., NATIONAL INSTITUTE FOR EARLY EDUCATION RESEARCH, THE STATE OF PRESCHOOL 2005, at 42 (2006), *available at* http://nieer.org/yearbook/pdf/yearbook.pdf.

40. *Id.* at 43.

41. *See id.* at 232.

42. *Id.* at 43.

43. *See id.* at 232.

44. U.S. Census Bureau, State and Local Government Finances 2003–04, http://www.census.gov/govs/www/estimate04.html (last visited Oct. 6, 2006) [hereinafter Government Finances].

45. *Id.*

Tax Revenue

Alaska collected approximately $2.4 billion in state and local tax revenue during fiscal year 2004.[46] As a result, Alaska residents paid $3,610 per capita in state and local taxes, an amount which ranked 14th nationally.[47] The different types of tax sources were approximately apportioned as follows:

Individual income taxes	0.0%
Property taxes	36.2%
General and selective sales taxes	15.1%
Corporate income and other taxes	48.7%
	100.0%[48]

Federal Funding

During fiscal year 2004, 22% of Alaska's total revenues came from the federal government.[49] For every dollar of federal taxes paid, Alaska received $1.87 in federal funding, an amount which ranked 2nd nationally and was far above the national average of $1.17.[50]

Lottery Revenues

Alaska does not operate a state lottery.

Legal Structures of Major Tax Sources

Income

Alaska does not collect individual income taxes.

Property

Overview

Alaska's property tax system taxes the value of property at the local level.[51] However, most of the real property in Alaska goes untaxed, with only 38 of the 163 incorporated

---

46. The total tax revenues were collected as follows: $1.4 billion by the state and $1 billion by local governments. *Id.*

47. *See id.*

48. *Id.*

49. Government Finances, *supra* note 44.

50. *See* The Tax Foundation, Federal Spending Received Per Dollar of Taxes Paid by State 2004, http://www.taxfoundation.org/taxdata/show/266.html (last visited Nov. 1, 2006).

51. *See* ALASKA STAT. § 29.45.

boroughs and municipalities authorized to levy property taxes actually doing so.[52] In addition to the local property tax system, there is a statewide tax on real and personal property used in oil and gas exploration, production, and pipeline transportation.[53] During fiscal year 2004, the state collected $47.4 million in property taxes and localities collected $811.7 million.[54] Alaska property owners paid $1,306 per capita in property taxes in 2004, an amount which ranked 12th nationally.[55]

Defining the Real Property Tax Base

Taxable property in Alaska is generally assessed at its "full and true value," which essentially means fair market value.[56] However, farmland, property used for oil and gas production or transportation, and private airports available for public use are granted special use assessment.[57] Property is assessed annually.[58]

Real Property Tax Rates

Real and personal property used in oil and gas exploration, production, and pipeline transportation is taxed by the state at a rate of 20 mills ($20 per $1,000).[59] Property tax rates for the principal Alaskan cities that levy property taxes range from 6 mills ($6 per $1,000) in Sitka to 20 mills ($20 per $1,000) in Fairbanks.[60] State law requires that municipal property taxes not exceed 3% of assessed value (30 mills, or $30 per $1,000) for most municipalities and 2% (20 mills, or $20 per $1,000) for "second class cities."[61]

---

52. ALASKA DEPARTMENT OF COMMERCE, COMMUNITY AND ECONOMIC DEVELOPMENT, ALASKA TAXABLE 2005, at 25 (2006), *available at* http://www.dced.state.ak.us/dca/osa/pub/05Taxable.pdf (last visited Apr. 1, 2006).

53. ALASKA STAT. § 43.56.

54. Government Finances, *supra* note 44.

55. *See id.*

56. *See* ALASKA STAT. §§ 43.56.060, 29.45.110.

57. *See id* . §§ 29.45.060, 43.56.060, 29.45.065. Qualifying farmland and private airports for public use are valued on the basis of their existing use, with penalties imposed if a landowner changes the use or sells the property to be used for other purposes. *See id.* Property used for the production of oil and gas is valued at actual cost, less depreciation, while property used for the transportation of oil and gas is valued according to the economic value of the property based on the estimated life of the reserves. *Id.* § 43.56.060.

58. ALASKA STAT. § 29.45.110.

59. *Id.* § 43.56.010.

60. CCH-EXP, AK-TAXRPTR ¶71-001, Rates in Principal Alaska Cities.

61. ALASKA STAT. §§ 29.45.090, 29.45.590. Alaska municipalities are broadly classified into home rule municipalities and general law municipalities. *See* ALASKA STAT. §§ 29.04.010 to .060. "A home rule municipality adopts a charter subject to voter approval and has all powers not prohibited by law or charter. A general law municipality is unchartered and its powers are granted by law." Alaska Division of Community Advocacy, Municipal Government Structure in Alaska, http://www.dced.state.ak.us/dca/LOGON/muni/muni-structure.htm (last visited Apr. 1, 2007) *citing* ALASKA CONST. art X, §§ 4, 7, 9, 10, 11; ALASKA STAT. §§ 29.04.010, .020. General law municipalities are further divided into first class boroughs, second class boroughs, third class boroughs, first class cities, and second class cities. ALASKA STAT. § 29.04.030. A primary factor that differentiates second class cities from first class cities is that a first class city must exercise

Personal and Intangible Property

Intangible personal property is not taxed in Alaska.[62] All tangible personal property used for oil and gas purposes is taxable at the state oil and gas tax rate of 20 mills.[63] In addition, municipalities are authorized to tax tangible personal property.[64] Municipal taxation of personal property may not exceed 3% of its assessed value.[65] Like real property, personal property is assessed at "full and true value."[66]

Exemptions

A homestead exemption of up to $150,000 is available for residents 65 or older, disabled veterans, and surviving spouses of one of the aforementioned who are over 60 years of age.[67] Other major real property exemptions include property used for nonprofit religious, charitable, cemetery, hospital, or educational purposes, as well as unharvested timber.[68] Additionally, municipalities are authorized to grant homestead exemptions without regard to the characteristics of the homeowner — but not to exceed $20,000 per residence.[69] Household goods are also exempt.[70] Furthermore, a municipality may exempt by ordinance any type of personal property.[71] A municipality that has exempted personal property may levy a flat tax on the exempted property.[72]

General and Selective Sales

General Sales

Although there is no sales tax at the state level, Alaska municipalities impose a general retail sales-and-use tax, which constituted 6.3% of the total state and local tax revenue during fiscal year 2004.[73] Municipalities are authorized to tax sales, rents, and services.[74] The power granted to the municipalities is very broad; the only statutory exemptions are those for food stamps, space flight vehicles, the physical transfer of refined fuel absent sale, and wholesale sales or transfer of fuel.[75] There is no statewide

---

education powers, while a second class city may not. Alaska Division of Community Advocacy, Municipal Government Structure in Alaska, http://www.dced.state.ak.us/dca/LOGON/muni/muni-structure.htm (last visited Apr. 1, 2007).

62. *See* ALASKA STAT. §§ 29.45.10, 29.71.800.

63. *See id.* § 43.56.010.

64. *See id.* § 29.45.010.

65. *Id.* § 29.45.090.

66. *Id.* § 29.45.110.

67. *Id.* § 29.45.030(e).

68. *Id.* § 29.45.030.

69. *Id.* § 29.45.050.

70. *See id.* § 29.45.030.

71. *Id.*

72. *Id.* § 29.45.055.

73. Government Finances, *supra* note 44.

74. ALASKA STAT. § 29.45.650.

75. *See id.* § 29.45.650.

exemption for food, other than the aforementioned exemption for food purchased with food stamps.[76] Localities have the power to grant exemptions by ordinance.[77] The local sales tax rates range from 1% to 7%.[78]

Selective Sales

Selective sales taxes made up 8.8% of Alaska's total state and local tax revenues during fiscal year 2004.[79] Of that amount, 2.1% was derived from taxes on tobacco products.[80] Alaska residents paid taxes of $65.71 per capita on tobacco product sales, an amount which ranked 12th nationally.[81] Alaska's tax rate on cigarettes is $2 per pack, effective July 1, 2007.[82]

Motor fuel taxes comprised 1.7% of the state's total tax revenue in 2004.[83] Alaska residents paid an average of $62 per capita in state motor fuel sales taxes in 2004, an amount which ranked 49th nationally and was well below the national average of $115.[84]

In 2004, taxes on alcoholic beverages comprised 1.5% of the state's total tax revenue.[85] Alaska residents paid $42.97 per capita in state alcoholic beverage sales taxes in 2004, an amount which ranked 1st nationally.[86]

The remainder of Alaska's selective sales taxes makes up 3.6% of its total tax revenue.[87] Of this amount, 0.2% represents taxes on utilities and the other 3.4% represents taxes on other specific commodities, businesses, or services not reported separately above (e.g., on contractors, lodging, lubricating oil, fuels other than motor fuel, motor vehicles, meals, soft drinks, margarine, etc.).[88]

Corporate Income and Other

Corporate Income

Alaska's corporate income tax constituted 14.3% of its total tax revenue during fiscal year 2004.[89] The starting point for Alaska's corporate income tax base is federal tax-

---

76. *See Id.*

77. *Id.*

78. Department of Commerce, Community and Economic Development at 12, *supra* note 52.

79. Government Finances, *supra* note 44.

80. *Id.*

81. STATE RANKINGS 2006, *supra* note 1, at 332.

82. *See* ALASKA STAT. § 43.50.090.

83. Government Finances, *supra* note 44.

84. STATE RANKINGS, *supra* note 1.

85. Government Finances, *supra* note 44.

86. STATE RANKINGS 2006, *supra* note 1, at 335.

87. Government Finances, *supra* note 44.

88. *See* GOVERNMENTS DIVISION, U.S. CENSUS BUREAU, GOVERNMENT FINANCE AND EMPLOYMENT CLASSIFICATION MANUAL, at ch.7 (2000), *available at* http://ftp2.census.gov/govs/class/classfull.pdf [hereinafter CLASSIFICATION MANUAL].

89. Government Finances, *supra* note 44.

able income, to which several adjustments are made.[90] The state corporate income tax applies to C corporations, while Alaska adopts the federal income tax pass-through treatment of S corporations, partnerships, and LLCs.[91] Rates are graduated from 1% to 9.4% in increments of $10,000 of taxable income.[92] The 9.4% maximum rate applies to taxable income of $90,000 and above.[93]

Other

During fiscal year 2004, the collection of all other taxes not previously mentioned generated $818.8 million, which comprised 34.4% of Alaska's total tax revenue.[94] Of this amount, $2.3 million was generated by the estate tax.[95] The estate tax is generally equal to the state death tax credit allowed under the federal estate tax laws; for Alaska residents, it is imposed on the same property that would be taxable under the federal laws.[96] Although the Alaska estate tax statutes remain in effect, the repeal of the federal death tax credit[97] has effectively eliminated Alaska's estate tax, and the state no longer requires that executors file estate tax returns.[98]

Alaska generates substantial revenue from petroleum tax. In addition to the property taxes imposed on oil and gas equipment, Alaska also imposes mining licensing taxes and severance taxes. [99] The mining license tax is imposed on net income and royalties at rates accelerating from 3% for taxable amounts under $50,000 to 7% for taxable amounts over $100,000.[100]

The "other taxes" category is further made up of various license taxes, documentary or stock transfer taxes, severance taxes, and all other taxes not listed separately or provided for in other categories.[101]

Burden Analysis

The overall state and local tax burden on Alaska's taxpayers is somewhat regressive. Taxpayers in the lowest quintile—those with incomes of less than $15,000—bear a tax burden equal to 3.8% of their income, while taxpayers in the top 1%—those with

---

90. *See* ALASKA STAT. § 43.20.021.
91. *Id.* § 43.20.021(a).
92. *Id.* § 43.20.011.
93. *Id.*
94. Government Finances, *supra* note 44.
95. *Id.*
96. *See* ALASKA STAT. § 43.31.011.
97. *See* Economic Growth and Tax Relief Reconciliation Act of 2001, Pub. L. No. 107-16 (2001).
98. Alaska Department of Revenue, Frequently Asked Questions, http://www.tax.state.ak.us/programs/other/faq.asp (last visited Apr. 1, 2007).
99. *See* ALASKA STAT. §§ 43.65.010, 43.55.011.
100. *Id.*
101. *See* CLASSIFICATION MANUAL, *supra* note 88, at ch.7.

incomes that exceed $273,000—bear a tax burden of just 2.8% of their income.[102] It is also worth noting that, although Alaska obviously has no control over federal tax policy, federal itemized deductions for state and local personal income and property taxes nonetheless further reduce the burden on taxpayers in the top 1% to 2.5%.[103] Furthermore, between 1989 and 2002, the tax burden on the bottom quintile rose by approximately 0.1%, while the burden on the top 1% fell by 0.8%.[104]

Alaska does not impose a personal income tax, but the state's corporate income tax burden across income groups is slightly progressive, with corporate taxpayers in the lowest quintile bearing a tax burden of 0.1% and those in the top 1% bearing a tax burden of 0.7%.[105] In contrast, the sales and excises taxes imposed by Alaska are slightly regressive, with taxpayers in the lowest quintile bearing a tax burden of 2.4% and those in the top 1% bearing a tax burden of just 0.2%.[106] Property taxes, on the other hand, are somewhat progressive, with taxpayers in the lowest quintile bearing a tax burden of 1.3% and those in the top quintile bearing an average tax burden of 2.2%.[107]

---

102. *See* ROBERT S. MCINTYRE ET AL., WHO PAYS? A DISTRIBUTIONAL ANALYSIS OF THE TAX SYSTEMS IN ALL 50 STATES 18 (2d ed. 2003), *available at* http://www.itepnet.org/wp2000/text.pdf. Taxpayers in the second quintile bear a 4.2% total tax burden on incomes between $15,000 and $31,000; those in the third quintile bear a 3.0% tax burden on incomes between $31,000 and $50,000; those in the fourth quintile bear a 3.2% tax burden on incomes between $50,000 and $80,000; those in the 80th–95th percentiles bear a 3.4% tax burden on incomes between $80,000 and $142,000; finally, those in the 96th–99th percentiles bear a 3.0% tax burden on incomes between $142,000 and $273,000. *Id.*

103. *Id.* Taxpayers in the lowest and second lowest quintiles did not receive any benefit from these federal offsets, while those in the third quintile were able to reduce their individual tax burdens by 0.1%, those in the fourth quintile by 0.3%, those in the 80th–95th percentiles by 0.5%, and those in the 96th–99th percentiles also by 0.5%. *Id.*

104. *Id.* at 19.

105. *See id.* at 18. Corporate taxpayers in the second, third, and fourth quintiles bear a 0.1% burden; those in the 80th–95th percentiles bear a 0.2% burden; finally, those in the 96th–99th percentiles bear a 0.3% burden. *Id.*

106. *See id.* Taxpayers in the second quintile bear a 1.6% sales-and-excise tax burden; those in the third quintile bear a 1.2% burden; those in the fourth quintile bear a 0.8% burden; those in the 80th–95th percentiles bear a 0.6% burden; finally, those in the 96th–99th percentiles bear a 0.4% burden. *Id.*

107. *See id.* Taxpayers in the second quintile bear a 2.5% property tax burden; those in the third quintile bear a 1.8% burden; those in the fourth quintile bear a 2.2% burden; those in the 80th–95th percentiles bear a 2.5% burden; those in the 96th–99th percentiles bear a 2.3% burden; finally, those in the top 1% bear a 1.9% burden. *Id.*

Arizona

General Information

Basic Profile – Geography, Population, and Industry

Admitted to the Union 1912, Arizona is known as the "Grand Canyon State."[1] It is located in the southwestern United States and is bordered by California on the west, Nevada on the northwest, Utah on the north, Colorado on the northeast, New Mexico on the east, and Mexico on the south. Arizona is located in the mountain time zone, and Phoenix is the state capital.

Arizona ranks 17th in population (approximately 5.6 million residents)[2] and 6th in total land and water area (113,998 square miles).[3] Its population is approximately 87.4% white, 5.1% American Indian and Alaska Native, and 3.6% black.[4] Additionally, 28.5% of its population identify themselves as persons of Hispanic or Latino origin.[5] The state is 29% Catholic, 43% Protestant, and 1% Jewish; 27% claim a religion outside the Judeo-Christian tradition or none at all.[6] Roughly 89% of Arizona's population lives in urban areas.[7] Major industries include aerospace, electronics, semiconductor manufacturing, tourism, business services, agriculture, mining, construction, and real estate and rental.[8]

---

1. State Rankings 2006, vi, 1 (Kathleen O'Leary Morgan & Scott Morgan eds., Morgan Quitno Press 2006).

2. *Id.* at 429.

3. *Id.* at 225.

4. Arizona Quick Facts from the U.S. Census Bureau, http://quickfacts.census.gov/qfd/states/54000.html (last visited Jan. 31, 2007). The remaining population is made up of 2.2% Asian persons; 0.2% Native Hawaiian and other Pacific Islanders; and 1.5% persons reporting two or more races. *Id.*

5. *Id.* Note that because Hispanics and Latinos may be of any race, they are also included within the other applicable race categories. *See id.*

6. Barry A. Kosmin, Egon Mayer & Ariela Keysar, American Religious Identification Survey 2001, at 41, *available at* http://www.gc.cuny.edu/faculty/research_studies/aris.pdf.

7. USDA Economic Research Service, Arizona Fact Sheet, http://www.ers.usda.gov/StateFacts/AZ.htm (last visited Oct. 16, 2006).

8. Arizona Department of Commerce, Arizona Economic Profile, http://www.commerce.state.az.us/doclib/prop/state_economic_profile.pdf (last visited Dec. 28, 2006).

Family Income and Poverty Indicators

In 2004, Arizona's per capita gross product was $34,836, which was below the national average of $39,725.[9] During this same period, although the median household income in Arizona was $42,590,[10] 13.8% of Arizona's population was living in poverty,[11] which was slightly above the national average of 12.4%.[12] More specifically, poverty affected 19.6% of Arizona's children,[13] 7.5% of its senior citizens,[14] and 10.9% of its families.[15] Of its female-headed households with children, 32.9% lived in poverty,[16] and 45.1% of the state's public elementary and secondary school students were eligible for free or reduced-price meals.[17] Of those living in poverty, approximately 4% were black, which represented 18% of Arizona's black population and 1% of its total population.[18] In an attempt to combat this poverty, Arizona spent approximately $3.29 billion on public welfare programs in 2002,[19] which made up 13% of its total government expenditures.[20]

Arizona's Public Elementary-Secondary School System

Overall Spending and Performance

For the 2003–2004 school year, Arizona spent $6,036 per pupil in its public elementary-secondary school system, which was substantially below the national average of $8,182.[21] Of this amount, 11.8% was provided by the federal government, 44.9% was provided by the state government, and 43.3% was provided by the local governments,[22] with property taxes making up 33.6% of the total funding.[23] Out of

---

9. STATE RANKINGS 2006, *supra* note 1, at 89.

10. *Id.* at 96.

11. *Id.* at 495.

12. *Id.* at 495.

13. *Id.* at 497.

14. *Id.* at 496.

15. *Id.* at 498.

16. *Id.* at 499.

17. *Id.* at 532.

18. *See* Fact Sheet, American FactFinder, http://factfinder.census.gov/home/saff/main.html?_lang=en (select "Arizona" under "Get a Fact Sheet for your community") (last visited Feb. 21, 2007). Note that these numbers are based on the 2000 census because more recent numbers were not available.

19. *Id.* at 500.

20. *Id.* at 502.

21. GOVERNMENTS DIVISION, U.S. CENSUS BUREAU, PUBLIC EDUCATION FINANCES 2004, at 8 tbl.8 (2006), *available at* http://www2.census.gov/govs/school/04f33pub.pdf.

22. *See id.* at 5 tbl.5.

23. *See id.* at 4 tbl.4.

these funds, Arizona paid its elementary and secondary school teachers an estimated average annual salary of $42,905 during the 2004–2005 school year,[24] but in 2003, it provided a student/teacher ratio of just 21.3, which was far worse than the national average of 15.9.[25]

In academic performance, Arizona's fourth and eighth grade students scored lower than the national average in mathematics,[26] reading,[27] science,[28] and writing.[29]

Equity Issues

In 2004, revenues spent per student in Arizona's highest poverty districts were determined to be $225 less than the revenues spent in its lowest poverty districts.[30] When adjustments were made for the additional costs of educating students growing up in poverty, however, the funding gap grew to $736.[31] Similarly, Arizona spent $230 less per student in its highest minority districts, and this amount grew to $680 when adjustments for low-income students were made.[32]

Fourth graders eligible for free or reduced-price school lunches had test scores that were 9% lower in mathematics,[33] 14% lower in reading,[34] and 15% lower in writing[35] than those of students who were not eligible. The results were generally similar for eighth graders eligible for free or reduced-price lunches; their test scores were 9% lower

24. Thomas D. Snyder et al., National Center for Education Statistics, Digest of Education Statistics 2005, at 116 tbl.77 (2006), *available at* http://nces.ed.gov/pubsearch/pubsinfo.asp?pubid=2006030.

25. *Id.* at 98 tbl.65.

26. National Center for Education Statistics, U.S. Department of Education, The Nation's Report Card: Mathematics 2005, at 14 fig.11, 16 fig.12 (2005), *available at* http://nces.ed.gov/nationsreportcard/pdf/main2005/ 2006453.pdf [hereinafter Mathematics 2005].

27. National Center for Education Statistics, U.S. Department of Education, The Nation's Report Card: Reading 2005, at 14 fig.11, 16 fig.12 (2005), *available at* http://nces.ed.gov/nationsreportcard/pdf/main2005/2006451.pdf [hereinafter Reading 2005].

28. National Center for Education Statistics, U.S. Department of Education, The Nation's Report Card: Science 2005, at 16 fig.12, 28 fig.22 (2006) *available at* http://nces.ed.gov/nationsreportcard//pdf/main2005/2006466.pdf [hereinafter Science 2005].

29. Hilary R. Persky et al., National Center for Education Statistics, U.S. Department of Education, The Nation's Report Card: Writing 2002, at 23 tbl.2.2, 24 tbl.2.3 (2003), *available at* http://nces.ed.gov/nationsreportcard/pdf/main2002/2003529.pdf [hereinafter Writing 2002].

30. The Education Trust, Funding Gaps 2006, at 7 tbl.3 (2006), *available at* http://www2.edtrust.org/NR/rdonlyres/CDEF9403-5A75-437E-93FF-EBF1174181FB/0/FundingGap2006.pdf.

31. *Id.*

32. *Id.* at 7 tbl.4.

33. Mathematics 2005, *supra* note 26, at 20 tbl.5.

34. Reading 2005, *supra* note 27, at 20 tbl.5.

35. Writing 2002, *supra* note 29, at 75 tbl.3.24.

in mathematics,[36] 9% lower in reading,[37] and 16% lower in writing[38] than those of students who were not eligible.

There have been a few, relatively recent instances of litigation challenging education funding in Arizona. In 2003, the Roosevelt Elementary School District brought suit against the state alleging a constitutional violation stemming from the legislature's failure to fund the Building Renewal Fund, which was part of Students FIRST legislation in Arizona. The state prevailed on appeal because the school district had failed to link its inadequate capital facilities with its students' academic performance.[39] Also in 2003, the Crane Elementary School District brought suit against the state alleging that underfunding at-risk student programs was a violation of the state constitution's education clause. In a similar 1998 case, parents filed suit seeking declaratory relief against the State of Arizona. Their complaint alleged that because of underfunding by the legislature, the State had failed to provide their children, who were students with limited English proficiency, with a uniform program of instruction. After a study was conducted, the court found that the levels of funding bore a rational relationship to the program needs and dismissed the case.[40]

Availability of Publicly Funded Prekindergarten Programs

Arizona's prekindergarten program primarily serves students four years of age, although it has no minimum age requirement. Rather than acting as a formal, state-sponsored program, the Arizona Early Childhood Block Grant simply funds supplemental prekindergarten services to students at local public schools.[41] Total enrollment in this state-funded program is 5,339,[42] which represents just 3% of Arizona's 182,647 three- and four-year-old children.[43] The federally funded Head Start program enrolls an additional 16,850 children,[44] which represents 9% of Arizona's three- and four-year-old children.[45]

Where Does Arizona Get Its Revenue?

At the end of fiscal year 2004, Arizona had total revenues of approximately $38.4 billion.[46] Of this amount, 43% was derived from state and local tax revenues and 20%

36. MATHEMATICS 2005, *supra* note 26, at 21 tbl.6.

37. READING 2005, *supra* note 27, at 21 tbl.6.

38. WRITING 2002, *supra* note 29, at 76 tbl.3.25.

39. Roosevelt Sch. Dist. No. 66 v. State, 205 Ariz. 584 (2003).

40. Flores v. Arizona, U.S. Dist. Lexis 23177 (2002).

41. W. STEVEN BARNETT ET AL., NATIONAL INSTITUTE FOR EARLY EDUCATION RESEARCH, THE STATE OF PRESCHOOL 2006, at 44 (2006), *available at* http://nieer.org/yearbook/pdf/yearbook.pdf.

42. *Id.* at 45.

43. *See id.* at 232.

44. *Id.* at 45.

45. *See id.* at 232.

46. U.S. Census Bureau, State and Local Government Finances - 2003–04, http://www.census.gov/govs/www/estimate04.html (last visited Oct. 16, 2006) [hereinafter Government Finances].

was received from the federal government.[47] The remaining 37% came from other sources, including the Arizona Lottery, insurance trust revenue, and revenue from government-owned utilities and other commercial or auxiliary enterprises.[48]

Tax Revenue

Arizona collected approximately $16.5 billion in state and local tax revenue during fiscal year 2004.[49] As a result, Arizona residents paid $2,871 per capita in state and local government taxes, an amount which ranked 36th nationally.[50] The different types of tax sources were approximately apportioned as follows:

Individual income taxes	14.1%
Property taxes	29.5%
General and selective sales taxes	48.5%
Corporate income and other taxes	7.9%
	100.0%[51]

Federal Funding

During fiscal year 2004, 20% of Arizona's total revenues came from the federal government.[52] For every dollar of federal taxes paid, Arizona received $1.30 in federal funding, an amount which ranked 19th nationally and was above the national average of $1.17.[53]

Lottery Revenues

The Arizona Lottery was created through the voter initiative process in 1980.[54] Lottery funds are used for various state purposes, with 2005 beneficiaries including the state's general fund, local transportation assistance, state parks and wildlife, county assistance, mass transit, and economic development.[55] In 2005, the Lottery had total operating revenues of $397.6 million and net income before transfers of $116.1 million.[56]

---

47. *Id.*

48. *Id.*

49. The total tax revenues were collected as follows: $9.6 billion by the state and $6.9 billion by local governments. *Id.*

50. *Id.*

51. *Id.*

52. *Id.*

53. *See* The Tax Foundation, Federal Spending Received Per Dollar of Taxes Paid by State, 2004, http://www.taxfoundation.org/taxdata/show/266.html (last visited Oct. 16, 2006).

54. The Arizona Lottery, 2005 Financial Statements, Introduction Section, http://www.arizonalottery.com/pdfs/ArizonaStateLottery_fs_2005.pdf (last visited Dec. 28, 2006).

55. The Arizona Lottery, "Where The Money Goes," http://www.arizonalottery.com/WhereTheMoneyGoes.asp (last visited Dec. 28, 2006).

56. *Id.*

Legal Structures of Major Tax Sources

Income

Arizona employs a broad-based income tax that uses adjusted gross income for federal income tax purposes as a starting point for determining the state's taxable income.[57] However, a fairly large number of adjustments may be available to various individuals in calculating this amount.[58] Arizona localities are prohibited from imposing income taxes as long as the Urban Revenue Sharing Fund, which distributes state-collected taxes to localities, is maintained as provided in the 1978 Arizona Tax Act.[59] During fiscal year 2004, Arizona collected personal income tax of $403 per capita, an amount which ranked 39th nationally.[60]

In Arizona, a typical family of four (i.e., married taxpayers who file jointly and have two dependent children) are not required to pay any income tax until their combined income exceeds $23,600, an amount which is above the national poverty line of $20,615.[61] For the tax year 2006, Arizona's income tax structure contained five tax brackets that imposed a minimum marginal rate of 2.73% and a maximum marginal rate of 4.79%.[62] When statutory exemptions and the standard deduction were taken into account, the maximum marginal rate applied to every dollar of income that exceeded $317,294.[63]

---

57. Ariz. Rev. Stat. Ann. §§ 43-102(A)(1), 43-1001.

58. *See id.* §§ 43-1021 to -1032.

59. *Id.* § 43-201. The Urban Revenue Sharing Fund consists of a percentage of the net proceeds of the state income tax, which must be distributed to incorporated cities and towns in amounts corresponding to the proportions of their individual populations to the total population. *See id.* § 43-206.

60. State Rankings 2006, *supra* note 1, at 321, *citing* U.S. Bureau of the Census, Governments Division "2004 State Government Tax Collections," *available a*t http://www.census.gov/govs/www/statetax04.html.

61. Jason A. Levitis, Center on Budget and Policy Priorities, The Impact of State Income Taxes on Low-Income Families in 2006, at 12 (2007). In 2006, Arizona taxpayers who were married and filing jointly were entitled to a standard deduction of $8,494 and personal and dependent exemptions of $4,200 and $2,300, respectively. Ariz. Rev. Stat. Ann. § 43-1041, 1043, & 1001. Note, however, that the threshold calculation of $23,600 was greater than the sum of these deductions and exemptions because it included additional tax benefits available to low-income families, such as the earned-income tax credit. *See* Levitis, *supra.*

62. Ariz. Rev. Stat. Ann. § 43-1011. Arizona's middle three rates were 3.04%, 3.55%, and 4.48%. *Id.* Note that for tax years 2007 and after, the brackets will remain the same, but the applicable rates will change to 2.59%, 2.88%, 3.36%, 4.24%, and 4.54%. *Id.*

63. The standard deduction and exemptions of $8,494 and $8,800, respectively, plus the threshold for the highest tax bracket of $300,000, equals $317,294. *See supra* notes 61–62.

Property

Overview

Arizona has a typical property tax system that taxes the value of real and tangible personal property mostly at the local level. Although property taxes are generally collected at the local level, certain property is assessed at the state level, including certain utility property and railroad property.[64] The state also assumes an advisory and supervisory role in the local assessment process.[65] During fiscal year 2004, Arizona localities collected more than $4.5 billion in property taxes, and the state collected $346.4 million.[66] As a result, Arizona residents paid $848 per capita in property taxes, an amount which ranked 35th nationally.[67]

Defining the Real Property Tax Base

Arizona real property is grouped into nine classes that are each subject to differing assessment ratios.[68] Class 1 property generally includes mines, standing timber, utilities, commercial property, and industrial property and was assessed at 24.5% for the 2006 tax year.[69] Class 2 generally consists of agricultural land, open-space land, vacant land, and real property owned by nonprofit organizations and is assessed at 16%.[70] Classes 3 and 4 encompass residential property and are both assessed at 10%.[71] Class 5 generally consists of railroads and airline flight property and is assessed at a ratio that is computed annually and is a weighted average of the assessment ratios for all other classes of commercial and industrial property.[72] Class 6 generally consists of noncommercial historic property, foreign trade zone property, military reuse zone property, and enterprise zone property and is assessed at 5%.[73] Class 7 consists of commercial historic property and is assessed at 25%, except that certain restoration modifications are assessed at 1% of full cash value for up to ten years.[74] Class 8 consists of residential historic property and is assessed at 10%, except that restoration modifications are assessed at 1% of full cash value for up to ten years.[75] Class 9 consists of improvements on government property and is assessed at 1%.[76]

---

64. *See* Ariz. Rev. Stat. Ann. §§ 42-14302, 42-14151, 42-14155.

65. *See id.* § 42-11051.

66. Government Finances, *supra* note 46 .

67. *See id.*

68. *See* Ariz. Rev. Stat. Ann. § 42-12001.

69. *Id.* §§ 42-12001, 42-15001. The Class 1 assessment ratio is scheduled to decrease by 0.5% per calendar year until 2014, when the rate will be 20%. *Id.* § 15001.

70. *Id.* §§ 42-12002, 42-15002.

71. *Id.* §§ 42-12003, 42-12004, 42-15003, 42-15004.

72. *See id.* §§ 42-12005, 42-15005.

73. *Id.* §§ 42-12006, 42-15006.

74. *Id.* §§ 42-12007, 42-15007.

75. *Id.* §§ 42-12008, 42-15008.

76. *Id* .§§ 42-12009, 42-15009.

Taxable real property in Arizona is generally valued at its "full cash value" or "limited property value."[77] "Full cash value" means market value unless another method is prescribed by statute.[78] "Limited property value" provides a means of implementing Arizona's statutory restriction on annual increases in property value. It is determined by first taking the limited property value of the preceding year and then by adding either (1) 10% of that value or (2) 25% of the difference between the full cash value of the parcel in the current year and the limited value in the preceding year, whichever is greater.[79] Special valuation methods are provided for shopping centers, golf courses, open-space land, and common areas.[80] Arizona has no specific statutory provisions regarding reappraisals.

Real Property Tax Rates

The primary rate levied by localities is limited by a formula created by statute.[81] Additionally, taxes on residential property are subject to a ceiling of 1% (10 mills) of limited value.[82] County or community college districts may, with voters' approval, levy additional property taxes that exceed the limitation on the primary rate.[83] Such levies must remain in place for at least two years but not more than seven years.[84]

Personal and Intangible Property

Household goods are exempt from Arizona property taxes, so generally only personal property used for business is taxable.[85] Intangibles are also exempt, according to an Arizona Supreme Court decision which held that there is no adequate method for equalization and collection of intangibles under the state's existing tax structure.[86] Personal property is valued at acquisition cost less depreciation.[87]

Exemptions

Arizona does not offer a general homestead exemption. However, disabled persons and all surviving spouses meeting certain income limitations and having property assessments not exceeding $20,000 are entitled to a property tax exemption of $3,000.[88]

---

77. *Id.* § 42-11001.
78. *Id.*
79. ARIZ. REV. STAT. ANN. § 42-14401.
80. *See id.* §§ 42-11114, 42-13152, 42-13204, 42-13293, 42-13403.
81. *Id.* § 42-17051.
82. *Id.* § 42-17052.
83. *Id.* § 42-17201 to -17202.
84. *Id.*
85. *See* ARIZ. CONST. art. 9, § 2.
86. See Maricopa County v. Trustees of Arizona Lodge No. 2, 80 P.2d 955 (Ariz. 1983).
87. ARIZ. REV. STAT. ANN. § 42-13054(A).
88. ARIZ. CONST. art. 9, § 2.3; ARIZ. REV. STAT. ANN. § 42-11111.

General and Selective Sales

General Sales

During fiscal year 2004, 38.7% of Arizona's total tax revenue was generated by a transaction privilege tax and a use excise tax.[89] The transaction privilege tax is imposed on the gross proceeds of sales and the gross income from business activity of persons engaged in business activities classified as taxable.[90] In addition to the general retail classification which covers the sale of tangible property, the business classifications upon which the tax is imposed include the following services: amusement, transportation, and intrastate telecommunications.[91] The transaction privilege tax rate is 5.6%, except for transient lodging and mining, which are taxed at 5.5% and 3.125%, respectively.[92] In addition to the foregoing statewide rates, counties and cities are authorized to levy additional transaction privilege taxes.[93] Combined state and county rates in effect at the end of 2006 ranged from 6.1% to 6.6% for retail businesses.[94] Additional city privilege tax rates in effect at the same time ranged generally from 2% to 3%.[95]

Generally, food purchased at an eligible grocery business is exempt from Arizona's transaction privilege tax, while food purchased at a restaurant is not.[96] Other exemptions include prescription drugs, prescription eyeglasses and contact lenses, hearing aids, certain medical supplies and equipment, motor fuel subject to the separate motor vehicle fuel tax, and college textbooks.[97]

Selective Sales

Selective sales taxes constituted 9.8% of Arizona's total tax revenue during fiscal year 2004.[98] Of that amount, 4.1% came from motor fuel sales taxes.[99] Arizona residents paid an average of $117 per capita in state motor fuel sales taxes in 2004, an amount which ranked 35th nationally and was above the national average of $115.[100]

The tobacco product sales tax made up 1.7% of Arizona's tax revenue during fiscal year 2004.[101] Arizona residents paid $47.86 per capita in state tobacco sales taxes in 2004, an amount which ranked 25th nationally.[102]

---

89. Government Finances, *supra* note 46.

90. ARIZ. REV. STAT. ANN. § 42-5008.

91. *Id.* §§ 42-5062, 42-5064, 42-5073.

92. *Id.* §§ 42-5010(A) & (G). The transaction privilege tax rate will change to 5% on July 1, 2021. *Id.*

93. ARIZ. CONST. art.13, § 2; ARIZ. REV. STAT. §§ 9-284, 42-6104, 42-6107, 48022.

94. CCH-EXP, AZ-TAXRPTR ¶ 61-735, Local Rates, Table I.

95. CCH-EXP, AZ-TAXRPTR ¶ 61-735, Local Rates, Table II.

96. *See* ARIZ. REV. STAT. ANN. § 42-5061.

97. *See id.*

98. Government Finances, *supra* note 46.

99. *Id.*

100. STATE RANKINGS 2006, *supra* note 1, at 327.

101. U.S. Census Bureau, *supra* note 4.

102. STATE RANKINGS 2006, *supra* note 1, at 332.

In 2004, sales taxes on alcoholic beverages made up 0.3% of Arizona's total tax revenue.[103] Arizona residents paid $9.75 per capita in state alcoholic beverage taxes in 2004, an amount which ranked 36th nationally.[104]

The remainder of Arizona's selective sales taxes constituted 3.7% of its total tax revenue in 2004.[105] Of that percentage, 1.1% represented taxes on utilities and the other 2.6% represented taxes on other specific commodities, businesses, or services not reported separately above (e.g., on contractors, lodging, lubricating oil, fuels other than motor fuel, motor vehicles, meals, soft drinks, margarine, etc.).[106]

Corporate Income and Other

Corporate Income

The corporate income tax comprised 3.2% of Arizona's total tax revenue during fiscal year 2004.[107] This broad-based tax is calculated with federal taxable income as the starting point.[108] The tax applies to C corporations, while S corporations and other business entities are generally treated under the federal pass-through rules.[109] The tax is imposed at a rate of 6.968%.[110]

Other

During fiscal year 2004, all other taxes not previously mentioned generated $782.5 million, which comprised 4.7% of Arizona's total tax revenue.[111] Of that amount, $42.3 million came from the estate tax, which for Arizona residents was generally equal to the federal credit for the state death tax.[112] Note that Arizona's estate tax was repealed, the statute having become effective in 2005.[113] The "other taxes" category is further made up of various license taxes, documentary or stock transfer taxes, severance taxes, and all other taxes not listed separately or provided for in other categories.[114]

---

103. Government Finances, *supra* note 46.

104. STATE RANKINGS 2006, *supra* note 1, at 335.

105. Government Finances, *supra* note 46.

106. *Id.*; *See also* GOVERNMENTS DIVISION, U.S. CENSUS BUREAU, GOVERNMENT FINANCE AND EMPLOYMENT CLASSIFICATION MANUAL, at ch.7 (2000), *available at* http://ftp2.census.gov/govs/class/classfull.pdf [hereinafter CLASSIFICATION MANUAL].

107. Government Finances, *supra* note 46.

108. *See* ARIZ. REV. STAT. ANN. § 43-1101(1).

109. *See id.*

110. *Id.* § 43-1126.

111. Government Finances, *supra* note 46.

112. ARIZ. REV. STAT. ANN. § 42-4001 to 4-102.

113. ARIZ. REV. STAT. ANN. § 262-3.

114. *See* CLASSIFICATION MANUAL, *supra* note 106, at ch.7.

Burden Analysis

The overall state and local tax burden on taxpayers in Arizona is extremely regressive. Taxpayers in the lowest quintile — those with incomes of less than $15,000 — bear a tax burden equal to 12.5% of their income, while taxpayers in the top 1% — those with incomes that exceed $237,000 — bear a tax burden of just 6.6% of their income.[115] It is also worth noting that, although Arizona obviously has no control over federal tax policy, federal itemized deductions for state and local personal income and property taxes nonetheless further reduce the burden on taxpayers in the top 1% to 4.9%.[116] Furthermore, between 1989 and 2002, the tax burden on the bottom quintile rose by approximately 2.1%, while the burden on the top 1% actually fell by 0.5%.[117]

In terms of the income tax, the burden across income groups in Arizona is slightly progressive, with taxpayers in the lowest quintile bearing a tax burden of 0.1% and those in the top 1% bearing a tax burden of 3.9%.[118] In contrast, however, the sales and excise taxes imposed by Arizona are extremely regressive, with taxpayers in the lowest quintile bearing a tax burden of 8.7% and those in the top 1% bearing a tax burden of just 1.2%.[119] Property taxes in Arizona are also regressive, with taxpayers in the lowest quintile bearing a tax burden of 3.7% and those in the top quintile bearing an average tax burden of 2.0%.[120]

---

115. *See* Robert S. McIntyre et al., Who Pays? A Distributional Analysis of the Tax Systems in All 50 States 20 (2d ed. 2003), *available at* http://www.itepnet.org/wp2000/text.pdf. Taxpayers in the second quintile bear a 10.8% total tax burden on incomes between $15,000 and $25,000; those in the third quintile bear a 9.7% tax burden on incomes between $25,000 and $39,000; those in the fourth quintile bear a 8.9% tax burden on incomes between $39,000 and $65,000; those in the 80th–95th percentiles bear a 7.9% tax burden on incomes between $65,000 and $127,000; finally, those in the 96th–99th percentiles bear a 7% tax burden on incomes between $127,000 and $237,000. *Id.*

116. *Id.* Taxpayers in the second lowest quintile did not receive any benefit from these federal offsets, while those in the lowest quintile were able to reduce their individual tax burdens by 0.1%, those in the third quintile by 0.2%, those in the fourth quintile by 0.4%, those in the 80th–95th percentiles by 0.9%, and those in the 96th–99th percentiles by 1.2%. *Id.*

117. *Id.* at 21.

118. *See id.* at 20. Taxpayers in the second quintile bear a 1.3% income tax burden; those in the third quintile bear a 1.7% burden; those in the fourth quintile bear a 1.9% burden; those in the 80th–95th percentiles bear a 2.2% burden; finally, those in the 96th–99th percentiles bear a 2.8% burden. *Id.* Note, however, that these percentages include both individual and corporate income tax burdens; that within the 96th–99th percentiles, corporate income taxes represent 0.1% of this burden; and that in the top 1%, they represent 0.2% of this burden. *Id.*

119. *See id.* Taxpayers in the second quintile bear a 7.3% sales-and-excise tax burden; those in the third quintile bear a 5.8% burden; those in the fourth quintile bear a 4.5% burden; those in the 80th–95th percentiles bear a 3.4% burden; finally, those in the 96th–99th percentiles bear a 2.2% burden. *Id.*

120. *Id.* Taxpayers in the second quintile bear a 2.2% property tax burden; those in the third quintile bear a 2.2% burden; those in the fourth quintile bear a 2.4% burden; those in the 80th–95th percentiles bear a 2.4% burden; those in the 96th–99th percentiles bear a 2.1% burden; finally, those in the top 1% bear a 1.5% burden. *Id.*

Arkansas

General Information

Basic Profile – Geography, Population, and Industry

Admitted to the Union in 1836, Arkansas is commonly referred to as the "Natural State."[1] Arkansas is located in the southeastern region of the United States and is bordered by Louisiana on the south; Texas and Oklahoma on the west; Missouri on the north; and Tennessee and Mississippi on the east. Arkansas is in the central time zone, and its capital is Little Rock.[2] Arkansas ranks 32nd in population (approximately 2.78 million residents) and 29th in total area (53,179 square miles).[3] Its population is 81.4% white and 15.7% black.[4] The state is approximately 7% Catholic; 74% Protestant (of which 50% are Baptist); and less than 0.5% Jewish; 19% claim a religion outside the Judeo-Christian tradition or no religion at all.[5] Approximately 58% of Arkansas's population lives in urban areas.[6] Major industries include manufacturing, agriculture, forestry, business services, and tourism.[7]

---

1. STATE RANKINGS 2006, vi, 1 (Kathleen O'Leary Morgan & Scott Morgan eds., Morgan Quitno Press 2006).

2. *Id.* at vi.

3. *Id.* at 429.

4. Arkansas Quick Facts from the U.S. Census Bureau, http://quickfacts.census.gov/qfd/states/05000.html (last visited Jan. 27, 2007). The remaining population is made up of 1.0% Asian persons; 0.7% American Indian and/or Alaska Native persons; and 1.2% persons reporting two or more races. *Id.* Additionally, 4.7% of Arkansas's total population identify themselves as persons of Hispanic or Latino origin. *Id.* (noting that because Hispanics may be of any race, they are included within the other applicable race categories).

5. BARRY A. KOSMIN, EGON MAYER & ARIELA KEYSAR, AMERICAN RELIGIOUS IDENTIFICATION SURVEY 2001, at 41, *available at* http://www.gc.cuny.edu/faculty/research_studies/aris.pdf.

6. USDA Economic Research Service, Arkansas Fact Sheet, http://www.ers.usda.gov/StateFacts/AR.htm (last visited Sept. 17, 2006). According to the latest estimates, approximately 1.2 million people live in rural areas, and 1.6 people live in urban areas. *Id.*

7. ARKANSAS USA, 5 ARKANSAS DEPARTMENT OF ECONOMIC DEVELOPMENT, Arkansas USA, 5, Arkansas Department of Economic Development, http://www.1800arkansas.com/data_demographics/files/Arkansas%20Profile2005.pdf, (Oct. 2005), (Last visited Oct.13, 2006).

Family Income and Poverty Indicators

In 2004, Arkansas's per capita gross product was $29,419, which ranked among the bottom ten states nationally and was below the national average of $39,725.[8] During this same period, while the median household income in Arkansas was $42,590,[9] 17.6% of the state's population was living in poverty, which was substantially above the national average of 12.4% and ranked among the top ten states nationally.[10] More specifically, poverty affected 25.3% of Arkansas's children,[11] 12.8% of its senior citizens,[12] and 14.1% of its families.[13] Of its female-headed households with children, 48.0% lived in poverty,[14] and 49.8% of the state's public elementary and secondary school students were eligible for free or reduced-price meals.[15] Of those living in poverty, approximately 32.6% were black, which represented 32.0% of Arkansas's black population and 5.0% of its total population.[16] In an attempt to combat this poverty, Arkansas spent approximately $2.6 billion on public welfare programs in 2002,[17] which made up 19.8% of its total government expenditures.[18]

Arkansas's Public Elementary-Secondary School System

Overall Spending and Performance

For the 2003–2004 school year, Arkansas spent $6,740 per pupil in its public elementary-secondary school system, which was substantially below the national average of $8,182.[19] Of this amount, 12.5% was provided by the federal government, 72.1% was provided by the state government, and 15.4% was provided by the local governments,[20] with property taxes making up 7.8% of the total funding.[21] Out of these funds, Arkansas paid its elementary and secondary school teachers an estimated average an-

---

8. STATE RANKINGS 2006, *supra* note 1, at 89.

9. *Id.* at 96.

10. *Id.* at 495.

11. *Id.* at 497.

12. *Id.* at 496.

13. *Id.* at 498.

14. *Id.* at 499.

15. *Id.* at 532.

16. *See* Fact Sheet, American FactFinder, http://factfinder.census.gov/home/saff/main.html?_lang=en (select "Arkansas" under "Get a Fact Sheet for your community") (last visited Feb. 16, 2007). Note that these numbers are based on the 2000 census because more recent numbers were not available.

17. STATE RANKINGS 2006, *supra* note 1, at 500.

18. *Id.* at 502.

19. GOVERNMENTS DIVISION, U.S. CENSUS BUREAU, PUBLIC EDUCATION FINANCES 2004, at 8 tbl.8 (2006).

20. *See id.* at 5 tbl.5.

21. *See id.* at 4 tbl.4.

nual salary of $40,495 during the 2004–2005 school year,[22] and it provided a student/teacher ratio of 14.7, which was better than the national average of 15.9.[23]

In academic performance, Arkansas's fourth grade students scored lower than the national average in mathematics,[24] science,[25] and writing[26] and equal to the national average in reading,[27] while Arkansas's eighth graders scored lower than the national average in mathematics,[28] reading,[29] science,[30] and writing.[31]

Equity Issues

In 2004, revenues spent per student in Arkansas's highest poverty districts were determined to be $158 less than the revenues spent in its lowest poverty districts.[32] When adjustments were made for the additional costs of educating students growing up in poverty, however, the funding gap grew to $500.[33] On the other hand, Arkansas spent $445 more per student in its highest minority districts, although this amount fell to $253 when adjustments for low-income students were made.[34]

Fourth graders eligible for free or reduced-price school lunches had test scores that were 8.5% lower in mathematics,[35] 10.4% lower in reading,[36] and 12.2% lower in writing[37] than those of students who were not eligible. The results were generally better for eighth graders eligible for free or reduced-price lunches; their test scores were 7.8%

---

22. Thomas D. Snyder et al., National Center for Education Statistics, Digest of Education Statistics 2005, at 116 tbl.77 (2006).

23. *Id.* at 98 tbl.65.

24. National Center for Education Statistics, U.S. Department of Education, The Nation's Report Card: Mathematics 2005, at 14 fig.11 (2005), *available at* http://nces.ed.gov/nationsreportcard/pdf/main2005/ 2006453.pdf [hereinafter Mathematics 2005].

25. National Center for Education Statistics, U.S. Department of Education, The Nation's Report Card: Science 2005, at 16 fig.12 (2006), *available at* http://nces.ed.gov/nationsreportcard//pdf/main2005/2006466.pdf [hereinafter Science 2005].

26. Hilary R. Persky et al., National Center for Education Statistics, U.S. Department of Education, The Nation's Report Card: Writing 2002, at 23 tbl.2.2 (2003), *available at* http://nces.ed.gov/nationsreportcard/pdf/main2002/2003529.pdf [hereinafter Writing 2002].

27. National Center for Education Statistics, U.S. Department of Education, The Nation's Report Card: Reading 2005, at 14 fig.11 (2005), *available at* http://nces.ed.gov/nationsreportcard/pdf/main2005/2006451.pdf [hereinafter Reading 2005].

28. Mathematics 2005, *supra* note 24, at 16 fig.12.

29. Reading 2005, *supra* note 27, at 16 fig.12.

30. Science 2005, *supra* note25, at 28 fig.22.

31. Writing 2002, *supra* note 26, at 24 tbl.2.3.

32. The Education Trust, Funding Gaps 2006, at 7 tbl.3 (2006), *available at* http://www2.edtrust.org/NR/rdonlyres/CDEF9403-5A75-437E-93FF-EBF1174181FB/0/FundingGap 2006.pdf.

33. *Id.*

34. *Id.* at 7 tbl.4.

35. Mathematics 2005, *supra* note 24, at 20 tbl.5.

36. Reading 2005, *supra* note 27, at 20 tbl.5.

37. Writing 2002, *supra* note 26, at 75 tbl.3.24.

lower in mathematics,[38] 7.8% lower in reading,[39] and 12.7% lower in writing[40] than those of students who were not eligible.

In 2005, the Arkansas State Supreme Court found that the Arkansas public school-funding system was inadequate and unconstitutional, but it stayed the mandate that it be corrected until December 1, 2006.[41] Because the state legislature held a special session to increase school funding in April of 2006, the court decided to retain jurisdiction over the case for an additional six months and appointed two Special Masters to evaluate and examine the legislature's action and how it addressed the court's constitutional concerns.[42]

Availability of Publicly Funded Prekindergarten Programs

The Arkansas Better Chance (ABC) program currently serves children from birth until aged five who are from low-income families or are considered at risk, while the Arkansas Better Chance for School Success (ABCSS) program currently serves three-year-old and four-year-old children from families at or below 200 percent of the federal poverty level.[43] Total enrollment in these state-funded programs is 11,820.[44] The federally funded Head Start program enrolls an additional 9,377 children,[45] which represents 8.6% of Arkansas's three- and four-year-old children.[46]

Where Does Arkansas Get Its Revenue?

At the end of fiscal year 2004, Arkansas had total revenues of approximately $18 billion.[47] Of this amount, 39% was derived from state and local tax revenues and 24% was received from the federal government.[48] The remaining 37% came from other sources, including insurance trust revenue and revenue from government-owned utilities and other commercial or auxiliary enterprises.[49]

---

38. MATHEMATICS 2005, *supra* note 24, at 21 tbl.6.

39. READING 2005, *supra* note 27, at 21 tbl.6.

40. WRITING 2002, *supra* note 26, at 76 tbl.3.25.

41. Lake View Sch. Dist. No. 25 v. Huckabee, No. 01-836, 2005 Ark. LEXIS 776, at *33 (Ark. Dec. 15, 2005).

42. Lake View Sch. Dist. No. 25 v. Huckabee, No. 01-836, 2006 Ark. LEXIS 601, at *4 (Ark. Nov. 30, 2006).

43. W. STEVEN BARNETT ET AL., NATIONAL INSTITUTE FOR EARLY EDUCATION RESEARCH, THE STATE OF PRESCHOOL 2006, at 148 (2006), *available at* http://nieer.org/yearbook/pdf/yearbook.pdf.

44. *Id.*

45. *Id.*

46. *See id.* at 232.

47. U.S. Census Bureau, State and Local Government Finances 2003–04, http://www.census.gov/govs/www/estimate04.html (last visited Oct. 6, 2006) [hereinafter Government Finances].

48. *Id.*

49. *Id.*

Tax Revenue

Arkansas collected approximately $7 billion in state and local tax revenue during fiscal year 2004.[50] As a result, Arkansas residents paid $2,536 per capita in state and local taxes, an amount which ranked 48th nationally.[51] The different types of tax sources were apportioned as follows:

Individual income taxes	24.2%
Property taxes	15.8%
General and selective sales taxes	53.3%
Corporate income and other taxes	6.7%
	100.0%[52]

Federal Funding

During fiscal year 2004, 24% of Arkansas's total revenues came from the federal government.[53] For every dollar of federal taxes paid, Arkansas received $1.47 in federal expenditures, an amount which ranked 12th nationally[54] and was well above the national median of $1.17.[55]

Lottery

Arkansas does not operate a state lottery.

Legal Structure of Major Tax Sources

Income

Arkansas has a broad-based income tax imposed on individuals[56] that, while incorporating many aspects of the federal Internal Revenue Code, uses its own definition of adjusted gross income—which includes income from any source,[57] with certain listed exclusions such as gifts, discharges on indebtedness, etc.[58]—as a starting point for determining the state's taxable income.[59] All local governments have the power to impose

---

50. The total tax revenues were collected as follows: $5.6 billion by the state and 1.4 billion by local governments. *Id.*

51. *Id.*

52. *Id.*

53. *Id.*

54. The Tax Foundation, Federal Spending Received Per Dollar of Taxes Paid by State 2004, http://www.taxfoundation.org/taxdata/show/266.html (last visited Sept. 17, 2006).

55. *See id.*

56. Ark. Code Ann. § 26-51-201.

57. *Id.* § 26-51-404.

58. *Id.*

59. *Id.*

an income tax under Arkansas law.[60] During fiscal year 2004, Arkansas collected individual income tax of $613 per capita, an amount which ranked 31st nationally.[61]

In Arkansas, a typical family of four (i.e., married taxpayers who file jointly and have two dependent children) are not required to pay any income tax until their combined income exceeds $16,000, an amount which is below the national poverty line of $20,615.[62] Arkansas has a dual income tax–rate structure.[63] The first allows taxpayers who make under $16,600 and who do not take certain exemptions[64] to pay reduced amounts of income tax.[65] The second, Arkansas's regular income tax structure, contains six tax brackets that impose a minimum tax rate of 1% and a maximum tax rate of 7%.[66] When statutory exemptions and the standard deduction are taken into account, the maximum marginal rate applies to every dollar of income exceeding $34,100.[67]

Property

Overview

Arkansas has a typical property tax system that taxes the value of real estate and tangible personal property at the local level. Arkansas is constitutionally prohibited from levying a statewide property tax, but the state is able to collect uniform local levies for distribution to the localities.[68] During fiscal year 2004, Arkansas collected approximately $581 million dollars in property tax at the local level and approximately $520 million

---

60. *Id.* § 26-73-104.

61. STATE RANKINGS 2006, *supra* note 1, at 321.

62. JASON A. LEVITIS, CENTER ON BUDGET AND POLICY PRIORITIES, THE IMPACT OF STATE INCOME TAXES ON LOW-INCOME FAMILIES IN 2006, AT 12 (2007). In 2006, Arkansas taxpayers who were married and who were filing jointly could claim a standard deduction of $4,000. Arkansas provides a $22 credit per person instead of personal and dependent exemptions. ARK. CODE ANN. §§ 26-51-430, 26-51-501. Note, however, that the threshold calculation of $16,000 is greater than the sum of these deductions and exemptions because it includes additional tax benefits available to low-income families, such as the earned-income tax credit. *See* LEVITIS, *supra*.

63. ARK. CODE ANN. §§ 26-51-201, 26-51-301.

64. Choosing the Correct Table, http://www.state.ar.us/dfa/income_tax/documents/600-ChoosingTheCorrectTable.pdf (last visited April 4, 2007). Taxpayers taking either the $6,000 or $9,000 exemption for military income or the $6,000 exemption for employer-sponsored pension and/or qualified IRA distributions do not qualify for the reduced-rate table. *Id.*

65. ARK. CODE ANN. § 26-51-302. Arkansas's reduced rates are defined as follows: $0 for income up to $15,500; $80 for income between $15,501 and $15,600; $81 for income between $15,601 and $15,700; $83 for income between $15,701 and $15,800; $84 for income between $15,801 and $15,900; $86 for income between $15,901 and $16,000; $116 for income between $16,001 and $16,100; and $118 for income between $16,101 and $16,200. *Id.*

66. *Id.* § 26-51-202. Arkansas's middle rates are 2.5%, 3.5%, 4.5%, and 6.0%. *Id.*

67. The standard deduction of $4,000 and personal/dependent credits of $88, plus the threshold of taxable income for the highest tax bracket of $30,100, equals $34,188. *See supra* notes 62–66.

68. ARK. CONST. amend. 47.

in uniform local property tax at the state level, an amount which was then distributed to the localities.[69] In 2004, Arkansas residents paid $400 per capita in state and local property taxes, an amount which ranked 49th nationally.[70]

Defining the Real Property Tax Base

Arkansas does not have statutory classifications for real property. Agricultural land, pastureland, timberland, vacant residential property, and commercial land are valued at 20% of their productive-use value.[71] All other real property, including residential property used solely as the principal residence of the owner, is assessed at 20% of true and full market value or actual value.[72] True market value is generally determined by the application of standard appraisal methods, including the cost method, the income method, and the market-data method, all of which are commonly used throughout the country.[73] State law requires that all real property be reappraised at least once every three years, but any county that has completed a reappraisal from 2002 through 2004 is required to appraise all real property normally assessed by the county assessor at least once every five years from the previous assessment.[74] Principal places of residence and utility properties are subject to an assessment limitation formula which limits the total increase statewide to 10%, except for principal places of residence used as homesteads, the rates for which are capped at 5%.[75]

Real Property Tax Rates

Real property tax rates, composed of county, city, school district, and special levies, vary and are set by each locality. In 2003, the tax rates per $1,000 of assessed value ranged from $0.25 in Waldo School District in Columbia County to $0.58 in Umpire School District # 8 in Howard County.[76]

Personal and Intangible Property

Arkansas taxes personal property at 20% of its usual selling price.[77] Household goods, unless held for sale or rental or for commercial use, are constitutionally exempt from taxation.[78] Intangible personal property is exempt from tax at both the state and local levels.[79]

---

69. Government Finances, *supra* note 47.

70. STATE RANKINGS 2006, *supra* note 1, at 294.

71. ARK. CODE ANN. §§ 26-26-407, 26-26-303.

72. ARK. CODE ANN. §§ 26-26-1202, 26-26-303.

73. CCH-EXP, AR-TAXRPTR ¶ 20-615, Valuation Methods in General.

74. ARK. CODE ANN. § 26-26-1902.

75. ARK. CONST. amend. 79.

76. *Id.*

77. ARK. CODE ANN. § 26-26-201.

78. ARK. CONST. amend. 71.

79. ARK. CODE ANN. § 26-3-302.

Exemptions

The Arkansas Homestead Property Tax Refund Act allows certain lower-income residents 62 years old and older, disabled persons as defined in Title XIX of the Social Security Act, and non-service-connected disabled veterans who own and reside in their homes to receive a refund of part or all of real estate taxes paid up to $300.[80]

General and Selective Sales

General Sales

Arkansas imposes a general retail sales-and-use tax, which makes up 40.6% of the state's total revenue.[81] The Arkansas constitution grants the state the right to impose sales taxes and grants local governments the right to impose local sales taxes, subject to limitations imposed by the state.[82] This tax is imposed on all tangible personal property and certain enumerated services, including utilities and lodging.[83] The state sales-tax rate is set at 6%.[84] Local tax rates vary from a low of 0.0% in Monroe County to a high of 5% in the town of Dermott.[85] Major categories of exemptions from Arkansas sales tax include items purchased with food stamps and prescription drugs.[86] Arkansas does not exempt food purchased without food stamps or over-the-counter medications.

Selective Sales

Selective sales taxes make up 12.7% of Arkansas's total revenue.[87] Of that amount, 6.5% is made up of a motor fuel sales tax imposed at a rate of $0.215 per gallon of gasoline.[88] Arkansas residents paid an average of $165 per capita in state motor fuel sales taxes in 2004, an amount which ranked 7th nationally and was above the national average of $115.[89]

In 2004, sales taxes on alcoholic beverages made up 0.6% of Arkansas's total tax revenue.[90] Arkansas residents paid $15.00 per capita in state alcoholic beverage sales taxes in 2004, an amount which ranked 22nd nationally.[91]

---

80. *Id.* § 26-26-1118.
81. Government Finances, *supra* note 47.
82. Ark. Const. art. 2 § 23, art. 12, § 4.
83. Ark. Code Ann. § 26-52-112.
84. Ark. Code Ann. §§ 26-52-302, 26-52-107.
85. CCH-EXP, AR-TAXRPTR ¶ 61-735, Rates of Tax.
86. Ark. Code Ann. §§ 26-52-401, 26-52-406.
87. Government Finances, *supra* note 47.
88. CCH-EXP, AR-TAXRPTR ¶ 40-120, Tax Rates and Fees.
89. State Rankings 2006, *supra* note 1, at 327.
90. Government Finances, *supra* note 47.
91. State Rankings 2006 , *supra* note 1, at 335.

The tobacco product sales tax makes up 2.1%[92] of Arkansas's tax revenues. It is imposed at a rate of 32% of the wholesale price of all tobacco products[93] except for cigarettes, which are taxed at 29.5 mills ($0.59) per pack of 20.[94] Arkansas residents paid $53.25 per capita in state tobacco sales taxes in 2004, an amount which ranked 20th nationally.[95]

The remainder of Arkansas's selective sales taxes makes up 3.4% of its total tax revenue. Of this amount, 1.2% represents taxes on utilities and the other 2.2% represents taxes on other specific commodities, businesses, or services not reported separately above (e.g., on contractors, lodging, lubricating oil, fuels other than motor fuel, motor vehicles, meals, soft drinks, margarine, etc.). [96]

Corporate Income and Other

Corporate Income

The corporate income tax makes up 2.6% of Arkansas's total tax revenue.[97] Arkansas does not use Federal Taxable Income; rather, it provides its own definition of taxable income—which is income from all sources, minus statutory deductions.[98] The state's broad-based corporate income tax is imposed on the Arkansas net income of corporations doing business within Arkansas or receiving income from property in the state.[99] The marginal rate ranges from 1% to 6.5%, with the highest rate applying to every dollar above $100,000.[100]

Arkansas follows the federal income tax treatment of S corporations. Thus they do not pay Arkansas's corporate income tax; rather, income and losses flow through to their shareholders.[101] A similar treatment is afforded to limited partnerships, limited liability partnerships, [102] and limited liability companies, assuming they are treated as a partnership for federal tax purposes.[103] If, however, a limited liability company is treated as a corporation for federal income tax purposes, the entity is subject to Arkansas's corporate income tax.[104]

---

92. Government Finances, *supra* note 47.

93. CCH-EXP, AR-TAXRPTR ¶ 55-120, Rates.

94. *Id.*

95. State Rankings 2006, *supra* note 1, at 332.

96. U.S. Census Bureau, Classification Manual, Description of Tax Categories, http://ftp2 .census.gov/govs/class/classrev.pdf (last visited Sept. 26, 2006) [hereinafter Classification Manual].

97. *Id.*

98. Ark. Code Ann. § 26-51-404.

99. *Id.* § 26-51-205.

100. *Id.* Rates are 1% on the first $3,000 of income; 2% on the next $3,000; 3% on the next $5,000; 5% on the next $14,000; $940 plus 6% of excess over $25,000 on the next $75,000; and $5,440 plus 6.5% on the excess of $100,000 on all income over $100,000.

101. Ark. Code Ann. § 26-51-402.

102. *Id.*

103. *Id.*

104. *Id.*

Other

During fiscal year 2004, the collection of all other taxes not previously mentioned accounted for 4.1% of Arkansas's total tax revenue.[105] Of this amount, $21 million[106] was generated by the estate tax, which has been repealed in conjunction with the federal repeal of a credit for state estate taxes.[107] Part of the "other" taxes is generated by a separate franchise tax on a corporation's outstanding capital stock that is apportioned to Arkansas, which is taxed at a rate of 0.3%.[108] The "other taxes" category is also made up of motor vehicle license taxes, documentary and stock transfer taxes, severance taxes, and all other taxes not listed separately or provided for in other categories, such as taxes on land based on a specified rate per acre (rather than on assessed value).[109]

Burden Analysis

The overall state and local tax burden on Arkansas's taxpayers is very regressive. Taxpayers in the lowest quintile—those with incomes of less than $12,000—bear a tax burden equal to 10.7% of their income, while taxpayers in the top 1%—those with incomes that exceed $242,000—bear a tax burden of just 7.8% of their income.[110] It is also worth noting that, although Arkansas obviously has no control over federal tax policy, federal itemized deductions for state and local personal income and property taxes nonetheless further reduce the burden on taxpayers in the top 1% to 5.8%.[111]Furthermore, between 1989 and 2002, the tax burden on the bottom quintile rose by approximately 1.9%, while the burden on the top 1% rose by only 0.3%.[112]

In terms of the income tax, the burden across income groups in Arkansas is slightly progressive, with taxpayers in the lowest quintile bearing a tax burden of 0.2% and

---

105. Government Finances, *supra* note 47.

106. U.S. Census Bureau, State Government Tax Collections: Arkansas, http://www.census.gov/govs/statetax/0404arstax.html (Last visited Oct. 11, 2006).

107. Ark. Code Ann. § 26-59-55.

108. *Id.*§ 25-54-104.

109. *See* Classification Manual, *supra* note 96, at ch.7.

110. *See* Robert S. McIntyre et al., Who Pays? A Distributional Analysis of the Tax Systems in All 50 States 22 (2d ed. 2003), *available at* http://www.itepnet.org/wp2000/text.pdf. Taxpayers in the second quintile bear a 10.9% total tax burden on incomes between $12,000 and $20,000; those in the third quintile bear a 10.5% tax burden on incomes between $20,000 and $33,000; those in the fourth quintile bear a 9.6% tax burden on incomes between $33,000 and $55,000; those in the 80th–95th percentiles bear a 9.4% tax burden on incomes between $55,000 and $100,000; finally, those in the 96th–99th percentiles bear a 8.8% tax burden on incomes between $100,000 and $242,000. *Id.*

111. *Id.* Taxpayers in the lowest quintile did not receive any benefit from these federal offsets, while those in the second quintile were able to reduce their individual tax burdens by 0.1%, those in the third quintile by 0.0%, those in the fourth quintile by 0.2%, those in the 80th–95th percentiles by 0.7%, and those in the 96th–99th percentiles by 1.4%. *Id.*

112. *Id.* at 23.

those in the top 1% bearing a tax burden of 5.3%.[113] In sharp contrast, however, the sales and excises taxes imposed by Arkansas are extremely regressive, with taxpayers in the lowest quintile bearing a tax burden of 8.6% and those in the top 1% bearing a tax burden of just 1.4%.[114] Property taxes in Arkansas are also regressive, with taxpayers in the lowest quintile bearing a tax burden of 1.9% and those in the top quintile bearing an average tax burden of 1.3%.[115]

---

113. *See id.* at 22. Taxpayers in the second quintile bear a 1.4% income tax burden; those in the third quintile bear a 2.4% burden; those in the fourth quintile bear a 2.8% burden; those in the 80th–95th percentiles bear a 3.9% burden; finally, those in the 96th–99th percentiles bear a 4.6% burden. *Id.* Note, however, that these percentages include both individual and corporate income tax burdens; that within the second quintile, corporate income taxes represent 0.1% of this burden; that within the third quintile, they represent 0.0% of this burden; that within the fourth quintile, they represent 0.1% of this burden; that within the 80th–95th percentiles, they represent 0.0% of this burden; that within the 96th–99th percentiles, they represent 0.1% of this burden; and that in the top 1%, they represent 0.2% of this burden. *Id.*

114. *See id.* Taxpayers in the second quintile bear a 7.8% sales-and-excise tax burden; those in the third quintile bear a 6.9% burden; those in the fourth quintile bear a 5.2% burden; those in the 80th–95th percentiles bear a 4.1% burden; finally, those in the 96th–99th percentiles bear a 2.7% burden. *Id.*

115. *See id.* Taxpayers in the second quintile bear a 1.6% property tax burden; those in the third quintile bear a 1.2% burden; those in the fourth quintile bear a 1.5% burden; those in the 80th–95th percentiles bear a 1.4% burden; those in the 96th–99th percentiles bear a 1.5% burden; finally, those in the top 1% bear a 1.1% burden. *Id.*

California

General Information

Basic Profile – Geography, Population, and Industry

California was admitted to the Union in 1850. The "Golden State" is located on the Pacific Coast and is bordered by the Oregon on the north, Nevada on the east, Arizona on the southeast, and Mexico on the south. California is located in the Pacific time zone, and Sacramento is the state capital.

California ranks 1st in population (approximately 36.1 million residents)[1] and 3rd in total land and water area (163,696 square miles).[2] Its population is approximately 77.0% white, 6.7% black, and 12.2% Asian.[3] Additionally, 35.2% of its population identify themselves as persons of Hispanic or Latino origin.[4] The state is approximately 32% Catholic, 35% Protestant, and 2% Jewish; 31% claim a religion outside the Judeo-Christian tradition or no religion at all.[5] Roughly 98% of California's population lives in urban areas.[6] Major industries include real estate, rental, and leasing; professional and technical services; retail trade; information; finance and insurance; durable goods manufacturing; and health care and social assistance.[7]

---

1. STATE RANKINGS 2006, vi, 429 (Kathleen O'Leary Morgan & Scott Morgan eds., Morgan Quitno Press 2006).

2. *Id.* at 225.

3. California Quick Facts from the U.S. Census Bureau, http://quickfacts.census.gov/qfd/states/06000.html (last visited Jan. 31, 2007). The remaining population is made up of 1.2% American Indian and Alaska Native persons, 0.4% Native Hawaiian and other Pacific Islanders, and 2.4% persons reporting two or more races. *Id.*

4. *Id.* (noting that because Hispanics and Latinos may be of any race, they are also included within the other applicable race categories).

5. *See* BARRY A. KOSMIN, EGON MAYER & ARIELA KEYSAR, AMERICAN RELIGIOUS IDENTIFICATION SURVEY 2001, at 39, *available at* http://www.gc.cuny.edu/faculty/research_studies/aris.pdf.

6. USDA Economic Research Service, California Fact Sheet, http://www.ers.usda.gov/StateFacts/CA.htm (last visited Oct. 16, 2006).

7. *See* U.S. Department of Commerce Bureau of Economic Analysis, Gross Domestic Product by State, http://www.bea.gov/bea/newsrelarchive/2006/gsp1006.xls (last visited Apr. 1, 2006).

Family Income and Poverty Indicators

In 2004, California's per capita gross product was $43,266, which was above the national average of $39,725.[8] During this same period, although the median household income in California was $49,894,[9] 13.2% of California's population was living in poverty, which was above the national average of 12.4%.[10] More specifically, poverty affected 18.5% of California's children,[11] 7.8% of its senior citizens,[12] and 10.5% of its families.[13] Of its female-headed households with children, 34.2% lived in poverty,[14] and 47.9% of the state's public elementary and secondary school students were eligible for free or reduced-price meals.[15] Of those living in poverty, approximately 10% were black, which represented 20.8% of California's black population and 1.4% of its total population.[16] In an attempt to combat this poverty, California spent approximately $35.5 billion on public welfare programs in 2002,[17] which made up 15.1% of its total government expenditures.[18]

California's Public Elementary-Secondary School System

Overall Spending and Performance

For the 2003–2004 school year, California spent $7,748 per pupil in its public elementary-secondary school system, which was slightly below the national average of $8,182.[19] Of this amount, 11.4% was provided by the federal government, 54.5% was provided by the state government, and 34.1% was provided by the local governments,[20] with property taxes making up 24.9% of the total funding.[21] Out of these funds, California paid its elementary and secondary school teachers an estimated average annual

---

8. STATE RANKINGS 2006, *supra* note 1, at 89.

9. *Id.* at 96.

10. *Id.* at 495.

11. *Id.* at 497.

12. *Id.* at 496.

13. *Id.* at 498.

14. *Id.* at 499.

15. *Id.* at 532.

16. *See* Fact Sheet, American FactFinder, http://factfinder.census.gov/home/saff/main.html?_lang=en (select "California" under "Get a Fact Sheet for your community") (last visited Feb. 16, 2007). Note that these numbers are based on the 2000 census because more recent numbers were not available.

17. *Id.* at 500.

18. *Id.* at 502.

19. GOVERNMENTS DIVISION, U.S. CENSUS BUREAU, PUBLIC EDUCATION FINANCES 2004, at 8 tbl.8 (2006), *available at* http://www2.census.gov/govs/school/04f33pub.pdf.

20. *See id.* at 5 tbl.5.

21. *See id.* at 4 tbl.4.

salary of $57,876 during the 2004–2005 school year,[22] but in 2003, it provided a student/teacher ratio of just 21.1, which was far worse than the national average of 15.9.[23]

In academic performance, California's fourth and eighth grade students scored lower than the national average in mathematics,[24] reading,[25] science,[26] and writing.[27]

Equity Issues

In 2004, the funding per student in California's highest poverty districts actually exceeded that in its lowest poverty districts by $218.[28] When adjustments were made for the additional costs of educating students growing up in poverty, however, the funding in high poverty districts actually declined by $259.[29] On the other hand, California spent $160 less per student in its highest minority districts, and this amount grew to $499 when adjustments for low-income students were made.[30]

Fourth graders eligible for free or reduced-price school lunches had test scores that were 10% lower in mathematics,[31] 14% lower in reading,[32] and 17% lower in writing[33] than those of students who were not eligible. The results were somewhat better for eighth graders eligible for free or reduced-price lunches; their test scores were 10% lower in mathematics,[34] 9% lower in reading,[35] and 16% lower in writing[36] than those of students who were not eligible.

---

22. Thomas D. Snyder et al., National Center for Education Statistics, Digest of Education Statistics 2005, at 116 tbl.77 (2006), *available at* http://nces.ed.gov/pubsearch/pubs info.asp?pubid=2006030.

23. *Id.* at 98 tbl.65.

24. National Center for Education Statistics, U.S. Department of Education, The Nation's Report Card: Mathematics 2005, at 14 fig.11, 16 fig.12 (2005), *available at* http:// nces.ed.gov/nationsreportcard/pdf/main2005/ 2006453.pdf [hereinafter Mathematics 2005].

25. National Center for Education Statistics, U.S. Department of Education, The Nation's Report Card: Reading 2005, at 14 fig.11, 16 fig.12 (2005), *available at* http://nces.ed .gov/nationsreportcard/pdf/main2005/2006451.pdf [hereinafter Reading 2005].

26. National Center for Education Statistics, U.S. Department of Education, The Nation's Report Card: Science 2005, at 16 fig.12, 28 fig.22 (2006), *available at* http://nces.ed .gov/nationsreportcard//pdf/main2005/2006466.pdf [hereinafter Science 2005].

27. Hilary R. Persky et al., National Center for Education Statistics, U.S. Department of Education, The Nation's Report Card: Writing 2002, at 23 tbl.2.2, 24 tbl.2.3 (2003), *available at* http://nces.ed.gov/nationsreportcard/pdf/main2002/2003529.pdf [hereinafter Writing 2002].

28. The Education Trust, Funding Gaps 2006, at 7 tbl.3 (2006), *available at* http://www2 .edtrust.org/NR/rdonlyres/CDEF9403-5A75-437E-93FF-EBF1174181FB/0/FundingGap2006.pdf.

29. *Id.*

30. *Id.* at 7 tbl.4.

31. Mathematics 2005, *supra* note 24, at 20 tbl.5.

32. Reading 2005, *supra* note 25, at 20 tbl.5.

33. Writing 2002, *supra* note 27, at 75 tbl.3.24.

34. Mathematics 2005, *supra* note 24, at 21 tbl.6.

35. Reading 2005, *supra* note 25, at 21 tbl.6.

36. Writing 2002, *supra* note 27, at 76 tbl.3.25.

In *Serrano v. Priest I*, generally regarded, along with its succeeding case,[37] as the first of the modern-era education finance litigation decisions,[38] the Supreme Court of California held that the state's public school financing system violated equal protection provisions of the state constitution by conditioning the availability of school revenues upon district wealth, resulting in disparities in school revenue, and by making the quality of education dependent upon the level of district expenditure.[39] After the *Serrano* cases, various voter-initiated constitutional amendments and responsive pieces of legislation were aimed at directing funds to schools and at limiting the budgetary discretion of state lawmakers.[40] In 1999, California's school financing system was again attacked in *Williams v. California*, a case which was resolved by a settlement under which the state agreed to implement accountability measures, extra financial support, and other measures for low-performing schools.[41] An investigative report issued by Public Advocates in August 2006 indicated that a number of public schools were not complying with their obligations under the *Williams* settlement.[42]

Availability of Publicly Funded Prekindergarten Programs

The California State Preschool Program serves three-to-five-year-old children whose families have incomes below 230% of the federal poverty level or who have experienced or are at risk of abuse, neglect, or exploitation.[43] Additionally, the state funds various other programs that serve children younger than five but that are not distinct prekindergarten programs.[44] Total enrollment in the state-funded Preschool Program is 79,621,[45] which represents just 7% of California's 1,067,730 three- and four-year-old children.[46] The federally funded Head Start program enrolls an additional 89,355 children,[47] which represents 8% of California's three- and four-year-old children.[48]

---

37. Serrano v. Priest, 487 P.2d 1241 (Cal. 1971).

38. National Access Network, State by State, California, http://www.schoolfunding.info/states/ca/lit_ca.php3 (last visited Mar. 16, 2007).

39. *Serrano*, 557 P.2d 929 (Cal. 1976).

40. *See* Edsource, California School Finance Website, California School Finance History, http://www.californiaschoolfinance.org/FinanceSystem/History/tabid/68/Default.aspx (last visited Apr. 1, 2007).

41. *Id.*; *see* National Access Network *supra* note 38.

42. PUBLIC ADVOCATES, INC., SARD INVESTIGATION REPORT (2006), *available at* http://www.publicadvocates.org/SARC%20Investigation%20Report%2008-17-06%20(final).pdf (last visited Apr. 1, 2007).

43. W. STEVEN BARNETT ET AL., NATIONAL INSTITUTE FOR EARLY EDUCATION RESEARCH, THE STATE OF PRESCHOOL 2006, at 48 (2006), *available at* http://nieer.org/yearbook/pdf/yearbook.pdf.

44. *Id.*

45. *Id.* at 49.

46. *See id.* at 232.

47. *Id.* at 49.

48. *See id.* at 232.

Where Does California Get Its Revenue?

At the end of fiscal year, California had total revenues of approximately $358.7 billion.[49] Of this amount, 37% was derived from state and local tax revenues and 15% was received from the federal government.[50] The remaining 48% came from other sources, including the California Lottery, insurance trust revenue, and revenue from government-owned utilities and other commercial or auxiliary enterprises.[51]

Tax Revenue

California collected approximately $133.9 billion in state and local tax revenue during fiscal year 2004.[52] As a result, California residents paid $3,736 per capita in state and local government taxes, an amount which ranked 11th nationally.[53] The different types of tax sources were approximately apportioned as follows:

Individual income taxes	27.2%
Property taxes	25.8%
General and selective sales taxes	33.8%
Corporate income and other taxes	13.2%
	100.0%[54]

Federal Funding

During fiscal year 2004, 15% of California's total revenues came from the federal government.[55] For every dollar of federal taxes paid, California received $0.79 in federal funding, an amount which ranked 43rd nationally and was well below the national average of $1.17.[56]

Lottery Revenues

The California Lottery was born in 1984, when 58% of the state's voters approved the California State Lottery Act.[57] The Act requires that at least 34% of gross revenues

---

49. U.S. Census Bureau, State and Local Government Finances 2003-04, http://www.census .gov/govs/www/estimate04.html (last visited Oct. 6, 2006) [hereinafter Government Finances].

50. *Id.*

51. *Id.*

52. The total tax revenues were collected as follows: $85.7 billion by the state and 48.2 billion by local governments. *Id.*

53. *Id.*

54. *Id.*

55. Government Finances, *supra* note 49.

56. *See* The Tax Foundation, Federal Spending Received Per Dollar of Taxes Paid by State 2004, http://www.taxfoundation.org/taxdata/show/266.html (last visited Oct. 16, 2006).

57. The California Lottery, About the Lottery, http://www.calottery.com/Media/Facts/About/ (last visited Dec. 18, 2006).

(before payment of prizes) be used for public education.[58] In 2005, the Lottery had gross revenues of $3.4 billion and transferred roughly $1.2 billion to the state's education fund.[59]

Legal Structures of Major Tax Sources

Income

California employs a broad-based income tax that uses adjusted gross income for federal income tax purposes as a starting point for determining the state's taxable income.[60] However, a fairly large number of adjustments may be available to various individuals in calculating this amount.[61] Localities in California are denied the power to impose income taxes.[62] During fiscal year 2004, California collected personal income tax of $1,016 per capita, an amount which ranked 6th nationally.[63]

In California, a typical family of four (i.e., married taxpayers who file jointly and have two dependent children) are not required to pay any income tax until their combined income exceeds $44,700, an amount which is well above the national poverty line of $20,615 and ranks 1st nationally.[64] California's income tax structure contains six tax brackets that impose a minimum marginal rate of 1% and a maximum marginal rate of 9.3%.[65] When the standard deduction is taken into account, the maximum marginal rate applies to every dollar of income exceeding $93,754.[66]

Beginning in 2005, California began imposing an additional 1% personal income tax on the portion of a taxpayer's income in excess of $1 million, with revenues from this tax used to support local government mental health services.[67]

---

58. *See* Cal. Rev. & Tax Code § 17071.

59. The California Lottery, 2005 Comprehensive Annual Financial Report, http://www.calottery.com/Media/Publications/Financials/ (follow "2005 Comprehensive Annual Report" link) (last visited Apr. 1, 2007).

60. *See* Cal. Rev. & Tax Code § 17071.

61. *See id.* §§ 17081–17168.

62. *Id.* § 17041.5.

63. State Rankings 2006, *supra* note 1, at 321.

64. Jason A. Levitis, Center on Budget and Policy Priorities, The Impact of State Income Taxes on Low-Income Families in 2006, at 12 (2007). In 2006, California taxpayers who were married and filing jointly could claim a standard deduction of $6,820, a combined personal exemption *credit* of $182, and dependent exemption *credits* of $285 for each dependent. Cal. Rev. & Tax Code §§ 17073, 17054; California Franchise Tax Board, 2006 Form 540 (2006), *available at* http://www.ftb.ca.gov/forms/06_forms/06_540.pdf?refresh=39099 (last visited Mar. 26, 2007). Note, however, that the threshold calculation of $44,700 is greater than the standard deduction because it includes additional tax benefits available to low-income families, such as the earned-income tax credit. *See* Levitis, *supra*.

65. Cal. Rev. & Tax Code § 17041. The rates applied to California's middle four brackets are 2%, 4%, 6%, and 8%. *Id.*

66. The standard deduction of $6,820, plus the threshold of taxable income for the highest tax bracket of $86,934, equals $93,754. *See supra* notes 64–65.

67. *See* Cal. Rev. & Tax Code § 17043.

Property

Overview

California has a typical property tax system that taxes the value of real and tangible personal property at the local and state levels. California localities collected roughly $32.4 billion in property taxes during fiscal year 2004, and the state collected $2.1 billion.[68] As a result, California residents paid $963 per capita in property taxes, an amount which ranked 29th nationally.[69]

Defining the Real Property Tax Base

Although a California statute requires that real property be assessed at 100% of full value,[70] an acquisition value system was implemented in 1978 by Proposition 13.[71] Under this system, property is assessed at "full cash value," which means (a) its fair market value on March 1, 1975 or (b) for property which is purchased, newly constructed, or changes ownership after March 1, 1975, its fair market value on either (i) the date the purchase or change in ownership occurs or (ii) the date on which the new construction is completed, or if uncompleted, on the lien date.[72] The fair market value in the year of acquisition under Proposition 13 becomes the "base year value" and can be increased for inflation up to a maximum rate of 2% per year.[73] The following types of transfers are deemed not to constitute a "change in ownership" and thus do not trigger a revaluation: spousal transfers, certain parent-child transfers, certain grandparent-grandchild transfers, and transfers caused by government action.[74] Similarly, certain taxpayers are permitted to carry over the assessed value of their property to newly acquired property. Such taxpayers include persons whose property was damaged by misfortune or calamity; persons over 55 in some counties; and severely or permanently disabled persons in some counties.[75]

Real Property Tax Rates

The maximum state and local tax on real property is constitutionally limited to 1% of full cash value (10 mills or $10 per $1,000).[76] However, this limitation does not apply when voters approve a higher rate required to service local government bond debt.[77]

---

68. Government Finances, *supra* note 49.
69. *See id.*
70. Cal. Rev. & Tax Code § 401.
71. *See* Cal Const. art. XIIIA, § 1, 2; Cal. Rev. & Tax Code § 51.
72. *Id.*
73. Cal. Rev. & Tax Code § 110.
74. *Id.* §§ 63, 63.1, 68.
75. *Id.* §§ 69, 69.5.
76. Cal Const. art. XIIIA, § 1.
77. *Id.*

Personal and Intangible Property

Intangible property is statutorily exempt from taxation.[78] All tangible personal property is taxable unless specifically exempt[79] and is valued at current fair market value.[80] The aforementioned 1% constitutional rate ceiling for real property applies indirectly to personal property because the state constitution also requires that the tax rate on personal property cannot be higher than the rate on real property.[81]

Exemptions

California permits a homestead exemption of $7,000.[82] Additionally, homeowners and renters with qualifying income levels who are older than 62, blind, or disabled are eligible to claim property tax reimbursement payments of a percentage of property taxes assessed on the first $34,000 of the home's value.[83] All veterans and their surviving spouses are eligible for a property tax exemption of $4,000 if they own property valued at less than $10,000 if married or $5,000 if single.[84] Certain disabled veterans are entitled to a homestead exemption of $100,000, or of $150,000 if that veteran's income does not exceed $40,000.[85] Other exemptions from property taxes include household items and personal property, intangibles, and motor vehicles subject to registration.[86]

General and Selective Sales

General Sales

California imposes a general retail sales-and-use tax, which makes up 25.6% of the state's total tax revenue.[87] This tax is imposed on the sale of tangible personal property.[88] Service transactions are not generally subject to the tax, except for certain fabrication services.[89] The statewide sales-and-use tax rate is currently 7.25%, which includes a 1% local component.[90] Local taxing districts, which overlap in some areas but

---

78. Cal Const. art. XIII, § 2; Cal. Rev. & Tax Code § 212.
79. Cal Const. art. XIII, § 2.
80. Cal. Rev. & Tax Code § 401.
81. Cal Const. art. XIII, § 2.
82. *Id.* § 3; Cal. Rev. & Tax Code § 218.
83. Cal. Rev. & Tax Code § 20542. The percentage varies inversely with total household income, ranging from 139% to 6%. *Id.* § 20543.
84. Cal Const. art. XIII, §§ 3, 3.5; Cal. Rev. & Tax Code § 205.1.
85. Cal. Rev. & Tax Code § 205.5.
86. Cal. Rev. & Tax Code §§ 224, 212, 10758.
87. Government Finances, *supra* note 49.
88. Cal. Rev. & Tax Code § 6051.
89. *Id* § 6006(b).
90. California State Board of Equalization, Detailed Description of the Sales and Use Tax Rate, http://www.boe.ca.gov/news/sp111500att.htm (last visited Apr. 1, 2007).

are not present in others, may add rates ranging from 0.10% to 1.0% per district.[91] Sales-and-use tax rates in effect in California cities in 2007 ranged from 7.25% to 8.75%.[92] Exemptions from the sales-and-use tax include food products,[93] certain utilities,[94] certain medical devices and equipment,[95] and prescription medicines.[96]

Selective Sales

Selective sales taxes constituted 8.1% of California's total tax revenue during fiscal year 2004.[97] Of that amount, 2.5% came from motor fuel sales taxes.[98] California residents paid an average of $93 per capita in state motor fuel sales taxes in 2004, an amount which ranked 45th nationally and was below the national average of $115.[99]

The tobacco product sales tax made up 0.8% of California's tax revenue during fiscal year 2004.[100] The state's residents paid $30.18 per capita in state tobacco sales taxes in 2004, an amount which ranked 34th nationally.[101]

In 2004, sales taxes on alcoholic beverages made up 0.2% of California's total tax revenue.[102] California residents paid $8.73 per capita in state alcoholic beverage sales taxes in 2004, an amount which ranked 39th nationally.[103]

The remainder of California's selective sales taxes constituted 4.6% of its total tax revenue in 2004.[104] Of that percentage, 2.1% represented taxes on utilities and the other 2.5% represented taxes on other specific commodities, businesses, or services not reported separately above (e.g., on contractors, lodging, lubricating oil, fuels other than motor fuel, motor vehicles, meals, soft drinks, margarine, etc.).[105]

---

91. California State Board of Equalization, California City and County Sales and Use Taxes, http://www.boe.ca.gov/sutax/pam71.htm (last visited Apr. 1, 2007).

92. California State Board of Equalization, Publication 71, California City and County sales and Use Tax Rates at 4–18 (2007), *available at* http://www.boe.ca.gov/pdf/pub71.pdf (last visited Apr. 1, 2006).

93. Cal. Rev. & Tax Code § 6359. The exemption does not generally apply to food products served as meals, sold for immediate consumption, or sold through a vending machine. *Id.*

94. Cal. Rev. & Tax Code §§ 6353.

95. *Id.* §§ 6108.7, 6369.1, 6369.2, 6369.5.

96. *Id.* §§ 6359(c), 6369, 6368.1.

97. Government Finances, *supra* note 49.

98. *Id.*

99. State Rankings 2006, *supra* note 1, at 327.

100. Government Finances, *supra* note 49.

101. State Rankings 2006, *supra* note 1, at 332.

102. Government Finances, *supra* note 49.

103. State Rankings 2006, *supra* note 1, at 335.

104. Government Finances, *supra* note 49.

105. *Id. See also* Governments Division, U.S. Census Bureau, Government Finance and Employment Classification Manual, at ch.7 (2000), *available at* http://ftp2.census.gov/govs/class/classfull.pdf [hereinafter Classification Manual].

Corporate Income and Other

Corporate Income

The corporate franchise and income taxes comprise 5.2% of California's total tax revenue.[106] The corporate franchise tax applies to applicable entities that are doing business in California, are incorporated in California, or have obtained a certificate of qualification to transact intrastate business; the corporate income tax applies to corporations that are not subject to the franchise tax but derive income from California sources.[107] These broad-based taxes are calculated with federal taxable income as the starting point,[108] although taxpayers with no federal filing requirement or that maintain separate records for state purposes may choose an alternate computation method.[109] The franchise and income taxes apply to C corporations,[110] but California generally adopts the federal income tax pass-through treatment of partnerships and limited liability companies.[111] California does impose an entity level tax on S corporations, although the rate is much lower than that for C corporations and income and losses still flow through to S corporation shareholders.[112] The current franchise and corporate income tax rates are as follows: 10.84% for C corporations that are financial institutions; 8.84% for other C corporations; 3.5% for S corporations that are financial institutions; and 1.5% for other S corporations.[113]

Other

During fiscal year 2004, the collection of all other taxes not previously mentioned generated $10.9 billion, which comprised 8.1% of California's total tax revenue.[114] Of that amount, $574.5 million came from estate taxes, which are equal to the maximum amount of the federal credit allowable for state death taxes.[115] Although the California estate tax statutes are still in effect, the repeal of the federal credit for state death taxes[116] has effectively eliminated the California estate taxes.[117] The "other taxes" category is further made up of various license taxes, documentary or stock transfer

---

106. Government Finances, *supra* note 49.

107. *See* Cal. Rev. & Tax Code §§ 23151, 13501.

108. *See id.* § 24271.

109. *See* State of California Franchise Tax Board, 2006 Form 100 Booklet (2006), *available at* http://www.ftb.ca.gov/forms/06_forms/06_100bk.pdf (last visited Jan. 3, 2007).

110. Cal. Rev. & Tax Code § 23151.

111. *See id.* §§ 17851, 23038(b).

112. *Id.* § 23800(a).

113. *Id.* §§ 23151, 23186, 23802, 23186.

114. Government Finances, *supra* note 49.

115. Cal. Rev. & Tax Code § 13302.

116. *See* Economic Growth and Tax Relief Reconciliation Act of 2001, Pub. L. No. 107-16 (2001).

117. *See* California State Controller, California Estate Tax, http://www.sco.ca.gov/col/tax-info/estate/index.shtml (last visited Jan. 29, 2007).

taxes, severance taxes, and all other taxes not listed separately or provided for in other categories.[118]

Burden Analysis

The overall state and local tax burden on California's taxpayers is somewhat regressive, although California is one of the nation's least regressive states.[119] Taxpayers in the lowest quintile—those with incomes of less than $18,000—bear a tax burden of 11.3% of their income, while taxpayers in the top 1%—those with incomes that exceed $567,000—bear a tax burden of just 10.6% of their income.[120] It is also worth noting that, although California obviously has no control over federal tax policy, federal itemized deductions for state and local personal income and property taxes nonetheless further reduce the burden on taxpayers in the top 1% to 7.2%.[121] Furthermore, between 1989 and 2002, the tax burden on the bottom quintile rose by approximately 1.1%, while the burden on the top 1% fell by 0.2%.[122]

In terms of the income tax, the burden across income groups in California is moderately progressive, with taxpayers in the lowest quintile bearing a tax burden of 0.2% and those in the top 1% bearing a tax burden of 8.4%.[123] In sharp contrast, however, the sales and excise taxes imposed by California are extremely regressive, with taxpayers in the lowest quintile bearing a tax burden of 8.6% and those in the top 1% bear-

---

118. *See* CLASSIFICATION MANUAL, *supra* note 105, at ch.7.

119. *See* ROBERT S. MCINTYRE ET AL., WHO PAYS? A DISTRIBUTIONAL ANALYSIS OF THE TAX SYSTEMS IN ALL 50 STATES 24 (2d ed. 2003), *available at* http://www.itepnet.org/wp2000/text.pdf.

120. *See id.* Taxpayers in the second quintile bear a 10.2% total tax burden on incomes between $18,000 and $30,000; those in the third quintile bear a 9.4% tax burden on incomes between $30,000 and $47,000; those in the fourth quintile bear a 9.3% tax burden on incomes between $47,000 and $80,000; those in the 80th–95th percentiles bear a 9.6% tax burden on incomes between $80,000 and $168,000; finally, those in the 96th–99th percentiles bear a 9.8% tax burden on incomes between 168,000 and $567,000. *Id.*

121. *Id.* Taxpayers in the lowest quintile did not receive any benefit from these federal offsets, while those in the second quintile were able to reduce their individual tax burdens by 0.1%, those in the third quintile by 0.3%, those in the fourth quintile by 0.7%, those in the 80th–95th percentiles by 1.5%, and those in the 96th–99th percentiles by 2.2%. *Id.*

122. *Id.* at 25.

123. *See id.* at 24. Taxpayers in the second quintile bear a 0.8% income tax burden; those in the third quintile bear a 1.7% burden; those in the fourth quintile bear a 2.7% burden; those in the 80th–95th percentiles bear a 4% burden; finally, those in the 96th–99th percentiles bear a 5.6% burden. *Id.* Note, however, that these percentages include both individual and corporate income tax burdens; that within the fourth quintile, corporate income taxes represent 0.1% of this burden; that within the 80th–95th percentiles, they represent 0.1% of this burden; that within the 96th–99th percentiles, they represent 0.1% of this burden; and that in the top 1%, they represent 0.4% of this burden. *Id.*

ing a tax burden of just 1.2%.[124] Property taxes in California are also regressive, with taxpayers in the lowest quintile bearing a tax burden of 2.5% and those in the top quintile bearing an average tax burden of 1.9%.[125]

---

124. *See id.* at 24. Taxpayers in the second quintile bear a 7.3% sales-and-excise tax burden; those in the third quintile bear a 5.6% burden; those in the fourth quintile bear a 4.4% burden; those in the 80th–95th percentiles bear a 3.2% burden; finally, those in the 96th–99th percentiles bear a 2.1% burden. *Id.*

125. *See id.* at 24. Taxpayers in the second quintile bear a 2.1% property tax burden; those in the third quintile bear a 2.2% burden; those in the fourth quintile bear a 2.3% burden; those in the 80th–95th percentiles bear a 2.4% burden; those in the 96th–99th percentiles bear a 2.1% burden; finally, those in the top 1% bear a 1.1% burden. *Id.*

Colorado

General Information

Basic Profile – Geography, Population, and Industry

Admitted to the Union in 1876, Colorado is known as the "Centennial State."[1] It is located in the eastern Rocky Mountains and is bordered by Wyoming on the north; Nebraska, Oklahoma, and Kansas on the east; New Mexico and Arizona on the south; and Utah on the west. Colorado is located in the mountain time zone, and its capital is Denver.

Colorado and ranks 8th in size (104,094 square miles)[2] but 22nd in population (approximately 4.7 million residents).[3] Its population is approximately 90.3% white and 4.1% black.[4] The state is approximately 23% Catholic; 45% Protestant; and 1% Jewish; 31% claim a religion outside the Judeo-Christian tradition or no religion at all.[5] Nearly 86.0% of Colorado's population lives in urban areas.[6] Major industries include manufacturing, mining, tourism, and agriculture.[7]

Family Income and Poverty Indicators

In 2004, Colorado's per capita gross product was $43,454, which ranked 10th nationally and was above the national average of $39,725.[8] During this same period, while

---

1. STATE RANKINGS 2006, vi & 1 (Kathleen O'Leary Morgan & Scott Morgan, eds. Morgan Quitno Press, 2006).

2. *Id.* at 225.

3. *Id.* at 429.

4. Colorado Quick Facts from the U.S. Census Bureau, http://quickfacts.census.gov/qfd/states/54000.html (last visited Jan. 27, 2007). The remaining population is made up of 1.1% American Indian and Alaska Native persons; 2.6% Asian persons; 0.1% Native Hawaiian and other Pacific Islanders; and 1.8% persons reporting two or more races. *Id.* Additionally, 19.5% of Colorado's population identify themselves as persons of Hispanic or Latino origin. *Id.* (noting that because Hispanics may be of any race, they are included within the other applicable race categories).

5. BARRY A. KOSMIN, EGON MAYER & ARIELA KEYSAR, AMERICAN RELIGIOUS IDENTIFICATION SURVEY 2001, at 39, *available at* http://www.gc.cuny.edu/faculty/research_studies/aris.pdf.

6. USDA Economic Research Service, Colorado Fact Sheet, http://www.ers.usda.gov/StateFacts/CO.htm (last visited Feb. 17, 2007). According to the latest estimates, approximately 655,179 people live in rural areas 4 million people live in urban areas. *Id.*

7. Colorado.gov, http://www.co.gov/colorado-doing-business/ (last visited Sept. 17, 2006).

8. STATE RANKINGS 2006, *supra* note 1, at 89.

the median household income in Colorado was $51,022,[9] 9.8% of the state's population was living in poverty,[10] which was below the national average of 12.4%.[11] More specifically, poverty affected 14.2% of Colorado's children,[12] 7.6% of its senior citizens,[13] and 8.6% of its families.[14] Of its female-headed households with children, 34.2% lived in poverty,[15] and 30.2% of the state's public elementary and secondary school students were eligible for free or reduced-price meals.[16] Of those living in poverty approximately 6.3% were black, which represented 14.7% of Colorado's black population and 0.6% of its total population.[17] In an attempt to combat this poverty, Colorado spent approximately $2.8 billion on public welfare programs in 2002,[18] which made up 10.4% of its total government expenditures.[19]

Colorado's Public Elementary-Secondary School System

Overall Spending and Performance

For the 2003–2004 school year, Colorado spent $7,412 per pupil in its public elementary-secondary school system, which was slightly below the national average of $8,182.[20] Of this amount, 6.7% was provided by the federal government, 43.7% was provided by the state government, and 49.6% was provided by the local governments,[21] with property taxes making up 40.2% of the total funding.[22] Out of these funds, Colorado paid its elementary and secondary school teachers an estimated average annual salary of $44,161 during the 2004–2005 school year,[23] but during the fall of 2003, it provided a worse-than-average student/teacher ratio of 16.9.[24]

---

9. *Id.* at 96.

10. *Id.* at 495.

11. *Id.*

12. *Id.* at 497.

13. *Id.* at 496.

14. *Id.* at 498.

15. *Id.* at 499.

16. *Id.* at 532.

17. *See* Fact Sheet, American FactFinder, http://factfinder.census.gov/home/saff/main.html?_lang=en (select "Colorado" under "Get a Fact Sheet for your community") (last visited Feb. 16, 2007). Note that these numbers are based on the 2000 census because more recent numbers were not available.

18. *Id.* at 500.

19. *Id.* at 502.

20. GOVERNMENTS DIVISION, U.S. CENSUS BUREAU, PUBLIC EDUCATION FINANCES 2004, at 8 tbl.8 (2006).

21. *See id.* at 5 tbl.5.

22. *See id.* at 4 tbl.4.

23. THOMAS D. SNYDER ET AL., NATIONAL CENTER FOR EDUCATION STATISTICS, DIGEST OF EDUCATION STATISTICS 2005, at 116 tbl.77 (2006).

24. *Id.* at 98 tbl.65.

In academic performance, however, Colorado's fourth grade students scored higher than the national average in mathematics,[25] reading,[26] science,[27] and writing.[28] The state's eighth graders also scored higher than the national average in mathematics,[29] reading,[30] science,[31] and writing.[32]

Equity Issues

In 2004, revenues spent per student in Colorado's highest poverty districts were determined to be $70 less than the revenues spent in its lowest poverty districts.[33] When adjustments were made for the additional costs of educating students growing up in poverty, however, the funding gap grew to $440.[34] Similarly, Colorado spent $799 less per student in its highest minority districts, although this amount grew to $1,032 when adjustments for low-income students were made.[35]

Fourth graders eligible for free or reduced-price school lunches had test scores that were 9.7% lower in mathematics[36] and 10.3% lower in reading[37] than those of students who were not eligible. The results were generally the same for eighth graders eligible for free or reduced-price lunches; their test scores were 10% lower in mathematics,[38] 8.8% lower in reading,[39] and 16.5% lower in writing[40] than those of students who were not eligible.

---

25. NATIONAL CENTER FOR EDUCATION STATISTICS, U.S. DEPARTMENT OF EDUCATION, THE NATION'S REPORT CARD: MATHEMATICS 2005, at 14 fig.11 (2005), *available at* http://nces.ed.gov/nationsreportcard/pdf/main2005/ 2006453.pdf [hereinafter MATHEMATICS 2005].

26. NATIONAL CENTER FOR EDUCATION STATISTICS, U.S. DEPARTMENT OF EDUCATION, THE NATION'S REPORT CARD: READING 2005, at 14 fig.11 (2005), *available at* http://nces.ed.gov/nationsreportcard/pdf/main2005/2006451.pdf [hereinafter READING 2005].

27. NATIONAL CENTER FOR EDUCATION STATISTICS, U.S. DEPARTMENT OF EDUCATION, THE NATION'S REPORT CARD: SCIENCE 2005, at 16 fig.12 (2006), *available at* http://nces.ed.gov/nationsreportcard//pdf/main2005/2006466.pdf [hereinafter SCIENCE 2005].

28. HILARY R. PERSKY ET AL., NATIONAL CENTER FOR EDUCATION STATISTICS, U.S. DEPARTMENT OF EDUCATION, THE NATION'S REPORT CARD: WRITING 2002, at 23 tbl.2.2 (2003), *available at* http://nces.ed.gov/nationsreportcard/pdf/main2002/2003529.pdf [hereinafter WRITING 2002].

29. MATHEMATICS 2005, *supra* note 25, at 16 fig.12.

30. READING 2005, *supra* note 26, at 16 fig.12.

31. SCIENCE 2005, *supra* note 27, at 28 fig.22.

32. WRITING 2002, *supra* note 28, at 24 tbl.2.3.

33. THE EDUCATION TRUST, FUNDING GAPS 2006, at 7 tbl.3 (2006), *available at* http://www2.edtrust.org/NR/rdonlyres/CDEF9403-5A75-437E-93FF-EBF1174181FB/0/FundingGap2006.pdf.

34. *Id.*

35. *Id.* at 7 tbl.4.

36. MATHEMATICS 2005, *supra* note 25, at 20 tbl.5.

37. READING 2005, *supra* note 26, at 20 tbl.5.

38. MATHEMATICS 2005, *supra* note 25, at 21 tbl.6.

39. READING 2005, *supra* note 26, at 21 tbl.6.

40. WRITING 2002, *supra* note 28, at 76 tbl.3.25.

The funding of Colorado's public elementary and secondary school systems was challenged on state constitutional grounds based on the substantial disparity between the funding of the wealthiest and the funding of the poorest school districts.[41] In *Lujan v. Colorado State Bd. of Education*, the Supreme Court of Colorado held that the Colorado constitution did not mandate absolute equality in educational services or expenditures. Furthermore, the court held that the children had not established that, as low-income persons, they were a distinct and insular suspect class. However, this litigation is credited with the enactment of the 1988 and 1994 Public School Finance Acts.[42] These initiatives require a state-guaranteed minimum funding threshold for all school districts.[43]

Availability of Publicly Funded Prekindergarten Programs

The Colorado Preschool Program currently serves four-year-old children who are considered at risk by meeting one of the state-provided criteria; three-year-olds are eligible if they meet three of the at-risk criteria.[44] Total enrollment in this state-funded program is 12,358,[45] which represents just 2% of Colorado's three-year-old children and 14% of its four-year-old children.[46] The federally funded Head Start program enrolls an additional 8,102 children,[47] which represents 4% of Colorado's three-year-old children and 7% of its four-year-old children.[48]

Where Does Colorado Get Its Revenue?

At the end of fiscal year 2004, Colorado had total revenues of approximately $38.7 billion.[49] Of this amount, 38% was derived from state and local tax revenues and 13% was received from the federal government.[50] The remaining 49% came from other sources, including the Colorado Lottery, insurance trust revenue, revenue from government-owned utilities, and other commercial or auxiliary enterprises.[51]

---

41. Lujan v. Colorado State Bd. of Education, 649 P.2d 1005 (Colo. 1982).

42. *Id.*

43. COLO. CONST. art. IX, §§ 1-17.

44. W. STEVEN BARNETT ET AL., NATIONAL INSTITUTE FOR EARLY EDUCATION RESEARCH, THE STATE OF PRESCHOOL 2006, at 50 (2007), *available at* http://nieer.org/yearbook/pdf/yearbook.pdf.

45. *Id.* at 51.

46. *See id.*

47. *Id.*

48. *See id.*

49. U.S. Census Bureau, State and Local Government Finances - 2003–04, http://www.census.gov/govs/www/estimate04.html (last visited Oct. 6, 2006) [hereinafter Government Finances].

50. *Id.*

51. *Id.*

Tax Revenue

Colorado collected approximately $14.6 billion in state and local tax revenue during fiscal year 2004.[52] As a result, Colorado residents paid $3,169 per capita in state and local taxes, an amount which ranked 25th nationally.[53] The different types of tax sources were approximately apportioned as follows:

Individual income taxes	23.4%
Property taxes	32.4%
General and selective sales taxes	37.0%
Corporate income and other taxes	7.2%
	100.0%[54]

Federal Funding

During fiscal year 2004, 13% of Colorado's total revenues came from the federal government.[55] For every dollar of federal taxes paid, Colorado received $0.79 in federal funding, an amount which ranked 41st nationally[56] and was far below the national average of $1.17.[57]

Lottery Revenue

The Colorado Lottery has been in operation since 1982. Under Colorado's constitution, all Colorado Lottery profits are to be used for the maintenance and preservation of Colorado's state parks and for educational purposes.[58] At the end of fiscal year 2006, the Lottery had total revenues of $445 million and net proceeds of $114 million.[59]

Legal Structures of Major Tax Sources

Income

Colorado employs a broad-based income tax[60] that uses adjusted gross income for federal income tax purposes as a starting point for determining the state's taxable in-

---

52. The total tax revenues were collected as follows: $14.2 billion by the state and 10.8 billion by local governments. *Id.*

53. *Id.*

54. *Id.*

55. *Id.*

56. The Tax Foundation, Federal Spending Received Per Dollar of Taxes Paid by State 2004, http://www.taxfoundation.org/taxdata/show/266.html (last visited Sept. 17, 2006).

57. *See id.*

58. Colo. Rev. Stat. §§ 24-35-202, 24-35-210.

59. The Colorado Lottery: Where the Money Goes, http://www.coloradolottery.com/about/proceeds.cfm?location=41 (last visited Feb. 17, 2006).

60. Colo. Rev. Stat. § 39-22-104.

come.[61] Taxes are collected only at the state level, and there are no exemptions, per se, to Colorado's personal income tax.[62] However, the state allows the same deductions as the federal government for determining taxable income.[63] During fiscal year 2004, Colorado collected individual income tax of $742 per capita, an amount which ranked 18th nationally.[64]

In Colorado, a typical family of four (i.e., married taxpayers who file jointly and have two dependent children) are not required to pay any income tax until their combined income exceeds $23,500, an amount which is above the national poverty line of $20,615.[65] Colorado's income tax structure employs a flat rate of 4.63% on all income after deductions.[66] When the standard deduction is taken into account, this flat rate applies to every dollar of income exceeding $10,300.[67]

Property

Overview

Colorado has a property tax system that taxes the value of real estate and limited personal property at the local level, with the state publishing the rates of the localities.[68] During fiscal year 2004, Colorado collected approximately $4.7 billion dollars in property tax at the local level.[69] As a result, Colorado residents paid $1,026 per capita in state and local property taxes, an amount which ranked 23rd nationally.[70]

Defining the Real Property Tax Base

Other than mining and oil and gas properties, for which special valuation rules apply,[71] Colorado has two classifications for real property valuation: residential property, which is assessed at 7.96% of actual value, and other property, which is assessed at 29% of actual value.[72] Actual value is generally determined by the application of stan-

---

61. *Id.*

62. *Id.* § 39-22-106.

63. *Id.* 39-22-104.

64. State Rankings 2006, *supra* note 1, at 321.

65. Jason A. Levitis & Nicholas Johnson, Center on Budget and Policy Priorities, The Impact of State Income Taxes on Low-Income Families in 2006, at 12 (2007). Colorado allows for a standard deduction of $10,300 but does not allow for any exemptions. *See* Levitis & Johnson, *supra*.

66. Colo. Rev. Stat. § 39-22-102 (includes dividends and capital gains as regular income).

67. The standard deduction, plus the threshold of income for the flat tax rate, equals $10,300. *See supra* notes 65–66.

68. Colo. Rev. Stat. §§ 39-1-101, 39-1-103; Colo. Const. art. X, § 3.

69. Government Finances, *supra* note 49.

70. *See id.*

71. Colo. Rev. Stat. §§ 39-1-102, 39-1-103, 39-1-106. The assessment ratio for residential property is set by the legislature every two years on the basis of a constitutionally mandated formula, and the 7.96% ratio applies for tax years 2005–2006. *Id.* § 39-1-104.2.

72. *Id.* § 39-1-104.

dard appraisal methods, including the cost method, the income method, and the market-data method.[73] All property is required to be reassessed every two years.[74]

Real Property Tax Rates

The tax rates imposed on real property vary and are set by each locality. However, the state requires that the rate imposed in any given year cannot exceed an amount that will generate revenues 5.5% greater than those in the preceding year.[75] The Colorado constitution allows each locality to vote to change the rate by referendum and permits appeals to exceed the maximum rate if need can be shown.[76]

Personal and Intangible Property

Colorado considers all non-real property as personal property.[77] Because of the provisions defining "property," however, most individual taxpayers are not required to pay taxes on personal property. Household goods, automobiles, and up to $2,500 of other items are exempt.[78] Intangible personal property is exempt from taxation.[79]

Exemptions

For individuals, household goods, automobiles, and up to $2,500 of other items are exempted.[80] For businesses, inventory is excluded.[81] Colorado offers a property tax deferment for homesteads of military personnel on active deployment[82] and for the low-income elderly.[83]

General and Selective Sales

General Sales

Colorado imposes a general retail sales-and-use tax, which makes up 37.0% of the state's total tax revenue.[84] This tax is imposed on the sale, distribution, renting, or furnishing of tangible personal property, as well as specified services.[85] These services include (1) provision of meals consumed on the premises and (2) lodging for fewer than sixty days.[86] The state sales-tax rate is 2.9%, and all localities may impose a local rate

---

73. CCH-EXP, PROP-TAX-GUIDE CO ¶ 20-615, Valuation Methods in General.
74. Colo. Rev. Stat. § 39-1-104.
75. *Id.* § 29-1-301.
76. Colo. Const. art. X, § 20.
77. Colo. Rev. Stat. § 39-1-102.
78. *Id.* § 39-1-102, 39-1-119.
79. *Id.* § 39-3-118.
80. *Id.* § 39-1- 119.
81. *Id.* § 39-1-121.
82. *Id.* § 39-3.5-101.
83. *Id.* § 39-3.5-102.
84. Government Finances, *supra* note 49.
85. Colo. Rev. Stat. § 39-26-104.
86. *Id.*

that has been approved by local referendum.[87] The highest local rate is 5% in Rico County and the lowest is 1% in five counties—for a maximum total of 7.9% and a minimum total of 3.9% at both the state and local levels.[88] Exemptions from Colorado's sales-and-use tax include, among other items, prescription and nonprescription drugs, food (not including prepared food) and food containers, school lunches, advertising materials, and textbooks.[89]

Selective Sales

Selective sales taxes make up 8.4% of Colorado's total revenue.[90] Of that amount, 4.1%[91] comes from a motor fuel sales tax imposed at a rate of $0.215 per gallon of gasoline.[92] Colorado residents paid an average of $130 per capita in state motor fuel sales taxes in 2004, an amount which ranked 23rd nationally and was above the national average of $115.[93]

In 2004, sales taxes on alcoholic beverages made up 0.2% of Colorado's total tax revenue.[94] Colorado residents paid $6.81 per capita in state alcoholic beverage sales taxes in 2004, an amount which ranked 42nd nationally.[95]

The tobacco product sales tax makes up 0.4% of Colorado's tax revenue and is imposed at a rate of $0.20 per pack of cigarettes.[96] Colorado residents paid $14.16 per capita in state tobacco sales taxes in 2004, an amount which ranked 46th nationally.[97]

The remainder of Colorado's selective sales taxes makes up 3.7% of its total tax revenue. Of this amount, 0.9% represents taxes on utilities and the other 2.8% represents taxes on other specific commodities, businesses, or services not reported separately above (e.g., on contractors, lodging, lubricating oil, fuels other than motor fuel, motor vehicles, meals, soft drinks, margarine, etc.).[98]

Corporate Income and Other

Corporate Income

The corporate income tax makes up 1.6% of Colorado's total tax revenue.[99] The state's broad-based corporate income tax is imposed at a flat rate of 4.63% on a cor-

---

87. *Id.* § 39-26-106.

88. CCH-EXP, CO-TAXRPTR ¶ 61-735.

89. Colo. Rev. Stat. § 39-26-701 – 39-26-721.

90. Government Finances, *supra* note 49.

91. *Id.*

92. Colo. Rev. Stat. § 39-27-102.

93. State Rankings 2006, *supra* note 1, at 327.

94. Government Finances, *supra* note 49.

95. State Rankings 2006, *supra* note 1, at 335.

96. Colo. Rev. Stat. § 39-28-103.

97. State Rankings 2006, *supra* note 1, at 335.

98. *See* Governments Division, U.S. Census Bureau, Government Finance and Employment Classification Manual, at ch.7 (2000), *available at* http://ftp2.census.gov/govs/class/classfull.pdf [hereinafter Classification Manual].

99. Government Finances, *supra* note 49.

poration's Colorado taxable income,[100] which is based on the corporation's federal taxable income.[101]

Colorado follows the federal income tax treatment of S corporations. Thus, they do not pay Colorado's corporate income tax; rather, income and losses flow through to their shareholders.[102] A similar treatment is afforded to limited partnerships and limited liability partnerships, as well as limited liability companies, assuming they are treated as a partnership for federal tax purposes.[103] However, if a limited liability company is treated as a corporation for federal income tax purposes, the entity is subject to Colorado's corporate income tax.[104]

Other

During fiscal year 2004, the collection of all other taxes not previously mentioned accounted for 5.6% of Colorado's total tax revenue. Of this amount, approximately $50.1 million was generated by the estate and gift tax,[105] which is calculated on the basis of the federal credit for state death taxes allowable by § 2011 of the Internal Revenue Code and is subject to the same flat rate as the state individual income tax.[106] The "other taxes" category is also made up of motor vehicle license taxes, documentary and stock transfer taxes, severance taxes, and all other taxes not listed separately or provided for in other categories.[107]

Burden Analysis

The overall state and local tax burden on Colorado taxpayers is very regressive. Taxpayers in the lowest quintile—those with incomes of less than $17,000—bear a tax burden equal to 9.9% of their income, while taxpayers in the top 1%—those with incomes that exceed $692,000—bear a tax burden of just 6.1% of their income.[108] It is also worth noting that, although Colorado obviously has no control over federal tax policy, federal itemized deductions for state and local personal income and property

---

100. Colo. Rev. Stat. § 39-22-101.

101. Id.

102. CCH-EXP, CO-TAXRPTR ¶ 10-240, Limited Liability Companies (LLCs)

103. Id.

104. Id.

105. Government Finances, supra note 49.

106. Colo. Rev. Stat. § 39-26-104.

107. See Classification Manual, supra note 98, at ch.7.

108. See Robert S. McIntyre et al., Who Pays? A Distributional Analysis of the Tax Systems in All 50 States 26 (2d ed. 2003), available at http://www.itepnet.org/wp2000/text.pdf. Taxpayers in the second quintile bear a 9.7% total tax burden on incomes between $17,000 and $30,000; those in the third quintile bear a 9.1 % tax burden on incomes between $30,000 and $47,000; those in the fourth quintile bear a 8.5% tax burden on incomes between $47,000 and $78,000; those in the 80th–95th percentiles bear a 8.0% tax burden on incomes between $78,000 and $154,000; finally, those in the 96th–99th percentiles bear a 6.8% tax burden on incomes between $154,000 and $692,000. Id.

taxes nonetheless further reduce the burden on taxpayers in the top 1% to 4.4%.[109] Furthermore, between 1989 and 2002, the tax burden on the bottom quintile rose by approximately 0.7%, while the burden on the top 1% actually fell by 0.2%.[110]

In terms of the income tax, the burden across income groups in Colorado is slightly progressive, with taxpayers in the lowest quintile bearing a tax burden of 1.0% and those in the top 1% bearing a tax burden of 4.1%.[111] In contrast, however, the sales and excises taxes imposed by Colorado are very regressive, with taxpayers in the lowest quintile bearing a tax burden of 6% and those in the top 1% bearing a tax burden of just 1.0%.[112] Property taxes in Colorado are also regressive, with taxpayers in the lowest quintile bearing a tax burden of 2.9% and those in the remaining quintiles bearing an average tax burden of 1.5%.[113]

---

109. *Id.* Taxpayers in the second lowest quintile were able to reduce their individual tax burdens by 0.1%, those in the third quintile by 0.4%, those in the fourth quintile by 0.7%, those in the 80th–95th percentiles by 1.2%, and those in the 96th–99th percentiles by 1.4%. *Id.*

110. *Id.* at 27.

111. *See id.* at 26. Taxpayers in the second quintile bear a 2.1% income tax burden; those in the third quintile bear a 2.8% burden; those in the fourth quintile bear a 3.1% burden; those in the 80th–95th percentiles bear a 3.4% burden; finally, those in the 96th–99th percentiles bear a 3.5% burden. *Id.* Note, however, that of the total income tax burden borne by the top 1% of taxpayers, 4.0% represents individual income taxes and 0.1% represents corporate income taxes. *Id.*

112. *See id.* Taxpayers in the second quintile bear a 5.4% sales-and-excise tax burden; those in the third quintile bear a 4.2% burden; those in the fourth quintile bear a 3.5% burden; those in the 80th–95th percentiles bear a 2.7% burden; finally, those in the 96th–99th percentiles bear a 1.7% burden. *Id.*

113. *See id.* at 26. Taxpayers in the second quintile bear a 2.2% property tax burden; those in the third quintile bear a 2.1% burden; those in the fourth quintile bear a 1.9% burden; those in the 80th–95th percentiles bear a 2.0% burden; those in the 96th–99th percentiles bear a 1.5% burden; finally, those in the top 1% bear a 1.0% burden. *Id.*

Connecticut

General Information

Basic Profile – Geography, Population, and Industry

Admitted to the Union in 1788, Connecticut is commonly referred to as the "Constitution State."[1] It is located in the northeastern region of the United States and is bordered by Massachusetts, New York, and Rhode Island. Connecticut is located in the eastern time zone, and its capital is Hartford.[2]

In 2005, Connecticut ranked 29th in population (approximately 3.51 million residents); the state ranks 48th in total area (5,543 square miles).[3] Connecticut's population is 84.9% white and 10.1% black.[4] Additionally, 10.9% of its population identify themselves as persons of Hispanic or Latino origin.[5] The state is approximately 44% Protestant; 32% Catholic; and 1% Jewish; 23% claim a religion outside the Judeo-Christian tradition or no religion at all.[6] Connecticut is mostly urban, with 91% of the population living in cities and towns.[7] Major industries include manufacturing, financial services, telecommunication and information, health care services, high technology, and tourism.[8]

---

1. STATE RANKINGS 2006, vi, 1 (Kathleen O'Leary Morgan & Scott Morgan eds., Morgan Quitno Press 2006).

2. *Id.* at vi.

3. *Id.* at 429.

4. Connecticut Quick Facts from the U.S. Census Bureau, http://quickfacts.census.gov/qfd/states/09000.html (last visited Jan. 27, 2007). The remaining population is made up of 3.2% Asian persons; 0.3% American Indian and/or Alaska Native persons; 0.1% Native Hawaiian and other Pacific Islanders, and 1.4% persons reporting two or more races. *Id.*

5. *Id.* (noting that because Hispanics may be of any race, they are included within the other applicable race categories).

6. BARRY A. KOSMIN, EGON MAYER & ARIELA KEYSAR, AMERICAN RELIGIOUS IDENTIFICATION SURVEY 2001, at 41, *available at* http://www.gc.cuny.edu/faculty/research_studies/aris.pdf.

7. USDA Economic Research Service, Connecticut Fact Sheet, http://www.ers.usda.gov/StateFacts/CT.htm (last visited Sept. 17, 2006). According to the latest estimates, approximately 0.3 million people live in rural areas, and 3.2 million people live in urban areas. *Id.*

8. "Connecticut Industry Clusters," Connecticut Department of Economic and Community Development, http://www.ct.gov/ecd/cwp/view.asp?a=1100&Q=249794&ecdNav=%7C, (Last visited Nov. 12, 2006).

Family Income and Poverty Indicators

In 2004, Connecticut's per capita gross product was $53,102, which ranked among the top ten states nationally and was above the national average of $39,725.[9] During this same period, although the median household income in Connecticut was $55,970,[10] 8.8% of Connecticut's population was living in poverty, which was substantially below the national average of 12.4% and ranked among the bottom ten states nationally.[11] More specifically, poverty affected 10.1% of Connecticut's children,[12] 6.6% of its senior citizens,[13] and 6.2% of its families.[14] Of its female-headed households with children, 30.0% lived in poverty,[15] and 25.4% of the state's public elementary and secondary school students were eligible for free or reduced-price meals.[16] Of those living in poverty, approximately 21% were black, which represented 18% of Connecticut's black population and 2% of its total population.[17] In an attempt to combat this poverty, Connecticut spent approximately $3.5 billion on public welfare programs in 2002,[18] which made up 14.3% of its total government expenditures.[19]

Connecticut's Public Elementary-Secondary School System

Overall Spending and Performance

For the 2003–2004 school year, Connecticut spent $10,788 per pupil in its public elementary-secondary school system, which was substantially above the national average of $8,182.[20] Of this amount, 5% was provided by the federal government, 35.3% was provided by the state government, and 59.7% was provided by the local governments,[21] with property taxes making up a substantial part of the total funding.[22] Out of these

---

9. STATE RANKINGS 2006, *supra* note 1, at 89.

10. *Id.* at 96.

11. *Id.* at 495.

12. *Id.* at 497.

13. *Id.* at 496.

14. *Id.* at 498.

15. *Id.* at 499.

16. *Id.* at 532.

17. *See* Fact Sheet, American FactFinder, http://factfinder.census.gov/home/saff/main.html?_lang=en (select "Connecticut" under "Get a Fact Sheet for your community") (last visited Feb. 16, 2007). Note that these numbers are based on the 2000 census because more recent numbers were not available.

18. STATE RANKINGS 2006, *supra* note 1, at 500.

19. *Id.* at 502.

20. GOVERNMENTS DIVISION, U.S. CENSUS BUREAU, PUBLIC EDUCATION FINANCES 2004, at 8 tbl.8 (2006).

21. *See id.* at 5 tbl.5.

22. Although none of the total funding has been specifically designated as provided by property taxes, 53.7% of the total funding comes from "Parent Government Contributions." *See id.* at 4 tbl.4., which is defined as "tax receipts and other amounts appropriated by a parent government and transferred to its dependent school system." *Id.* at app. A-1. This amount, how-

funds, Connecticut paid its elementary and secondary school teachers an estimated average annual salary of \$58,688 during the 2004–2005 school year,[23] and it provided a student/teacher ratio of 13.6, which was better than the national average of 15.9.[24]

In academic performance, Connecticut's fourth grade students scored higher than the national average in mathematics,[25] reading,[26] science,[27] and writing,[28] and Connecticut's eighth graders scored higher than the national average in mathematics,[29] reading,[30] science,[31] and writing.[32]

In 2005, the State of Connecticut challenged the No Child Left Behind Act as an unfunded federal government mandate.[33] A federal district court dismissed three of Connecticut's four claims, citing lack of subject matter jurisdiction.[34] The fourth claim, which asserted that the Department of Education arbitrarily and capriciously denied the state's requests for plan amendments, in violation of the federal Administrative Procedures Act (APA), because it failed to provide an adequate hearing before rejecting the state's requests, is still in litigation.[35]

Equity Issues

In 2004, the funding per student in Connecticut's highest poverty districts actually exceeded that in its lowest poverty districts by \$666,[36] although when adjustments were

ever, "[e]xcludes intergovernmental revenue, current charges, and miscellaneous general revenue." *Id.*

23. Thomas D. Snyder et al., National Center for Education Statistics, Digest of Education Statistics 2005, at 116 tbl.77 (2006).

24. *Id.* at 98 tbl.65.

25. National Center for Education Statistics, U.S. Department of Education, The Nation's Report Card: Mathematics 2005, at 14 fig.11 (2005), *available at* http://nces.ed.gov/nationsreportcard/pdf/main2005/ 2006453.pdf [hereinafter Mathematics 2005].

26. National Center for Education Statistics, U.S. Department of Education, The Nation's Report Card: Reading 2005, at 14 fig.11 (2005), *available at* http://nces.ed.gov/nationsreportcard/pdf/main2005/2006451.pdf [hereinafter Reading 2005].

27. National Center for Education Statistics, U.S. Department of Education, The Nation's Report Card: Science 2005, at 16 fig.12 (2006), *available at* http://nces.ed.gov/nationsreportcard//pdf/main2005/2006466.pdf [hereinafter Science 2005].

28. Hilary R. Persky et al., National Center for Education Statistics, U.S. Department of Education, The Nation's Report Card: Writing 2002, at 23 tbl.2.2 (2003), *available at* http://nces.ed.gov/nationsreportcard/pdf/main2002/2003529.pdf [hereinafter Writing 2002].

29. Mathematics 2005, *supra* note 25, at 16 fig.12.

30. Reading 2005, *supra* note 26, at 16 fig.12.

31. Science 2005, *supra* note 27, at 28 fig.22.

32. Writing 2002, *supra* note 28, at 24 tbl.2.3.

33. Conn. v. Spellings, 453 F.Supp. 2d 459 (D. Conn. 2006).

34. *Id.*

35. *Id.* at 502.

36. The Education Trust, Funding Gaps 2006, at 7 tbl.3 (2006), *available at* http://www2.edtrust.org/NR/rdonlyres/CDEF9403-5A75-437E-93FF-EBF1174181FB/0/FundingGap2006.pdf

made for the additional costs of educating students growing up in poverty, that excess narrowed to $59.[37] On the other hand, Connecticut spent $74 less per student in its highest minority districts, and this amount grew to $602 when adjustments for low-income students were made.[38]

Fourth graders eligible for free or reduced-price school lunches had test scores that were 10.4% lower in mathematics,[39] 14% lower in reading,[40] and 14.9% lower in writing[41] than those of students who were not eligible. The results were generally worse for eighth graders eligible for free or reduced-price lunches; their test scores were 12.7% lower in mathematics,[42] 10.7% lower in reading,[43] and 17.8% lower in writing[44] than those of students who were not eligible.

Availability of Publicly Funded Prekindergarten Programs

The Connecticut School Readiness program currently serves three-year-old and four-year-old children in priority school districts and in school districts with severe needs.[45] Total enrollment in this state-funded program is 7,392,[46] which represents just 8.7% of Connecticut's 85,220 three- and four-year-old children.[47] The federally funded Head Start program enrolls an additional 5,945 children,[48] which represents 7% of Connecticut's three- and four-year-old children.[49]

Where Does Connecticut Get Its Revenue?

At the end of fiscal year 2004, Connecticut had total revenues of approximately $29.3 billion.[50] Of this amount, 59% was derived from state and local tax revenues and 15% was received from the federal government.[51] The remaining 26% came from other

37. *Id.*

38. *Id.* at 7 tbl.4.

39. Mathematics 2005, *supra* note 25, at 20 tbl.5.

40. Reading 2005, *supra* note 26, at 20 tbl.5.

41. Writing 2002, *supra* note 28, at 75 tbl.3.24.

42. Mathematics 2005, *supra* note 25, at 21 tbl.6.

43. Reading 2005, *supra* note 26, at 21 tbl.6.

44. Writing 2002, *supra* note 28, at 76 tbl.3.25.

45. W. Steven Barnett et al., National Institute for Early Education Research, The State of Preschool 2006, at 148 (2006), *available at* http://nieer.org/yearbook/pdf/yearbook.pdf.

46. *Id.* at 53.

47. *See id.* at 232.

48. *Id.* at 53.

49. *See id.* at 232.

50. U.S. Census Bureau, State and Local Government Finances 2003–04, http://www.census.gov/govs/www/estimate04.html (last visited Oct. 6, 2006) [hereinafter Government Finances].

51. *Id.*

sources, including the Connecticut Lottery, insurance trust revenue, and revenue from government-owned utilities and other commercial or auxiliary enterprises.[52]

Tax Revenue

Connecticut collected approximately $17.22 billion in state and local tax revenue during fiscal year 2004.[53] As a result, Connecticut residents paid $4,921 per capita in state and local taxes, an amount which ranked 2nd nationally.[54] The different types of tax sources were apportioned as follows:

Individual income taxes	25.1%
Property taxes	39.5%
General and selective sales taxes	28.5%
Corporate income and other taxes	6.9%
	100.0%[55]

Federal Funding

During fiscal year 2004, 15% of Connecticut's total revenues came from the federal government.[56] For every dollar of federal taxes paid, Connecticut received $0.67 in federal funding, an amount which ranked 49th nationally[57] and was well below the national average of $1.17.[58]

Lottery

Connecticut has operated the "CT Lottery" since 1972.[59] Its proceeds are deposited into the state's general fund.[60] In 2005, the CT Lottery had operating revenues of $933 million and a net income of $268.5 million.[61] In 2005, the CT Lottery transferred $268.5 million to the Connecticut General Fund.[62]

---

52. *Id.*

53. The total tax revenues were collected as follows: $17.4 billion by the state and $12.0 billion by local governments. *Id.*

54. *Id.*

55. *Id.*

56. *Id.*

57. The Tax Foundation, Federal Spending Received Per Dollar of Taxes Paid by State 2004, http://www.taxfoundation.org/taxdata/show/266.html (last visited Sept. 17, 2006).

58. *See id.*

59. CT Lottery History, http://www.ctlottery.org/history.htm (last visited Nov. 12, 2006).

60. Conn. Gen. Stat. § 12-812.

61. CT Lottery Comprehensive Annual Financial Report Fiscal Year 2005, 24, *available at* http://www.ctlottery.org/images/CAFR-FY05.pdf (last visited Nov. 12, 2006).

62. *Id.*

Legal Structure of Major Tax Sources

Income

Connecticut employs a broad-based income tax imposed on individuals[63] that uses adjusted gross income for federal income tax purposes, with very few adjustments, as a starting point for determining the state's taxable income.[64] Connecticut has no provisions authorizing a local income tax.[65] During fiscal year 2004, Connecticut collected individual income tax of $1,235 per capita, an amount which ranked 3rd nationally.[66]

On the basis of the relevant statutory exemptions, a typical family of four (i.e., married taxpayers who file jointly and have two dependent children) are not required to pay any income tax until their combined income exceeds $24,100, an amount which is above the national poverty line of $20,615.[67] Each filing status contains two tax brackets that impose a minimum marginal rate of 3% and a maximum marginal rate of 5%.[68] When statutory exemptions are taken into account, the maximum marginal rate applies to every dollar of income exceeding $44,000. [69]

Property

Overview

Connecticut has a typical property tax system that taxes the value of real estate and personal property at the local level. During fiscal year 2004, Connecticut collected approximately $6.8 billion dollars in property tax at the local level.[70] In 2004, Connecticut residents paid $1,944 per capita in local property taxes, an amount which ranked 2nd nationally.[71]

---

63. Conn. Gen. Stat. § 12-700.

64. *Id.* § 12-701.

65. CCH-EXP, CT-TAXRPTR ¶ 15-040, Local Power to Tax.

66. State Rankings 2006, *supra* note 1, at 321.

67. Jason A. Levitis, Center on Budget and Policy Priorities, The Impact of State Income Taxes on Low-Income Families in 2006, at 12 (2007). In 2006, Connecticut taxpayers who were married and filing jointly could claim a personal exemption of $24,500 (reduced by $1,000 for each $1,000 the taxpayer's AGI exceeded $48,000), but Connecticut law does not provide a standard deduction or dependent exemptions. Conn. Gen. Stat. § 12-702. Note, however, that the threshold calculation of $24,100 is greater than the sum of these exemptions because it includes additional tax benefits available to low-income families, such as the earned-income tax credit. *See* Levitis, *supra*.

68. Conn. Gen. Stat. § 12-700.

69. The exemptions of $24,500, plus the threshold of taxable income for the highest tax bracket of $10,000, equals $34,500. *See supra* notes 67–68.

70. Government Finances, *supra* note 50.

71. *See id.*

Defining the Real Property Tax Base

Connecticut has four classifications of real property: farm, forest, open space, and unclassified.[72] Real property is assessed at 70% of the true and actual value, while farm, forest, and open-space properties are each assessed according to its current use.[73] "True and actual value" is not statutorily defined, but it is generally determined by the application of standard appraisal methods, including the cost method, the income method, and the market-data method.[74] State law requires that all real property be assessed every ten years.[75]

Real Property Tax Rates

The real property tax rates, which are composed of municipality, city, school district, and special levies, vary and are set by each locality. Taxes are levied in terms of dollars per $1,000 of taxable value and are collected locally.[76] In 2005, the tax rates per $1,000 of assessed value ranged from $14.02 in Darien to $65.00 in Bridgeport.[77]

Personal and Intangible Property

Connecticut imposes a tax on personal property unless it is exempt.[78] Personal property is assessed at 70% of the true and actual value.[79] "True and actual value" is not statutorily defined, but it is generally determined by the application of standard appraisal methods, including the cost method, the income method, and the market-data method, all of which are commonly used throughout the country.[80] Personal property is taxed at a separate rate from real property. The personal property tax rates, which are composed of municipality, city, school district, and special levies, vary and are set by each locality. Taxes are levied in terms of dollars per $1,000 of taxable value and are collected locally.[81] In 2005, the tax rates per $1,000 of assessed value ranged from $14.02 in Darien to $65.00 in Bridgeport.[82] Because Connecticut's property tax extends only to real[83] and personal property,[84] intangible personal property is not subject to tax.

---

72. CONN. GEN. STAT. § 12-63.
73. *Id.*
74. CCH-EXP, CT-TAXRPTR ¶ 20-615, Valuation Methods in General.
75. CONN. GEN. STAT. § 12-62.
76. *Id.* § 12-142.
77. CCH-EXP, CT-TAXRPTR ¶ 20-405, Rates of Tax.
78. CONN. GEN. STAT. § 12-43.
79. *Id.* § 12-71.
80. CCH-EXP, CT-TAXRPTR ¶ 20-615, Valuation Methods in General.
81. CONN. GEN. STAT. § 12-142.
82. CCH-EXP, CT-TAXRPTR ¶ 20-405, Rates of Tax.
83. CONN. GEN. STAT. § 12-64.
84. *Id.* § 12-43.

Exemptions

Personal property exempt from tax includes clothing,[85] household furniture,[86] computer software,[87] and aircraft.[88] There is also a reduction in property tax for certain qualifying senior citizens.[89] In addition, Connecticut has a homestead exemption that exempts the first $75,000 of value from taxation.[90]

General and Selective Sales

General Sales

Connecticut imposes a general retail sales-and-use tax, which makes up 18.2% of its total revenue.[91] This tax is imposed on all tangible personal property[92] and taxable services.[93] The state sales tax rate is set at 6%, except in enumerated circumstances.[94] Localities do not have the power to impose additional sales taxes.[95] Exemptions from Connecticut sales tax include food; food stamps; drugs; certain enumerated farm and agricultural equipment, supplies, and livestock; equipment and computers; certain meals; and clothing.[96]

Selective Sales

Selective sales taxes make up 10.3% of Connecticut's total revenue.[97] Of that amount, 2.7% comes from a motor fuel sales tax that is imposed at a rate of $0.25 per gallon of gasoline.[98] Connecticut residents paid an average of $131 per capita in state motor fuel sales taxes in 2004, an amount which ranked 22nd nationally and was above the national average of $115.[99]

The tobacco product sales tax makes up 1.6%[100] of Connecticut's tax revenues and is imposed at a rate of 20% of the wholesale price of all tobacco products[101] except for

---

85. CONN. GEN. STAT. § 12-81.
86. *Id.*
87. CONN. GEN. STAT. § 12-71.
88. *Id.*
89. CONN. GEN. STAT. § 12-170.
90. *Id* § 52-352b.
91. Government Finances, *supra* note 50.
92. CONN. GEN. STAT. § 12-411.
93. *Id.*
94. CONN. GEN. STAT. § 12-408.
95. CCH-EXP, CT-TAXRPTR ¶ 61-710, Local Power to Tax.
96. CONN. GEN. STAT. § 12-412. By definition, "food" does not include prepared food, soft drinks, tobacco, alcoholic beverages, dietary supplements, food from vending machines, or candy.
97. Government Finances, *supra* note 50.
98. CONN. GEN. STAT. § 12-458.
99. STATE RANKINGS 2006, *supra* note 1, at 327.
100. Government Finances, *supra* note 50.
101. CONN. GEN. STAT. § 12-330.

cigarettes and little cigars, which are taxed at 77.5 mills ($1.51) per pack of 20.[102] Connecticut residents paid $79.26 per capita in state tobacco sales taxes in 2004, an amount which ranked 6th nationally.[103]

In 2004, sales taxes on alcoholic beverages made up 0.3% of Connecticut's total tax revenue.[104] Connecticut residents paid $12.58 per capita in state alcoholic beverage sales taxes in 2004, an amount which ranked 28th nationally.[105]

The remainder of Connecticut's selective sales taxes makes up 5.7% of its total tax revenue. Of this amount, 1.1% represents taxes on utilities and the other 4.6% represents taxes on other specific commodities, businesses, or services not reported separately above (e.g., on contractors, lodging, lubricating oil, fuels other than motor fuel, motor vehicles, meals, soft drinks, etc.). [106]

Corporate Income and Other

Corporate Income

The corporate income tax makes up 2.2% of Connecticut's total tax revenue.[107] The state's broad-based corporate income tax is imposed at a rate of 7.5%[108] on the Connecticut net income of corporations doing business within Connecticut or receiving income from property in the state.[109]

Connecticut follows the federal income tax treatment of S corporations. Thus, they do not pay Connecticut's corporate income tax; rather, income and losses flow through to their shareholders.[110] A similar treatment is afforded to limited partnerships and limited liability partnerships, [111] as well as limited liability companies, assuming they are treated as a partnership for federal tax purposes.[112] However, if a limited liability company is treated as a corporation for federal income tax purposes, the entity is subject to Connecticut's corporate income tax.[113]

---

102. *Id.* § 12-296.

103. State Rankings 2006, *supra* note 1, at 332.

104. Government Finances, *supra* note 50.

105. State Rankings 2006, *supra* note 1, at 335.

106. *See* Governments Division, U.S. Census Bureau, Government Finance and Employment Classification Manual, at ch.7 (2000), *available at* http://ftp2.census.gov/govs/class/classfull.pdf [hereinafter Classification Manual].

107. Government Finances, *supra* note 50.

108. Conn. Gen. Stat. § 12-214.

109. *Id.* § 12-216.

110. *Id.* § 12-214.

111. CCH-EXP, CT-TAXRPTR ¶ 10-225, Limited Partnerships, Limited Liability Partnerships.

112. Conn. Gen. Stat. § 34-113.

113. *Id.*

Other

In 2004, the collection of all other taxes not previously mentioned accounted for 4.8% of Connecticut's total tax revenue.[114] Of this amount, $50 million[115] was generated by the succession and transfer tax, the estate tax, and the gift tax. The succession and transfer tax was phased out in 2005.[116] As of January 1, 2005, the estate tax is imposed only on taxable estates valued at more than $2 million.[117] The gift tax is imposed on taxable gift transfers after 1991.[118] The "other taxes" category is also made up of motor vehicle license taxes, documentary and stock transfer taxes, severance taxes, and all other taxes not listed separately or provided for in other categories, such as taxes on land based on a specified rate per acre (rather than on assessed value).[119]

Burden Analysis

The overall state and local tax burden on Connecticut's taxpayers is very regressive. Taxpayers in the lowest quintile — those with incomes of less than $21,000 — bear a tax burden equal to 10.3% of their income, while taxpayers in the top 1% — those with incomes that exceed $471,000 — bear a tax burden of just 6.4% of their income.[120] It is also worth noting that, although Connecticut obviously has no control over federal tax policy, federal itemized deductions for state and local personal income and property taxes nonetheless further reduce the burden on taxpayers in the top 1% to 4.4%.[121] Furthermore, between 1989 and 2002, the tax burden on the bottom quintile rose by approximately 0.6%, while the burden on the top 1% rose by only 0.8%.[122]

---

114. Government Finances, *supra* note 50.

115. *Id.*

116. CONN. GEN. STAT. § 12-344.

117. *Id.* § 12-391. *See also*, 2007 Tax Guide, State Taxes Connecticut, http://www.bankrate.com/brm/itax/edit/state/profiles/state_tax_conn.asp.

118. *Id* § 12-642.

119. *See* CLASSIFICATION MANUAL, *supra* note 106, at ch.7.

120. *See* ROBERT S. McINTYRE ET AL., WHO PAYS? A DISTRIBUTIONAL ANALYSIS OF THE TAX SYSTEMS IN ALL 50 STATES 28 (2d ed. 2003), *available at* http://www.itepnet.org/wp2000/text.pdf. Taxpayers in the second quintile bear a 10.3% total tax burden on incomes between $21,000 and $37,000; those in the third quintile bear a 10.4% tax burden on incomes between $37,000 and $60,000; those in the fourth quintile bear a 10.7% tax burden on incomes between $60,000 and $97,000; those in the 80th–95th percentiles bear a 9.8% tax burden on incomes between $97,000 and $220,000; finally, those in the 96th–99th percentiles bear a 8.6% tax burden on incomes between $220,000 and $471,000. *Id.*

121. *Id.* Taxpayers in the lowest quintile were able to reduce their individual tax burdens by 0.1% with federal offsets, while those in the second quintile were able to reduce their individual tax burdens by 0.3%, those in the third quintile by 0.8%, those in the fourth quintile by 1.5%, those in the 80th–95th percentiles by 2.0%, and those in the 96th–99th percentiles by 2.1%. *Id.*

122. *Id.* at 29.

In terms of the income tax, the burden across income groups in Connecticut is slightly progressive, with taxpayers in the lowest quintile bearing a tax burden of 0.3% and those in the top 1% bearing a tax burden of 4.7%.[123] In sharp contrast, however, the sales and excise taxes imposed by Connecticut are very regressive, with taxpayers in the lowest quintile bearing a tax burden of 6.3% and those in the top 1% bearing a tax burden of just 0.8%.[124] Property taxes in Connecticut are also regressive, with taxpayers in the lowest quintile bearing a tax burden of 3.8% and those in the top quintile bearing an average tax burden of 2.5%.[125] However, the most onerous burden is actually placed on the middle class, who pay an average of 4.3% of their income in property taxes.[126]

---

123. *See id.* at 28. Taxpayers in the second quintile bear a 1.2% income tax burden; those in the third quintile bear a 2.5% burden; those in the fourth quintile bear a 3.3% burden; those in the 80th–95th percentiles bear a 3.9% burden; finally, those in the 96th–99th percentiles bear a 4.2% burden. *Id.* Note, however, that these percentages include both individual and corporate income tax burdens and that within the top 1%, corporate income taxes represent 0.1% of this burden. *Id.*

124. *See id.* Taxpayers in the second quintile bear a 4.7% sales-and-excise tax burden; those in the third quintile bear a 3.7% burden; those in the fourth quintile bear a 3.1% burden; those in the 80th–95th percentiles bear a 2.2% burden; finally, those in the 96th–99th percentiles bear a 1.5% burden. *Id.*

125. *See id.* Taxpayers in the second quintile bear a 4.4% property tax burden; those in the third quintile bear a 4.1% burden; those in the fourth quintile bear a 4.3% burden; those in the 80th–95th percentiles bear a 3.7% burden; those in the 96th–99th percentiles bear a 2.9% burden; finally, those in the top 1% bear a 1.0% burden. *Id.*

126. *See id.*

Delaware

General Information

Basic Profile – Geography, Population, and Industry

Admitted to the Union in 1787, Delaware is known as the "First State."[1] It is located in the Mid-Atlantic region and is bordered by Pennsylvania and New Jersey on the north; the Atlantic Ocean on the east; and Maryland on the south and west. The state is located in the eastern time zone, and its capital is Dover.

Delaware ranks 49th in total area (2,489 square miles);[2] in 2005, the state ranked 45th in population (approximately 843,524 residents).[3] Delaware's population is approximately 74.9% white and 20.7% black.[4] The state is approximately 9% Catholic; 57% Protestant; and 1% Jewish; 33% claim a religion outside the Judeo-Christian tradition or no religion at all.[5] Nearly 79.1% of Delaware's population lives in urban areas.[6] Major industries include chemicals and engineering, exports, and banking and finance.[7]

Family Income and Poverty Indicators

In 2004, Delaware's per capita gross product was $65,385, which ranked 1st nationally and was well above the national average of $39,725.[8] During this same period, while

---

1. STATE RANKINGS 2006, vi & 1 (Kathleen O'Leary Morgan & Scott Morgan, eds. Morgan Quitno Press, 2006).

2. *Id.* at 225.

3. *Id.* at 429.

4. Delaware Quick Facts from the U.S. Census Bureau, http://quickfacts.census.gov/qfd/states/54000.html (last visited Jan. 27, 2007). The remaining population is made up of 0.4% American Indian and Alaskan Native; 2.7% Asian persons; 0.1% Native Hawaiian other Pacific Islanders; and 1.4% persons reporting two or more races. *Id.* Additionally, 19.5% of Delaware's total population identify themselves as persons of Hispanic or Latino origin. *Id.* (noting that because Hispanics may be of any race, they are included within the other applicable race categories).

5. BARRY A. KOSMIN, EGON MAYER & ARIELA KEYSAR, AMERICAN RELIGIOUS IDENTIFICATION SURVEY 2001, at 39, *available at* http://www.gc.cuny.edu/faculty/research_studies/aris.pdf.

6. USDA Economic Research Service, Delaware Fact Sheet, http://www.ers.usda.gov/StateFacts/DE.htm (last visited Feb. 17, 2007). According to the latest estimates, approximately 176,548 people live in rural areas, 666,976 people live in urban areas. *Id.*

7. Delaware Facts and Symbols, http://www.state.de.us/gic/delfacts/ (last visited Feb. 17, 2007).

the median household income in Delaware was $50,152,[9] 8.5% of the state's population was living in poverty,[10] which was below the national average of 12.4%.[11] More specifically, poverty affected 13.6% of Delaware's children,[12] 7.2% of its senior citizens,[13] and 7.6% of its families.[14] Of its female-headed households with children, 32.9% of them lived in poverty,[15] and 33.8% of the state's public elementary and secondary school students were eligible for free or reduced-price meals.[16] Of those living in poverty, approximately 37.7% were black, which represented 17.5% of Delaware's black population and 3.3% of its total population.[17] In an attempt to combat this poverty, Delaware spent approximately $659 million on public welfare programs in 2002,[18] which made up 12.3% of its total government expenditures.[19]

Delaware's Public Elementary-Secondary School System

Overall Spending and Performance

For the 2003–2004 school year, Delaware spent $10,228 per pupil in its public elementary-secondary school system, which was substantially above the national average of $8,182.[20] Of this amount, 8.1% was provided by the federal government, 64.0% was provided by the state government, and 27.9% was provided by the local governments,[21] with property taxes making up 22.6% of the total funding.[22] Out of these funds, Delaware paid its elementary and secondary school teachers an estimated average annual salary of $50,869 during the 2004–2005 school year,[23] and it provided a student/teacher ratio of 15.2, which was better than the national average of 15.9.[24]

---

8. STATE RANKINGS 2006, *supra* note 1, at 89.

9. *Id.* at 96.

10. *Id.* at 495.

11. *Id.*

12. *Id.* at 497.

13. *Id.* at 496.

14. *Id.* at 498.

15. *Id.* at 499.

16. *Id.* at 532.

17. *See* Fact Sheet, American FactFinder, http://factfinder.census.gov/home/saff/main.html?_lang=en (select "Delaware" under "Get a Fact Sheet for your community") (last visited Feb. 16, 2007). Note that these numbers are based on the 2000 census because more recent numbers where not available.

18. *Id.* at 500.

19. *Id.* at 502.

20. GOVERNMENTS DIVISION, U.S. CENSUS BUREAU, PUBLIC EDUCATION FINANCES 2004, at 8 tbl.8 (2006).

21. *See id.* at 5 tbl.5.

22. *See id.* at 4 tbl.4.

23. THOMAS D. SNYDER ET AL., NATIONAL CENTER FOR EDUCATION STATISTICS, DIGEST OF EDUCATION STATISTICS 2005, at 116 tbl.77 (2006).

24. *Id.* at 98 tbl.65.

In academic performance, Delaware's fourth grade students scored higher than the national average in mathematics,[25] reading,[26] science,[27] and writing.[28] Delaware's eighth graders also scored higher than the national average in mathematics,[29] reading,[30] writing [31] and science.[32]

Equity Issues

In 2004, revenues spent per student in Delaware's highest poverty districts were determined to be $207 less than the revenues spent in its lowest poverty districts.[33] When adjustments were made for the additional costs of educating students growing up in poverty, however, the funding gap grew to $371.[34] On the other hand, Delaware spent $408 more per student in its highest minority districts, although this amount fell to $353 when adjustments for low-income students were made.[35]

In Delaware, fourth graders eligible for free or reduced-price school lunches had test scores that were 7.3% lower in mathematics,[36] 8.2% lower in reading,[37] and 12.9% lower in writing[38] than those of students who were not eligible. The results were generally the same for eighth graders eligible for free or reduced-price lunches; their test scores were 8.0% lower in mathematics,[39] 6.3% lower in reading,[40] and 15.0% lower in writing[41] than those of students who were not eligible.

---

25. NATIONAL CENTER FOR EDUCATION STATISTICS, U.S. DEPARTMENT OF EDUCATION, THE NATION'S REPORT CARD: MATHEMATICS 2005, at 14 fig.11 (2005), *available at* http://nces.ed.gov/nationsreportcard/pdf/main2005/ 2006453.pdf [hereinafter MATHEMATICS 2005].

26. NATIONAL CENTER FOR EDUCATION STATISTICS, U.S. DEPARTMENT OF EDUCATION, THE NATION'S REPORT CARD: READING 2005, at 14 fig.11 (2005), *available at* http://nces.ed.gov/nationsreportcard/pdf/main2005/2006451.pdf [hereinafter READING 2005].

27. NATIONAL CENTER FOR EDUCATION STATISTICS, U.S. DEPARTMENT OF EDUCATION, THE NATION'S REPORT CARD: SCIENCE 2005, at 16 fig.12 (2006), *available at* http://nces.ed.gov/nationsreportcard//pdf/main2005/2006466.pdf [hereinafter SCIENCE 2005].

28. HILARY R. PERSKY ET AL., NATIONAL CENTER FOR EDUCATION STATISTICS, U.S. DEPARTMENT OF EDUCATION, THE NATION'S REPORT CARD: WRITING 2002, at 23 tbl.2.2 (2003), *available at* http://nces.ed.gov/nationsreportcard/pdf/main2002/2003529.pdf [hereinafter WRITING 2002].

29. MATHEMATICS 2005, *supra* note 25, at 16 fig.12.

30. READING 2005, *supra* note 26, at 16 fig.12.

31. WRITING 2002, *supra* note 28, at 24 tbl.2.3.

32. SCIENCE 2005, *supra* note 27, at 28 fig.22.

33. THE EDUCATION TRUST, FUNDING GAPS 2006, at 7 tbl.3 (2006), *available at* http://www2.edtrust.org/NR/rdonlyres/CDEF9403-5A75-437E-93FF-EBF1174181FB/0/Funding-Gap2006.pdf.

34. *Id.*

35. *Id.* at 7 tbl.4.

36. MATHEMATICS 2005, *supra* note 25, at 20 tbl.5.

37. READING 2005, *supra* note 26, at 20 tbl.5.

38. WRITING 2002, *supra* note 28, at 75 tbl.3.24.

39. MATHEMATICS 2005, *supra* note 25, at 21 tbl.6.

40. READING 2005, *supra* note 26, at 21 tbl.6.

Although Delaware has seen little litigation regarding the equity of education funding, two recent decisions have focused on the funding for special needs education.[42]

Availability of Publicly Funded Prekindergarten Programs

The Delaware Early Childhood Assistance Program currently serves four-year-old children who are considered at risk but does not serve three-year-old children.[43] Total enrollment in this state-funded program is 843,[44] which represents just 3.9% of Delaware's 21,817 three- and four-year-old children.[45] The federally funded Head Start program enrolls an additional children 1,538,[46] which represents 7% of Delaware's three- and four-year-old children.[47]

Where Does Delaware Get Its Revenue?

At the end of fiscal year 2004, Delaware had total revenues of approximately $7.1 billion.[48] Of this amount, 42.2% was derived from state and local tax revenues and 15.4% was received from the federal government.[49] The remaining 42.4% came from other sources, including the Delaware Lottery, insurance trust revenue, revenue from government-owned utilities, and other commercial or auxiliary enterprises.[50]

Tax Revenue

Delaware collected approximately $3 billion in state and local tax revenue during fiscal year 2004.[51] As a result, Delaware residents paid $3,608 per capita in state and

---

41. WRITING 2002, *supra* note 28, at 76 tbl.3.25.

42. *See* Fisher v. Bd. of Educ. of the Christina Sch. Dist., 856 A.2d 552 (Del. 2004) (the court held that the lower court's deference to a report recommending public funding for the private education of a special needs child was proper) and Raymond v. Red Clay Consol. Sch. Dist., 765 A.2d 952 (Del. 2000) (parents failed to meet the burden of showing deprivation of education by placing their special needs child in private school after being fed up with the public school "red tape").

43. W. STEVEN BARNETT ET AL., NATIONAL INSTITUTE FOR EARLY EDUCATION RESEARCH, THE STATE OF PRESCHOOL 2006, at 54 (2007), *available at* http://nieer.org/yearbook/pdf/yearbook.pdf.

44. *Id.* at 55.

45. *See id.*

46. *Id.*

47. *See id.*

48. U.S. Census Bureau, State and Local Government Finances 2003–04, http://www.census.gov/govs/www/estimate04.html (last visited Oct. 6, 2006) [hereinafter Government Finances].

49. *Id.*

50. *Id.*

51. The total tax revenues were collected as follows: $14.2 billion by the state and 10.8 billion by local governments. *Id.*

local taxes, an amount which ranked 16th nationally.[52] The different types of tax sources were approximately apportioned as follows:

Individual income taxes	27.7%
Property taxes	15.1%
General and selective sales taxes	13.2%
Corporate income and other taxes	<u>44.0%</u>
	100.0%[53]

Federal Funding

During fiscal year 2004, 15.4% of Delaware's total revenues came from the federal government.[54] For every dollar of federal taxes paid, Delaware received $0.79 in federal funding, an amount which ranked 40th nationally[55] and was well below the national average of $1.17.[56]

Lottery Revenue

The Delaware Lottery has been in operation since 1975. Under Delaware's constitution, all Delaware Lottery profits are to be used to supplement the state's general fund.[57] A portion of the proceeds from the state's video lottery program supplements the horseracing business in Delaware.[58] No less than 45% of the gross proceeds can fund future awards, and no less than 30% of the gross proceeds can supplement the general fund.[59] During fiscal year 2006, the Lottery had total revenues of $689 million and net proceeds of $298 million.[60]

Legal Structures of Major Tax Sources

Income

Delaware employs a broad-based income tax[61] that uses adjusted gross income for federal income tax purposes as a starting point for determining the state's taxable in-

---

52. *Id.*

53. *Id.*

54. *Id.*

55. The Tax Foundation, Federal Spending Received Per Dollar of Taxes Paid by State, 2004 http://www.taxfoundation.org/taxdata/show/266.html (last visited Sept. 17, 2006).

56. *See Id.*

57. DEL. CODE. ANN. tit. 29, § 4801.

58. *Id.* § 4802.

59. *Id.* § 4801.

60. "The Delaware Lottery 2005 Annual Report," http://lottery.state.de.us/pdf/2005annual-report.pdf.

61. DEL. CODE. ANN. tit. 30, § 1102.

come.[62] Numerous adjustments, however, may be available to various individuals in calculating this amount.[63] Localities with at least 50,000 residents may impose a local income tax.[64] The maximum amount that can be imposed is 1.25%, and only the city of Wilmington meets this criterion.[65] During fiscal year 2004,, Delaware collected individual income tax of $941 per capita, an amount which ranked 9th nationally.[66]

In Delaware, a typical family of four (i.e., married taxpayers who file jointly and have two dependent children) are not required to pay any income tax until their combined income exceeds $28,600, an amount which is above the national poverty line of $20,615.[67] Delaware's income tax structure contains six tax brackets that impose a minimum marginal tax rate of 2.2% and a maximum marginal tax rate of 5.95%.[68] When statutory exemptions and the standard deduction are taken into account, the maximum marginal rate applies to every dollar of income exceeding $66,940.[69]

Property

Overview

Delaware has a property tax system that relegates all property tax issues to the counties and offers virtually no oversight by the state department of revenue.[70] The state does, however, strictly prohibit the taxation of personal property, whether tangible or intangible.[71] During fiscal year 2004, Delaware collected approximately $453 million dollars in property taxes at the local level.[72] As a result, Delaware residents paid $546 per capita in property taxes, an amount which ranked 43rd nationally.[73]

---

62. Id. § 1105.

63. Id. §§ 1108–1117.

64. Id. tit. 22, § 901.

65. Id.

66. STATE RANKINGS 2006, *supra* note 1, at 321.

67. JASON A. LEVITIS & NICHOLAS JOHNSON, CENTER ON BUDGET AND POLICY PRIORITIES, THE IMPACT OF STATE INCOME TAXES ON LOW-INCOME FAMILIES IN 2006, at 12 (2007). Note also that Delaware taxpayers who are married and filing jointly are entitled to a standard deduction of $6,500 and personal and dependent exemptions of $110 each. 30 Del. C. § 1108. Note, however, that the threshold calculation of $23,000 is greater than the sum of these deductions and exemptions because it includes additional tax benefits available to low-income families, such as the earned-income tax credit. *See* LEVITIS & JOHNSON, *supra*.

68. DEL. CODE. ANN. tit. 30, § 1102. Delaware's middle four tax rates are 3.9%, 4.8%, 5.2%, and 5.5%. *Id.*

69. This total incorporates the standard deductions and exemptions allowable for a family of four at $6,940, plus the threshold of income for the highest tax bracket, $60,000. *See supra* notes 67–68.

70. DEL. CODE ANN. tit. 9, § 8101.

71. *Id.* § 8103.

72. Government Finances, *supra* note 48.

73. *See id.*

Defining the Real Property Tax Base

Delaware has only one classification for real property: both residential and commercial properties are assessed at 100% of the estimated fair market value. The taxes are collected on a date specified by the individual county.[74] "Fair market value" is generally determined by the application of standard appraisal methods, including the cost method, the capitalization-of-income method, and the market or comparable-sales method.[75] In general, cities are required to reassess property annually.[76]

Real Property Tax Rates

The tax rates imposed on real property vary and are set by each locality without limitation.[77] However, the state requires that the rate imposed after reassessment cannot exceed an amount that will generate revenues 15% greater than those of the previous year.[78]

Personal and Intangible Property

The state strictly prohibits the taxation of personal property, whether tangible or intangible.[79]

Exemptions

Delaware provides exemptions to property tax based on both use and ownership.[80] These include cemeteries, college fraternities, civil organizations, commercial forests, land used to store manure or other agricultural nutrients, and lands owned by veterans associations.[81] Delaware also allows a homestead exemption of $5,000 for residents over the age of 65 who have less than $3,000 in taxable income and have lived in the same residence for at least three years.[82]

General and Selective Sales

General Sales

Delaware does not impose a general sales tax.

---

74. DEL. CODE. ANN. tit. 9, §§ 8101, 8601. Agricultural, horticultural, and forest land may be eligible for current use valuation if certain requirements are met. Id. § 8329.

75. CCH-EXP, PROP-TAX-GUIDE DE ¶ 20-615, Valuation Methods in General.

76. DEL. CODE. ANN. tit. 9, § 8301.

77. See, e.g., id. §§ 8102, 1134, 7001.

78. Id. § 8002.

79. Id. § 8103.

80. Id. §§ 8105–8111.

81. Id.

82. Id. § 8131.

Selective Sales

Selective sales taxes make up 13.2% of Delaware's total revenue.[83] Of that amount, 3.8%[84] comes from a motor fuel sales tax imposed at a rate of $0.11 per gallon of gasoline.[85] Delaware residents paid an average of $135 per capita in state motor fuel sales taxes in 2004, an amount which ranked 19th nationally and was above the national average of $115.[86]

In 2004, sales taxes on alcoholic beverages made up 0.4% of Delaware's total tax revenue.[87] Delaware residents paid $16.13 per capita in state alcoholic beverage sales taxes in 2004, an amount which ranked 20th nationally.[88]

The tobacco product sales tax makes up 2.5% of Delaware's tax revenues and is imposed at a rate of $0.55 per pack of cigarettes.[89] Delaware residents paid $90.93 per capita in state tobacco sales taxes in 2004, an amount which ranked 3rd nationally.[90]

The remainder of Delaware's selective sales taxes makes up 6.5% of its total tax revenue. Of this amount, 1.3% represents taxes on utilities and the other 5.2% represents taxes on other specific commodities, businesses, or services not reported separately above (e.g., on contractors, lodging, lubricating oil, fuels other than motor fuel, motor vehicles, meals, soft drinks, margarine, etc.).[91]

Corporate Income and Other

Corporate Income

The corporate income tax makes up 7.3% of Delaware's total tax revenue.[92] Delaware's broad-based corporate income tax is imposed at a flat rate of 8.7% on a corporation's Delaware taxable income,[93] which is based on the corporation's federal taxable income.[94]

Delaware follows the federal income tax treatment of S corporations. Thus, they do not pay Delaware's corporate income tax; rather income and losses flow through to their shareholders.[95] A similar treatment is afforded to limited partnerships and lim-

---

83. Government Finances, *supra* note 48.

84. *Id.*

85. DEL. CODE. ANN. tit. 30, § 5110.

86. STATE RANKINGS 2006, *supra* note 1, at 327.

87. Government Finances, *supra* note 48.

88. STATE RANKINGS 2006, *supra* note 1, at 335.

89. DEL. CODE ANN. tit. 30, § 5305.

90. STATE RANKINGS 2006, *supra* note 1, at 332.

91. U.S. Census Bureau, Classification Manual, Description of Tax Categories, http://ftp2 .census.gov/govs/class/classrev.pdf (last visited Sept. 26, 2006) [hereinafter CLASSIFICATION MANUAL].

92. Government Finances, *supra* note 48.

93. DEL. CODE. ANN. tit. 30, § 1902.

94. *Id.*

95. CCH-EXP, DE-TAXRPTR ¶ 10-240, Limited Liability Companies (LLCs).

ited liability partnerships, as well as limited liability companies, assuming they are treated as a partnership for federal tax purposes.[96] However, if a limited liability company is treated as a corporation for federal income tax purposes, the entity is subject to Delaware's corporate income tax.[97]

Other

During fiscal year 2004, the collection of all other taxes not previously mentioned accounted for 36.8% of Delaware's total tax revenue. Of this amount, approximately $149 million was generated by the estate and gift tax,[98] which is calculated on the basis of the entire taxable income of the estate.[99] The "other taxes" category is made up of various license taxes and fees, including motor vehicle licenses, occupational licenses, and utility and telephone fees.[100] The final component of the "other taxes" category includes fees imposed on affiliated finance companies[101] and those imposed on corporate headquarters.[102]

Burden Analysis

The overall state and local tax burden on Delaware taxpayers is somewhat progressive. Taxpayers in the lowest quintile—those with incomes of less than $15,000—bear a tax burden equal to 4.7% of their income, while taxpayers in the top 1%—those with incomes that exceed $923,600—bear a tax burden of just 6.9% of their income.[103] It is also worth noting that, although Delaware obviously has no control over federal tax policy, federal itemized deductions for state and local personal income and property taxes nonetheless further reduce the burden on taxpayers in the top 1% to 4.8%.[104] Fur-

---

96. *Id.*

97. *Id.*

98. Government Finances, *supra* note 48.

99. DEL. CODE. ANN. tit. 30, § 1631.

100. *See id.* §§ 2101–4307.

101. *Id.* § 6301-6306 (those that primarily issue commercial paper and other debt obligations).

102. *Id.* § 6401-6407 (equal to the greater of 8.7% of income from the headquarters or $5,000).

103. *See* ROBERT S. McINTYRE ET AL., WHO PAYS? A DISTRIBUTIONAL ANALYSIS OF THE TAX SYSTEMS IN ALL 50 STATES 30 (2d ed. 2003), *available at* http://www.itepnet.org/wp2000/text.pdf. Taxpayers in the second quintile bear a 4.7% total tax burden on incomes between $15,000 and $26,000; those in the third quintile bear a 5.4% tax burden on incomes between $26,000 and $45,000; those in the fourth quintile bear a 5.6% tax burden on incomes between $45,000 and $74,000; those in the 80th–95th percentiles bear a 6.1% tax burden on incomes between $74,000 and $136,000; finally those in the 96th–99th percentiles bear a 6.1% tax burden on incomes between $136,000 and $923,000. *Id.*

104. *Id.* In 2004, taxpayers in the lowest and second lowest quintiles saw no reduction; those in the third quintile saw a reduction of 0.3%; those in the fourth quintile saw a reduction of 0.5%; those in the 80th–95th percentiles saw a reduction of 0.9%; and those in the 96th–99th percentiles saw a reduction of 1.4%. *Id.*

thermore, between 1989 and 2002, the tax burden on the bottom quintile rose by ap-proximately 0.4%, while the burden on the top 1% actually fell by the same amount.[105]

In terms of the income tax, the burden across income groups in Delaware is slightly progressive, with taxpayers in the lowest quintile bearing a tax burden of 0.4% and those in the top 1% bearing a tax burden of 5.9%.[106] In contrast, however, the sales and excises taxes imposed by Delaware are slightly regressive, with taxpayers in the lowest quintile bearing a tax burden of 2.3% and those in the top 1% bearing a tax burden of just 0.2%.[107] Property taxes in Delaware are also regressive, with taxpayers in the low-est quintile bearing a tax burden of 1.9% and those in the remaining quintiles bearing an average tax burden of 1.2%.[108]

---

105. *Id.* at 31.

106. *See id.* at 30. Taxpayers in the second quintile bear a 1.8% income tax burden; those in the third quintile bear a 2.6% burden; those in the fourth quintile bear a 3.2% burden; those in the 80th–95th percentiles bear a 3.8% burden; finally, those in the 96th–99th percentiles bear a 4.3% burden. *Id.* Note, however, that of the total income tax burden born by the top 1%, 4.8% represents individual income taxes and 1.1% represents corporate income taxes. *Id.*

107. *See id.* Taxpayers in the second quintile bear a 1.8% sales-and-excise tax burden; those in the third quintile bear a 1.3% burden; those in the fourth quintile bear a 1.1% burden; those in the 80th–95th percentiles bear a 0.8% burden; finally, those in the 96th–99th percentiles bear a 0.5% burden. *Id.*

108. *See id.* Taxpayers in the second quintile bear a 1.1% property tax burden; those in the third quintile bear a 1.5% burden; those in the fourth quintile bear a 1.3% burden; those in the 80th–95th percentiles bear a 1.4% burden; those in the 96th–99th percentiles bear a 1.3% bur-den: finally, those in the top 1% bear a 0.7% burden. *Id.*

Florida

General Information

Basic Profile – Geography, Population and Industry

Admitted to the Union in 1845, Florida is commonly referred to as the "Sunshine State."[1] It is located in the southeast region and is bordered by Georgia and Alabama on the north; the Atlantic Ocean on the south and east; and the Gulf of Mexico on the west. The eastern portion of the state is located in the eastern time zone, while the western side of the panhandle is located in the central time zone. The state capital is Tallahassee.[2]

Florida ranks 22nd in total land and water area (approximately 66,000 square miles);[3] in 2005, the state ranked 4th in population (approximately 17.8 million residents).[4] Florida's population is approximately 80.4% white and 15.7% black.[5] Additionally, 19.5% of its population identify themselves as persons of Hispanic or Latino origin.[6] The state is approximately 26% Catholic, 49% Protestant, and 3% Jewish; 22% claim a religion outside the Judeo-Christian tradition or no religion at all.[7] In 2005, approximately 94% of Florida's citizens lived in urban areas.[8] Major industries include tourism, agriculture, and electronics.[9]

---

1. STATE RANKINGS 2006, vi, 1 (Kathleen O'Leary Morgan & Scott Morgan eds., Morgan Quitno Press, 2006).

2. *Id.*

3. *Id.* at 225.

4. *Id.* at 429.

5. Florida Quick Facts from the U.S. Census Bureau, http://quickfacts.census.gov/qfd/states/12000.html (last visited Jan. 31, 2007). The remaining population is made up of 2.1% Asian persons, 0.4% American Indian and/or Alaska Native persons, 0.1% Native Hawaiian persons and other Pacific Islanders, and 1.2% persons reporting two or more races. *Id.*

6. *Id.* (noting that because Hispanics and Latinos may be of any race, they are also included within the other applicable race categories). *Id.*

7. BARRY A. KOSMIN, EGON MAYER & ARIELA KEYSAR, AMERICAN RELIGIOUS IDENTIFICATION SURVEY 2001, at 39, *available at* http://www.gc.cuny.edu/faculty/research_studies/aris.pdf.

8. USDA Economic Research Service, Florida Fact Sheet, http://www.ers.usda.gov/StateFacts/FL.htm (last visited Nov. 17, 2006). According to the latest estimates, approximately 1.1 million people live in rural areas, and 16.7 million people live in urban areas. *Id.*

9. Florida Facts, http://www.floridasmart.com/facts/index.htm (last visited Nov. 17, 2006).

Family Income and Poverty Indicators

In 2004, Florida's per capita gross product was $34,458, which was below the national average of $39,725.[10] During this same period, while the median household income in Florida was $40,171,[11] 12.3% of the state's population was living in poverty, which was just below the national average of 12.4%.[12] More specifically, poverty affected 17.2% of Florida's children,[13] 9.7% of its senior citizens,[14] and 9.1% of its families.[15] Of its female-headed households with children, 32.5% of them lived in poverty,[16] and 46% of the state's public elementary and secondary school students were eligible for free or reduced-price meals.[17] Of those living in poverty, approximately 29% were black, which represented 24% of Florida's black population and 3.6% of its total population.[18] In an attempt to combat this poverty, Florida spent approximately $12.5 billion on public welfare programs in 2002,[19] which made up 14.4% of its total government expenditures.[20]

Florida's Public Elementary-Secondary School System

Overall Spending and Performance

For the 2003–2004 school year, Florida spent $6,784 per pupil in its public elementary-secondary school system, which was substantially below the national average of $8,182.[21] Of this amount, 10.1% was provided by the federal government, 44.4% was provided by the state government, and 45.6% was provided by the local governments,[22] with property taxes making up 36.9% of the total funding.[23] Out of these funds, Florida paid its elementary and secondary school teachers an estimated average annual salary

---

10. STATE RANKINGS 2006, *supra* note 1, at 89.

11. *Id.* at 96.

12. *Id.* at 495.

13. *Id.* at 497.

14. *Id.* at 496.

15. *Id.* at 498.

16. *Id.* at 499.

17. *Id.* at 532.

18. *See* Fact Sheet, American FactFinder, http://factfinder.census.gov/home/saff/main.html?_lang=en (select "Florida" under "Get a Fact Sheet for your community") (last visited Feb. 22, 2007). Note that these numbers are based on the 2000 census because more recent numbers were not available.

19. STATE RANKINGS 2006, *supra* note 1, at 500.

20. *Id.* at 502.

21. GOVERNMENTS DIVISION, U.S. CENSUS BUREAU, PUBLIC EDUCATION FINANCES 2004, at 8 tbl.8 (2006).

22. *See id.* at 5 tbl.5.

23. *See id.* at 4 tbl.4.

of \$41,081 during the 2004–2005 school year,[24] but in 2003, it provided a student/teacher ratio of only 17.9, which was worse than the national average of 15.9.[25]

In academic performance, Florida's fourth grade students scored higher than the national average in mathematics,[26] reading,[27] science,[28] and writing,[29] while its eighth graders scored higher than the national average in writing[30] but lower than the national average in mathematics,[31] reading,[32] and science.[33]

Equity Issues

In 2004, revenues spent per student in Florida's highest poverty districts were determined to be \$272 less than the revenues spent in its lowest poverty districts.[34] When adjustments were made for the additional costs of educating students growing up in poverty, however, the funding gap grew to \$461.[35] On the other hand, Florida spent \$17 more per student in its highest minority districts, although this amount actually declined by \$106 when adjustments for low-income students were made.[36]

Fourth graders eligible for free or reduced-price school lunches had test scores that were 8% lower in mathematics,[37] 9% lower in reading,[38] and 12% lower in writing[39] than those of students who were not eligible. The results were generally the same for eighth graders eligible for free or reduced price lunches; their test scores were 9% lower

---

24. THOMAS D. SNYDER ET AL., NATIONAL CENTER FOR EDUCATION STATISTICS, DIGEST OF EDUCATION STATISTICS 2005, at 116 tbl.77 (2006).

25. *Id.* at 98 tbl.65.

26. NATIONAL CENTER FOR EDUCATION STATISTICS, U.S. DEPARTMENT OF EDUCATION, THE NATION'S REPORT CARD: MATHEMATICS 2005, at 14 fig.11 (2005), *available at* http://nces.ed.gov/ nationsreportcard/pdf/main2005/ 2006453.pdf [hereinafter MATHEMATICS 2005].

27. NATIONAL CENTER FOR EDUCATION STATISTICS, U.S. DEPARTMENT OF EDUCATION, THE NATION'S REPORT CARD: READING 2005, at 14 fig.11 (2005), *available at* http://nces.ed.gov/na-tionsreportcard/pdf/main2005/2006451.pdf [hereinafter READING 2005].

28. NATIONAL CENTER FOR EDUCATION STATISTICS, U.S. DEPARTMENT OF EDUCATION, THE NATION'S REPORT CARD: SCIENCE 2005, at 16 fig.12 (2006), *available at* http://nces.ed.gov/na-tionsreportcard//pdf/main2005/2006466.pdf [hereinafter SCIENCE 2005].

29. HILARY R. PERSKY ET AL., NATIONAL CENTER FOR EDUCATION STATISTICS, U.S. DE-PARTMENT OF EDUCATION, THE NATION'S REPORT CARD: WRITING 2002, at 23 tbl.2.2 (2003), *available at* http://nces.ed.gov/nationsreportcard/pdf/main2002/2003529.pdf [hereinafter WRIT-ING 2002].

30. WRITING 2002, *supra* note 29, at 24 tbl.2.3.

31. MATHEMATICS 2005, *supra* note 26, at 16 fig.12.

32. READING 2005, *supra* note 27, at 16 fig.12.

33. SCIENCE 2005, *supra* note 28, at 28 fig.22.

34. THE EDUCATION TRUST, FUNDING GAPS 2006, at 7 tbl.3 (2006), *available at* http://www2.edtrust.org/NR/rdonlyres/CDEF9403-5A75-437E-93FF-EBF1174181FB/0/Fund-ingGap2006.pdf.

35. *Id.*

36. *Id.* at 7 tbl.4.

37. MATHEMATICS 2005, *supra* note 26, at 20 tbl.5.

38. READING 2005, *supra* note 27, at 20 tbl.5.

39. WRITING 2002, *supra* note 29, at 75 tbl.3.24.

in mathematics,[40] 7% lower in reading,[41] and 13% lower in writing[42] than those of students who were not eligible.

In June 2004, the School Board of Miami-Dade County filed a complaint against the Florida Department of Education, the State Board of Education, and the president of the Florida Senate, among others, seeking a declaratory judgment regarding the 2004–2005 District Cost Differential (DCD), which is used to determine funding of salaries for school personnel.[43] The School Board alleged, among other things, that the revised DCD calculation "violated *Article IX, section 1, of the Florida Constitution* because 'it results in the arbitrary, capricious, non-uniform and discriminatory distribution of education funds'" and because it denies the students in the Miami-Dade County school district a "uniform, safe and high quality education to which they are guaranteed."[44] The trial court granted the defendants' motion for involuntary dismissal, and the appellate court affirmed the trial court's ruling on the basis that the original complaint had failed to state a proper cause of action and instead "merely challenged the method of distribution of state education funds."[45]

Availability of Publicly Funded Prekindergarten Programs

The Florida Voluntary Prekindergarten Program, which began in 2005, is available to all four-year-old children in the state but is not available to three-year-old children.[46] Total enrollment in this state-funded program is 105,896,[47] which represents 24% of Florida's 448,285 three- and four-year-old children.[48] The federally funded Head Start program enrolls an additional 32,509,[49] which represents 7% of Florida's three- and four-year-old children.[50]

Where Does Florida Get Its Revenue?

At the end of fiscal year 2004, Florida had total revenues of approximately $129.7 billion.[51] Of this amount, 41% was derived from state and local tax revenues and 15%

---

40. MATHEMATICS 2005, *supra* note 26, at 21 tbl.6.

41. READING 2005, *supra* note 27, at 21 tbl.6.

42. WRITING 2002, *supra* note 29, at 76 tbl.3.25.

43. Sch. Bd. v. King, 940 So. 2d 593, 597 (Fla. Dist. Ct. App. 1996).

44. *Id.* at 598.

45. *Id.* at 602.

46. W. STEVEN BARNETT ET AL., NATIONAL INSTITUTE FOR EARLY EDUCATION RESEARCH, THE STATE OF PRESCHOOL 2006, at 56 (2006), *available at* http://nieer.org/yearbook/pdf/yearbook.pdf.

47. *Id.* at 57.

48. *See id.* at 232.

49. *Id.* at 57.

50. *See id.* at 232.

51. U.S. Census Bureau, State and Local Government Finances 2003–04, http://www.census.gov/govs/www/estimate04.html (last visited Nov. 16, 2006) [hereinafter Government Finances].

was received from the federal government.[52] The remaining 44% came from other sources, including the Florida Lottery, insurance trust revenue, and revenue from government-owned utilities and other commercial or auxiliary enterprises.

Tax Revenue

Florida collected approximately $53.8 billion in state and local tax revenue during fiscal year 2004.[53] As a result, Florida residents paid $3,094 per capita in state and local taxes, an amount which ranked 27th nationally.[54] The different types of tax sources were approximately apportioned as follows:

Individual income taxes	00.0%
Property taxes	34.4%
General and selective sales taxes	51.0%
Corporate income and other taxes	14.6%
	100.0%[55]

Federal Funding

During fiscal year 2004, 15% of Florida's total revenues came from the federal government.[56] For every dollar of federal taxes paid, Florida received $1.02 in federal funding, an amount which ranked 30th nationally[57] and was below the national average of $1.17.[58]

Lottery Revenue

The Florida Education Lottery was created in 1986 through the passage of an amendment to Florida's constitution.[59] Net proceeds derived from the Lottery are deposited into the State Education Lotteries Trust Fund and are appropriated by the legislature.[60] During fiscal year 2005, the Lottery had total revenues of $3.5 billion and net income available for transfer of $1.1 billion.[61]

---

52. *Id.*

53. *Id.* The total tax revenues were collected as follows: $30.5 billion by the state and $23.3 billion by local governments. *Id.*

54. *Id.*

55. *Id.*

56. *Id.*

57. The Tax Foundation, Federal Spending Received Per Dollar of Taxes Paid by State 2004, http://www.taxfoundation.org/taxdata/show/266.html (last visited Sept. 17, 2006).

58. *See id.*

59. Official Home of the Florida Lottery, http://www.flalottery.com/inet/about-history-Main.do (last visited Sept. 27, 2006).

60. FLA. CONST. art. X, § 15.

61. Florida Lottery Annual Report 2004–2005, http://www.flalottery.com/inet/downloads/yearlyreport04-05.pdf (last visited Sept. 27, 2006).

Legal Structures of Major Tax Sources

Income

Florida does not impose personal income taxes.

Property

Overview

Florida has a typical property tax system that taxes the value of real property and tangible personal property almost entirely at the local level.[62] During fiscal year 2004, Florida collected approximately $18.2 billion dollars in property taxes at the local level and approximately $277 million at the state level.[63] As a result, Florida residents paid $1,064 per capita in state and local property taxes, an amount which ranked 19th nationally.[64]

Defining the Real Property Tax Base

Real property in Florida is classified according to the assessment basis of the land into one of the following categories: residential, commercial and industrial, agricultural, nonagricultural, high-water recharge, historic property, exempt property, centrally assessed, leasehold interests, time-share property, and other.[65] All real property is assessed at 100% of the just value of the property, which is determined on the basis of its present value, the highest and best use of the property, the historical cost of the property, the income from the property, or the net proceeds from the sale of the property.[66] Property classified as agricultural is assessed on the sole basis of its agricultural use.[67] Real property is assessed each calendar year according to its just value on January 1.[68]

Real Property Tax Rates

The tax rates imposed on real property vary and are set by each locality. The county commissioners are responsible for determining the amount to be raised for all county purposes, other than county school purposes.[69] Counties and municipalities are lim-

---

62. FLA. STAT. ANN. § 196.001.
63. Government Finances, *supra* note 51.
64. *See id.*
65. FLA. STAT. ANN. § 195.073.
66. *Id.* § 193.011.
67. *Id.* § 193.461.
68. *Id.* § 192.042. The reassessment of real property that is further classified as homestead property is limited to an increase in any given year of 3% of the assessed value for the prior year or the percentage of change in the Consumer Price Index for All Urban Consumers, U.S. City Average. *Id.* § 193.155. This assessment-increase limitation applies only to real property and taxpayers eligible for homestead status. *Id.*
69. *Id.* § 200.011.

ited to a tax rate of 10 mills (i.e., 1 mill equals 1 dollar per thousand; therefore 10 mills equals 10 dollars per thousand) unless otherwise voted on by the citizens of the county.[70] Any city or county that provides both municipal and county services can levy up to 20 mills for such services.[71] School districts are allowed to levy a millage rate up to the minimum rate necessary to provide the district-required local effort as certified by the Commissioner of Education.[72] In 2005, the tax rates per $1,000 of assessed value ranged from $6.79 in Monroe County to $20.54 in Franklin County.[73]

Personal and Intangible Property

Tangible personal property is subject to local taxation unless specifically exempt.[74] Tangible personal property is defined as all goods, chattels, and other articles of value (other than vehicles) capable of manual possession.[75] Tangible personal property is valued at its just value[76] and is subject to rates as determined for that county, municipality, and/or school district. Intangible personal property is not subject to tax at either the state or local level since the provisions regarding the taxation of intangible personal property were repealed effective January 1, 2007.[77]

Exemptions

Household goods, personal effects,[78] all items of inventory,[79] and all property up to the value of $500 of every widow, widower, blind person, or permanently disabled person[80] are exempt from property tax. Citizens of Florida are allowed a homestead exemption of up to $25,000 of the gross assessed value of the home if they are permanent residents of the state.[81] In addition, Florida taxpayers over the age of 65 who qualify for the homestead exemption are allowed an additional exemption of up to $25,000 of the gross assessed value of their home, subject to certain household income requirements, if this exemption is adopted by the board of county commissioners or the governing authority of the municipality.[82]

---

70. *Id.* § 200.071.
71. *Id.* § 200.141.
72. *Id.* § 1011.71.
73. CCH-EXP, PROP-TAX-GUIDE FL ¶ 20-405, Rates of Tax.
74. FLA. STAT. ANN. § 195.073.
75. *Id.* § 192.001.
76. *Id.* § 193.011.
77. *Id.* § 193.032.
78. *Id.* § 196.181.
79. *Id.* § 196.185.
80. *Id.* § 196.202.
81. *Id.* § 196.031.
82. *Id.* § 196.075.

General and Selective Sales

General Sales

Florida imposes a general retail sales-and-use tax, which makes up 33.5% of its total tax revenue.[83] This tax is imposed at a rate of 6% on tangible personal property sold at retail, selected services, and gross proceeds from the lease or rental of tangible personal property.[84] Counties may impose additional discretionary sales taxes and local option taxes on all transactions occurring in the county which are subject to the state sales tax.[85] The total sales tax rate imposed by the state and each county generally ranges from 6% to as high as 7.5% in Escambia, Jackson, Leon, Madison, and Monroe counties.[86] Exemptions from Florida's sales-and-use tax include food products for human consumption (i.e., groceries), prescription drugs and medical supplies, and food stamp purchases.[87]

Selective Sales

Selective sales taxes make up 17.5% of Florida's total revenue.[88] Of that amount, 5.0%[89] comes from a motor fuel sales tax that is imposed at a rate of between $0.225 per gallon of gasoline and $0.335 per gallon of gasoline, depending on the county.[90] Florida residents paid an average of $105 per capita in state motor fuel sales taxes in 2004, an amount which ranked 43rd nationally and was below the national average of $115.[91]

In 2004, sales taxes on alcoholic beverages made up 1.1% of Florida's total tax revenue.[92]

---

83. Government Finances, *supra* note 51.

84. FLA. STAT. ANN. § 212.05.

85. *Id.* § 212.054. Discretionary sales taxes that may be imposed by counties include the following: charter county transit system surtax; local government infrastructure surtax; small county surtax; indigent care and trauma center surtax; county public hospital surtax; school capital outlay surtax; and voter-approved indigent care surtax, depending on circumstances. *Id.* § 212.055. Local option sales taxes that may be imposed by counties include the following: tourist development tax, tourist impact tax, convention development tax, food and beverage tax, and municipal parking facility surcharge. *Id.* §§ 125.0104, 125.0108, 212.0305, 212.0306, 166.271.

86. CCH-EXP, SALES-TAX-GUIDE FL ¶ 61-735, Local Rates. Note that the tax on living and sleeping accommodations generally ranges from 7% to as high as 14% in Dade county, a percentage which is higher than the sales tax generally imposed because of the imposition of local option taxes on living and sleeping accommodations. *Id.*

87. FLA. STAT. ANN. § 212.08. The exemption does not apply to food products sold as meals for consumption on or off the premises of the dealer who is selling the meal. *Id.*

88. Government Finances, *supra* note 51.

89. *Id.*

90. 2007 State Taxes, Ninth-Cent, Local Option, Additional Local Option and SCETS Motor Fuel Taxes, http://dor.myflorida.com/dor/pdf/06b05-04.pdf (last visited Jan. 5, 2007).

91. STATE RANKINGS 2006, *supra* note 1, at 327.

92. Government Finances, *supra* note 51.

Florida residents paid $34.03 per capita in state alcoholic beverage sales taxes in 2004, an amount which ranked 3rd nationally.[93]

The tobacco product sales tax makes up 0.8% of Florida's tax revenues and is imposed at a rate of $0.339 per pack of cigarettes.[94]

The remainder of Florida's selective sales taxes makes up 10.6% of its total tax revenue. Of this amount, 6.6% represents taxes on utilities and the other 4% represents taxes on other specific commodities, businesses, or services not reported separately above (e.g., on contractors, lodging, lubricating oil, fuels other than motor fuel, motor vehicles, meals, soft drinks, margarine, etc.).[95]

Corporate Income and Other

Corporate Income

The corporate income tax makes up 2.6% of Florida's total tax revenue.[96] Florida's broad-based corporate income tax is imposed at a rate of 5.5% on a corporation's Florida net income,[97] which is based on the corporation's federal taxable income.[98]

Florida follows the federal income tax treatment of S corporations, limited partnerships, limited liability partnerships, as well as limited liability companies, assuming they are treated as a partnership for federal tax purposes.[99]

Other

During fiscal year 2004, the collection of all other taxes not previously mentioned accounted for 12.0% of Florida's total tax revenue. Of this amount, approximately $387 million was generated by the estate and gift tax,[100] which is calculated on the basis of the federal credit for state death taxes allowable under the Internal Revenue Code.[101] The "other taxes" category is also made up of motor vehicle license taxes, documentary and stock transfer taxes, severance taxes, and all other taxes not listed separately or provided for in other categories, such as taxes on land based on a specified rate per acre (rather than on assessed value).[102]

---

93. STATE RANKINGS 2006, *supra* note 1, at 335.

94. *Id.* at 333.

95. *See* GOVERNMENTS DIVISION, U.S. CENSUS BUREAU, GOVERNMENT FINANCE AND EMPLOYMENT CLASSIFICATION MANUAL, at ch. 7 (2000), *available at* http://ftp2.census.gov/govs/class/classfull.pdf [hereinafter CLASSIFICATION MANUAL].

96. Government Finances, *supra* note 51.

97. FLA. STAT. ANN. § 220.11.

98. *Id.* § 220.12.

99. *Id.* § 220.13.

100. Government Finances, *supra* note 51.

101. FLA. STAT. ANN. § 198.02. Note, however, that the federal credit for state death taxes was phased out for all deaths occurring after December 31, 2004, so Florida does not currently have an estate tax. Florida Department of Revenue, Florida's Estate Tax, http://dor.myflorida.com/dor/taxes/estate_tax.html (last visited Feb. 25, 2007).

102. See CLASSIFICATION MANUAL, *supra* note 95, at ch. 7.

Burden Analysis

The overall state and local tax burden on taxpayers in Florida is extremely regressive; in fact, the state has one of the ten most regressive tax systems in the nation.[103] Taxpayers in the lowest quintile—those with incomes of less than $15,000—bear a tax burden of 14.4% of their income, while taxpayers in the top 1%—those with incomes that exceed $289,000 - - bear a tax burden of just 3.0% of their income.[104] It is also worth noting that, although Florida obviously has no control over federal tax policy, federal itemized deductions for state and local personal income and property taxes nonetheless further reduce the burden on those in the top 1% to 2.7%.[105] Furthermore, between 1989 and 2002, the tax burden on the bottom quintile rose by approximately 1.4%, while the burden on the top 1% rose by only approximately 0.1%.[106]

One of the regressive features of Florida's tax system is that it does not employ an income tax. Moreover, the sales and excise taxes imposed by the state are extremely regressive, with taxpayers in the lowest quintile bearing a tax burden of 11.1% and those in the top 1% bearing a tax burden of just 1.3%.[107] Property taxes in Florida are also regressive, with taxpayers in the lowest quintile bearing a tax burden of 3.3% and those in the top quintile bearing an average tax burden of 2.1%.[108]

---

103. *See* ROBERT S. MCINTYRE ET AL., WHO PAYS? A DISTRIBUTIONAL ANALYSIS OF THE TAX SYSTEMS IN ALL 50 STATES 34 (2d ed. 2003), *available at* http://www.itepnet.org/wp2000/text.pdf.

104. *See id.* at 34. Taxpayers in the second quintile bear an 11.3% total tax burden on incomes between $15,000 and $24,000; those in the third quintile bear a 9.9% tax burden on incomes between $24,000 and $38,000; those in the fourth quintile bear an 8.2% tax burden on incomes between $38,000 and $64,000; those in the 80th–95th percentiles bear a 6.9% tax burden on incomes between $64,000 and $133,000; finally, those in the 96th–99th percentiles bear a 5.0% tax burden on incomes between $133,000 and $289,000. *Id.*

105. *Id.* Taxpayers in the lowest and second lowest quintiles did not receive any benefit from these federal offsets, while those in the third quintile were able to reduce their individual tax burdens by 0.1%, those in the fourth quintile by 0.2%, those in the 80th–95th percentiles by 0.4%, and those in the 96th–99th percentiles by 0.5%. *Id.*

106. *Id.* at 35.

107. *See id.* at 34. Taxpayers in the second quintile bear a 9.4% sales-and-excise tax burden; those in the third quintile bear a 7.7% burden; those in the fourth quintile bear a 6.0% burden; those in the 80th–95th percentiles bear a 4.4% burden; finally, those in the 96th–99th percentiles bear a 2.7% burden. *Id.*

108. *See id.* Taxpayers in the second quintile bear a 1.9% property tax burden; those in the third quintile bear a 2.3% burden; those in the fourth quintile bear a 2.3% burden; those in the 80th–95th percentiles bear a 2.5% burden; those in the 96th–99th percentiles bear a 2.3% burden; finally, those in the top 1% bear a 1.6% burden. *Id.*

Georgia

General Information

Basic Profile – Geography, Population and Industry

Admitted to the Union in 1788, Georgia is commonly referred to as the "Peach State."[1] It is located in the southeast region and is bordered by Tennessee and South Carolina on the north; the Atlantic Ocean on the east; Florida on the south; and Alabama on the west. The state is located in the eastern time zone, and its capital is Atlanta.[2]

Georgia ranks 24th in total land and water area (approximately 59,000 square miles);[3] in 2005, the state ranked 9th in population (approximately 9.1 million residents).[4] Georgia's population is approximately 66.1% white and 29.8% black.[5] The state is approximately 8% Catholic, 71% Protestant (of which 52% are Baptist), and less than 0.5% Jewish; 21% claim a religion outside the Judeo-Christian tradition or no religion at all.[6] As of 2005, approximately 81% of Georgia's citizens lived in urban areas.[7] Major industries include textile manufacturing, mining, production of peanuts and pecans, and automobile manufacturing.[8]

---

1. STATE RANKINGS 2006, vi, 1 (Kathleen O'Leary Morgan & Scott Morgan eds., Morgan Quitno Press 2006).

2. *Id.*

3. *Id.* at 225.

4. *Id.* at 429.

5. Georgia Quick Facts from the U.S. Census Bureau, http://quickfacts.census.gov/qfd/states/13000.html (last visited Jan. 31, 2007). The remaining population is made up of 2.7% Asian persons, 0.3% American Indian and/or Alaska Native persons, 0.1% Native Hawaiian persons and other Pacific Islanders, and 1% persons reporting two or more races. *Id.* Additionally, 7.1% of Georgia's total population identify themselves as persons of Hispanic or Latino origin. *Id.* (noting that because Hispanics may be of any race, they are included within the other applicable race categories).

6. BARRY A. KOSMIN, EGON MAYER & ARIELA KEYSAR, AMERICAN RELIGIOUS IDENTIFICATION SURVEY 2001, at 39, *available at* http://www.gc.cuny.edu/faculty/research_studies/aris.pdf (last visited Jan. 31, 2007).

7. USDA Economic Research Service, Georgia Fact Sheet, http://www.ers.usda.gov/StateFacts/GA.htm (last visited Sept. 17, 2006). According to the latest estimates, approximately 7.3 million people live in urban areas, approximately 1.8 million people live in rural areas. *Id.*

8. Georgia, http://www.netstate.com/states/links/ga_links.htm (last visited Dec. 7, 2006).

Family Income and Poverty Indicators

In 2004, Georgia's per capita gross product was $38,475, which was below the national average of $39,725.[9] During this same period, while the median household income in Georgia was $43,217,[10] 12.0% of Georgia's population was living in poverty, which was just below the national average of 12.4%.[11] More specifically, poverty affected 20.9% of Georgia's children,[12] 13.2% of its senior citizens,[13] and 12.0% of its families.[14] Of its female-headed households with children, 42.6% lived in poverty,[15] and 46.4% of the state's public elementary and secondary school students were eligible for free or reduced-price meals.[16] Of those living in poverty, approximately 50% were black, which represented 22% of Georgia's black population and 6% of its total population.[17] In an attempt to combat this poverty, Georgia spent approximately $6.2 billion on public welfare programs in 2002,[18] which made up 13.7% of its total government expenditures.[19]

Georgia's Public Elementary-Secondary School System

Overall Spending and Performance

For the 2003–2004 school year, Georgia spent $7,733 per pupil in its public elementary-secondary school system, which was slightly below the national average of $8,182.[20] Of this amount, 8.5% was provided by the federal government, 44.8% was provided by the state government, and 46.7% was provided by the local governments,[21] with property taxes making up 30.8% of the total funding.[22] Out of these funds, Georgia paid its elementary and secondary school teachers an estimated average annual

---

9. STATE RANKINGS 2006, *supra* note 1, at 89.

10. *Id.* at 96.

11. *Id.* at 495.

12. *Id.* at 497.

13. *Id.* at 496.

14. *Id.* at 498.

15. *Id.* at 499.

16. *Id.* at 532.

17. *See* Fact Sheet, American FactFinder, http://factfinder.census.gov/home/saff/main.html?_lang=en (select Georgia under "Get a Fact Sheet for your community") (last visited Feb. 22, 2007). Note that these numbers are based on the 2000 census because more recent numbers were not available.

18. STATE RANKINGS 2006, *supra* note 1, at 500.

19. *Id.* at 502.

20. GOVERNMENTS DIVISION, U.S. CENSUS BUREAU, PUBLIC EDUCATION FINANCES 2004, at 8 tbl.8 (2006).

21. *See id.* at 5 tbl.5.

22. *See id.* at 4 tbl.4.

salary of $46,526 during the 2004–2005 school year,[23] and in 2003, it provided a student/teacher ratio of 15.7, which was slightly better than the national average of 15.9.[24]

In academic performance, Georgia's fourth and eighth grade students scored lower than the national average in mathematics,[25] reading,[26] science,[27] and writing.[28]

Equity Issues

In 2004, the funding per student in Georgia's highest poverty districts actually exceeded that in its lowest poverty districts by $156.[29] When adjustments were made for the additional costs of educating students growing up in poverty, however, the funding in high poverty districts actually declined by $292.[30] On the other hand, Georgia spent $566 more per student in its highest minority districts, although this amount fell to $271 when adjustments for low-income students were made.[31]

Fourth graders eligible for free or reduced-price school lunches had test scores that were 9% lower in mathematics,[32] 12% lower in reading,[33] and 14% lower in writing[34] than those of students who were not eligible. The results were generally the same for eighth graders eligible for free or reduced price lunches; their test scores were 10% lower in mathematics,[35] 10% lower in reading,[36] and 14% lower in writing[37] than those of students who were not eligible.

---

23. Thomas D. Snyder et al., National Center for Education Statistics, Digest of Education Statistics 2005, at 116 tbl.77 (2006).

24. *Id.* at 98 tbl.65.

25. National Center for Education Statistics, U.S. Department of Education, The Nation's Report Card: Mathematics 2005, at 14 fig.11, 16 fig.12 (2005), *available at* http://nces.ed.gov/nationsreportcard/pdf/main2005/ 2006453.pdf [hereinafter Mathematics 2005].

26. National Center for Education Statistics, U.S. Department of Education, The Nation's Report Card: Reading 2005, at 14 fig.11, 16 fig.12 (2005), *available at* http://nces.ed.gov/nationsreportcard/pdf/main2005/2006451.pdf [hereinafter Reading 2005].

27. National Center for Education Statistics, U.S. Department of Education, The Nation's Report Card: Science 2005, at 16 fig.12, 28 fig.22 (2006), *available at* http://nces.ed.gov/nationsreportcard//pdf/main2005/2006466.pdf [hereinafter Science 2005].

28. Hilary R. Persky et al., National Center for Education Statistics, U.S. Department of Education, The Nation's Report Card: Writing 2002, at 23 tbl.2.2, 24 tbl.2.3 (2003), *available at* http://nces.ed.gov/nationsreportcard/pdf/main2002/2003529.pdf [hereinafter Writing 2002].

29. The Education Trust, Funding Gaps 2006, at 7 tbl.3 (2006), *available at* http://www2.edtrust.org/NR/rdonlyres/CDEF9403-5A75-437E-93FF-EBF1174181FB/0/FundingGap2006.pdf.

30. *Id.*

31. *Id.* at 7 tbl.4.

32. Mathematics 2005, *supra* note 25, at 20 tbl.5.

33. Reading 2005, *supra* note 26, at 20 tbl.5.

34. Writing 2002, *supra* note 28, at 75 tbl.3.24.

35. Mathematics 2005, *supra* note 25, at 21 tbl.6.

36. Reading 2005, *supra* note 26, at 21 tbl.6.

37. Writing 2002, *supra* note 28, at 76 tbl.3.25.

In September 2004, the Consortium for Adequate School Funding in Georgia (CASFG), which consists of 51 rural school systems, filed suit against the State of Georgia on the basis that the state had denied the children of Georgia an equal opportunity for an adequate education and had violated the equal education requirements of the Georgia constitution by having failed to provide adequate funding.[38] Specifically, the complaint alleged that the Georgia school funding system had failed "to provide school districts ... with the resources needed to educate their students to meet contemporary educational standards...."[39] On November 21, 2006, the Superior Court of Fulton County issued an order regarding the standard that should be used to determine the question of adequacy.[40] In the order, Judge Long stated that "if the plaintiffs are able to produce evidence that shows that the current State funding for public education is so low that 'it deprives students in any particular school district of basic educational opportunities,'[41] then they will have made their case."[42] The case is still pending before the Superior Court of Fulton County.

Availability of Publicly Funded Prekindergarten Programs

The Georgia Pre-K Program is available to all four-year-old children in the state but is not available to three-year-old children.[43] The program is funded solely by proceeds from the Georgia Lottery.[44] Total enrollment in this state-funded program is 72,902,[45] which represents just 26% of Georgia's 275,412 three- and four-year-old children.[46] The federally funded Head Start program enrolls an additional 21,546 children,[47] which represents 8% of Georgia's three- and four-year-old children.[48]

---

38. Consortium for Adequate School Funding in Georgia, Inc. v. State of Georgia, Civil Action No. 2004CV91004, Complaint at 3 (Super. Ct. of Fulton County, Georgia, Sept. 14, 2004) *available at* http://www.casfg.org/litigation/Ga_School_Finance_Complaint.pdf.

39. *Id.*

40. Consortium for Adequate School Funding in Georgia, Inc. v. State of Georgia, Civil Action No. 2004CV91004, Order (Super. Ct. of Fulton County, Georgia, Nov. 21, 2006) *available at* http://www.casfg.org/litigation/Order_on_Adequacy_Standard_11.21.06.pdf.

41. *Quoting* McDaniel v. Thomas, 285 S.E.2d 156, 166 (Ga. 1981).

42. *Consortium, supra* note 40, at 3.

43. W. STEVEN BARNETT ET AL., NATIONAL INSTITUTE FOR EARLY EDUCATION RESEARCH, THE STATE OF PRESCHOOL 2006, at 58 (2006), *available at* http://nieer.org/yearbook/pdf/yearbook.pdf.

44. *Id.*

45. *Id.* at 59.

46. *See id.* at 232.

47. *Id.* at 59.

48. *See id.* at 232.

Where Does Georgia Get Its Revenue?

At the end of fiscal year 2004, Georgia had total revenues of approximately $57.9 billion.[49] Of this amount, 44% was derived from state and local tax revenues and 17% was received from the federal government.[50] The remaining 39% came from other sources, including the Georgia Lottery, insurance trust revenue, and revenue from government-owned utilities and other commercial or auxiliary enterprises.

Tax Revenue

Georgia collected approximately $25.7 billion in state and local tax revenue during fiscal year 2004.[51] As a result, Georgia residents paid $2,877 per capita in state and local taxes, an amount which ranked 35th nationally.[52] The different types of tax sources were approximately apportioned as follows:

Individual income taxes	26.6%
Property taxes	30.6%
General and selective sales taxes	36.7%
Corporate income and other taxes	6.1%
	100.0%[53]

Federal Funding

During fiscal year 2004, 17% of Georgia's total revenues came from the federal government.[54] For every dollar of federal taxes paid, Georgia received $0.96 in federal funding, an amount which ranked 35th nationally[55] and was far below the national average of $1.17.[56]

Lottery Revenue

The Georgia Lottery was officially created in 1992 when the voters of Georgia approved a constitutional amendment which allowed the general assembly to operate and

---

49. U.S. Census Bureau, State and Local Government Finances 2003–04, http://www.census.gov/govs/www/estimate04.html (last visited Oct. 16, 2006) [hereinafter Government Finances].

50. *Id.*

51. *Id.* The total tax revenues were collected as follows: $14.6 billion by the state and $11.1 billion by local governments.

52. *Id.*

53. *Id.*

54. *Id.*

55. The Tax Foundation, Federal Spending Received Per Dollar of Taxes Paid by State 2004, http://www.taxfoundation.org/taxdata/show/266.html (last visited Sept. 17, 2006).

56. *See id.*

regulate lotteries on behalf of the state.[57] The Georgia Lottery sold its first lottery ticket in 1993.[58] Under Georgia's constitution, all proceeds from the Georgia Lottery are to be used solely for educational programs and educational purposes.[59] During fiscal year 2005, the Lottery had total revenues of $2.9 billion and net proceeds of $800 million, which were to be transferred to the Lottery for Education Account.[60]

Legal Structures of Major Tax Sources

Income

Georgia employs a broad-based income tax that uses adjusted gross income for federal income tax purposes as a starting point for determining the state's taxable net income.[61] However, a fairly large number of adjustments may be available to various individuals in calculating this amount.[62] Counties and municipalities may impose a 1% tax on Georgia's taxable net income of every resident in the taxing subdivision.[63] During fiscal year 2004, Georgia collected individual income tax of $766 per capita, an amount which ranked 16th nationally.[64]

In Georgia, a typical family of four (i.e., married taxpayers who file jointly and have two dependent children) are not required to pay any income tax until their combined exceeds $15,900, an amount which is well below the national poverty line of $20,615.[65] Georgia's income tax structure contains six tax brackets that impose a minimum marginal tax rate of 1% and a maximum marginal tax rate of 6%.[66] When statutory ex-

---

57. Official Home of the Georgia Lottery, Georgia Lottery Timeline, http://www.galottery .com/stc/aboutus/timeline.jsp (last visited Dec. 7, 2006).

58. *Id.*

59. GA. CONST. art. I, § II, ¶ VIII. Specifically, proceeds from the Georgia Lottery are used for tuition grants, scholarships, or loans to citizens of the state to attend colleges and universities within the state; voluntary prekindergarten programs; education shortfall reserves of not less than 10% of the net proceeds of the Lottery; and capital outlay projects for educational facilities. *Id.*

60. Official Home of the Georgia Lottery, Lottery Reports, Georgia Lottery 2005 Annual Report, http://www.galottery.com/gen/aboutUs/lotteryReports.jsp (last visited Dec. 7, 2006).

61. GA. CODE ANN. § 48-7-27.

62. *Id.*

63. GA. CODE ANN. § 48-7-141. Any county or municipality income tax levy requires a majority vote of the qualified electors in the taxing subdivision. *Id.* § 48-7-142.

64. STATE RANKINGS 2006, *supra* note 1, at 321.

65. JASON A. LEVITIS, CENTER ON BUDGET AND POLICY PRIORITIES, THE IMPACT OF STATE INCOME TAXES ON LOW-INCOME FAMILIES IN 2006, at 12 (2007), *available at* http://www .cbpp.org/2-22-06sfp.pdf. In 2006, Georgia taxpayers who were married and filing jointly could claim a standard deduction of $3,000, a personal exemption of $5,400 (combined for taxpayer and spouse), and dependent exemptions of $3,000 each. GA. CODE ANN. §§ 48-7-27, 48-7-26. Note, however, that the threshold calculation of $15,900 is greater than the sum of these deductions and exemptions because it includes additional tax benefits available to low-income families, such as the earned-income tax credit. *See* LEVITIS, *supra*.

66. GA. CODE ANN. § 48-7-20. Georgia's middle four tax brackets are 2%, 3%, 4% and 5%. *Id.*

emptions and the standard deduction are taken into account, the maximum marginal rate applies to every dollar of income exceeding $24,400.[67]

Property

Overview

Georgia has a typical property tax system that taxes the value of real estate, including leaseholds, and all personal property almost entirely at the local level, unless otherwise provided for by law.[68] During fiscal year 2004, Georgia collected approximately $7.8 billion dollars in property tax at the local level and approximately $65 million at the state level.[69] As a result, Georgia residents paid $880 per capita in state and local property taxes, an amount which ranked 34th nationally.[70]

Defining the Real Property Tax Base

Georgia classifies all real property into one of the following categories: 1) Residential, 2) Residential Transitional, 3) Agricultural, 4) Preferential, 5) Conservation Use, 6) Environmentally Sensitive, 7) Commercial, 8) Historic, 9) Industrial, and 10) Utility.[71] Real property classified as Residential, Commercial, Historic, Industrial, and Utility is assessed at 40% of the fair market value of the property.[72] Real property classi-

---

67. The standard deduction of $3,000 and the personal and dependent exemptions of $5,400 and $6,000, respectively, plus the threshold of taxable income for the highest tax bracket of $10,000, equals $24,400. *See supra* note 65.

68. GA. CODE ANN. § 48-5-3.

69. Government Finances, *supra* note 49.

70. *See Id.*

71. GA. COMP. R. & REGS. r. 560-11-2-.20. Residential property is 1) all land utilized, or best suited to be utilized, as a single-family home site and 2) all personal property owned by individuals. Residential Transitional property includes a residential improvement and no more than five acres of land underneath the improvement. Agricultural property, limited to 2,000 acres and owned by one or more individuals or a family-farm corporation, includes all real and personal property currently utilized, or best suited to be utilized, as an agricultural unit. Preferential property includes all land and improvements primarily used for bona fide agricultural purposes and receiving preferential assessment. Conservation Use property includes all land and improvements used in the good-faith production of agricultural products or timber. Environmentally Sensitive property includes all land certified as such by the Georgia Department of Natural Resources. Commercial property includes all real and personal property utilized as a business unit involved in the exchange of goods and services. Historic property includes up to two acres of land and improvements designated as a rehabilitated historic property or landmark historic property and receiving preferential assessment. Industrial property includes all real and personal property utilized as a business unit involved in manufacturing or processing goods. Utility property includes all real and personal property of railroad companies, public utility companies, and the flight equipment of airline companies. *Id.*

72. GA. CODE ANN. § 48-5-7.

fied as Residential Transitional, Conservation Use, and Environmentally Sensitive is assessed at 40% of the current use value of the property.[73] Real property classified as Agricultural and Preferential is assessed at 30% of the fair market value of the property.[74] Standing timber is assessed, once it is harvested or sold, at 100% of its fair market value.[75] All real property is valued on January 1 of each year.[76]

Real Property Tax Rates

The tax rates imposed on real property vary and are set by each taxing jurisdiction. Counties may levy and collect taxes for public purposes, including the payment of county police, the building and repairing of public buildings and bridges, and the payment of the administrative expenses of the county government.[77] Municipalities are authorized to levy a tax for their school system, which may not exceed 20 mills per dollar.[78] The average county and municipal tax millage rate in Georgia is around 30 mills (i.e., 1 mill equals 1 dollar per thousand; therefore 30 mills equals 30 dollars per thousand)[79]

Personal and Intangible Property

As mentioned previously, all personal property is subject to taxation at the local level, unless otherwise provided for by law.[80] Tangible personal property is classified as either Residential, Agricultural, Commercial, Industrial, or Utility and is assessed in the same manner as real property in these categories.[81] Intangible personal property is not subject to tax since the provisions regarding the taxation of intangible personal property were repealed in 1996.[82] Motor vehicles and mobile homes are subject to the property tax on the basis of the assessment level and the millage rate levied by the taxing authority on other tangible property.[83]

Exemptions

All personal clothing and effects, household furniture, equipment, and other property used within the home are exempt, as well as the tools and implements of the trade

---

73. *Id.*

74. *Id.*

75. *Id.* § 48-5-7.5.

76. *Id.* § 48-5-10.

77. *Id.* § 48-5-220.

78. Ga. Const. art. VIII, § VI, ¶ I.

79. Georgia Department of Revenue, Property Tax Guide for The Georgia Taxpayer, http://www.etax.dor.ga.gov/ptd/adm/taxguide/gen/rate.shtml (last visited Jan. 7, 2006).

80. Ga. Code Ann. § 48-5-3.

81. Ga. Comp. R. & Regs. r. 560-11-2-20.

82. *See* Ga. Code Ann. §§ 48-6-20 through -44 (which was repealed in 1996).

83. *Id.* § 48-5-443.

of manual laborers that do not exceed $2,500.[84] Citizens of Georgia are allowed a homestead exemption of up to $2,000 of the value of a homestead which is occupied by the taxpayer/owner as a residence.[85] The homestead exemption does not apply to taxes levied by municipalities.[86]

General and Selective Sales

General Sales

Georgia imposes a general retail sales-and-use tax, which makes up 27.7% of its total tax revenue.[87] This tax is imposed on the retail purchase, retail sale, storage, use, and consumption of tangible personal property and limited services.[88] These services include (1) telecommunications,[89] (2) custom printing,[90] and (3) lodging for less than 90 days.[91] The state sales tax rate is 4%,[92] and all counties and municipalities in the state may impose additional taxes at a rate of 1% as follows: joint county and municipal sales-and-use tax,[93] homestead options sales-and-use tax,[94] special county sales-and-use tax,[95] and the educational local option sales-and-use tax.[96] Total sales taxes in Georgia typically range from 6% to 7%.[97] Exemptions from its sales-and-use tax include, among other items, prescription drugs and prescription eye glasses, school lunches, food stamp purchases, machinery and equipment used for the irrigation of farm crops, and equipment used in the harvesting of pecans.[98]

Selective Sales

Selective sales taxes make up approximately 9% of Georgia's total revenue.[99] Of that amount, 2.9%[100] comes from a motor fuel sales tax that is imposed at a rate of 3%.[101] Georgia residents paid an average of $85 per capita in state motor fuel sales taxes in

---

84. *Id.* § 48-5-42.
85. *Id.* § 48-5-44.
86. *Id.*
87. Government Finances, *supra* note 49.
88. Ga. Code Ann. § 48-8-1.
89. Ga. Comp. R. & Regs. r. 560-12-2-.24.
90. Ga. Comp. R. & Regs. r. 560-12-2-.75.
91. *Id.* at 560-12-2-.51.
92. Ga. Code Ann. § 48-8-30.
93. *Id.* § 48-8-82.
94. *Id.* § 48-8-102.
95. *Id.* § 48-8-110.1.
96. *Id.* § 48-8-141.
97. CCH-EXP, SALES-TAX-GUIDE GA ¶ 61-735, Local Rates.
98. Ga. Code Ann. § 48-8-3.
99. Government Finances, *supra* note 49.
100. *Id.*
101. Ga. Code Ann. § 48-9-14.

2004, an amount which ranked 46th nationally and was below the national average of $115.[102]

In 2004, sales taxes on alcoholic beverages made up 1% of Georgia's total tax revenue.[103] Georgia residents paid $16.80 per capita in state alcoholic beverage sales taxes in 2004, an amount which ranked 18th nationally.[104]

The tobacco product sales tax makes up 0.9%[105] of Georgia's tax revenues and is imposed at a rate of $0.37 per pack of cigarettes.[106]

The remainder of Georgia's selective sales taxes makes up 4.2% of its total tax revenue. Of this amount, 0.9% represents taxes on utilities and the other 3.3% represents taxes on other specific commodities, businesses, or services not reported separately above (e.g., on contractors, lodging, lubricating oil, fuels other than motor fuel, motor vehicles, meals, soft drinks, margarine, etc.).[107]

Corporate Income and Other

Corporate Income

The corporate income tax makes up 2.0% of Georgia's total tax revenue.[108] Georgia's broad-based corporate income tax is imposed at a rate of 6% on a corporation's Georgia taxable net income, which is based on the corporation's federal taxable income.[109]

Georgia follows the federal income tax treatment of S corporations. Thus, they do not pay Georgia's corporate income tax as long as all shareholders are subject to Georgia income tax on their portion of income.[110] Georgia also follows the federal income tax treatment of limited partnerships, limited liability partnerships,[111] as well as limited liability companies, assuming they are treated as a partnership for federal tax purposes;[112] therefore, they do not pay Georgia's corporate income tax. However, if a limited liability company is treated as a corporation for federal income tax purposes, the entity is subject to Georgia's corporate income tax.[113]

---

102. STATE RANKINGS 2006, *supra* note 1, at 327.

103. Government Finances, *supra* note 49.

104. STATE RANKINGS 2006, *supra* note 1, at 335.

105. Government Finances, *supra* note 49.

106. STATE RANKINGS 2006, *supra* note 1, at 333.

107. *See* GOVERNMENTS DIVISION, U.S. CENSUS BUREAU, GOVERNMENT FINANCE AND EMPLOYMENT CLASSIFICATION MANUAL, at ch. 7 (2000), *available at* http://ftp2.census.gov/govs/class/classfull.pdf [hereinafter CLASSIFICATION MANUAL].

108. Government Finances, *supra* note 49.

109. GA. CODE ANN. §48-7-21.

110. *Id.* Note, however, that S corporations "doing business or owning property" in Georgia must pay an annual corporate net worth tax "for the privilege of carrying on a business within this state in the corporate form." *Id.* §48-13-72.

111. GA. CODE ANN. §48-7-23.

112. *Id.* §14-11-1104.

113. *Id.*

Other

During fiscal year 2004, the collection of all other taxes not previously mentioned accounted for 4.1% of Georgia's total tax revenue. Of this amount, approximately $66 million was generated by the estate and gift tax,[114] which is calculated on the basis of the federal credit for state death taxes allowable by § 2011 of the Internal Revenue Code of 1986.[115] The "other taxes" category is also made up of motor vehicle license taxes, documentary and stock transfer taxes, severance taxes, and all other taxes not listed separately or provided for in other categories, such as taxes on land based on a specified rate per acre (rather than on assessed value).[116]

Burden Analysis

The overall state and local tax burden on Georgia's taxpayers is very regressive. Taxpayers in the lowest quintile — those with incomes of less than $15,000 — bear a tax burden equal to 11.9% of their income, while taxpayers in the top 1% — those with incomes that exceed $281,000 — bear a tax burden of just 7.5% of their income.[117] It is also worth noting that, although Georgia obviously has no control over federal tax policy, federal itemized deductions for state and local personal income and property taxes nonetheless further reduce the burden on taxpayers in the top 1% to 5.4%.[118] Furthermore, between 1989 and 2002, the tax burden on the bottom quintile rose by approximately 2%, while the burden on the top 1% fell by approximately 0.2%.[119]

In terms of the income tax, the burden across income groups in Georgia is slightly progressive, with taxpayers in the lowest quintile bearing a tax burden of 0.6% and those in the top 1% bearing a tax burden of 4.9%.[120] In sharp contrast, however, the

---

114. Government Finances, *supra* note 49.

115. Ga. Code Ann. § 48-12-2. Note, however, that the Georgia estate tax does not apply to any estate with a date of death in a year in which the federal credit for state death taxes is not in force. *Id.* § 48-12-1.1.

116. *See* Classification Manual, *supra* note 107, at ch. 7.

117. *See* Robert S. McIntyre et al., Who Pays? A Distributional Analysis of the Tax Systems in All 50 States 36 (2d ed. 2003), *available at* http://www.itepnet.org/wp2000/text.pdf. Taxpayers in the second quintile bear a 11.3% total tax burden on incomes between $15,000 and $26,000; those in the third quintile bear a 10.6% tax burden on incomes between $26,000 and $41,000; those in the fourth quintile bear a 10.1% tax burden on incomes between $41,000 and $69,000; those in the 80th–95th percentiles bear a 9.5% tax burden on incomes between $69,000 and $142,000; finally, those in the 96th–99th percentiles bear a 8.7% tax burden on incomes between $142,000 and $281,000. *Id.*

118. *Id.* Taxpayers in the lowest and second lowest quintiles did not receive any benefit from these federal offsets, while those in the third quintile were able to reduce their individual tax burdens by 0.3%, those in the fourth quintile by 0.6%, those in the 80th–95th percentiles by 1.3%, and those in the 96th–99th percentiles by 1.8%. *Id.*

119. *Id.* at 37.

120. *See id.* at 36. Taxpayers in the second quintile bear a 2.1% income tax burden; those in the third quintile bear a 3.0% burden; those in the fourth quintile bear a 3.5% burden; those in

sales and excise taxes imposed by Georgia are extremely regressive, with taxpayers in the lowest quintile bearing a tax burden of 8.1% and those in the top 1% bearing a tax burden of just 1.1%.[121] Property taxes in Georgia are also regressive, with taxpayers in the lowest quintile bearing a tax burden of 3.3% and those in the top quintile bearing an average tax burden of 2.0%.[122]

the 80th–95th percentiles bear a 3.9% burden; finally, those in the 96th–99th percentiles bear a 4.3% burden. *Id.* Note, however, that these percentages include both individual and corporate income tax burdens; that within the 96th–99th percentiles, corporate income taxes represent 0.1% of this burden; and that in the top 1%, they represent 0.2% of this burden. *Id.*

121. *See Id.* Taxpayers in the second quintile bear a 6.9% sales-and-excise tax burden; those in the third quintile bear a 5.6% burden; those in the fourth quintile bear a 4.6% burden; those in the 80th–95th percentiles bear a 3.3% burden; finally, those in the 96th–99th percentiles bear a 2.1% burden. *Id.*

122. *See id.* Taxpayers in the second quintile bear a 2.3% property tax burden; those in the third quintile bear a 2.0% burden; those in the fourth quintile bear a 2.0% burden; those in the 80th–95th percentiles bear a 2.3% burden; those in the 96th–99th percentiles bear a 2.3% burden; finally, those in the top 1% bear a 1.5% burden. *Id.*

Hawaii

General Information

Basic Profile – Geography, Population, and Industry

Hawaii achieved statehood in 1959. The "Aloha State" is situated in the North Pacific Ocean, approximately 2,300 miles from the mainland United States. Honolulu is the state capital. It is located in the Hawaii-Aleutian time zone, which is five hours behind eastern standard time. Honolulu is the state capital.[1]

Hawaii ranks 42nd in population (approximately 1.3 million residents)[2] and 43rd in total land and water area (10,931 square miles).[3] Its population is approximately 26.8% white, 2.3% black, 41.5% Asian, and 9.0% Native Hawaiian and other Pacific Islander.[4] The state is approximately 20% Catholic, 12% Protestant, less than 1% Jewish, and 67% other.[5] Roughly 71% of Hawaii's population lives in urban areas.[6] Major industries include tourism; real estate, rental, and leasing; accommodation and food services; retail trade; construction; and health care and social assistance.[7]

---

1. Hawaii Visitors & Convention Bureau, Hawaii FAQs, http://www.gohawaii.com/about_hawaii/learn/faq (last visited Mar. 27, 2007).

2. STATE RANKINGS 2006, vi, 429 (Kathleen O'Leary Morgan & Scott Morgan eds., Morgan Quitno Press 2006).

3. *Id.* at 225.

4. Hawaii Quick Facts from the U.S. Census Bureau, http://quickfacts.census.gov/qfd/states/15000.html (last visited Jan. 31, 2007). The remaining population is made up of 0.3% American Indian and Alaska Native persons and 20.1% persons reporting two or more races. *Id.* Additionally, 8.0% of Hawaii's total population identify themselves as persons of Hispanic or Latino origin. *Id.* (noting that because Hispanics and Latinos may be of any race, they are also included within the other applicable race categories). *See id.*

5. DALE E. JONES ET AL., ASSOCIATION OF STATISTICIANS OF AMERICAN RELIGIOUS BODIES, RELIGIOUS CONGREGATIONS & MEMBERSHIP: 2000 (2000), *available at* http://www.thearda.com/mapsReports/reports/state/02_2000.asp (last visited Mar. 26, 2007). Note that Hawaii and Alaska were not included in the religious identification survey that is cited in the other chapters of this book. *See* BARRY A. KOSMIN, EGON MAYER & ARIELA KEYSAR, AMERICAN RELIGIOUS IDENTIFICATION SURVEY 2001, at 42, *available at* http://www.gc.cuny.edu/faculty/research_studies/aris.pdf.

6. *See* USDA Economic Research Service, Hawaii Fact Sheet, http://www.ers.usda.gov/StateFacts/HI.htm (last visited Oct. 16, 2006).

7. *See* U.S. Department of Commerce Bureau of Economic Analysis, Gross Domestic Product by State, http://www.bea.gov/bea/newsrelarchive/2006/gsp1006.xls (last visited Nov. 10, 2006).

Family Income and Poverty Indicators

In 2004, Hawaii's per capita gross product was $39,871, which was just above the national average of $39,725.[8] During this same period, although the median household income in Hawaii was $53,123,[9] 9.7% of Hawaii's population was living in poverty, which was below the national average of 12.4%.[10] More specifically, poverty affected 13.6% of Hawaii's children,[11] 8.3% of its senior citizens,[12] and 7.9% of its families.[13] Of its female-headed households with children, 29% lived in poverty,[14] and 42.5% of the state's public elementary and secondary school students were eligible for free or re-duced-price meals.[15] Of those living in poverty, approximately 1.3% were black, which represented 7.3% of Hawaii's black population and 0.1% of its total population.[16] Hawaii spent approximately $1.1 billion on public welfare programs in 2002,[17] which made up 13.8% of its total government expenditures.[18]

Hawaii's Public Elementary-Secondary School System

Overall Spending and Performance

For the 2003–2004 school year, Hawaii spent $8,533 per pupil in its public elemen-tary-secondary school system, which hovered around the national average of $8,182.[19] Of this amount, 11.1% was provided by the federal government, 86.6% was provided by the state government, and 2.4% was provided by the local governments.[20] Out of these funds, Hawaii paid its elementary and secondary school teachers an estimated average annual salary of $44,273 during the 2004–2005 school year,[21] and in 2003, it

---

8. STATE RANKINGS 2006, *supra* note 2, at 89.

9. *Id.* at 96.

10. *Id.* at 495.

11. *Id.* at 497.

12. *Id.* at 496.

13. *Id.* at 498.

14. *Id.* at 499.

15. *Id.* at 532.

16. *See* Fact Sheet, American FactFinder, http://factfinder.census.gov/home/saff/main.html?_lang=en (select "Hawaii" under "Get a Fact Sheet for your community") (last visited Feb. 16, 2007). Note that these numbers are based on the 2000 census because more recent numbers were not available.

17. *Id.* at 500.

18. *Id.* at 502.

19. GOVERNMENTS DIVISION, U.S. CENSUS BUREAU, PUBLIC EDUCATION FINANCES 2004, at 8 tbl.8 (2006), *available at* http://www2.census.gov/govs/school/04f33pub.pdf.

20. *See id.* at 5 tbl.5.

21. THOMAS D. SNYDER ET AL., NATIONAL CENTER FOR EDUCATION STATISTICS, DIGEST OF EDUCATION STATISTICS 2005, at 116 tbl.77 (2006), *available at* http://nces.ed.gov/pubsearch/pubs info.asp?pubid=2006030.

provided a student/teacher ratio of 16.5, which was worse than the national average of 15.9.[22]

In academic performance, Hawaii's fourth and eighth grade students scored lower than the national average in mathematics,[23] reading,[24] science,[25] and writing.[26]

Equity Issues

Fourth graders eligible for free or reduced-price school lunches had test scores that were 8% lower in mathematics,[27] 11% lower in reading,[28] and 12% lower in writing[29] than those of students who were not eligible. The results were similar for eighth graders eligible for free or reduced price lunches; their test scores were 9% lower in mathematics,[30] 7% lower in reading,[31] and 14% lower in writing[32] than those of students who were not eligible.

Hawaii is one of the five states in which no litigation has been filed challenging school funding.[33] However, a 2005 study commissioned by the Hawaii Department of Education found that the state's school system was grossly underfunded and made recommendations for improvement.[34] In 2004, the Hawaii legislature enacted the Reinventing Education Act of 2004, which provides for the implementation of weighted student funding beginning with the 2006–2007 school year, along with other reforms.[35]

---

22. *Id.* at 98 tbl.65.

23. NATIONAL CENTER FOR EDUCATION STATISTICS, U.S. DEPARTMENT OF EDUCATION, THE NATION'S REPORT CARD: MATHEMATICS 2005, at 14 fig.11, 16 fig.12 (2005), *available at* http://nces.ed.gov/nationsreportcard/pdf/main2005/ 2006453.pdf [hereinafter MATHEMATICS 2005].

24. NATIONAL CENTER FOR EDUCATION STATISTICS, U.S. DEPARTMENT OF EDUCATION, THE NATION'S REPORT CARD: READING 2005, at 14 fig.11, 16 fig.12 (2005), *available at* http://nces.ed.gov/nationsreportcard/pdf/main2005/2006451.pdf [hereinafter READING 2005].

25. NATIONAL CENTER FOR EDUCATION STATISTICS, U.S. DEPARTMENT OF EDUCATION, THE NATION'S REPORT CARD: SCIENCE 2005, at 16 fig.12, 28 fig.22 (2006), *available at* http://nces.ed.gov/nationsreportcard//pdf/main2005/2006466.pdf [hereinafter SCIENCE 2005].

26. HILARY R. PERSKY ET AL., NATIONAL CENTER FOR EDUCATION STATISTICS, U.S. DEPARTMENT OF EDUCATION, THE NATION'S REPORT CARD: WRITING 2002, at 23 tbl.2.2, 24 tbl.2.3 (2003), *available at* http://nces.ed.gov/nationsreportcard/pdf/main2002/2003529.pdf [hereinafter WRITING 2002].

27. MATHEMATICS 2005, *supra* note 23, at 20 tbl.5.

28. READING 2005, *supra* note 24, at 20 tbl.5.

29. WRITING 2002, *supra* note 26, at 75 tbl.3.24.

30. MATHEMATICS 2005, *supra* note 23, at 21 tbl.6.

31. READING 2005, *supra* note 24, at 21 tbl.6.

32. WRITING 2002, *supra* note 26, at 76 tbl.3.25.

33. National Access Network, State by State, Hawaii, http://www.schoolfunding.info/states/hi/lit_hi.php3 (last visited Mar. 19, 2007).

34. National Access Network, State by State, Hawaii, http://www.schoolfunding.info/news/policy/10-11-05HIadequacystudy.php3 (last visited Mar. 19, 2007).

35. S.B. 3238, 22nd Leg. (Haw. 2004) (amended).

Availability of Publicly Funded Prekindergarten Programs

Hawaii does not have a standard state-funded prekindergarten program, although the state does offer funding for initiatives that provide some support for prekindergarten education.[36] The federally funded Head Start program enrolls 2,478 children,[37] which represents 7% of Hawaii's 35,412 three- and four-year-old children.[38]

Where Does Hawaii Get Its Revenue?

At the end of fiscal year 2004, Hawaii had total revenues of approximately $9.98 billion.[39] Of this amount, 48% was derived from state and local tax revenues and 18% was received from the federal government.[40] The remaining 34% came from other sources, including insurance trust revenue, as well as revenue from government-owned utilities and other commercial or auxiliary enterprises.[41]

Tax Revenue

Hawaii collected approximately $4.8 billion in state and local tax revenue during fiscal year 2004.[42] As a result, Hawaii residents paid $3,813 per capita in state and local government taxes in 2004, an amount which ranked 8th nationally.[43] The different types of tax sources were approximately apportioned as follows:

Individual income taxes	24.3%
Property taxes	15.0%
General and selective sales taxes	54.1%
Corporate income and other taxes	6.6%
	100.0%[44]

---

36. W. STEVEN BARNETT ET AL., NATIONAL INSTITUTE FOR EARLY EDUCATION RESEARCH, THE STATE OF PRESCHOOL 2006, at 60 (2006), *available at* http://nieer.org/yearbook/pdf/yearbook.pdf.

37. *Id.* at 61.

38. *See id.* at 232.

39. U.S. Census Bureau, State and Local Government Finances 2003–04, http://www.census.gov/govs/www/estimate04.html (last visited Oct. 6, 2006) [hereinafter Government Finances].

40. *Id.*

41. *Id.*

42. The total tax revenues were collected as follows: $3.8 billion by the state and just under $1 billion by local governments. *Id.*

43. *Id.*

44. *Id.*

Federal Funding

During fiscal year 2004, 18% of Hawaii's total revenues came from the federal government.[45] For every dollar of federal taxes paid, Hawaii received $1.60 in federal funding, an amount which ranked 8th nationally and was well above the national average of $1.17.[46]

Lottery Revenues

Hawaii does not operate a state lottery.

Legal Structures of Major Tax Sources

Income

Hawaii employs a broad-based income tax that uses adjusted gross income for federal income tax purposes as a starting point for determining the state's taxable income.[47] However, a fairly large number of adjustments may be available to various individuals in calculating this amount.[48] Although the state legislature can delegate the state's taxing power to counties,[49] it has not done so in regard to income taxes. During fiscal year 2004, Hawaii collected personal income tax of $926 per capita, an amount which ranked 10th nationally.[50]

In Hawaii, a typical family of four (i.e., married taxpayers who file jointly and have two dependent children) are not required to pay any income tax until their combined income exceeds $11,500, an amount which ranks 47th nationally and is well below the national poverty line of $20,615.[51] Hawaii's income tax structure contains nine tax brackets that impose a minimum marginal rate of 1.4% and a maximum marginal rate of 8.25%.[52] When statutory exemptions and the standard deduction are taken into account, the maximum marginal rate applies to every dollar of income exceeding

---

45. Government Finances, *supra* note 39.

46. *See* The Tax Foundation, Federal Spending Received Per Dollar of Taxes Paid by State 2004, http://www.taxfoundation.org/taxdata/show/266.html (last visited Oct. 16, 2006).

47. *See* Haw. Rev. Stat. §§ 235-1, 235-2.3.

48. *See id.* § 235-7.

49. Haw. Const. art. VIII, § 3.

50. State Rankings 2006, *supra* note 2, at 321.

51. Jason A. Levitis, Center on Budget and Policy Priorities, The Impact of State Income Taxes on Low-Income Families in 2006, at 12 (2007). In 2006, Hawaii taxpayers who were married and filing jointly could claim a combined standard deduction of $4,000, as well as personal and dependent exemptions of $1,040 for each available federal exemption. Haw. Rev. Stat. §§ 235-2.4, 235-54(a). Note, however, that the threshold calculation of $11,500 is greater than the sum of these deductions and exemptions because it includes additional tax benefits available to low-income families, such as the earned-income tax credit. *See* Levitis *supra.*

52. Haw. Rev. Stat. § 235.51. The rates applied to Hawaii's middle seven tax brackets are 3.2%, 5.5%, 6.4%, 6.8%, 7.2%, 7.6%, and 7.9%. *Id.*

$88,160.[53] Hawaii is one of the few states that give preferable treatment to capital gains—by taxing them at an alternate rate of 7.25% when the taxpayer has ordinary income that is taxed at a rate over 7.25%.[54] However, this preferential treatment is not nearly as liberal as the federal system's treatment of capital gains, given that the highest marginal rate imposed by Hawaii's income tax system is 8.25%.[55]

Property

Overview

Hawaii has a typical property tax system that taxes the value of real property at the local level. Property taxes were levied by the state until the 1978 Constitutional Convention adopted a constitutional amendment that transferred the power to tax property to the counties. During fiscal year 2004, Hawaii localities collected property taxes of $720.8 million.[56] As a result, Hawaii residents paid $571 per capita in property taxes, an amount which ranked 42nd nationally.[57]

Defining the Real Property Tax Base

Real property in Hawaii is classified into the following general categories: (a) single-family and two-family residential; (b) three-or-more family residential, apartment, hotel and resort; (c) commercial; (d) industrial; (e) agricultural; and (f) conservation.[58] County ordinances generally provide for the assessment of real property at 100% of fair market value.[59] However, as discussed below, the rates of tax may vary for different categories of property.[60] Real property used for agricultural purposes is granted current use valuation.[61] Furthermore, a landowner who dedicates his or her land for certain agricultural or ranching uses for twenty years may receive a special assessment ratio of 50%.[62] Hawaii has no specific statutory provisions concerning the reappraisal of property. Property taxes are assessed on an annual basis.[63]

---

53. The standard deduction and exemptions of $4,000 and $4,160, respectively, plus the threshold of taxable income for the highest tax bracket of $80,000, equals $88,160. See supra notes 51–52. Note, however, that for tax years beginning after 2006, the threshold of taxable income for the highest tax bracket is increased to $96,000. Id.

54. Haw. Rev. Stat. § 235-51(f).

55. See id. § 235-51.

56. Government Finances, supra note 39.

57. State Rankings 2006, supra note 2, at 294.

58. Haw. Rev. Stat. § 246-10.

59. CCH-EXP, HI-TAXRPTR ¶ 20-605, Overview.

60. Id.

61. Haw. Rev. Stat. § 246-10.

62. Id. § 246-12.

63. Id. § 246-3.

Real Property Tax Rates

The rate of tax for each category of property is set at the county level.[64] The counties currently levy rates for different property categories ranging from $3.44 per $1,000 (3.44 mills) to $11.37 per $1,000 (11.37 mills).[65]

Personal and Intangible Property

Hawaii does not tax personal or intangible property.

Exemptions

Although an active state statute sets a general homestead exemption in Hawaii,[66] the maximum exemptions available to qualifying Hawaiian homeowners are generally set by county ordinances, which provide for higher exemptions than the state statute. In Hawaii County, the homestead exemption is $40,000 for most taxpayers, $80,000 for taxpayers aged 60 to 69, and $100,000 for taxpayers over 70.[67] In the City and County of Honolulu, the homestead exemption is $80,000 for most taxpayers and $120,000 for taxpayers aged 65 and older.[68] In Kauai County, the homestead exemption is $48,000 for most taxpayers, $96,000 for taxpayers aged 60 to 69, and $120,000 for taxpayers aged 70 and older.[69] In Maui County, the homestead exemption is $300,000.[70] Furthermore, a Hawaii statute gives disabled veterans or their unmarried surviving spouses

---

64. *Id.* § 246A-2.

65. CCH-EXP, HI-TAXRPTR ¶ 20-405, Rates of Tax. Honolulu County imposes rates ranging from 3.75 mills for improved residential and apartment property to 11.37 mills for hotel and resort, commercial, and industrial property. *Id.* Maui County imposes rates ranging from 3.50 mills for homeowner property to 8.30 mills for resort property. *Id.* Hawaii County imposes a rate of 5.55 mills for homeowner property, a rate of 9.10 mills for improved residential property, and a rate of 9.85 mills for all other categories. *Id.* Kauai County imposes rates ranging from 3.44 mills for homestead property to 7.95 mills for hotel and resort, apartment, commercial, and industrial property. *Id.*

66. *See* HAW. REV. STAT. § 246-26.

67. HAWAII COUNTY, HAW., CODE § 19-71, *available at* http://www.hawaii-county.com/countycode/chapter19.pdf (last visited Apr. 1, 2007).

68. HONOLULU, HAW., REVISED ORDINANCES § 8-10.4, *available at* http://www.honolulu.gov/refs/roh/8a10.htm (last visited Apr. 1, 2007). Furthermore, taxpayers aged 75 and older with qualifying low levels of income are eligible for increased homestead exemptions as follows: $140,000 for taxpayers aged 75 to 79, $160,000 for taxpayers aged 80 to 84, $ 180,000 for taxpayers aged 85 to 89, and $200,000 for taxpayers aged 90 and over. *Id.*

69. County of Kauai, Department of Finance, Real Property Assessment Section, http://www.kauai.gov/Government/Departments/Finance/RealProperty/ExemptionInformation/tabid/95/Default.aspx (last visited Mar. 27, 2007). Homeowners with income levels below $40,000 are entitled to an additional $55,000 homestead exemption. *Id.*

70. MAUI COUNTY, HAW., CODE, § 3.48.450, *available at* http://ordlink.com/codes/maui/index.htm (last visited Apr. 1, 2007).

an exemption of the entire value of their homestead.[71] A state statute also provides an exemption of $25,000 of *any* real property (in addition to any homestead exemption) owned by individuals who are blind, deaf, totally disabled, or afflicted with Hansen's disease.[72]

General and Selective Sales

General Sales

Hawaii imposes a general excise tax, which made up 39.5% of Hawaii's total tax revenue in 2004.[73] This tax applies to the sale of tangible personal property, the renting of personal property, and the rendering of services to end-consumers by one engaged in a business.[74] The tax also applies to all other business activities in the state, including manufacturing, contracting, and acting as a sales representative or purchasing agent.[75] The general excise tax is levied and assessed against the retailer or service provider,[76] although the tax may be passed on to the consumer by contract.[77] Hawaii's general excise tax is imposed on all services unless an exemption applies.[78]

Hawaii retailers are typically charged a general excise tax rate of 4%, while wholesalers and manufacturers are generally charged a rate of 0.5%.[79] Insurance producers are charged a rate of 1.15%.[80] Legislation passed in 2005 authorized counties meeting certain requirements to adopt a local general excise-and-use tax surcharge of up to 0.5%.[81] In order to take advantage of this delegation of taxing authority, a county had to adopt an ordinance before December 31, 2005; not levy any taxes before January 1, 2007; and schedule the surcharge to be repealed on December 31, 2022.[82] The City and County of Honolulu satisfied the requirements and adopted a 0.5% county surcharge on the island of Oahu, effective January 1, 2007.[83]

---

71. HAW. REV. STAT. § 246-29.

72. *Id.* §§ 246-30 to 31. At least two counties, Hawaii and Kauai, have increased the amount of this exemption to $50,000. County of Kauai, *supra* note 69; HAWAII COUNTY, HAW., CODE § 19-74 to 75, *available at* http://www.hawaii-county.com/countycode/chapter19.pdf (last visited Apr. 1, 2007).

73. Government Finances, *supra* note 39.

74. HAW. REV. STAT. §§ 237-13 to 18.

75. *Id.*

76. *Id.*

77. *See* Hawaii Department of Taxation, Tax Facts 96-1, General Excise vs. Sales Tax, http://www.hawaii.gov/tax/taxfacts/tf96-01.pdf (last visited Dec. 28, 2006).

78. HAW. REV. STAT. § 237-13.

79. *See id.*

80. *Id.*

81. *See id.* § 46-16-8.

82. *Id.*

83. *See* HONOLULU, HAW., REVISED ORDINANCES § 6-60, *available at* http://www.honolulu.gov/refs/roh/6.htm (last visited Apr. 1, 2007).

Some exemptions to the general excise tax include food purchased with food stamps and WIC vouchers (but not other food), prescription drugs (but not nonprescription drugs), and prosthetic devices.[84]

Selective Sales

Selective sales taxes constituted 14.7% of Hawaii's total tax revenue during fiscal year 2004.[85] Of that amount, 3.3% came from motor fuel sales taxes.[86] Hawaii residents paid an average of $67 per capita in state motor fuel sales taxes in 2004, an amount which ranked 47th nationally and was well below the national average of $115.[87]

The tobacco product sales tax made up 1.6% of Hawaii's tax revenue during fiscal year 2004.[88] The state's residents paid $62.90 per capita in state tobacco sales taxes in 2004, an amount which ranked 13th nationally.[89]

Sales taxes on alcoholic beverages made up 0.9% of Hawaii's total tax revenue during fiscal year 2004.[90] Hawaii residents paid $32.68 per capita in state alcoholic beverage sales taxes in 2004, an amount which ranked 4th nationally.[91]

The remainder of Hawaii's selective sales taxes constituted 8.8% of its total tax revenue in 2004.[92] Of that percentage, 3.3% represented taxes on utilities and the other 5.5% represented taxes on other specific commodities, businesses, or services not reported separately above (e.g., on contractors, lodging, lubricating oil, fuels other than motor fuel, motor vehicles, meals, soft drinks, margarine, etc.).[93]

Corporate Income and Other

Corporate Income

The corporate income tax comprised 1.2% of Hawaii's total tax revenue during fiscal year 2004.[94] This broad-based income tax is calculated with federal taxable income as the starting point.[95] The corporate income tax applies only to C corporations, since Hawaii follows the federal pass-through treatment of partnerships, S corporations, and limited liability companies.[96] The corporation income tax structure contains three tax brackets that impose a minimum marginal rate of 4.4% and a maximum marginal rate

---

84. Haw. Rev. Stat. § 237-24, 24.3.
85. Government Finances, *supra* note 39.
86. *Id.*
87. State Rankings 2006, *supra* note 2, at 327.
88. Government Finances, *supra* note 39.
89. State Rankings 2006, *supra* note 2, at 332.
90. Government Finances, *supra* note 39.
91. State Rankings 2006, *supra* note 2, at 335.
92. Government Finances, *supra* note 39.
93. *Id.*; *see* Governments Division, U.S. Census Bureau, Government Finance and Employment Classification Manual, at ch. 7 (2000), *available at* http://ftp2.census.gov/govs/class/classfull.pdf [hereinafter Classification Manual].
94. Government Finances, *supra* note 39.
95. *See* Haw. Rev. Stat. § 235-1, 235-2.3.
96. *See id.* §§ 235-2.3, 235-95.

of 6.4%.[97] The maximum marginal rate applies to every dollar of income exceeding $100,000.[98]

Other

During fiscal year 2004, the collection of all other taxes not previously mentioned generated $259.2 million, which comprised 5.4% of Hawaii's total tax revenue.[99] Of that amount, $9.8 million came from estate taxes, which are generally imposed in an amount equal to the federal credit for state death taxes, with subtractions for decedents who die owning property in other states.[100] Although the Hawaii estate tax statutes are still in effect, the repeal of the federal credit for state death taxes[101] has effectively eliminated the Hawaii estate tax. The "other taxes" category is further made up of various license taxes, documentary or stock transfer taxes, severance taxes, and all other taxes not listed separately or provided for in other categories.[102]

Burden Analysis

The overall state and local tax burden on Hawaii's taxpayers is very regressive. Taxpayers in the lowest quintile—those with incomes of less than $14,000—bear a tax burden equal to 12.6% of their income, while taxpayers in the top 1%—those with incomes that exceed $238,000—bear a tax burden of just 8% of their income.[103] It is also worth noting that, although Hawaii obviously has no control over federal tax policy, federal itemized deductions for state and local personal income and property taxes nonetheless further reduce the burden on taxpayers in the top 1% to 5.8%.[104] Fur-

---

97. *Id.* § 235-71(a).

98. *Id.* Corporate income is taxed at a rate of 4.4% up to $25,000; a rate of 5.4% from $25,000 to $100,000; and a rate of 6.4% above $100,000. *Id.*

99. Government Finances, *supra* note 39.

100. *See* Haw. Rev. Stat. § 236D-1.

101. *See* Economic Growth and Tax Relief Reconciliation Act of 2001, Pub. L. No. 107-16 (2001).

102. *See* Classification Manual, *supra* note 93, at ch.7.

103. *See* Robert S. McIntyre et al., Who Pays? A Distributional Analysis of the Tax Systems in All 50 States 38 (2d ed. 2003), *available at* http://www.itepnet.org/wp2000/text.pdf. Taxpayers in the second quintile bear a 12.3% total tax burden on incomes between $14,000 and $27,000; those in the third quintile bear a 11.2% tax burden on incomes between $27,000 and $42,000; those in the fourth quintile bear a 10% tax burden on incomes between $42,000 and $68,000; those in the 80th–95th percentiles bear a 9.2% tax burden on incomes between $68,000 and $124,000; finally, those in the 96th–99th percentiles bear a 8.4% tax burden on incomes between $124,000 and $238,000. *Id.*

104. *Id.* Taxpayers in the lowest and second lowest quintiles did not receive any benefit from these federal offsets, while those in the third quintile were able to reduce their individual tax burdens by 0.2%, those in the fourth quintile by 0.5%, those in the 80th–95th percentiles by 1%, and those in the 96th–99th percentiles by 1.6%. *Id.*

thermore, between 1989 and 2002, while the tax burden on the bottom quintile fell by approximately 0.2%, the burden on the top 1% fell by approximately 1.2%.[105]

In terms of the income tax, the burden across income groups in Hawaii is slightly progressive, with taxpayers in the lowest quintile bearing a tax burden of 1.3% and those in the top 1% bearing a tax burden of 5.7%.[106] In sharp contrast, however, the sales and excises taxes imposed by Hawaii are extremely regressive, with taxpayers in the lowest quintile bearing a tax burden of 9.8% and those in the top 1% bearing a tax burden of just 1.4%.[107] Property taxes in Hawaii are also regressive, with taxpayers in the lowest quintile bearing a tax burden of 1.5% and those in the top quintile bearing an average tax burden of 1.1%.[108]

---

105. *Id.* at 39.

106. *See id.* at 38. Taxpayers in the second quintile bear a 3.5% income tax burden; those in the third quintile bear a 4% burden; those in the fourth quintile bear a 4.4% burden; those in the 80th–95th percentiles bear a 4.6% burden; finally, those in the 96th–99th percentiles bear a 4.9% burden. *Id.* Note, however, that these percentages include both individual and corporate income tax burdens and that within the top 1%, corporate income taxes represent 0.1% of the income tax burden. *Id.*

107. *See id.* Taxpayers in the second quintile bear a 7.9% sales-and-excise tax burden; those in the third quintile bear a 6.1% burden; those in the fourth quintile bear a 4.7% burden; those in the 80th–95th percentiles bear a 3.6% burden; finally, those in the 96th–99th percentiles bear a 2.4% burden. *Id.*

108. *See id.* Taxpayers in the second quintile bear a 0.8% property tax burden; those in the third quintile bear a 1.1% burden; those in the fourth quintile bear a 0.9% burden; those in the 80th–95th percentiles bear a 1.1% burden; those in the 96th–99th percentiles bear a 1.2% burden; finally, those in the top 1% bear a 0.9% burden. *Id.*

Idaho

General Information

Basic Profile – Geography, Population, and Industry

Admitted to the Union in 1890, Idaho is commonly referred to as the "Gem State."[1] It is located in the western region of the United States and is bordered by Washington and Oregon on the west, Nevada and Utah on the south, and Wyoming and Montana on the east. Idaho is split between the Pacific and mountain time zones, and its capital is Boise.[2]

In 2005, Idaho ranked 39th in population (approximately 1.43 million residents); the state ranks 14th in total area (83,570 square miles).[3] Its population is 95.5% white and 0.6% black.[4] Additionally, 9.1% of its population identify themselves as persons of Hispanic or Latino origin.[5] The state is 15% Catholic; 58% Protestant; and less than 0.5% Jewish; 27% claim a religion outside the Judeo-Christian tradition or no religion at all.[6] Idaho is mostly urban, with 64% of the population living in cities and towns.[7] Major industries include manufacturing, agriculture, tourism, food and similar products, lumber products, mining, and technology.[8]

---

1. State Rankings 2006, vi, 1 (Kathleen O'Leary Morgan & Scott Morgan eds., Morgan Quitno Press 2006).

2. *Id.* at vi.

3. *Id.* at 429.

4. Idaho Quick Facts from the U.S. Census Bureau, http://quickfacts.census.gov/qfd/states/16000.html (last visited Jan. 27, 2007). The remaining population is made up of 1.0% Asian persons; 1.4% American Indian and/or Alaska Native persons; 0.1% Native Hawaiian and other Pacific Islanders; and 1.3% persons reporting two or more races. *Id.*

5. *Id.* (noting that because Hispanics may be of any race, they are included within the other applicable race categories).

6. Barry A. Kosmin, Egon Mayer & Ariela Keysar, American Religious Identification Survey 2001, at 41, *available at* http://www.gc.cuny.edu/faculty/research_studies/aris.pdf.

7. USDA Economic Research Service, Idaho Fact Sheet, http://www.ers.usda.gov/StateFacts/ID.htm (last visited Sept. 17, 2006). According to the latest estimates, approximately 0.5 million people live in rural areas, 0.9 million people live in urban areas. *Id.*

8. Discover Idaho, Idaho Official Website, http://gov.idaho.gov/fyi/kidbook/KidBook.pdf, (Last visited Nov. 12, 2006).

Family Income and Poverty Indicators

In 2004, Idaho's per capita gross product was $31,231, which ranked among the bottom ten states nationally and was below the national average of $39,725.[9] During this same period, although the median household income in Idaho was $42,519,[10] 10.5% of Idaho's population was living in poverty, which was below the national average of 12.4%.[11] More specifically, poverty affected 19.1% of Idaho's children,[12] 7.2% of its senior citizens,[13] and 11.1% of its families.[14] Of its female-headed households with children, 43.4% lived in poverty,[15] and 37.0% of the state's public elementary and secondary school students were eligible for free or reduced-priced meals.[16] Of those living in poverty, approximately 0.6% were black, which represented 15.7% of Idaho's black population and 0.1% of its total population.[17] In an attempt to combat this poverty, Idaho spent approximately $1.0 billion on public welfare programs in 2002,[18] which made up 15.2% of its total government expenditures.[19]

Idaho's Public Elementary-Secondary School System

Overall Spending and Performance

For the 2003–2004 school year, Idaho spent $6,028 per pupil in its public elementary-secondary school system, which was substantially below the national average of $8,182.[20] Of this amount, 10.2% was provided by the federal government, 58.2% was provided by the state government, and 31.6% was provided by the local governments,[21] with property taxes making up 27.9% of the total funding.[22] Out of these funds, Idaho paid its elementary and secondary school teachers an estimated average annual salary

---

9. STATE RANKINGS 2006, *supra* note 1, at 89.

10. *Id.* at 96.

11. *Id.* at 495.

12. *Id.* at 497.

13. *Id.* at 496.

14. *Id.* at 498.

15. *Id.* at 499.

16. *Id.* at 532.

17. *See* Fact Sheet, American FactFinder, http://factfinder.census.gov/home/saff/main.html?_lang=en (select "Idaho" under "Get a Fact Sheet for your community") (last visited Feb. 16, 2007). Note that these numbers are based on the 2000 census because more recent numbers were not available.

18. STATE RANKINGS 2006, *supra* note 1, at 500.

19. *Id.* at 502.

20. GOVERNMENTS DIVISION, U.S. CENSUS BUREAU, PUBLIC EDUCATION FINANCES 2004, at 8 tbl.8 (2006).

21. *See id.* at 5 tbl.5.

22. *See id.* at 4 tbl.4.

of $42,122 during the 2004–2005 school year,[23] but during the fall of 2003, it provided a student/teacher ratio of 17.9, which was worse than the national average of 15.9.[24]

In academic performance, Idaho's fourth grade students scored lower than the national average in writing[25] and higher than the national average in mathematics,[26] reading,[27] and science,[28] while Idaho's eighth graders scored lower than the national average in writing[29] and higher than the national average in mathematics,[30] reading,[31] and science.[32]

Equity Issues

In 2004, revenues spent per student in Idaho's highest poverty districts were determined to be $55 less than the revenues spent in its lowest poverty districts.[33] When adjustments were made for the additional costs of educating students growing up in poverty, however, the funding gap grew to $257.[34] Similarly, Idaho spent $836 less per student in its highest minority districts, and this amount grew to $849 when adjustments for low-income students were made.[35]

Fourth graders eligible for free or reduced-price school lunches had test scores that were 5.6% lower in mathematics,[36] 8.7% lower in reading,[37] and 10.8% lower in writ-

23. THOMAS D. SNYDER ET AL., NATIONAL CENTER FOR EDUCATION STATISTICS, DIGEST OF EDUCATION STATISTICS 2005, at 116 tbl.77 (2006).

24. *Id.* at 98 tbl.65.

25. HILARY R. PERSKY ET AL., NATIONAL CENTER FOR EDUCATION STATISTICS, U.S. DEPARTMENT OF EDUCATION, THE NATION'S REPORT CARD: WRITING 2002, at 23 tbl.2.2 (2003), *available at* http://nces.ed.gov/nationsreportcard/pdf/main2002/2003529.pdf [hereinafter WRITING 2002].

26. NATIONAL CENTER FOR EDUCATION STATISTICS, U.S. DEPARTMENT OF EDUCATION, THE NATION'S REPORT CARD: MATHEMATICS 2005, at 14 fig.11 (2005), *available at* http://nces.ed.gov/nationsreportcard/pdf/main2005/ 2006453.pdf [hereinafter MATHEMATICS 2005].

27. NATIONAL CENTER FOR EDUCATION STATISTICS, U.S. DEPARTMENT OF EDUCATION, THE NATION'S REPORT CARD: READING 2005, at 14 fig.11 (2005), *available at* http://nces.ed.gov/nationsreportcard/pdf/main2005/2006451.pdf [hereinafter READING 2005].

28. NATIONAL CENTER FOR EDUCATION STATISTICS, U.S. DEPARTMENT OF EDUCATION, THE NATION'S REPORT CARD: SCIENCE 2005, at 16 fig.12 (2006), *available at* http://nces.ed.gov/nationsreportcard//pdf/main2005/2006466.pdf [hereinafter SCIENCE 2005].

29. WRITING 2002, *supra* note 25, at 24 tbl.2.3.

30. MATHEMATICS 2005, *supra* note 26, at 16 fig.12.

31. READING 2005, *supra* note 27, at 16 fig.12.

32. SCIENCE 2005, *supra* note 28, at 28 fig.22.

33. THE EDUCATION TRUST, FUNDING GAPS 2006, at 7 tbl.3 (2006), *available at* http://www2.edtrust.org/NR/rdonlyres/CDEF9403-5A75-437E-93FF-EBF1174181FB/0/FundingGap2006.pdf.

34. *Id.*

35. *Id.* at 7 tbl.4.

36. MATHEMATICS 2005, *supra* note 26, at 20 tbl.5.

37. READING 2005, *supra* note 27, at 20 tbl.5.

ing[38] than those of students who were not eligible. The results were generally better for eighth graders eligible for free or reduced-price lunches; their test scores were 4.9% lower in mathematics,[39] 4.8% lower in reading,[40] and 10.3% lower in writing[41] than those of students who were not eligible.

In 2005, the Idaho Supreme Court upheld a district court's decision that the state public-school funding system was inadequate and unconstitutional.[42] The Idaho legislature increased school funding in the spring of 2006 in response to this ruling.[43]

Availability of Publicly Funded Prekindergarten Programs

Idaho does not have a standard state-funded prekindergarten program.[44] The federally funded Head Start program enrolls 3,150 children,[45] which represents 7.7% of Idaho's 41,157 three- and four-year-old children."[46]

Where Does Idaho Get Its Revenue?

At the end of fiscal year 2004, Idaho had total revenues of approximately $9.8 billion.[47] Of this amount, 39% was derived from state and local tax revenues and 19% was received from the federal government.[48] The remaining 42% came from other sources, including the Idaho Lottery, insurance trust revenue, and revenue from government-owned utilities and other commercial or auxiliary enterprises.[49]

Tax Revenue

Idaho collected approximately $3.81 billion in state and local tax revenue during fiscal year 2004.[50] As a result, Idaho residents paid $2,728 per capita in state and local

---

38. WRITING 2002, *supra* note 25, at 75 tbl.3.24.

39. MATHEMATICS 2005, *supra* note 26, at 21 tbl.6.

40. READING 2005, *supra* note 27, at 21 tbl.6.

41. WRITING 2002, *supra* note 25, at 76 tbl.3.25.

42. Idaho Schs. for Equal Educ. Opportunity v. State, 129 P.3d 1199 (Idaho 2005).

43. Litigation Update: Arkansas, Arizona, and Idaho, *available at* http://www.schoolfunding.info/news/litigation/12-12-06litupdate.php3 (last visited April 4, 2007).

44. W. STEVEN BARNETT ET AL., NATIONAL INSTITUTE FOR EARLY EDUCATION RESEARCH, THE STATE OF PRESCHOOL 2006, at 148 (2006), *available at* http://nieer.org/yearbook/pdf/yearbook.pdf.

45. *Id.* at 63.

46. *See id.* at 232.

47. U.S. Census Bureau, State and Local Government Finances 2003–04, http://www.census.gov/govs/www/estimate04.html (last visited Oct. 6, 2006) [hereinafter Government Finances].

48. *Id.*

49. *Id.*

50. The total tax revenues were collected as follows: $5.3 billion by the state and $4.0 billion by local governments. *Id.*

taxes, an amount which ranked 42nd nationally.[51] The different types of tax sources were apportioned as follows:

Individual income taxes	23.9%
Property taxes	28.5%
General and selective sales taxes	37.5%
Corporate income and other taxes	10.1%
	100.0%[52]

Federal Funding

During fiscal year 2004, 19% of Idaho's total revenues came from the federal government.[53] For every dollar of federal taxes paid, Idaho received $1.28 in federal funding, an amount which ranked 21st nationally[54] and was well above the national average of $1.17.[55]

Lottery

Idaho has operated a state lottery named the "Idaho Lottery" since 1989.[56] Idaho's Lottery proceeds are deposited into Idaho's Permanent Building Fund and Public Schools Building Fund.[57] In 2005, the Idaho Lottery had operating revenues of $113.5 million and a net income of $26 million.[58] In 2005, the Idaho Lottery transferred $13 million to the Idaho State Permanent Building Fund and $13 million to the Idaho State Public Schools Building Fund.[59]

Legal Structure of Major Tax Sources

Income

Idaho has a broad-based income tax[60] that uses adjusted gross income for federal income tax purposes as a starting point for determining the state's taxable income.[61]

---

51. *Id.*

52. *Id.*

53. *Id.*

54. The Tax Foundation, Federal Spending Received Per Dollar of Taxes Paid by State 2004, http://www.taxfoundation.org/taxdata/show/266.html (last visited Sept. 17, 2006).

55. *See id.*

56. Idaho Lottery History, http://www.idaholottery.com/lothist.html (last visited Nov. 12, 2006).

57. IDAHO CODE ANN. §67-7434.

58. Idaho Lottery Annual Report Fiscal Year 2005, 28, *available at* http://www.idaholottery.com/annualreport05.pdf (last visited Nov.12, 2006).

59. *Id.*

60. IDAHO CODE ANN. §63-3024.

61. *Id.*

However, a fairly large number of adjustments may be available to various individuals in calculating this amount. [62] Idaho has no provisions authorizing a local income tax.[63] During fiscal year 2004, Idaho collected individual income tax of $651 per capita, an amount which ranked 27th nationally.[64]

On the basis of relevant statutory exemptions and standard deductions, a typical family of four (i.e., married taxpayers who file jointly and have two dependent children) are not required to pay any income tax until their combined income exceeds $23,600 or more, an amount which is above the national poverty line of $20,615.[65] Idaho's income tax structure contains eight tax brackets that impose a minimum marginal tax rate of 1.6% and a maximum marginal rate of 7.8%.[66] When statutory exemptions and the standard deduction are taken into account, the maximum marginal rate applies to every dollar of income exceeding $72,226.[67]

Property

Overview

Idaho has a typical property tax system that taxes the value of real and personal property at the local level. The Idaho state property tax has been suspended since 1965.[68] During fiscal year 2004, Idaho collected approximately $1.1 billion dollars in property taxes at the local level.[69] As a result, Idaho residents paid $1,395 per capita in local property taxes, an amount which ranked 36th nationally.[70]

Defining the Real Property Tax Base

Idaho classifies property for the determination of value subject to taxation. The state classifies property into three categories: real property, personal property, and operat-

---

62. *Id.* § 67-7439.

63. CCH-EXP, ID-TAXRPTR ¶ 15-015, Local Power to Tax.

64. STATE RANKINGS 2006, *supra* note 1, at 321.

65. JASON A. LEVITIS, CENTER ON BUDGET AND POLICY PRIORITIES, THE IMPACT OF STATE INCOME TAXES ON LOW-INCOME FAMILIES IN 2006, AT 12 (2007). In 2006, Idaho taxpayers who were married and filing jointly could claim a standard deduction of $10,700, personal exemptions of $3,400 each, and dependent exemptions of $3,400 each. IDAHO CODE ANN. § 63-3022P, IDAHO CODE ANN. § 63-3004. Note, however, that the threshold calculation of $23,600 is greater than the sum of these deductions and exemptions because it includes additional tax benefits available to low-income families, such as the earned-income tax credit. *See* LEVITIS, *supra*.

66. IDAHO CODE ANN. § 63-3024. Idaho's middle brackets are 3.6%, 4.1%, 5.1%, 6.1%, 7.1%, and 7.4. *Id.*

67. The standard deduction and the four exemptions of $10,700 and $3,400, respectively, plus the threshold of taxable income for the highest tax bracket of $23,964, equals $48,264. *See supra* notes 65–66.

68. CCH-EXP, ID-TAXRPTR ¶ 20-010, Overview.

69. Government Finances, *supra* note 47.

70. *See id.*

ing property.[71] All property is assessed at 100% of market value,[72] except for mining properties, which are valued at purchase price;[73] forest property over five contiguous acres, which can choose between the productivity-valuation method or the bare-use-and-yield method;[74] agricultural property, which is valued using the income method; and public utilities and railroads, which are subject to a licensing tax instead of a property tax.[75] Fair market value is generally determined by the application of standard appraisal methods, including the cost method and the income method.[76] State law requires that all real property be assessed at least once every five years.[77]

Real Property Tax Rates

The real property tax rates, composed of county, city, school district, and special levies, vary and are set by each locality. Taxes are levied according to the percentage of taxable value and are collected locally.[78] In 2005, the tax rates ranged from 2.386% in Power County ($23.86 per $1,000 of assessed value) to 0.249% in Custer County ($2.49 per $1,000 of assessed value).[79]

Personal and Intangible Property

Idaho taxes all personal property unless it is specifically exempt from taxation.[80] Taxes are levied according to the percentage of taxable value and are collected locally.[81] In 2005, the tax rates ranged from 2.386% in Power County ($23.86 per $1,000 of assessed value) to 0.249% in Custer County ($2.49 per $1,000 of assessed value).[82]

Intangible personal property is exempt from tax at both the state and local levels.[83]

Exemptions

Household goods, furniture, furnishings,[84] and properly registered automobiles[85] are exempt from taxation. Idaho provides a homeowner's exemption for the lesser of the first $75,000 of the market value of the homestead or 50% of the market value of the

---

71. IDAHO CODE ANN. § 63-204. These categories are broken down into additional categories by the state tax commission.
72. *Id.* § 63-205.
73. *Id.* § 63-2801.
74. *Id.* § 63-1705.
75. *Id.* § 63-3502.
76. *Id.* § 63-208.
77. *Id.* § 63-301.
78. CCH-EXP, ID-TAXRPTR ¶ 20-405, Rates of Tax.
79. *Id.*
80. IDAHO CODE ANN. § 63-203.
81. CCH-EXP, ID-TAXRPTR ¶ 20-405, Rates of Tax.
82. *Id.*
83. IDAHO CODE ANN. § 63-602L.
84. *Id.* § 63-602I.
85. *Id.* § 63-602J.

homestead.[86] The exemption applies if the residence is occupied and used as the primary dwelling place of the owner as of January 1 or if the owner occupies the residence after January 1 but before April 15 and no other property tax reductions have been claimed.[87]

General and Selective Sales

General Sales

Idaho imposes a general retail sales-and-use tax, which makes up 27.2% of its total revenue.[88] This tax is imposed on tangible personal property and certain enumerated services.[89] The state sales tax rate is 6%.[90] Idaho authorizes certain "resort" cities and counties with a large number of travelers for recreation to impose a sales tax.[91] The local tax rates range from a low of 0.0% in all nonresort areas to a high of 3% in Sun Valley.[92] Major exemptions from Idaho sales tax include items purchased with food stamps;[93] prescription drugs and medical equipment;[94] and certain enumerated farm equipment, supplies, and livestock.[95] Idaho does not exempt food purchases without food stamps or over-the-counter medications.

Selective Sales

Selective sales taxes make up 10.2% of Idaho's total revenue.[96] Of that amount, 5.7% comes from a motor fuel sales tax imposed at a rate of $.025 per gallon.[97] Idaho residents paid an average of $156 per capita in state motor fuel sales taxes in 2004, an amount which ranked 11th nationally and was above the national average of $115.[98]

The tobacco product sales tax makes up 1.4%[99] of Idaho's tax revenues. It is imposed at a rate of 40% of the wholesale price of all tobacco products[100] except for cigarettes, which are taxed at 28.5 mills ($0.57) per pack of 20.[101] Idaho residents paid $37.47 per capita in state tobacco sales taxes in 2004, an amount which ranked 6th nationally.[102]

---

86. *Id.* § 63-602G.

87. *Id.*

88. Government Finances, *supra* note 47.

89. IDAHO CODE ANN. § 63-3619.

90. *Id.*

91. *Id.* § 63-2602.

92. CCH-EXP, ID-TAXRPTR ¶ 61-735, Rates of Tax.

93. IDAHO CODE ANN. § 63-3622FF.

94. *Id.* § 63-3622N.

95. *Id.* § 63-3622D.

96. Government Finances, *supra* note 47.

97. IDAHO CODE ANN. § 63-2402.

98. STATE RANKINGS 2006, *supra* note 1, at 327.

99. Government Finances, *supra* note 47.

100. IDAHO CODE ANN. § 63-2552.

101. *Id.* § 62-2506.

102. STATE RANKINGS 2006, *supra* note 1, at 332.

In 2004, sales taxes on alcoholic beverages made up 0.2% of Idaho's total tax revenue.[103] Idaho residents paid $4.74 per capita in state alcoholic beverage sales taxes in 2004, an amount which ranked 28th nationally.[104]

The remainder of Idaho's selective sales taxes makes up 3.0% of its total tax revenue. Of this amount, 0.4% represents taxes on utilities and the other 2.6% represents taxes on other specific commodities, businesses, or services not reported separately above (e.g., on contractors, lodging, lubricating oil, fuels other than motor fuel, motor vehicles, meals, soft drinks, margarine, etc.). [105]

Corporate Income and Other

Corporate Income

The corporate income tax makes up 2.7% of Idaho's total tax revenue.[106] The state's broad-based corporate income tax is imposed on the Idaho net income of corporations doing business within Idaho or receiving income from property in the state.[107] Idaho imposes a flat rate of 7.6% on Idaho corporate income, with a minimum tax of $20.[108]

Idaho follows the federal income tax treatment of S corporations. Thus, they do not pay Idaho's corporate income tax; rather income and losses flow through to their shareholders.[109] A similar treatment is afforded to limited partnerships and limited liability partnerships, [110] as well as limited liability companies, assuming they are treated as a partnership for federal tax purposes.[111] However, if a limited liability company is treated as a corporation for federal income tax purposes, the entity is subject to Idaho's corporate income tax.[112]

Other

During fiscal year 2004, the collection of all other taxes not previously mentioned accounted for 7.4% of Idaho's total tax revenue.[113] Of this amount, $7.4 million[114] was generated by the estate tax. The estate tax is set at 100% of the maximum federal credit

---

103. Government Finances, *supra* note 47.

104. STATE RANKINGS 2006 , *supra* note 1, at 335.

105. *See* GOVERNMENTS DIVISION, U.S. CENSUS BUREAU, GOVERNMENT FINANCE AND EMPLOYMENT CLASSIFICATION MANUAL, at ch.7 (2000), *available at* http://ftp2.census.gov/govs/class/classfull.pdf [hereinafter CLASSIFICATION MANUAL].

106. *Id.*

107. IDAHO CODE ANN. § 63-3025.

108. *Id.*

109. *Id.* § 63-3022.

110. *Id.* § 63-3004.

111. *Id.* § 63-3006A.

112. *Id.*

113. Government Finances, *supra* note 47.

114. *Id.*

for state inheritance taxes paid, which was phased out in 2005.[115] The "other taxes" category is also made up of motor vehicle license taxes, documentary and stock transfer taxes, severance taxes, and all other taxes not listed separately or provided for in other categories, such as taxes on land based on a specified rate per acre (rather than on assessed value).[116]

Burden Analysis

The overall state and local tax burden on Idaho's taxpayers is very regressive. Taxpayers in the lowest quintile—those with incomes of less than $14,000—bear a tax burden equal to 9.7% of their income, while taxpayers in the top 1%—those with incomes that exceed $273,000—bear a tax burden of just 8.7% of their income.[117] It is also worth noting that, although Idaho obviously has no control over federal tax policy, federal itemized deductions for state and local personal income and property taxes nonetheless further reduce the burden on taxpayers in the top 1% to 6.1%.[118] Furthermore, between 1989 and 2002, the tax burden on the bottom quintile rose by approximately 1.4%, while the burden on the top 1% fell by 0.4%.[119]

In terms of the income tax, the burden across income groups in Idaho is slightly progressive, with taxpayers in the lowest quintile bearing a tax burden of 0.1% and those in the top 1% bearing a tax burden of 6.5%.[120] In sharp contrast, however, the

---

115. IDAHO CODE ANN. § 14-403.

116. *See* CLASSIFICATION MANUAL, *supra* note 105, at ch.7.

117. *See* ROBERT S. MCINTYRE ET AL., WHO PAYS? A DISTRIBUTIONAL ANALYSIS OF THE TAX SYSTEMS IN ALL 50 STATES 40 (2d ed. 2003), *available at* http://www.itepnet.org/wp2000/text.pdf. Taxpayers in the second quintile bear a 9.7% total tax burden on incomes between $14,000 and $25,000; those in the third quintile bear a 9.3% tax burden on incomes between $25,000 and $42,000; those in the fourth quintile bear a 9.0% tax burden on incomes between $42,000 and $64,000; those in the 80th–95th percentiles bear a 9.2% tax burden on incomes between $64,000 and $119,000; finally, those in the 96th–99th percentiles bear a 9.2% tax burden on incomes between $119,000 and $273,000. *Id.*

118. *Id.* Taxpayers in the lowest quintile did not receive any benefit from these federal offsets, while those in the second quintile were able to reduce their individual tax burdens by 0.1%, those in the third quintile by 0.2%, those in the fourth quintile by 0.6%, those in the 80th–95th percentiles by 1.2%, and those in the 96th–99th percentiles by 1.7%. *Id.*

119. *Id.* at 41.

120. *See id.* at 40. Taxpayers in the second quintile bear a 1.5% income tax burden; those in the third quintile bear a 2.8% burden; those in the fourth quintile bear a 3.5% burden; those in the 80th–95th percentiles bear a 4.5% burden; finally, those in the 96th–99th percentiles bear a 5.6% burden. *Id.* Note, however, that these percentages include both individual and corporate income tax burdens; that within the bottom quintile, corporate income taxes represent 0.1% of this burden; that within the second quintile, corporate income taxes represent 0.0% of this burden; that within the third quintile, corporate income taxes represent 0.0% of this burden; that within the fourth quintile, corporate income taxes represent 0.0% of this burden; that within the 80th–95th percentiles, corporate income taxes represent 0.0% of this burden; that within the 96th–99th percentiles, corporate income taxes represent 0.1% of this burden; and that in the top 1%, corporate income taxes represent 0.2% of this burden. *Id.*

sales and excise taxes imposed by Idaho are very regressive, with taxpayers in the lowest quintile bearing a tax burden of 6.1% and those in the top 1% bearing a tax burden of just 0.9%.[121] Property taxes in Idaho are also regressive, with taxpayers in the lowest quintile bearing a tax burden of 3.5% and those in the top quintile bearing an average tax burden of 1.7%.[122]

---

121. *See id.* Taxpayers in the second quintile bear a 5.3% sales-and-excise tax burden; those in the third quintile bear a 4.5% burden; those in the fourth quintile bear a 3.6% burden; those in the 80th–95th percentiles bear a 2.7% burden; finally, those in the 96th–99th percentiles bear a 1.8% burden. *Id.*

122. *See id.* Taxpayers in the second quintile bear a 2.9% property tax burden; those in the third quintile bear a 2.0% burden; those in the fourth quintile bear a 1.9% burden; those in the 80th–95th percentiles bear a 1.9% burden; those in the 96th–99th percentiles bear a 1.9% burden; finally, those in the top 1% bear a 1.3% burden. *Id.*

Illinois

General Information

Basic Profile – Geography, Population, and Industry

Admitted to the Union in 1818,[1] Illinois is known as the "Prairie State."[2] It is located in the Midwest and is bordered by Wisconsin on the north, Michigan on the northeast, Indiana on the east, Kentucky on the southeast, Missouri on the southwest, and Iowa on the northwest.[3] Illinois is located in the central time zone, and the state capital is Springfield.[4]

In 2005, Illinois ranked 5th in population (over 12.7 million residents);[5] it ranks 25th in total area (57,914 square miles).[6] Its population is 79.4% white and 15.1% black.[7] The state is approximately 29% Catholic; 46% Protestant; and 1% Jewish; 24% claim a religion outside the Judeo-Christian tradition or no religion at all.[8] Illinois is primarily urban, with 86.8% living in cities and towns.[9] Major industries include agriculture, finance, manufacturing, technology, warehousing, and distribution.[10]

---

1. STATE RANKINGS 2006, vi, 1 (Kathleen O'Leary Morgan & Scott Morgan, eds., Morgan Quitno Press, 2006).

2. State of Illinois – Illinois Facts Section, http://www.illinois.gov/facts/ (go to "Symbols" link on top right of page) (last visited October 17, 2006) (hereinafter Illinois Facts).

3. *Id.* (go to "Geography" link on top right of page); *see also* Map of United States, http://www.united-states-map.com/us-map.htm (last visited October 17, 2006).

4. STATE RANKINGS 2006, *supra* note 1, at vi.

5. *Id.* at 429.

6. *Id.* at 225.

7. Illinois QuickFacts from the U.S. Census Bureau, http://quickfacts.census.gov/qfd/states/17000.html (last visited January 31, 2007). Other races include 4.1% Asian persons; 0.3% American Indian and Alaska Native persons; and 1.1% persons reporting two or more races. Persons reporting Hispanic or Latino origin make up 14.3% of the population and are accounted for in the other groups. *Id.* (noting that because Hispanics may be of any race, they are included within the other applicable race categories).

8. BARRY A. KOSMIN, EGON MAYER & ARIELA KEYSAR, AMERICAN RELIGIOUS IDENTIFICATION SURVEY 2001, at 39, *available at* http://www.gc.cuny.edu/faculty/research_studies/aris.pdf.

9. USDA Economic Research Service, Illinois Fact Sheet, http://www.ers.usda.gov/StateFacts/IL.htm (last visited Sept. 17, 2006).

10. State of Illinois Business Portal – Illinois – Access to Key Industries, http://business.illinois.gov/io_keyIndustries.cfm (last visited October 17, 2006).

Family Income and Poverty Indicators

In 2004, Illinois's per capita gross product was $41,056, which was above the national average of $39,725.[11] During this same period, although the median household income in Illinois was $45,787,[12] 12.5% of the state's population was living in poverty, which was just above the national average of 12.4%.[13] More specifically, poverty affected 16.5% of Illinois's children,[14] 8.4% of its senior citizens,[15] and 9.0% of its families.[16] Of its female-headed households with children, 37.9% lived in poverty, [17] and 36.9% of the state's public elementary and secondary school students were eligible for free or reduced-price meals.[18] Of those living in poverty, approximately 35.8% were black, which represented 24.7% of Illinois's black population and 3.7% of its total population.[19] In an attempt to combat this poverty, Illinois spent approximately $9.9 billion on public welfare programs in 2002,[20] which made up 13.4% of its total government expenditures.[21]

Illinois's Public Elementary-Secondary School System

Overall Spending and Performance

For the 2003–2004 school year Illinois spent $8,656 per pupil in its public elementary-secondary school system, which was slightly above the national average of $8,182.[22] Of this amount, 8.6% was provided by the federal government, 35.5% was provided by the state government, and 56.0% was provided by the local governments,[23] with property taxes making up 51.3% of the total funding.[24] Out of these funds, Illinois paid its elementary and secondary school teachers an estimated average annual salary of $55,629

---

11. STATE RANKINGS 2006, *supra* note 1, at 89.

12. *Id.* at 96.

13. *Id.* at 495.

14. *Id.* at 497.

15. *Id.* at 496.

16. *Id.* at 498.

17. *Id.* at 499.

18. *Id.* at 532.

19. *See* Fact Sheet, American FactFinder, http://factfinder.census.gov/home/saff/main.html?_lang=en (select "Illinois" under "Get a Fact Sheet for your community") (last visited Feb. 16, 2007). Note that these numbers are based on the 2000 census because more recent numbers were not available.

20. *Id.* at 500.

21. *Id.* at 502.

22. GOVERNMENTS DIVISION, U.S. CENSUS BUREAU, PUBLIC EDUCATION FINANCES 2004, at 8 tbl.8 (2006).

23. *See id.* at 5 tbl.5.

24. *See id.* at 4 tbl.4.

during the 2004–2005 school year,[25] but during the fall of 2003, it provided a student teacher ratio of 16.5, which was worse than the national average of 15.9.[26]

In academic performance, Illinois's fourth grade students scored lower than the national average in mathematics,[27] reading,[28] and science,[29] while its eighth graders scored at the national average in mathematics[30] and higher than the national average in reading[31] and science.[32]

Equity Issues

In 2004, revenues spent per student in Illinois's highest poverty districts were determined to be $1,924 less than the revenues spent in its lowest poverty districts.[33] When adjustments were made for the additional costs of educating students growing up in poverty, however, the funding gap grew to $2,355.[34] Similarly, Illinois spent $1,223 less per student in its highest minority districts, and this amount grew to $1,524 when adjustments for low-income students were made.[35]

Fourth graders eligible for free or reduced-price school lunches had test scores that were 11.0% lower in mathematics[36] and 13.9% lower in reading[37] than those of students who were not eligible. The results were generally better for eighth graders eligible for free or reduced-price lunches; their test scores were 7.6% lower in mathematics[38] and 9.2% lower in reading[39] than those of students who were not eligible.

Illinois has not been receptive to challenges to its education finance system. In the 1996 case *Committee for Educational Rights v. Edgar*,[40] the Illinois Supreme Court ruled

---

25. THOMAS D. SNYDER ET AL., NATIONAL CENTER FOR EDUCATION STATISTICS, DIGEST OF EDUCATION STATISTICS 2005, at 116 tbl.77 (2006).

26. *Id.* at 98 tbl.65.

27. NATIONAL CENTER FOR EDUCATION STATISTICS, U.S. DEPARTMENT OF EDUCATION, THE NATION'S REPORT CARD: MATHEMATICS 2005, at 14 fig.11 (2005), *available at* http://nces.ed.gov/nationsreportcard/pdf/main2005/2006453.pdf [hereinafter MATHEMATICS 2005].

28. NATIONAL CENTER FOR EDUCATION STATISTICS, U.S. DEPARTMENT OF EDUCATION, THE NATION'S REPORT CARD: READING 2005, at 14 fig.11 (2005), *available at* http://nces.ed.gov/nationsreportcard/pdf/main2005/2006451.pdf [hereinafter READING 2005].

29. NATIONAL CENTER FOR EDUCATION STATISTICS, U.S. DEPARTMENT OF EDUCATION, THE NATION'S REPORT CARD: SCIENCE 2005, at 16 fig.12 (2006) *available at* http://nces.ed.gov/nationsreportcard//pdf/main2005/2006466.pdf [hereinafter SCIENCE 2005].

30. MATHEMATICS 2005, *supra* note 27, at 16 fig.12.

31. READING 2005, *supra* note 28, at 16 fig.12.

32. SCIENCE 2005, *supra* note 29, at 28 fig.22.

33. THE EDUCATION TRUST, FUNDING GAPS 2006, at 7 tbl.3 (2006), *available at* http://www2.edtrust.org/NR/rdonlyres/CDEF9403-5A75-437E-93FF EBF1174181FB/0/FundingGap2006.pdf.

34. *Id.*

35. *Id.* at 7 tbl.4.

36. MATHEMATICS 2005, *supra* note 27, at 20 tbl.5.

37. READING 2005, *supra* note 28, at 20 tbl.5.

38. MATHEMATICS 2005, *supra* note 27, at 21 tbl.6.

39. READING 2005, *supra* note 28, at 21 tbl.6.

40. 672 N.E.2d 1178 (Ill. 1996).

against the plaintiff on the grounds that the reform of educational funding "must be undertaken in a legislative forum rather than the courts."[41] The court ruled against a plaintiff's challenge to the Illinois education finance system on the same grounds in 1999 in *Lewis E. v. Spagnolo*.[42]

Availability of Publicly Funded Prekindergarten Programs

The Prekindergarten Program for At-Risk Children is available to all at-risk children in Illinois between the ages of three and five.[43] Total enrollment in this state-funded program is 72,152,[44] which represents just 20.1% of Illinois's 358,299 three- , four- , and five-year-old children.[45] The federally funded Head Start program enrolls an additional 33,035 children,[46] which represents 9.2% of Illinois's three- and four-year-old children."[47]

Where Does Illinois Get Its Revenue?

At the end of fiscal year 2004, Illinois had total revenues of approximately $100.2 billion.[48] Of this amount, 45% was derived from state and local tax revenues and 16% was received from the federal government.[49] The remaining 39% came from other sources, including the Illinois Lottery, insurance trust revenue, and revenue from government-owned utilities and other commercial or auxiliary enterprises.[50]

Tax Revenue

Illinois collected approximately $45.2 billion in state and local tax revenue during fiscal year 2004.[51] As a result, Illinois residents paid $3,555 per capita in state and local

---

41. *Id.* at 1196. The court stated that "[w]hile the present school funding scheme might be thought unwise, undesirable or unenlightened from the standpoint of contemporary notions of social justice, these objections must be presented to the General Assembly." *Id.*

42. 710 N.E.2d 798, 800 (Ill. 1999).

43. W. Steven Barnett et al., National Institute for Early Education Research, The State of Preschool 2006, at 64 (2007), *available at* http://nieer.org/yearbook/pdf/yearbook.pdf.

44. *Id.* at 64.

45. *See id.* at 232.

46. *Id.* at 64.

47. *See id.* at 232.

48. U.S. Census Bureau, State and Local Government Finances 2003–04, http://www.census.gov/govs/www/estimate04.html (last visited Oct. 17, 2006) [hereinafter Government Finances].

49. *Id.*

50. *Id.*

51. *Id.*

government taxes, an amount which ranked 17th nationally.[52] The different types of tax sources were apportioned as follows:

Individual income taxes	16.0%
Property taxes	39.6%
General and selective sales taxes	34.0%
Corporate income and other taxes	10.4%
	100.0%[53]

Federal Funding

During fiscal year 2004, 16% of Illinois's total revenues came from the federal government.[54] For every dollar of federal taxes paid, Illinois received $0.73 in federal funding, an amount which ranked 23rd nationally[55] and was well below the national average of $1.17.[56]

Lottery

The Illinois Lottery was established in 1974 by the Illinois Lottery Law.[57] In 1985, the Illinois legislature amended the law to institute the purpose of using Lottery proceeds for Illinois's Common School Fund (CSF).[58] During fiscal year 2005, the Illinois Lottery had total revenues of approximately $1.8 billion and net operating income of $621.5 million; also, it raised approximately $619 million for the CSF.[59]

Legal Structure of Major Tax Sources

Income

Illinois has a broad-based income tax which uses adjusted gross income for federal income tax purposes, with very few adjustments, as a starting point for determining

---

52. *Id.*

53. *Id.*

54. *Id.*

55. The Tax Foundation, Federal Spending Received Per Dollar of Taxes Paid by State, 2004, http://www.taxfoundation.org/taxdata/show/266.html (last visited Oct. 10, 2006).

56. *Id.*

57. Illinois Lottery, Proceeds, http://www.illinoislottery.com/subsections/News01Text.htm (last visited October 18, 2006); *see also* 20 ILL. COMP. STAT. 1605/2 (1974).

58. Illinois Lottery, Proceeds, *supra* note 57; *see also* 20 ILL. COMP. STAT. 1605/2 (1985).

59. Illinois Lottery, Proceeds, *supra* note 57; Illinois Lottery, 2005 Annual Report 4, *available at* http://www.illinoislottery.com/subsections/PR/FY05AnRpt.pdf.

the state's taxable income.[60] During fiscal year 2004, Illinois collected individual income tax of $640 per capita, an amount which ranked 21st nationally.[61] No Illinois localities have been authorized to levy an income tax,[62] although home-rule units have the authority to do so.[63]

In Illinois, a typical family of four (i.e., married taxpayers who file jointly and have two dependent children) are not required to pay any income tax until their combined income exceeds $15,600, an amount which is below the national poverty line of $20,615.[64] Illinois's income tax structure contains a flat tax of 3% imposed on all levels of income.[65] When statutory exemptions are taken into account, the income tax applies to every dollar of income exceeding $8,000.[66]

Property

Overview

Illinois's property tax system taxes the value of real property at the local level.[67] During fiscal year 2004, the property tax raised over $17.8 billion at the local level and almost $57.1 million at the state level.[68] As a result, Illinois residents paid property taxes of $1,407 per capita, an amount which ranked 9th nationally.[69]

---

60. Illinois Department of Revenue, Individual Income Tax, http://www.revenue.state.il.us/Businesses/TaxInformation/Income/individual.htm (last visited October 18, 2006) (contains a concise, simple explanation of the minor changes to the federal tax base); 35 ILL. COMP. STAT. 5/203.

61. STATE RANKINGS 2006, *supra* note 1, at 321.

62. CCH-EXP, IL-TAXRPTR ¶ 15-011, Local Power to Tax.

63. ILL. CONST. art. VII, § 6(e).

64. JASON A. LEVITIS & NICHOLAS JOHNSON, CENTER ON BUDGET AND POLICY PRIORITIES, THE IMPACT OF STATE INCOME TAXES ON LOW-INCOME FAMILIES IN 2006, at 12 (2007). In 2006, Illinois taxpayers who were married and filing jointly could not claim a standard deduction but could claim personal exemptions of $2,000 (for each spouse) and dependent exemptions of $2,000. 35 ILL. COMP. STAT. 5/204. Note, however, that the threshold calculation of $15,600 is greater than the sum of these exemptions because it includes additional tax benefits available to low-income families, such as the earned-income tax credit. *See* LEVITIS & JOHNSON, *supra*. Illinois's personal exemptions remain unchanged for 2007. 35 ILL. COMP. STAT. 5/204; Individual Income Tax, *supra* note 61.

65. 35 ILL. COMP. STAT. 5/201(b)(3).

66. The personal and dependent exemptions of $4,000 (for both spouses combined) and $4,000 (for two children), respectively, equals $8,000, an amount at which Illinois begins taxing income, because the state employs a flat rate system. *See supra* notes 64–65.

67. Illinois Department of Revenue, *The Illinois Property Tax System: A General Guide to the Local Property Tax Cycle* 5, *available at* http://www.revenue.state.il.us/Publications/LocalGovernment/PTAX1004.pdf (hereinafter *Illinois Property Tax System*). The local level includes counties, municipalities, and school districts, for example.

68. Government Finances, *supra* note 48. Property taxes constitute a large majority (approximately 83.0%) of all taxes raised at the local level. *See id.*

69. *See id.*

Defining the Real Property Tax Base

Illinois has one classification of real property, which is valued according to its market value; this is determined by using one of three valuation methods: market-data, cost, or income.[70] The assessment rate used to determine the tax base for most real property is 33 1/3%.[71] Land that has been used for agricultural purposes for two years, otherwise known as farmland, is assessed at 33 1/3% of its "agricultural economic value." This is determined according to the net return of land to farmland having the same soil productivity.[72] Real property, other than farmland, must be reappraised once every four years.[73]

Real Property Tax Rates

Illinois localities determine property tax rates first by determining a tax levy in dollars and then by dividing that levy amount by the tax base.[74] Maximum limitations can be placed on these tax rates in certain smaller cities and counties.[75] In 2003, the average property tax rate for Illinois counties was 7.3%, ranging from 5.32% in Hardin County to 10.12% in Alexander County.[76]

Personal and Intangible Property

Personal property is not taxed in Illinois; rather, business entities must pay a personal-property-tax-replacement income tax, which is distributed to local governments of the state.[77]

---

70. ILL. CONST. OF 1970, art. IX, § 4; 35 ILL. COMP. STAT. 200/1-50; *Illinois Property Tax System, supra* note 67, at 10–11.

71. 35 ILL. COMP. STAT. 200/9-145; *Illinois Property Tax System, supra* note 67, at 11. In counties with a population of 200,000 or more, real property may be classified for assessment. Currently, Cook County is the only county that classifies and assesses real property; it has thirteen categories, with assessment levels ranging from 16% of market value for residential property to 38% of market value for commercial property. *Id.*

72. 35 ILL. COMP. STAT. 200/10-115; For a concise explanation of this process, see *Illinois Property Tax System, supra* note 67, at 11–12.

73. 35 ILL. COMP. STAT. 200/9-225; *Illinois Property Tax System, supra* note 67, at 12. Real property in Cook County is reassessed once every three years. *Id.*

74. *Illinois Property Tax System, supra* note 67, at 18–21.

75. 35 ILL. COMP. STAT. 200/18-45. Home-rule cities and counties are not subject to limitations on their property tax rates. *Illinois Property Tax System, supra,* note 67, at 20. Home-rule municipalities are those which have more than 25,000 people or which elect by referendum to become home-rule units. ILL. CONST. OF 1970 SECTION 6. Cook County is a home-rule county. *Illinois Property Tax System, supra,* note 67, at 20. The tax rate limitations can be found in the annual *Illinois Property Tax Rate and Levy Manual,* the 2006 version of which is available at http://www.commerce.state.il.us/NR/rdonlyres/983E76B4-63D7-426C-894A-5B23094CA04C/0/TaxRateManual2006.pdf.

76. Illinois Department of Revenue, Table 8, Average Tax Rates, 1999–2003, *available at* http://www.revenue.state.il.us/Publications/LocalGovernment/PtaxStats/2003/table8.pdf. Cook County had an average property tax rate of 7.56%.

77. 35 ILL. COMP. STAT. 5/201(c)-(d); *Illinois Property Tax System, supra,* note 67, at 5. The

Exemptions

Illinois allows a general homestead exemption of up to $5,000 in all counties, but a county may adopt an alternative general homestead exemption of up to $20,000.[78] Homeowners are also allowed a homestead improvement exemption of up to $75,000 for increases in the value of their homes because of home improvements.[79]

General and Selective Sales

General Sales

Illinois imposes a general retail sales-and-use tax, which makes up 17.5% of the state's total tax revenue.[80] This tax "is imposed on a seller's receipts from sales of tangible personal property for use or consumption."[81] The base state sales tax rate is 1% for "qualifying food, drugs and medical appliances" and 6.25% for vehicles and "other general merchandise."[82] Localities may impose additional taxes or fees.[83] For instance, the City of Chicago imposes a 9.00% general merchandise sales tax rate, a 2.00% qualifying food, drugs, and medical appliances sales tax rate, and a 7.00% vehicle sales tax rate.[84]

Selective Sales

Selective sales taxes make up 16.5% of Illinois's total revenue.[85] Of that amount, 3.5%[86] comes from a motor fuel sales tax imposed at a rate of $0.201 per gallon of gaso-

---

rate is 2.5% for C corporations and 1.5% for S corporations, trusts, and partnerships. 35 ILL. COMP. STAT. 5/201(d). See *infra* Section D. 1., second paragraph.

78. 35 ILL. COMP. STAT. 200/15-175 (general homestead exemption); 35 ILL. COMP. STAT. 200/15-176 (alternative general homestead exemption).

79. *Id.* 200/15-180.

80. Government Finances, *supra* note 48.

81. Illinois Department of Revenue, Sales & Use Taxes, http://www.revenue.state.il.us/Businesses/TaxInformation/Sales/rot.htm (last visited October 20, 2006) (hereinafter Sales & Use Taxes). "The term 'sales tax' actually refers to several tax acts. Sales tax is a combination of 'occupation' taxes that are imposed on sellers' receipts and 'use' taxes that are imposed on amounts paid by purchasers. Sellers owe the occupation tax to the department; they reimburse themselves for this liability by collecting use tax from the buyers. 'Sales tax' is the combination of all state, local, mass transit, water commission, home rule occupation and use, non-home rule occupation and use, park district, and county public safety taxes." *Id. See also* Use Tax Act, 35 ILL. COMP. STAT. 105/; Service Use Tax Act, 35 ILL. COMP. STAT. 110/; Service Occupation Tax Act, 35 ILL. COMP. STAT. 115/; Retailers' Occupation Tax Act, 35 ILL. COMP. STAT. 120/.

82. Sales & Use Taxes, *supra* note 81; 35 ILL. COMP. STAT. 120/2-10. Qualifying food is "food for human consumption that is to be consumed off the premises where it is sold (other than alcoholic beverages, soft drinks, and food that has been prepared for immediate consumption)." *Id.*

83. Sales & Use Taxes, *supra* note 81.

84. For a listing of all sales tax rates in Illinois by municipality and county as of July 1, 2006, see Illinois Department of Revenue, *Illinois Sales Tax Rate Reference Manual, available at* http://www.revenue.state.il.us/Publications/Sales/strrm/07012006/st25.pdf.

85. Government Finances, *supra* note 48.

86. *Id.*

line.[87] During fiscal year 2004, Illinois residents paid $112 per capita in state motor fuel sales taxes, an amount which was just below the national average of $115.[88]

Sales taxes on tobacco products make up 1.8% of Illinois's total revenue[89] and are imposed at a rate of $0.98 per pack of cigarettes.[90] Illinois residents paid an average of $59.80 per capita in state tobacco sales taxes in 2004, an amount which ranked 14th nationally.[91]

Sales taxes on alcoholic beverages make up 0.4% of Illinois's total revenue.[92] Illinois residents paid $11.63 per capita in state alcoholic beverage sales taxes in 2004, an amount which ranked 31st nationally.[93]

The remainder of Illinois's selective sales taxes makes up 10.7% of its total tax revenue.[94] Of this amount, 5.9% represents taxes on utilities and the other 4.8% represents taxes on other specific commodities, businesses, or services not reported separately above (e.g., on contractors, lodging, lubricating oil, fuels other than motor fuel, motor vehicles, meals, soft drinks, margarine, etc.).[95]

Corporate Income and Other

Corporate

The corporate income tax makes up 2.8% of Illinois's total revenue.[96] It is a broad-based income tax imposed on corporations (other than S corporations).[97] The tax base for the Illinois corporate income tax is federal taxable income with certain minor adjustments.[98] The tax rate for corporate income is a flat 4.8%.[99] While they are not subject to the corporate income tax, trusts are taxed at a 3% flat rate.[100] S corporations and partnerships are not subject to the corporate income tax.[101] Limited liability compa-

---

87. State Rankings 2006, *supra* note 1, at 328.

88. *Id.* at 327.

89. Government Finances, *supra* note 48.

90. State Rankings 2006, *supra* note 1, at 333.

91. *Id.* at 332.

92. Government Finances, *supra* note 48.

93. State Rankings 2006, *supra* note 1, at 335.

94. Government Finances, *supra* note 48.

95. *See* Governments Division, U.S. Census Bureau, Government Finance and Employment Classification Manual, at ch.7 (2000), *available at* http://ftp2.census.gov/govs/class/classfull.pdf [hereinafter Classification Manual].

96. *Id.*

97. 35 Ill. Comp. Stat. 5/201(b). For an overview, see Illinois Department of Revenue, Business Income Tax, http://www.revenue.state.il.us/Businesses/TaxInformation/Income/corporate.htm (last visited October 20, 2006) (hereinafter Business Income Tax). S corporations are not taxed because taxes are applied at the shareholder level. Illinois Department of Revenue, Subchapter S, http://www.revenue.state.il.us/Businesses/TaxInformation/Income/subchapters.htm (last visited October 20, 2006).

98. 35 Ill. Comp. Stat. 5/203(b); Business Income Tax, *supra* note 97.

99. 35 Ill. Comp. Stat. 5/201(b)(8).

100. *Id.* 5/201(b)(3).

101. *Id.* 5/205(b)-(c).

nies are not subject to the corporate income tax unless they are treated as corporations for federal income tax purposes.[102]

Business entities in Illinois are also subject to the personal-property-tax-replacement income tax, which supplements the income of Illinois localities.[103] This tax is imposed on the net income of C corporations, S corporations, partnerships, and trusts at the corporate level.[104] The tax rate for C corporations is 2.5%, while the tax rate for S corporations, partnerships, limited liability companies,[105] and trusts is 1.5%.[106]

Other

During fiscal year 2004, the collection of all other taxes not previously mentioned accounted for 7.7% of Illinois's total tax revenue.[107] Of this amount, $221.7 million was generated by the estate and gift tax.[108] This tax is calculated on the basis of the amount equal to the maximum federal credit allowable for state death taxes.[109] The "other taxes" category is further made up of various license taxes, documentary or stock transfer taxes, severance taxes, and all other taxes not listed separately or provided for in other categories.[110]

Burden Analysis

The overall state and local tax burden on Illinois's taxpayers is extremely regressive. In fact, Illinois is one of the ten most regressive states. Taxpayers in the lowest quintile—those with incomes of less than $16,000—bear a tax burden equal to 13.1% of their income, while taxpayers in the top 1%—those with incomes that exceed $295,000—bear a tax burden of just 5.8% of their income.[111] It is also worth noting that, although Illinois obviously has no control over federal tax policy, federal itemized deductions for state and local personal income and property taxes nonetheless further

---

102. *Id.* 5/1501(a)(4).

103. *Id.* 5/201(c)-(d).

104. *Id.*

105. Unless treated as a corporation for federal income tax purposes.

106. 35 ILL. COMP. STAT. 5/201(c)-(d).

107. Government Finances, *supra* note 48. This calculation includes "Other Taxes" and "Motor Vehicle License" taxes.

108. *Id.*

109. *See* 35 ILL. COMP. STAT. 405/3; *see also* 35 ILL. COMP. STAT. 405/2.

110. *See* CLASSIFICATION MANUAL, *supra* note 95, at ch.7.

111. *See* ROBERT S. MCINTYRE ET AL., WHO PAYS? A DISTRIBUTIONAL ANALYSIS OF THE TAX SYSTEMS IN ALL 50 STATES 42 (2d ed. 2003), *available at* http://www.itepnet.org/wp2000/text.pdf. Taxpayers in the second quintile bear a 11.3% total tax burden on incomes between $16,000 and $30,000; those in the third quintile bear a 10.4% tax burden on incomes between $30,000 and $48,000; those in the fourth quintile bear a 9.9% tax burden on incomes between $48,000 and $77,000; those in the 80th–95th percentiles bear a 8.9% tax burden on incomes between $77,000 and $148,000; finally, those in the 96th–99th percentiles bear a 7.6% tax burden on incomes between $148,000 and $295,000. *Id.*

reduce the burden on those in the top 1% to 4.6%.[112] Furthermore, between 1989 and 2002, the tax burden on the bottom quintile rose by approximately 1.6%, while the burden on the top 1% rose by only 0.1%.[113]

In terms of the income tax, the burden across income groups in Illinois is almost flat, with taxpayers in the lowest quintile bearing a tax burden of 1.5% and those in the top 1% bearing a tax burden of 3.1%.[114] In contrast, however, the sales and excise taxes imposed by Illinois are very regressive, with taxpayers in the lowest quintile bearing a tax burden of 7.8% and those in the top 1% bearing a tax burden of just 1.0%.[115] Property taxes in Illinois are also regressive, with taxpayers in the lowest quintile bearing a tax burden of 3.8% and those in the top quintile bearing an average tax burden of 1.7%.[116]

---

112. *Id.* Taxpayers in the lowest quintile did not receive any benefit from these federal offsets, while those in the second quintile were able to reduce their individual tax burdens by 0.2%, those in the third quintile by 0.4%, those in the fourth quintile by 0.7%, those in the 80th–95th percentiles by 1.2%, and those in the 96th–99th percentiles by 1.4%. *Id.*

113. *Id.* at 43.

114. *See id.* at 42. Taxpayers in the second quintile bear a 2.1% income tax burden; those in the third quintile bear a 2.3% burden; those in the fourth quintile bear a 2.3% burden; those in the 80th–95th percentiles bear a 2.5% burden; finally, those in the 96th–99th percentiles bear a 2.6% burden. *Id.* Note, however, that these percentages include both individual and corporate income tax burdens; that within the third and fourth quintiles, corporate income taxes represent 0.1% of this burden; that within the 80th–95th percentiles, corporate income taxes represent 0.1% of this burden; that within the 96th–99th percentiles, corporate income taxes represent 0.2% of this burden; and that in the top 1%, corporate income taxes represent 0.5% of this burden. *Id.*

115. *See id.* Taxpayers in the second quintile bear a 6.0% sales-and-excise tax burden; those in the third quintile bear a 4.7% burden; those in the fourth quintile bear a 3.9% burden; those in the 80th–95th percentiles bear a 2.9% burden; finally, those in the 96th–99th percentiles bear a 1.9% burden. *Id.*

116. *See id.* Taxpayers in the second quintile bear a 3.2% property tax burden; those in the third quintile bear a 3.3% burden; those in the fourth quintile bear a 3.7% burden; those in the 80th–95th percentiles bear a 3.5% burden; and those in the 96th–99th percentiles bear a 3.0% burden. *Id.*

Indiana

General Information

Basic Profile – Geography, Population, and Industry

Admitted to the Union in 1816, Indiana is known as the "Hoosier State."[1] It is located in the Great Lakes region and is bordered by Lake Michigan and Michigan on the north, Ohio on the east, Kentucky on the south, and Illinois on the west. Most of Indiana is located in the eastern time zone, although the northwestern and southwestern parts of the state are located in the central time zone. The state capital is Indianapolis.

In 2005, Indiana ranked 15th in population (approximately 6.3 million residents);[2] it ranks 38th in total area (36,418 square miles).[3] Its population is 88.6% white and 8.8% black.[4] The state is approximately 20% Catholic; 56% Protestant; and 1% Jewish; 23% claim a religion outside the Judeo-Christian tradition or no religion at all.[5] Approximately 77.7% of Indiana's population lives in urban areas.[6] Major industries include manufacturing (automotive, plastics, and steel), life sciences, service industries, and information technology.[7]

Family Income and Poverty Indicators

In 2004, Indiana's per capita gross product was $36,548, which was below the national average of $39,725.[8] During this same period, although the median household

---

1. STATE RANKINGS 2006, vi & 1 (Kathleen O'Leary Morgan & Scott Morgan, eds. Morgan Quitno Press, 2006).

2. *Id.* at 429.

3. *Id.* at 225.

4. Indiana Quick Facts from the U.S. Census Bureau, http://quickfacts.census.gov/qfd/states/27000.html (last visited January 24, 2007). Other races include 1.2% Asian persons; 0.3% American Indian and Alaska Native persons; and 1.1% people reporting two or more races. Persons of Hispanic or Latino origin make up 4.5% of the population. *Id.* (noting that because Hispanics may be of any race, they are included within the other applicable race categories).

5. BARRY A. KOSMIN, EGON MAYER & ARIELA KEYSAR, AMERICAN RELIGIOUS IDENTIFICATION SURVEY 2001, at 39, *available at* http://www.gc.cuny.edu/faculty/research_studies/aris.pdf.

6. USDA Economic Research Service, Indiana Fact Sheet, http://www.ers.usda.gov/StateFacts/IN.htm (last visited December 20, 2006).

7. Indiana Economic Development Corporation, *Informed: The Cost of Doing Business in Indiana* 2–3, *available at* http://www.in.gov/iedc/pdfs/Informed.pdf.

8. STATE RANKINGS 2006, *supra* note 1, at 89.

income in Indiana was $43,003,[9] 10.2% of the state's population was living in poverty, which was somewhat below the national poverty rate of 12.4%.[10] More specifically, poverty affected 14.4% of Indiana's children,[11] 7.3% of its senior citizens,[12] and 7.9% of its families.[13] Of its female-headed households with children, 37.4% lived in poverty, [14] and 34.4% of the state's public elementary and secondary school students were eligible for free or reduced-price meals.[15] Of those living in poverty, approximately 19.9% were black, which represented 21.8% of Indiana's black population and 1.8% of its total population.[16] In an attempt to combat this poverty, Indiana spent approximately $5.3 billion on public welfare programs in 2002,[17] which made up 16.2% of its total government expenditures.[18]

Indiana's Public Elementary-Secondary School System

Overall Spending and Performance

For the 2003–2004 school year, Indiana spent $8,280 per pupil in its public elementary-secondary school system, which hovered around the national average of $8,182.[19] Of this amount, 6.4% was provided by the federal government, 49.6% was provided by the state government, and 44.0% was provided by the local governments,[20] with property taxes making up 35.3% of the total funding.[21] Out of these funds, Indiana paid its elementary and secondary school teachers an estimated average annual salary of $46,851 during the 2004–2005 school year,[22] but during the fall of 2003, it provided a student/teacher ratio of 16.9, which was worse than the national average of 15.9.[23]

---

9. *Id.* at 96.

10. *Id.* at 495.

11. *Id.* at 497.

12. *Id.* at 496.

13. *Id.* at 498.

14. *Id.* at 499.

15. *Id.* at 532.

16. *See* Fact Sheet, American FactFinder, http://factfinder.census.gov/home/saff/main.html?_lang=en (select "Indiana" under "Get a Fact Sheet for your community") (last visited Feb. 16, 2007). Note that these numbers are based on the 2000 census because more recent numbers were not available.

17. *Id.* at 500.

18. *Id.* at 502.

19. Governments Division, U.S. Census Bureau, Public Education Finances 2004, at 8 tbl.8 (2006).

20. *See id.* at 5 tbl.5.

21. *See id.* at 4 tbl.4.

22. Thomas D. Snyder et al., National Center for Education Statistics, Digest of Education Statistics 2005, at 116 tbl.77 (2006).

23. *Id.* at 98 tbl.65.

In academic performance, Indiana's fourth grade students scored higher than the national average in mathematics,[24] reading,[25] science,[26] and writing,[27] while Indiana's eighth graders scored lower than the national average in writing[28] and higher than the national average in mathematics,[29] reading,[30] and science.[31]

Equity Issues

In 2004, the funding per student in Indiana's highest poverty districts actually exceeded that in its lowest poverty districts by $518,[32] although when adjustments were made for the additional costs of educating students growing up in poverty, that excess narrowed to $93.[33] Similarly, Indiana spent $1,345 more per student in its highest minority districts, although this amount fell to $1,096 when adjustments for low-income students were made.[34]

Fourth graders eligible for free or reduced-price school lunches had test scores that were 6.5% lower in mathematics,[35] 8.8% lower in reading,[36] and 11.9% lower in writing[37] than those of students who were not eligible. The results were generally the same for eighth graders eligible for free or reduced-price lunches; their test scores were 7.6% lower in mathematics,[38] 6.7% lower in reading,[39] and 11.0% lower in writing[40] than those of students who were not eligible.

---

24. NATIONAL CENTER FOR EDUCATION STATISTICS, U.S. DEPARTMENT OF EDUCATION, THE NATION'S REPORT CARD: MATHEMATICS 2005, at 14 fig.11 (2005), *available at* http://nces.ed.gov/nationsreportcard/pdf/main2005/ 2006453.pdf [hereinafter MATHEMATICS 2005].

25. NATIONAL CENTER FOR EDUCATION STATISTICS, U.S. DEPARTMENT OF EDUCATION, THE NATION'S REPORT CARD: READING 2005, at 14 fig.11 (2005), *available at* http://nces.ed.gov/nationsreportcard/pdf/main2005/2006451.pdf [hereinafter READING 2005].

26. NATIONAL CENTER FOR EDUCATION STATISTICS, U.S. DEPARTMENT OF EDUCATION, THE NATION'S REPORT CARD: SCIENCE 2005, at 16 fig.12 (2006), *available at* http://nces.ed.gov/nationsreportcard//pdf/main2005/2006466.pdf [hereinafter SCIENCE 2005].

27. HILARY R. PERSKY ET AL., NATIONAL CENTER FOR EDUCATION STATISTICS, U.S. DEPARTMENT OF EDUCATION, THE NATION'S REPORT CARD: WRITING 2002, at 23 tbl.2.2 (2003), *available at* http://nces.ed.gov/nationsreportcard/pdf/main2002/2003529.pdf [hereinafter WRITING 2002].

28. WRITING 2002, *supra* note 27, at 24 tbl.2.3.

29. MATHEMATICS 2005, *supra* note 24, at 16 fig.12.

30. READING 2005, *supra* note 25, at 16 fig.12.

31. SCIENCE 2005, *supra* note 26, at 28 fig.22.

32. THE EDUCATION TRUST, FUNDING GAPS 2006, at 7 tbl.3 (2006), *available at* http://www2.edtrust.org/NR/rdonlyres/CDEF9403-5A75-437E-93FF-EBF1174181FB/0/FundingGap2006.pdf.

33. *Id.*

34. *Id.* at 7 tbl.4.

35. MATHEMATICS 2005, *supra* note 24, at 20 tbl.5.

36. READING 2005, *supra* note 25, at 20 tbl.5.

37. WRITING 2002, *supra* note 27, at 75 tbl.3.24.

38. MATHEMATICS 2005, *supra* note 24, at 21 tbl.6.

39. READING 2005, *supra* note 25, at 21 tbl.6.

40. WRITING 2002, *supra* note 27, at 76 tbl.3.25.

The first challenge to Indiana's education finance system occurred in the April 2006 case *Bonner v. Daniels*.[41] In late January 2007, the Indiana Supreme Court granted the state's motion to dismiss the complaint on the grounds that school funding is an issue for the legislature rather than the courts and that the complaint did not address how the State Board of Education implemented the formula.[42]

Availability of Publicly Funded Prekindergarten Programs

Indiana does not provide any type of preschool program, but the federally funded Head Start program enrolls 12,090 children,[43] which represents 7.0% of Indiana's 172,536 three- and four-year-old children.[44]

Where Does Indiana Get Its Revenue?

At the end of fiscal year 2004, Indiana had total revenues of approximately $41.0 billion.[45] Of this amount, 46% was derived from state and local tax revenues and 18% was received from the federal government.[46] The remaining 36% came from other sources, including the Hoosier Lottery, insurance trust revenue, and revenue from government-owned utilities and other commercial or auxiliary enterprises.[47]

Tax Revenue

Indiana collected approximately $18.7 billion in state and local tax revenue during fiscal year 2004.[48] As a result, Indiana residents paid $2,999 per capita in state and local taxes, an amount which ranked 29th nationally.[49] The different types of tax sources were apportioned as follows:

---

41. This case is unpublished. A copy of the complaint is available at http://www.startingat3.org/news/Sa3news_060429_BonnerComplaint.pdf. *See also* Staci Hupp, Teachers plan suit over financing; Union wants more cash to meet stricter standards, **Indianapolis Star**, February 23, 2007, at 1B; see also Indiana, STARTINGAT3.ORG, http://www.startingat3.org/state_laws/StatelawINdetail.htm.

42. Indiana, STARTINGAT3.ORG, *supra* note 41.

43. W. STEVEN BARNETT ET AL., NATIONAL INSTITUTE FOR EARLY EDUCATION RESEARCH, THE STATE OF PRESCHOOL 2006, at 66–67 (2007), *available at* http://nieer.org/yearbook/pdf/yearbook.pdf.

44. *See id.* at 232.

45. U.S. Census Bureau, State and Local Government Finances - 2003–04, http://www.census.gov/govs/www/estimate04.html (last visited Oct. 17, 2006) [hereinafter Government Finances].

46. *Id.*

47. *Id.*

48. *Id.*

49. *Id.*

Individual income taxes	22.7%
Property taxes	32.5%
General and selective sales taxes	37.4%
Corporate income and other taxes	7.4%
	100.0%[50]

Federal Funding

During fiscal year 2004, 18% of Indiana's total revenues came from the federal government.[51] For every dollar of federal taxes paid, Indiana received $0.97 in federal funding, an amount which ranked 33rd nationally[52] and was below the national average of $1.17.[53]

Lottery Revenues

The Hoosier Lottery has been in operation since 1989.[54] Under Indiana law, $30 million of lottery profits are distributed to the Indiana State Teachers' Retirement Fund, $30 million to the Police and Fire Pension Relief Fund, and the remainder to the Build Indiana Fund.[55] During fiscal year 2005, the Lottery had total revenues of approximately $739.6 million and net income of approximately $189.0 million.[56]

Legal Structures of Major Tax Sources

Income

Indiana employs a broad-based income tax that uses adjusted gross income for federal income tax purposes as a starting point for determining Indiana gross income.[57] However, a fairly large number of adjustments may be available to various individuals in calculating this amount.[58] Indiana counties may impose an additional income tax on ad-

---

50. *Id.*

51. *Id.*

52. The Tax Foundation, Federal Spending Received Per Dollar of Taxes Paid by State, 2004 http://www.taxfoundation.org/taxdata/show/266.html (last visited December 17, 2006).

53. *See id.*

54. Hoosier Lottery, Distribution of Hoosier Lottery Profits, http://www.in.gov/hoosierlottery/where_money_goes/profitdistribution.asp (December 20, 2006).

55. *Id.*; IND. CODE § 4-30-16.

56. Hoosier Lottery, *2005 Annual Report* 4, *available at* http://www.in.gov/hoosierlottery/where_money_goes/05Hoosierlottery.pdf.

57. IND. CODE § 6-3-1-3.5.

58. *Id.*

justed gross income.[59] During fiscal year 2004, Indiana collected individual income tax of $612 per capita, an amount which ranked 32nd nationally.[60]

In Indiana, a typical family of four (i.e., married taxpayers who file jointly and have two dependent children) are not required to pay any income tax until their combined income exceeds $15,000, an amount which is below the national poverty line of $20,615.[61] Indiana's income tax structure contains a flat tax of 3.4% on all levels of income.[62] Counties may impose an additional income tax rate of 0.5%, 0.75%, or 1.0% on Indiana adjusted gross income, depending on the county.[63] When statutory exemptions and certain specific deductions are taken into account, the income tax applies to every dollar of income exceeding $7,000.[64]

Property

Overview

Indiana has a typical property tax system that taxes the value of real estate and tangible personal property at the local level.[65] Intangible personal property is specifically exempt.[66] During fiscal year 2004, Indiana collected approximately $6.1 billion at the local level and approximately $9.0 million at the state level.[67] As a result, Indiana resi-

---

59. *Id.* § 6-3.5-1.1-2.

60. STATE RANKINGS 2006, *supra* note 1, at 321 *citing* U.S. Bureau of the Census, Governments Division "2004 State Government Tax Collections" *available at* http://www.census.gov/govs/www/statetax04.html.

61. JASON A. LEVITIS & NICHOLAS JOHNSON, CENTER ON BUDGET AND POLICY PRIORITIES, THE IMPACT OF STATE INCOME TAXES ON LOW-INCOME FAMILIES IN 2006, at 11 (2007). In 2006, Indiana taxpayers who were married and filing jointly could claim personal exemptions of $2,000 (for taxpayer and spouse combined) and dependent exemptions of $2,500 for each dependent child. IND. CODE § 6-3-1-3.5(a)(3)-(4). Indiana does not allow for a standard deduction. Rather, it allows for certain specific deductions from adjusted gross income for federal income tax purposes when determining Indiana adjusted gross income. Indiana Department of Revenue, Indiana Deductions from Individual Income, http://www.in.gov/dor/individual/deductions.html (last visited December 23, 2006). Note, however, that the threshold calculation of $15,000 is greater than the sum of these deductions and exemptions because it includes additional tax benefits available to low-income families, such as the earned-income tax credit. *See* LEVITIS & JOHNSON, *supra*. Indiana's personal exemptions remain unchanged for 2007. IND. CODE § 6-3-1-3.5(a)(3)-(4).

62. IND. CODE § 6-3-2-1(a).

63. *Id.* § 6-3.5-1.1-2.

64. The personal and dependent exemptions of $2,000 and $5,000 (for two children) combined equal $7,000, which serves as the threshold because the flat tax applies to every dollar of income. *See supra* notes 61–63.

65. IND. CONST. art. 10, § 1(a); Indiana Department of Local Government Finance, Taxpayer Information, http://www.in.gov/dlgf/taxpayer/ (last visited December 23, 2006).

66. IND. CONST. art. 10, § 1(a).

67. Government Finances, *supra* note 45.

dents paid $975 per capita in state and local property taxes, an amount which ranked 26th in the nation.[68]

Defining the Real Property Tax Base

In Indiana, a property's assessed value serves as its property tax base.[69] For the purpose of assessing its value and taxability, property is classified as real, or personal and tangible, or intangible.[70] The assessed value of real property is 100% of its "true tax value,"[71] which is determined according to the rules of the Department of Local Government Finance.[72] Real property is assessed once every four years.[73]

Real Property Tax Rates

The State of Indiana may impose a tax rate of up to $0.0033 per $100 of assessed valuation of the property.[74] Political subdivisions of the State of Indiana may impose a tax rate of up to $0.4167 per $100 of assessed valuation in areas outside the corporate limits of a city or town and $0.6667 per $100 of assessed value in areas inside the corporate limits of a city or town.[75] District tax rates range from $1.2468 in Turkey Creek Township to $8.9474 in the Gary Corp. Calumet Township (Gary School District) per $100 of assessed value.[76]

Personal and Intangible Property

Indiana taxes tangible personal property, but intangible personal property is exempt.[77] Tangible personal property is assessed at 100% of its true tax value.[78]

Exemptions

Exemptions from personal property taxation include, among other items, low-income housing,[79] free medical clinics, [80] and household goods.[81] A taxpayer is entitled to a credit against property taxes payable on his or her homestead equal to a percent-

---

68. *Id.*
69. Taxpayer Information, *supra* note 65.
70. 50 Ind. Admin. Code 4.2-4-10; Ind. Code § 6-1.1-31-6; Ind. Code § 6-1.1-31-7.
71. Ind. Code § 6-1.1-1-3(a)(2).
72. *Id.* § 6-1.1-31-6(c).
73. *Id.* § 6-1.1-4-4.
74. *Id.* § 6-1.1-18-2.
75. *Id.* § 6-1.1-18-3.
76. Department of Local Government Finance, Certified Tax Rates – 2006, *available at* http://www.in.gov/dlgf/pdfs/2006_tax_rates_06092006.pdf.
77. Ind. Const. art. 10, § 1(a).
78. Ind. Code § 6-1.1-1-3.
79. *Id.* § 6-1.1-10-16.7.
80. *Id.* § 6-1.1-10-28.
81. 50 Ind. Admin. Code 4.3-1-1.

age of the taxpayer's tax liability for the homestead property.[82] The credit percentage is equal to 28% for 2006 and 20% for 2007 and thereafter.[83] Additionally, taxpayers who are entitled to the homestead credit are also eligible for a deduction from the assessed value of their homestead property equal to the lesser of (1) one-half of the assessed value or (2) $45,000 for the 2007 tax year.[84]

General and Selective Sales

General Sales

Indiana imposes a general retail sales-and-use tax, which makes up 25.5% of its total tax revenue.[85] The tax is imposed on retail transactions, which include the sale of personal property and certain taxable services.[86] Taxable services include services that are furnished together with items of tangible personal property.[87] Indiana's state sales tax rate is 6%.[88] Localities are not authorized to impose a separate sales tax, but those that meet certain population requirements may impose a food-and-beverage tax.[89] Exemptions to Indiana's sales tax include, among other items, food, grocery items,[90] and prescription drugs.[91]

Selective Sales

Selective sales taxes make up 12.0% of Indiana's total tax revenue.[92] Of that amount, 4.3%[93] comes from a motor fuel sales tax that is imposed at a rate of $0.18 per gallon of gasoline.[94] Indiana residents paid an average of $129 per capita in state motor fuel sales taxes in 2004, an amount which ranked 25th nationally.[95]

Sales taxes on tobacco products make up 1.8% of Indiana's total tax revenue[96] and are imposed at a rate of $0.555 per pack of cigarettes.[97] Indiana residents paid an average of $54.40 per capita in state tobacco sales taxes in 2004, an amount which ranked 19th nationally.[98]

---

82. IND. CODE §6-1.1-20.9-2.
83. *Id.*
84. *Id.* §6-1.1-12-37.
85. Government Finances, *supra* note 45.
86. IND. CODE §6-2.5-2-2; 45 IND. ADMIN. CODE §2.2-1-1.
87. 45 IND. ADMIN. CODE §2.2-1-1.
88. IND. CODE §6-2.5-2-2.
89. *Id.* §6-9-33-3; *Id.* 6-9-24-1 to -9; *Id.* §6-9-27-1 to -10.
90. 45 IND. ADMIN. CODE 2.2-5-38.
91. IND. CODE §6-2.5-5-19.
92. Government Finances, *supra* note 45.
93. *Id.*
94. STATE RANKINGS 2006, *supra* note 1, at 328.
95. *Id.* at 327.
96. Government Finances, *supra* note 45.
97. STATE RANKINGS 2006, *supra* note 1, at 333.
98. *Id.* at 332.

In 2004, sales taxes on alcoholic beverages made up 0.2% of Indiana's total tax revenue.[99] Indiana residents paid $6.18 per capita in state alcoholic beverage sales taxes in 2004, an amount which ranked 43rd nationally and was well below the national average of $15.74.[100]

The remainder of Indiana's selective sales taxes makes up 5.6% of its total tax revenue.[101] Of this amount, 0.1% represents taxes on utilities and the other 5.5% represents taxes on other specific commodities, businesses, or services not reported separately above (e.g., on contractors, lodging, lubricating oil, fuels other than motor fuel, motor vehicles, meals, soft drinks, margarine, etc.).[102]

Corporate Income and Other

Corporate Income

The corporate income tax makes up 3.5% of Indiana's total tax revenue.[103] Indiana's broad-based corporate income tax is imposed at a rate of 8.5% on a corporation's taxable income,[104] which is based on the corporation's federal taxable income before the net operating loss deduction subject to certain modifications.[105]

Indiana follows the federal income tax treatment of S corporations, and thus they do not pay Indiana's corporate income tax.[106] A similar treatment is afforded to general partnerships,[107] limited partnerships, limited liability partnerships,[108] and limited liability companies.[109] However, if a limited liability company is treated as a corporation for federal income tax purposes, the entity is subject to Indiana's corporate income tax.[110]

Indiana also employs a franchise tax on financial institutions, which is imposed at a rate of 8.5% on the taxpayer institution's apportioned income for the privilege of transacting the business of a financial institution in Indiana.[111] An institution that is subject to the financial institutions tax is exempt from the corporate income tax.[112]

---

99. Government Finances, *supra* note 45.

100. STATE RANKINGS 2006, *supra* note 1, at 335.

101. Government Finances, *supra* note 45.

102. *See* GOVERNMENTS DIVISION, U.S. CENSUS BUREAU, GOVERNMENT FINANCE AND EMPLOYMENT CLASSIFICATION MANUAL, at ch.7 (2000), *available at* http://ftp2.census.gov/govs/class/classfull.pdf [hereinafter CLASSIFICATION MANUAL].

103. Government Finances, *supra* note 45.

104. IND. CODE § 6-3-2-1(b).

105. *Id.* § 6-3-1-3.5(b).

106. 45 IND. ADMIN. CODE § 3.1-1-66.

107. IND. CODE § 6-3-4-11(a).

108. *Id.* § 23-4-1-6.

109. *Id.* § 6-3-1-19(a).

110. *Id.*

111. *Id.*

112. *Id.* § 6-5.5-9-4.

Other

During fiscal year 2004, the collection of all other taxes not previously mentioned accounted for 3.9% of Indiana's total tax revenue.[113] Of this amount, approximately $140.0 million was generated by the estate and gift tax.[114] This tax is based on the difference between the maximum state death tax credit allowable by federal law and the amount paid in state inheritance tax.[115] The "other taxes" category is further made up of various license taxes, documentary or stock transfer taxes, severance taxes, and all other taxes not listed separately or provided for in other categories.[116]

Burden Analysis

The overall state and local tax burden on Indiana's taxpayers is very regressive. Taxpayers in the lowest quintile—those with incomes of less than $16,000—bear a tax burden equal to 11.7% of their income, while taxpayers in the top 1%—those with incomes that exceed $279,000—bear a tax burden of just 6.3% of their income.[117] It is also worth noting that, although Indiana obviously has no control over federal tax policy, federal itemized deductions for state and local personal income and property taxes nonetheless further reduce the burden on taxpayers in the top 1% to 4.7%.[118] Furthermore, between 1989 and 2002, the tax burden on the bottom quintile rose by approximately 0.7%, while the burden on the top 1% fell by 0.7%.[119]

In terms of the income tax, the burden across income groups in Indiana is slightly progressive, with taxpayers in the lowest quintile bearing a tax burden of 2.5% and those in the top 1% bearing a tax burden of 3.9%.[120] In contrast, however, the sales and

---

113. Government Finances, *supra* note 45.

114. *Id.*

115. Indiana Department of Revenue, Miscellaneous Tax Rates, http://www.in.gov/dor/tax-types/rates.html (last visited December 25, 2006).

116. *See* Classification Manual, *supra* note 102, at ch.7.

117. *See* Robert S. McIntyre et al., Who Pays? A Distributional Analysis of the Tax Systems in All 50 States 44 (2d ed. 2003), *available at* http://www.itepnet.org/wp2000/text.pdf. Taxpayers in the second quintile bear a 10.8% total tax burden on incomes between $16,000 and $28,000; those in the third quintile bear a 9.9% tax burden on incomes between $28,000 and $45,000; those in the fourth quintile bear a 9.3% tax burden on incomes between $45,000 and $69,000; those in the 80th–95th percentiles bear a 8.6% tax burden on incomes between $69,000 and $122,000; finally, those in the 96th–99th percentiles bear a 7.5% tax burden on incomes between $122,000 and $279,000. *Id.*

118. *Id.* Taxpayers in the lowest quintile did not receive any benefit from these federal offsets, while those in the second quintile were able to reduce their individual tax burdens by 0.1%, those in the third quintile by 0.2%, those in the fourth quintile by 0.6%, those in the 80th–95th percentiles by 1.1%, and those in the 96th–99th percentiles by 1.3%. *Id.*

119. *Id.* at 45.

120. *See id.* at 44. Taxpayers in the second quintile bear a 3.3% income tax burden; those in the third quintile bear a 3.4% burden; those in the fourth quintile bear a 3.7% burden; those in the 80th–95th percentiles bear a 3.9% burden; finally, those in the 96th–99th percentiles bear a

excise taxes imposed by Indiana are very regressive, with taxpayers in the lowest quintile bearing a tax burden of 6.8% and those in the top 1% bearing a tax burden of just
1.0%.[121] Property taxes in Indiana are also regressive, with taxpayers in the lowest quintile bearing a tax burden of 2.4% and those in the top quintile bearing an average tax
burden of 1.4%.[122]

3.9% burden. *Id.* Note, however, that these percentages include both individual and corporate
income tax burdens; that within the 96th–99th percentiles, corporate income taxes represent
0.1% of the income tax burden; and that in the top 1%, corporate income taxes represent 0.2%
of the income tax burden. *Id.*

121. *See id.* Taxpayers in the second quintile bear a 5.7% sales-and-excise tax burden; those
in the third quintile bear a 4.5% burden; those in the fourth quintile bear a 3.8% burden; those
in the 80th–95th percentiles bear a 2.9% burden; finally, those in the 96th–99th percentiles bear
a 1.8% burden. *Id.*

122. *See id.* Taxpayers in the second quintile bear a 1.8% property tax burden; those in the
third quintile bear a 1.9% burden; those in the fourth quintile bear a 1.8% burden; those in the
80th–95th percentiles bear a 1.8% burden; and those in the 96th–99th percentiles bear a 1.8%
burden. *Id.*

Iowa

General Information

Basic Profile – Geography, Population, and Industry

Admitted to the Union in 1846, Iowa is commonly referred to as the "Hawkeye State."[1] It is located in the Midwest and is bordered by Minnesota on the north; Wisconsin and Illinois on the east; Missouri on the south; and South Dakota and Nebraska on the west. Iowa is located in the central time zone, and its capital is Des Moines.[2]

Iowa ranks 30th in population (approximately 2.97 million residents) and 26th in total area (56,272 square miles).[3] Its population is 94.9% white and 2.3% black.[4] The state is approximately 23% Catholic; 53% Protestant; and less than 0.5% Jewish; 24% claim a religion outside the Judeo-Christian tradition or no religion at all.[5] Iowa is almost evenly split between urban and rural, with 55% of the population living in cities and towns and 45% living in rural areas.[6] Major industries include agriculture, advanced manufacturing, biotechnology, finance and insurance services, and food processing.[7]

---

1. STATE RANKINGS 2006, vi, 1 (Kathleen O'Leary Morgan & Scott Morgan eds., Morgan Quitno Press 2006).

2. *Id.* at vi.

3. *Id.* at 429.

4. Iowa Quick Facts from the U.S. Census Bureau, http://quickfacts.census.gov/qfd/states/19000.html (last visited Jan. 27, 2007). The remaining population is made up of 1.4% Asian persons; 0.3% American Indian and/or Alaska Native persons; and 0.9% persons reporting two or more races. *Id.* Additionally, 3.7% of Iowa's total population identify themselves as persons of Hispanic or Latino origin. *Id.* (noting that because Hispanics may be of any race, they are included within the other applicable race categories) (last visited Jan. 31, 2007).

5. BARRY A. KOSMIN, EGON MAYER & ARIELA KEYSAR, AMERICAN RELIGIOUS IDENTIFICATION SURVEY 2001, at 41, *available at* http://www.gc.cuny.edu/faculty/research_studies/aris.pdf.

6. USDA Economic Research Service, Iowa Fact Sheet, http://www.ers.usda.gov/StateFacts/IA.htm (last visited Sept. 17, 2006). According to the latest estimates, approximately 1.3 million people live in rural areas, and 1.6 people live in urban areas. *Id.*

7. "Major Industries in Iowa," Iowa Department of Economic Development, http://www.iowalifechanging.com/downloads/iaindustries.pdf#search=%22iowa%20major%20industries%22, (last visited Oct. 2, 2006).

Family Income and Poverty Indicators

In 2004, Iowa's per capita gross product was $37,629, which was below the national average of $39,725.[8] During this same period, although the median household income in Iowa was $43,042,[9] 9.7% of Iowa's population was living in poverty, which was below the national average of 12.4% and ranked among the bottom ten states nationally.[10] More specifically, poverty affected 12.1% of Iowa's children,[11] 7.8% of its senior citizens,[12] and 6.8% of its families.[13] Of its female-headed households with children, 34.2% lived in poverty,[14] and 30.0% of the state's public elementary and secondary school students were eligible for free or reduced-price meals.[15] Of those living in poverty, approximately 6.8% were black, which represented 28.4% of Iowa's black population and 0.6% of its total population.[16] In an attempt to combat this poverty, Iowa spent approximately $2.0 billion on public welfare programs in 2002,[17] which made up 15.6% of its total government expenditures.[18]

Iowa's Public Elementary-Secondary School System

Overall Spending and Performance

For the 2003–2004 school year Iowa spent $7,631 per pupil in its public elementary-secondary school system, which was slightly below the national average of $8,182.[19] Of this amount, 8.3% was provided by the federal government, 46.2% was provided by the state government, and 45.5% was provided by the local governments,[20] with property taxes making up 34.5% of the total funding.[21] Out of these funds, Iowa paid its elementary and secondary school teachers an estimated average annual salary of $40,347

---

8. STATE RANKINGS 2006, *supra* note 1, at 89.

9. *Id.* at 96.

10. *Id.* at 495.

11. *Id.* at 497.

12. *Id.* at 496.

13. *Id.* at 498.

14. *Id.* at 499.

15. *Id.* at 532.

16. *See* Fact Sheet, American FactFinder, http://factfinder.census.gov/home/saff/main.html?_lang=en (select "Iowa" under "Get a Fact Sheet for your community") (last visited Feb. 16, 2007). Note that these numbers are based on the 2000 census because more recent numbers were not available.

17. STATE RANKINGS 2006, *supra* note 1, at 500.

18. *Id.* at 502.

19. GOVERNMENTS DIVISION, U.S. CENSUS BUREAU, PUBLIC EDUCATION FINANCES 2004, at 8 tbl.8 (2006).

20. *See id.* at 5 tbl.5.

21. *See id.* at 4 tbl.4.

during the 2004–2005 school year,[22] and it provided a student/teacher ratio of 13.8, which was above the national average of 15.9.[23]

In academic performance, Iowa's fourth grade students scored higher than the national average in mathematics,[24] reading,[25] and writing,[26] while Iowa's eighth graders scored higher than the national average in mathematics[27] and reading.[28] Iowa did not participate in the national average for fourth grade students in science[29] and the national average for eighth grade students in science[30] and writing.[31]

Equity Issues

In 2004, the funding per student in Iowa's highest poverty districts actually exceeded that in its lowest poverty districts by $82.[32] When adjustments were made for the additional costs of educating students growing up in poverty, however, the funding in high poverty districts actually declined by $176.[33] On the other hand, Iowa spent $327 less per student in its highest minority districts, and this amount grew to $414 when adjustments for low-income students were made.[34]

Fourth graders eligible for free or reduced-price school lunches had test scores that were 5.3% lower in mathematics,[35] 8.4% lower in reading,[36] and 11.3% lower in writ-

22. Thomas D. Snyder et al., National Center for Education Statistics, Digest of Education Statistics 2005, at 116 tbl.77 (2006).

23. *Id.* at 98 tbl.65.

24. National Center for Education Statistics, U.S. Department of Education, The Nation's Report Card: Mathematics 2005, at 14 fig.11 (2005), *available at* http://nces.ed.gov/nationsreportcard/pdf/main2005/ 2006453.pdf [hereinafter Mathematics 2005].

25. National Center for Education Statistics, U.S. Department of Education, The Nation's Report Card: Reading 2005, at 14 fig.11 (2005), *available at* http://nces.ed.gov/nationsreportcard/pdf/main2005/2006451.pdf [hereinafter Reading 2005].

26. Hilary R. Persky et al., National Center for Education Statistics, U.S. Department of Education, The Nation's Report Card: Writing 2002, at 23 tbl.2.2 (2003), *available at* http://nces.ed.gov/nationsreportcard/pdf/main2002/2003529.pdf [hereinafter Writing 2002].

27. Mathematics 2005, *supra* note 24, at 16 fig.12.

28. Reading 2005, *supra* note 25, at 16 fig.12.

29. National Center for Education Statistics, U.S. Department of Education, The Nation's Report Card: Science 2005, at 16 fig.12 (2006), *available at* http://nces.ed.gov/nationsreportcard//pdf/main2005/2006466.pdf [hereinafter Science 2005].

30. Science 2005, *supra* note 29, at 28 fig.22.

31. Writing 2002, *supra* note 26, at 24 tbl.2.3.

32. The Education Trust, Funding Gaps 2006, at 7 tbl.3 (2006), *available at* http://www2.edtrust.org/NR/rdonlyres/CDEF9403-5A75-437E-93FF-EBF1174181FB/0/FundingGap2006.pdf.

33. *Id.*

34. *Id.* at 7 tbl.4.

35. Mathematics 2005, *supra* note 24, at 20 tbl.5.

36. Reading 2005, *supra* note 25, at 20 tbl.5.

ing[37] than those of students who were not eligible. The results were generally the same for eighth graders eligible for free or reduced-price lunches; their test scores were 7.2% lower in mathematics[38] and 6.3% lower in reading[39] than those of students who were not eligible.

In 2002, Iowa school districts and individuals sued, alleging that the school funding system violated the Iowa constitution's education clause because it created significant disparities in educational resources and did not provide sufficient resources for many districts to be able to offer an adequate education to students.[40] Iowa's legislature changed the school funding statutes, and the case was withdrawn without prejudice after a settlement was reached.[41] Currently, no court has decided that Iowa's state school funding system violates the state constitution.

Availability of Publicly Funded Prekindergarten Programs

Iowa's Shared Visions program currently serves children between the ages of three and five who are from low-income families or who are considered at risk.[42] Total enrollment in this state-funded program is 2,322,[43] which represents just 3.3% of Iowa's 70,546 three-, four-, and five-year-old children.[44] The federally funded Head Start program enrolls an additional 6,278 children,[45] which represents 8.9% of Iowa's three- and four-year-old children.[46]

Where Does Iowa Get Its Revenue?

At the end of fiscal year 2004, Iowa had total revenues of approximately $22.5 billion.[47] Of this amount, 40% was derived from state and local tax revenues and 19% was received from the federal government.[48] The remaining 41% came from other

---

37. WRITING 2002, *supra* note 26, at 75 tbl.3.24.

38. MATHEMATICS 2005, *supra* note 24, at 21 tbl.6.

39. READING 2005, *supra* note 25, at 21 tbl.6.

40. Iowa Suit Seeks Equitable and Adequate School Funding, *available at* http://www.schoolfunding.info/states/ia/lit_ia.php3 (last visited April 8, 2007).

41. *Id.*

42. W. STEVEN BARNETT ET AL., NATIONAL INSTITUTE FOR EARLY EDUCATION RESEARCH, THE STATE OF PRESCHOOL 2006, at 148 (2006), *available at* http://nieer.org/yearbook/pdf/yearbook.pdf.

43. *Id.* at 69.

44. *See id.* at 232.

45. *Id.* at 69.

46. *See id.* at 232.

47. U.S. Census Bureau, State and Local Government Finances 2003–04, http://www.census.gov/govs/www/estimate04.html (last visited Oct. 6, 2006) [hereinafter Government Finances].

48. *Id.*

sources, including the Iowa Lottery, insurance trust revenue, and revenue from government-owned utilities and other commercial or auxiliary enterprises.[49]

Tax Revenue

Iowa collected approximately $9 billion in state and local tax revenue during fiscal year 2004.[50] As a result, Iowa residents paid $3,054 per capita in state and local taxes, an amount which ranked 28th nationally.[51] The different types of tax sources were apportioned as follows:

Individual income taxes	22.3%
Property taxes	35.4%
General and selective sales taxes	33.4%
Corporate income and other taxes	8.9%
	100.0%[52]

Federal Funding

During fiscal year 2004, 19% of Iowa's total revenues came from the federal government.[53] For every dollar of federal taxes paid, Iowa received $1.11 in federal funding, an amount which ranked 25th nationally[54] and was just below the national median of $1.17.[55]

Lottery

The Iowa Lottery has been in operation since 1986.[56] The proceeds of the Iowa Lottery are deposited into Iowa's general fund.[57] In 2005, the Iowa Lottery had operating revenues of $211 million and a net income of $52 million,[58] $50 million of which was transferred to the Iowa State General Fund.[59]

---

49. *Id.*

50. The total tax revenues were collected as follows: $5.2 billion by the state and $3.8 billion by local governments. *Id.*

51. *Id.*

52. *Id.*

53. *Id.*

54. The Tax Foundation, Federal Spending Received Per Dollar of Taxes Paid by State 2004, http://www.taxfoundation.org/taxdata/show/266.html (last visited Sept. 17, 2006).

55. *See id.*

56. Iowa Lottery History, http://www.ialottery.com/AboutUs/history.html (last visited Sept. 7, 2006).

57. Iowa Code § 99G.2.

58. Iowa Lottery Annual Report Fiscal Year 2005, 9, *available at* http://www.ialottery.com/AboutUs/AnnualReport.html (last visited Oct. 13, 2006).

59. *Id.*

Legal Structure of Major Tax Sources

Income

Iowa employs a broad-based income tax[60] that uses adjusted gross income for federal income tax purposes as a starting point for determining the state's taxable income.[61] However, a fairly large number of adjustments may be available to various individuals in calculating this amount.[62] Iowa allows a deduction for 100% of federal income tax paid.[63] Iowa counties can impose two approved local income taxes, one for school districts, which is limited to 20%, [64] and one for emergency medical services, which is limited to 1% or the difference between other local income tax surcharges and the maximum cumulative rate of 20%.[65] The local tax rates vary from no tax at all in Corning to a high of 20% in English Valleys.[66] During fiscal year 2004, Iowa collected individual income tax of $663 per capita, an amount which 24th nationally.[67]

On the basis of the relevant statutory exemptions and standard deductions, a typical family of four (i.e., married taxpayers who file jointly and have two dependent children) are not required to pay any income tax until their combined income exceeds $18,300, an amount which is below the national poverty line of $20,615.[68] Iowa's income tax structure contains nine tax brackets that impose a minimum marginal rate of 0.36% and a maximum marginal rate of 8.98%.[69] When statutory credits and the standard deduction are taken into account, the maximum marginal rate applies to every dollar of income exceeding $64,556.[70]

---

60. Iowa Code § 422.5.

61. *Id.* § 422.7.

62. *Id.*

63. *Id.* § 422.9.

64. *Id.* § 257.19.

65. *Id.* § 422D.1.

66. CCH-EXP, IA-TAXRPTR ¶ 16-205, Rates of Tax.

67. State Rankings 2006, *supra* note 1, at 321.

68. Jason A. Levitis, Center on Budget and Policy Priorities, The Impact of State Income Taxes on Low-Income Families in 2006, at 12 (2007). In 2006, Iowa taxpayers who were married and filing jointly could claim a standard deduction of $4,060. Iowa provides a *credit* of $40 per person instead of personal and dependent exemptions . Iowa Code § 422.9 and Iowa Code § 422.12. Note, however, that the threshold calculation of $18,300 is greater than the sum of these deductions and credits because it includes additional tax benefits available to low-income families, such as the earned-income tax credit. *See* Levitis, *supra*.

69. Iowa Code § 422.5. Iowa's middle 7 brackets are 0.72%, 2.43%, 4.5%, 6.12%, 6.48%, 6.80%, and 7.92%. *Id.*

70. The standard deduction of $4,060 and four credits, plus the threshold of taxable income for the highest tax bracket of $60,436, equals $64,556. *See supra* notes 68–69.

Property

Overview

Iowa has a typical property tax system that taxes the value of real property at the local level. During fiscal year 2004, Iowa collected approximately $3.2 billion dollars in property tax at the local level.[71] As a result, Iowa residents paid $1,080 per capita in state and local property taxes, an amount which ranked 18th nationally.[72]

Defining the Real Property Tax Base

Iowa has five classifications of real property: (1) residential; (2) agricultural; (3) commercial; (4) industrial; and (5) utilities/railroads.[73] Residential, commercial, and industrial properties are assessed at 100% of market value, while agricultural property is assessed according to its productivity.[74] Computers and industrial machinery and equipment acquired before January 1, 1994, are classified as real property.[75] They are exempt if acquired after December 31, 1993. The base for computers and industrial machinery and equipment is assessed as a percentage of its acquisition cost (22% for 1999). Fair market value is generally determined by the application of standard appraisal methods, including the cost method, the income method, and the market-data method, all of which are commonly used throughout the country.[76] State law requires that all real property be assessed every two years in odd-numbered years.[77] Railroads and public utilities, which are assessed by the Iowa Department of Revenue, are assessed every year.[78] Residential and agricultural properties are subject to an assessment limitation formula which limits the total increase statewide to 4%.[79]

Real Property Tax Rates

The real property tax rates, composed of county, city, school district, and special levies, vary and are set by each locality. Taxes are levied in terms of dollars per $1,000

---

71. Government Finances, *supra* note 47.

72. *See id.*

73. http://www.state.ia.us/tax/educate/78573.html (last visited Oct. 11, 2006). Several taxing authorities are supported by the property tax, including K–12 schools, which receive 45% of the taxes collected; cities, which receive 28%; counties, which receive 21%; hospitals, which receive 2%; merged areas, which receive 2%; assessors, which receive 1%; and others, which receive 1%. The property tax is paid as follows: residential property pays 47% of the property tax; commercial property pays 29%; agricultural land and buildings pay 16%; industrial property pays 5%; and public utilities and railroads pay 3%.

74. *Id.*

75. *Id.*

76. *Id.*

77. Iowa Code § 428.4.

78. http://www.state.ia.us/tax/educate/78573.html (last visited Oct. 11, 2006).

79. *Id.*

of taxable value and are collected locally.[80] In 2005, the tax rates per $1,000 of assessed value ranged from $0.32 in Benton County to $4.90 in Montgomery County.[81]

Personal and Intangible Property

Because the property tax statutorily applies only to real property, Iowa does not tax tangible or intangible personal property.[82]

Exemptions

Iowa has adopted a homestead credit to encourage home ownership through property tax relief.[83] The current credit is equal to the actual tax levy on the first $4,850 of actual value.[84] Furthermore, a taxpayer must own and occupy the property as a homestead on July 1 of each year, declare residency in Iowa for income tax purposes, and occupy the property for at least six months each year.[85]

General and Selective Sales

General Sales

Iowa imposes a general retail sales-and-use tax, which makes up 22.6% of the state's total tax revenue.[86] This tax is imposed on all tangible personal property, [87] utilities, and certain enumerated services, such as hotel and motel stays and automobile rentals.[88] The state sales tax rate is set at 5%.[89] Local jurisdictions can impose a sales tax of up to 2% through Iowa's two local-option sales taxes.[90] The local-option sales tax of up to 1% began in 1986 and allows each city or unincorporated area to elect to impose the tax.[91] The school infrastructure sales tax of up to 1% began in 1998 and allows each county to elect to impose the tax.[92] Major exemptions from Iowa sales tax include defined food and food ingredients (mostly grocery); items purchased with food stamps; prescription drugs and prescribed medical equipment or devices; certain enumerated farm and agricultural equipment, supplies, and livestock; equipment and com-

---

80. *Id.*

81. CCH-EXP, IA-TAXRPTR ¶ 20-405, Rates of Tax.

82. Iowa Code § 427A.2.

83. http://www.state.ia.us/tax/taxlaw/PropertyTaxCredits.html#Homestead (last visited Oct. 7, 2006).

84. Iowa Code § 425.1.

85. *Id.* § 425.2.

86. Government Finances, *supra* note 47.

87. Iowa Code § 423.2.

88. *Id.* §§ 423A, 423C.

89. *Id.*

90. *Id.* § 423B.5, 423E.1.

91. *Id.* § 423B.5.

92. *Id.* § 423E.1.

puters; the sale of tangible personal property to enumerated nonprofit corporations or organizations; and clothing under $100 for one week in August.[93]

Selective Sales

Selective sales taxes make up 10.8% of Iowa's total revenue.[94] Of that amount, 4.8% comes from a motor fuel sales tax imposed at a rate of $0.205 per gallon of gasoline.[95] Iowa residents paid an average of $121 per capita in state motor fuel sales taxes in 2004, an amount which ranked 32nd nationally and was above the national average of $115.[96]

In 2004, sales taxes on alcoholic beverages made up 0.1% of Iowa's total tax revenue.[97] Iowa residents paid $4.30 per capita in state alcoholic beverage sales taxes in 2004, an amount which ranked 48th nationally.[98]

The tobacco product sales tax makes up 1.0% of Iowa's tax revenues.[99] It is imposed at a rate of 22% of the wholesale price of all tobacco products[100] except for cigarettes and small cigars, which are taxed at 18 mills ($0.36) per pack of 20.[101] Iowa residents paid $31.93 per capita in state tobacco sales taxes in 2004, an amount which ranked 33rd nationally.[102]

The remainder of Iowa's selective sales taxes makes up 4.9% of its total tax revenue. Of this amount, 0.5% represents taxes on utilities and the other 4.4% represents taxes on other specific commodities, businesses, or services not reported separately above (e.g., on contractors, lodging, lubricating oil, fuels other than motor fuel, motor vehicles, meals, soft drinks, margarine, etc.). [103]

Corporate Income and Other

Corporate Income

The corporate income tax made up only 1.0% of Iowa's total tax revenue during fiscal year 2004.[104] Iowa's broad-based corporate income tax is imposed on the Iowa net

---

93. *Id.* § 423.3. Food is defined as not including prepared food, soft drinks, tobacco, alcoholic beverages, dietary supplements, food from vending machines, or candy.

94. Government Finances, *supra* note 47.

95. Iowa Code §§ 452A.1–452A.86.

96. State Rankings 2006, *supra* note 1, at 327.

97. Government Finances, *supra* note 47.

98. State Rankings 2006 , *supra* note 1, at 335.

99. Government Finances, *supra* note 47.

100. Iowa Code § 453A.43.

101. *Id.* § 453A.8.

102. State Rankings 2006, *supra* note 1, at 332.

103. *See* Governments Division, U.S. Census Bureau, Government Finance and Employment Classification Manual, at ch.7 (2000), *available at* http://ftp2.census.gov/govs/class/classfull.pdf [hereinafter Classification Manual].

104. Government Finances, *supra* note 47.

income of corporations doing business within Iowa or receiving income from property in the state.[105] The rate is 6% for the lowest bracket and 12% for the highest bracket.[106]

Iowa follows the federal income tax treatment of S corporations. Thus, they do not pay Iowa's corporate income tax; rather, income and losses flow through to their shareholders.[107] A similar treatment is afforded to limited partnerships, limited liability partnerships,[108] and limited liability companies, assuming they are treated as a partnership for federal tax purposes.[109] However, if a limited liability company is treated as a corporation for federal income tax purposes, the entity is subject to Iowa's corporate income tax.[110]

Other

During fiscal year 2004, the collection of all other taxes not previously mentioned accounted for 8% of Iowa's total tax revenue.[111] Of this amount, $67 million[112] was generated by the inheritance tax, which is calculated on the basis of the fair market value of the property.[113] The rate of tax depends on the relation to the deceased and the amount passed; there is no minimum marginal rate, and the maximum marginal rate is 15%.[114] The "other taxes" category is also made up of motor vehicle license taxes, documentary and stock transfer taxes, severance taxes, and all other taxes not listed separately or provided for in other categories, such as taxes on land based on a specified rate per acre (rather than on assessed value).[115]

Burden Analysis

The overall state and local tax burden on Iowa's taxpayers is very regressive. Taxpayers in the lowest quintile—those with incomes of less than $14,000—bear a tax

---

105. Iowa Code §§ 422.32–422.41.

106. *Id.* § 422.33. Iowa's corporate rates are as follows: 6% on the first $25,000 of taxable income; 8% on the next $75,000; 10% on the next $150,000; and 12% on all income over $250,000. *Id.*

107. CCH-EXP, IA-TAXRPTR ¶ 10-215.40, Exempt Organization.

108. CCH-EXP, IA-TAXRPTR ¶ 10-225, Limited Partnerships, Limited Liability Partnerships.

109. CCH-EXP, IA-TAXRPTR ¶ 10-240, Limited Liability Companies (LLCs).

110. *Id.*

111. Government Finances, *supra* note 47.

112. Id.

113. Iowa Code § 450.37.

114. *Id.* § 450.10. Property passing to the surviving spouse, parents, grandparents, great-grandparents, and other lineal ascendants, as well as to children, stepchildren, grandchildren, great-grandchildren, and other lineal descendants, is not taxed. If the property passes to a brother, sister, son-in-law, or daughter-in law, the rates are as follows: 5% up to $12,500; 6% between $12,501 and $25,000; 7% between $25,001 and $75,000; 8% between $75,001 and $100,000; 9% between $100,001 and $150,000; and 10% over $150,000. Property passing to a for-profit organization is taxed at 15%. Property passing to charitable, educational, religious, or cemetery associations is taxed at 10%. Property passing to all other organizations is taxed at the following rates: 10% up to $50,000; 12% between $50,001 and $100,000, and 15% over $100,000. *Id.*

115. *See* CLASSIFICATION MANUAL, *supra* note 103, at ch.7.

burden of 10.6% of their income, while taxpayers in the top 1% — those with incomes that exceed $257,000 — bear a tax burden of just 7.9% of their income.[116] It is also worth noting that, although Iowa obviously has no control over federal tax policy, federal itemized deductions for state and local personal income and property taxes nonetheless further reduce the burden on taxpayers in the top 1% to 5.8%.[117] Furthermore, between 1989 and 2002, the tax burden on the bottom quintile rose by approximately 0.2%, while the burden on the top 1% fell by 0.8%.[118]

In terms of the income tax, the burden across income groups in Iowa is slightly progressive, with taxpayers in the lowest quintile bearing a tax burden of 0.7% and those in the top 1% bearing a tax burden of 5.2%.[119] In sharp contrast, however, the sales and excise taxes imposed by Iowa are very regressive, with taxpayers in the lowest quintile bearing a tax burden of 6.9% and those in the top 1% bearing a tax burden of just 1.2%.[120] Property taxes in Iowa are also regressive, with taxpayers in the lowest quintile bearing a tax burden of 3.0% and those in the top quintile bearing an average tax burden of 2.2%.[121]

---

116. *See* ROBERT S. MCINTYRE ET AL., WHO PAYS? A DISTRIBUTIONAL ANALYSIS OF THE TAX SYSTEMS IN ALL 50 STATES 46 (2d ed. 2003), *available at* http://www.itepnet.org/wp2000/text.pdf. Taxpayers in the second quintile bear a 10.5% total tax burden on incomes between $14,000 and $28,000; those in the third quintile bear a 10.6% tax burden on incomes between $28,000 and $44,000; those in the fourth quintile bear a 10.3% tax burden on incomes between $44,000 and $65,000; those in the 80th–95th percentiles bear a 9.8% tax burden on incomes between $65,000 and $110,000; finally. those in the 96th–99th percentiles bear a 8.7% tax burden on incomes between $110,000 and $257,000. *Id.*

117. *Id.* Taxpayers in the lowest quintile did not receive any benefit from these federal offsets, while those in the second quintile were able to reduce their individual tax burdens by 0.1%, those in the third quintile by 0.2%, those in the fourth quintile by 0.4%, those in the 80th–95th percentiles by 1.0%, and those in the 96th–99th percentiles by 1.5%. *Id.*

118. *Id.* at 47.

119. *See id.* at 46. Taxpayers in the second quintile bear a 2.7% income tax burden: those in the third quintile bear a 3.3% burden: those in the fourth quintile bear a 3.7% burden; those in the 80th–95th percentiles bear a 4.0% burden; finally, those in the 96th–99th percentiles bear a 4.2% burden. *Id.* Note, however, that these percentages include both individual and corporate income tax burdens and that within the top 1%, corporate income taxes represent 0.1% of the income tax burden. *Id.*

120. *See id.* Taxpayers in the second quintile bear a 5.7% sales-and-excise tax burden; those in the third quintile bear a 4.9% burden; those in the fourth quintile bear a 4.1% burden; those in the 80th–95th percentiles bear a 3.2% burden; finally, those in the 96th–99th percentiles bear a 2.1% burden. *Id.*

121. *See id.* Taxpayers in the second quintile bear a 2.1% property tax burden; those in the third quintile bear a 2.5% burden; those in the fourth quintile bear a 2.5% burden; those in the 80th–95th percentiles bear a 2.6% burden; those in the 96th–99th percentiles bear a 2.4% burden, finally, those in the top 1% bear a burden. *Id.*

Kansas

General Information

Basic Profile – Geography, Population, and Industry

Admitted to the Union in 1861,[1] Kansas is known as the "Sunflower State."[2] Kansas is located in the Great Plains region and is bordered by Nebraska on the north, Missouri on the east, Oklahoma on the south, and Colorado on the west. Kansas is located in the central time zone , and its capital is Topeka.[3]

In 2005, Kansas ranked 33rd in population (over 2.7 million residents);[4] it ranks 15th in total area (82,277 square miles).[5] Its population is 89.4% white and 5.9% black.[6] The state is 20% Catholic; 52% Protestant; and 1% Jewish; 27% claim a religion outside the Judeo-Christian tradition or none at all.[7] Kansas is primarily urban, with 63.0% of the population living in cities and towns.[8] The state's major industries include aircraft manufacturing, agriculture, and education.[9]

Family Income and Poverty Indicators

In 2004, Kansas's per capita gross product was $36,195, which was below the national average of $39,725.[10] During this same period, although the median household

---

1. STATE RANKINGS 2006, vi, 1 (Kathleen O'Leary Morgan & Scott Morgan, eds., Morgan Quitno Press, 2006).

2. *Id.* at vi.

3. *Id.*

4. *Id.* at 429.

5. *Id.* at 225.

6. Kansas QuickFacts from the U.S. Census Bureau, http://quickfacts.census.gov/qfd/states/20000.html (last visited January 30, 2007). Other races include 2.1% Asian persons; 0.9% American Indian and Alaska Native persons; 0.1% Native Hawaiian persons and other Pacific Islanders; and 1.6% persons reporting two or more races. *Id.* Persons of Hispanic or Latino origin make up 8.3% of the population. *Id.* (noting that because Hispanics may be of any race, they are included within the other applicable race categories).

7. BARRY A. KOSMIN, EGON MAYER & ARIELA KEYSAR, AMERICAN RELIGIOUS IDENTIFICATION SURVEY 2001, at 39, *available at* http://www.gc.cuny.edu/faculty/research_studies/aris.pdf.

8. USDA Economic Research Service, Kansas Fact Sheet, http://www.ers.usda.gov/StateFacts/KS.htm (last visited Sept. 17, 2006).

9. Kansas Office of the Governor, Kansas Quick Facts, http://www.governor.ks.gov/Facts/quickfacts.htm (last visited November 10, 2006).

10. STATE RANKINGS 2006, *supra* note 1, at 89.

income in Kansas was $43,725,[11] 10.7% of its population was living in poverty, which was somewhat below the national average of 12.4%.[12] More specifically, poverty affected 11.6% of Kansas's children,[13] 8.2% of its senior citizens,[14] and 6.8% of its families.[15] Of its female-headed households with children, 28.3% lived in poverty ,[16] and 37.4% of the state's public elementary and secondary school students were eligible for free or reduced-price meals.[17] Of those living in poverty, approximately 12.6% were black, which represented 21% of Kansas's black population and 1.2% of its total population.[18] In an attempt to combat this poverty, Kansas spent approximately $2.0 billion on public welfare programs in 2002,[19] which made up 13.5% of its total government expenditures.[20]

Kansas's Public Elementary-Secondary School System

Overall Spending and Performance

For the 2003–2004 school year, Kansas spent $7,518 per pupil in its public elementary-secondary school system, which was slightly below the national average of $8,182.[21] Of this amount, 7.8% was provided by the federal government, 51.4% was provided by the state government, and 40.8% was provided by the local governments,[22] with property taxes making up 33.3% of the total funding.[23] Out of these funds, Kansas paid its elementary and secondary school teachers an estimated average annual salary of $39,190 during the 2004–2005 school year,[24] and it provided a student/teacher ratio of 14.4, which was better than the national average of 15.9.[25]

---

11. *Id.* at 96.

12. *Id.* at 495.

13. *Id.* at 497.

14. *Id.* at 496.

15. *Id.* at 498.

16. *Id.* at 499.

17. *Id.* at 532.

18. *See* Fact Sheet, American FactFinder, http://factfinder.census.gov/home/saff/main.html?_lang=en (select "Kansas" under "Get a Fact Sheet for your community") (last visited Feb. 16, 2007). Note that these numbers are based on the 2000 census because more recent numbers where not available.

19. State Rankings 2006, *supra* note 1, at 500.

20. *Id.* at 502.

21. Governments Division, U.S. Census Bureau, Public Education Finances 2004, at 8 tbl. 8 (2006).

22. *See id.* at 5 tbl.5.

23. *See id.* at 4 tbl.4.

24. Thomas D. Snyder et al., National Center for Education Statistics, Digest of Education Statistics 2005, at 116 tbl.77 (2006).

25. *Id.* at 98 tbl.65.

In academic performance, Kansas's fourth grade students scored lower than the national average in reading[26] and higher than the national average in mathematics[27] and writing,[28] while Kansas's eighth graders scored higher than the national average in mathematics,[29] reading,[30] and writing.[31]

Equity Issues

In 2004, revenues spent per student in Kansas's highest poverty districts were determined to be $549 less than the revenues spent in its lowest poverty districts.[32] When adjustments were made for the additional costs of educating students growing up in poverty, however, the funding gap grew to $885.[33] Similarly, Kansas spent $1,514 less per student in its highest minority districts, and this amount grew to $1,630 when adjustments for low-income students were made.[34]

Fourth graders eligible for free or reduced-price school lunches had test scores that were 7.5% lower in mathematics,[35] 9.6% lower in reading,[36] and 13.3% lower in writing[37] than those of students who were not eligible. The results were generally better for eighth graders eligible for free or reduced-price lunches; their test scores were 7.8% lower in mathematics,[38] 7.6% lower in reading,[39] and 12.5% lower in writing[40] than those of students who were not eligible.

In the 2006 decision *Montoy v. State*,[41] the Kansas Supreme Court held that the state legislature had complied with orders to "provide annual increased funding by the

---

26. National Center for Education Statistics, U.S. Department of Education, The Nation's Report Card: Reading 2005, at 14 fig.11 (2005), *available at* http://nces.ed.gov/nationsreportcard/pdf/main2005/2006451.pdf [hereinafter Reading 2005].

27. National Center for Education Statistics, U.S. Department of Education, The Nation's Report Card: Mathematics 2005, at 14 fig.11 (2005), *available at* http://nces.ed.gov/nationsreportcard/pdf/main2005/ 2006453.pdf [hereinafter Mathematics 2005].

28. Hilary R. Persky et al., National Center for Education Statistics, U.S. Department of Education, The Nation's Report Card: Writing 2002, at 23 tbl.2.2 (2003), *available at* http://nces.ed.gov/nationsreportcard/pdf/main2002/2003529.pdf [hereinafter Writing 2002].

29. Mathematics 2005, *supra* note 27, at 16 fig.12.

30. Reading 2005, *supra* note 26, at 16 fig.12.

31. Writing 2002, *supra* note 28, at 24 tbl.2.3.

32. The Education Trust, Funding Gaps 2006, at 7 tbl.3 (2006), *available at* http://www2.edtrust.org/NR/rdonlyres/CDEF9403-5A75-437E-93FF-EBF1174181FB/0/FundingGap2006.pdf.

33. *Id.*

34. *Id.* at 7 tbl.4.

35. Mathematics 2005, *supra* note 27, at 20 tbl.5.

36. Reading 2005, *supra* note 26, at 20 tbl.5.

37. Writing 2002, *supra* note 28, at 75 tbl.3.24.

38. Mathematics 2005, *supra* note 27, at 21 tbl.6.

39. Reading 2005, *supra* note 26, at 21 tbl.6.

40. Writing 2002, *supra* note 28, at 76 tbl.3.25.

41. 138 P.3d 755 (Kan. 2006).

2008–09 school year of $755.6 million."[42] This constituted an increase of 26% over the funding provided by the state for the 2004–2005 school year.[43]

Availability of Publicly Funded Prekindergarten Programs

The At-Risk Four-Year-Old Children Preschool program serves four-year-old children who meet eligibility requirements such as "developmental delay, having a single or teen parent, English Language Learner or migrant status, free lunch eligibility, or referral from another agency." [44] Total enrollment in this state-funded program is 5,375,[45] which represents just 7.3% of Kansas's 74,046 three- and four-year-old children.[46] The federally funded Head Start program enrolls an additional 6,455 children,[47] which represents 8.7% of Kansas's three- and four-year-old children.[48]

Where Does Kansas Get Its Revenue?

At the end of fiscal year 2004, Kansas had total revenues of approximately $18.5 billion.[49] Of this amount, 50% was derived from state and local tax revenues and 17% was received from the federal government.[50] The remaining 33% came from other sources, including the Kansas Lottery, insurance trust revenue, and revenue from government-owned utilities and other commercial or auxiliary enterprises.[51]

Tax Revenue

Kansas collected approximately $9.2 billion in state and local tax revenue during fiscal year 2004.[52] As a result, Kansas residents paid $3,380 per capita in state and local government taxes, an amount which ranked 22nd nationally.[53] The different types of tax sources were apportioned as follows:

---

42. *Id.*

43. Access: Education Finance Litigation, School Funding Policy and Advocacy, July 31, 2006, http://www.schoolfunding.info/news/litigation/7-31-06kansasdecision.php3.

44. W. Steven Barnett et al., National Institute for Early Education Research, The State of Preschool 2006, at 70 (2007), *available at* http://nieer.org/yearbook/pdf/yearbook.pdf. Another program, Parents as Teachers (PAT), is provided by the state for children aged three and younger. *Id.*

45. *Id.* at 71.

46. *See id.* at 232.

47. *Id.* at 71.

48. *See id.* at 232.

49. U.S. Census Bureau, State and Local Government Finances - 2003–04, http://www.census.gov/govs/www/estimate04.html (last visited Oct. 10, 2006) [hereinafter Government Finances].

50. *Id.*

51. *Id.*

52. *Id.*

53. *Id.*

Individual income taxes	20.7%
Property taxes	35.1%
General and selective sales taxes	37.1%
Corporate income and other taxes	7.1%
	100.0%[54]

Federal Funding

During fiscal year 2004, 17% of Kansas's total revenues came from the federal government.[55] For every dollar of federal taxes paid, Kansas received $1.12 in federal funding, an amount which ranked 23rd nationally[56] and was slightly below the national average of $1.17.[57]

Lottery Revenue

The Kansas Lottery Act, which established the Kansas Lottery,[58] was authorized by a constitutional amendment passed in November 1986.[59] The Lottery revenue is allocated by first transferring $80,000 to the Problem Gambling Fund, and then transferring 85% of the balance to the Economic Development Initiatives Fund (EDIF), 10% to the Correctional Institutions Building Fund, and 5% to the Juvenile Detention Facilities Fund; any receipts in excess of $50 million are transferred to the State General Fund.[60] During fiscal year 2005, the Kansas Lottery brought in almost $62.3 million and paid $65.4 million to the State of Kansas.[61]

Legal Structures of Major Tax Sources

Income

Kansas employs a broad-based income tax that uses adjusted gross income for federal income tax purposes as a starting point for determining the state's taxable in-

---

54. *Id.*

55. *Id.*

56. The Tax Foundation, Federal Spending Received Per Dollar of Taxes Paid by State, 2004, http://www.taxfoundation.org/taxdata/show/266.html (last visited Oct. 10, 2006).

57. *Id.*

58. Kansas Lottery, About the Kansas Lottery, http://www.kslottery.com/LotteryInfo/AboutUs.htm (last visited October 18, 2006).

59. *Id.*

60. Kansas Lottery, Where the Money Goes, http://www.kslottery.com/WhereTheMoneyGoes/WhereTheMoneyGoes.htm (last visited Oct. 5, 2006). The primary responsibilities of the agencies receiving money from the EDIF are business and community development, stimulation of new technologies and related private-public technologies, and strategic planning. *Id.*

61. Kansas Lottery, Kansas Lottery Annual Report 2005 6, *available at* http://www.kslottery.com/LotteryInfo/AnnualReport05.pdf (last visited Oct. 10, 2006).

come.[62] However, a fairly large number of adjustments may be available to various individuals in calculating this amount.[63] During fiscal year 2004, Kansas collected individual income tax of $701 per capita, an amount which ranked 20th nationally.[64] Kansas localities do not have the power to impose income taxes.[65]

In Kansas, a typical family of four (i.e., married taxpayers who file jointly and have two dependent children) are not required to pay any income tax until their combined income exceeds $26,100, an amount which is above the national poverty line of $20,615.[66] Kansas's income tax structure contains three tax brackets that impose a minimum marginal rate of 3.5% and a maximum marginal rate of 6.45%.[67] When statutory exemptions and the standard deduction are taken into account, the maximum marginal rate applies to every dollar of income exceeding $65,000.[68]

Property

Overview

Kansas collects taxes on both real and tangible personal property for use at the state and local levels.[69] During fiscal year 2004, Kansas collected almost $3.2 billion at the local level and just under $57.6 million at the state level.[70] As a result, Kansas residents paid $1,187 per capita in state and local property taxes, an amount which ranked 14th nationally.[71]

Defining the Real Property Tax Base

Property in Kansas is valued by using its fair market value in money as of January 1 of each year.[72] "Fair market value" is defined as the amount that an informed seller

---

62. KAN. STAT. ANN. § 79-32,117; Kansas Department of Revenue, Form K-40 Line-By-Line Instructions, *available at* http://www.ksrevenue.org/pdf/forms/k-40inst05.pdf.

63. KAN. STAT. ANN. § 79-32,117.

64. STATE RANKINGS 2006, *supra* note 1, at 321.

65. KAN. STAT. ANN. § 12-140; KAN. STAT. ANN. § 19-101a.

66. JASON A. LEVITIS & NICHOLAS JOHNSON, CENTER ON BUDGET AND POLICY PRIORITIES, THE IMPACT OF STATE INCOME TAXES ON LOW-INCOME FAMILIES IN 2006, at 11 (2007). In 2006, Kansas taxpayers who were married and filing jointly could claim a standard deduction of $6,000, personal exemptions of $2,250 each for taxpayer and spouse, and dependent exemptions of $2,250. KAN. STAT. ANN. § 79-32,119; KAN. STAT. ANN. § 79-32,121. Note, however, that the threshold calculation of $26,100 is greater than the sum of these deductions and exemptions because it includes additional tax benefits available to low-income families, such as the earned-income tax credit. *See* LEVITIS & JOHNSON, *supra*. Kansas's standard deduction and personal exemptions remain unchanged for 2007. KAN. STAT. ANN. § 79-32,119; KAN. STAT. ANN. § 79-32,121.

67. KAN. STAT. ANN. § 79-32,110. Kansas's middle tax bracket is 6.25%. *Id.*

68. The standard deduction and exemptions of $6,000 and $9,000, respectively, plus the threshold of taxable income for the highest tax bracket of $50,000, equals $65,000. *See supra* notes 66–67.

69. KAN. STAT. ANN. § 79-101.

70. Government Finances, *supra* note 49.

71. *See id.*

72. *See* KAN. STAT. ANN. § 79-503a.

would accept and the amount an informed buyer would pay for the property;[73] it is determined by various methods, including the replacement-cost method, the capitalization-of-income method, and the sales method.[74] Property used for agricultural purposes is valued according to its current use.[75] Real property is divided into seven subclasses, and each subclass's tax base is assessed as a different percentage of its overall value. The seven subclasses are (a) land for residential use, which is assessed at 11.5%; (b) land for agricultural use, which is assessed at 30%; (c) vacant lots, which are assessed at 12%; (d) real property owned and operated by a nonprofit organization, which is assessed at 12%; (e) public-utility real property, which is assessed at 33%; (f) land for commercial and industrial use, which is assessed at 25%; and (g) other real property not specifically classified, which is assessed at 30%.[76]

Real Property Tax Rates

Kansas has a permanent state tax levy of 1 mill ($1 per $1,000 of value) which is used for the benefit of state institutions of higher education.[77] Kansas also has a state tax levy of .5 mill ($0.50 per $1,000 of value) which is used for the benefit of institutions for care of the disabled.[78] School districts in Kansas are required to levy a property tax of 20 mills ($20 per $1,000 of value) for the school years 2005–2006 and 2006–2007 in order to support public schools, [79] but $20,000 of residential property is exempt from this levy.[80] During fiscal year 2005, average county tax rates per $1,000 of value ranged from $68.999 in Coffey County to $165.567 in Smith County.[81]

Personal and Intangible Property

Tangible personal property is subject to taxation in Kansas.[82] It is divided into six subclasses, and each subclass's tax base is assessed as a different percentage of its overall value. The six subclasses are (a) mobile homes used as residences, which are assessed at 11.5%; (b) mineral leasehold interests, which are assessed at 30% (except for oil and natural gas leasehold interests whose average daily production is 100 mcf or less, which are assessed at 25%); (c) public-utility tangible personal property, which is assessed at 33%; (d) motor vehicles and off-road motor vehicles, which are assessed at 30%; (e) commercial and industrial machinery and equipment, which are assessed at 25%; and

---

73. *Id.* §79-503a; *see also* §79-101. Factors to be considered in determining the fair market value in money of a piece of property are listed in §79-503a.

74. CCH-EXP, PROP-TAX-GUIDE KS ¶20-615, Valuation Methods in General.

75. Kan. Stat. Ann. §79-1476.

76. *Id.* §79-1439.

77. *Id.* §76-6b01.

78. *Id.* §76-6b04.

79. *Id.* §72-6431.

80. *Id.* §79-201x.

81. Kansas Department of Revenue, Average County Levies on Tangible Property Valuation, http://www.ksrevenue.org/pdf/03-05tableivavglevies.pdf.

82. Kan. Stat. Ann. §79-501.

(f) other tangible personal property not specifically classified, which is assessed at 30%.[83]

Exemptions

Household goods, the inventories of merchants and manufacturers, farm machinery and equipment, and machinery used for business that costs less than $400 are exempt from property tax.[84] Kansas does not have a homestead exemption, but it allows a homestead property tax refund for the disabled, the elderly, and families and individuals with children.[85] The refunds, which are only available to low-income households, start with a 4% property tax deduction when household income exceeds $6,000 and gradually increase to a 95% deduction when household income reaches a maximum of $27,600.[86]

General and Selective Sales

General Sales

Kansas imposes a retail sales tax of 5.3%,[87] which makes up 26.9% of the state's total tax revenue.[88] This tax is imposed on the: "[(1)] Retail sale, rental or lease of tangible personal property; [(2)] Labor services to install, apply, repair, service, alter, or maintain tangible personal property; and [(3)]Admissions to entertainment, amusement, or recreation places in Kansas."[89] Cities and counties in Kansas may impose additional retail sales taxes at various rates specified by statute.[90] Most cities and counties may add up to an additional 1% sales tax, but for some specific counties, the amount of additional tax that may be imposed has been increased by statute.[91] Cities and counties in Kansas are also authorized to impose a transient guest tax of up to 2% on the gross receipts of hotels, motels, or tourist courts from transient guests for sleeping accommodations.[92] Prescription drugs, as well as food purchased with food stamps, are exempt from Kansas retail sales tax.[93]

---

83. *Id.* § 79-1439.

84. *Id.* § 79-201c; § 79-201m; § 79-201p; § 79-201j; § 79-201w. For a more comprehensive listing, see KAN. STAT. ANN. ch. 79, art. 2.

85. *Id.* § 79-4502.

86. 2006 Kan. Sess. Laws 205 (H.B. 2583) (amending KAN. STAT. ANN. § 79-4508).

87. KAN. STAT. ANN. § 79-3603.

88. Government Finances, *supra* note 49.

89. Kansas Department of Revenue, Business Tax Types – Sales (Retailers), http://www.ksrevenue.org/bustaxtypessales.htm (last visited Oct. 2, 2006); *see also* KAN. STAT. ANN. § 79-3603.

90. *See* 2006 Kan. Sess. Laws 9 (H.B. 2698) (amending KAN. STAT. ANN. § 12-187 and § 12-189); *see also* KAN. STAT. ANN. § 12-189, which was amended minimally by the previously cited session law in parts which have no bearing on the information provided.

91. *See* 2006 Kan. Sess. Laws 9 (H.B. 2698) (amending KAN. STAT. ANN. § 12-187 and § 12-189); *see also* KAN. STAT. ANN. § 12-189, which was amended minimally by the previously cited session law in parts which have no bearing on the information provided.

92. KAN. STAT. ANN. § 12-1697.

93. *Id.* § 79-3606(dd) (food purchased with food stamps exempt); KAN. STAT. ANN. § 79-3606(p) (prescription drugs exempt); *see also* Kansas Department of Revenue, Kansas Exemp-

Selective Sales

Selective sales taxes make up 10.2% of Kansas's total tax revenue.[94] Of that amount, 4.7%[95] comes from a motor fuel sales tax that is imposed at a rate of $0.24 per gallon of gasoline.[96] Kansas residents paid $157 per capita in state motor fuel sales taxes in 2004, an amount which ranked 10th nationally.[97]

The tobacco product sales tax makes up 1.3% of Kansas's total tax revenue[98] and is imposed at a rate of $0.79 per pack of cigarettes.[99] Kansas residents paid an average of $45.57 per capita in state tobacco sales taxes in 2004, an amount which ranked 26th nationally.[100]

Sales taxes on alcoholic beverages make up 0.9% of Kansas's total tax revenue.[101] Kansas residents paid $32.06 per capita in state alcoholic beverage sales taxes in 2004, an amount which ranked 5th nationally and was well above the national average of $15.74.[102]

The remainder of Kansas's selective sales taxes makes up 3.3% of its total tax revenue.[103] Of this amount, 1.4% represents taxes on utilities and the other 1.9% represents taxes on other specific commodities, businesses, or services not reported separately above (e.g., on contractors, lodging, lubricating oil, fuels other than motor fuel, motor vehicles, meals, soft drinks, margarine, etc.).[104]

Corporate Income and Other

Corporate Income

The corporate income tax makes up 1.8% of Kansas's total revenue.[105] Kansas has a broad-based corporate income tax that is "imposed upon the Kansas taxable income of every corporation doing business within [Kansas] or deriving income from sources within [Kansas]."[106] The corporate income tax base is the amount of federal taxable in-

---

tion Certificates 7, *available at* http://www.ksrevenue.org/pdf/forms/pub1520.pdf (last visited Oct. 2, 2006). For a comprehensive list of all items exempt from Kansas's retail sales tax, see Kan. Stat. Ann. § 79-3606.

94. Government Finances, *supra* note 49.

95. *Id.*

96. State Rankings 2006, *supra* note 1, at 328.

97. *Id.* at 327.

98. Government Finances, *supra* note 49.

99. State Rankings 2006, *supra* note 1, at 333.

100. *Id.* at 332.

101. Government Finances, *supra* note 49.

102. State Rankings 2006, *supra* note 1, at 335.

103. Government Finances, *supra* note 49.

104. *See* Governments Division, U.S. Census Bureau, Government Finance and Employment Classification Manual, at ch.7 (2000), *available at* http://ftp2.census.gov/govs/class/classfull.pdf [hereinafter Classification Manual].

105. *Id.*

106. Kan. Stat. Ann. § 79-32,110(c).

come apportioned to business activity in Kansas.[107] The corporate income tax rate is 4.0% of total taxable income, plus a 3.35% surtax on taxable income over $50,000.[108] S corporations, partnerships, and limited liability companies are not covered by the corporate income tax; rather, they must withhold tax at a rate equal to the maximum individual rate.[109]

Other

During fiscal year 2004, the collection of all other taxes not previously mentioned accounted for 5.3% of Kansas's total tax revenue.[110] Of this amount, $48.1 million was generated by the estate and gift tax.[111] This tax is calculated as the amount equal to the maximum federal credit allowable for state death taxes.[112] The "other taxes" category is further made up of various license taxes, documentary or stock transfer taxes, severance taxes, and all other taxes not listed separately or provided for in other categories.[113]

Burden Analysis

The overall state and local tax burden on Kansas's taxpayers is moderately regressive. Taxpayers in the lowest quintile—those with incomes of less than $14,000—bear a tax burden equal to 11.5% of their income, while taxpayers in the top 1%—those with incomes that exceed $292,000—bear a tax burden of just 8.0% of their income.[114] It is also worth noting that, although Kansas obviously has no control over federal tax policy, federal itemized deductions for state and local personal income and property taxes nonetheless further reduce the burden on taxpayers in the top 1% to 5.7%.[115] Fur-

---

107. Kansas Department of Revenue, Kansas Corporate Income Tax Booklet Forms and Instructions 2005 9-11, *available at* http://www.ksrevenue.org/pdf/forms/corpbook2005.pdf (last visited Oct. 8, 2006).

108. *Id.*

109. KAN. STAT. ANN. § 79-32,100c.

110. Government Finances, *supra* note 49. This calculation includes "Other Taxes" and "Motor Vehicle License" taxes.

111. *Id.*

112. KAN. STAT. ANN. § 79-15,102.

113. *See* CLASSIFICATION MANUAL, *supra* note 104, at ch.7.

114. *See* ROBERT S. MCINTYRE ET AL., WHO PAYS? A DISTRIBUTIONAL ANALYSIS OF THE TAX SYSTEMS IN ALL 50 STATES 48 (2d ed. 2003), *available at* http://www.itepnet.org/wp2000/text.pdf. Taxpayers in the second quintile bear a 10.8% total tax burden on incomes between $14,000 and $27,000; those in the third quintile bear a 10.4% tax burden on incomes between $27,000 and $44,000; those in the fourth quintile bear a 10.2% tax burden on incomes between $44,000 and $69,000; those in the 80th–95th percentiles bear a 9.9% tax burden on incomes between $69,000 and $126,000; finally, those in the 96th–99th percentiles bear a 9.0% tax burden on incomes between $126,000 and $292,000. *Id.*

115. *Id.* Taxpayers in the lowest quintile did not receive any benefit from these federal offsets, while those in the second and third quintiles were able to reduce their individual tax bur-

thermore, between 1989 and 2002, the tax burden on the bottom quintile rose by approximately 2.4%, while the burden on the top 1% rose by only 0.5%.[116]

In terms of the income tax, the burden across income groups in Kansas is moderately progressive, with taxpayers in the lowest quintile bearing a tax burden of 0.3% and those in the top 1% bearing a tax burden of 5.4%.[117] In sharp contrast, however, the sales and excise taxes imposed by Kansas are extremely regressive, with taxpayers in the lowest quintile bearing a tax burden of 8.8% and those in the top 1% bearing a tax burden of just 1.2%.[118] Property taxes in Kansas are also regressive, with taxpayers in the lowest quintile bearing a tax burden of 3.0% and those in the top quintile bearing an average tax burden of 2%.[119]

---

dens by 0.1%, those in the fourth quintile by 0.4%, those in the 80th–95th percentiles by 1.2%, and those in the 96th–99th percentiles by 1.8%. *Id.*

116. *Id.* at 49.

117. *See id.* at 48. Taxpayers in the second quintile bear a 1.5% income tax burden; those in the third quintile bear a 2.5% burden; those in the fourth quintile bear a 3.1% burden; those in the 80th–95th percentiles bear a 3.8% burden; finally, those in the 96th–99th percentiles bear a 4.5% burden. *Id.* Note, however, that these percentages include both individual and corporate income tax burdens; that within the 96th–99th percentiles, corporate income taxes make up 0.1% of this burden; and that in the top 1%, corporate income taxes represent 0.2% of this burden. *Id.*

118. *See id.* Taxpayers in the second quintile bear a 7.2% sales-and-excise tax burden; those in the third quintile bear a 5.9% burden; those in the fourth quintile bear a 4.9% burden; those in the 80th–95th percentiles bear a 3.7% burden; finally, those in the 96th–99th percentiles bear a 2.4% burden. *Id.*

119. *See id.* Taxpayers in the second quintile bear a 2.1% property tax burden; those in the third quintile bear a 2.0% burden; those in the fourth quintile bear a 2.2% burden; those in the 80th–90th percentiles bear a 2.4% burden; those in the 96th–99th percentiles bear a 2.2% burden; finally those in the top 1% bear a 1.4% burden. *Id.*

Kentucky

General Information

Basic Profile – Geography, Population, and Industry

Kentucky, known as "The Bluegrass State," was admitted to the Union in 1792.[1] It is located in the south central region, along the west side of the Appalachian Mountains, and straddles both the central and eastern time zones. The state is bordered by Illinois, Indiana, Ohio, Tennessee, West Virginia, Virginia, and Missouri. Its capital is Frankfort.

Kentucky ranks 37th in total land and water area (40,409 square miles).[2] In 2005, the state ranked 26th in population (approximately 4.2 million residents).[3] Its population is approximately 90.4% white and 7.5% black.[4] The state is approximately 14% Catholic; 62% Protestant (of which 53% are Baptist); and less than 0.5% Jewish; 24% claim a religion outside the Judeo-Christian tradition or no religion at all.[5] Of Kentucky's population, 43.28% live in rural areas and 56.72% live in urban areas.[6] Major industries include exports of transportation equipment, chemicals, computer electronic products, machinery, and livestock.[7]

Family Income and Poverty Indicators

In 2004, Kentucky's per capita gross product was $32,943, which ranked among the bottom ten states nationally and was below the national average of $39,725.[8] During

---

1. STATE RANKINGS 2006, vi, 1 (Kathleen O'Leary Morgan & Scott Morgan eds., Morgan Quitno Press, 2006).

2. *Id.* at 225.

3. *Id.* at 429.

4. Kentucky Quick Facts from the U.S. Census Bureau, http://quickfacts.census.gov/qfd/states/54000.html (last visited Jan. 30, 2007). The remaining population is made up of 0.9% Asian persons; 0.2 % American Indian and Alaska Native persons; and 1.0% persons two or more races. *Id.* Additionally, 2% of Kentucky's total population identify themselves as persons of Hispanic or Latino origin. *Id.* (noting that because Hispanics may be of any race, they are included within the other applicable race categories).

5. BARRY A. KOSMIN, EGON MAYER & ARIELA KEYSAR, AMERICAN RELIGIOUS IDENTIFICATION SURVEY 2001, at 39, *available at* http://www.gc.cuny.edu/faculty/research_studies/aris.pdf.

6. United States Department of Agriculture, A Economic Research Service, Kentucky Fact Sheet, http://www.ers.usda.gov/StateFacts/KY.htm (last visited Sept. 17, 2006).

7. Think Kentucky: Kentucky Facts, http://www.thinkkentucky.com (last visited Sept. 20, 2006).

8. STATE RANKINGS 2006, *supra* note 1, at 89.

this same period, the median household income in Kentucky was $37,396,[9] In addition, 15.4% of the state's population was living in poverty, which ranked among the top ten states nationally and was far above the national average of 12.4%.[10] More specifically, poverty affected 24.6% of Kentucky's children,[11] 12.6% of its senior citizens,[12] and 13.9% of its families.[13] Of its female-headed households with children, 48.7% lived in poverty.[14] Of those living in poverty approximately 12.5% were black, which represented 26.2% of Kentucky's black population and 1.9% of its total population.[15] In an attempt to combat this poverty, Kentucky spent approximately $4.8 billion on public welfare programs in 2002,[16] which made up 22.3% of its total government expenditures.[17]

Kentucky's Public Elementary-Secondary School System

Overall Spending and Performance

For the 2003–2004 school year, Kentucky spent $6,888 per pupil in its public elementary-secondary school system, which was substantially below the national average of $8,182.[18] Of this amount, 11.8% was provided by the federal government, 57.8% was provided by the state government, and 30.4% was provided by the local governments,[19] with property taxes making up 20.8% of the total funding.[20] Out of these funds, Kentucky paid its elementary and secondary school teachers an estimated average annual salary of $41,002 during the 2004–2005 school year,[21] but in 2003, it provided a student/teacher ratio of 16.1, which was slightly worse than the national average of 15.9.[22]

---

9. *Id.* at 96.

10. *Id.* at 495.

11. *Id.* at 497.

12. *Id.* at 496.

13. *Id.* at 498.

14. *Id.* at 499.

15. *See* Fact Sheet, American FactFinder, http://factfinder.census.gov/home/saff/main.html?_lang=en (select "Kentucky" under "Get a Fact Sheet for your community") (last visited Feb. 16, 2007). Note that these numbers are based on the 2000 census because more recent numbers were not available.

16. *Id.* at 500.

17. *Id.* at 502.

18. Governments Division, U.S. Census Bureau, Public Education Finances 2004, at 8 tbl.8 (2006), *available at* http://www2.census.gov/govs/school/04f33pub.pdf.

19. *See id.* at 5 tbl.5.

20. *See id.* at 4 tbl.4.

21. Thomas D. Snyder et al., National Center for Education Statistics, Digest of Education Statistics 2005, at 116 tbl.77 (2006) *available at* http://nces.ed.gov/pubsearch/pubsinfo.asp?pubid=2006030.

22. *Id.* at 98 tbl.65.

In academic performance, Kentucky's fourth grade students scored lower than the national average in mathematics[23] but higher than the national average in reading,[24] science,[25] and writing.[26] Kentucky's eighth graders, on the other hand, scored lower than the national average in mathematics[27] and writing[28] but higher than the national average in reading[29] and science.[30]

Equity Issues

In 2004, the funding per student in Kentucky's highest poverty districts actually exceeded that in its lowest poverty districts by $852,[31] although when adjustments were made for the additional costs of educating students growing up in poverty, that excess narrowed to $448.[32] Similarly, Kentucky spent $150 more per student in its highest minority districts, and this amount grew to $274 when adjustments for low-income students were made.[33]

Fourth graders eligible for free or reduced-price school lunches had test scores that were 7% lower in mathematics,[34] 7% lower in reading,[35] and 13% lower in writing[36] than those of students who were not eligible. The results were generally the same for eighth graders eligible for free or reduced price lunches; their test scores were 7% lower in mathematics,[37] 6% lower in reading,[38] and 13% lower in writing[39] than those of students who were not eligible.

---

23. NATIONAL CENTER FOR EDUCATION STATISTICS, U.S. DEPARTMENT OF EDUCATION, THE NATION'S REPORT CARD: MATHEMATICS 2005, at 14 fig.11 (2005), *available at* http://nces.ed.gov/ nationsreportcard/pdf/main2005/ 2006453.pdf [hereinafter MATHEMATICS 2005].

24. NATIONAL CENTER FOR EDUCATION STATISTICS, U.S. DEPARTMENT OF EDUCATION, THE NATION'S REPORT CARD: READING 2005, at 14 fig.11 (2005), *available at* http://nces.ed.gov/nationsreportcard/pdf/main2005/2006451.pdf [hereinafter READING 2005].

25. NATIONAL CENTER FOR EDUCATION STATISTICS, U.S. DEPARTMENT OF EDUCATION, THE NATION'S REPORT CARD: SCIENCE 2005, at 16 fig.12 (2006), *available at* http://nces.ed.gov/nationsreportcard//pdf/main2005/2006466.pdf [hereinafter SCIENCE 2005].

26. HILARY R. PERSKY ET AL., NATIONAL CENTER FOR EDUCATION STATISTICS, U.S. DEPARTMENT OF EDUCATION, THE NATION'S REPORT CARD: WRITING 2002, at 23 tbl.2.2 (2003), *available at* http://nces.ed.gov/nationsreportcard/pdf/main2002/2003529.pdf [hereinafter WRITING 2002].

27. MATHEMATICS 2005, *supra* note 23, at 16 fig.12.

28. WRITING 2002, *supra* note 26, at 24 tbl.2.3.

29. READING 2005, *supra* note 24, at 16 fig.12.

30. SCIENCE 2005, *supra* note 25, at 28 fig.22.

31. THE EDUCATION TRUST, FUNDING GAPS 2006, at 7 tbl.3 (2006), *available at* http://www2 .edtrust.org/NR/rdonlyres/CDEF9403-5A75-437E-93FF-EBF1174181FB/0/FundingGap2006.pdf.

32. *Id.*

33. *Id.* at 7 tbl.4.

34. MATHEMATICS 2005, *supra* note 23, at 20 tbl.5.

35. READING 2005, *supra* note 24, at 20 tbl.5.

36. WRITING 2002, *supra* note 26, at 75 tbl.3.24.

37. MATHEMATICS 2005, *supra* note 23, at 21 tbl.6.

38. READING 2005, *supra* note 24, at 21 tbl.6.

39. WRITING 2002, *supra* note 26, at 76 tbl.3.25.

After the Kentucky Supreme Court ruled that Kentucky's entire system of school-ing—including financing, governance, and curriculum—was unconstitutional in the 1989 decision *Rose v. Council for Better Education*,[40] the Kentucky General Assembly re-sponded with the Kentucky Education Reform Act of 1990 (KERA).[41] While KERA made great strides in reforming education, Support Education and Excellence Kentucky (SEEK) has further reformed Kentucky's education system.[42] SEEK adjusts equalizing grants and property assessments so that poorer districts receive a larger share of state aid, and it has changed the aid formula so that state funding is calculated on a per-pupil basis.[43] The SEEK formula requires a minimum local tax effort for local school districts of 30 cents per $100 of assessed property valuation.[44] School districts may raise the rev-enues through any combination of the property tax, motor vehicle tax, and three op-tional taxes, and districts may exceed the required minimum under a two-tier system that limits local support.[45] After the enactment of KERA and the subsequent establish-ment of SEEK, further litigation ensued in *Young v. Williams*.[46] This litigation, based on the *Rose* case, argued that the state should determine a systematic method for school funding.[47] On February 13, 2007, *Young v. Williams* was dismissed on the basis of the separation-of-powers clause of the Kentucky constitution and because there was no "ob-jective evidence of shortcomings in Kentucky's education system."[48]

Availability of Publicly Funded Prekindergarten Programs

The Kentucky Preschool Program currently serves all three- and four-year-olds with disabilities and all four-year-olds from low-income families.[49] Total enrollment in this state-funded program is 21,519,[50] which represents 20% of Kentucky's 106,275 three-and four-year-old children.[51] The federally funded Head Start program enrolls an ad-ditional 14,665 children,[52] which represents 14% of Kentucky's three- and four-year-old children.[53]

---

40. Rose v. Council for Better Education, 790 S.W.2d 186 (Ky 1989).

41. Sheila E. Murray, Kentucky, at 13, *available at* http://nces.ed.gov/edfin/pdf/StFi-nance/Kentucky.pdf.

42. Kentucky Department of Education, http://www.kde.state.ky.us/KDE/Administrative +Resources/Finance+and+ Funding/School+Finance/SEEK+and+Tax+Rates (last visited Feb. 21, 2007).

43. *Id.*

44. *Id.*

45. *Id.*

46. Young v. Williams, Franklin Circuit Court, Civil Action No. 03- CI-00055 and 03-CI-01152.

47. *Id.*

48. *Id.*

49. W. Steven Barnett et al., National Institute for Early Education Research, The State of Preschool 2006, at 72 (2006), *available at* http://nieer.org/yearbook/pdf/yearbook.pdf.

50. *Id* at 73.

51. *See id.* at 232.

52. *Id.* at 73.

53. *Id.* at 27.

Where Does Kentucky Gets Its Revenue?

At the end of fiscal year 2004, Kentucky had total revenues of approximately $26.8 billion.[54] Of this amount, 43% was derived from state and local tax revenues and 23% was received from the federal government.[55] The remaining 34% came from other sources, including the Kentucky Lottery, insurance trust revenue, and revenue from government-owned utilities and other commercial or auxiliary enterprises.[56]

Tax Revenue

Kentucky collected approximately $11.5 billion in state and local tax revenue during fiscal year 2004.[57] As a result, Kentucky residents paid $2,767 per capita in state and local taxes, an amount which ranked 39th nationally.[58] The different types of tax sources were approximately apportioned as follows:

Individual income taxes	31.7%
Property taxes	18.6%
General and selective sales taxes	37.6%
Corporate income and other taxes	12.1%
	100.0%[59]

Federal Funding

During fiscal year 2004, 23% of Kentucky's total revenues came from the federal government.[60] For every dollar of federal taxes paid, Kentucky received $1.45 in federal funding, an amount which ranked 14th nationally[61] and was above the national average of $1.17.[62]

Lottery Revenue

The Kentucky Lottery was created in 1989.[63] Monies from the Lottery are divided among the following: education (in the form of scholarships, grants, and childhood

---

54. U.S. Census Bureau, State and Local Government Finances - 2003–04, http://www.census.gov/govs/www/estimate04.html (last visited Oct. 6, 2006) [hereinafter Government Finances].

55. *Id.*

56. *Id.*

57. The total tax revenues were collected as follows: $8.5 billion by the state and $3.0 billion by local governments. *Id.*

58. *Id.*

59. *Id.*

60. *Id.*

61. The Tax Foundation, Federal Spending Received Per Dollar of Taxes Paid by State, 2004 http://www.taxfoundation.org/news/show/266.html (last visited Sept. 17,2006).

62. *See id.*

63. Ky. Rev. Stat. Ann. § 154A.060.

reading and adult literacy programs); Vietnam Veterans; The Affordable Housing Trust Fund; and the General Fund.[64] The total gross proceeds from the Kentucky Lottery during fiscal year 2006 were $742.3 million, $204 million of which was transferred to the Commonwealth.[65]

Legal Structures of Major Tax Sources

Income

Kentucky employs a broad-based income tax that uses adjusted gross income for federal income tax purposes as a starting point for determining the state's taxable income.[66] Numerous adjustments, however, may be available to various individuals in calculating this amount.[67] Kentucky law gives cities the authority to levy taxes based on income.[68] During fiscal year 2004, Kentucky collected individual income tax of $681 per capita.[69]

In Kentucky, a typical family of four (i.e., married taxpayers who file jointly and have two dependent children) are not required to pay any income tax until their combined income exceeds $19,900, an amount which is below the national poverty line of $20,615.[70] Kentucky's income tax structure consists of six tax brackets that impose a minimum marginal tax rate of 2% and a maximum marginal tax rate of 6%.[71] When statutory credits and the standard deduction are taken into account, the maximum marginal rate applies to every dollar of income exceeding $76,970.[72]

---

64. Kentucky Lottery, http://www.kylottery.com/where_money_goes.html (last visited September 19, 2006).

65. Kentucky Lottery, http://www.kylottery.com/show_news_story.html?news_id=e962ad394 83c8e740ac21b184c60e8ed, (last visited September 19, 2006).

66. KY. REV. STAT. ANN. § 141.020.

67. *See, e.g.,* KY. REV. STAT. ANN. § 141.020.

68. KY. REV. STAT. ANN. §§ 91.260(1); 92.281(1).

69. STATE RANKINGS 2006, *supra* note 1, at 321.

70. JASON A. LEVITIS, CENTER ON BUDGET AND POLICY PRIORITIES, THE IMPACT OF STATE INCOME TAXES ON LOW-INCOME FAMILIES IN 2006, at 12 (2007). In 2006, Kentucky taxpayers who were married and filing jointly could claim a standard deduction of $1,970 and personal and dependent credits of $20 each. KY. REV. STAT. ANN. §§ 141.020(3); 141.081(2). Note, however, that the threshold calculation of $19,900 is greater than the sum of these deductions and credits because it includes additional tax benefits available to low-income families, such as the earned-income tax credit. *See* LEVITIS, *supra.* Note also that in 2007, Kentucky increased the standard deduction for taxpayers who are married and filing jointly to $2,050, while the personal and dependent credits have remained $20 each. Commonwealth of Kentucky: Department of Revenue, "What's new for 2007?" (2007); http://revenue.ky.gov/NR/rdonlyres/523F946F-B7E5-49E6-AE5B-3BD27BBDE2F4/0/42A740S4.pdf (last visited March 25, 2007).

71. KY. REV. STAT. ANN. § 141.020. Kentucky's middle tax brackets are as follows: 3%, 4%, 5%, and 5.8%. *Id.*

72. The standard deduction of $1,970, plus the threshold of taxable income for the highest tax bracket of $75,000, equals $76,970. *See supra* notes 70–71.

Property

Overview

Kentucky has a typical property tax system that taxes the value of property at both the state and local levels. During fiscal year 2004, Kentucky collected $2.14 billion in property taxes.[73] Of this amount, Kentucky localities collected $1.68 billion and the state collected $455.5 million.[74] As a result, Kentucky residents paid $516 per capita in property taxes, an amount which ranked 45th nationally.[75]

Defining the Real Property Tax Base

Kentucky classifies property as real property and personal property, either tangible or intangible.[76] Kentucky also has the following classes of political subdivisions that impose taxes on property: (1) the state; (2) counties; (3) cities (there are six classes of cities); and (4) local taxing districts.[77] The basis of real and personal property tax is determined by the property's true cash value estimated at the price it would bring through a voluntary sale.[78] Kentucky uses several methods in order to determine this value, including the capitalization-income approach, the market- or sales-comparison approach, and the cost approach.[79] The property valuation administrator assesses all real property, which is revalued during each year at its fair cash value and is physically examined at least once every four years.[80]

Real Property Tax Rates

The real property state tax rate per $100 valuation in 2006 was 12.8 cents,[81] as compared with 16.3 cents just ten years ago.[82] Other than for school purposes, the maximum tax rate that a county can impose is 50 cents per $100.[83] In cities, maximum tax rates per $100 vary according to population: in a city with a population of more than 15,000, its residents may be taxed up to $1.50 per $1000; in a city with a population of less than 10,000, its residents may be taxed only up to $.75 per $100.[84] A cap on property tax levied for school purposes in each school district is $1.50 annually on each $100 of property subject to local taxation.[85]

---

73. Government Finances, *supra* note 54.
74. *Id.*
75. *See id.*
76. Ky. Rev. Stat. Ann. § 132.200.
77. Ky. Const. of 1891, § 156.
78. *Id.* § 172.
79. CCH-EXP, PROP-TAX-GUIDE KY ¶ 20-615, Valuation Methods in General.
80. Ky. Rev. Stat. Ann. § 132.690.
81. CCH-EXP, KY-TAXRPTR ¶ 20-405, Rates of Tax.
82. *Id.*
83. Ky. Const. of 1891, § 157.
84. *Id.*
85. Ky. Rev. Stat. Ann. § 160.475.

Personal and Intangible Property

All personal property is subject to taxation in Kentucky, unless otherwise exempted by the constitution or by statute.[86] The intangible property tax was eliminated on January 1, 2006.[87]

Exemptions

Exemptions include, among other types of real property, real property maintained as the permanent residence of an owner who is sixty-five years of age or older or who is classified as totally disabled.[88] To qualify as totally disabled, the property owner must have received disability payments pursuant to the disability classification, maintain the disability classification for the entire tax period, and file with the appropriate local assessor by December 31 of the taxable period.[89] No other homestead exemptions are currently offered in Kentucky.

Personal property exemptions include, among other items, household goods as well as crops grown in the year in which the assessment is made.[90]

General and Selective Sales

General Sales

Kentucky imposes a general retail sales-and-use tax, which makes up 21.6% of the state's total tax revenue.[91] This tax is imposed on retail sales or rentals of tangible personal property and specified services.[92] Services subject to sales tax include the rental of hotel and motel rooms for a period of less than 30 days, admission charges, sales of nonresidential utility services (sewer services, electricity, and water and gas), and interstate and intrastate communications services.[93] Sales taxes are imposed on all retailers at the rate of 6% of gross receipts or purchase price.[94] The Kentucky constitution provides that legislation may be enacted authorizing cities and towns to impose taxation for municipal purposes, but the Kentucky General Assembly has not yet enacted any local sales-and-use tax laws.[95]

Food for human consumption and prescription drugs are exempt from sales tax.[96] The statute states that "'[f]ood and food ingredients shall not include: alco-

---

86. Ky. Rev. Stat. Ann. § 132.190.
87. Ch. 168 (H.B. 272), Laws 2005.
88. Id.
89. Id.
90. Ky. Const. of 1891, § 170.
91. State and Local Government Finances, *supra* note 54.
92. Ky. Rev. Stat. Ann. § 139.090.
93. Id. § 139.100.
94. Ky. Rev. Stat. Ann. § 139.200.
95. Ky. Const. of 1891, § 181.
96. Ky. Rev. Stat. Ann. § 139.485.

holic beverages; tobacco; candy; dietary supplements; soft drinks; and prepared food."[97]

Selective Sales

Selective sales taxes make up 16.0% of Kentucky's total revenue.[98] Of that amount, 4.2% is comes from motor fuel sales taxes.[99] Such taxes include those on gasoline, liquefied petroleum, and special fuels.[100] Kentucky residents paid an average of $115 per capita in state motor fuel sales taxes in 2004, an amount which ranked 37th nationally and was equal to the national average of $115.[101]

In 2004, Sales taxes on alcoholic beverages made up 0.7% of Kentucky's tax revenues.[102] Kentucky residents paid $19.10 per capita in state alcoholic beverage sales taxes in 2004, an amount which ranked 16th nationally.[103]

The tobacco product sales tax makes up 0.2%[104] of Kentucky's total tax revenue and is imposed on cigarettes at a rate of $0.30 per pack.[105] Other tobacco products (e.g., cigars, chewing tobacco, etc.) are taxed at the rate of 7.5% of gross receipts.[106] Snuff is taxed at rate of $0.95 per 1.5 ounces.[107]

The remainder of Kentucky's selective sales taxes makes up 11.0% of its total tax revenue. Of this amount, 1.8% represents taxes on utilities and the other 9.2% represents taxes on other specific commodities, businesses, or services not reported separately above (e.g., on contractors, lodging, lubricating oil, fuels other than motor fuel, motor vehicles, meals, soft drinks, etc.).[108]

Corporate and Income and Other

Corporate Income

Kentucky has a broad-based corporate income tax[109] that makes up 3.3% of Kentucky's total tax revenue.[110] In 2005, the Kentucky General Assembly enacted legisla-

---

97. *Id.* For further explanations of exempt transactions, see Ky. Rev. Stat. Ann. § 139.470.

98. Government Finances, *supra* note 54.

99. *Id.*

100. Kentucky Department of Revenue, http://revenue.ky.gov/business/motorfuels.htm (last visited on March 1, 2007).

101. State rankings 2006, *supra* note 1, at 327.

102. Government Finances, *supra* note 54.

103. State rankings 2006, *supra* note 1, at 335.

104. Government Finances, *supra* note 54.

105. State rankings 2006, *supra* note 1, at 333.

106. *Id.*

107. *Id.*

108. *See* Governments Division, U.S. Census Bureau, Government Finance and Employment Classification Manual, at ch.7 (2000), *available at* http://ftp2.census.gov/govs/class/classfull.pdf [hereinafter Classification Manual].

109. Kentucky Department of Revenue, http://revenue.ky.gov/business/corptax.htm (last visited on Nov. 21,2006).

110. Government Finances, *supra* note 54.

tion that defines "'Corporation' to include a C Corporation, S Corporation, Limited Partnership, Limited Liability Partnership (LLP), Limited Liability Company (LLC), Professional Limited Company (PLLC), Real Estate Investment Trust (REIT), Regulated Investment Company (RIC), Real Estate Mortgage Investment Conduit (REMIC), Financial Asset Securitization Investment Trust (FASIT), or similar entities created with limited liability for the partners, members, or shareholders."[111] The entities defined above are subject to the Kentucky Corporation Income Tax beginning on or after January 1, 2005, regardless of how they file with the Internal Revenue Service.[112]

Kentucky's corporate income tax structure contains three brackets, ranging from 4% to 6%, with the top rate of 6% applying after net income reaches $100,000.[113]

Other

During fiscal year 2004, the collection of all other taxes not previously mentioned accounted for 8.7% of Kentucky's total tax revenue.[114] Of this amount, $67 million was generated by the inheritance and gift taxes.[115] The inheritance tax is calculated by using the fair cash value of all real and personal property as of the date of the death of the grantor or donor of the property.[116] Although Kentucky previously imposed an estate tax based on the state death tax credit under federal estate tax law, it has been phased out and no longer applies. The "other taxes" category is further made up of various license taxes, documentary or stock transfer taxes, severance taxes, and all other taxes not listed separately or provided for in other categories.[117]

Burden Analysis

The overall state and local tax burden on Kentucky's taxpayers is very regressive. Taxpayers in the lowest quintile—those with incomes of less than $12,000—bear a tax burden equal to 9.8% of their income, while taxpayers in the top 1%—those with incomes that exceed $243,000—bear a tax burden of just 7.8% of their income.[118] It is also worth noting that, although Kentucky obviously has no control over federal tax

---

111. *Id.*

112. *Id.*

113. For further calculation and computation of the corporate income tax for tax years ending before and after January 1, 2007, see Kentucky 2006 Session Laws 2006 Regular Session: Chapter 252 that creates the updated Kentucky Revised Statute Section 141.040.

114. Government Finances, *supra* note 54.

115. *Id.*

116. KY. REV. STAT. ANN. § 140.010.

117. *See* CLASSIFICATION MANUAL, *supra* note 108, at ch.7.

118. *See* ROBERT S. MCINTYRE ET AL., WHO PAYS? A DISTRIBUTIONAL ANALYSIS OF THE TAX SYSTEMS IN ALL 50 STATES 50 (2d ed. 2003), *available at* http://www.itepnet.org/wp2000/text.pdf. Taxpayers in the second quintile bear a 10.0% total tax burden on incomes between $12,000 and $23,000; those in the third quintile bear a 10.2% tax burden on incomes between $23,000 and $38,000; those in the fourth quintile bear a 10.1% tax burden on incomes between $38,000 and $61,000; those in the 80th–95th percentiles bear a 9.7% tax burden on incomes between $61,000

policy, federal itemized deductions for state and local personal income and property taxes nonetheless further reduce the burden on taxpayers in the top 1% to 5.6%.[119] Furthermore, between 1989 and 2002, the tax burden on the bottom quintile rose by approximately 1.5%, while the burden on the top 1% rose by only 0.7%.[120]

In terms of the income tax, the burden across income groups in Kentucky is slightly progressive, with taxpayers in the lowest quintile bearing a tax burden of 1.4% and those in the top 1% bearing a tax burden of 5.7%.[121] In contrast, however, the sales and excise taxes imposed by Kentucky are very regressive, with taxpayers in the lowest quintile bearing a tax burden of 4.9% and those in the top 1% bearing a tax burden of just 1.0%.[122] Property taxes in Kentucky are also regressive, with taxpayers in the lowest quintile bearing a tax burden of 3.5% and those in the top quintile bearing an average burden of 1.5%.[123] However, the middle class receives somewhat of a break, with taxpayers in the three middle quintiles bearing the same average burden as those in the top quintile.[124]

---

and $113,000; finally, those in the 96th–99th percentiles bear a 8.8% tax burden on incomes between $113,000 and $243,000. *Id.*

119. *Id.* Taxpayers in the lowest and second lowest quintiles did not receive any benefit from these federal offsets, while those in the third quintile were able to reduce their individual tax burdens by 0.1%, those in the fourth quintile by 0.5%, those in the 80th–95th percentiles by 1.2%, and those in the 96th–99th percentiles by 1.8%. *Id.*

120. *Id.* at 51.

121. *See id.* at 50. Taxpayers in the second quintile bear a 3.4% income tax burden; those in the third quintile bear a 4.5% burden; those in the fourth quintile bear a 5.0% burden; those in the 80th–95th percentiles bear a 5.3% burden; finally, those in the 96th–99th percentiles bear a 5.4% burden. *Id.* Note, however, that of the total income tax burden borne by those in the 96th–99th percentiles, corporate income taxes represent 0.1% of the income tax burden and that of the total income tax burden borne by the top 1%, corporate income taxes represent 0.2% of the income tax burden. *Id.*

122. *See id.* Taxpayers in the second quintile bear a 5.3% sales-and-excise tax burden; those in the third quintile bear a 4.3% burden; those in the fourth quintile bear a 3.5% burden; those in the 80th–95th percentiles bear a 2.7% burden; finally, those in the 96th–99th percentiles bear a 1.8% burden. *Id.*

123. *See id.* Taxpayers in the second quintile bear a 1.3% property tax burden; those in the third quintile bear a 1.5% burden; those in the fourth quintile bear a 1.6% burden; those in the 80th–95th percentiles bear a 1.7% burden; those in the 96th–99th percentiles bear a 1.6% burden; finally, those in the top 1% bear a 1.2% burden. *Id.*

124. *Id.*

Louisiana

General Information

Basic Profile – Geography, Population and Industry

Admitted to the Union in 1812, Louisiana is commonly referred to as the "Pelican State."[1] It is located in the southeast region and is bordered by Arkansas on the north; Mississippi on the east; the Gulf of Mexico on the south; and Texas on the west. The state is part of the central time zone and its capital is Baton Rouge.[2]

Louisiana ranks 31st nationally in total land and water area (approximately 52,000 square miles).[3] In 2005, Louisiana ranked 24th in population (approximately 4.5 million residents).[4] Its population is approximately 64.1% white and 33.1% black.[5] The state is approximately 28% Catholic; 54% Protestant (of which 65% are Baptist); and less than 0.5% Jewish; 18% claim a religion outside the Judeo-Christian tradition or no religion at all.[6] As of 2005, approximately 75% of Louisiana's population lived in urban areas.[7] Major industries include oil and natural gas production, petroleum refining, chemical production, and commercial fishing.[8]

---

1. STATE RANKINGS 2006, vi, 1 (Kathleen O'Leary Morgan & Scott Morgan eds., Morgan Quitno Press 2006).

2. *Id.*

3. *Id.* at 225.

4. *Id.* at 429.

5. Louisiana Quick Facts from the U.S. Census Bureau, http://quickfacts.census.gov/qfd/states/22000.html (last visited Jan. 31, 2007). The remaining population is made up of 1.4% Asian persons, 0.6% American Indian and/or Alaska Native persons, and 0.8% persons reporting two or more races. *Id.* Additionally, 2.8% of Louisiana's total population identify themselves as persons of Hispanic or Latino origin. *Id.* (noting that because Hispanics may be of any race, they are included within the other applicable race categories).

6. BARRY A. KOSMIN, EGON MAYER & ARIELA KEYSAR, AMERICAN RELIGIOUS IDENTIFICATION SURVEY 2001, at 39, *available at* http://www.gc.cuny.edu/faculty/research_studies/aris.pdf (last visited Jan. 31, 2007).

7. USDA Economic Research Service, Louisiana Fact Sheet, http://www.ers.usda.gov/StateFacts/LA.htm (last visited Sept. 17, 2006). According to the latest estimates, approximately 3.4 million people live in urban areas, and approximately 1.1 million people live in rural areas. *Id.*

8. About Louisiana, History & Culture, http://www.doa.state.la.us/about_economy.htm (last visited Nov. 17, 2006).

Family Income and Poverty Indicators

In 2004, Louisiana's per capita gross product was $33,937, which was below the national average of $39,725.[9] During this same period, while the median household income in Louisiana was $35,523,[10] 17.0% of Louisiana's population was living in poverty, which was substantially above the national average of 12.4% and ranked among the top ten states nationally.[11] More specifically, poverty affected 29.5% of Louisiana's children,[12] 14.7% of its senior citizens,[13] and 14.9% of its families.[14] Of its female-headed households with children, 49.7% of them lived in poverty,[15] and 61.4% of the state's public elementary and secondary school students were eligible for free or reduced-price meals.[16] Of those living in poverty, approximately 59% were black, which represented 35% of Louisiana's black population and 11% of its total population.[17] In an attempt to combat this poverty, Louisiana spent approximately $3.4 billion on public welfare programs in 2002,[18] which made up 13.8% of its total government expenditures.[19]

Louisiana's Public Elementary-Secondary School System

Overall Spending and Performance

For the 2003–2004 school year Louisiana spent $7,209 per pupil in its public elementary-secondary school system, which was substantially below the national average of $8,182.[20] Of this amount, 13.8% was provided by the federal government, 48% was provided by the state government, and 38.2% was provided by the local governments,[21] with property taxes making up 14.6% of the total funding.[22] Out of these funds, Louisiana paid its elementary and secondary school teachers an estimated average annual salary of

---

9. STATE RANKINGS 2006, *supra* note 1, at 89.

10. *Id.* at 96.

11. *Id.* at 495.

12. *Id.* at 497.

13. *Id.* at 496.

14. *Id.* at 498.

15. *Id.* at 499.

16. *Id.* at 532.

17. *See* Fact Sheet, American FactFinder, http://factfinder.census.gov/home/saff/main.html?_lang=en (select "Louisiana" under "Get a Fact Sheet for your community") (last visited Feb. 22, 2007). Note that these numbers are based on the 2000 census because more recent numbers were not available.

18. STATE RANKINGS 2006, *supra* note 1, at 500.

19. *Id.* at 502.

20. GOVERNMENTS DIVISION, U.S. CENSUS BUREAU, PUBLIC EDUCATION FINANCES 2004, at 8 tbl.8 (2006).

21. *See id.* at 5 tbl.5.

22. *See id.* at 4 tbl.4.

$38,880 during the 2004–2005 school year,[23] and in 2003, it provided a student/teacher ratio of 16.6, which was slightly worse than the national average of 15.9.[24]

In academic performance, Louisiana's fourth and eighth grade students scored lower than the national average in mathematics,[25] reading,[26] science,[27] and writing.[28]

Equity Issues

In 2004, revenues spent per student in Louisiana's highest poverty districts were determined to be $200 less than the revenues spent in its lowest poverty districts.[29] When adjustments were made for the additional costs of educating students growing up in poverty, however, the funding gap grew to $481.[30] On the other hand, Louisiana spent $355 more per student in its highest minority districts, although this amount fell to $111 when adjustments for low-income students were made.[31]

Fourth graders eligible for free or reduced-price school lunches had test scores that were 8% lower in mathematics,[32] 12% lower in reading,[33] and 13% lower in writing[34] than those of students who were not eligible. The results were generally the same for eighth graders eligible for free or reduced-price lunches; their test scores were 8% lower in mathematics,[35] 8% lower in reading,[36] and 14% lower in writing[37] than those of students who were not eligible.

In December 2003, Louisiana's education funding formula, developed by the Louisiana State Board of Elementary and Secondary Education (BESE), was challenged

---

23. Thomas D. Snyder et al., National Center for Education Statistics, Digest of Education Statistics 2005, at 116 tbl.77 (2006).

24. *Id.* at 98 tbl.65.

25. National Center for Education Statistics, U.S. Department of Education, The Nation's Report Card: Mathematics 2005, at 14 fig.11, 16 fig.12 (2005), *available at* http:// nces.ed.gov/nationsreportcard/pdf/ main2005/2006453.pdf [hereinafter Mathematics 2005].

26. National Center for Education Statistics, U.S. Department of Education, The Nation's Report Card: Reading 2005, at 14 fig.11, 16 fig.12 (2005), *available at* http:// nces.ed.gov/nationsreportcard/pdf/main2005/2006451.pdf [hereinafter Reading 2005].

27. National Center for Education Statistics, U.S. Department of Education, The Nation's Report Card: Science 2005, at 16 fig.12, 28 fig.22 (2006), *available at* http:// nces.ed.gov/nationsreportcard//pdf/main2005/2006466.pdf [hereinafter Science 2005].

28. Hilary R. Persky et al., National Center for Education Statistics, U.S. Department of Education, The Nation's Report Card: Writing 2002, at 23 tbl.2.2, 24 tbl.2.3 (2003), *available at* http://nces.ed.gov/nationsreportcard/pdf/main2002/2003529.pdf [hereinafter Writing 2002].

29. The Education Trust, Funding Gaps 2006, at 7 tbl.3 (2006), *available at* http:// www2 .edtrust.org/NR/rdonlyres/CDEF9403-5A75-437E-93FF-EBF1174181FB/0/FundingGap 2006.pdf.

30. *Id.*

31. *Id.* at 7 tbl.4.

32. Mathematics 2005, *supra* note 25, at 20 tbl.5.

33. Reading 2005, *supra* note 26, at 20 tbl.5.

34. Writing 2002, *supra* note 28, at 75 tbl.3.24.

35. Mathematics 2005, *supra* note 25, at 21 tbl.6.

36. Reading 2005, *supra* note 26, at 21 tbl.6.

37. Writing 2002, *supra* note 28, at 76 tbl.3.25.

on the grounds that it violated the Louisiana constitution.[38] In *Jones v. Bese*, the plaintiffs alleged that the education funding formula violated article 1, section 13 of the Louisiana constitution by failing to consider the cost of capital outlay funding for school buildings in the funding formula.[39] The Louisiana Court of Appeals, in affirming the defendant's motion for summary judgment, stated that the "BESE is only required to annually develop and adopt a formula."[40] The court further stated that the Louisiana constitution "does not require any particular items be included in the formula nor does it require that the formula be based on actual costs."[41]

Availability of Publicly Funded Prekindergarten Programs

Louisiana has four preschool education programs available to four-year-old children, but it does not have programs available to three-year-old children.[42] The four programs are the 8(g) Student Enhancement Block Grant Program, LA4, Starting Points, and the Nonpublic Schools Early Childhood Development Program (NSECD).[43] The 8(g) Student Enhancement Block Grant Program is available only to at-risk four-year-olds, and the NSECD program provides tuition reimbursements for state-approved private preschools only to families with income which is twice the federal poverty level.[44] Total enrollment in this state-funded program is 13,791,[45] which represents just 11% of Louisiana's 126,711 three- and four-year-old children.[46] The federally funded Head Start program enrolls an additional 18,375 children,[47] which represents 15% of Louisiana's three- and four-year-old children.[48]

Where Does Louisiana Get Its Revenue?

At the end of fiscal year 2004, Louisiana had total revenues of approximately $34 billion.[49] Of this amount, 38% was derived from state and local tax revenues and 22%

---

38. Jones v. State Bd. of Elem. & Secondary Educ., 927 So.2d 426 (La. Ct. App. 2005).

39. *Id.* at 428.

40. *Id.* at 431 *citing* Charlet v. Legislature of the State of Louisiana, 713 So.2d 1199, 1207 (La. 1998).

41. *Id.* at 431.

42. W. Steven Barnett et al., National Institute for Early Education Research, The State of Preschool 2006, at 74 (2006), *available at* http://nieer.org/yearbook/pdf/yearbook.pdf.

43. *Id.*

44. *Id.*

45. *Id.* at 75.

46. *See id.* at 232.

47. *Id.* at 76.

48. *See id.* at 232.

49. U.S. Census Bureau, State and Local Government Finances 2003–04, http://www.census.gov/govs/www/estimate04.html (last visited Oct. 16, 2006) [hereinafter Government Finances].

was received from the federal government.[50] The remaining 40% came from other sources, including the Louisiana Lottery, insurance trust revenue, and revenue from government-owned utilities and other commercial or auxiliary enterprises.

Tax Revenue

Louisiana collected approximately $13 billion in state and local tax revenue during fiscal year 2004.[51] As a result, Louisiana residents paid $2,899 per capita in state and local taxes, an amount which ranked 33rd nationally.[52] The different types of tax sources were approximately apportioned as follows:

Individual income taxes	16.8%
Property taxes	17.3%
General and selective sales taxes	55.4%
Corporate income and other taxes	10.5%
	100.0%[53]

Federal Funding

During fiscal year 2004, 22% of Louisiana's total revenues came from the federal government.[54] For every dollar of federal taxes paid, Louisiana received $1.45 in federal funding, an amount which ranked 13th nationally[55] and was far above the national average of $1.17.[56]

Lottery Revenue

The Louisiana Lottery Corporation was created in 1990 when the voters of Louisiana approved a constitutional amendment allowing the legislature to create a state lottery.[57] The Louisiana Lottery began operations in 1991.[58] Net proceeds from the Lottery are deposited into the Lottery Proceeds Fund, from which the legislature annually appropriates funds only for the purposes of the minimum foundation program for educa-

---

50. *Id.*

51. *Id.* The total tax revenues were collected as follows: $7.7 billion by the state and $5.3 billion by local governments. *Id.*

52. *Id.*

53. *Id.*

54. *Id.*

55. The Tax Foundation, Federal Spending Received Per Dollar of Taxes Paid by State 2004, http://www.taxfoundation.org/taxdata/show/266.html (last visited Sept. 17, 2006).

56. *See id.*

57. Official Home of the Louisiana Lottery Corporation, About the Lottery, http://www.louisianalottery.com/index.cfm?md=pagebuilder&tmp=home&navID=15&cpID=43&cfmID=0&catID=0 (last visited Nov. 17, 2006).

58. *Id.*

tion.[59] During fiscal year 2006, the Lottery had total revenues of $333 million and net payments to the state treasury of $119 million.[60]

Legal Structures of Major Tax Sources

Income

Louisiana employs a broad-based income tax that uses adjusted gross income for federal income tax purposes, with very few adjustments, as a starting point for determining the state's taxable income.[61] During fiscal year 2004, Louisiana collected individual income tax of $485 per capita, an amount which ranked 38th nationally.[62]

In Louisiana, a typical family of four (i.e., married taxpayers who file jointly and have two dependent children) are not required to pay any income tax until their combined income exceeds $16,900, an amount which is well below the national poverty line of $20,615.[63] Louisiana's income tax structure contains three tax brackets that impose a minimum marginal rate of 2% and a maximum marginal rate of 6%.[64] When statutory exemptions and the standard deduction are taken into account, the maximum marginal rate applies to every dollar of income exceeding $61,000.[65] It is also noteworthy that Louisiana is one of the very few states that provide a deduction for federal taxes paid.[66]

Property

Overview

Louisiana has a typical property tax system that taxes the assessed value of all property situated in the state, unless expressly exempt, almost entirely at the local

---

59. La. Const. art. XII, § 6.

60. Official Home of the Louisiana Lottery Corporation, Lottery Financials, Comprehensive Financial Report for the Fiscal Years Ended June 30, 2006 and 2005, http://www.louisianalottery.com/assets/docs/Financial/CAFR.pdf (last visited Nov. 17, 2006).

61. La. Rev. Stat. Ann. § 47:293.

62. State Rankings 2006, supra note 1.

63. Jason A. Levitis, Center on Budget and Policy Priorities, The Impact of State Income Taxes on Low-Income Families in 2006, at 12 (2007). http://www.cbpp.org/2-22-06sfp.pdf. In 2006, Louisiana taxpayers who were married and filing jointly could claim a combined standard deduction and personal exemption of $9,000 (combined for taxpayer and spouse) and dependent exemptions of $1,000 each. La. Rev. Stat. Ann. § 47:294. Note, however, that the threshold calculation of $16,900 is greater than the sum of these deductions and exemptions because it includes additional tax benefits available to low-income families, such as the earned-income tax credit. See Levitis, supra.

64. La. Rev. Stat. Ann. § 47:32. Louisiana's middle tax bracket is 4%. Id.

65. The combined standard deduction/personal exemption and dependent exemptions of $9,000 and $2,000, respectively, plus the threshold of taxable income for the highest tax bracket of $50,000, equals $61,000. See supra note 63.

66. La. Rev. Stat. Ann. § 47:293.

level.[67] During fiscal year 2004, Louisiana collected approximately $2.2 billion dollars in property taxes at the local level and approximately $40 million at the state level.[68] As a result, Louisiana residents paid $502 per capita in state and local property taxes, an amount which ranked 46th nationally.[69]

Defining the Real Property Tax Base

Real property in Louisiana is classified as land, residential improvements,[70] electric cooperatives (excluding land), and public-service properties (excluding land).[71] Land is further classified as land, agricultural land, horticultural land, marshland, and timberland.[72] Land (excluding the above-mentioned subclassifications), residential improvements, electric cooperatives (excluding land), and public-service properties (excluding land) are all valued at their fair market value.[73] Land qualifying as agricultural land, horticultural land, marshland, or timberland is valued at the land's use value.[74] Residential improvements, land, agricultural land, horticultural land, marshland, and timberland are assessed at 10% of their determined values.[75] Electric cooperatives (excluding land) are assessed at 15% of their fair market value, and public-service properties (excluding land) are assessed at 25% of their fair market value.[76] In general, real property reassessments are required to take place every four years.[77]

Real Property Tax Rates

The tax rates imposed on real property vary and are set by each locality. Parishes in Louisiana can levy a property tax for general purposes not to exceed 4 mills on the dollar of assessed value[78] (i.e., 1 mill equals 1 dollar per thousand; therefore 4 mills equals

---

67. La. Rev. Stat. Ann. § 47:1951.

68. Government Finances, *supra* note 49.

69. *See id.*

70. Residential improvements include those made to single-family dwellings, duplexes, triplexes, fourplexes, apartment buildings, condominiums, and mobile homes used as a residence. La. Rev. Stat. Ann. § 47:2322.

71. La. Const. art. VII, § 18.

72. La. Rev. Stat. Ann. § 47:2322.

73. La. Const. art. VII, § 18. Fair market value is the highest price the property will bring in a sale on the open market between a willing and informed buyer and a willing and informed seller. La. Rev. Stat. Ann. § 47:2321.

74. La. Const. art. VII, § 18. Use value is calculated by dividing estimated net income by a capitalization rate as determined by the Louisiana Tax Commission. La. Rev. Stat. Ann. § 47:2307.

75. La. Const. art. VII, § 18.

76. *Id.*

77. La. Rev. Stat. Ann. § 47:2331.

78. La. Const. art. VII, § 26. Orleans Parish is allowed a maximum millage rate for general purposes of 7 mills, and Jackson Parish is limited to five mills. *Id.* Orleans Parish is also allowed an additional millage rate of 5 mills each for fire and police protection. *Id.* In addition, all parishes may impose additional millage increases for specific purposes as long as the additional proceeds are used solely for those purposes. *Id.*

4 dollars per thousand). Municipalities in Louisiana can levy a property tax for general purposes not to exceed 7 mills on the dollar of assessed value.[79] In addition, any taxing entity maintaining public schools can impose an additional tax not to exceed an aggregate of 70 mills.[80] In 2005, millage rates ranged from 56.9 mills in Avoyelles Parish to 182.1 mills in LaSalle Parish.[81]

Personal and Intangible Property

As stated above, all property situated in Louisiana, unless otherwise exempt, is subject to local taxation.[82] Personal property includes all tangible property that is capable of being moved or removed from real property, including inventory, furniture, fixtures, machinery, and equipment.[83] Tangible property is valued at its fair market value and is assessed at 15% of that value.[84] Intangible personal property is not subject to tax at either the state or local level.[85] Taxes are imposed at rates determined by the taxing entities, as discussed above.

Exemptions

Personal property used in the home, agricultural machinery, farm animals, motor vehicles used on public highways, and commercial vessels used for gathering seafood for human consumption are all exempt from the property tax.[86] Louisiana also allows a $7,500 exemption from state, parish, and special ad valorem taxes for taxpayers with a bona fide homestead.[87]

General and Selective Sales

General Sales

Louisiana imposes a general retail sales-and-use tax, which makes up 40.8% of Louisiana's total tax revenue.[88] This tax is imposed on the sale at retail, the use, the consumption, the distribution, and the storage for use or consumption of each item of tangible personal property[89] as well as on certain services,[90] unless otherwise exempt. These services include (1) the furnishing of sleeping rooms, cottages, or cabins by ho-

---

79. LA. CONST. art. VII, § 27. In addition, all municipalities may impose additional millage increases for specific purposes as long as the additional proceeds are used solely for those purposes. *Id.*

80. LA. REV. STAT. ANN. § 39:812.

81. CCH-EXP, PROP-TAX-GUIDE LA ¶ 20-405, Rates of Tax.

82. LA. REV. STAT. ANN. § 47:1951.

83. *Id* § 47:2322.

84. LA. CONST. art. VII, § 18.

85. LA. REV. STAT. ANN. § 47:1709.

86. LA. CONST. art. VII, § 21.

87. LA. REV. STAT. ANN. § 47:1703; LA. CONST. ART. VII, § 20.

88. Government Finances, *supra* note 49.

89. LA. REV. STAT. ANN. § 47:302.

90. *Id.* § 47:301.

tels; (2) the furnishing of storage or parking privileges by parking lots; (3) the furnishing of laundry and cleaning services; (4) telecommunications, and (5) the furnishing of repairs to tangible property.[91] The state sales tax rate is 4%,[92] and municipalities, parishes and school boards may levy a tax in addition to the state sales tax. Municipalities may impose a local rate of up to 2.5%[93] if approved by a majority of the voters in the municipality, and parishes and school boards may impose an additional tax of up to 5% if approved by a majority of the voters in the parish or school district.[94] Total sales taxes in Louisiana typically range from 6% in unincorporated areas within LaSalle Parish to 11% in Lake Providence.[95] Exemptions from Louisiana's sales-and-use tax include, among other items, prescription drugs, pesticides used for agricultural purposes, purchases made with food stamps, and school lunches.[96]

Selective Sales

Selective sales taxes make up 14.6% of Louisiana's total tax revenue.[97] Of that amount, 4.3%[98] comes from a motor fuel sales tax imposed at a rate of $0.13 per gallon of gasoline and $0.16 per gallon of diesel fuel.[99] Louisiana residents paid an average of $124 per capita in state motor fuel sales taxes in 2004, an amount which ranked 29th nationally and was just above the national average of $115.[100]

In 2004, sales taxes on alcoholic beverages made up 0.4% of Louisiana's total tax revenue.[101] Louisiana residents paid $11.85 per capita in state alcoholic beverage sales taxes in 2004, an amount which ranked 29th nationally.[102]

The tobacco product sales tax makes up 0.8%[103] of Louisiana's tax revenues and is imposed at a rate of $0.36 per pack of cigarettes.[104]

The remainder of Louisiana's selective sales taxes makes up 9.1% of its total tax revenue. Of this amount, 1.3% represents taxes on utilities and the other 7.8% represents taxes on other specific commodities, businesses, or services not reported separately above (e.g., on contractors, lodging, lubricating oil, fuels other than motor fuel, motor vehicles, meals, soft drinks, margarine, etc.).[105]

---

91. *Id.*

92. *Id.* § 47:302.

93. *Id.* § 33:2711.

94. *Id.* § 33:2721.6.

95. CCH-EXP, SALES-TAX-GUIDE LA ¶ 61-735, Local Rates.

96. La. Rev. Stat. Ann. § 47:305.

97. Government Finances, *supra* note 49.

98. *Id.*

99. La. Rev. Stat. Ann. § 47:818.12.

100. State Rankings 2006, *supra* note 1, at 327.

101. Government Finances, *supra* note 49.

102. State Rankings 2006, *supra* note 1, at 335.

103. Government Finances, *supra* note 49.

104. State Rankings 2006, *supra* note 1, at 333.

105. *See* Governments Division, U.S. Census Bureau, Government Finance And Employment Classification Manual, at ch. 7 (2000), *available at* http://ftp2.census.gov/govs/class/classfull.pdf [hereinafter Classification Manual].

Corporate Income and Other

Corporate Income

The corporate income tax makes up 1.8% of Louisiana's total tax revenue.[106] Louisiana's broad-based corporate income tax is imposed in five tax brackets ranging from 5% to 8% on a corporation's Louisiana taxable income,[107] which is based on the corporation's federal gross income.[108]

Louisiana follows the federal income tax treatment of S corporations to the extent that income and losses flow through to their shareholders who pay taxes on the income in Louisiana.[109] Limited partnerships and limited liability partnerships,[110] as well as limited liability companies, assuming they are treated as a partnership for federal tax purposes,[111] are treated as they are for federal income tax purposes and therefore do not pay Louisiana's corporate income tax. However, if a limited liability company is treated as a corporation for federal income tax purposes, the entity is subject to Louisiana's corporate income tax.[112]

Other

During fiscal year 2004, the collection of all other taxes not previously mentioned accounted for 8.7% of Louisiana's total tax revenue. Of this amount, approximately $46 million was generated by the estate and gift tax,[113] which is calculated on basis of the federal credit for state death taxes allowable by the Internal Revenue Code.[114] The "other taxes" category is also made up of motor vehicle license taxes, documentary and stock transfer taxes, severance taxes, and all other taxes not listed separately or provided for in other categories, such as taxes on land based on a specified rate per acre (rather than on assessed value).[115]

Burden Analysis

The overall state and local tax burden on Louisiana's taxpayers is extremely regressive. Taxpayers in the lowest quintile—those with incomes of less than $12,000—bear a tax burden equal to 11.5% of their income, while taxpayers in the top 1%—those

---

106. Government Finances, *supra* note 49.

107. La. Rev. Stat. Ann. § 47:287.12.

108. *Id.* § 47:287.61.

109. *Id.* § 47:287.732.

110. *Id.* § 9:3431.

111. *Id.* § 12:1368.

112. *Id.*

113. Government Finances, *supra* note 49.

114. La. Rev. Stat. Ann. § 47:2432. Note, however, that the federal credit for state death taxes was phased out for all deaths occurring after December 31, 2004, so Louisiana does not currently have an estate tax.

115. *See* Classification Manual, supra note 105, at ch. 7 (2000).

with incomes that exceed $248,000—bear a tax burden of just 6.0% of their income.[116] It is also worth noting that, although Louisiana obviously has no control over federal tax policy, federal itemized deductions for state and local personal income and property taxes nonetheless further reduce the burden on taxpayers in the top 1% to 4.9%.[117] Between 1989 and 2002, however, the tax burden on the bottom quintile fell by approximately 0.4%, while the burden on the top 1% rose by approximately 0.2%.[118]

In terms of the income tax, the burden across income groups in Louisiana is slightly progressive, with taxpayers in the lowest quintile bearing a tax burden of 0.3% and those in the top 1% bearing a tax burden of 3.4%.[119] In sharp contrast, however, the sales and excise taxes imposed by Louisiana are extremely regressive, with taxpayers in the lowest quintile bearing a tax burden of 9.9% and those in the top 1% bearing a tax burden of just 1.5%.[120] Property taxes in Louisiana are also mostly regressive, with taxpayers in the lowest quintile bearing a tax burden of 1.4% and those in the top quintile bearing an average tax burden of 0.9%.[121]

---

116. *See* ROBERT S. MCINTYRE ET AL., WHO PAYS? A DISTRIBUTIONAL ANALYSIS OF THE TAX SYSTEMS IN ALL 50 STATES 52 (2d ed. 2003), *available at* http://www.itepnet.org/wp2000/text.pdf. Taxpayers in the second quintile bear a 10.6% total tax burden on incomes between $12,000 and $20,000; those in the third quintile bear a 9.5% tax burden on incomes between $20,000 and $33,000; those in the fourth quintile bear a 8.7% tax burden on incomes between $33,000 and $59,000; those in the 80th–95th percentiles bear a 7.5% tax burden on incomes between $59,000 and $107,000; finally those in the 96th–99th percentiles bear a 6.6% tax burden on incomes between $107,000 and $248,000. *Id.*

117. *Id.* Taxpayers in the lowest, second lowest, and third lowest quintiles did not receive any benefit from these federal offsets, while those in the fourth quintile were able to reduce their individual tax burdens by 0.1%, those in the 80th–95th percentiles by 0.4%, and those in the 96th–99th percentiles by 0.8%. *Id.*

118. *Id.* at 53.

119. *See id.* at 52. Taxpayers in the second quintile bear a 0.8% income tax burden; those in the third quintile bear a 1.4% burden; those in the fourth quintile bear a 2.0% burden; those in the 80th–95th percentiles bear a 2.4% burden; finally those in the 96th–99th percentiles bear a 2.7% burden. *Id.* Note, however, that these percentages include both individual and corporate income tax burdens; that within the fourth quintile, corporate income taxes represent 0.1% of this burden; that within the 80th–95th percentiles, corporate income taxes represent 0.1% of this burden; that within the 96th–99th percentiles, corporate income taxes represent 0.1% of this burden; and that in the top 1%, corporate income taxes represent 0.2% of this burden. *Id.*

120. *See id.* Taxpayers in the second quintile bear a 8.8% sales-and-excise tax burden; those in the third quintile bear a 7.5% burden; those in the fourth quintile bear a 6.1% burden; those in the 80th–95th percentiles bear a 4.4% burden; finally, those in the 96th–99th percentiles bear a 2.7% burden. *Id.*

121. *See id.* Taxpayers in the second quintile bear a 1.0% property tax burden; those in the third quintile bear a 0.7% burden; those in the fourth quintile bear a 0.6% burden; those in the 80th–95th percentiles bear a 0.7% burden; those in the 96th–99th percentiles bear a 1.1% burden; finally, those in the top 1% bear a 1.0% burden. *Id.*

Maine

General Information

Basic Profile – Geography, Population, and Industry

Maine, known as "The Pine Tree State," was admitted to the Union in 1820.[1] It is located in the extreme northeastern corner of the United States and is bordered on the north by the Canadian provinces of Quebec and New Brunswick; on the east by the province of New Brunswick; on the south by the Atlantic Ocean; and on the west by New Hampshire and the province of Quebec. Maine is located in the eastern time zone, and its capital is Augusta.

Maine ranks 39th in total land and water area (35,385 square miles);[2] and in 2005, the state ranked 40th in population (approximately 1.32 million residents.[3] Its population is approximately 96.9% white and 0.8% black.[4] The state is approximately 44% Catholic; 25% Protestant; and 2% Jewish; 29% claim a religion outside the Judeo-Christian tradition or no religion at all.[5] Maine's population is fairly split, with 41.78% living in rural areas and 58.22% in urban areas.[6] Major industries include fishing, forestry, dairy farming, and fruit farming. Tourism also plays a considerable role in the economy.[7]

Family Income and Poverty Indicators

In 2004, Maine's per capita gross product was $32,956, which ranked among the ten lowest states in the country and below the national average of $39,725.[8] During this

---

1. State Rankings 2006, vi, 1 (Kathleen O'Leary Morgan & Scott Morgan eds., Morgan Quitno Press 2006).

2. *Id.* at 225.

3. *Id.* at 429.

4. Maine Quick Facts from the U.S. Census Bureau, http://quickfacts.census.gov/qfd/states/54000.html (last visited Jan. 30, 2007). The remaining population is made up of 0.8% Asian persons; 0.6% American Indian and/or Alaska Native persons; and 0.9% persons reporting two or more races. *Id.* Additionally, 1% of Maine's total population identify themselves as persons of Hispanic or Latino origin. *Id.* (noting that because Hispanics may be of any race, they are included within the other applicable race categories).

5. Barry A. Kosmin, Egon Mayer & Ariela Keysar, American Religious Identification Survey 2001, at 42, *available at* http://www.gc.cuny.edu/faculty/research_studies/aris.pdf.

6. *See* http://www.ers.usda.gov/StateFacts/KY.htm.

7. http://www.maine.gov/portal/facts_history/facts.html

8. State Rankings 2006, *supra* note 1, at 89.

same period, although the median household income in Maine was $39,395,[9] 12.2% of Maine's population lived in poverty,[10] which was slightly below the national average of 12.4%.[11] More specifically, poverty affected 16.7% of Maine's children,[12] 9.5% of its senior citizens,[13] and 9.5% of its families.[14] Of its female-headed households with children, 44.4% lived in poverty,[15] and 30.1% of the state's public elementary and secondary school students were eligible for free or reduced-price meals.[16] Of those living in poverty, approximately 1% were black, which represented 22% of Maine's black population and 0.1% of its total population.[17] In an attempt to combat this poverty, Maine spent approximately $1.8 billion on public welfare programs in 2002,[18] which made up 22.5% of its total government expenditures.[19]

Maine's Public Elementary-Secondary School System

Overall Spending and Performance

For the 2003–2004 school year Maine spent $9,534 per pupil in its public elementary-secondary school system, which was slightly above the national average of $8,182.[20] Of this amount, 8.9% was provided by the federal government, 40.7% was provided by the state government, and 50.4% was provided by the local governments,[21] with property taxes making up 20.2% of the total funding.[22] Out of these funds, Maine paid its elementary and secondary school teachers an estimated average annual salary of $40,940 during the 2004–2005 school year,[23] and in 2003 it provided a student/teacher ratio of 11.5, which was far better than the national average of 15.9.[24]

---

9. *Id.* at 96.

10. *Id.* at 495.

11. *Id.* at 495.

12. *Id.* at 497.

13. *Id.* at 496.

14. *Id.* at 498.

15. *Id.* at 499.

16. *Id.* at 532.

17. *See* Fact Sheet, American FactFinder, http://factfinder.census.gov/home/saff/main.html?_lang=en (select "Maine" under "Get a Fact Sheet for your community") (last visited Feb. 16, 2007). Note that these numbers are based on the 2000 census because more recent numbers were not available.

18. STATE RANKINGS 2006, *supra* note 1, at 500.

19. *Id.* at 502.

20. GOVERNMENTS DIVISION, U.S. CENSUS BUREAU, PUBLIC EDUCATION FINANCES 2004, at 8 tbl.8 (2006), *available at* http://www2.census.gov/govs/school/04f33pub.pdf.

21. *See id.* at 5 tbl.5.

22. *See id.* at 4 tbl.4.

23. THOMAS D. SNYDER ET AL., NATIONAL CENTER FOR EDUCATION STATISTICS, DIGEST OF EDUCATION STATISTICS 2005, at 116 tbl.77 (2006), *available at* http://nces.ed.gov/pubsearch/pubsinfo.asp?pubid=2006030.

24. *Id.* at 98 tbl.65.

In academic performance, Maine's fourth and eighth grade students scored higher than the national average in mathematics,[25] reading,[26] science,[27] and writing.[28]

Equity Issues

In 2004, revenues spent per student in Maine's highest poverty districts were determined to be $137 less than the revenues spent in its lowest poverty districts.[29] When adjustments were made for the additional costs of educating students growing up in poverty, however, the funding gap grew to $543.[30] Similarly, Maine spent $817 less per student in its highest minority districts, and this amount grew to $874 when adjustments for low-income students were made.[31]

Fourth graders eligible for free or reduced-price school lunches had test scores that were 6% lower in mathematics,[32] 8% lower in reading,[33] and 14% lower in writing[34] than those of students who were not eligible. The results were just slightly better for eighth graders eligible for free or reduced-price lunches; their test scores were 6% lower in mathematics,[35] 5% lower in reading,[36] and 13% lower in writing[37] than those of students who were not eligible.

Education finance litigation has been rare in Maine: the most recent cases occurred during the mid-1990s. In 1994, school funding cuts led several students and school districts to bring suit against the state on equal protection grounds. The court found for the state for two primary reasons. First, Maine's state constitution bestows responsi-

---

25. National Center for Education Statistics, U.S. Department of Education, The Nation's Report Card: Mathematics 2005, at 14 fig.11, 16 fig.12 (2005), *available at* http://nces.ed.gov/nationsreportcard/pdf/ main2005/2006453.pdf [hereinafter Mathematics 2005].

26. National Center for Education Statistics, U.S. Department of Education, The Nation's Report Card: Reading 2005, at 14 fig.11, 16 fig.12 (2005), *available at* http://nces.ed.gov/nationsreportcard/pdf/main2005/2006451.pdf [hereinafter Reading 2005].

27. National Center for Education Statistics, U.S. Department of Education, The Nation's Report Card: Science 2005, at 16 fig.12, 28 fig.22 (2006), *available at* http://nces.ed.gov/nationsreportcard//pdf/main2005/2006466.pdf [hereinafter Science 2005].

28. Hilary R. Persky et al., National Center for Education Statistics, U.S. Department of Education, The Nation's Report Card: Writing 2002, at 23 tbl.2.2, 24 tbl.2.3 (2003), *available at* http://nces.ed.gov/nationsreportcard/pdf/main2002/2003529.pdf [hereinafter Writing 2002].

29. The Education Trust, Funding Gaps 2006, at 7 tbl.3 (2006), *available at* http://www2.edtrust.org/NR/rdonlyres/CDEF9403-5A75-437E-93FF-EBF1174181FB/0/FundingGap2006.pdf.

30. *Id.*

31. *Id.* at 7 tbl.4.

32. Mathematics 2005, *supra* note 25, at 20 tbl.5.

33. Reading 2005, *supra* note 26, at 20 tbl.5.

34. Writing 2002, *supra* note 28, at 75 tbl.3.24.

35. Mathematics 2005, *supra* note 25, at 21 tbl.6.

36. Reading 2005, *supra* note 26, at 21 tbl.6.

37. Writing 2002, *supra* note 28, at 76 tbl.3.25.

bility for school funding on "towns" rather than the state. Second, the plaintiff school districts and students had failed to show that the funding cuts had resulted in any students receiving an inadequate education.[38]

Availability of Publicly Funded Prekindergarten Programs

The Maine Two Year Kindergarten Initiative serves students four years of age and is operated voluntarily by local school districts.[39] Total enrollment in this state-funded program is 2,088,[40] which represents 8% of Maine's three- and four-year-old children.[41] Federally funded and state-funded Head Start programs enroll an additional 2,882 and 461 children, respectively,[42] which represents 11% and 2%, respectively, of Maine's three- and four-year-old children.[43]

Where Does Maine Gets Its Revenue?

At the end of fiscal year 2004, Maine had total revenues of approximately $11.1 billion.[44] Of this amount, 45% was derived from state and local tax revenues and 24% was received from the federal government.[45] The remaining 31% came from other sources, including the Maine State Lottery, insurance trust revenue, and revenue from government-owned utilities and other commercial or auxiliary enterprises.[46]

Tax Revenue

Maine collected approximately $5 billion in state and local tax revenue during fiscal year 2004.[47] As a result, Maine residents paid $3,789 per capita in state and local taxes, an amount which ranked 10th nationally.[48] The different types of tax sources were approximately apportioned as follows:

---

38. School Administrative District No. 1 v. Commissioner, 659 A.2d 854

39. W. STEVEN BARNETT ET AL., NATIONAL INSTITUTE FOR EARLY EDUCATION RESEARCH, THE STATE OF PRESCHOOL 2006, at 80 (2006), *available at* http://nieer.org/yearbook/pdf/yearbook.pdf.

40. *Id.* at 81.

41. *See id.* at 232.

42. *Id.* at 81.

43. *See id.* at 232.

44. U.S. Census Bureau, State and Local Government Finances - 2003–04, http://www.census.gov/govs/www/estimate04.html (last visited Oct. 19, 2006) [hereinafter Government Finances].

45. *Id.*

46. *Id.*

47. The total tax revenues were collected as follows: $2.9 million by the state and $2.1 billion by local governments. *Id.*

48. *Id.*

Individual income taxes	23.3%
Property taxes	42.1%
General and selective sales taxes	26.8%
Corporate income and other taxes	7.8%
	100.0%[49]

Federal Funding

During fiscal year ended 2004, 24% of Maine's total revenues came from the federal government.[50] For every dollar of federal taxes paid, Maine received $1.40 in federal funding, an amount which ranked 16th nationally[51] and was above the national average of $1.17.[52]

Lottery Revenue

The Maine State Lottery was established in 1974.[53] Maine's lottery profits go directly to the General Fund[54] and are then redistributed to over 200 various state agencies.[55] During fiscal year 2005, the Maine State Lottery generated $200 million in gross proceeds, $50 million of which was transferred to the state's general fund.[56] Maine is also involved in a Tri-State Lotto under a tristate compact with Vermont and New Hampshire.[57]

Legal Structures of Major Tax Sources

Income

Maine employs a broad-based income tax[58] that uses adjusted gross income for federal income tax purposes as a starting point for determining the state's taxable income.[59] However, a fairly large number of adjustments may be available to various individuals in calculating this amount.[60] Maine currently has no statutes or constitutional

---

49. *Id.*

50. *Id.*

51. The Tax Foundation, Federal Spending Received Per Dollar of Taxes Paid by State, 2004 http://www.taxfoundation.org/news/show/266.html (last visited Sept. 17, 2006).

52. *See id.*

53. http://www.naspl.org/Contacts/index.cfm?fuseaction=view&ID=15

54. *Id.*

55. *Id.*

56. http://www.maine.gov/tools/whatsnew/index.php?topic=Lottery_News&id=13748&v=Article

57. Me. Rev. Stat. Ann. tit. 8, § 405

58. Me. Rev. Stat. Ann. tit. 36, § 5121.

59. *Id.* § 5111.

60. *See, e.g.,* Me. Rev. Stat. Ann. tit. 36, § 5111.

law regarding the ability of localities to tax personal income.[61] During fiscal year 2004, Maine collected individual income tax of $882 per capita, an amount which ranked 12th nationally.[62]

In Maine, a typical family of four (i.e., married taxpayers who file jointly and have two dependent children) are not required to pay any income tax until their combined income exceeds $26,400, an amount which is above the national poverty line of $20,615.[63] Maine's income tax structure contains four tax brackets that impose a minimum marginal rate of 2% and the maximum marginal rate is 8.5%.[64] When statutory exemptions and the standard deduction are taken into account, the maximum marginal rate applies to every dollar of income exceeding $56,550.[65]

Property

Overview

Maine has a property tax system that taxes the value of real and tangible personal property mostly at the local level; some taxes, however, are also collected at the state level.[66] During fiscal year 2004, Maine collected a total of $2.1 billion in property taxes.[67] Of this amount, Maine localities collected $2.05 billion, while the state collected $45 million.[68] As a result, Maine residents paid $1,596 per capita in property taxes, an amount which ranked 6th nationally.[69]

Defining the Real Property Tax Base

"Real property" in Maine is defined "as all land located in the state, and all buildings, mobile homes, and other things affixed to the land."[70] Unlike most state property-

---

61. CCH-EXP, ME-TAXRPTR ¶ 15-015, Local Power to Tax.

62. State Rankings 2006, *supra* note 1, at 321.

63. Jason A. Levitis, Center on Budget and Policy Priorities, The Impact of State Income Taxes on Low-Income Families in 2006, at 12 (2007). In 2006, Maine taxpayers who were married and filing jointly could claim a standard deduction of $8,600 and personal and dependent exemptions of $2,850 each. (*Maine Tax Alert*, Vol. 15 No. 8, Maine Revenue Services, October 1, 2005.) Note, however, that the threshold calculation of $26,400 is greater than the sum of these deductions and exemptions because it includes additional tax benefits available to low-income families, such as the earned-income tax credit. *See* Levitis, *supra*. Note also that in 2007, Maine taxpayers who are married and filing jointly are entitled to an increased standard deduction of $8,900, while personal and dependent exemptions remain $2,850 each. (*Maine Tax Alert*, Vol. 16, No. 7, Maine Revenue Services, October 1, 2006); Me. Rev. Stat. Ann. tit. 36, § 5126.

64. Me. Rev. Stat. Ann. tit. 36, § 5111. Maine's middle two tax brackets are 4.5% and 7%. *Id.*

65. The standard deduction and exemptions of $8,600 and $11,400, respectively, plus the threshold of taxable income for the highest tax bracket of $36,550, equals $56,550. *See supra* notes 63–64.

66. Me. Rev. Stat. Ann. tit. 36, § 502.

67. Government Finances, *supra* note 44.

68. *Id.*

69. *Id.*

70. Me. Rev. Stat. Ann. tit. 36, § 551.

tax schemes, Maine does not apply an assessment percentage to property valuations.[71] It uses a variety of valuation methods to determine the value of real property, which include the capitalization-of-income approach, the comparable-sales-or market approach, and the replacement-cost approach.[72] For valuation purposes, however, certain types of real property are specially treated in that they are valued at current use rather than at the highest and best use.[73] These categories include wildlife sanctuaries, open space, and farm properties.[74]

Real Property Tax Rates

Although different types of property may be treated differently for valuation purposes, all property within a jurisdiction is basically taxed at a single rate.[75] Furthermore, Maine does not apply any assessment percentage to valuations, so all rates of tax are applied equally to all property.[76]

Personal and Intangible Property

Personal property is reported by the owner to municipal and county assessors and is valued by the assessors as of April 1 of the current tax year, like real property.[77] Although the Maine constitution authorizes the taxation of intangibles, such property is exempt from taxation.[78] A state tax is imposed on telecommunications personal property, which includes transmission of any interactive two-way communications by way of voice, image, data, and information, at the rate of 27 mills times the value of the property.[79]

Exemptions

Maine provides property tax exemptions for certain property, including, among other types of property, business and agricultural inventories and the household goods of individuals,[80] as well as most intangible property.[81]

In addition, homesteads are afforded an exemption of up to $13,000, provided the owner is a permanent resident of Maine and has owned the property for 12 months preceding the use of the exemption.[82]

---

71. CCH-EXP, ME-TAXRPTR ¶ 20-700. In other words, 100% of the property's value is included in the tax base. *Id.*

72. Me. Rev. Stat. Ann. tit. 36, § 751.

73. Me Const., art. IX, § 8 (1978).

74. *Id.*

75. *Id.*

76. Me. Rev. Stat. Ann. tit. 36, § 502.

77. *Id.* § 601.

78. *Id.*

79. *Id.* § 457.

80. *Id.* § 603.

81. *Id.* tit. 9B, § 241. Assets held by financial institutions are subject to an excise tax, however, in order to offset administrative costs of supervision. *Id.*

82. *Id.* tit. 36, § 683.

General and Selective Sales

General Sales

Maine imposes a general retail sales-and-use tax, which makes up 18.4% of its total tax revenue.[83] This tax is imposed on all tangible personal property and certain taxable services at a general rate of 5%.[84] "Taxable services include rental of living quarters in any hotel, rooming house, tourist or trailer; rental or lease of an automobile; transmittal and distribution of electricity; and prepaid calling arrangements."[85] Maine taxes the rental of automobiles for less than one year at a rate of 10%, liquor sales at 7%, rentals of rooms or shelter at 7%, and the total value of all prepared food by a retailer at 7%.[86] There are currently no specific provisions for local sales-and-use taxes. Maine provides sales-and-use tax exemptions for, among other items, food stamp purchases, prescription drugs, and 95% of the sales price of fuel and electricity purchased for use at a manufacturing facility.[87] In addition, food products are exempt from sales tax if they are deemed "grocery staples."[88]

Selective Sales

Selective sales taxes make up 8.4% of Maine's total revenue.[89] Of that amount, 4.4% comes from motor fuel sales taxes.[90] Maine residents paid an average of $168 per capita in state motor fuel sales taxes in 2004, an amount which ranked 6th nationally and was well above the national average of $115.[91]

The tobacco product sales tax made up 1.9%[92] of Maine's total tax revenue in 2004 and was imposed at a rate of $1.00 per pack of cigarettes.[93]

In 2004, sales taxes on alcoholic beverages made up 0.3% of Maine's tax revenue.[94] Maine residents paid $29.87 per capita in state alcoholic beverage sales taxes in 2004, an amount which ranked 8th nationally.[95]

The remainder of Maine's selective sales taxes makes up 1.9% of its total tax revenue. Of this amount, 0.2% represents taxes on utilities and the other 1.7% represents

---

83. Government Finances, *supra* note 44.

84. *Id.*

85. Me. Rev. Stat. Ann. tit. 36, § 1752(17-B).

86. *Id.* § 1811.

87. *Id.* § 1760(5).

88. *Id.* § 1760(3). "Grocery staples" do not include products such as candy and confections, prepared food, and most beverages, such as soft drinks, spirits, and bottled water. *Id.*

89. U.S. Census Bureau, "State and Local Government Finances - 2003–04", http://www.census.gov/govs/www/estimate04.html (last visited Oct. 22, 2006).

90. *Id.*

91. State Rankings 2006, *supra* note 1, at 327.

92. U.S. Census Bureau, *supra* note 4.

93. State Rankings 2006, *supra* note 1, at 333.

94. U.S. Census Bureau, *supra* note 4.

95. State Rankings 2006, *supra* note 1, at 335.

taxes on other specific commodities, businesses, or services not reported separately above (e.g., on contractors, lodging, lubricating oil, fuels other than motor fuel, motor vehicles, meals, soft drinks, etc.).[96]

Corporate and Income and Other

Corporate Income

The corporate income tax makes up 2.2% of Maine's total tax revenue.[97] "Maine imposes a corporate income tax on domestic and foreign corporations carrying on a trade or business in, or deriving income from sources within, the state."[98] The Maine Income Tax Law imposes an income tax on "'taxable corporations,'"[99] meaning any corporation, including certain S corporations, that realizes Maine net income at any time during the tax year."[100] Maine follows the federal income tax treatment of LLC's and LLP's.[101] Maine's income tax treatment of such corporations is accorded the same treatment as the federal one. The corporation's federal taxable income for the year is the starting point for determining the amount of state net income.[102] Maine's corporate income tax structure has four brackets, with the highest rate 8.93%, plus $19,418 for income of $250,000 or more.[103]

Other

During fiscal year 2004, the collection of all other taxes not previously mentioned accounted for 5.5% of Maine's total tax revenue.[104] Of this amount, $32 million was generated by the estate tax. [105] Although Maine's estate tax is computed on the basis of

---

96. *See* GOVERNMENTS DIVISION, U.S. CENSUS BUREAU, GOVERNMENT FINANCE AND EMPLOYMENT CLASSIFICATION MANUAL, at ch.7 (2000), *available at* http://ftp2.census.gov/govs/class/classfull.pdf [hereinafter CLASSIFICATION MANUAL].

97. Government Finances, *supra* note 44.

98. ME. REV. STAT. ANN. tit. 36, § 5200.

99. *Id.*

100. *Id.* § 5102.

101. *Id.* § 5190.

102. *Id.* § 5200.

103. *Id.* A tax is imposed for each taxable year at the following rates on each taxable corporation or group of corporations that derives income from a unitary business carried on by two or more members of an affiliated group:

If the Maine income is:	The tax is:
Not over $25,000	3.5% of Maine income
$25,000 but not over $75,000	$875 plus 7.93% of excess over $25, 000
$75,000 but not over $250,000	$4,840 plus 8.33% of excess over $75, 000
$250,000 or more	$19,418 plus 8.93% of excess over $250,000.

104. Government Finances, *supra* note 44.

105. *Id.*

the federal state death tax credit,[106] Maine has survived the federal government's elimination of this credit by calculating the tax on the basis of the Internal Revenue Code in effect on December 31, 2002.[107] The "other taxes" category is further made up of various license taxes, documentary or stock transfer taxes, severance taxes, and all other taxes not listed separately or provided for in other categories.[108]

Burden Analysis

The overall state and local tax burden on Maine's taxpayers is somewhat regressive. Taxpayers in the lowest quintile—those with incomes of less than $15,000—bear a tax burden equal to 10% of their income, while taxpayers in the top 1%—those with incomes that exceed $262,000—bear a tax burden of 9.7% of their income.[109] It is also worth noting that, although Maine obviously has no control over federal tax policy, federal itemized deductions for state and local personal income and property taxes nonetheless further reduce the burden on taxpayers in the top 1% to 6.8%.[110] Furthermore, between 1989 and 2002, the tax burden on the bottom quintile rose by approximately 1.1%, while the burden on the top 1% actually fell by 0.3%.[111]

In terms of the income tax, the burden across income groups in Maine is slightly progressive, with taxpayers in the lowest quintile bearing a tax burden of 0.4% and those in the top 1% bearing a tax burden of 6.9%.[112] In contrast, however, the sales and excise taxes imposed by Maine are very regressive, with taxpayers in the lowest quin-

---

106. ME. REV. STAT. ANN. tit. 36, § 4063.

107. *Id.* § 4062.

108. *See* CLASSIFICATION MANUAL, *supra* note 96, at ch.7.

109. *See* ROBERT S. MCINTYRE ET AL., WHO PAYS? A DISTRIBUTIONAL ANALYSIS OF THE TAX SYSTEMS IN ALL 50 STATES 54 (2d ed. 2003), *available at* http://www.itepnet.org/wp2000/text.pdf. Taxpayers in the second quintile bear a 10.3% total tax burden on incomes between $15,000 and $26,000; those in the third quintile bear a 10.2% tax burden on incomes between $26,000 and $40,000; those in the fourth quintile bear a 10.5% tax burden on incomes between $40,000 and $63,000; those in the 80th–95th percentiles bear a 10.9% tax burden on incomes between $63,000 and $116,000; finally, those in the 96th–99th percentiles bear a 10.5% tax burden on incomes between $116,000 and $262,000. *Id.*

110. *Id.* Taxpayers in the lowest quintile did not receive any benefit from these federal offsets, while those in the second quintile were able to reduce their individual tax burdens by 0.1%, those in the third quintile by 0.3%, those in the fourth quintile by 0.5%, those in the 80th–95th percentiles by 1.4%, and those in the 96th–99th percentiles by 2.1%. *Id.*

111. *Id.* at 55.

112. *See id.* at 54. Taxpayers in the second quintile bear a 1.6% income tax burden; those in the third quintile bear a 2.5% burden; those in the fourth quintile bear a 3.4% burden; those in the 80th–95th percentiles bear a 4.6% burden; finally, those in the 96th–99th percentiles bear a 5.6% burden. *Id.* Note, however, that these percentages include both individual and corporate income tax burdens; that within the 96th–99th percentiles, corporate income taxes represent 0.1% of this burden; and that in the top 1%, corporate income taxes represent 0.1% of this burden. *Id.*

tile bearing a tax burden of 6.4% and those in the top 1% bearing a tax burden of just 0.9%.[113] Although not purely regressive, property taxes in Maine place a somewhat higher burden on the middle class, who bear an average tax burden of 3.3% compared with taxpayers in the lowest quintile, who bear a burden of 3.2%, and compared with taxpayers in the top quintile, who bear an average burden 2.8%.[114]

---

113. *See id.* Taxpayers in the second quintile bear a 5.4% sales-and-excise tax burden; those in the third quintile bear a 4.4% burden; those in the fourth quintile bear a 3.7% burden; those in the 80th–95th percentiles bear a 2.9% burden; finally, those in the 96th–99th percentiles bear a 1.8% burden. *Id.*

114. *Id.* Taxpayers in the second quintile bear a 3.2% property tax burden; those in the third quintile bear a 3.3% burden; those in the fourth quintile bear a 3.5% burden; those in the 80th–95th percentiles bear a 3.4% burden; those in the 96th–99th percentiles bear a 3.1% burden; finally, those in the top 1% bear a 2% burden. *Id.*

Maryland

General Information

Basic Profile – Geography, Population, and Industry

Admitted to the Union in 1788, Maryland is known as the "Free State."[1] It is located in the Mid-Atlantic region and is bordered by Pennsylvania and Delaware on the north; Nebraska, Delaware, and the Atlantic Ocean on the east; Virginia and the District of Colombia on the south; and West Virginia on the west. The state is located in the eastern time zone, and its capital is Annapolis.

Maryland ranks 42nd in total land and water area (12,407 square miles);[2] in 2005, the state ranked 19th in population (approximately 5.6 million residents).[3] Maryland's population is approximately 64.0% white and 29.3% black.[4] The state is approximately 22% Catholic; 53% Protestant; and 3% Jewish; 22% claim a religion outside the Judeo-Christian tradition or no religion at all.[5] Nearly 94.8% of Maryland's population lives in urban areas.[6] Major industries include manufacturing, exports, tourism, and agriculture.[7]

---

1. STATE RANKINGS 2006, vi, 1 (Kathleen O'Leary Morgan & Scott Morgan eds., Morgan Quitno Press 2006).

2. *Id.* at 225.

3. *Id.* at 429.

4. Maryland Quick Facts from the U.S. Census Bureau, http://quickfacts.census.gov/qfd/states/54000.html (last visited Jan. 27, 2007). The remaining population is made up of 4.8% Asian persons; 0.3% American Indian and/or Alaskan Native persons; 0.1% Native Hawaiian and/or other Pacific Islanders; and 1.5% persons reporting two or more races. *Id.* Additionally, 5.7% of Maryland's total population identify themselves as persons of Hispanic or Latino origin. *Id.* (noting that because Hispanics may be of any race, they are included within the other applicable race categories).

5. BARRY A. KOSMIN, EGON MAYER & ARIELA KEYSAR, AMERICAN RELIGIOUS IDENTIFICATION SURVEY 2001, at 41, *available at* http://www.gc.cuny.edu/faculty/research_studies/aris.pdf.

6. USDA Economic Research Service, Maryland Fact Sheet, http://www.ers.usda.gov/StateFacts/MD.htm (last visited Feb. 17, 2007). According to the latest estimates, approximately 293,982 people live in rural areas, and 5.3 million people live in urban areas. *Id.*

7. Business – MD.gov, http://www.maryland.gov/portal/server.pt?space=CommunityPage&cached=true&parentname =MyPage&parentid=0&in_hi_userid=1333&control=SetCommunity &CommunityID=201&PageID=0&portal=md (last visited Feb. 17, 2007).

Family Income and Poverty Indicators

In 2004, Maryland's per capita gross product was $40,996, which ranked 15th nationally and was above the national average of $39,725.[8] During this same period, while the median household income in Maryland was $56,763,[9] 8.6% of the state's population was living in poverty,[10] which was far below the national average of 12.4%.[11] More specifically, poverty affected 11.0% of Maryland's children,[12] 7.8% of its senior citizens,[13] and 5.8% of its families.[14] Of its female-headed households with children, 22.1% lived in poverty,[15] and 31.4% of the state's elementary and secondary school students were eligible for free or reduced-price meals.[16] Of those living in poverty approximately 48% were black, which represented 14% of Maryland's black population and 4% of its total population.[17] In an attempt to combat this poverty, Maryland spent approximately $4.7 billion on public welfare programs in 2002,[18] which made up 14.9% of its total government expenditures.[19]

Maryland's Public Elementary-Secondary School System

Overall Spending and Performance

For the 2003–2004 school year, Maryland spent $9,212 per pupil in its public elementary-secondary school system, which was slightly above the national average of $8,182.[20] Of this amount, 6.4% was provided by the federal government, 37.7% was provided by the state government, and 55.9% was provided by the local governments,[21] with property taxes making up a substantial part of the total funding.[22] Out of these funds, Maryland paid its elementary and secondary school teachers an estimated av-

---

8. STATE RANKINGS 2006, *supra* note 1, at 89.

9. *Id.* at 96.

10. *Id.* at 495.

11. *Id.* at 495.

12. *Id.* at 497.

13. *Id.* at 496.

14. *Id.* at 498.

15. *Id.* at 499.

16. *Id.* at 532.

17. *See* Fact Sheet, American FactFinder, http://factfinder.census.gov/home/saff/main.html?_lang=en (select "Maryland" under "Get a Fact Sheet for your community") (last visited Feb. 16, 2007). Note that these numbers are based on the 2000 census because more recent numbers were not available.

18. *Id.* at 500.

19. *Id.* at 502.

20. GOVERNMENTS DIVISION, U.S. CENSUS BUREAU, PUBLIC EDUCATION FINANCES 2004, at 8 tbl.8 (2006), *available at* http://www2.census.gov/govs/school/04f33pub.pdf.

21. *See id.* at 5 tbl.5.

22. Although none of the total funding has been specifically designated as provided by property taxes, 51.9% comes from "Parent Government Contributions," *see id.* at 4 tbl.4., which are defined as "tax receipts and other amounts appropriated by a parent government and trans-

erage annual salary of $52,331 during the 2004–2005 school year,[23] and in 2003, it provided a student/teacher ratio of 15.8, which was slightly better than the national average of 15.9.[24]

In academic performance, fourth grade students in Maryland scored above the national average in mathematics,[25] reading,[26] and writing[27] and equal to the national average in science.[28] Eighth grade students fared similarly, scoring above the national average in both reading[29] and writing,[30] equal to the national average in mathematics,[31] and just below the national average in science.[32]

Equity Issues

In 2004, revenues spent per student in Maryland's highest poverty districts were determined to be $123 less than the revenues spent in its lowest poverty districts.[33] When adjustments were made for the additional costs of educating students growing up in poverty, however, the funding gap grew to $432.[34] Similarly, Maryland spent $302 less per student in its highest minority districts, and this amount grew to $454 when adjustments for low-income students were made.[35]

Fourth graders eligible for free or reduced-price school lunches had test scores

---

ferred to its dependent school system." *Id.* at app. A-1. This amount, however, "[e]xcludes intergovernmental revenue, current charges, and miscellaneous general revenue." *Id.*

23. THOMAS D. SNYDER ET AL., NATIONAL CENTER FOR EDUCATION STATISTICS, DIGEST OF EDUCATION STATISTICS 2005, at 116 tbl.77 (2006), *available at* http://nces.ed.gov/pubsearch/pubsinfo.asp?pubid=2006030.

24. *Id.* at 98 tbl.65.

25. NATIONAL CENTER FOR EDUCATION STATISTICS, U.S. DEPARTMENT OF EDUCATION, THE NATION'S REPORT CARD: MATHEMATICS 2005, at 14 fig.11 (2005), *available at* http://nces.ed.gov/nationsreportcard/pdf/main2005/ 2006453.pdf [hereinafter MATHEMATICS 2005].

26. NATIONAL CENTER FOR EDUCATION STATISTICS, U.S. DEPARTMENT OF EDUCATION, THE NATION'S REPORT CARD: READING 2005, at 14 fig.11 (2005), *available at* http://nces.ed.gov/nationsreportcard/pdf/main2005/2006451.pdf [hereinafter READING 2005].

27. HILARY R. PERSKY ET AL., NATIONAL CENTER FOR EDUCATION STATISTICS, U.S. DEPARTMENT OF EDUCATION, THE NATION'S REPORT CARD: WRITING 2002, at 23 tbl.2.2 (2003), *available at* http://nces.ed.gov/nationsreportcard/pdf/main2002/2003529.pdf [hereinafter WRITING 2002].

28. NATIONAL CENTER FOR EDUCATION STATISTICS, U.S. DEPARTMENT OF EDUCATION, THE NATION'S REPORT CARD: SCIENCE 2005, at 16 fig.12 (2006), *available at* http://nces.ed.gov/nationsreportcard//pdf/main2005/2006466.pdf [hereinafter SCIENCE 2005].

29. READING 2005, *supra*, note 26.

30. WRITING 2002, *supra*, note 27.

31. MATHEMATICS 2005, *supra* note 25.

32. SCIENCE 2005, *supra*, note 28.

33. THE EDUCATION TRUST, FUNDING GAPS 2006, at 7 tbl.3 (2006), *available at* http://www2.edtrust.org/NR/rdonlyres/CDEF9403-5A75-437E-93FF-EBF1174181FB/0/FundingGap2006.pdf.

34. *Id.*

35. *Id.* at 7 tbl.4.

that were 11% lower in mathematics,[36] 14% lower in reading,[37] and 12% lower in writing[38] than those of students who were not eligible. The results were generally similar for eighth graders eligible for free or reduced-price lunches; their test scores were 10% lower in mathematics,[39] 10% lower in reading,[40] and 15% lower in writing[41] than those of students who were not eligible.

School funding litigation in Maryland has centered on two primary cases. In the 1983 case *Hornbeck v. Somerset County Board of Education*, the Maryland Supreme Court held that the state constitution did not require equal per-student spending levels in each school district. The court did hold, however, that Maryland's state constitution required that students be provided "an adequate education measured by contemporary educational standards."[42] Such "educational standards" led to the 1994 case *Bradford v. Maryland State Board of Education*, in which the Baltimore City Public School District alleged that inadequate funding was keeping students from receiving an adequate education. Although the parties settled by agreeing that the state should provide slightly increased funding, the plaintiffs returned to court in 2000 because the schools had not improved. As a result of this litigation, the legislature enacted a more modern, standards-based approach to school funding, which has diverted more funds to high-need school districts.

Availability of Publicly Funded Prekindergarten Programs

The Maryland Pre-kindergarten Program began as a pilot program in two counties and now serves students four years of age in school districts across the state.[43] Total enrollment in this state-funded program is 24,219,[44] which represents 16% of Maryland's 151,970 three- and four-year-old children.[45] Federally funded and state-funded Head Start programs enroll an additional 9,174 and 338 children, respectively,[46] which represents 6% and 0.2%, respectively, of Maryland's three- and four-year-old children.[47]

---

36. MATHEMATICS 2005, *supra* note 25, at 20 tbl.5.

37. READING 2005, *supra* note 26, at 20 tbl.5.

38. WRITING 2002, *supra* note 27, at 75 tbl.3.24.

39. MATHEMATICS 2005, *supra* note 25, at 21 tbl.6.

40. READING 2005, *supra* note 26, at 21 tbl.6.

41. WRITING 2002, *supra* note 27, at 76 tbl.3.25.

42. Hornbeck v. Somerset County Board of Education, 295 Md. 597 (M.D. 1983).

43. W. STEVEN BARNETT ET AL., NATIONAL INSTITUTE FOR EARLY EDUCATION RESEARCH, THE STATE OF PRESCHOOL 2006, at 82 (2006), *available at* http://nieer.org/yearbook/pdf/yearbook.pdf.

44. *Id.* at 41.

45. *See id.* at 232.

46. *Id.* at 41.

47. *See id.* at 232.

Where Does Maryland Get Its Revenue?

At the end of fiscal year 2004, Maryland had total revenues of approximately $44.3 billion.[48] Of this amount, 50.4% was derived from state and local tax revenues and 16.4% was received from the federal government.[49] The remaining 33.2% came from other sources, including the Maryland Lottery, insurance trust revenue, revenue from government-owned utilities, and other commercial or auxiliary enterprises.[50]

Tax Revenue

Maryland collected approximately $22.3 billion in state and local tax revenue during fiscal year 2004.[51] As a result, Maryland residents paid $4,016 per capita in state and local taxes, an amount which ranked 6th nationally.[52] The different types of tax sources were approximately apportioned as follows:

Individual income taxes	37.1%
Property taxes	27.0%
General and selective sales taxes	24.4%
Corporate income and other taxes	11.5%
	100.0%[53]

Federal Funding

During fiscal year 2004, 16.4% of Maryland's total revenues came from the federal government.[54] For every dollar of federal taxes paid, Maryland received $1.55 in federal funding, an amount which ranked 14th nationally[55] and was far above the national average of $1.17.[56]

Lottery Revenue

The Maryland Lottery has been in operation since 1957. Under Maryland's constitution, all Maryland Lottery profits are to be used to supplement the state's general

---

48. U.S. Census Bureau, State and Local Government Finances - 2003–04, http://www.census.gov/govs/www/estimate04.html (last visited Oct. 6, 2006). [hereinafter Government Finances]

49. Id.

50. Id.

51. The total tax revenues were collected as follows: $14.2 billion by the state and 10.8 billion by local governments. Id.

52. Id.

53. Id.

54. Id.

55. The Tax Foundation, Federal Spending Received Per Dollar of Taxes Paid by State, 2004 http://www.taxfoundation.org/taxdata/show/266.html (last visited Sept. 17, 2006).

56. See Id.

fund.[57] Additionally, all of Maryland's sports-related lottery games are used to fund the upkeep of professional sports arenas in the state.[58] During fiscal year 2006, the Lottery had total revenues of $1.49 billion and net proceeds of $477 million.[59]

Legal Structures of Major Tax Sources

Income

Maryland employs a broad based-income tax[60] that uses adjusted gross income for federal income tax purposes as a starting point for determining the state's taxable income.[61] A few adjustments, however, may be available to various individuals in calculating this amount.[62] By statute, Maryland allows counties to impose a general income tax.[63] This local income tax is limited to a minimum of 1% and a maximum of 3.2%.[64] Rates that exceed 2.6% must be approved by a local referendum.[65] During fiscal year 2004, Maryland collected individual income tax of $949 per capita, an amount which ranked 6th nationally.[66]

In Maryland, a typical family of four (i.e., married taxpayers who file jointly and have two dependent children) are not required to pay any income tax until their combined income exceeds $31,000, an amount which is above the national poverty line of $20,615.[67] Maryland's income tax structure contains four tax brackets that impose a minimum marginal rate of 2% and a maximum marginal rate of 4.75%.[68] When statu-

---

57. MD. CODE ANN., STATE GOV'T at §§ 9-103 – 9-104.

58. *Id.*

59. 2005 Annual Report Maryland State Lottery Agency, http://www.mdlottery.com/ (last checked Dec. 18, 2006).

60. MD. CODE ANN., TAX-GEN. § 10-102.

61. *Id.* § 10-107.

62. *Id.* § 10-104.

63. *Id.* § 10-103.

64. *Id.* § 10-106.

65. *Id.*

66. STATE RANKINGS 2006, *supra* note 1, at 321 *citing* U.S. Bureau of the Census, Governments Division "2004 State Government Tax Collections" *available at* http://www.census.gov/govs/www/statetax04.html.

67. JASON A. LEVITIS, CENTER ON BUDGET AND POLICY PRIORITIES, THE IMPACT OF STATE INCOME TAXES ON LOW-INCOME FAMILIES IN 2006, at 12 (2007). In 2006, Maryland taxpayers who were married and filing jointly could claim a standard deduction of $4,000, a personal exemption of $2,400 (both spouses combined), and dependent exemptions of $2,400 each. MD. CODE ANN., TAX-GEN. §§ 10-208, 10-211. Note, however, that the threshold calculation of $31,000 is greater than the sum of these deductions and exemptions because it includes additional tax benefits available to low-income families, such as the earned-income tax credit. *See* LEVITIS, *supra.*

68. MD. CODE ANN., TAX-GEN. § 10-105. Maryland's middle two tax brackets are 3.9% and 4%. *Id.*

tory exemptions and the standard deduction are taken into account, the maximum marginal rate applies to every dollar of income exceeding $16,600.[69]

Property

Overview

Maryland has a property tax system that taxes the value of real estate and tangible personal property at the state and local levels.[70] This system includes the taxation of stock held in business and held by out-of-state trustees for an in-state beneficiary.[71] During fiscal year 2004, Maryland collected approximately $5.5 billion dollars in property tax at the local level and approximately $478 million at the state level.[72] As a result, Maryland residents paid $1,082 per capita in state and local property taxes, an amount which ranked 17th nationally.[73]

Defining the Real Property Tax Base

Maryland has eleven classifications of real property and seven classifications of personal property.[74] Real property is assessed at 100% of its "phased in value,"[75] with a few limited exceptions.[76] Fair market value is generally determined by the application of

---

69. The standard deduction and exemptions of $4,000 and $9,600, respectively, plus the threshold for taxable income for the highest tax bracket of $3,000, equals $16,600. *See supra* notes 67–68.

70. MD. CODE ANN., TAX-PROP. § 5-102.

71. *Id.*

72. Government Finances, *supra* note 48.

73. *See id.*

74. MD. CODE ANN., TAX-PROP. § 8-101 (real property includes "(1) land that is actively devoted to farm or agricultural use, assessed under § 8-209 of this title; (2) marshland, assessed under § 8-210 of this title; (3) woodland, assessed under § 8-211 of this title; (4) land of a country club or golf course, assessed under §§ 8-212 through 8-217 of this title; (5) land that is used for a planned development, assessed under §§ 8-220 through 8-225 of this title; (6) rezoned real property that is used for residential purposes, assessed under §§ 8-226 through 8-228 of this title; (7) operating real property of a railroad; (8) operating real property of a public utility; (9) property valued under § 8-105(a)(3) of this subtitle; (10) conservation property, assessed under § 8-209.1 of this title; and (11) all other real property that is directed by this article to be assessed." Personal property includes "(1) stock in business; (2) distilled spirits; (3) operating personal property of a railroad; (4) operating personal property of a public utility that is machinery or equipment used to generate electricity or steam for sale; (5) all other operating personal property of a public utility; (6) machinery and equipment, other than operating personal property of a public utility, that is used to generate (i) electricity or steam for sale or (ii) hot or chilled water for sale that is used to heat or cool a building; and (7) all other personal property that is directed by this article to be assessed.") *Id.*

75. "Phased in value" covers a three year cycle and is defined as "the prior value of real property increase by one-third, two-thirds, or the full amount by which the value increased over the prior value … or if the value has not increased, the value determined by the most recent valuation." MD. CODE ANN., TAX-PROP. § 8-103(a)(3).

76. MD. CODE ANN., TAX-PROP. § 8-103 (assessed at 50%: (i) farm or agricultural use land; (ii) marshland; (iii) woodland; (iv) country club property; and (v) planned development land.

standard appraisal methods, including the cost method, the income method, and the market-data method.[77] In general, assessments occur annually.[78]

Real Property Tax Rates

The tax rates imposed on real property vary and are set by each locality. During fiscal year 2006, the state tax rate per $1,000 of assessed value was $1.12 for real property and $2.80 for utility operating real property.[79] The highest county rate for real property is an additional amount of $11.10 per $1,000 value in Baltimore County, and the lowest county rate is $6,24 per $1,000 value in Montgomery County.[80]

Personal and Intangible Property

Tax is imposed on stock ownership, machinery used in production of utilities, and the fair value of distilled spirits on the property of production.[81] Other intangible personal property is not subject to tax at either the state or local level.[82]

Exemptions

Generally, personal property such as automobiles, household goods, and most other tangible property is exempt from property tax.[83] Agricultural supplies, cemeteries, nature conservancy, and student housing is also exempt.[84] Additionally, Maryland provides a homestead exemption in the form of a credit against Maryland property tax equal to the total real property tax of a dwelling less a percentage of the taxpayer's gross income.[85]

General and Selective Sales

General Sales

Maryland imposes a general retail sales-and-use tax, which makes up 12.1% of Maryland's total tax revenue.[86] This tax is imposed on the sale, distribution, renting, or furnishing of tangible personal property, as well as specified services.[87] These ser-

---

However, the assessment of the operating real property of a public utility equals its value). Note that agricultural land is assessed on the basis of its use value. MD. CODE ANN., TAX-PROP. § 8-209.

77. CCH-EXP, PROP-TAX-GUIDE MD ¶ 20-615, Valuation Methods in General.
78. MD. CODE ANN., TAX-PROP. §§ 8-201–8-204.
79. CCH-EXP, PROP-TAX-GUIDE MD ¶ 20-405, Rates of Tax.
80. *Id.*
81. CCH-EXP, PROP-TAX-GUIDE MD ¶ 20-95, Personal Property.
82. MD. CODE ANN., TAX-PROP. § 6-101.
83. *Id.* §§ 7-301, 7-227, 7-230.
84. *Id.* § 7-201–7-241.
85. *Id.* § 9-104.
86. Government Finances, *supra* note 48.
87. MD. CODE ANN., TAX-GEN. § 11-104.

vices include (1) printing and packaging; (2) cleaning and repair; and (3) credit assistance performed by credit-assistance corporations.[88] The state-imposed sales tax rate is 5%.[89] Under state law localities may not impose a separate sales tax.[90] Exemptions from Maryland's sales-and-use tax include, among other items, prescription and non-prescription drugs, unprepared food and pet food, school lunches, and thrift shop purchases.[91]

Selective Sales

Selective sales taxes make up 12.2% of Maryland's total revenue.[92] Of that amount, 3.3%[93] comes from a motor fuel sales tax imposed at a rate of $0.235 per gallon of gasoline.[94] Maryland residents paid an average of $134 per capita in state motor fuel sales taxes in 2004, an amount which ranked 21st nationally and was above the national average of $115.[95]

In 2004, sales taxes on alcoholic beverages made up 0.1% of Maryland's total tax revenue.[96] Maryland residents paid $4.83 per capita in state alcoholic beverage sales taxes in 2004, an amount which ranked 45th nationally.[97]

The tobacco product sales tax makes up 1.2% of Maryland's tax revenues and is imposed at a rate of $1.00 per pack of cigarettes.[98] Maryland residents paid $48.92 per capita in state tobacco sales taxes in 2004, an amount which ranked 22nd nationally.[99]

The remainder of Maryland's selective sales taxes makes up 7.6% of its total tax revenue. Of this amount, 2.2% represents taxes on utilities and the other 5.4% represents taxes on other specific commodities, businesses, or services not reported separately above (e.g., on contractors, lodging, lubricating oil, fuels other than motor fuel, motor vehicles, meals, soft drinks, margarine, etc.).[100]

---

88. *Id.* § 11-101.
89. *Id.* § 11- 104.
90. *Id.* § 11- 102.
91. *Id.* §§ 201 – 11-229.
92. Government Finances, *supra* note 48.
93. *Id.*
94. Md. Code Ann., Tax-Gen. § 9-305.
95. State Rankings 2006, *supra* note 1, at 327.
96. Government Finances, *supra* note 48.
97. State Rankings 2006, *supra* note 1, at 335.
98. Md. Code Ann., Tax-Gen. § 12-105
99. State Rankings 2006, *supra* note 1, at 332.

100. *See* Governments Division, U.S. Census Bureau, Government Finance and Employment Classification Manual, at ch.7 (2000), *available at* http://ftp2.census.gov/govs/class/classfull.pdf [hereinafter Classification Manual].

Corporate Income and Other

Corporate Income

The corporate income tax makes up 11.5% of Maryland's total tax revenue.[101] Maryland's broad-based corporate income tax is imposed at a rate of 7% on a corporation's taxable income,[102] which is based on the corporation's federal taxable income.[103]

Maryland follows the federal income tax treatment of S corporations. Thus, they do not pay Maryland's corporate income tax; rather, income and losses flow through to their shareholders.[104] A similar treatment is afforded to limited partnerships and limited liability partnerships, as well as limited liability companies, assuming they are treated as a partnership for federal tax purposes.[105] However, if a limited liability company is treated as a corporation for federal income tax purposes, the entity is subject to Maryland's corporate income tax.[106]

Other

During fiscal year 2004, the collection of all other taxes not previously mentioned accounted for 9.0% of Maryland's total tax revenue. Of this amount, approximately $152.3 million was generated by the estate and gift tax,[107] the liability of which is determined by the county register of the decedent.[108] The "other taxes" category is also made up of motor vehicle license taxes, documentary and stock transfer taxes, severance taxes, and all other taxes not listed separately or provided for in other categories, such as taxes on land based on a specified rate per acre (rather than on assessed value).[109]

Burden Analysis

The overall state and local tax burden on Maryland taxpayers is very regressive. Taxpayers in the lowest quintile—those with incomes of less than $19,000—bear a tax burden equal to 9.4% of their income, while taxpayers in the top 1%—those with incomes that exceed $301,000—bear a tax burden of just 7.6% of their income.[110] It is

---

101. Government Finances, *supra* note 48.
102. MD. CODE ANN., TAX-GEN. § 10-105.
103. *Id.*
104. CCH-EXP, MD-TAXRPTR ¶ 10-240, Limited Liability Companies (LLCs).
105. *Id.*
106. *Id.*
107. Government Finances, *supra* note 48.
108. MD. CODE ANN., TAX-GEN. §§ 7-101–7-309.
109. *See* CLASSIFICATION MANUAL, *supra* note 100, at ch.7.
110. *See* ROBERT S. MCINTYRE ET AL., WHO PAYS? A DISTRIBUTIONAL ANALYSIS OF THE TAX SYSTEMS IN ALL 50 STATES 56 (2d ed. 2003), *available at* http://www.itepnet.org/wp2000/text.pdf. Taxpayers in the second quintile bear a 9.0% total tax burden on incomes between $19,000 and $33,000; those in the third quintile bear a 9.5% tax burden on incomes between $33,000 and

also worth noting that, although Maryland obviously has no control over federal tax policy, federal itemized deductions for state and local personal income and property taxes nonetheless further reduce the burden on taxpayers in the top 1% to 5.1%.[111] Furthermore, between 1989 and 2002, the tax burden on the bottom quintile rose by approximately 1.0%, while the burden on the top 1% actually fell by 0.4%.[112]

In terms of the income tax, the burden across income groups in Maryland is slightly progressive, with taxpayers in the lowest quintile bearing a tax burden of 2.3% and those in the top 1% bearing a tax burden of 6.0%.[113] In contrast, however, the sales and excises taxes imposed by Maryland are very regressive, with taxpayers in the lowest quintile bearing a tax burden of 5.1% and those in the top 1% bearing a tax burden of just 0.6%.[114] Although not purely regressive, property taxes in Maryland place a somewhat higher burden on the middle class, who bear an average tax burden of 2.1% compared with taxpayers in the lowest quintile, who bear a burden of 2.0%, and compared with taxpayers in the highest quintile, who bear an average burden of 1.7%.[115]

$51,000; those in the fourth quintile bear a 9.6% tax burden on incomes between $51,000 and $84,000; those in the 80th–95th percentiles bear a 9.2% tax burden on incomes between $84,000 and $160,000; finally, those in the 96th–99th percentiles bear a 8.6% tax burden on incomes between $160,000 and $301,000. *Id.*

111. *Id.* Taxpayers in the lowest quintile did not receive any benefit from these federal offsets, while those in the second quintile were able to reduce their individual tax burdens by 0.2%, those in the third quintile by 0.7%, those in the fourth quintile by 1.2%, those in the 80th–95th percentiles by 1.8%, and those in the 96th–99th percentiles by 2.2%. *Id.*

112. *Id.* at 57.

113. *See id.* at 56. Taxpayers in the second quintile bear a 3.4% income tax burden; those in the third quintile bear a 4.5% burden; those in the fourth quintile bear a 4.9% burden; those in the 80th–95th percentiles bear a 5.3% burden; finally, those in the 96th–99th percentiles bear a 5.5% burden. *Id.* Note, however, that these percentages include both individual and corporate income tax burdens; that within the 96th–99th percentiles, corporate income taxes represent 0.1% of this burden; and that in the top 1%, corporate income taxes represent 0.1% of this burden. *Id.*

114. *See id.*.Taxpayers in the second quintile bear a 3.7% sales-and-excise tax burden; those in the third quintile bear a 2.9% burden; those in the fourth quintile bear a 2.3% burden; those in the 80th–95th percentiles bear a 1.7% burden; finally, those in the 96th–99th percentiles bear a 1.2% burden. *Id.*

115. *See id.* Taxpayers in the second quintile bear a 1.8% property tax burden; those in the third quintile bear a 2.1% burden; those in the fourth quintile bear a 2.4% burden; those in the 80th–95th percentiles bear a 2.2% burden; those in the 96th–99th percentiles bear a 1.9% burden; finally, those in the top 1% bear a 1.0% burden. *Id.*

Massachusetts

General Information

Basic Profile – Geography, Population, and Industry

Admitted to the Union in 1788, Massachusetts is commonly referred to as the "Bay State."[1] It is located in the northeastern region and is bordered by New Hampshire and Vermont on the north; New York on the west; Connecticut and Rhode Island on the south; and the Atlantic Ocean on the east. Massachusetts is located in the eastern time zone, and its capital is Boston.[2]

Massachusetts ranks 14th in population (approximately 6.4 million residents) and 44th in total area (10,555 square miles).[3] Its population is 86.7% white and 6.9% black.[4] The state is 44% Catholic; 25% Protestant; and 2% Jewish; 29% claim a religion outside the Judeo-Christian tradition or no religion at all.[5] Massachusetts is almost entirely urban, with 99.6% of the population living in cities and towns.[6] Major industries include agriculture, forestry, and fishing; construction; manufacturing; transportation and public utilities; wholesale and retail trade; finance, insurance, and real estate; and services.[7]

---

1. State Rankings 2006, vi, 1 (Kathleen O'Leary Morgan & Scott Morgan eds., Morgan Quitno Press 2006).

2. *Id.* at vi.

3. *Id.* at 429.

4. Massachusetts Quick Facts from the U.S. Census Bureau, http://quickfacts.census.gov/qfd/states/25000.html (last visited Jan. 27, 2007). The remaining population is made up of 4.7% Asian persons; 0.3% American Indian and/or Alaska Native persons; 0.1% Native Hawaiian and other Pacific Islanders; and 1.3% persons reporting two or more races. *Id.* Additionally, 7.9% of Massachusetts's total population identify themselves as persons of Hispanic or Latino origin. *Id.* (noting that because Hispanics may be of any race, they are included within the other applicable race categories.

5. Barry A. Kosmin, Egon Mayer & Ariela Keysar, American Religious Identification Survey 2001, at 41, *available at* http://www.gc.cuny.edu/faculty/research_studies/aris.pdf.

6. USDA Economic Research Service, Massachusetts Fact Sheet, http://www.ers.usda.gov/StateFacts/MA.htm (last visited Sept. 17, 2006). According to the latest estimates, approximately 0.3 million people live in rural areas, and 6.4 people live in urban areas. *Id.*

7. "Massachusetts Occupational Injuries and Illnesses 2002," Massachusetts Department of Occupational Safety, http://www.mass.gov/dos/stats/osh2002_private_industy.pdf (last visited Nov. 12, 2006).

Family Income and Poverty Indicators

In 2004, Massachusetts's per capita gross product was $49,599, which ranked among the top ten states nationally and was above the national average of $39,725.[8] During this same period, although the median household income in Massachusetts was $52,354,[9] 9.8% of Massachusetts's population was living in poverty, which was below the national average of 12.4%.[10] More specifically, poverty affected 12.2% of Massachusetts's children,[11] 8.7% of its senior citizens,[12] and 7.1% of its families.[13] Of its female-headed households with children, 35.1% lived in poverty,[14] and 27.2% of the state's public elementary and secondary school students were eligible for free or reduced-price meals.[15] Of those living in poverty, approximately 11.9% were black, which represented 19.8% of Massachusetts's black population and 1.1% of its total population.[16] In an attempt to combat this poverty, Massachusetts spent approximately $5.7 billion on public welfare programs in 2002,[17] which made up 13.5% of its total government expenditures.[18]

Massachusetts's Public Elementary-Secondary School System

Overall Spending and Performance

For the 2003–2004 school year, Massachusetts spent $10,693 per pupil in its public elementary-secondary school system, which was substantially above the national average of $8,182.[19] Of this amount, 6.5% was provided by the federal government, 39.8% was provided by the state government, and 53.6% was provided by the local governments,[20] with property taxes making up a substantial part of the total funding.[21] Out of these

---

8. State Rankings 2006, *supra* note 1, at 89.

9. *Id.* at 96.

10. *Id.* at 495.

11. *Id.* at 497.

12. *Id.* at 496.

13. *Id.* at 498.

14. *Id.* at 499.

15. *Id.* at 532.

16. *See* Fact Sheet, American FactFinder, http://factfinder.census.gov/home/saff/main.html?_lang=en (select "Massachusetts" under "Get a Fact Sheet for your community") (last visited Feb. 16, 2007). Note that these numbers are based on the 2000 census because more recent numbers were not available.

17. State Rankings 2006, *supra* note 1, at 500.

18. *Id.* at 502.

19. Governments Division, U.S. Census Bureau, Public Education Finances 2004, at 8 tbl.8 (2006).

20. *See id.* at 5 tbl.5.

21. Although none of the total funding has been specifically designated as provided by property taxes, 43% of the total funding comes from "Parent Government Contributions," *see id.* at 4 tbl.4., which are defined as "tax receipts and other amounts appropriated by a parent government

funds, Massachusetts paid its elementary and secondary school teachers an estimated average annual salary of $54,596 during the 2004–2005 school year,[22] and it provided a student/teacher ratio of 13.6, which was better than the national average of 15.9.[23]

In academic performance, Massachusetts's fourth grade students scored higher than the national average in mathematics,[24] reading,[25] science,[26] and writing,[27] and its eighth graders scored higher than the national average in mathematics,[28] reading,[29] science,[30] and writing.[31]

Equity Issues

In 2004, the funding per student in Massachusetts's highest poverty districts actually exceeded that in its lowest poverty districts by $1,299,[32] although when adjustments were made for the additional costs of educating students growing up in poverty that excess narrowed to $694.[33] Similarly, Massachusetts spent $1,663 more per student in its highest minority districts, although this amount fell to $1,139 when adjustments for low-income students were made.[34]

Fourth graders eligible for free or reduced-price school lunches had test scores that were 9% lower in mathematics,[35] 11.7% lower in reading,[36] and 14.7% lower in writing[37] than those of students who were not eligible. The results were generally better for

---

and transferred to its dependent school system." *Id.* at app. A-1. This amount, however, "[e]xcludes intergovernmental revenue, current charges, and miscellaneous general revenue." *Id.*

22. Thomas D. Snyder et al., National Center for Education Statistics, Digest of Education Statistics 2005, at 116 tbl.77 (2006).

23. *Id.* at 98 tbl.65.

24. National Center for Education Statistics, U.S. Department of Education, The Nation's Report Card: Mathematics 2005, at 14 fig.11 (2005), *available at* http://nces.ed.gov/nationsreportcard/pdf/main2005/ 2006453.pdf [hereinafter Mathematics 2005].

25. National Center for Education Statistics, U.S. Department of Education, The Nation's Report Card: Reading 2005, at 14 fig.11 (2005), *available at* http://nces.ed.gov/nationsreportcard/pdf/main2005/2006451.pdf [hereinafter Reading 2005].

26. National Center for Education Statistics, U.S. Department of Education, The Nation's Report Card: Science 2005, at 16 fig.12 (2006), *available at* http://nces.ed.gov/nationsreportcard//pdf/main2005/2006466.pdf [hereinafter Science 2005].

27. Hilary R. Persky et al., National Center for Education Statistics, U.S. Department of Education, The Nation's Report Card: Writing 2002, at 23 tbl.2.2 (2003), *available at* http://nces.ed.gov/nationsreportcard/pdf/main2002/2003529.pdf [hereinafter Writing 2002].

28. Mathematics 2005, *supra* note 24, at 16 fig.12.

29. Reading 2005, *supra* note 25, at 16 fig.12.

30. Science 2005, *supra* note 26, at 28 fig.22.

31. Writing 2002, *supra* note 27, at 24 tbl.2.3.

32. The Education Trust, Funding Gaps 2006, at 7 tbl.3 (2006), *available at* http://www2.edtrust.org/NR/rdonlyres/CDEF9403-5A75-437E-93FF-EBF1174181FB/0/FundingGap2006.pdf.

33. *Id.*

34. *Id.* at 7 tbl.4.

35. Mathematics 2005, *supra* note 24, at 20 tbl.5.

36. Reading 2005, *supra* note 25, at 20 tbl.5.

37. Writing 2002, *supra* note 27, at 75 tbl.3.24.

eighth graders eligible for free or reduced-price lunches; their test scores were 8.7% lower in mathematics,[38] 8.6% lower in reading,[39] and 18.4% lower in writing[40] than those of students who were not eligible.

The 1993 Education Reform Act in Massachusetts greatly increased the responsibility of the Massachusetts Commonwealth for financing education spending.[41] In 2004, public school students sued the Commissioner of Education in Massachusetts, alleging that the state was not meeting its constitutional duty to educate children, especially in poor communities.[42] The Massachusetts Supreme Court rejected this assertion and held that the state was meeting its education obligations.[43] Despite this ruling for the defendants, legislators in Massachusetts have continued to reform the state's school funding system.

Availability of Publicly Funded Prekindergarten Programs

The Massachusetts Community Partnerships for Children program focuses on serving three- and four-year-old children from working families.[44] Total enrollment in this state-funded program is 17,350,[45] which represents just 10.9% of Massachusetts's 159,162 three- and four-year-old children.[46] The federally funded Head Start program enrolls an additional 10,567 children,[47] which represents 6.6% of Massachusetts's three- and four-year-old children.[48]

Where Does Massachusetts Get Its Revenue?

At the end of fiscal year 2004, Massachusetts had total revenues of approximately $60.8 billion.[49] Of this amount, 44% was derived from state and local tax revenues and 17% was received from the federal government.[50] The remaining 39% came from other

---

38. MATHEMATICS 2005, *supra* note 24, at 21 tbl.6.

39. READING 2005, *supra* note 25, at 21 tbl.6.

40. WRITING 2002, *supra* note 27, at 76 tbl.3.25.

41. PUBLIC SCHOOL FUNDING IN MASSACHUSETTS (2002), at 2, *available at* http://www.mass-budget.org/publicschool.pdf.

42. Hancock v. Comm'r of Educ., 822 N.E. 2d 1134, 1138 (Mass. 2005).

43. *Id.* at 1137.

44. W. STEVEN BARNETT ET AL., NATIONAL INSTITUTE FOR EARLY EDUCATION RESEARCH, THE STATE OF PRESCHOOL 2006, at 148 (2007), *available at* http://nieer.org/yearbook/pdf/year-book.pdf.

45. *Id.* at 85.

46. *See id.* at 232.

47. *Id.* at 85.

48. *See id.* at 232.

49. U.S. Census Bureau, State and Local Government Finances 2003–04, http://www.census.gov/govs/www/estimate04.html (last visited Oct. 6, 2006) [hereinafter Government Finances].

50. *Id.*

sources, including the Massachusetts Lottery, insurance trust revenue, and revenue from government-owned utilities and other commercial or auxiliary enterprises.[51]

Tax Revenue

Massachusetts collected approximately $27 billion in state and local tax revenue during fiscal year 2004.[52] As a result, Massachusetts residents paid $4,217 per capita in state and local taxes, an amount which ranked 5th nationally.[53] The different types of tax sources were apportioned as follows:

Individual income taxes	32.7%
Property taxes	36.3%
General and selective sales taxes	21.2%
Corporate income and other taxes	9.8%
	100.0%[54]

Federal Funding

During fiscal year 2004, 17% of Massachusetts's total revenues came from the federal government.[55] For every dollar of federal taxes paid, Massachusetts received $0.77 in federal funding, an amount which ranked 44th nationally[56] and was well below the national median of $1.17.[57]

Lottery

The Massachusetts Lottery has been in operation since 1971.[58] The proceeds of the Lottery are deposited into the Massachusetts Lottery Fund, which disburses the net balance to the Local Aid Fund and the state's general fund.[59] In 2005, the Massachusetts Lottery had operating revenues of $1.02 billion and a net income of $936 million,[60]

---

51. *Id.*

52. The total tax revenues were collected as follows: $16.9 billion by the state and 10.1 billion by local governments. *See id.*

53. *See id.*

54. *Id.*

55. *Id.*

56. The Tax Foundation, Federal Spending Received Per Dollar of Taxes Paid by State 2004, http://www.taxfoundation.org/taxdata/show/266.html (last visited Sept. 17, 2006).

57. *See id.*

58. Massachusetts State Lottery Commission Information Packet, http://www.masslottery .com/StudentGuide/studentpack.htm (last visited Dec. 16, 2006).

59. Mass. Gen. Laws Ann. ch. 10, §35.

60. Massachusetts State Lottery Annual Report FY2005, 6, *available at* http://www.masslottery .com/pdfs/AnnualReport2005.pdf (last visited Dec. 16, 2006).

$736 million of which was transferred to the Local Aid Fund and $200 million of which was transferred to the general fund.[61]

Legal Structure of Major Tax Sources

Income

Massachusetts has a broad-based income tax that uses adjusted gross income for federal income tax purposes, with very few adjustments, [62] as a starting point for determining the state's taxable income.[63] Massachusetts has no provisions authorizing a local income tax.[64] During fiscal year 2004, Massachusetts collected individual income tax of $1,378 per capita, an amount which ranked 1st nationally.[65]

On the basis of the relevant statutory exemptions, a typical family of four (i.e., married taxpayers who file jointly and have two dependent children) are not required to pay any income tax until their combined income exceeds $26,200, an amount which is above the national poverty line of $20,615.[66]

Massachusetts's income tax structure contains three types of income: Part A gross income comprised of taxable interest (except interest received by pawnbrokers and Massachusetts bank interest), dividends, and capital gains income (comprised of gains from the sale or exchange of capital assets held for one year or less); Part C gross income comprised of capital gains income comprised of gains from the sale or exchange of capital assets held for more than one year; and Part B gross income comprised of income which is not Part A gross income or Part C gross income.[67] Massachusetts applies a flat tax rate to each type of income, which is currently 5.3% for all income (Part B, Part C, and Part A interest and dividends), except for Part A capital gains income, which is taxed at 12%.[68] When statutory exemptions and the filing threshold are taken into account, the flat rate applies to every dollar of income exceeding $25,550.[69]

---

61. *Id* at 8.

62. Mass. Gen. Laws Ann. ch. 62, § 2 .

63. *Id.* § 1.

64. CCH-EXP, MA-TAXRPTR ¶ 18-510, Local Power to Tax.

65. State Rankings 2006, *supra* note 1, at 321.

66. Jason A. Levitis, Center on Budget and Policy Priorities, The Impact of State Income Taxes on Low-Income Families in 2006, at 12 (2007). In 2006, Massachusetts taxpayers who were married and filing jointly were subject to a filing threshold of $15,300 and could claim, personal exemptions of $4,125 each and dependent exemptions of $1,000 each. Mass. Gen. Laws Ann. ch. 62, § 5. There is no standard deduction offered in Massachusetts. Note, however, that the threshold calculation of $26,200 is greater than the sum of these exemptions because it includes additional tax benefits available to low-income families, such as the earned-income tax credit. *See* Levitis, *supra*.

67. CCH-EXP, MA-TAXRPTR ¶ 15-001, Overview.

68. Mass. Gen. Laws Ann. ch. 62, § 4.

69. The filing threshold, two exemptions, and two dependent exemptions of $15,300, $4,125 and $1,000, respectively, equals $25,500. *See supra* notes 66–68.

Property

Overview

Massachusetts has a typical property tax system that taxes the value of real estate and tangible personal property mainly at the local level.[70] During fiscal year 2004, Massachusetts collected approximately $9.8 billion dollars in property taxes at the local level and $51,000 at the state level.[71] As a result, Massachusetts residents paid $1,532 per capita in state and local property taxes, an amount which ranked 7th nationally.[72]

Defining the Real Property Tax Base

Massachusetts has four classifications for real property: residential, open space, commercial, and industrial.[73] Real property is assessed at 100% fair cash value, but current use value is used for qualifying property, such as agricultural property.[74] Fair cash value is generally determined by the application of standard appraisal methods, including the cost method, the income method, and the market-data method, all of which are commonly used throughout the country.[75] State law requires that all real property be assessed every year.[76]

Real Property Tax Rates

Real property tax rates, composed of state, county, city, and district rates, vary and are set by each locality.[77] Taxes are levied as a percentage of the fair cash value and are collected at the local level.[78] Total taxes on real and personal property within a particular city or town must not, in any fiscal year, exceed 2.5% of the full and fair cash value of the property.[79] The real property tax rates vary according to locality. During fiscal year 2004, for residential property, the highest rate was 18.08% in Heath, and the lowest rate was 1.87% in Chilmark; for open-space property, the highest rate was 14.25% in Pittsfield, compared with no tax at all in Lenox; for commercial property, the highest rate was 32.59% in West Springfield, and the lowest rate was 1.87% in Chilmark; for industrial property, the highest rate was 32.59% in West Springfield, and the lowest rate was 1.87% in Chilmark.[80]

---

70. MASS. GEN. LAWS ANN. ch. 59, §§ 2,5.
71. Government Finances, *supra* note 49.
72. *See id.*
73. MASS. GEN. LAWS ANN. ch. 59, § 2A.
74. *Id.*, MASS. GEN. LAWS ANN. ch. 61A, § 4.
75. *Id.* ch. 59, § 2A.
76. *Id.*
77. *Id.* § 26.
78. *Id.* ch. 60, § 2.
79. *Id.* ch. 59, § 21C.
80. Massachusetts Department of Revenue Division of Local Services Communities with Approved Tax Rates for FY 2007 as of 12/16/06, http://www.dls.state.ma.us/TaxRates/taxrate.pdf (last visited Dec. 17, 2006). [hereinafter Approved Tax Rates].

Personal and Intangible Property

Massachusetts imposes a tax on personal property at the fair cash value of the property.[81] Intangible personal property is not subject to tax at either the state or local level.[82] The personal property tax rate varies according to locality, with the highest personal property rate 32.59% in West Springfield and the lowest 1.87% in Chilmark.[83]

Exemptions

Household goods are exempt from tax as long as the goods are in the residence that is the taxpayer's domicile[84] Massachusetts does not provide for a general homestead exemption, but cities and towns may allow an exemption for the personal residence of a taxpayer equal to not more than 20% (30% in the cities of Cambridge, Somerville, and Boston) of the average assessed valuation of all Class One residential parcels in the city or town.[85]

General and Selective Sales

General Sales

Massachusetts imposes a general retail sales-and-use tax, which makes up 13.9% of Massachusetts's total revenue.[86] This tax is imposed on all tangible personal property, services,[87] and hotel and motel stays.[88] The state sales tax rate is set at 5%.[89] Massachusetts has no provisions authorizing a local sales tax.[90] Major exemptions from Massachusetts sales tax include food products (except those sold in restaurants); clothing up to $175; purchases made on food stamps; prescription drugs and prescribed medical equipment or devices; certain enumerated farm and agricultural equipment, supplies, and livestock; and equipment and computers.[91]

Selective Sales

Selective sales taxes make up 7.4% of Massachusetts's total revenue.[92] Of that amount, 2.5% comes from a motor fuel sales tax imposed at a rate of $0.229 per gal-

---

81. MASS. GEN. LAWS ANN. ch. 59, § 18, CCH-EXP, MA-TAXRPTR ¶ 20-295, Personal Property.

82. MASS. GEN. LAWS ANN..ch. 59, § 5.

83. Approved Tax Rates, *supra* note 80.

84. MASS. GEN. LAWS ANN. ch. 59, § 5.

85. *Id.* § 5C.

86. Government Finances, *supra* note 49.

87. MASS. GEN. LAWS ANN. ch. 64H, § 2; *Id.* ch. 64I, § 2.

88. MASS. GEN. LAWS ANN. ch. 64G, § 3.

89. MASS. GEN. LAWS ANN. ch. 64H, § 2; *Id.* ch. 64I, § 2.

90. CCH-EXP, MA-TAXRPTR ¶ 61-710, Local Power to Tax.

91. MASS. GEN. LAWS ANN. ch. 64G, § 6.

92. Government Finances, *supra* note 49.

lon of gasoline.[93] Massachusetts residents paid an average of $107 per capita in state motor fuel sales taxes in 2004, an amount which ranked 41st nationally and was below the national average of $115.[94]

In 2004, sales taxes on alcoholic beverages made up 0.3% of Massachusetts's total tax revenue.[95] Massachusetts residents paid $10.69 per capita in state alcoholic beverage sales taxes in 2004, an amount which ranked 32nd nationally.[96]

The tobacco product sales tax makes up 1.6%[97] of Massachusetts's total tax revenue and is imposed at a rate of 90% of the wholesale sale price of smokeless tobacco products.[98] Cigars and loose tobacco are taxed at 30% of the wholesale price, while cigarettes are taxed at 75.5 mills ($1.51) per pack of 20.[99] Massachusetts residents paid $66.40 per capita in state tobacco sales taxes in 2004, an amount which ranked 11th nationally.[100]

The remainder of Massachusetts's selective sales taxes makes up 3.0% of its total tax revenue. This amount represents taxes on other specific commodities, businesses, or services not reported separately above (e.g., on contractors, lodging, lubricating oil, fuels other than motor fuel, motor vehicles, meals, soft drinks, margarine, etc.).[101]

Corporate Income and Other

Corporate Income

Massachusetts does not impose a corporate income tax; rather, it imposes a corporate excise tax for the privilege of doing business in the state, which is partly based on income and partly based on net worth.[102] The corporate excise tax makes up 4.8% of Massachusetts's total tax revenue.[103] The income portion of the corporate excise tax is imposed at a rate of 9.5% on the Massachusetts-sourced net income of corporations doing business within Massachusetts or receiving income from property located in Massachusetts.[104] The property portion of the tax is imposed at the rate of $2.60 per $1,000 of value subject to tax, which is the average value of real and tangible property owned or rented and used in Massachusetts, divided by the average value of real and tangible property owned or rented and used everywhere else.[105]

---

93. MASS. GEN. LAWS ANN. ch. 64A, § 1.

94. STATE RANKINGS 2006, *supra* note 1, at 327.

95. Government Finances, *supra* note 49.

96. STATE RANKINGS 2006, *supra* note 1, at 334.

97. Government Finances, *supra* note 49.

98. MASS. GEN. LAWS ANN. ch. 64C, § 6; *Id.* § 7A.

99. *Id.*

100. STATE RANKINGS 2006, *supra* note 1, at 332.

101. *See* GOVERNMENTS DIVISION, U.S. CENSUS BUREAU, GOVERNMENT FINANCE AND EMPLOYMENT CLASSIFICATION MANUAL, at ch.7 (2000), *available at* http://ftp2.census.gov/govs/class/classfull.pdf [hereinafter CLASSIFICATION MANUAL].

102. CCH-EXP, MA-TAXRPTR ¶ 10-005, Overview.

103. Government Finances, *supra* note 49.

104. MASS. GEN. LAWS ANN. ch. 63, § 32; *Id.* § 39.

105. *Id.* § 31B.

Massachusetts follows the federal income tax treatment of S corporations. Thus, they are not subject to the income portion of the corporate excise tax; rather, income and losses flow through to their shareholders.[106] S corporations are, however, subject to the property portion of the excise tax. The corporation excise tax does not apply to limited partnerships, limited liability partnerships,[107] or limited liability companies, assuming they are treated as a partnership for federal tax purposes.[108] If, however, a limited liability company is treated as a corporation for federal income tax purposes, the entity is subject to Massachusetts's corporate excise tax.[109]

Other

During fiscal year 2004, the collection of all other taxes not previously mentioned accounted for 4.9% of Massachusetts's total tax revenue.[110] Of this amount, $195 million[111] was generated by the estate tax. The estate tax is applied to all estates over $1,000,000 in value in years after 2006 and is not based on the federal credit.[112] The maximum marginal rate for the estate tax is 16%.[113] The "other taxes" category is also made up of motor vehicle license taxes, documentary and stock transfer taxes, severance taxes, and all other taxes not listed separately or provided for in other categories, such as taxes on land based on a specified rate per acre (rather than on assessed value).[114]

Burden Analysis

The overall state and local tax burden on Massachusetts's taxpayers is very regressive. Taxpayers in the lowest quintile—those with incomes of less than $19,000—bear a tax burden equal to 9.3% of their income, while taxpayers in the top 1%—those with incomes that exceed $413,000—bear a tax burden of just 6.8% of their income.[115] It

---

106. MASS. GEN. LAWS ANN. ch. 63, § 32D.

107. *Id.* ch. 62, § 17.

108. *Id.*

109. *Id.*

110. Government Finances, *supra* note 49.

111. *Id.*

112. MASS. GEN. LAWS ANN. ch. 65, §§ 1,25,26.

113. *Id.* § 2. The marginal tax rate applies as follows: 5% up to $50,000; 7% between $50,001 and $100,000; 9% between $100,001 and $200,000; 10% between $200,001 and $400,000; 11% between $400,001 and $600,000; 12% between $600,001 and $800,000; 13% between $800,001 and 1,000,000; 14% between $1,000,001 and $2,000,000; 15% between $2,000,001 and $4,000,000; and 16% over $4,000,000. *Id.*

114. *See* CLASSIFICATION MANUAL, *supra* note 101, at ch.7.

115. *See* ROBERT S. MCINTYRE ET AL., WHO PAYS? A DISTRIBUTIONAL ANALYSIS OF THE TAX SYSTEMS IN ALL 50 STATES 58 (2d ed. 2003), *available at* http://www.itepnet.org/wp2000/text.pdf. Taxpayers in the second quintile bear a 9.2% total tax burden on incomes between $19,000 and $34,000; those in the third quintile bear a 9.2% tax burden on incomes between $34,000 and $56,000; those in the fourth quintile bear a 9.3% tax burden on incomes between $56,000 and

is also worth noting that, although Massachusetts obviously has no control over federal tax policy, federal itemized deductions for state and local personal income and property taxes nonetheless further reduce the burden on taxpayers in the top 1% to 4.6%.[116] Furthermore, between 1989 and 2002, the tax burden on the bottom quintile rose by approximately 0.2%, while the burden on the top 1% fell by 1.5%.[117]

In terms of the income tax, the burden across income groups in Massachusetts is slightly progressive, with taxpayers in the lowest quintile bearing a tax burden of 0.9% and those in the top 1% bearing a tax burden of 5.1%.[118] In contrast, however, the sales and excises taxes imposed by Massachusetts are very regressive, with taxpayers in the lowest quintile bearing a tax burden of 5.4% and those in the top 1% bearing a tax burden of just 0.6%.[119] Property taxes in Massachusetts are also regressive, with taxpayers in the lowest quintile bearing a tax burden of 3.0% and those in the top quintile bearing an average tax burden of 2.1%.[120]

$90,000; those in the 80th–95th percentiles bear a 8.8% tax burden on incomes between $90,000 and $182,000; and those in the 96th–99th percentiles bear a 8.2% tax burden on incomes between $182,000 and $413,000. *Id.*

116. *Id.* Taxpayers in the lowest quintile did not receive any benefit from these federal offsets, while those in the second quintile were able to reduce their individual tax burdens by 0.1%, those in the third quintile by 0.6%, those in the fourth quintile by 1.1%, those in the 80th–95th percentiles by 1.6%, and those in the 96th–99th percentiles by 2.0%. *Id.*

117. *Id.* at 59.

118. *See id.* at 58. Taxpayers in the second quintile bear a 2.9% income tax burden; those in the third quintile bear a 3.5% burden; those in the fourth quintile bear a 3.8% burden; those in the 80th–95th percentiles bear a 4.3% burden; finally, those in the 96th–99th percentiles bear a 4.6% burden. *Id.* Note, however, that these percentages include both individual and corporate income tax burdens; that within the 96th–99th percentiles, corporate income taxes represent 0.1% of this burden; and that in the top 1%, corporate income taxes represent 0.2% of this burden. *Id.*

119. *See id.* Taxpayers in the second quintile bear a 3.9% sales-and-excise tax burden; those in the third quintile bear a 2.9% burden; those in the fourth quintile bear a 2.3% burden; those in the 80th–95th percentiles bear a 1.8% burden; finally, those in the 96th–99th percentiles bear a 1.2% burden. *Id.*

120. *See id.* Taxpayers in the second quintile bear a 2.5% property tax burden; those in the third quintile bear a 2.8% burden; those in the fourth quintile bear a 3.1% burden; those in the 80th–95th percentiles bear a 2.8% burden; those in the 96th–99th percentiles bear a 2.4% burden; finally, those in the top 1% bear a 1.1% burden. *Id.*

Michigan

General Information

Basic Profile – Geography, Population, and Industry

Admitted to the Union in 1837,[1] Michigan is known as the "Great Lake State,"[2] but it is also sometimes called "the Wolverine State."[3] Michigan is located in the Great Lakes region and is made up of two peninsulas.[4] It is bordered on the north by Lake Superior (and beyond that, Canada); on the east by Ontario, Canada, Lake Huron, and Lake Erie; on the south by Ohio and Indiana; and on the west by Lake Michigan and Wisconsin.[5] All of Michigan, except for four counties in the Upper Peninsula that border Wisconsin, is located in the eastern time zone; the four counties—Gogebic, Iron, Dickinson, and Menominee—are located in the central time zone.[6] The state capital is Lansing.[7]

In 2005, Michigan ranked 8th in population (approximately 10.1 million residents);[8] it ranks 11th in total area (approximately 96,715 square miles).[9] Its population is 81.3% white and 14.3% black.[10] The state is 23% Catholic; 52% Protestant; and 1% Jewish;

---

1. STATE RANKINGS 2006, vi, 1 (Kathleen O'Leary Morgan & Scott Morgan, eds., Morgan Quitno Press, 2006).

2. *Id.*

3. Michigan Historic Arts and Libraries, Michigan FAQ, http://www.michigan.gov/hal/0,1607,7-160-15481_20826_20829-54118—,00.html (last visited November 2, 2006).

4. *Id.* These peninsulas are referred to as the Upper and Lower Peninsulas.

5. *Id.*

6. *Id.*

7. *Id.*

8. STATE RANKINGS 2006, *supra* note 1, at 429

9. *Id.* at 225. Of this total area, 56,804 square miles is land area and the remainder is water area. U.S. Census Bureau, State and County Quick Facts, http://quickfacts.census.gov/qfd/index.html (last visited November 2, 2006) (click on "Michigan" on the map and scroll to bottom). Michigan, on the other hand, claims a total area of 97,990 square miles, the difference being that Michigan claims 58,110 square miles of land area. Michigan Historic Arts and Libraries, Michigan in Brief, http://www.michigan.gov/hal/0,1607,7-160-15481_20826_20829-56001-,00.html (last visited November 2, 2006) (hereinafter Michigan in Brief).

10. Michigan QuickFacts from the U.S. Census Bureau, http://quickfacts.census.gov/qfd/states/26000.html (last visited January 29, 2007). Other races include 0.6% American Indian and Alaska Native persons; 2.2% Asian persons; and 1.6% persons reporting two or more races. *Id.* Persons of Hispanic or Latino origin make up 3.8% of the population. *Id.* (noting that because Hispanics may be of any race, they are included within the other applicable race categories).

24% claim a religion outside the Judeo-Christian tradition or no religion at all.[11] Michigan is primarily urban, with approximately 84.1% living in cities and towns.[12] Major industries include auto and other manufacturing, tourism, and agriculture.[13]

Family Income and Poverty Indicators

In 2004, Michigan's per capita gross product was $36,833, which was below the national average of $39,725.[14] During this same period, although the median household income in Michigan was $44,476,[15] 12.1% of the state's population was living in poverty, which was just below the national poverty rate of 12.4%.[16] More specifically, poverty affected 17.2% of Michigan's children,[17] 7.9% of its senior citizens,[18] and 9.0% of its families.[19] Of its female-headed households with children, 37.4% lived in poverty,[20] and 32.5% of the state's public elementary and secondary school students were eligible for free or reduced-price meals.[21] Of those living in poverty, approximately 33.1% were black, which represented 24.0% of Michigan's black population and 3.4% of its total population.[22] In an attempt to combat this poverty, Michigan spent approximately $9.8 billion on public welfare programs in 2002,[23] which made up 16.2% of its total government expenditures.[24]

Michigan's Public Elementary-Secondary School System

Overall Spending and Performance

For the 2003–2004 school year Michigan spent $9,072 per pupil in its public elementary-secondary school system, which was slightly above the national average of

---

11. BARRY A. KOSMIN, EGON MAYER & ARIELA KEYSAR, AMERICAN RELIGIOUS IDENTIFICATION SURVEY 2001, at 40, *available at* http://www.gc.cuny.edu/faculty/research_studies/aris.pdf.

12. USDA Economic Research Service, Michigan Fact Sheet, http://www.ers.usda.gov/StateFacts/MI.htm (last visited Sept. 17, 2006).

13. Michigan in Brief, *supra* note 9.

14. STATE RANKINGS 2006, *supra* note 1, at 89.

15. *Id.* at 96.

16. *Id.* at 495.

17. *Id.* at 497.

18. *Id.* at 496.

19. *Id.* at 498.

20. *Id.* at 499.

21. *Id.* at 532.

22. *See* Fact Sheet, American FactFinder, http://factfinder.census.gov/home/saff/main.html?_lang=en (select "Michigan" under "Get a Fact Sheet for your community") (last visited Feb. 16, 2007). Note that these numbers are based on the 2000 census because more recent numbers were not available.

23. *Id.* at 500.

24. *Id.* at 502.

$8,182.[25] Of this amount, 7.9% was provided by the federal government, 62.0% was provided by the state government, and 30.0% was provided by the local governments,[26] with property taxes making up 24.4% of the total funding.[27] Out of these funds, Michigan paid its elementary and secondary school teachers an estimated average annual salary of $54,412 during the 2004–2005 school year,[28] but during the fall of 2003, it provided a student teacher ratio of 18.1, which was worse than the national average of 15.9.[29]

In academic performance, Michigan's fourth grade students scored lower than the national average in writing[30] and higher than the national average in mathematics,[31] reading,[32] and science,[33] while Michigan's eighth graders scored lower than the national average in mathematics[34] and writing,[35] and higher than the national average in reading[36] and science.[37]

Equity Issues

In 2004, revenues spent per student in Michigan's highest poverty districts were determined to be $573 less than the revenues spent in its lowest poverty districts.[38] When adjustments were made for the additional costs of educating students growing up in poverty, however, the funding gap grew to $1,072.[39] On the other hand, Michigan spent

---

25. GOVERNMENTS DIVISION, U.S. CENSUS BUREAU, PUBLIC EDUCATION FINANCES 2004, at 8 tbl.8 (2006).

26. *See id.* at 5 tbl.5.

27. *See id.* at 4 tbl.4.

28. THOMAS D. SNYDER ET AL., NATIONAL CENTER FOR EDUCATION STATISTICS, DIGEST OF EDUCATION STATISTICS 2005, at 116 tbl.77 (2006).

29. *Id.* at 98 tbl.65.

30. HILARY R. PERSKY ET AL., NATIONAL CENTER FOR EDUCATION STATISTICS, U.S. DEPARTMENT OF EDUCATION, THE NATION'S REPORT CARD: WRITING 2002, at 23 tbl.2.2 (2003), *available at* http://nces.ed.gov/nationsreportcard/pdf/main2002/2003529.pdf [hereinafter WRITING 2002].

31. NATIONAL CENTER FOR EDUCATION STATISTICS, U.S. DEPARTMENT OF EDUCATION, THE NATION'S REPORT CARD: MATHEMATICS 2005, at 14 fig.11 (2005), *available at* http://nces.ed.gov/nationsreportcard/pdf/main2005/ 2006453.pdf [hereinafter MATHEMATICS 2005].

32. NATIONAL CENTER FOR EDUCATION STATISTICS, U.S. DEPARTMENT OF EDUCATION, THE NATION'S REPORT CARD: READING 2005, at 14 fig.11 (2005), *available at* http://nces.ed.gov/nationsreportcard/pdf/main2005/2006451.pdf [hereinafter READING 2005].

33. NATIONAL CENTER FOR EDUCATION STATISTICS, U.S. DEPARTMENT OF EDUCATION, THE NATION'S REPORT CARD: SCIENCE 2005, at 16 fig.12 (2006) *available at* http://nces.ed.gov/nationsreportcard//pdf/main2005/2006466.pdf [hereinafter SCIENCE 2005].

34. MATHEMATICS 2005, *supra* note 31, at 16 fig.12.

35. WRITING 2002, *supra* note 30, at 24 tbl.2.3.

36. READING 2005, *supra* note 32, at 16 fig.12.

37. SCIENCE 2005, *supra* note 33, at 28 fig.22.

38. THE EDUCATION TRUST, FUNDING GAPS 2006, at 7 tbl.3 (2006), *available at* http://www2 .edtrust.org/NR/rdonlyres/CDEF9403-5A75-437E-93FF-EBF1174181FB/0/FundingGap2006.pdf.

39. *Id.*

$68 more per student in its highest minority districts, although this amount fell to $251 when adjustments for low-income students were made.[40]

Fourth graders eligible for free or reduced-price school lunches had test scores that were 9.3% lower in mathematics,[41] 11.4% lower in reading,[42] and 14.6% lower in writing[43] than those of students who were not eligible. The results were generally better for eighth graders eligible for free or reduced-price lunches; their test scores were 9.5% lower in mathematics,[44] 7.9% lower in reading,[45] and 11.0% lower in writing[46] than those of students who were not eligible.

In the 1984 case *East Jackson Public Schools v. State of Michigan*,[47] the Michigan Court of Appeals held that: "(1) Education is not a fundamental right under Michigan's Constitution of 1963; (2) the state's obligation to provide a system of free public education under Const 1963, art 8, § 2, is not synonymous with the claimed obligation to provide equal educational (financial) support; and (3) the challenged statutory financing system for Michigan's public elementary and secondary schools does not deny plaintiff students equal protection of the laws in violation of Const 1963, art 1, § 2."[48] The court also held that the plaintiff school districts lacked standing to bring the constitutional challenges because the school districts are creations of the state.[49] Since *East Jackson Public Schools*, there have been no other major challenges to Michigan's education financing system.

Availability of Publicly Funded Prekindergarten Programs

The Michigan School Readiness Program provides preschool education services to at-risk four-year-olds.[50] Total enrollment in this state-funded program is 21,571,[51] which represents just 8.2% of Michigan's 262,212 three- and four-year-old children.[52] The federally funded Head Start program enrolls an additional 31,577 children,[53] which represents 12.0% of Michigan's three- and four-year-old children.[54]

---

40. *Id.* at 7 tbl.4.

41. MATHEMATICS 2005, *supra* note 31, at 20 tbl.5.

42. READING 2005, *supra* note 32, at 20 tbl.5.

43. WRITING 2002, *supra* note 30, at 75 tbl.3.24.

44. MATHEMATICS 2005, *supra* note 31, at 21 tbl.6.

45. READING 2005, *supra* note 32, at 21 tbl.6.

46. WRITING 2002, *supra* note 30, at 76 tbl.3.25.

47. 348 N.W.2d 303 (Mich. App. 1984).

48. *Id.* at 305–06.

49. *Id.* at 306.

50. W. STEVEN BARNETT ET AL., NATIONAL INSTITUTE FOR EARLY EDUCATION RESEARCH, THE STATE OF PRESCHOOL 2006, at 86 (2007), *available at* http://nieer.org/yearbook/pdf/yearbook.pdf.

51. *Id.* at 87.

52. *See id.* at 232.

53. *Id.* at 87.

54. *See id.* at 232.

Where Does Michigan Get Its Revenue?

At the end of fiscal year 2004, Michigan had total revenues of approximately $80.2 billion.[55] Of this amount, 42% was derived from state and local tax revenues and 19% was received from the federal government.[56] The remaining 39% came from other sources, including the Michigan Lottery, insurance trust revenue, and revenue from government-owned utilities and other commercial or auxiliary enterprises.[57]

Tax Revenue

Michigan collected approximately $33.4 billion in state and local tax revenue during fiscal year 2004.[58] As a result, Michigan residents paid $3,313 per capita in state and local taxes, an amount which ranked 24th nationally.[59] The different types of tax sources were apportioned as follows:

Individual income taxes	19.0%
Property taxes	35.8%
General and selective sales taxes	33.1%
Corporate income and other taxes	12.1%
	100.0%[60]

Federal Funding

During fiscal year 2004, 19% of Michigan's total revenues came from the federal government.[61] For every dollar of federal taxes paid, Michigan received $0.85 in federal funding, an amount which ranked 14th nationally[62] and was far below the national average of $1.17.[63]

---

55. U.S. Census Bureau, State and Local Government Finances - 2003–04, http://www.census.gov/govs/www/estimate04.html (last visited Oct. 10, 2006) [hereinafter Government Finances].

56. *Id.*

57. *Id.*

58. The total tax revenues were collected as follows: $22.6 billion by the state and 10.8 billion by local governments. *Id.*

59. *Id.*

60. *Id.*

61. *Id.*

62. The Tax Foundation, Federal Spending Received Per Dollar of Taxes Paid by State, 2004 http://www.taxfoundation.org/taxdata/show/266.html (last visited Sept. 17, 2006).

63. *See id.*

Lottery Revenue

The Michigan Lottery has been in operation since 1972.[64] Since 1981, revenues from the Michigan Lottery have been earmarked for the School Aid Fund.[65] During fiscal year 2005, the Michigan Lottery had sales of $2.07 billion and net revenues of $667.7 million.[66]

Legal Structures of Major Tax Sources

Income

Michigan employs a broad-based income tax[67] that uses adjusted gross income for federal income tax purposes as a starting point for determining the state's taxable income.[68] However, a fairly large number of adjustments may be available to various individuals in calculating this amount.[69] Michigan allows cities to impose an income tax of up to 1% on city residents and 0.5% on nonresidents.[70] During fiscal year 2004, Michigan collected individual income tax of $651 per capita, an amount which ranked 23rd nationally.[71]

In Michigan, a typical family of four (i.e., married taxpayers who file jointly and have two dependent children) are not required to pay any income tax until their combined income exceeds $14,400, an amount which is below the national poverty line of $20,615.[72] Michigan's income tax structure contains a flat tax of 3.9% imposed on all

---

64. Michigan Lottery, Michigan Lottery Through the Years, http://www.michigan.gov/lottery/0,1607,7-110-29196-4130-,00.html (last visited November 2, 2006). "On May 16, 1972, voters approve a constitutional amendment by a 2-to-1 margin, enabling the establishment of a state lottery." *Id.*

65. *Id.*

66. Michigan Lottery, Fast Facts and Figures, http://www.michigan.gov/lottery/0,1607,7-110-29196_29198—-,00.html (last visited November 2, 2006).

67. Mich. Comp. Laws § 206.110.

68. *Id.* § 206.30.

69. *Id.*

70. *Id.* at § 206.611. For a list of cities that impose these taxes, see Michigan Department of Treasury, What Cities Impose an Income Tax?, http://www.michigan.gov/taxes/0,1607,7-238-43715-153955—F,00.html (last visited January 30, 2007). Four cities—Detroit, Grand Rapids, Highland Park, and Saginaw—impose higher rates; Detroit's 2006 tax of 2.5% on residents and 1.25% on nonresidents is the highest. *Id.*; *see also* Mich. Comp. Laws § 141.503c.

71. State Rankings 2006, *supra* note 1, at 321.

72. Jason A. Levitis & Nicholas Johnson, Center on Budget and Policy Priorities, The Impact of State Income Taxes on Low-Income Families in 2006, at 12 (2007). In 2006, Michigan taxpayers who were married and filing jointly could claim personal exemptions of $3,300 (for each spouse), and dependent exemptions of $3,300 each. Michigan Department of Treasury, Taxes – New Developments for Tax Year 2006, http://www.michigan.gov/taxes/0,1607,7-238-43513_44135-159097-,00.html (last visited January 30, 2007). Note, however, that the threshold calculation of $14,400 is greater than the sum of these deductions and exemptions because it includes additional tax benefits available to low-income families, such as the

levels of income.[73] When statutory exemptions are taken into account, the income tax applies to every dollar of income exceeding $13,200.[74]

Property

Overview

Michigan has a typical property tax system that taxes the value of real estate and tangible personal property at the state and local levels.[75] During fiscal year 2004, Michigan collected approximately $9.9 billion in property tax at the local level and approximately $2.1 billion at the state level.[76] As a result, Michigan residents paid $1,186 per capita in state and local property taxes, an amount which ranked 15th in the nation.[77]

Defining the Real Property Tax Base

Real property is classified into six categories: (1) agricultural real property; (2) commercial real property; (3) developmental real property; (4) industrial real property; (5) residential real property; and (6) timber-cutover real property.[78] It is generally assessed at 50% of its true cash value.[79] The true cash value of real property is determined by the application of standard appraisal methods, including the cost method, the income method, and the market-data method.[80] Property must be valued according to the same method as other property in its category.[81]

Real Property Tax Rates

At the state level, Michigan levies a state education tax of 6 mills (1 mill = $1 per $1,000 of assessed value).[82] Tax rates imposed on real property at the local level vary by locality. In 2005, the tax rates per $1,000 of assessed value ranged from $25.04 on principal residences and $42.87 on nonprincipal residence property in Grand Rapids to $53.72 on principal residences and $71.27 on nonprincipal residence property in

---

earned-income tax credit. *See* Levitis & Johnson, *supra*. The personal and dependent exemptions are adjusted yearly for inflation. Mich. Comp. Laws § 206.30(7).

73. Mich. Comp. Laws § 206.51e.

74. Four personal and dependent exemptions of $3,300 each equal $13,200. Because Michigan has a flat tax on all levels of income, every resident starts being taxed at this point. *See supra* notes 72–73.

75. Mich. Comp. Laws. § 211.1.

76. Government Finances, *supra* note 55.

77. *Id.*

78. Mich. Comp. Laws § 211.34c(2)(a)-(f).

79. *Id.* § 211.27a(1).

80. CCH-EXP, PROP-TAX-GUIDE MI ¶ 20-615, Valuation Methods in General; True cash value is defined as "the usual selling price at the place where the property to which the term is applied is at the time of assessment, being the price that could be obtained for the property at private sale." Mich. Comp. Laws § 211.27(1).

81. Mich. Comp. Laws § 211.27(5).

82. *Id.* § 211.903. One mill equals $1 per $,1000 of assessed value.

Detroit.[83] Michigan imposes a constitutional limitation of 15 mills on localities, but counties may elect by a majority of qualified electors to impose separate limitations on the county and its townships and school districts which may not exceed 50 mills for a 20-year period.[84] These limitations do not apply to localities that have tax limitations which are provided by charter or general law.[85] School district boards may not levy taxes above 18 mills.[86]

Personal and Intangible Property

Tangible personal property is subject to taxation unless specifically exempt.[87] It is classified into five categories: (1) agricultural personal property; (2) commercial personal property; (3) industrial personal property; (4) residential personal property; and (5) utility personal property.[88] Intangible personal property is exempt from taxation.[89] Tangible personal property is valued and taxed like real property, as explained above.

Exemptions

Property owned and occupied by nonprofit religious or educational organizations and used exclusively for religious or educational purposes is constitutionally exempt from real and personal property taxation.[90] Generally, principal residences and qualified agricultural property are exempt from the school district board levies.[91] The principal residence of indigent persons[92] and a householder's personal property[93] are both exempt from property tax levies.

General and Selective Sales

General Sales

Michigan imposes a general retail sales-and-use tax, which makes up 23.6% of the state's total tax revenue.[94] The tax is imposed on all sales, leases, or rentals of tangible personal property for any purpose other than resale, sublease, or subrent.[95] Services are

---

83. CCH-EXP, PROP-TAX-GUIDE MI ¶ 20-405, Rates of Tax.

84. MICH. CONST of 1963, art. IX, § 6 (1978).

85. Id.

86. MICH. COMP. LAWS § 380.1211.

87. Id. § 211.1.

88. Id. § 211.34c(3).

89. Id. § 211.9e.

90. MICH. CONST. art. IX, § 4.

91. MICH. COMP. LAWS § 211.7cc; Id. § 211.7ee. There is no general homestead exemption, however.

92. Id. § 211.7u. "The principal residence of persons who, in the judgment of the supervisor and board of review, by reason of poverty, are unable to contribute toward the public charges is eligible for exemption in whole or in part from taxation under this act. This section does not apply to the property of a corporation." Id. § 211.7u(1).

93. MICH. COMP. LAWS § 211.9(f).

94. Government Finances, *supra* note 55.

95. MICH. COMP. LAWS § 205.51.

generally not subject to the tax,[96] but the tax is specifically imposed on lodging, telecommunications services, and the laundering or cleaning of textiles under a sale, rental, or service agreement with a term of at least five days.[97] Michigan has a statewide sales tax of 6%.[98] Until April 30, 1994, Michigan's constitution limited the statewide sales tax to 4%, but beginning May 1, 1994, it imposed an additional 2%, the proceeds of which are deposited in the state school aid fund.[99] Michigan does not have any local sales taxes.[100] Prescription drugs and unprepared food not intended for immediate consumption are constitutionally exempt from Michigan's sales-and-use tax,[101] and the residential use of electricity, natural gas, or home heating fuel is exempt from the additional 2% rate that was imposed in May 1994.[102]

Selective Sales

Selective sales taxes make up 9.5% of Michigan's total tax revenue.[103] Of that amount, 3.2%[104] comes from a motor fuel sales tax imposed at a rate of $0.19 per gallon of gasoline, $0.15 per gallon of diesel fuel, and $0.12 per gallon of gasoline that is at least 70% ethanol and diesel fuel that contains at least 5% biodiesel.[105] Michigan residents paid an average of $107 per capita in state motor fuel sales taxes in 2004, an amount which ranked 41st nationally and was just below the national average of $115.[106]

The tobacco products sales tax makes up 3.0% of Michigan's tax revenues[107] and is imposed at a rate of $2.00 per pack of 20 cigarettes and 32% of the wholesale price for cigars, noncigarette smoking tobacco, and smokeless tobacco.[108] Michigan residents paid an average of $98.26 per capita in tobacco sales taxes in 2004, an amount which ranked 2nd nationally and was well above the national average of $41.97.[109]

---

96. A sale of tangible personal property in addition to providing a service is subject to the sales tax. Michigan Department of Treasury, Sales Tax, http://www.michigan.gov/treasury/0,1607,7-121-1750_2143_2153-15477—,00.html (last visited November 5, 2006).

97. MICH. COMP. LAWS § 205.93a.

98. Id. § 205.52.

99. MICH. CONST. of 1963, art. IX, § 8 (1994). (This additional 2% does not include food ordered at a restaurant.)

100. Sales Tax, supra note 96.

101. MICH. CONST. art. IX, § 8.

102. MICH. COMP. LAWS § 205.54n; Id. § 205.94n.

103. Government Finances, supra note 55.

104. Id.

105. 2006 Mich. Pub. Acts 1074; MICH. COMP. LAWS § 207.1008. In addition to the motor fuel sales tax, the Michigan sales tax is applied to gasoline and diesel fuels. Id. § 207.1022.

106. STATE RANKINGS 2006, supra note 1, at 327.

107. Government Finances, supra note 55.

108. Mich. Comp. Laws § 205.427 (year). The $2.00 per pack of 20 cigarettes is the equivalent of the 100 mills per cigarette, or $0.10 per cigarette, imposed by the statute. The $2.00 tax on a pack of cigarettes is the third highest in the nation. STATE RANKINGS 2006, supra note 1, at 333.

109. STATE RANKINGS 2006, supra note 1, at 332.

In 2004, sales taxes on alcoholic beverages made up 0.5% of Michigan's total tax revenue.[110] Michigan residents paid $14.79 per capita in state alcoholic beverage sales taxes in 2004, an amount which ranked 23rd nationally and was just below the national average of $15.74.[111]

The remainder of Michigan's selective sales taxes make up 2.8% of its total tax revenue.[112] Of this amount, 0.3% represents taxes on utilities and the other 2.5% represents taxes on other specific commodities, businesses, or services not reported separately above (e.g., on contractors, lodging, lubricating oil, fuels other than motor fuel, motor vehicles, meals, soft drinks, margarine, etc.).[113]

Corporate Income and Other

Corporate Income

The corporate income tax makes up 5.5% of Michigan's total tax revenue.[114] The Michigan Single Business Tax is a value-added tax of 1.9%, which is imposed on "business activity," including the sale of real or personal property, property rental, and performance of a service for a fee.[115] C corporations, S corporations, partnerships, limited partnerships, and LLCs are subject to the Single Business Tax.[116]

Other

During fiscal year 2004, the collection of all other taxes not previously mentioned accounted for 6.6% of Michigan's total tax revenue.[117] Of this amount, approximately $75.5 million was generated by the estate and gift tax,[118] which is based on the maximum allowable federal credit for state death taxes paid.[119] For deaths occurring after

---

110. Government Finances, *supra* note 55.

111. STATE RANKINGS 2006, *supra* note 1, at 335.

112. Government Finances, *supra* note 55.

113. *See* GOVERNMENTS DIVISION, U.S. CENSUS BUREAU, GOVERNMENT FINANCE AND EMPLOYMENT CLASSIFICATION MANUAL, at ch.7 (2000), *available at* http://ftp2.census.gov/govs/class/classfull.pdf [hereinafter CLASSIFICATION MANUAL].

114. *Id.*

115. MICH. COMP. LAWS § 208.31; *See also* Michigan Department of Treasury, What is the Single Business Tax?, http://www.michigan.gov/treasury/0,1607,7-121-1750_2143_2153_3222-126184—,00.html (last visited November 5, 2006). The rate is to be phased out at 0.1% per year beginning January 1, 1999, but it is to be phased out only if the state's Budget Stabilization Fund balance for the fiscal year does not fall below $250 million. *Id.* The rate has stayed the same since 2003. *Id.* "When enacted in 1976 [the Single Business Tax] replaced seven separate business taxes, including the corporate income tax." *Id.*

116. MICH. COMP. LAWS § 208.6.

117. Government Finances, *supra* note 55.

118. *Id.*

119. Michigan Department of Treasury, *2005 Tax Text* 133, http://www.michigan.gov/documents/2005TTtIntroInternet_147210_7.pdf (click on "Estate Tax / Inheritance Tax" button) (last visited November 5, 2006).

December 31, 2004, Michigan will no longer apply an inheritance or estate tax.[120] The "other taxes" category is further made up of various license taxes, documentary or stock transfer taxes, severance taxes, and all other taxes not listed separately or provided for in other categories.[121]

Burden Analysis

The overall state and local tax burden on Michigan's taxpayers is extremely regressive. Taxpayers in the lowest quintile—those with incomes of less than $16,000—bear a tax burden equal to 13.3% of their income, while taxpayers in the top 1%—those with incomes that exceed $278,000—bear a tax burden of just 6.7% of their income.[122] It is also worth noting that, although Michigan obviously has no control over federal tax policy, federal itemized deductions for state and local personal income and property taxes nonetheless further reduce the burden on taxpayers in the top 1% to 5.0%.[123] Furthermore, between 1989 and 2002, the tax burden on the bottom quintile rose by approximately 2.9%, while the burden on the top 1% fell by 1.0%.[124]

In terms of the income tax, the burden across income groups in Michigan is slightly progressive, with taxpayers in the lowest quintile bearing a tax burden of 1.8% and those in the top 1% bearing a tax burden of 3.7%.[125] In contrast, however, the sales and excises taxes imposed by Michigan are extremely regressive, with taxpayers in the lowest quintile bearing a tax burden of 8.9% and those in the top 1% bearing a tax burden of just 1.4%.[126] Property taxes in Michigan are also regressive, with taxpayers in

---

120. *Id.*

121. *See* CLASSIFICATION MANUAL, *supra* note 113, at ch.7.

122. *See* ROBERT S. MCINTYRE ET AL., WHO PAYS? A DISTRIBUTIONAL ANALYSIS OF THE TAX SYSTEMS IN ALL 50 STATES 60 (2d ed. 2003), *available at* http://www.itepnet.org/wp2000/text.pdf. Taxpayers in the second quintile bear a 12.2% total tax burden on incomes between $16,000 and $29,000; those in the third quintile bear a 11.1% tax burden on incomes between $29,000 and $48,000; those in the fourth quintile bear a 10.4% tax burden on incomes between $48,000 and $76,000; those in the 80th–95th percentiles bear a 9.6% tax burden on incomes between $76,000 and $139,000; finally, those in the 96th–99th percentiles bear a 8.6% tax burden on incomes between $139,000 and $278,000. *Id.*

123. *Id.* Taxpayers in the lowest quintile did not receive any benefit from these federal offsets, while those in the second quintile were able to reduce their individual tax burdens by 0.1%, those in the third quintile by 0.4%, those in the fourth quintile by 0.7%, those in the 80th–95th percentiles by 1.3%, and those in the 96th–99th percentiles by 1.6%. *Id.*

124. *Id.* at 61.

125. *See id.* at 60. Taxpayers in the second quintile bear a 2.8% income tax burden; those in the third quintile bear a 3.1% burden; those in the fourth quintile bear a 3.4% burden; those in the 80th–95th percentiles bear a 3.6% burden; finally, those in the 96th–99th percentiles bear a 3.7% burden. *Id.*

126. *See id.* Taxpayers in the second quintile bear a 7.2% sales-and-excise tax burden; those in the third quintile bear a 5.5% burden; those in the fourth quintile bear a 4.3% burden; those in the 80th–95th percentiles bear a 3.3% burden; finally, those in the 96th–99th percentiles bear a 2.4% burden. *Id.*

the lowest quintile bearing a tax burden of 2.7% and those in the top quintile bearing an average tax burden of 1.6%.[127]

---

127. *See id.* Taxpayers in the second quintile bear a 2.2% property tax burden; those in the third quintile bear a 2.6% burden; those in the fourth quintile bear a 2.7% burden; those in the 80th–95th percentiles bear a 2.7% burden; and those in the 96th–99th percentiles bear a 2.5% burden. *Id.*

Minnesota

General Information

Basic Profile – Geography, Population, and Industry

Admitted to the Union in 1858, Minnesota is known as the "North Star State."[1] Minnesota is located in the Upper Midwest and is bordered by Canada on the north, Michigan through Lake Superior and Wisconsin on the east, Iowa on the south, and North Dakota and South Dakota on the west. The state is located in the central time zone, and its capital is St. Paul.

In 2005, Minnesota ranked 21st in population (approximately 5.1 million residents);[2] it ranks 12th in total area (86,939 square miles).[3] Its population is approximately 89.6% white and 4.3% black.[4] The state is 25% Catholic; 52% Protestant (of which 46% are Lutheran); and 1% Jewish; 22% claim a religion outside the Judeo-Christian tradition or no religion at all.[5] Approximately 72.5% of Minnesota's population lives in urban areas.[6] Major industries include agriculture (sugar beets, sweet corn, and green peas) and iron ore mining.[7]

Family Income and Poverty Indicators

In 2004, Minnesota's per capita gross product was $43,916, which ranked among the top ten states nationally and was above the national average of $39,725.[8] During

---

1. STATE RANKINGS 2006, vi & 1 (Kathleen O'Leary Morgan & Scott Morgan, eds. Morgan Quitno Press, 2006).

2. *Id.* at 429.

3. *Id.* at 225.

4. U.S. Census Bureau, Minnesota Quick Facts, http://quickfacts.census.gov/qfd/states/27000.html (last visited January 24, 2007). Other races include 3.4% Asian persons; 1.2% American Indian and Alaska Native persons; and 1.4% people reporting two or more races. *Id.* Persons of Hispanic or Latino origin make up 3.6% of the population. *Id.* (noting that because Hispanics may be of any race, they are included within the other applicable race categories).

5. BARRY A. KOSMIN, EGON MAYER & ARIELA KEYSAR, AMERICAN RELIGIOUS IDENTIFICATION SURVEY 2001, at 39, *available at* http://www.gc.cuny.edu/faculty/research_studies/aris.pdf.

6. USDA Economic Research Service, Minnesota Fact Sheet, http://www.ers.usda.gov/StateFacts/MN.htm (last visited December 19, 2006).

7. Minnesota Department of Employment and Economic Development, Wealth of Resources, http://www.deed.state.mn.us/whymn/resources.htm (last visited December 19, 2006).

8. STATE RANKINGS 2006, *supra* note 1, at 89.

this same period, although the median household income in Minnesota was $55,914,[9] 7.0% of Minnesota's population was living in poverty, which ranked among the bottom ten states nationally and was substantially below the national poverty rate of 12.4%.[10] More specifically, poverty affected 10.2% of Minnesota's children,[11] 7.7% of its senior citizens,[12] and 5.3% of its families.[13] Of its female-headed households with children, 25.5% lived in poverty ,[14] and 28.2% of the state's public elementary and secondary school students were eligible for free or reduced-price meals.[15] Of those living in poverty, approximately 11.3% were black, which represented 25.1% of Minnesota's black population and 0.9% of its total population.[16] In an attempt to combat this poverty, Minnesota spent approximately $7.5 billion on public welfare programs in 2002,[17] which made up 16.2% of its total government expenditures.[18]

Minnesota's Public Elementary-Secondary School System

Overall Spending and Performance

For the 2003–2004 school year, Minnesota spent $8,359 per pupil in its public elementary-secondary school system, which hovered around the national average of $8,182.[19] Of this amount, 6.0% was provided by the federal government, 71.4% was provided by the state government, and 22.6% was provided by the local governments,[20] with property taxes making up 13.0% of the total funding.[21] Out of these funds, Minnesota paid its elementary and secondary school teachers an estimated average annual salary of $46,906 during the 2004–2005 school year,[22] but during the fall of 2003, it provided a student/teacher ratio of 16.3, which was worse than the national average of 15.9.[23]

---

9. *Id.* at 96.

10. *Id.* at 495.

11. *Id.* at 497.

12. *Id.* at 496.

13. *Id.* at 498.

14. *Id.* at 499.

15. *Id.* at 532.

16. *See* Fact Sheet, American FactFinder, http://factfinder.census.gov/home/saff/main.html?_lang=en (select Minnesota under "Get a Fact Sheet for your community") (last visited Feb. 16, 2007). Note that these numbers are based on the 2000 census because more recent numbers where not available.

17. State Rankings 2006, *supra* note 1, at 500.

18. *Id.* at 502.

19. Governments Division, U.S. Census Bureau, Public Education Finances 2004, at 8 tbl.8 (2006).

20. *See id.* at 5 tbl.5.

21. *See id.* at 4 tbl.4.

22. Thomas D. Snyder et al., National Center for Education Statistics, Digest of Education Statistics 2005, at 116 tbl.77 (2006).

23. *Id.* at 98 tbl.65.

In academic performance, Minnesota's fourth grade students scored higher than the national average in mathematics,[24] reading,[25] science,[26] and writing,[27] while Minnesota's eighth graders scored higher than the national average in mathematics,[28] reading,[29] and science.[30]

Equity Issues

In 2004, the funding per student in Minnesota's highest poverty districts actually exceeded that in its lowest poverty districts by $1,349,[31] although when adjustments were made for the additional costs of educating students growing up in poverty, that excess narrowed to $950.[32] Similarly, Minnesota spent $898 more per student in its highest minority districts, and this amount fell to $623 when adjustments for low-income students were made.[33]

Fourth graders eligible for free or reduced-price school lunches had test scores that were 8.3% lower in mathematics,[34] 9.9% lower in reading,[35] and 8.7% lower in writing[36] than those of students who were not eligible. The results were generally the opposite for eighth graders eligible for free or reduced-price lunches; their test scores were 9.1% lower in mathematics[37] and 8.4% lower in reading[38] than those of students who were not eligible.

In the 1993 case *Skeen v. State*,[39] the plaintiff school districts and parents challenged the Minnesota education finance system on the basis that it did not "meet the state

24. NATIONAL CENTER FOR EDUCATION STATISTICS, U.S. DEPARTMENT OF EDUCATION, THE NATION'S REPORT CARD: MATHEMATICS 2005, at 14 fig.11 (2005), *available at* http://nces.ed.gov/nationsreportcard/pubs/main2005/2006453.asp [hereinafter MATHEMATICS 2005].

25. NATIONAL CENTER FOR EDUCATION STATISTICS, U.S. DEPARTMENT OF EDUCATION, THE NATION'S REPORT CARD: READING 2005, at 14 fig.11 (2005), *available at* http://nces.ed.gov/nationsreportcard/pdf/main2005/2006451.pdf [hereinafter READING 2005].

26. NATIONAL CENTER FOR EDUCATION STATISTICS, U.S. DEPARTMENT OF EDUCATION, THE NATION'S REPORT CARD: SCIENCE 2005, at 16 fig.12 (2006) *available at* http://nces.ed.gov/nationsreportcard//pdf/main2005/2006466.pdf [hereinafter SCIENCE 2005].

27. HILARY R. PERSKY ET AL., NATIONAL CENTER FOR EDUCATION STATISTICS, U.S. DEPARTMENT OF EDUCATION, THE NATION'S REPORT CARD: WRITING 2002, at 23 tbl.2.2 (2003), *available at* http://nces.ed.gov/nationsreportcard/pdf/main2002/2003529.pdf [hereinafter WRITING 2002].

28. MATHEMATICS 2005, *supra* note 24, at 16 fig.12.

29. READING 2005, *supra* note 25, at 16 fig.12.

30. SCIENCE 2005, *supra* note 26, at 28 fig.22.

31. THE EDUCATION TRUST, FUNDING GAPS 2006, at 7 tbl.3 (2006), *available at* http://www2.edtrust.org/NR/rdonlyres/CDEF9403-5A75-437E-93FF-EBF1174181FB/0/FundingGap2006.pdf.

32. *Id.*

33. *Id.* at 7 tbl.4.

34. MATHEMATICS 2005, *supra* note 24, at 20 tbl.5.

35. READING 2005, *supra* note 25, at 20 tbl.5.

36. WRITING 2002, *supra* note 27, at 75 tbl.3.24.

37. MATHEMATICS 2005, *supra* note 24, at 21 tbl.6.

38. READING 2005, *supra* note 25, at 21 tbl.6.

39. 505 N.W.2d 299.

constitutional requirement that the legislature 'establish a general and uniform system of public schools' and provide sufficient financing to 'secure a thorough and efficient system of public schools throughout the state.'"[40] The Minnesota Supreme Court held that although education is a fundamental right under the Minnesota constitution,[41] the current education funding system did not violate the education clause of the Minnesota constitution because the right to a "general and uniform system of education" is separate from the determination of whether the system's financing is "thorough and efficient."[42]

Availability of Publicly Funded Prekindergarten Programs

Minnesota funds a supplement to Head Start and Early Head Start programs that serves children from the age of three to the age of five, as well as children from birth to the age of three.[43] The School Readiness Program also provides various services for families with children of preschool age.[44] Total enrollment in this state-funded program is 2,641,[45] which represents just 2.0% of Minnesota's 130,486 three- and four-year-old children.[46] The federally funded Head Start program enrolls an additional 8,233 children,[47] which represents 6.3% of Minnesota's three- and four-year-old children."[48]

Where Does Minnesota Get Its Revenue?

At the end of fiscal year 2004, Minnesota had total revenues of approximately $43.0 billion.[49] Of this amount, 45% was derived from state and local tax revenues and 17%

---

40. *Id.* at 301.

41. *Id.* at 313.

42. *Id.* at 316 ("Thus, the evidence indicates that while strict scrutiny analysis should be applied in determining whether the legislature has met a student's fundamental right to a general and uniform *system* of public schools, a lesser standard, such as a rational basis test, should apply to the determination of whether the *financing* of such a system is 'thorough and efficient.'"). *See also* Minnesota, STARTINGAT3.ORG, http://www.startingat3.org/state_laws/statelawsMNdetail.html#toc44.

43. W. STEVEN BARNETT ET AL., NATIONAL INSTITUTE FOR EARLY EDUCATION RESEARCH, THE STATE OF PRESCHOOL 2006, at 88 (2007), *available at* http://nieer.org/yearbook/pdf/yearbook.pdf. Minnesota's programs follow federal Head Start performance standards.

44. *Id.*

45. *Id.* at 89.

46. *See id.* at 232.

47. *Id.* at 89.

48. *See id.* at 232.

49. U.S. Census Bureau, State and Local Government Finances - 2003–04, http://www.census.gov/govs/www/estimate04.html (last visited Oct. 17, 2006) [hereinafter Government Finances].

was received from the federal government.[50] The remaining 38% came from other sources, including the Minnesota State Lottery, insurance trust revenue, and revenue from government-owned utilities and other commercial or auxiliary enterprises.[51]

Tax Revenue

Minnesota collected approximately $19.4 billion in state and local tax revenue during fiscal year 2004.[52] As a result, Minnesota residents paid $3,811 per capita in state and local taxes, an amount which ranked 9th nationally.[53] The different types of tax sources were apportioned as follows:

Individual income taxes	29.4%
Property taxes	25.3%
General and selective sales taxes	33.8%
Corporate income and other taxes	11.5%
	100.0%[54]

Federal Funding

During fiscal year 2004, 17% of Minnesota's total revenues came from the federal government.[55] For every dollar of federal taxes paid, Minnesota received $0.69 in federal funding, an amount which ranked 46th nationally[56] and was well below the national average of $1.17.[57]

Lottery Revenue

The Minnesota State Lottery has been in operation since 1988.[58] By law, 40% of the Lottery profits are distributed to the Environment and Natural Resources Trust fund and 60% are distributed to the state's General Fund.[59] During fiscal year 2005, the Minnesota State Lottery had total operating revenues of $408 million and operating income of $78.9 million.[60]

---

50. *Id.*

51. *Id.*

52. *Id.*

53. *Id.*

54. *Id.*

55. *Id.*

56. The Tax Foundation, Federal Spending Received Per Dollar of Taxes Paid by State, 2004 http://www.taxfoundation.org/taxdata/show/266.html (last visited December 17, 2006).

57. *Id.*

58. Minnesota State Lottery, Milestones, http://www.mnlottery.com/mstones.html (last visited December 19, 2006).

59. Minnesota State Lottery, *2005 Annual Report* 6-10, *available at* http://www.mnlottery .com/ar05/AnnualReport05.pdf; Minn. Statutes § 349A.10 Subd. 5.

60. *Id.* at 27.

Legal Structure of Major Tax Sources

Income

Minnesota employs a broad-based income tax that uses adjusted gross income for federal income tax purposes as a starting point for determining the state's taxable income.[61] However, a fairly large number of adjustments may be available to various individuals in calculating this amount.[62] Localities do not have the power to impose an income tax.[63] During fiscal year 2004, Minnesota collected individual income tax of $1,120 per capita, an amount which ranked 5th nationally.[64]

In Minnesota, a typical family of four (i.e., married taxpayers who file jointly and have two dependent children) are not required to pay any income tax until their combined income exceeds $33,200, an amount which is above the national poverty line of $20,615.[65] Minnesota's income tax structure contains three tax brackets that impose a minimum marginal tax rate of 5.35% and a maximum marginal tax rate of 7.85%.[66] When statutory exemptions and the standard deduction are taken into account, the maximum marginal rate applies to every dollar of income exceeding $125,530.[67]

Property

Overview

Minnesota has a typical property tax system that taxes the value of real property at the state and local levels.[68] During fiscal year 2004, Minnesota collected approximately

---

61. MINN. STAT. § 290.01(19).

62. *Id.* §§ 290.01(19a), (19b).

63. *Id.* § 477A.016.

64. STATE RANKINGS 2006, *supra* note 1, at 321.

65. JASON A. LEVITIS & NICHOLAS JOHNSON, THE IMPACT OF STATE INCOME TAXES ON LOW-INCOME FAMILIES IN 2006 12 (2007), *available at* http://www.cbpp.org/2-22-06sfp.pdf. Minnesota does not provide for a standard deduction or personal exemptions because adjusted gross income for federal income tax purposes is the starting point; therefore, the federal standard deduction and personal exemptions are adopted. The federal standard deduction is adjusted yearly for inflation. Taxable Income Defined, 26 U.S.C.A. § 63 (year). The 2006 federal standard deduction for married couples filing jointly was $10,300. Internal Revenue Service, Publication 17 (2006), 20. Standard Deduction, http://www.irs.gov/publications/p17/ch20.html#d0e47713 (last visited January 28, 2007). The 2006 federal personal exemption was $3,300 each for taxpayer, spouse, and two dependents. Internal Revenue Service, Publication 17 (2006), 3. Personal Exemptions and Dependents, http://www.irs.gov/publications/p17/ch03.html#d0e10368 (last visited January 28, 2007). Note, however, that the threshold calculation of $33,200 is greater than the sum of these deductions and exemptions because it includes additional tax benefits available to low–income families, such as the earned-income tax credit. *See* LEVITIS & JOHNSON, *supra*.

66. MINN. STAT. § 290.06(2c). Minnesota's middle tax bracket is 7.05%. *Id.*

67. The standard deduction and exemptions of $10,300 and $13,200 (for four exemptions), respectively, plus the threshold of taxable income for the highest tax bracket of $102,030, equals $125,530. *See supra* notes 65–66.

$4.9 billion in property tax at the local level and approximately $608 million at the state level.[69] As a result, Minnesota residents paid $965 per capita in state and local property taxes, an amount which ranked 27th nationally.[70]

Defining Real Property Tax Base

Real property is divided into five classes, each of which contains various subclasses that are assessed at varying rates.[71] Market value of real property is generally determined by the application of standard appraisal methods, including the cost method, the capitalization-of-income method, the market-sales or comparison method, and the unit method.[72] Property in Minnesota must be appraised at least once every five years.[73] Minnesota's property tax system is based on the uniform valuation of property at its market value.[74]

---

68. MINN. STAT. § 272.01; MINN. STAT. § 272.02, subd. 1(8) (most personal property is exempt from taxation).

69. Government Finances, *supra* note 49.

70. *Id.*

71. MINN. STAT. § 273.13. Class 1 property is residential property, which has four subclasses: (1a) residential homestead property that is assessed at 1% of its first $500,000 of market value and at 1.25% of any additional market value; (1b) homestead property of a blind person, veteran, or certain disabled persons that is assessed at 0.45% of its first $32,000 of market value; the remaining market value is subject to the rates applicable to 1a or 2a property; (1c) commercial/residential use property abutting a shoreline that is assessed at 1% of its first $500,000 of market value and at 1% of its remaining market value, subject to certain limitations; and (1d) structures occupied by seasonal farm workers, which are subject to the same rates as class 1a property. *Id.* § 273.13 subd. 22. Class 2 property is agricultural property, which is divided into two subclasses: (2a) agricultural land that is a homestead, which is assessed at 0.55% of market value up to $600,000 and at 1% of remaining market value; and (2b) other agricultural land that is assessed at 1% of market value. *Id.* § 273.13 subd. 23. Class 3 property is commercial property, which is divided into two subclasses: (3a) commercial and industrial property and utility real and personal property that is assessed at 1.5% of the first $150,000 of market value and at 2.0% of any excess market value; and (3b) employment property that is assessed at the same rates as class 3a property. *Id.* § 273.13 subd. 24. Class 4 property is residential rental property, which is divided into five subclasses: (4a) apartments and certain nonexempt hospitals that are assessed at 1.25% of market value; (4b) residential real estate containing fewer than four units, manufactured homes, and unimproved residential property that is assessed at 1.25%; (4bb) nonhomestead single-unit residential real estate that is assessed at the same rate as class 1a property; (4c) real property that is occupied temporarily and seasonally that is assessed at 1.5% of market value; and (4d) qualifying low-income rental housing that is assessed at 1.25% of market value. *Id.* § 273.13 subd. 25. Class 5 property is miscellaneous property, which consists of all other unclassified property and is assessed at 2% of its market value. *Id.* § 273.13 subd. 31.

72. CCH-EXP, PROP-TAX-GUIDE MN ¶ 20-615, Valuation Methods in General.

73. MINN. STAT. § 273.01.

74. CCH-EXP, PROP-TAX-GUIDE MN ¶ 20-010, Overview.

Real Property Tax Rates

The tax rates imposed on real property vary and are set by each locality. The State of Minnesota levies a tax on certain types of property, a tax which varies from year to year.[75] In 2005, the state tax rate was 51.121%,[76] and the average county tax rates ranged from 63.333% in Cook county to 178.948% in Mahnomen county.[77]

Personal and Intangible Property

Most personal property in Minnesota is exempt from the property tax.[78] Taxable personal property includes, among other items, railroad docks, wharves, and manufactured homes.[79]

Exemptions

Household goods,[80] motor vehicles,[81] inventories,[82] and furnishings and fixtures are exempt from the Minnesota property tax.[83] Minnesota does not provide for a homestead exemption, but it does provide for certain refunds, including one which depends on household income[84] and another which depends on the amount of increase in property taxes on a homeowner's homestead.[85]

General and Selective Sales

General Sales

Minnesota imposes a general retail sales-and-use tax, which makes up 21.3% of Minnesota's total tax revenue.[86] The tax is imposed on the sale, lease, or rental of tan-

---

75. Minnesota Department of Revenue, Property Tax Fact Sheet #8: State General Levy, January 10, 2005, http://www.taxes.state.mn.us/taxes/property/publications/fact_sheets/html_content/state_levy_propfs8_onscreen.shtml.

76. *Id.* "This rate applies to the net tax capacity of the affected properties. Net tax capacity is a small percentage of a property's market value. The percentage varies by property class." *Id.*; *see also supra* note 71.

77. CCH-EXP, PROP-TAX-GUIDE MN ¶ 20-405, Rates of Tax.

78. MINN. STAT. § 272.02 subd. 9.

79. *Id.* § 272.02 subd. 9.

80. *Id.* § 272.02.

81. CCH-EXP, PROP-TAX-GUIDE MN ¶ 20-275, Motor Vehicles.

82. CCH-EXP, PROP-TAX-GUIDE MN ¶ 20-240, Inventories.

83. MINN. STAT. § 272.03.

84. *Id.* § 290A.04 subd. 1. If the amount of property taxes paid exceed a percentage of income specified by statute, the taxpayer is eligible for a refund. *Id.*

85. *Id.* § 290A.04 subd. 2h. If the amount of property taxes paid increase by 12% or more over the course of a year and that amount is at least $100, the taxpayer is eligible for a refund of 60% of the amount of the increase over 12% or $100, up to $1,000. *Id.*

86. Government Finances, *supra* note 49.

gible personal property and on specified services.[87] These services include (1) preparation of meals; (2) entertainment, admissions, and membership fees; (3) computer software; and (4) lodging.[88] The state sales tax rate is 6.5%,[89] and certain cities and counties are allowed to impose an additional sales-and-use tax that ranges from 0.5% to 1.0%.[90] Hennepin County is also authorized to impose an additional 0.15% sales-and-use tax to fund the construction of a new baseball stadium.[91] Exemptions from the Minnesota sales tax include, among other items, food and grocery items,[92] clothing,[93] and drugs for human use, including over-the-counter drugs.[94]

Selective Sales

Selective sales taxes make up 12.5% of Minnesota's total tax revenue.[95] Of that amount, 3.3%[96] comes from a motor fuel sales tax imposed at a rate of $0.20 per gallon of gasoline.[97] Minnesota residents paid an average of $127 per capita in state motor fuel sales taxes in 2004, an amount which ranked 26th nationally.[98]

Sales taxes on tobacco products make up 1.0% of Minnesota's total tax revenue[99] and are imposed at a rate of $0.48 per pack of cigarettes.[100] Minnesota residents paid an average of $37.30 per capita in state tobacco sales taxes in 2004, an amount which ranked 29th nationally.[101]

In 2004, sales taxes on alcoholic beverages made up 0.4% of Minnesota's total tax revenue.[102] Minnesota residents paid $13.64 per capita in state alcoholic beverage sales taxes in 2004, an amount which ranked 26th nationally and was well below the national average of $15.74.[103]

The remainder of Minnesota's selective sales taxes makes up 7.8% of its total tax revenue.[104] Of this amount, 0.3% represents taxes on utilities and the other 7.5% represents taxes on other specific commodities, businesses, or services not reported sepa-

---

87. MINN. STAT. § 297A.61(4); *Id.* § 297A.62.

88. MINN. STAT. §§ 297A.61(3)(g), (6).

89. *Id.* § 297A62(1).

90. CCH-EXP, SALES-TAX-GUIDE MN ¶ 61-735, Local Rates.

91. MINN. STAT. §§ 473.757(10), (11).

92. *Id.* § 297A.67(2). This does not include candy, soft drinks, prepared foods, dietary supplements, alcoholic beverages, or tobacco products. *Id.*

93. *Id.* § 297A.67(8).

94. *Id.* § 297A.67(7).

95. Government Finances, *supra* note 49.

96. *Id.*

97. STATE RANKINGS 2006, *supra* note 1, at 328.

98. *Id.* at 327.

99. Government Finances, *supra* note 49.

100. STATE RANKINGS 2006, *supra* note 1, at 333.

101. *Id.* at 332.

102. Government Finances, *supra* note 49.

103. STATE RANKINGS 2006, *supra* note 1, at 335.

104. Government Finances, *supra* note 49.

rately above (e.g., on contractors, lodging, lubricating oil, fuels other than motor fuel, motor vehicles, meals, soft drinks, margarine, etc.).[105]

Corporate Income and Other

Corporate Income

The corporate income tax makes up 3.3% of Minnesota's total tax revenue.[106] Minnesota's broad-based corporate income tax is imposed at a rate of 9.8% on a corporation's Minnesota taxable income,[107] which is based on federal taxable income.[108]

Minnesota follows the federal income tax treatment of S corporations,[109] partnerships,[110] limited partnerships,[111] and limited liability companies;[112] thus, income and losses flow through the entities to their shareholders. However, if a limited liability company is treated as a corporation for federal income tax purposes, the entity is subject to Minnesota's corporate income tax.[113]

Other

During fiscal year 2004, the collection of all other taxes not previously mentioned accounted for 8.2% of Minnesota's total tax revenue.[114] Of this amount, approximately $87 million was generated by the estate and gift tax.[115] This tax is calculated on the basis of the value of the decedent's estate.[116] The "other taxes" category is also made up of motor vehicle license taxes, documentary and stock transfer taxes, severance taxes, and all other taxes not listed separately or provided for in other categories, such as taxes on land based on a specified rate per acre (rather than on assessed value).[117]

---

105. *See* Governments Division, U.S. Census Bureau, Government Finance and Employment Classification Manual, at ch.7 (2000), *available at* http://ftp2.census.gov/govs/class/classfull.pdf [hereinafter Classification Manual].

106. Government Finances, *supra* note 49.

107. Minn. Stat. § 290.06(1).

108. *Id.* § 290.01(19).

109. *Id.* § 290.9725.

110. *Id.* § 290.01(3); *Id.* § 290.31(1).

111. Minn. Stat. § 290.31(1).

112. CCH-EXP, MCIT-GUIDE MN ¶ 10-240, Limited Liability Companies (LLCs).

113. *Id.*

114. Government Finances, *supra* note 49.

115. *Id.*

116. Minnesota Department of Revenue, Estate tax fact sheet: Tax issues for personal representatives, http://www.taxes.state.mn.us/taxes/estate_trust/publications/factsheets/html_content/estate_fact_sheet.shtml (last visited January 4, 2007).

117. *See* Classification Manual, *supra* note 105, at ch.7.

Burden Analysis

The overall state and local tax burden on Minnesota's taxpayers is slightly regressive. Taxpayers in the lowest quintile—those with incomes of less than $$19,000—bear a tax burden of 10.5% of their income, while taxpayers in the top 1%—those with incomes that exceed $556,000—bear a tax burden of 9.3% of their income.[118] It is also worth noting that, although Minnesota obviously has no control over federal tax policy, federal itemized deductions for state and local personal income and property taxes nonetheless further reduce the burden on taxpayers in the top 1% to 6.4%.[119] Furthermore, between 1989 and 2002, the tax burden on the bottom quintile fell by approximately 0.1%, while the burden on the top 1% fell by approximately 1.3%.[120]

In terms of the income tax, the burden across income groups in Minnesota is largely progressive, with taxpayers in the lowest quintile bearing a tax burden of 0.4% and those in the top 1% bearing a tax burden of 6.8%.[121] In sharp contrast, however, the sales and excises taxes imposed by Minnesota are very regressive, with taxpayers in the lowest quintile bearing a tax burden of 6.9% and those in the top 1% bearing a tax burden of just 1.0%.[122] Property taxes in Minnesota are also regressive, with taxpayers in the lowest quintile bearing a tax burden of 3.2% and those in the top 1% bearing an average tax burden of 1.6%.[123]

---

118. *See* ROBERT S. MCINTYRE ET AL., WHO PAYS? A DISTRIBUTIONAL ANALYSIS OF THE TAX SYSTEMS IN ALL 50 STATES 62 (2d ed. 2003), *available at* http://www.itepnet.org/wp2000/text.pdf. Taxpayers in the second quintile bear a 10.0% total tax burden on incomes between $19,000 and $$32,000; those in the third quintile bear a 10.4% tax burden on incomes between $32,000 and $50,000; those in the fourth quintile bear a 10.4% tax burden on incomes between $50,000 and $76,000; those in the 80th–95th percentiles bear a 10.3% tax burden on incomes between $76,000 and $147,000; finally, those in the 96th–99th percentiles bear a 9.8% tax burden on incomes between $147,000 and $556,000. *Id.*

119. *Id.* Taxpayers in the lowest quintile did not receive any benefit from these federal offsets, while those in the second quintile were able to reduce their individual tax burdens by 0.1%, those in the third quintile by 0.5%, those in the fourth quintile by 0.9%, those in the 80th–95th percentiles by 1.8%, and those in the 96th–99th percentiles by 2.2%. *Id.*

120. *Id.* at 63.

121. *See id.* at 62. Taxpayers in the second quintile bear a 2.5% income tax burden; those in the third quintile bear a 3.6% burden; those in the fourth quintile bear a 4.3% burden; those in the 80th–95th percentiles bear a 4.9% burden; finally, those in the 96th–99th percentiles bear a 5.6% income tax burden. *Id.* Note, however, that these percentages include both individual and corporate income tax burdens; that within the within the 96th–99th percentiles, corporate income taxes represent 0.1% of this burden; and that in the top 1%, corporate income taxes represent 0.3% of this burden. *Id.*

122. *See id.* at 62. Taxpayers in the second quintile bear a 5.1% sales-and-excise tax burden; those in the third quintile bear a 4.1% burden; those in the fourth quintile bear a 3.5% burden; those in the 80th–95th percentiles bear a 2.7% burden; finally, those in the 96th–99th percentiles bear a 1.8% burden. *Id.*

123. *See id.* at 62. Taxpayers in the second quintile bear a 2.3% property tax burden; those in the third quintile bear a 2.7% burden; those in the fourth quintile bear a 2.7% burden; those in the 80th–95th percentiles bear a 2.7% burden; and those in the 96th–99th percentiles bear a 2.4% burden. *Id.*

Mississippi

General Information

Basic Profile – Geography, Population and Industry

Mississippi was admitted to the Union in 1817 and is commonly referred to as the "Magnolia State".[1] It is located in the southeastern United States and is bordered by Alabama on the east, Louisiana and Arkansas on the west, and Tennessee on the north. The state is located in the central time zone, and its capital is Jackson.[2]

Mississippi ranks 32nd in total land and water area (approximately 48,000 square miles).[3] In 2005, Mississippi ranked 31st in population (approximately 2.9 million residents).[4] Its population is approximately 61.2% white and 36.9% black.[5] The state is approximately 5% Catholic; 81% Protestant (of which 68% are Baptist); and less than 0.5% Jewish; 14% claim a religion outside the Judeo-Christian tradition or no religion at all.[6] As of 2005, approximately 56% of Mississippi's residents lived in rural areas.[7] Major industries include agriculture (poultry/eggs, forestry products, cotton, soybeans and catfish), casino gaming, and manufacturing (upholstered products and industrial chemicals).[8]

---

1. STATE RANKINGS 2006, vi, 1(Kathleen O'Leary Morgan & Scott Morgan eds., Morgan Quitno Press, 2006).

2. *Id.*

3. *Id.* at 225.

4. *Id.* at 429.

5. Mississippi Quick Facts from the U.S. Census Bureau, http://quickfacts.census.gov/qfd/states/28000.html (last visited Jan. 31, 2007). The remaining population is made up of 0.7% Asian persons, 0.4% American Indian and/or Alaska Native persons and 0.6% persons reporting two or more races. *Id.* Additionally, 1.7% of Mississippi's total population identify themselves as persons of Hispanic or Latino origin. *Id.* (noting that because Hispanics may be of any race, they are included within the other applicable race categories).

6. BARRY A. KOSMIN, EGON MAYER & ARIELA KEYSAR, AMERICAN RELIGIOUS IDENTIFICATION SURVEY 2001, at 40, *available at* http://www.gc.cuny.edu/faculty/research_studies/aris.pdf (last visited Jan. 31, 2007).

7. USDA Economic Research Service, Oklahoma Fact Sheet, http://www.ers.usda.gov/StateFacts/MS.htm (last visited October 23, 2006). According to the latest estimates, approximately 1.6 million people live in rural areas, and 1.3 million people live in urban areas. *Id.*

8. Mississippi, http://www..netstate.com/states/links/ms_links.htm (last visited Oct. 23, 2006).

Family Income and Poverty Indicators

In 2004, Mississippi's per capita gross product was $26,257, which ranked among the bottom ten states nationally and was below the national average of $39,725.[9] During this same period, although the median household income in Mississippi was $33,659,[10] 17.7% of Mississippi's population was living in poverty, which was substantially above the national average of 12.4% and ranked among the top ten states nationally.[11] More specifically, poverty affected 30.8% of Mississippi's children,[12] 15.2% of its senior citizens,[13] and 17.6% of its families.[14] Of its female-headed households with children, 52.9% lived in poverty,[15] and 64.3% of the state's public elementary and secondary school students were eligible for free or reduced-price meals.[16] Of those living in poverty, approximately 63% were black, which represented 33% of Mississippi's black population and 12% of its total population.[17] In an attempt to combat this poverty, Mississippi spent approximately $3.2 billion on public welfare programs in 2002,[18] which made up 21.0% of its total government expenditures.[19]

Mississippi's Public Elementary-Secondary School System

Overall Spending and Performance

For the 2003–2004 school year, Mississippi spent $6,237 per pupil in its public elementary-secondary school system, which was substantially below the national average of $8,182.[20] Of this amount, 14.9% was provided by the federal government, 54.9% was provided by the state government, and 30.3% was provided by the local governments,[21] with property taxes making up 23.6% of the total funding.[22] Out of these funds, Mississippi paid its elementary and secondary school teachers an estimated av-

---

9. STATE RANKINGS 2006, *supra* note 1, at 89.

10. *Id.* at 96.

11. *Id.* at 495.

12. *Id.* at 497.

13. *Id.* at 496.

14. *Id.* at 498.

15. *Id.* at 499.

16. *Id.* at 532.

17. *See* Fact Sheet, American FactFinder, http://factfinder.census.gov/home/saff/main.html?_lang=en (select "Mississippi" under "Get a Fact Sheet for your community") (last visited Feb. 22, 2007). Note that these numbers are based on the 2000 census because more recent numbers were not available.

18. STATE RANKINGS 2006, *supra* note 1, at 500.

19. *Id.* at 502.

20. GOVERNMENTS DIVISION, U.S. CENSUS BUREAU, PUBLIC EDUCATION FINANCES 2004, at 8 tbl.8 (2006).

21. *See id.* at 5 tbl.5.

22. *See id.* at 4 tbl.4.

erage annual salary of $36,590 during the 2004–2005 school year,[23] and in 2003, it provided a student/teacher ratio of 15.1, which was slightly better than the national average of 15.9.[24]

In academic performance, Mississippi's fourth and eighth grade students scored lower than the national average in mathematics,[25] reading,[26] science,[27] and writing.[28]

Equity Issues

In 2004, the funding per student in Mississippi's highest poverty districts exceeded that in its lowest poverty districts by $207.[29] When adjustments were made for the additional costs of educating students growing up in poverty, however, the funding in high poverty districts actually declined by $191.[30] Similarly, Mississippi spent $413 more per student in its highest minority districts, although this amount fell to just $26 when adjustments for low-income students were made.[31]

Fourth graders eligible for free or reduced-price school lunches had test scores that were 8% lower in mathematics,[32] 12% lower in reading,[33] and 14% lower in writing[34] than those of students who were not eligible. The results were just slightly better for eighth graders eligible for free or reduced-price lunches; their test scores were 9% lower in mathematics,[35] 9% lower in reading,[36] and 12% lower in writing[37] than those of students who were not eligible.

23. THOMAS D. SNYDER ET AL., NATIONAL CENTER FOR EDUCATION STATISTICS, DIGEST OF EDUCATION STATISTICS 2005, at 116 tbl.77 (2006).

24. *Id.* at 98 tbl.65.

25. NATIONAL CENTER FOR EDUCATION STATISTICS, U.S. DEPARTMENT OF EDUCATION, THE NATION'S REPORT CARD: MATHEMATICS 2005, at 14 fig.11, 16 fig.12 (2005), *available at* http://nces.ed.gov/nationsreportcard/pdf/ main2005/2006453.pdf [hereinafter MATHEMATICS 2005].

26. NATIONAL CENTER FOR EDUCATION STATISTICS, U.S. DEPARTMENT OF EDUCATION, THE NATION'S REPORT CARD: READING 2005, at 14 fig.11, 16 fig.12 (2005), *available at* http://nces.ed.gov/nationsreportcard/pdf/main2005/2006451.pdf [hereinafter READING 2005].

27. NATIONAL CENTER FOR EDUCATION STATISTICS, U.S. DEPARTMENT OF EDUCATION, THE NATION'S REPORT CARD: SCIENCE 2005, at 16 fig.12, 28 fig.22 (2006), *available at* http://nces.ed.gov/nationsreportcard//pdf/main2005/2006466.pdf [hereinafter SCIENCE 2005].

28. HILARY R. PERSKY ET AL., NATIONAL CENTER FOR EDUCATION STATISTICS, U.S. DEPARTMENT OF EDUCATION, THE NATION'S REPORT CARD: WRITING 2002, at 23 tbl.2.2, 24 tbl.2.3 (2003), *available at* http://nces.ed.gov/nationsreportcard/pdf/main2002/2003529.pdf [hereinafter WRITING 2002].

29. THE EDUCATION TRUST, FUNDING GAPS 2006, at 7 tbl.3 (2006), *available at* http://www2 .edtrust.org/NR/rdonlyres/CDEF9403-5A75-437E-93FF-EBF1174181FB/0/FundingGap2006.pdf.

30. *Id.*

31. *Id.* at 7 tbl.4.

32. MATHEMATICS 2005, *supra* note 25, at 20 tbl.5.

33. READING 2005, *supra* note 26, at 20 tbl.5.

34. WRITING 2002, *supra* note 28, at 75 tbl.3.24.

35. MATHEMATICS 2005, *supra* note 25, at 21 tbl.6.

36. READING 2005, *supra* note 26, at 21 tbl.6.

37. WRITING 2002, *supra* note 28, at 76 tbl.3.25.

Mississippi is one of five states in which no cases have been filed challenging the state education finance system.[38]

Availability of Publicly Funded Prekindergarten Programs

Mississippi does not currently provide any state-funded prekindergarten programs for three- or four-year-old children.[39] However, the federally funded Head Start program enrolls 25,447 children,[40] which represents 31% of Mississippi's 82,698 three- and four-year-old children.[41]

Where Does Mississippi Get Its Revenue?

At the end of fiscal year 2004, Mississippi had total revenues of approximately $21 billion.[42] Of this amount, 34% was derived from state and local tax revenues and 27% was received from the federal government. The remaining 39% came from other sources, including insurance trust revenue and revenue from government-owned utilities and other commercial or auxiliary enterprises.[43]

Tax Revenue

Mississippi collected approximately $7.1 billion in state and local tax revenue during fiscal year 2004.[44] As a result, Mississippi residents paid $2,444 per capita in state and local government taxes, an amount which ranked 49th nationally.[45] The different types of tax sources were approximately apportioned as follows:

---

38. National Access Network, Education Finance Litigation, http://www.schoolfunding.info/states/ms/lit_ms.php3 (last visited Apr. 9, 2007).

39. W. STEVEN BARNETT ET AL., NATIONAL INSTITUTE FOR EARLY EDUCATION RESEARCH, THE STATE OF PRESCHOOL 2006, at 90 (2006), *available at* http://nieer.org/yearbook/pdf/yearbook.pdf.

40. *Id.* at 91.

41. *See id.* at 232.

42. U.S. Census Bureau, State and Local Government Finances 2003–04, http://www.census.gov/govs/www/estimate04.html (last visited Oct. 16, 2006) [hereinafter Government Finances].

43. *Id.*

44. *Id.* The total tax revenues were collected as follows: $5.1 billion by the state and $2.0 billion by local governments. *Id.*

45. *Id.*

Individual income taxes	15.0%
Property taxes	26.2%
General and selective sales taxes	48.8%
Corporate income and other taxes	10.0%
Total	100.0%[46]

Federal Funding

During fiscal year 2004, 27% of Mississippi's total revenues came from the federal government.[47] For every dollar of federal taxes paid, Mississippi received $1.77 in federal funding, a amount which ranked 4th nationally and was far above the national average of $1.17.[48]

Lottery Revenue

Mississippi does not currently have a state lottery.

Legal Structures of Major Tax Sources

Income

Mississippi employs a broad-based income tax that loosely uses adjusted gross income for federal income tax purposes as a starting point for determining the state's taxable income.[49] Numerous adjustments, however, may be available to various individuals in calculating this amount.[50] During fiscal year 2004, Mississippi collected individual income tax of $366 per capita, an amount which ranked 40th nationally.[51]

In Mississippi, a typical family of four (i.e., married taxpayers who file jointly and have two dependent children) are not required to pay any income tax until their combined income exceeds $19,600, an amount which is just below the national poverty line of $20,615.[52] Mississippi's income tax structure contains three tax brackets that impose

---

46. *Id.*

47. *Id.*

48. The Tax Foundation, Federal Spending Received per Dollar of Taxes Paid by State 2004, http://www.taxfoundation.org/taxdata/show/266.html (last visited Oct. 16, 2006).

49. Miss. Code Ann. § 27-7-15. Gross income in Mississippi is defined as "the income of a taxpayer derived from salaries, wages, fees or compensation for service, of whatever kind and in whatever form paid" unless otherwise specifically exempt from gross income. *Id.*

50. *Id.*

51. State Rankings 2006, *supra* note 1, at 321.

52. Jason A. Levitis, Center on Budget and Policy Priorities, The Impact of State Income Taxes on Low-Income Families in 2006, at 12 (2007). http://www.cbpp.org/2-22-06sfp.pdf. In 2006, Mississippi taxpayers who were married and filing jointly could claim a standard deduction of $4,600, a personal exemption of $12,000 (combined for taxpayer and spouse), and dependent exemptions of $1,500 each. Miss. Code Ann. §§ 27-7-17, 27-7-21. Note, however, that the threshold calculation of $19,600 is greater than the sum of these deductions and

a minimum marginal rate of 3% and a maximum marginal rate of 5.00%.[53] When statutory exemptions and the standard deduction are taken into account, the maximum marginal rate applies to every dollar of income exceeding $29,600.[54]

Property

Overview

Mississippi has a typical property tax system that taxes and collects the value of property almost entirely at the local level.[55] During fiscal year 2004, Mississippi localities collected approximately $1.8 billion in property taxes and the state collected approximately $40 million.[56] As a result, Mississippi residents paid $641 per capita in property taxes, an amount which ranked 40th nationally.[57]

Defining the Real Property Tax Base

Real property in the state of Mississippi is grouped into one of three classes.[58] Class I property consists of single-family, owner-occupied residential property.[59] Class II property consists of all other real property, except for real property included in Class I or Class IV.[60] Class IV property consists of public-utility property owned or used by public-service corporations.[61] All real property is valued at its true value according to the property's current use[62] and is valued on an annual basis.[63] True value is determined by using either the income-capitalization approach, the cost approach or the market-data approach.[64] Class I property is assessed at 10% of its true value; Class II property is assessed at 15% of its true value; and Class IV property is assessed at 30% of its true value.[65]

---

exemptions because it includes additional tax benefits available to low-income families, such as the earned-income tax credit. *See* LEVITIS, *supra*.

53. MISS. CODE ANN. § 27-7-5. Mississippi's middle tax bracket is 4%. *Id.*

54. The standard deduction and exemptions of $4,600 and $15,000, respectively, plus the threshold of taxable income for the highest tax bracket of $10,000, equals $29,600. *See supra* note 52.

55. MISS. CONST. art. IV, § 112.

56. Government Finances, *supra* note 42.

57. *See id.*

58. MISS. CONST. art. IV, § 112. The other two classes of property, III and V, subject to property tax encompass nonexempt personal property and motor vehicles. *See infra* notes 73 and 74 and accompanying text.

59. *Id.*

60. *Id.*

61. *Id.*

62. *Id.* True value is the amount that a willing buyer would pay a willing seller. MISS. CODE ANN. § 27-35-29.

63. MISS. CODE ANN. § 27-35-50.

64. *Id.*

65. MISS. CONST. art. IV, § 112.

Real Property Tax Rates

Tax rates are determined at the local level by the board of supervisors and can be levied at any rate necessary to fund general county purposes excluding roads and bridges and schools.[66] The board of supervisors for each county is required to levy a tax for each school district at no less than 28 mills (i.e., 1 mill equals 1 dollar per thousand; therefore 28 mills equals 28 dollars per thousand).[67] In addition, a county may levy additional taxes for the construction and maintenance of road and bridges,[68] a forest acreage tax,[69] a garbage collection tax,[70] and a Burn Care Fund tax.[71] Since each county and municipality can levy a different rate of tax, tax rates throughout the state vary. In 2005–2006, millage rates ranged from 47.50 mills in Tunica County to 133.61 mills in Jefferson County.[72]

Personal and Intangible Property

All personal property, except for motor vehicles and unless otherwise exempt, is included in Class III and is assessed at 15% of its true value.[73] Motor vehicles are included in Class V and are assessed at 30% of their true value.[74]

Exemptions

Wearing apparel, household goods, farming tools, implements, and machinery are all exempt from property tax.[75] Citizens of Mississippi are also allowed a homestead exemption equal to $7,500 of the assessed value of the homestead.[76]

General and Selective Sales

General Sales

Mississippi imposes a general sales-and-use tax, which makes up 35% of its total tax revenue.[77] The tax is levied and assessed for the privilege of doing business within the state and is imposed on the gross proceeds of sales or gross income or values.[78] Gener-

---

66. Miss. Code Ann. § 27-39-303.

67. *Id.* § 37-57-1.

68. *Id* § 27-39-305.

69. *Id.* § 49-19-115. The board of supervisors of each county is required to levy a tax of 9 cents per acre on all timbered and uncultivatable lands until June 30, 2008, at which time the statute is repealed. *Id.*

70. *Id.* § 19-5-21.

71. *Id.* § 27-39-332.

72. CCH-EXP, PROP-TAX-GUIDE MS ¶ 20-405, Rates of Tax.

73. Miss. Const. art. IV, § 112.

74. *Id.*

75. Miss. Code Ann. § 27-31-1.

76. *Id.* § 27-33-3.

77. Government Finances, *supra* note 42.

78. Miss. Code Ann. § 27-65-13.

ally, the tax is imposed on the sale of tangible personal property[79] and on certain services, including computer software services, burglar and fire alarm system services, and pest control services.[80] Mississippi sales tax is generally levied at 7 percent of the gross proceeds of the retail sales of a business.[81] However, certain retail sales are taxed at a lower rate. For example, retail sales of machinery used in the operation of structures and facilities within the state are taxed at 1.5%;[82] retail sales of tangible personal property upon any floating structure[83] are taxed at 3.5%;[84] and retail sales of farm tractors are taxed at 1%.[85] There are several exemptions from the sales tax, including retail sales of livestock,[86] sales to commercial fishermen of commercial fishing boats,[87] purchases made with food stamps,[88] and retail sales of prescription drugs and medications.[89] In addition to the state sales tax, counties and cities are authorized to impose limited occupancy taxes and limited taxes on restaurants and bars, which generally range from 1% to 3%.[90]

Selective Sales

Selective sales taxes make up 13.8% of Mississippi's total tax revenue.[91] Of that amount, 6.6% [92] comes from a motor fuel sales tax imposed at a rate of $0.18 per gallon of gasoline.[93] Mississippi residents paid $160 per capita in state motor fuel sales taxes in 2004, an amount which ranked 9th nationally and was just above the national average of $115.[94]

The tobacco products sales tax makes up 0.8%[95] of Mississippi's total tax revenue, and in 2005, it was imposed at a rate of $0.18 per pack of cigarettes.[96]

In 2004, sales tax on alcoholic beverages made up 0.6% of Mississippi's total tax revenue.[97] Mississippi residents paid $13.72 per capita in state alcoholic beverage sales taxes in 2004, an amount which ranked 25th nationally.[98]

---

79. *Id* § 27-65-17.

80. *Id.*§ 27-65-23.

81. *Id.*

82. *Id* § 27-65-20.

83. Floating structures consist mostly of casinos, restaurants, and hotels built upon floating structures. Miss. Code Ann. § 27-65-18.

84. *Id.*

85. *Id.* § 27-65-17.

86. *Id.* § 27-65-103.

87. *Id.* § 27-65-101.

88. *Id.* § 27-65-111.

89. *Id.*

90. CCH-EXP, PROP-TAX-GUIDE MS ¶ 60-480, Lodging.

91. Government Finances, *supra* note 42.

92. *Id.*

93. Miss. Code Ann. § 27-55-11.

94. State Rankings 2006, *supra* note 1, at 327.

95. Government Finances, *supra* note 42.

96. State Rankings 2006, *supra* note 1, at 333.

97. Government Finances, *supra* note 42.

98. State Rankings 2006, *supra* note 1, at 335.

The remainder of Mississippi's selective sales taxes makes up 5.8% of its total tax revenue.[99] Of this amount, 0.7% represents taxes on utilities and the other 5.1% represents taxes on other specific commodities, businesses, or services not reported separately above (e.g. on contractors, lodging, lubricating oil, fuels other than motor fuel, motor vehicles, meals, soft drinks, margarine, etc.).[100]

Corporate Income and Other

Corporate Income

The corporate income tax makes up 3.4% of Mississippi's tax revenue.[101] Mississippi has a broad-based corporate income tax which is imposed on the net income from every trade, business, or occupation carried on within the state.[102] The state's corporate income tax applies to C corporations. S corporations,[103] partnerships,[104] limited partnerships, and limited liability companies are treated as flow-through entities in accordance with the Internal Revenue Code. The corporate income tax is applied at a rate of 3% on the first $5,000 of taxable income, 4% on the next $5,000 of taxable income, and 5% on taxable income over $10,000.[105]

Other

During fiscal year 2004, the collection of all other taxes not previously mentioned accounted for 6.6% of Mississippi's total tax revenue.[106] Of this amount, approximately $15.4 million was generated by the estate and gift tax,[107] which is equal to the maximum amount of state death tax credit permissible as a credit or deduction in computing any federal estate tax payable by the estate.[108] The "other taxes" category is further made up of various license taxes, franchise taxes,[109] gaming fees and taxes,

---

99. Government Finances, *supra* note 42.

100. *See* GOVERNMENTS DIVISION, U.S. CENSUS BUREAU, GOVERNMENT FINANCE AND EMPLOYMENT CLASSIFICATION MANUAL, at ch. 7 (2000), *available at* http://ftp2.census.gov/govs/class/classfull.pdf [hereinafter CLASSIFICATION MANUAL].

101. Government Finances, *supra* note 42.

102. MISS. CODE ANN. § 27-7-5.

103. *Id.* § 27-8-7.

104. *Id.* § 27-7-25.

105. *Id.* § 27-7-5.

106. Government Finances, *supra* note 42.

107. *Id.*

108. MISS. CODE ANN. § 27-9-5. Note, however, that the federal credit for state death taxes was phased out for all deaths occurring after December 31, 2004, so Mississippi does not currently have an estate tax.

109. *Id.* § 27-13-5. The franchise tax is levied "every corporation, association or joint-stock company or partnership treated as a corporation under the income tax laws or regulations, organized or created for pecuniary gain, having privileges not possessed by individuals, and having authorized capital stock now existing in this state, or hereafter organized, created or established, under and by virtue of the laws of the State of Mississippi, equal to Two Dollars and Fifty Cents ($2.50) for each One Thousand Dollars ($1,000.00), or fraction thereof, of the value of

severance taxes, and all other taxes not listed separately or provided for in other categories.[110]

Burden Analysis

The overall state and local tax burden on Mississippi's taxpayers is very regressive. Taxpayers in the lowest quintile—those with incomes of less than $11,000—bear a tax burden equal to 10.0% of their income, while taxpayers in the top 1%—those with incomes that exceed $228,000—bear a tax burden of just 6.9% of their income.[111] It is also worth noting that, although Mississippi obviously has no control over federal tax policy, federal itemized deductions for state and local personal income and property taxes nonetheless further reduce the burden on taxpayers in the top 1% to 5.3%.[112] Furthermore, between 1989 and 2002, the tax burden on the bottom quintile rose by approximately 0.5%, while the burden on the top 1% rose by only approximately 0.2%.[113]

In terms of the income tax, the burden across income groups in Mississippi is slightly progressive, with taxpayers in the lowest quintile bearing a tax burden of 0.2% and those in the top 1% bearing a tax burden of 4.0%.[114] In sharp contrast, however,

---

the capital used, invested or employed in the exercise of any power, privilege or right enjoyed by such organization within this state." *Id.*

110. *See* CLASSIFICATION MANUAL, *supra* note 100, at ch. 7.

111. *See* ROBERT S. MCINTYRE ET AL., WHO PAYS? A DISTRIBUTIONAL ANALYSIS OF THE TAX SYSTEMS IN ALL 50 STATES 64 (2d ed. 2003), *available at* http://www.itepnet.org/wp2000/text.pdf. Taxpayers in the second quintile bear a 11.6% total tax burden on incomes between $11,000 and $19,000; those in the third quintile bear a 9.8% tax burden on incomes between $19,000 and $29,000; those in the fourth quintile bear a 8.8% tax burden on incomes between $29,000 and $53,000; those in the 80th–95th percentiles bear a 8.5% tax burden on incomes between $53,000 and $96,000; finally, those in the 96th–99th percentiles bear a 7.6% tax burden on incomes between $96,000 and $228,000. *Id.*

112. *Id.* Taxpayers in the three lowest quintiles did not receive any benefit from these federal offsets, while those in the fourth quintile were able to reduce their individual tax burdens by 0.1%, those in the 80th–95th percentiles by 0.5%, and those in the 96th–99th percentiles by 1.0%. *Id.*

113. *Id.* at 65. Note also that during this same period, the tax burden on the second quintile rose by approximately 2.5%. *Id.*

114. *See id.* at 64. Taxpayers in the second quintile bear a 0.6% income tax burden; those in the third quintile bear a 1.2% burden; those in the fourth quintile bear a 2.0% burden; those in the 80th–95th percentiles bear a 2.4% burden; finally, those in the 96th–99th percentiles bear a 3.1% burden. *Id.* Note, however, that these percentages include both individual and corporate income tax burdens; that within the bottom quintile, corporate income taxes represent 0.1% of this burden; that within the second quintile, corporate income taxes represent 0.1% of this burden; that within the third quintile, corporate income taxes represent 0.0% of this burden; that within the fourth quintile, corporate income taxes represent 0.1% of this burden; that within the 80th–95th percentiles, corporate income taxes represent 0.1% of this burden; that within the 96th–99th percentiles, corporate income taxes represent 0.1% of this burden; and that in the top 1%, corporate income taxes represent 0.2% of this burden. *Id.*

the sales and excise taxes imposed by Mississippi are very regressive, with taxpayers in the lowest quintile bearing a tax burden of 8.1% and those in the top 1% bearing a tax burden of just 1.3%.[115] The property tax burden in Mississippi, however, is relatively flat across all income levels and averages approximately 1.8%.[116] Note, however, that the most onerous burden is placed on taxpayers in the second quintile, who pay 2.9% of their income in property taxes.[117]

---

115. *See id.* Taxpayers in the second quintile bear a 8.0% sales-and-excise tax burden; those in the third quintile bear a 6.9% burden; those in the fourth quintile bear a 5.4% burden; those in the 80th–95th percentiles bear a 4.3% burden; finally, those in the 96th–99th percentiles bear a 2.7% burden. *Id.*

116. *See id.* Taxpayers in the bottom quintile bear a 1.7% property tax burden; those in the second quintile bear a 2.9% burden; those in the third quintile bear a 1.6% burden; those in the fourth quintile bear a 1.4% burden; those in the 80th–95th percentiles bear a 1.8% burden; those in the 96th–99th percentiles bear a 1.8% burden; finally, those in the top 1% bear a 1.5% burden. *Id.*

117. *Id.*

Missouri

General Information

Basic Profile – Geography, Population, and Industry

Admitted to the Union in 1821, Missouri is commonly referred to as the "Show Me State."[1] It is located in the Midwest and is bordered by Arkansas, Tennessee, Kentucky, Illinois, Iowa, Nebraska, Kansas, and Oklahoma. Missouri is located in the central time zone, and its capital is Jefferson City.[2]

In 2005, Missouri ranked 18th in population (approximately 5.8 million residents); the state ranks 21st in total area (69,704 square miles).[3] Its population is 85.4% white and 11.5% black.[4] The state is 19% Catholic; 58% Protestant; and less than 0.5% Jewish; 23% claim a religion outside the Judeo-Christian tradition or no religion at all.[5] Missouri is mostly urban, with 73% of the population living in cities and towns.[6] Major industries include manufacturing, financial activities, professional and business services, trade, transportation, and utilities.[7]

Family Income and Poverty Indicators

In 2004, Missouri's per capita gross product was $35,297, which was below the national average of $39,725.[8] During this same period, although the median household

---

1. STATE RANKINGS 2006, vi, 1 (Kathleen O'Leary Morgan & Scott Morgan eds., Morgan Quitno Press 2006).

2. *Id.* at vi.

3. *Id.* at 429.

4. Missouri Quick Facts from the U.S. Census Bureau, http://quickfacts.census.gov/qfd/states/29000.html (last visited Jan. 27, 2007). The remaining population is made up of 1.3% Asian persons; 0.4% American Indian and/or Alaska Native persons; 0.1% Native Hawaiian and other Pacific Islanders; and 1.3% persons reporting two or more races. *Id.* Additionally, 2.7% of Missouri's total population identify themselves as persons of Hispanic or Latino origin. *Id.* (noting that because Hispanics may be of any race, they are included within the other applicable race categories).

5. BARRY A. KOSMIN, EGON MAYER & ARIELA KEYSAR, AMERICAN RELIGIOUS IDENTIFICATION SURVEY 2001, at 41, *available at* http://www.gc.cuny.edu/faculty/research_studies/aris.pdf.

6. USDA Economic Research Service, Missouri Fact Sheet, http://www.ers.usda.gov/StateFacts/MO.htm (last visited Sept. 17, 2006). According to the latest estimates, approximately 1.6 million people live in rural areas, and 4.2 million people live in urban areas. *Id.*

7. "Missouri Gross State Product 2002 by Industry," Missouri Dept. of Economic Development, http://www.ded.mo.gov/pdfs/gsp2002g.pdf (last visited Nov. 12, 2006).

8. STATE RANKINGS 2006, *supra* note 1, at 89.

income in Missouri was $43,988,[9] 10.9% of Missouri's population was living in poverty, which is somewhat below the national average of 12.4%.[10] More specifically, poverty affected 15.8% of Missouri's children,[11] 9.5% of its senior citizens,[12] and 8.7% of its families.[13] Of its female-headed households with children, 33.3% lived in poverty,[14] and 38.0% of the state's public elementary and secondary school students were eligible for free or reduced-price meals.[15] Of those living in poverty, approximately 23.8% were black, which represented 24.1% of Missouri's black population and 2.7% of its total population.[16] In an attempt to combat this poverty, Missouri spent approximately $5.5 billion on public welfare programs in 2002,[17] which made up 19.0% of its total government expenditures.[18]

Missouri's Public Elementary-Secondary School System

Overall Spending and Performance

For the 2003–2004 school year, Missouri spent $7,331 per pupil in its public elementary-secondary school system, which was substantially below the national average of $8,182.[19] Of this amount, 7.9% was provided by the federal government, 44.2% was provided by the state government, and 47.9% was provided by the local governments,[20] with property taxes making up 35.9% of the total funding.[21] Out of these funds, Missouri paid its elementary and secondary school teachers an estimated average annual salary of $38,971 during the 2004–2005 school year,[22] and it provided a student/teacher ratio of 13.9, which was better than the national average of 15.9.[23]

---

9. *Id.* at 96.

10. *Id.* at 495.

11. *Id.* at 497.

12. *Id.* at 496.

13. *Id.* at 498.

14. *Id.* at 499.

15. *Id.* at 532.

16. *See* Fact Sheet, American FactFinder, http://factfinder.census.gov/home/saff/main.html?_lang=en (select "Missouri" under "Get a Fact Sheet for your community") (last visited Feb. 16, 2007). Note that these numbers are based on the 2000 census because more recent numbers where not available.

17. STATE RANKINGS 2006, *supra* note 1, at 500.

18. *Id.* at 502.

19. GOVERNMENTS DIVISION, U.S. CENSUS BUREAU, PUBLIC EDUCATION FINANCES 2004, at 8 tbl.8 (2006).

20. *See id.* at 5 tbl.5.

21. *See id.* at 4 tbl.4.

22. THOMAS D. SNYDER ET AL., NATIONAL CENTER FOR EDUCATION STATISTICS, DIGEST OF EDUCATION STATISTICS 2005, at 116 tbl.77 (2006).

23. *Id.* at 98 tbl.65.

In academic performance, Missouri's fourth grade students scored lower than the national average in mathematics[24] and writing[25] and higher than the national average in reading[26] and science,[27] while Missouri's eighth graders scored lower than the national average in mathematics,[28] reading,[29] and writing[30] and higher than the national average in science.[31]

Equity Issues

In 2004, the funding per student in Missouri's highest poverty districts exceeded that in its lowest poverty districts by $190.[32] When adjustments were made for the additional costs of educating students growing up in poverty, however, the funding in high poverty districts actually declined by $271.[33] Similarly, Missouri spent $795 more per student in its highest minority districts, although this amount fell to $662 when adjustments for low-income students were made.[34]

Fourth graders eligible for free or reduced-price school lunches had test scores that were 7.4% lower in mathematics,[35] 9.5% lower in reading,[36] and 12% lower in writing[37] than those of students who were not eligible. The results were generally the same for eighth graders eligible for free or reduced-price lunches; their test scores were 8.4%

---

24. National Center for Education Statistics, U.S. Department of Education, The Nation's Report Card: Mathematics 2005, at 14 fig.11 (2005), *available at* http://nces.ed.gov/nationsreportcard/pdf/main2005/ 2006453.pdf [hereinafter Mathematics 2005].

25. Hilary R. Persky et al., National Center for Education Statistics, U.S. Department of Education, The Nation's Report Card: Writing 2002, at 23 tbl.2.2 (2003), *available at* http://nces.ed.gov/nationsreportcard/pdf/main2002/2003529.pdf [hereinafter Writing 2002].

26. National Center for Education Statistics, U.S. Department of Education, The Nation's Report Card: Reading 2005, at 14 fig.11 (2005), *available at* http://nces.ed.gov/nationsreportcard/pdf/main2005/2006451.pdf [hereinafter Reading 2005].

27. National Center for Education Statistics, U.S. Department of Education, The Nation's Report Card: Science 2005, at 16 fig.12 (2006), *available at* http://nces.ed.gov/nationsreportcard//pdf/main2005/2006466.pdf [hereinafter Science 2005].

28. Mathematics 2005, *supra* note 24, at 16 fig.12.

29. Reading 2005, *supra* note 26, at 16 fig.12.

30. Writing 2002, *supra* note 25, at 24 tbl.2.3.

31. Science 2005, *supra* note 27, at 28 fig.22.

32. The Education Trust, Funding Gaps 2006, at 7 tbl.3 (2006), *available at* http://www2.edtrust.org/NR/rdonlyres/CDEF9403-5A75-437E-93FF-EBF1174181FB/0/FundingGap2006.pdf.

33. *Id.*

34. *Id.* at 7 tbl.4.

35. Mathematics 2005, *supra* note 24, at 20 tbl.5.

36. Reading 2005, *supra* note 26, at 20 tbl.5.

37. Writing 2002, *supra* note 25, at 75 tbl.3.24.

lower in mathematics,[38] 7% lower in reading,[39] and 12.7% lower in writing[40] than those of students who were not eligible.

In *Committee for Educational Equality v. State*, the state court in Missouri found the state's school funding unconstitutional in 1993.[41] The court held that the system was "unconstitutional because it failed to provide children living in low-wealth districts educational opportunities on par with those available to their counterparts in affluent districts."[42] The General Assembly responded by passing legislation to improve funding equity, to create standards for the school districts, and to increase funding overall.[43] In 2004, in another case, *Committee for Educational Equality v. State*, plaintiffs filed suit against the state, alleging that the Missouri school funding system was still unconstitutional.[44] After the suit was filed, the legislature enacted another school funding law in 2005, but the plaintiffs claimed that this was also inequitable.[45] Litigation is currently ensuing, which began in January 2007.[46]

Availability of Publicly Funded Prekindergarten Programs

The Missouri Preschool Project currently serves three- and four-year-old children, with priority grants given to children with special needs or from low-income families.[47] Total enrollment in this state-funded program is 4,609,[48] which represents just 3.1% of Missouri's 147,142 three- and four-year-old children.[49] The federally funded Head Start program enrolls an additional 14,026 children,[50] which represents 9.5% of Missouri's three- and four-year-old children."[51]

Where Does Missouri Get Its Revenue?

At the end of fiscal year 2004, Missouri had total revenues of approximately $40 billion.[52] Of this amount, 41% was derived from state and local tax revenues and 20%

---

38. MATHEMATICS 2005, *supra* note 24, at 21 tbl.6.

39. READING 2005, *supra* note 26, at 21 tbl.6.

40. WRITING 2002, *supra* note 25, at 76 tbl.3.25.

41. Committee for Educational Equality v. State, Mo. Cir. Ct. Cole County, No. CV190-1371CC, order dated Jan. 1993.

42. *Id.*

43. *Missouri,* STARTINGAT3.ORG, *http://www.startingat3.org/state_laws/StatelawMOdetail.htm.*

44. Committee for Educational Equality v. State, Mo. Cir. Ct. Cole County, No. _____, petition filed Jan. 2004.

45. *Id.*

46. *Id.*

47. W. STEVEN BARNETT ET AL., NATIONAL INSTITUTE FOR EARLY EDUCATION RESEARCH, THE STATE OF PRESCHOOL 2006, at 148 (2007), *available at* http://nieer.org/yearbook/pdf/yearbook.pdf.

48. *Id.* at 93.

49. *See id.* at 232.

50. *Id.* at 93.

51. *See id.* at 232.

52. U.S. Census Bureau, State and Local Government Finances 2003–04, http://www.census.gov/govs/www/estimate04.html (last visited Oct. 6, 2006) [hereinafter Government Finances].

was received from the federal government.[53] The remaining 39% came from other sources, including the Missouri Lottery, insurance trust revenue, and revenue from government-owned utilities and other commercial or auxiliary enterprises.[54]

Tax Revenue

Missouri collected approximately $16.26 billion in state and local tax revenue during fiscal year 2004.[55] As a result, Missouri residents paid $2,822 per capita in state and local taxes, an amount which ranked 38th nationally.[56] The different types of tax sources were apportioned as follows:

Individual income taxes	24.8%
Property taxes	26.5%
General and selective sales taxes	41.2%
Corporate income and other taxes	7.5%
	100.0%[57]

Federal Funding

During fiscal year 2004, 20% of Missouri's total revenues came from the federal government.[58] For every dollar of federal taxes paid, Missouri received $1.29 in federal funding, an amount which ranked 25th nationally[59] and was well above the national average of $1.17.[60]

Lottery

Missouri has operated a state lottery named the "Missouri Lottery" since 1985.[61] Missouri's lottery proceeds are deposited into Missouri's general revenue fund[62] solely to fund education.[63] In 2005, the Missouri Lottery had operating revenues of $786 mil-

---

53. *Id.*

54. *Id.*

55. The total tax revenues were collected as follows: $26.23 billion by the state and $18.8 billion by local governments. *Id.*

56. *Id.*

57. *Id.*

58. *Id.*

59. The Tax Foundation, Federal Spending Received Per Dollar of Taxes Paid by State 2004, http://www.taxfoundation.org/taxdata/show/266.html (last visited Sept. 17, 2006).

60. *See id.*

61. General Information, http://www.molottery.com/learnaboutus/generalinfo/general-info.shtm (last visited Nov. 12, 2006).

62. Mo. Ann. Stat. § 313.321.

63. Mo. Const. art. III, § 39(d).

lion and a net income of $220 million.[64] In 2005, the Missouri Lottery transferred $219 million to the State of Missouri.[65]

Legal Structure of Major Tax Sources

Income

Missouri has a broad-based income tax[66] that uses adjusted gross income for federal income tax purposes as a starting point for determining the state's taxable income.[67] However, a fairly large number of adjustments may be available to various individuals in calculating this amount. [68] Two cities, St. Louis[69] and Kansas City, [70] have a local income tax of 1%. During fiscal year 2004, Missouri collected individual income tax of $646 per capita, an amount which ranked 29th nationally.[71]

Based on the relevant statutory exemptions and standard deductions, a typical family of four (i.e., married taxpayers who file jointly and have two dependent children) are not required to pay any income tax until their combined income exceeds $17,000, an amount which is below the national poverty line of $20,615.[72]

Missouri's income tax structure contains ten tax brackets that impose a minimum marginal rate of 1.5% and a maximum marginal rate of 6.00%.[73] When statutory exemptions and the standard deduction are taken into account, the maximum marginal rate applies to every dollar of income exceeding $25,900.[74]

---

64. Missouri Lottery Annual Report Fiscal Year 2005, 9, *available at* http://www.molottery.com/learnaboutus/wherethemoneygoes/fy05_cafr.pdf (last visited Nov. 11, 2006).

65. *Id.*

66. Mo. Ann. Stat. § 143.011.

67. *Id.* § 143.121.

68. *Id.* § 143.124.

69. *Id.* § 92.120.

70. *Id.* § 92.230.

71. State Rankings 2006, *supra* note 1, at 321.

72. Jason A. Levitis, Center on Budget and Policy Priorities, The Impact of State Income Taxes on Low-Income Families in 2006, at 12 (2007). In 2006, Missouri taxpayers who were married and filing jointly could claim a standard deduction of $10,300, personal exemptions of $2,100 each, and dependent exemptions of $1,200 each. Mo. Ann. Stat. §§ 143.131, 143.161. Note, however, that the threshold calculation of $17,000 is greater than the sum of these deductions and exemptions because it includes additional tax benefits available to low-income families, such as the earned-income tax credit. *See* Levitis, *supra*.

73. Mo. Ann. Stat. § 143.021. Missouri's middle eight brackets are 2.0%, 2.5%, 3.0%, 3.5%, 4.0%, 4.5%, 5.0%, and 5.5%. *Id.*

74. The standard deduction, two personal exemptions, and two dependent exemptions of $10,300, $2,100 and $1,200, respectively, plus the threshold of taxable income for the highest tax bracket of $9,000, equals $25,900. *See supra* notes 72–73.

Property

Overview

Missouri has a typical property tax system that taxes the value of real and personal property at the state and local levels. During fiscal year 2004, Missouri collected approximately $4.3 billion dollars in property tax at the local level and $22 million at the state level.[75] As a result, Missouri residents paid $747 per capita in state and local property taxes, an amount which ranked 37th nationally.[76]

Defining the Real Property Tax Base

Missouri has three classifications of real property: residential; agricultural and horticultural; and utility, industrial, commercial, railroad, and all other.[77] All real property is assessed according to its true value in money, but different assessment rates apply according to property classification.[78] Residential property is assessed at 19%; agricultural and horticultural property is assessed at 12%; and utility, industrial, commercial, railroad, and all other property is assessed at 32%.[79] True value in money is generally determined by the application of standard appraisal methods, including the cost method, the income method, and the market-data method.[80] There is no statutory provision for the reappraisal of property.[81]

Real Property Tax Rates

The Missouri state property tax rate is currently $0.30 per $1,000 of property value.[82] The real property tax rates, composed of county, city, school district, and special levies, vary and are set by each locality. Taxes are levied in terms of dollars per $1,000 of taxable value and are collected locally.[83] In 2005, the tax rates per $1,000 of assessed value ranged from $41.46 in Benton City to $64.86 in Moberly City.[84]

Personal and Intangible Property

Missouri has seven classifications of personal property: grain and unprocessed crops; livestock; farm machinery; vehicles, not including residential mobile homes; residential mobile homes; historic motor vehicles; and all other taxable personal property.[85]

---

75. Government Finances, *supra* note 52.

76. *See id.*

77. Mo. Ann. Stat. § 137.016.

78. Mo. Ann. Stat. § 137.115. The true value of agricultural and horticultural property is based on the use of the property. *Id* § 137.017.

79. *Id.*

80. CCH-EXP, MO-TAXRPTR ¶ 20-615, Valuation Methods in General.

81. CCH-EXP, MO-TAXRPTR ¶ 20-665, Reappraisals.

82. Mo. Const. art. III, § 38(b).

83. CCH-EXP, MO-TAXRPTR ¶ 20-405, Rates of Tax.

84. *Id.*

85. Mo. Ann. Stat. § 137.080.

All personal property is assessed according to its true value in money, but different assessment rates apply according to property classification.[86] Grain is assessed at 0.5%; livestock is assessed at 12%; farm machinery is assessed at 12%; historic motor vehicles and aircraft are assessed at 5%; poultry is assessed at 12%; pollution control and retooling equipment is assessed at 25%; and other personal property is assessed at 33.33%.[87] True value in money is generally determined by the application of standard appraisal methods, including the cost method, the income method, and the market-data method.[88] Intangible personal property is not subject to tax at either the state or local level.[89]

Exemptions

Missouri does not tax manufacturers' and merchants' inventories and the household goods of individuals.[90] Missouri provides a tax credit for senior citizens and disabled persons for an increase in their taxes that exceeds 5% in a reassessment year and 2.5% in a year without a general reassessment.[91] Missouri has authorized a homestead exemption but has not yet enacted a general homestead exemption.[92]

General and Selective Sales

General Sales

Missouri imposes a general retail sales-and-use tax, which makes up 28.6% of Missouri's total revenue.[93] This tax is imposed on all tangible personal property[94] and certain enumerated services.[95] The state sales tax rate is 4.225%.[96] Local jurisdictions can impose a sales tax.[97] Qualified retail sales of food are subject to a reduced rate of 1.225%.[98] Major exemptions from Missouri sales tax include items purchased with food stamps;[99] prescription drugs and medical equipment or devices;[100] and certain enumerated farm and agricultural equipment, supplies, and livestock.[101]

---

86. *Id* § 137.115.
87. *Id.*
88. CCH-EXP, MO-TAXRPTR ¶ 20-615, Valuation Methods in General.
89. *Id.*
90. CCH-EXP, MO-TAXRPTR ¶ 20-010, Overview.
91. Mo. Ann. Stat. § 137.106.
92. Mo. Const. art. X, § 6(a).
93. Government Finances, *supra* note 52.
94. Mo. Ann. Stat. § 144.020.
95. *Id.* § 144.021.
96. CCH-EXP, MO-TAXRPTR ¶ 60-110, Rate of Tax.
97. CCH-EXP, MO-TAXRPTR ¶ 61-735, Local Rates.
98. Mo. Ann. Stat. § 144.010. Food is defined as only those products and types of food for which food stamps may be redeemed pursuant to the federal Food Stamp Program, including food dispensed through vending machines. It does not include prepared food.
99. Mo. Ann. Stat. § 144.037.
100. *Id.* § 144.030.
101. *Id.*

Selective Sales

Selective sales taxes make up 12.6% of Missouri's total revenue.[102] Of that amount, 4.5% comes from a motor fuel sales tax imposed at a rate of $0.17 per gallon of gasoline.[103] Missouri residents paid an average of $126 per capita in state motor fuel sales taxes in 2004, an amount which ranked 27th nationally and was above the national average of $115.[104]

The tobacco product sales tax makes up 0.8%[105] of Missouri's tax revenues and is imposed at a rate of 10% of the manufacturer's invoice price before discounts and deals on all tobacco products[106] except for cigarettes, which are taxed at 8.5 mills ($0.17) per pack of 20.[107] Missouri residents paid $19.04 per capita in state tobacco sales taxes in 2004, an amount which ranked 44th nationally.[108]

In 2004, sales taxes on alcoholic beverages made up 0.2% of Missouri's total tax revenue.[109] Missouri residents paid $4.87 per capita in state alcoholic beverage sales taxes in 2004, an amount which ranked 44th nationally.[110]

The remainder of Missouri's selective sales taxes makes up 7.2% of its total tax revenue. Of this amount, 2.2% represents taxes on utilities and the other 5.0% represents taxes on other specific commodities, businesses, or services not reported separately above (e.g., on contractors, lodging, lubricating oil, fuels other than motor fuel, motor vehicles, meals, soft drinks, margarine, etc.). [111]

Corporate Income and Other

Corporate Income

The corporate income tax makes up 1.4% of Missouri's total tax revenue.[112] Missouri's broad-based corporate income tax is imposed on the Missouri net income of corporations doing business within Missouri or receiving income from property in the state.[113] The rate is a flat rate of 6.25% on all Missouri corporate income.[114]

Missouri follows the federal income tax treatment of S corporations. Thus, they do not pay Missouri's corporate income tax; rather, income and losses flow through to

---

102. Government Finances, *supra* note 52.

103. Mo. Ann. Stat. § 142.803.

104. State Rankings 2006, *supra* note 1, at 327.

105. Government Finances, *supra* note 52.

106. Mo. Ann. Stat. § 149.160.

107. *Id.* § 149.015.

108. State Rankings 2006, *supra* note 1, at 332.

109. Government Finances, *supra* note 52.

110. State Rankings 2006 , *supra* note 1, at 335.

111. *See* Governments Division, U.S. Census Bureau, Government Finance and Employment Classification Manual, at ch.7 (2000), *available at* http://ftp2.census.gov/govs/class/classfull.pdf [hereinafter Classification Manual].

112. *Id.*

113. Mo. Ann. Stat. § 143.431.

114. *Id.* § 143.071.

their shareholders.[115] A similar treatment is afforded to limited partnerships and limited liability partnerships, [116] as well as limited liability companies, assuming they are treated as a partnership for federal tax purposes.[117] However, if a limited liability company is treated as a corporation for federal income tax purposes, the entity is subject to Missouri's corporate income tax.[118]

Other

During fiscal year 2004, the collection of all other taxes not previously mentioned accounted for 6.1% of Missouri's total tax revenue.[119] Of this amount, $70 million[120] was generated by the estate and gift tax. This tax is calculated as the federal credit for state death taxes.[121] The "other taxes" category is also made up of motor vehicle license taxes, documentary and stock transfer taxes, severance taxes, and all other taxes not listed separately or provided for in other categories, such as taxes on land based on a specified rate per acre (rather than on assessed value).[122]

Burden Analysis

The overall state and local tax burden on Missouri's taxpayers is very regressive. Taxpayers in the lowest quintile—those with incomes of less than $15,000—bear a tax burden of 10.0% of their income, while taxpayers in the top 1%—those with incomes that exceed $271,000—bear a tax burden of just 7.4% of their income.[123] It is also worth noting that, although Missouri obviously has no control over federal tax policy, federal itemized deductions for state and local personal income and property taxes nonetheless further reduce the burden on taxpayers in the top 1% to 5.3%.[124] Fur-

---

115. *Id.* § 143.471.2.

116. *Id.* § 143.401.

117. *Id.*

118. *Id.*

119. Government Finances, *supra* note 52.

120. *Id.*

121. Mo. Ann. Stat. § 145.011.

122. *See* Classification Manual, *supra* note 111, at ch.7.

123. *See* Robert S. McIntyre et al. Who Pays? A Distributional Analysis of the Tax Systems in All 50 States 66 (2d ed. 2003), *available at* http://www.itepnet.org/wp2000/text.pdf. Taxpayers in the second quintile bear a 9.5% total tax burden on incomes between $15,000 and $25,000; those in the third quintile bear a 9.5% tax burden on incomes between $25,000 and $41,000; those in the fourth quintile bear a 9.6% tax burden on incomes between $41,000 and $67,000; those in the 80th–95th percentiles bear a 9.0% tax burden on incomes between $67,000 and $123,000; finally, those in the 96th–99th percentiles bear a 8.4% tax burden on incomes between $123,000 and $271,000. *Id.*

124. *Id.* Taxpayers in the lowest quintile did not receive any benefit from these federal offsets, while those in the second quintile were able to reduce their individual tax burdens by 0.1%, those in the third quintile by 0.2%, those in the fourth quintile by 0.5%, those in the 80th–95th percentiles by 1.2%, and those in the 96th–99th percentiles by 1.6%. *Id.*

thermore, between 1989 and 2002, the tax burden on the bottom quintile rose by approximately 0.6%, while the burden on the top 1% rose by 0.7%.[125]

In terms of the income tax, the burden across income groups in Missouri is slightly progressive, with taxpayers in the lowest quintile bearing a tax burden of 0.5% and those in the top 1% bearing a tax burden of 5.0%.[126] In sharp contrast, however, the sales and excises taxes imposed by Missouri are very regressive, with taxpayers in the lowest quintile bearing a tax burden of 7.1% and those in the top 1% bearing a tax burden of just 1.1%.[127] Property taxes in Missouri are also regressive, with taxpayers in the lowest quintile bearing a tax burden of 2.4% and those in the top quintile bearing an average tax burden of 1.8%.[128]

---

125. *Id.* at 67.

126. *See id.* at 66. Taxpayers in the second quintile bear a 1.6% income tax burden; those in the third quintile bear a 2.3% burden; those in the fourth quintile bear a 3.2% burden; those in the 80th–95th percentiles bear a 3.7% burden; finally, those in the 96th–99th percentiles bear a 4.3% burden. *Id.* Note, however, that these percentages include both individual and corporate income tax burdens; that within the 96th–99th percentiles, corporate income taxes represent 0.1% of this burden; and that in the top 1%, corporate income taxes represent 0.1% of this burden. *Id.*

127. *See id.* Taxpayers in the second quintile bear a 6.0% sales-and-excise tax burden; those in the third quintile bear a 5.0% burden; those in the fourth quintile bear a 4.2% burden; those in the 80th–95th percentiles bear a 3.1% burden; finally, those in the 96th–99th percentiles bear a 2.1% burden. *Id.*

128. *See id.* Taxpayers in the second quintile bear a 1.9% property tax burden; those in the third quintile bear a 2.2% burden; those in the fourth quintile bear a 2.1% burden; those in the 80th–95th percentiles bear a 2.2% burden; those in the 96th–99th percentiles bear a 2.0% burden; finally, those in the top 1% bear a 1.3% burden. *Id.*

Montana

General Information

Basic Profile – Geography, Population, and Industry

Admitted to the Union in 1889, Montana is commonly referred to as the "Treasure State."[1] Montana is located in the western region and is bordered by North Dakota, South Dakota, Wyoming, and Idaho. Montana is located in the mountain time zone, and its capital is Helena.[2]

In 2005, Montana ranked 44th in population (approximately 940,000 residents); the state ranks 4th in total area (147,042 square miles).[3] Its population is 91.1% white, 0.4% black, and 6.5% American Indian and Alaska Native.[4] The state is 22% Catholic; 51% Protestant; and less than 0.5% Jewish; 27% claim a religion outside the Judeo-Christian tradition or no religion at all.[5] Montana is mostly rural, with 65% of the population living in rural areas.[6] Major industries include agriculture, timber, mineral production, and tourism.[7]

Family Income and Poverty Indicators

In 2004, Montana's per capita gross product was $29,649, which ranked among the bottom ten states nationally and was below the national average of $39,725.[8] During

---

1. State Rankings 2006, vi, 1 (Kathleen O'Leary Morgan & Scott Morgan eds., Morgan Quinto Press 2006).

2. *Id.* at vi.

3. *Id.* at 429.

4. Montana Quick Facts from the U.S. Census Bureau, http://quickfacts.census.gov/qfd/states/30000.html (last visited Jan. 27, 2007). The remaining population is made up of 0.5% Asian persons and 1.5% persons reporting two or more races. *Id.* Additionally, 2.4% of Montana's total population identify themselves as persons of Hispanic or Latino origin. *Id.* (noting that because Hispanics may be of any race, they are included within the other applicable race categories).

5. Barry A. Kosmin, Egon Mayer & Ariela Keysar, American Religious Identification Survey 2001, at 41, *available at* http://www.gc.cuny.edu/faculty/research_studies/aris.pdf.

6. USDA Economic Research Service, Montana Fact Sheet, http://www.ers.usda.gov/StateFacts/MT.htm (last visited Sept. 17, 2006). According to the latest estimates, approximately 0.6 million people live in rural areas and 0.3 million people live in urban areas. *Id.*

7. "The Economy," Montana Historical Society, A division of the Official Montana State Website mt.gov, http://www.montanahistoricalsociety.org/education/studentguide/default.asp (last visited Nov. 12, 2006).

8. State Rankings 2006, *supra* note 1, at 89.

this same period, although the median household income in Montana was $35,201,[9] 14.3% of Montana's population was living in poverty, which was above the national average of 12.4%.[10] More specifically, poverty affected 18.7% of Montana's children,[11] 8.8% of its senior citizens,[12] and 10.5% of its families.[13] Of its female-headed households with children, 45.4% lived in poverty,[14] and 33.7% of the state's public elementary and secondary school students were eligible for free or reduced-price meals.[15] Of those living in poverty, approximately 0.5% were black, which represented 21.5% of Montana's black population and 0.1% of its total population.[16] In an attempt to combat this poverty, Montana spent approximately $671 million on public welfare programs in 2002,[17] which made up 13.3% of its total government expenditures.[18]

Montana's Public Elementary-Secondary School System

Overall Spending and Performance

For the 2003–2004 school year, Montana spent $7,763 per pupil in its public elementary-secondary school system, which was slightly below the national average of $8,182.[19] Of this amount, 15.2% was provided by the federal government, 44.4% was provided by the state government, and 40.4% was provided by the local governments,[20] with property taxes making up 25.3% of the total funding.[21] Out of these funds, Montana paid its elementary and secondary school teachers an estimated average annual salary of $38,485 during the 2004–2005 school year,[22] and it provided a student/teacher ratio of 14.4, which was better than the national average of 15.9.[23]

---

9. *Id.* at 96.

10. *Id.* at 495.

11. *Id.* at 497.

12. *Id.* at 496.

13. *Id.* at 498.

14. *Id.* at 499.

15. *Id.* at 532.

16. *See* Fact Sheet, American FactFinder, http://factfinder.census.gov/home/saff/main.html?_lang=en (select Montana under "Get a Fact Sheet for your community") (last visited Feb. 16, 2007). Note that these numbers are based on the 2000 census because more recent numbers were not available.

17. STATE RANKINGS 2006, *supra* note 1, at 500.

18. *Id.* at 502.

19. GOVERNMENTS DIVISION, U.S. CENSUS BUREAU, PUBLIC EDUCATION FINANCES 2004, at 8 tbl.8 (2006).

20. *See id.* at 5 tbl.5.

21. *See id.* at 4 tbl.4.

22. THOMAS D. SNYDER ET AL., NATIONAL CENTER FOR EDUCATION STATISTICS, DIGEST OF EDUCATION STATISTICS 2005, at 116 tbl.77 (2006).

23. *Id.* at 98 tbl.65.

In academic performance, Montana's fourth grade students scored lower than the national average in writing[24] and higher than the national average in mathematics,[25] reading,[26] and science,[27] while Montana's eighth graders scored at the national average in writing[28] and higher than the national average in mathematics,[29] reading,[30] and science.[31]

Equity Issues

In 2004, revenues spent per student in Montana's highest poverty districts were determined to be $789 less than the revenues spent its lowest poverty districts.[32] When adjustments were made for the additional costs of educating students growing up in poverty, however, the funding gap grew to $1,148.[33] Similarly, Montana spent $1,787 less per student in its highest minority districts, and this amount grew to $1,838 when adjustments for low-income students were made.[34]

Fourth graders eligible for free or reduced-price school lunches had test scores that were 6.4% lower in mathematics,[35] 8.6% lower in reading,[36] and 11.4% lower in writing[37] than those of students who were not eligible. The results were generally worse for eighth graders eligible for free or reduced-price lunches; their test scores were 7.2% lower in mathematics,[38] 7.7% lower in reading,[39] and 15.1% lower in writing[40] than those of students who were not eligible.

---

24. HILARY R. PERSKY ET AL., NATIONAL CENTER FOR EDUCATION STATISTICS, U.S. DEPARTMENT OF EDUCATION, THE NATION'S REPORT CARD: WRITING 2002, at 23 tbl.2.2 (2003), *available at* http://nces.ed.gov/nationsreportcard/pdf/main2002/2003529.pdf [hereinafter WRITING 2002].

25. NATIONAL CENTER FOR EDUCATION STATISTICS, U.S. DEPARTMENT OF EDUCATION, THE NATION'S REPORT CARD: MATHEMATICS 2005, at 14 fig.11 (2005), *available at* http://nces.ed.gov/nationsreportcard/pdf/main2005/ 2006453.pdf [hereinafter MATHEMATICS 2005].

26. NATIONAL CENTER FOR EDUCATION STATISTICS, U.S. DEPARTMENT OF EDUCATION, THE NATION'S REPORT CARD: READING 2005, at 14 fig.11 (2005), *available at* http://nces.ed.gov/nationsreportcard/pdf/main2005/2006451.pdf [hereinafter READING 2005].

27. NATIONAL CENTER FOR EDUCATION STATISTICS, U.S. DEPARTMENT OF EDUCATION, THE NATION'S REPORT CARD: SCIENCE 2005, at 16 fig.12 (2006) *available at* http://nces.ed.gov/nationsreportcard//pdf/main2005/2006466.pdf [hereinafter SCIENCE 2005].

28. WRITING 2002, *supra* note 24, at 24 tbl.2.3.

29. MATHEMATICS 2005, *supra* note 25, at 16 fig.12.

30. READING 2005, *supra* note 26, at 16 fig.12.

31. SCIENCE 2005, *supra* note 27, at 28 fig.22.

32. THE EDUCATION TRUST, FUNDING GAPS 2006, at 7 tbl.3 (2006), *available at* http://www2.edtrust.org/NR/rdonlyres/CDEF9403-5A75-437E-93FF-EBF1174181FB/0/FundingGap2006.pdf.

33. *Id.*

34. *Id.* at 7 tbl.4.

35. MATHEMATICS 2005, *supra* note 25, at 20 tbl.5.

36. READING 2005, *supra* note 26, at 20 tbl.5.

37. WRITING 2002, *supra* note 24, at 75 tbl.3.24.

38. MATHEMATICS 2005, *supra* note 25, at 21 tbl.6.

39. READING 2005, *supra* note 26, at 21 tbl.6.

40. WRITING 2002, *supra* note 24, at 76 tbl.3.25.

In 2005, the Montana Supreme Court upheld the decision of the district court that the Montana public school funding system was unconstitutional.[41] In response, the Montana legislature increased school funding in its 2005 regular session.[42]

Availability of Publicly Funded Prekindergarten Programs

Montana has no state publicly funded prekindergarten programs.[43] The federally funded Head Start program enrolls 3,929 children,[44] which represents 18.8% of Montana's 20,853 three- and four-year-old children.[45]

Where Does Montana Get Its Revenue?

At the end of fiscal year 2004, Montana had total revenues of approximately $7.1 billion.[46] Of this amount, 34% was derived from state and local tax revenues and 27% was received from the federal government.[47] The remaining 39% came from other sources, including the Montana Lottery, insurance trust revenue, and revenue from government-owned utilities and other commercial or auxiliary enterprises.[48]

Tax Revenue

Montana collected approximately $2.43 billion in state and local tax revenue during fiscal year 2004.[49] As a result, Montana residents paid $2,623 per capita in state and local taxes, an amount which ranked 45th nationally.[50] The different types of tax sources were apportioned as follows:

---

41. Columbia Falls Elem. Sch. Dist. No. 6 v. State, 109 P.3d 257 (Mont. 2005).

42. Litigation Update: Compliance in Kansas and Montana, Decision in New Jersey, Appeals in New York, *available at* http://www.schoolfunding.info/news/litigation/6-27-06litupdate (last visited April 4, 2007).

43. W. STEVEN BARNETT ET AL., NATIONAL INSTITUTE FOR EARLY EDUCATION RESEARCH, THE STATE OF PRESCHOOL 2006, at 148 (2007), *available at* http://nieer.org/yearbook/pdf/yearbook.pdf.

44. *Id.* at 95.

45. *See id.* at 232.

46. U.S. Census Bureau, State and Local Government Finances 2003–04, http://www.census.gov/govs/www/estimate04.html (last visited Oct. 6, 2006) [hereinafter Government Finances].

47. *Id.*

48. *Id.*

49. The total tax revenues were collected as follows: $1.6 billion by the state and $0.8 billion by local governments. *Id.*

50. *Id.*

Individual income taxes	24.9%
Property taxes	39.4%
General and selective sales taxes	18.1%
Corporate income and other taxes	<u>17.6%</u>
	100.0%[51]

Federal Funding

During fiscal year 2004, 27% of Montana's total revenues came from the federal government.[52] For every dollar of federal taxes paid, Montana received $1.58 in federal funding, an amount which ranked 9th nationally[53] and was well above the national median of $1.17.[54]

Lottery

Montana has operated a state lottery named the "Montana Lottery" since 1986.[55] Montana's lottery proceeds are deposited into Montana's general fund.[56] In 2005, the Montana Lottery had operating revenues of $10.4 million and a net income of $6.2 million.[57] In 2005, the Montana Lottery transferred $6.2 million to the Montana State General Fund.[58]

Legal Structure of Major Tax Sources

Income

Montana has a broad-based income tax[59] that uses adjusted gross income for federal income tax purposes, with very few adjustments, as a starting point for determining the state's taxable income.[60] Montana allows a deduction for 100% of federal income taxes paid up to $5,000 if single or $10,000 if married and filing jointly.[61] Montana has no statutes authorizing a local income tax.[62] During fiscal year 2004,

---

51. *Id.*

52. *Id.*

53. The Tax Foundation, Federal Spending Received Per Dollar of Taxes Paid by State 2004, http://www.taxfoundation.org/taxdata/show/266.html (last visited Sept. 17, 2006).

54. *See id.*

55. Montana Lottery History, http://www.montanalottery.com/history.xsp (last visited Nov.11, 2006).

56. MONT. CODE ANN. § 23-7-402.

57. Montana Lottery Annual Report 2005, 10, *available at* http://www.montanalottery.com/reports_forms/annual_report_2005.pdf (last visited Nov. 11, 2006).

58. *Id.*

59. MONT. CODE ANN. § 15-30-101.

60. *Id.* § 15-30-111.

61. *Id.* § 15-30-121.

62. CCH-EXP, MT-TAXRPTR ¶ 15-020, Local Power to Tax.

Montana collected individual income tax of $653 per capita, an amount which ranked 26th nationally.[63]

On the basis of the relevant statutory exemptions and standard deductions, a typical family of four (i.e., married taxpayers who file jointly and have two dependent children) are not required to pay any income tax until their combined income exceeds $11,300, an amount which is well below the national poverty line of $20,615.[64] Montana's income tax structure contains seven tax brackets that impose a minimum marginal rate of 1.0% and a maximum marginal rate of 6.9%.[65] When statutory exemptions and the standard deduction are taken into account, the maximum marginal rate applies to every dollar of income exceeding $29,540.[66]

Property

Overview

Montana has a typical property tax system that taxes the value of real and personal property at the state and local levels. During fiscal year 2004, Montana collected approximately $775 million dollars in property tax at the local level and $184 million at the state level.[67] As a result, Montana residents paid $1,034 per capita in state and local property taxes, an amount which ranked 20th nationally.[68]

Defining the Real Property Tax Base

Montana currently has twelve property classifications (but only eleven of them are used for real property), which are assessed at different rates.[69]

---

63. STATE RANKINGS 2006, *supra* note 1, at 321.

64. JASON A. LEVITIS, CENTER ON BUDGET AND POLICY PRIORITIES, THE IMPACT OF STATE INCOME TAXES ON LOW-INCOME FAMILIES IN 2006, AT 12 (2007). In 2006, Montana taxpayers who were married and filing jointly could claim a standard deduction of 20% of their adjusted gross income, with a minimum deduction of $3,160 and a maximum deduction of $7,120, personal exemptions of $1,980 each, and dependent exemptions of $1,980 each. MONT. CODE ANN. §§ 15-30-122, 15-30-112. Note, however, that the threshold calculation of $11,300 is greater than the sum of these deductions and exemptions because it includes additional tax benefits available to low-income families, such as the earned-income tax credit. *See* LEVITIS, *supra*.

65. MONT. CODE ANN. § 15-30-103. Montana's middle five brackets are 1%, 2%, 3%, 4%, 5%, and 6%. *Id.*

66. The maximum standard deduction and the exemptions of $7,120 and $1,980, respectively, plus the threshold of taxable income for the highest tax bracket of $14,500, equals $29,540. *See supra* notes 64–65.

67. Government Finances, *supra* note 46.

68. *See id.*

69. http://www.state.ia.us/tax/educate/78573.html (last visited Oct. 11, 2006). Categories six and eleven have been repealed. Montana uses the following classes: Class one is mining property, excluding metal mines; class two is metal mines; class three includes agricultural property; class four includes residential property and commercial and industrial land; class five property is property owned by certain electric and telephone companies, new industrial property, and certain pollution-control equipment; class seven property is property owned by certain coop-

Market value is generally determined by the application of standard appraisal methods, including the cost method, the income method, and the market-data method.[70] State law requires that all real property be assessed every year, except property in classes three, four and ten, which are reassessed according to programs developed by the Department of Revenue.[71]

Real Property Tax Rates

The real property tax rates, composed of county, city, school district, and special levies, vary and are set by each locality. Taxes are levied in terms of dollars per $1,000 of assessed taxable value and are collected locally.[72] Class one property is assessed at 100% of net proceeds;[73] class two is assessed at 3% of annual gross proceeds;[74] class three is assessed at the same rate as class four;[75] class four is assessed at 3.22% in 2005, 3.14% in 2006, 3.07% in 2007, 3.01% in years after 2007 of market value;[76] class five is assessed at 3% of market value;[77] class seven is assessed at 8% of market value;[78] class nine is assessed at 12% of market value;[79] class ten is initially assessed at 0.79% of its forest productivity value;[80] class twelve is assessed at the lesser of 12% of market value or the ratio of taxable value to market value of commercial property;[81] class thirteen is assessed at 6% of market value;[82] and class fourteen is assessed at 3% of market value.[83] All other real property is assessed at 100% of market value.[84] In 2006, the statewide average millage rate was 583 mills.[85]

---

erative rural electrical associations and specified property of noncentrally assessed public utilities; class nine property consists of certain property of centrally assessed utilities; class ten is forest property; class twelve property is railroad and airline transportation property; class thirteen property is the property of centrally assessed telecommunications service companies; and class fourteen property is wind-generation facilities. MONT. CODE ANN. §§ 15-6-131, 15-6-132, 15-6-133, 15-6-134, 15-6-135, 15-6-137, 15-6-141, 15-6-141, 15-6-143, 15-6-145,15-6-156, 15-6-157. Class eight property covers personal property subject to the property tax. *See infra* note 87 and accompanying text.

70. CCH-EXP, MT-TAXRPTR ¶ 20-615, Valuation Methods in General.

71. MONT. CODE ANN. § 15-7-111.

72. CCH-EXP, MT-TAXRPTR ¶ 20-405, Rates of Tax.

73. MONT. CODE ANN. § 15-6-131.

74. *Id.* § 15-6-132.

75. *Id.* § 15-6-133.

76. *Id.* § 15-6-134.

77. *Id.* § 15-6-135.

78. *Id.* § 15-6-137.

79. *Id.* § 15-6-141.

80. MONT. CODE ANN. § 15-6-143. The initial assessment rate is reduced by 0.11% annually until the assessment rate reaches 0.35% of forest productivity value. *Id.*

81. *Id.* § 15-6-145.

82. *Id.* § 15-6-156.

83. *Id.* § 15-6-157.

84. *Id.* § 15-8-111.

85. Montana Tax Rates: 1996–2006. Montana Taxpayers Association. http://www.montax.org/index.php?pr=doug. (last visited: Feb. 12, 2007).

Personal and Intangible Property

Montana has one classification for personal property, which is class eight.[86] Class eight property is taxed at 3% of its market value.[87] Intangible personal property is not subject to tax at either the state or local level.[88]

Exemptions

Household goods are exempt from property tax.[89] Montana also provides a residential property tax credit for certain taxpayers who are over the age of 62, have resided in the state for at least 9 months, have occupied one or more dwellings in the state for at least 6 months of the claim period, and have less than $45,000 of gross household income.[90]

General and Selective Sales

General Sales

Montana imposes no general retail sales-and-use tax.[91] Special sales-and-use taxes are imposed at the following rates: 4% for accommodations,[92] 3% for campgrounds,[93] 4% for lodging facilities,[94] and 4% for rental vehicles.[95] Certain localities are authorized to impose a "resort" tax of up to 3%.[96]

Selective Sales

Selective sales taxes make up 18.1% of Montana's total tax revenue.[97] Of that amount, 8.1% comes from a motor fuel sales tax imposed at a rate of $0.27 per gallon of gasoline.[98] Montana residents paid an average of $213 per capita in state motor fuel sales taxes in 2004, an amount which ranked 1st nationally and was well above the national average of $115.[99]

The tobacco product sales tax makes up 1.9%[100] of Montana's tax revenues and is imposed at a rate of 50% of the wholesale price of all tobacco products[101] except for ciga-

---

86. MONT. CODE ANN. § 15-6-138.
87. *Id.*
88. *Id.* § 15-6-218.
89. *Id.* § 15-6-119.
90. *Id.* § 15-30-172.
91. CCH-EXP, MT-TAXRPTR ¶ 60-010, Overview.
92. MONT. CODE ANN. § 15-65-111.
93. *Id.* § 15-68-102.
94. *Id.* § 15-65-111.
95. *Id.* § 15-68-102.
96. *Id.* § 7-6-1501 et seq.
97. Government Finances, *supra* note 46.
98. MONT. CODE ANN. § 15-70-204.
99. STATE RANKINGS 2006, *supra* note 1, at 327.
100. Government Finances, *supra* note 46.
101. MONT. CODE ANN. § 16-11-202.

rettes, which are taxed at 85 mills ($1.70) per pack of 20.[102] Montana residents paid $48.77 per capita in state tobacco sales taxes in 2004, an amount which ranked 23rd nationally.[103]

In 2004, sales taxes on alcoholic beverages made up 0.8% of Montana's total tax revenue.[104] Montana residents paid $22.19 per capita in state alcoholic beverage sales taxes in 2004, an amount which ranked 12th nationally.[105]

The remainder of Montana's selective sales taxes makes up 7.3% of its total tax revenue. Of this amount, 1.2% represents taxes on utilities and the other 6.1% represents taxes on other specific commodities, businesses, or services not reported separately above (e.g., on contractors, lodging, lubricating oil, fuels other than motor fuel, motor vehicles, meals, soft drinks, margarine, etc.). [106]

Corporate Income and Other

Corporate Income

The corporate income tax makes up 2.8% of Montana's total tax revenue.[107] Montana's broad-based corporate income tax is imposed on the Montana net income of corporations doing business within Montana or receiving income from property in the state.[108] The rate is a flat 6.75% on all corporate income over $50.[109]

Montana follows the federal income tax treatment of S corporations. Thus, they do not pay Montana's corporate income tax; rather, income and losses flow through to their shareholders.[110] A similar treatment is afforded to limited partnerships and limited liability partnerships, [111] as well as limited liability companies, assuming they are treated as a partnership for federal tax purposes.[112] However, if a limited liability company is treated as a corporation for federal income tax purposes, the entity is subject to Montana's corporate income tax.[113]

Other

During fiscal year 2004, the collection of all other taxes not previously mentioned accounted for 14.88% of Montana's total tax revenue.[114] Of this amount, $11.4 mil-

---

102. *Id.* § 16-11-111.

103. STATE RANKINGS 2006, *supra* note 1, at 332.

104. Government Finances, *supra* note 46.

105. STATE RANKINGS 2006, *supra* note 1, at 335.

106. *See* GOVERNMENTS DIVISION, U.S. CENSUS BUREAU, GOVERNMENT FINANCE AND EMPLOYMENT CLASSIFICATION MANUAL, at ch.7 (2000), *available at* http://ftp2.census.gov/govs/class/classfull.pdf [hereinafter CLASSIFICATION MANUAL].

107. *Id.*

108. MONT. CODE ANN. § 15-31-101.

109. *Id.* § 15-31-121.

110. *Id.* § 15-30-1102.

111. CCH-EXP, MT-TAXRPTR ¶ 10-225, Limited Partnerships, Limited Liability Partnerships.

112. CCH-EX, MT-TAXRPTR ¶ 10-240, Limited Liability Companies (LLCs).

113. *Id.*

114. Government Finances, *supra* note 46.

lion[115] was generated by the estate tax. The estate tax is set at 100% of the maximum federal credit for state inheritance taxes paid, which was phased out in 2005.[116] The "other taxes" category is also made up of motor vehicle license taxes, documentary and stock transfer taxes, severance taxes, and all other taxes not listed separately or provided for in other categories, such as taxes on land based on a specified rate per acre (rather than on assessed value).[117]

Burden Analysis

The overall state and local tax burden on Montana's taxpayers is somewhat progressive. In fact, Montana is one of the least regressive states. Taxpayers in the lowest quintile—those with incomes of less than $12,000—bear a tax burden of 6.1% of their income, while taxpayers in the top 1%—those with incomes that exceed $264,000—bear a tax burden of just 7.2% of their income.[118] It is also worth noting that, although Montana obviously has no control over federal tax policy, federal itemized deductions for state and local personal income and property taxes nonetheless further reduce the burden on taxpayers in the top 1% to 5.2%.[119] Furthermore, between 1989 and 2002, the tax burden on the bottom quintile fell by approximately 0.7%, while the burden on the top 1% fell by approximately 0.8%.[120]

In terms of the income tax, the burden across income groups in Montana is slightly progressive, with taxpayers in the lowest quintile bearing a tax burden of 1.2% and those in the top 1% bearing a tax burden of 5.5%.[121] The sales and excises taxes im-

---

115. *Id.*

116. Mont. Code Ann. § 72-16-905

117. *See* Classification Manual, *supra* note 106, at ch.7.

118. *See* Robert S. McIntyre et al., Who Pays? A Distributional Analysis of the Tax Systems in All 50 States 68 (2d ed. 2003), *available at* http://www.itepnet.org/wp2000/text.pdf. Taxpayers in the second quintile bear a 6.8% total tax burden on incomes between $12,000 and $22,000; those in the third quintile bear a 7.0% tax burden on incomes between $22,000 and $35,000; those in the fourth quintile bear a 7.2% tax burden on incomes between $35,000 and $59,000; those in the 80th–95th percentiles bear a 7.1% tax burden on incomes between $59,000 and $102,000; finally, those in the 96th–99th percentiles bear a 7.4% tax burden on incomes between $102,000 and $264,000. *Id.*

119. *Id.* Taxpayers in the lowest quintile did not receive any benefit from these federal offsets, while those in the second quintile were able to reduce their individual tax burdens by 0.1%, those in the third quintile by 0.3%, those in the fourth quintile by 0.5%, those in the 80th–95th percentiles by 0.9%, and those in the 96th–99th percentiles by 1.5%. *Id.*

120. *Id.* at 69.

121. *See id.* at 68. Taxpayers in the second quintile bear a 1.8% income tax burden; those in the third quintile bear a 2.5% burden; those in the fourth quintile bear a 3.0% burden; those in the 80th–95th percentiles bear a 3.5% burden; finally, those in the 96th–99th percentiles bear a 4.7% burden. *Id.* Note, however, that these percentages include both individual and corporate income tax burdens; that within the bottom quintile, corporate income taxes represent 0.1% of this burden; that within the second quintile, corporate income taxes represent 0.1% of this burden; that within the third quintile, corporate income taxes represent 0.0% of this burden; that

posed by Montana are slightly regressive, with taxpayers in the lowest quintile bearing a tax burden of 1.5% and those in the top 1% bearing a tax burden of just 0.1%.[122] Property taxes in Montana are also regressive, with taxpayers in the lowest quintile bearing a tax burden of 3.5% and those in the top quintile bearing an average tax burden of 2.4%.[123]

---

within the fourth quintile, corporate income taxes represent 0.1% of this burden; that within the 80th–95th percentiles, corporate income taxes represent 0.0% of this burden; that within the 96th–99th percentiles, corporate income taxes represent 0.1% of this burden; and that in the top 1%, corporate income taxes represent 0.2% of this burden. *Id.*

122. *See id.* at 68. Taxpayers in the second quintile bear a 1.6% sales-and-excise tax burden; those in the third quintile bear a 1.1% burden; those in the fourth quintile bear a 0.9% burden; those in the 80th–95th percentiles bear a 0.6% burden; and finally, those in the 96th–99th percentiles bear a 0.3% burden. *Id.*

123. *See id.* at 68. Taxpayers in the second quintile bear a 3.3% property tax burden; those in the third quintile bear a 3.5% burden; those in the fourth quintile bear a 3.3% burden; those in the 80th–95th percentiles bear a 3.1% burden; those in the 96th–99th percentiles bear a 2.4% burden; finally, those in the top 1% bear a 1.6% burden. *Id.*

Nebraska

General Information

Basic Profile – Geography, Population, and Industry

Nebraska was admitted to the Union in 1867. The "Cornhusker State" is located in the Great Plains and is bordered by South Dakota on the north, Iowa and Missouri on the east. Kansas on the south, Colorado on the southwest, and Wyoming on the west. Lincoln is the state capital. Most of Nebraska is located in the central time zone; a western portion of the state is located in the mountain time zone.

Nebraska ranks 38th in population (approximately 1.76 million residents)[1] and 16th in total land and water area (77,354 square miles).[2] Its population is approximately 92.0% white and 4.3% black.[3] The state is approximately 27% Catholic; 54% Protestant; and less than 0.5% Jewish; 19% claim a religion outside the Judeo-Christian tradition or no religion at all.[4] Roughly 57% of Nebraska's population lives in urban areas.[5] The state's economy revolves around agriculture, although manufacturing, health services, and business services are also prominent industries.[6]

Family Income and Poverty Indicators

In 2004, Nebraska's per capita gross product was $39,013, which was just below the national average of $39,725.[7] During this same period, although the median household

---

1. STATE RANKINGS 2006, vi, 429 (Kathleen O'Leary Morgan & Scott Morgan eds., Morgan Quitno Press 2006).

2. *Id.* at 225.

3. Nebraska Quick Facts from the U.S. Census Bureau, http://quickfacts.census.gov/qfd/states/31000.html (last visited Apr. 1, 2007). The remaining population is made up of 0.9% American Indian and Alaska Native persons; 1.6% Asian persons; 0.1% Native Hawaiian persons and other Pacific Islanders; and 1.1% persons reporting two or more races. *Id.* Additionally, 7.1% of Nebraska's total population identify themselves as persons of Hispanic or Latino origin. *Id.* (noting that because Hispanics and Latinos may be of any race, they are also included within the other applicable race categories). *See id.*

4. *See* BARRY A. KOSMIN, EGON MAYER & ARIELA KEYSAR, AMERICAN RELIGIOUS IDENTIFICATION SURVEY 2001, at 40, *available at* http://www.gc.cuny.edu/faculty/research_studies/aris.pdf.

5. USDA Economic Research Service, Nebraska Fact Sheet, http://www.ers.usda.gov/StateFacts/NE.htm (last visited Oct. 16, 2006).

6. NEBRASKA UNICAMERAL INFORMATION OFFICE, NEBRASKA BLUE BOOK, 38-40 (2004–2005), *available at* http://www.unicam.state.ne.us/web/public/bluebook (last visited Oct. 16, 2006).

7. STATE RANKINGS 2006, *supra* note 1, at 89.

income in Nebraska was $44,623,[8] 9.9% of Nebraska's population was living in poverty, which was below the national average of 12.4%.[9] More specifically, poverty affected 12.7% of Nebraska's children,[10] 7.7% of its senior citizens,[11] and 7.7% of its families.[12] Of its female-headed households with children, 38.6% lived in poverty,[13] and 33.9% of the state's public elementary and secondary school students were eligible for free or reduced-price meals.[14] Of those living in poverty, approximately 10.9% were black, which represented 25.6% of Nebraska's black population and 1% of its total population.[15] In an attempt to combat this poverty, Nebraska spent approximately $1.7 billion on public welfare programs in 2002,[16] which made up 17.5% of its total government expenditures.[17]

Nebraska's Public Elementary-Secondary School System

Overall Spending and Performance

For the 2003–2004 school year, Nebraska spent $8,032 per pupil in its public elementary-secondary school system, which hovered around the national average of $8,182.[18] Of this amount, 9% was provided by the federal government, 32.8% was provided by the state government, and 58.2% was provided by the local governments,[19] with property taxes making up 46.3% of the total funding.[20] Out of these funds, Nebraska paid its elementary and secondary school teachers an estimated average annual salary of $39,456 during the 2004–2005 school year,[21] and in 2003, it provided a student/teacher ratio of 13.6, which was better than the national average of 15.9.[22]

---

8. *Id.* at 96.

9. *Id.* at 495.

10. *Id.* at 497.

11. *Id.* at 496.

12. *Id.* at 498.

13. *Id.* at 499.

14. *Id.* at 532.

15. *See* Fact Sheet, American FactFinder, http://factfinder.census.gov/home/saff/main.html?_ lang=en (select "Nebraska" under "Get a Fact Sheet for your community") (last visited Feb. 16, 2007). Note that these numbers are based on the 2000 census because more recent numbers were not available.

16. *Id.* at 500.

17. *Id.* at 502.

18. GOVERNMENTS DIVISION, U.S. CENSUS BUREAU, PUBLIC EDUCATION FINANCES 2004, at 8 tbl.8 (2006), *available at* http://www2.census.gov/govs/school/04f33pub.pdf.

19. *See id.* at 5 tbl.5.

20. *See id.* at 4 tbl.4.

21. THOMAS D. SNYDER ET AL., NATIONAL CENTER FOR EDUCATION STATISTICS, DIGEST OF EDUCATION STATISTICS 2005, at 116 tbl.77 (2006) *available at* http://nces.ed.gov/pubsearch/pubsinfo.asp?pubid=2006030.

22. *Id.* at 98 tbl.65.

In academic performance, Nebraska's fourth and eighth grade students scored higher than the national average in mathematics,[23] reading,[24] and writing.[25] Nebraska's test scores for science were unavailable.[26]

Equity Issues

In 2004, the funding per student in Nebraska's highest poverty districts exceeded that in its lowest poverty districts by $515,[27] although when adjustments were made for the additional costs of educating students growing up in poverty, that excess narrowed to $210.[28] On the other hand, Nebraska spent $1,280 less per student in its highest minority districts, and this amount grew to $1,374 when adjustments for low-income students were made.[29]

Fourth graders eligible for free or reduced-price school lunches had test scores that were 9% lower in mathematics,[30] 12% lower in reading,[31] and 12% lower in writing[32] than those students who were not eligible. The results were just slightly better for eighth graders eligible for free or reduced-price lunches; their test scores were 8% lower in mathematics,[33] 8% lower in reading,[34] and 13% lower in writing[35] than those of students who were not eligible.

In the 1993 case *Gould v. Orr*, the Nebraska Supreme Court rejected the plaintiffs' equal protection challenge of the education funding system, holding that the complaint failed to state facts sufficient to constitute a cause of action because it did not allege that unequal funding of schools affected quality of education.[36] Two lawsuits filed in

---

23. NATIONAL CENTER FOR EDUCATION STATISTICS, U.S. DEPARTMENT OF EDUCATION, THE NATION'S REPORT CARD: MATHEMATICS 2005, at 14 fig.11, 16 fig.12 (2005), *available at* http:// nces.ed.gov/nationsreportcard/pdf/ main2005/2006453.pdf [hereinafter MATHEMATICS 2005].

24. NATIONAL CENTER FOR EDUCATION STATISTICS, U.S. DEPARTMENT OF EDUCATION, THE NATION'S REPORT CARD: READING 2005, at 14 fig.11, 16 fig.12 (2005), *available at* http:// nces.ed.gov/nationsreportcard/pdf/main2005/2006451.pdf [hereinafter READING 2005].

25. HILARY R. PERSKY ET AL., NATIONAL CENTER FOR EDUCATION STATISTICS, U.S. DEPARTMENT OF EDUCATION, THE NATION'S REPORT CARD: WRITING 2002, at 23 tbl.2.2, 24 tbl.2.3 (2003), *available at* http://nces.ed.gov/nationsreportcard/pdf/main2002/2003529.pdf [hereinafter WRITING 2002].

26. *See* NATIONAL CENTER FOR EDUCATION STATISTICS, U.S. DEPARTMENT OF EDUCATION, THE NATION'S REPORT CARD: SCIENCE 2005, at 16 fig.12, 28 fig.22 (2006), *available at* http://nces.ed.gov/nationsreportcard//pdf/main2005/2006466.pdf [hereinafter SCIENCE 2005].

27. THE EDUCATION TRUST, FUNDING GAPS 2006, at 7 tbl.3 (2006), *available at* http://www2 .edtrust.org/NR/rdonlyres/CDEF9403-5A75-437E-93FF-EBF1174181FB/0/FundingGap2006.pdf.

28. *Id.*

29. *Id.* at 7 tbl.4.

30. MATHEMATICS 2005, *supra* note 23, at 20 tbl.5.

31. READING 2005, *supra* note 24, at 20 tbl.5.

32. WRITING 2002, *supra* note 25, at 75 tbl.3.24.

33. MATHEMATICS 2005, *supra* note 23, at 21 tbl.6.

34. READING 2005, *supra* note 24, at 21 tbl.6.

35. WRITING 2002, *supra* note 25, at 76 tbl.3.25.

36. N.W. 2d 349 (Neb. 1993).

2003 challenging the adequacy of Nebraska's school funding system are currently pending.[37]

Availability of Publicly Funded Prekindergarten Programs

Nebraska's Early Child Grant Program serves primarily three- and four-year-old children, and most of its funds are used for children meeting at least one of the following four criteria: children eligible for free or reduced-priced lunches; English Language Learners; children born prematurely or with low birth weight; and children of teen parents who have not completed high school.[38] Total enrollment in this state-funded program is 1,483 (of which only 123 are younger than three years of age),[39] which represents 3% of Nebraska's 47,830 three- and four-year-old children.[40] The federally funded Head Start program enrolls an additional 4,146 children,[41] which represents 9% of Nebraska's three- and four-year-old children.[42]

Where Does Nebraska Get Its Revenue?

At the end of fiscal year 2004, Nebraska had total revenues of approximately $15.5 billion.[43] Of this amount, 41% was derived from state and local tax revenues and 16% was received from the federal government.[44] The remaining 43% came from other sources, including the Nebraska Lottery, insurance trust revenue, and revenue from government-owned utilities and other commercial or auxiliary enterprises.[45]

Tax Revenue

Nebraska collected approximately $6.3 billion in state and local tax revenue during fiscal year 2004.[46] As a result, Nebraska residents paid $3,609 per capita in state and

---

37. *See* National Access Network, Litigation Update, http://www.schoolfunding.info/news/litigation/2-20-07litupdate.php3 (Mar. 19, 2007).

38. W. Steven Barnett et al., National Institute for Early Education Research, The State of Preschool 2006, at 96 (2006), *available at* http://nieer.org/yearbook/pdf/yearbook.pdf.

39. *Id.* at 97.

40. *See id.* at 232.

41. *Id.* at 97.

42. *See id.* at 232.

43. U.S. Census Bureau, State and Local Government Finances 2003–04, http://www.census.gov/govs/www/estimate04.html (last visited Oct. 6, 2006) [hereinafter Government Finances].

44. *Id.*

45. *Id.*

46. The total tax revenues were collected as follows: $3.6 billion by the state and 2.7 billion by local governments. *Id.*

local government taxes, an amount which ranked 15th nationally.[47] The different types of tax sources were approximately apportioned as follows:

Individual income taxes	19.7%
Property taxes	31.8%
General and selective sales taxes	37.0%
Corporate income and other taxes	11.5%
	100.0%[48]

Federal Funding

During fiscal year 2004, 16% of Nebraska's total revenues came from the federal government.[49] For every dollar of federal taxes paid, Nebraska received $1.07 in federal funding, an amount which ranked 28th nationally and was below the national average of $1.17.[50]

Lottery Revenues

The Nebraska Lottery has operated since 1993, when voters approved a constitutional amendment authorizing the creation of a lottery and the legislature passed enabling legislation.[51] The bulk of the profits earned by the Lottery are allocated to education and an environmental trust fund.[52] In 2005, the Lottery had total revenues of roughly $100.9 million and transferred approximately $22.1 million to its various beneficiary funds.[53]

Legal Structures of Major Tax Sources

Income

Nebraska employs a broad-based income tax that uses adjusted gross income for federal income tax purposes as a starting point for determining the state's taxable in-

---

47. *Id.*

48. *Id.*

49. *Id.*

50. *See* The Tax Foundation, Federal Spending Received Per Dollar of Taxes Paid by State 2004, http://www.taxfoundation.org/taxdata/show/266.html (last visited Oct. 16, 2006).

51. *See* NEB. REV. STAT §§ 9-801–9-841.

52. Pursuant to a constitutional amendment passed in 2004, lottery profits are allocated as follows: Education, as determined by the Legislature (44.5%); Nebraska Environmental Trust Fund (44.5%); Nebraska State Fair (10%); Compulsive Gamblers Assistance Fund (1%, plus the first $500,000 in fund proceeds each fiscal year). *See* NEB. CONST. ART. III, § 24.

53. NEBRASKA LOTTERY, 2005 ANNUAL REPORT (2006), *available at* http://www.nelottery .com/media/annualreport2005.pdf (last visited Oct. 16, 2006).

come.[54] However, a fairly large number of adjustments may be available to various individuals in calculating this amount.[55] Nebraska localities have the authority to levy income taxes for some purposes, but none have done so.[56] During fiscal year 2004, Nebraska collected personal income tax of $711 per capita, an amount which ranked 19th nationally.[57]

In Nebraska, a typical family of four (i.e., married taxpayers who file jointly and have two dependent children) are not required to pay any income tax until their combined income exceeds $25,600, an amount which is above the national poverty line of $20,615.[58] Nebraska's income tax structure contains four tax brackets that impose a minimum marginal rate of 2.56% and a maximum marginal rate of 6.84%.[59] When statutory exemptions and the standard deduction are taken into account, the maximum marginal rate applies to every dollar of income exceeding $55,330.[60]

Property

Overview

Nebraska has a typical property tax system that taxes the value of real and tangible personal property at the local level.[61] The state is constitutionally prohibited from collecting property taxes for state purposes,[62] although taxes for certain types of property, such as the operating property of railroad companies, are collected at the state level and then distributed to localities.[63] Nebraska localities collected more than $2 billion in property taxes during fiscal year 2004, while the state collected only $2.3 million.[64]

---

54. NEB. REV. STAT. § 77-2715(2).

55. *See id.* § 77-216.

56. CCH-EXP, NE-TAXRPTR ¶ 15-020, Local Power to Tax.

57. STATE RANKINGS 2006, *supra* note 1, at 321.

58. JASON A. LEVITIS, CENTER ON BUDGET AND POLICY PRIORITIES, THE IMPACT OF STATE INCOME TAXES ON LOW-INCOME FAMILIES IN 2006, at 12 (2007). In 2006, Nebraska taxpayers who were married and filing jointly could claim a standard deduction of $8,580 and personal and dependent exemption *credits* of $106 for each federal exemption available. NEB. REV. STAT. § 77-2716.01; NEBRASKA DEPARTMENT OF REVENUE, 2006 FORM 1040N INSTRUCTIONS (2006), *available at* http://www.revenue.ne.gov/tax/current/f_1040n_inst.pdf (last visited Feb. 1, 2007). Note, however, that the threshold calculation of $25,600 is greater than the sum of these deductions and exemptions because it includes additional tax benefits available to low-income families, such as the earned-income tax credit. *See* LEVITIS, *supra*.

59. *See* NEB. REV. STAT. §§ 77-2701.01, 77-2715.02. The rates applied to Nebraska's middle two tax brackets are 3.57% and 5.12%. *Id.*

60. The standard deduction of $8,580, plus the threshold of taxable income for the highest tax bracket of $46,750, equals $55,330. *See supra* notes 58–59.

61. *See* NEB. REV. STAT. § 77-201.

62. NEB. CONST. art. VIII, § 1A.

63. *See* NEB. REV. STAT. §§ 77-603–606, 77-683–684.

64. Government Finances, *supra* note 43.

As a result, Nebraska residents paid $1,148 per capita in property taxes, an amount which ranked 16th nationally.[65]

Defining the Real Property Tax Base

Taxable property in Nebraska is generally divided into two classes: real property and tangible personal property. Real property is assessed at 100% of actual value, except for agricultural and horticultural land, which is assessed at 80% of actual value.[66] In addition, historically significant real property that meets certain criteria may be taxed at special values lower than actual value.[67] "Actual value" for purposes of Nebraska property taxation means the market value of real property in the ordinary course of trade and may be determined by methods including, but not limited to, the following: (1) the sales-comparison approach, (2) the income approach, and (3) the cost approach.[68] Nebraska real property is assessed annually.[69]

Real Property Tax Rates

Nebraska localities are authorized to levy property taxes at maximum rates ranging from $1.50 per $100 of taxable property for educational service units to $0.07 per $100 for community colleges.[70] Average property tax rates levied in 2005 ranged from $1.22 per $100 (12.2 mills or $12.20 per $1,000) in Sioux County to $2.18 per $100 (21.8 mills or $21.80 per $1,000) in Douglas County.[71] There is no general state property tax rate, since the state collects taxes only on certain types of atypical property, such as the operating property of railroad companies.[72]

Personal and Intangible Property

Intangible property is not taxed in Nebraska.[73] Only tangible personal property that is depreciable and used in the course of a business for producing income is subject to taxation.[74] Such tangible personal property is valued at its net book value[75] and is taxed at rates set by Nebraska localities. Motor vehicles are exempt from the personal property tax, but Nebraska imposes a separate motor vehicle tax in addition to a registration fee and other fees.[76]

---

65. *See id.*
66. NEB. REV. STAT § 77-201.
67. *Id.*
68. NEB. REV. STAT. § 77-112.
69. *See id.* § 77-1301.
70. *Id.* § 77-3442.
71. CCH-EXP, NE-TAXRPTR ¶ 20-405, Rates of Tax.
72. *See supra* note 63.
73. *See* NEB. REV. STAT. § 77-201.
74. *See id.* §§ 77-202, 77-119.
75. *Id.* § 77-201(3).
76. *Id.* §§ 77-202(4), 60-3002.

Exemptions

Although there is no general homestead exemption,[77] Nebraska provides homestead exemptions to persons over 65, certain disabled individuals, and surviving spouses of deceased veterans.[78] The exemptions are limited both by the value of the homestead and the income of the claimant.[79] Other exemptions from real property tax include cemeteries, charities, government and public property, Native American land, religious organizations, livestock, and schools.[80]

General and Selective Sales

General Sales

Nebraska imposes a general retail sales-and-use tax, which during fiscal year 2004, constituted 27.9% of Nebraska's total revenue.[81] This tax is imposed on tangible personal property and selected services.[82] Examples of taxable services include building maintenance and security, utilities, some construction contractor services, installing and applying personal property the sale of which is subject to sales tax, and repairing or maintaining tangible personal property except for motor vehicles.[83] The Nebraska state sales-and-use tax rate is 5.5%.[84] In addition, counties are authorized to impose sales taxes at rates of .5%, 1%, or 1.5%.[85]

Exemptions from the sales tax include gasoline, prescription medicines, medical equipment and supplies, and most food and food ingredients.[86] Only the following types of foods are subject to the sales tax: prepared foods (such as restaurant meals), food sold in vending machines, food sold by concessionaires, and food prepared by caterers for immediate consumption.[87] Other exemptions include agricultural chemicals, machinery, and equipment; energy and water for irrigation and farming; and energy and water for manufacturing, processing, or refining.[88]

Selective Sales

Selective sales taxes constituted 9.1% of Nebraska's total tax revenue during fiscal year 2004.[89] Of that amount, 4.8% came from motor fuel sales taxes.[90] Nebraska resi-

---

77. *See* NEB. REV. STAT. §§ 77-201 to 212, 77-3501 to 3530.
78. *See id.* §§ 77-3507 to 3509.
79. *See id.*
80. *See id.* § 77-202.
81. Government Finances, *supra* note 43.
82. *See* NEB. REV. STAT. § 77-2703.
83. *Id.* § 77-2701.16.
84. *Id.* § 77-2701.02.
85. *Id.* § 13-319.
86. *Id.* §§ 77-2704.09, 77-2704.13, 77-2704.24.
87. *Id.* § 77-2704.24.
88. *Id.* § 77-2704.
89. Government Finances, *supra* note 43.
90. *Id.*

dents paid an average of $173 per capita in state motor fuel sales taxes in 2004, an amount which ranked 4th nationally and was above the national average of $115.[91]

In 2004, sales taxes on alcoholic beverages made up 0.4% of Nebraska's total tax revenue.[92] Nebraska residents paid $13.25 per capita in state alcoholic beverage sales taxes in 2004, an amount which ranked 27th nationally.[93]

The tobacco product sales tax made up 1.1% of Nebraska's tax revenue during fiscal year 2004.[94] The cigarette tax is $0.64 per pack of 20 cigarettes and $0.80 per pack of 25 cigarettes.[95]

The remainder of Nebraska's selective sales taxes constituted 2.8% of its total tax revenue in 2004.[96] Of that percentage, 1.3% represented taxes on utilities and the other 1.5% represented taxes on other specific commodities, businesses, or services not reported separately above (e.g., on contractors, lodging, lubricating oil, fuels other than motor fuel, motor vehicles, meals, soft drinks, margarine, etc.).[97]

Corporate Income and Other

Corporate Income

The corporate income tax comprises 2.7% of Nebraska's total tax revenue.[98] This broad-based corporate income tax is calculated with federal taxable income as the starting point.[99] The tax applies to C corporations doing business in Nebraska. Partnerships, subchapter S corporations, and LLCs are treated under the federal pass-through rules.[100]

The corporate income tax rates are calculated as a percentage of the primary individual rate, which is 3.7%.[101] The first $50,000 of taxable corporate income is subject to a rate of 150.8% of the primary rate, and the excess is subject to a rate of 211% of the primary rate.[102] Application of those percentages to the primary individual rate results in current corporate income rates of 5.58% and 7.81%, respectively.[103] In 2004, Nebraska's corporate income tax generated $167.4 million, an amount which ranked 33rd nationally.[104]

---

91. STATE RANKINGS 2006, *supra* note 1, at 327.

92. Government Finances, *supra* note 43.

93. STATE RANKINGS 2006, *supra* note 1, at 334.

94. Government Finances, *supra* note 43.

95. NEB. REV. STAT. § 77-2602.

96. Government Finances, *supra* note 43.

97. *Id. See also* GOVERNMENTS DIVISION, U.S. CENSUS BUREAU, GOVERNMENT FINANCE AND EMPLOYMENT CLASSIFICATION MANUAL, at ch.7 (2000), *available at* http://ftp2.census.gov/govs/class/classfull.pdf [hereinafter Classification Manual].

98. *Id.*

99. *See* NEB. REV. STAT. § 77-2734.04(6).

100. *See id.* §§ 77-2734.04, 77-2727, 21-2633.

101. *Id.* §§ 77-2734.02, 77-2701.01.

102. *Id.*

103. *See id.*

104. STATE RANKINGS 2006, *supra* note 1, at 322.

Other

During fiscal year 2004, the collection of all other taxes not previously mentioned generated $556.8 million, which comprised 8.8% of Nebraska's total tax revenue.[105] Of that amount, $26.4 million came from inheritance taxes.[106] Inheritance taxes are calculated on the basis of three classes of beneficiaries: immediate relatives, remote relatives, and other beneficiaries.[107] Transfers to a surviving spouse are exempt from tax.[108] Transfers to immediate relatives are granted a $10,000 exemption for each beneficiary and are subject to a rate of 1% on amounts above the exemption.[109] Transfers to remote relatives receive an exemption of $2,000 and are subject to graduated rates of 6% and 9% thereafter.[110] The exemption for other beneficiaries is $500, with graduated rates ranging from 6% to 18%.[111]

Nebraska imposes an "occupation tax," which is measured by paid-up capital stock for domestic corporations and by the value of "property and credits" within Nebraska for out-of-state corporations.[112] In lieu of the corporate income tax, Nebraska imposes a franchise tax on financial institutions based on average deposits.[113]

The "other taxes" category is further made up of various license taxes, documentary or stock transfer taxes, severance taxes, and all other taxes not listed separately or provided for in other categories.[114]

Burden Analysis

The overall state and local tax burden on Nebraska's taxpayers is somewhat regressive. Taxpayers in the lowest quintile—those with incomes of less than $17,000—bear a tax burden of 10.2% of their income, while taxpayers in the top 1%—those with incomes that exceed $299,000—bear a tax burden of 9.3% of their income.[115] It is also worth noting that, although Nebraska obviously has no control over federal tax pol-

---

105. Government Finances, supra note 43.

106. *Id.*

107. *See* NEB. REV. STAT. §§ 77-2004–2006.

108. *Id.*

109. *Id.*

110. *Id.*

111. *Id.*

112. *See* NEB. REV. STAT. §§ 21-301–306.

113. *See id.* § 77-3802.

114. *See* CLASSIFICATION MANUAL, *supra* note 97, at ch.7.

115. *See* ROBERT S. MCINTYRE ET AL., WHO PAYS? A DISTRIBUTIONAL ANALYSIS OF THE TAX SYSTEMS IN ALL 50 STATES 70 (2d ed. 2003), *available at* http://www.itepnet.org/wp2000/text.pdf. Taxpayers in the second quintile bear a 9.5% total tax burden on incomes between $17,000 and $28,000; those in the third quintile bear a 10% tax burden on incomes between $28,000 and $42,000; those in the fourth quintile bear a 9.6% tax burden on incomes between $42,000 and $64,000; those in the 80th–95th percentiles bear a 9.7% tax burden on incomes between $64,000 and $111,000; finally, those in the 96th–99th percentiles bear a 9.5%% tax burden on incomes between $111,000 and $299,000. *Id.*

icy, federal itemized deductions for state and local personal income and property taxes nonetheless further reduce the burden on taxpayers in the top 1% to 6.4%.[116] Furthermore, between 1989 and 2002, the tax burden on the bottom quintile rose by approximately 1.4%, while the burden on the top 1% fell by 1.4%.[117]

In terms of the income tax, the burden across income groups in Nebraska is slightly progressive, with taxpayers in the lowest quintile bearing a tax burden of 0.7% and those in the top 1% bearing a tax burden of 6.8%.[118] In sharp contrast, however, the sales and excises taxes imposed by Nebraska are very regressive, with taxpayers in the lowest quintile bearing a tax burden of 6.5% and those in the top 1% bearing a tax burden of just 0.9%.[119] Property taxes in Nebraska are also regressive, with taxpayers in the lowest quintile bearing a tax burden of 3% and those in the top quintile bearing an average tax burden of 2.5%.[120]

---

116. *Id.* Taxpayers in the lowest quintile did not receive any benefit from these federal offsets, while those in the second quintile were able to reduce their individual tax burdens by 0.1%, those in the third quintile by 0.2%, those in the fourth quintile by 0.5%, those in the 80th–95th percentiles by 1.2%, and those in the 96th–99th percentiles by 2%. *Id.*

117. *Id.* at 71.

118. *See id.* at 70. Taxpayers in the second quintile bear a 1.4% income tax burden; those in the third quintile bear a 2.2% burden; those in the fourth quintile bear a 2.7% burden; those in the 80th–95th percentiles bear a 3.7% burden; finally, those in the 96th–99th percentiles bear a 4.7% burden. *Id.* Note, however, that these percentages include both individual and corporate income tax burdens and that within the top 1%, corporate income taxes represent 0.1% of the income tax burden. *Id.*

119. *See id.* Taxpayers in the second quintile bear a 5.6% sales-and-excise tax burden; those in the third quintile bear a 4.8% burden; those in the fourth quintile bear a 3.8% burden; those in the 80th–95th percentiles bear a 3% burden; finally, those in the 96th–99th percentiles bear a 1.9% burden. *Id.*

120. *See id.* Taxpayers in the second quintile bear a 2.5% property tax burden; those in the third quintile bear a 3% burden; those in the fourth quintile bear a 3% burden; those in the 80th–95th percentiles bear a 3% burden; those in the 96th–99th percentiles bear a 2.8% burden; finally, those in the top 1% bear a 1.6% burden. *Id.*

Nevada

General Information

Basic Profile – Geography, Population, and Industry

Nevada was admitted to the Union in 1864. The "Sagebrush State" is located in the West and is bordered by California on the west, Idaho and Oregon on the north, Utah on the east, and Arizona on the southeast. Nevada is located in the Pacific time zone, and Carson City is the state capital.

Nevada ranks 35th in population (approximately 2.4 million residents)[1] and 7th in total area (110,561 square miles).[2] Its population is approximately 82.0% white, 7.7% black, and 5.7% Asian.[3] Additionally, 23.5% of its population identify themselves as persons of Hispanic or Latino origin.[4] The state is approximately 24% Catholic; 50% Protestant; and 2% Jewish; 24% claim a religion outside the Judeo-Christian tradition or no religion at all.[5] Eighty-nine percent of Nevada's population lives in urban areas.[6] Nevada is well known for gaming and tourism; its prominent industries also include construction, retail trade, accommodation and food services, and mining.[7]

Family Income and Poverty Indicators

In 2004, Nevada's per capita gross product was $43,001, which was above the national average of $39,725.[8] During this same period, although the median household

---

1. STATE RANKINGS 2006, vi, 429 (Kathleen O'Leary Morgan & Scott Morgan eds., Morgan Quitno Press 2006).

2. *Id.* at 225.

3. Nevada Quick Facts from the U.S. Census Bureau, http http://quickfacts.census.gov/qfd/states/32000.html (last visited Jan. 31, 2007). The remaining population is made up of 1.4% American Indian and Alaska Native persons; 0.5% Native Hawaiian persons and other Pacific Islanders; and 2.6% persons reporting two or more races. *Id.*

4. *Id.* (noting that because Hispanics and Latinos may be of any race, they are also included within the other applicable race categories). *See id.*

5. *See* BARRY A. KOSMIN, EGON MAYER & ARIELA KEYSAR, AMERICAN RELIGIOUS IDENTIFICATION SURVEY 2001, at 40, *available at* http://www.gc.cuny.edu/faculty/research_studies/aris.pdf.

6. USDA Economic Research Service, Nevada Fact Sheet, http://www.ers.usda.gov/StateFacts/NV.htm (last visited Sept. 17, 2006).

7. *See* U.S. Department of Commerce Bureau of Economic Analysis, Gross Domestic Product by State, http://www.bea.gov/bea/newsrelarchive/2006/gsp1006.xls (last visited Nov. 10, 2006).

8. STATE RANKINGS 2006, supra note 1, at 89.

income in Nevada was $46,984,[9] 10.2% of Nevada's population was living in poverty, which was below than the national average of 12.4%.[10] More specifically, poverty affected 18.5% of Nevada's children,[11] 6.4% of its senior citizens,[12] and 10% of its families.[13] Of its female-headed households with children, 36% lived in poverty,[14] and 33.7% of the state's public elementary and secondary school students were eligible for free or reduced-price meals.[15] Of those living in poverty approximately 12.7% were black, which represented 19.2% of Nevada's black population and 1.3% of its total population.[16] In an attempt to combat this poverty, Nevada spent approximately $1.1 billion on public welfare programs in 2002,[17] which made up 9.5% of its total government expenditures.[18]

Nevada's Public Elementary-Secondary School System

Overall Spending and Performance

For the 2003–2004 school year, Nevada spent $6,399 per pupil in its public elementary-secondary school system, which was substantially below the national average of $8,182.[19] Of this amount, 7.2% was provided by the federal government, 60.4% was provided by the state government, and 32.4% was provided by the local governments,[20] with property taxes making up 27.4% of the total funding.[21] Out of these funds, Nevada paid its elementary and secondary school teachers an estimated average annual salary of $43,394 during the 2004–2005 school year,[22] but in 2003, it provided a student/teacher ratio of just 19.0, which was far worse than the national average of 15.9.[23]

---

9. *Id.* at 96.

10. *Id.* at 495.

11. *Id.* at 497.

12. *Id.* at 496.

13. *Id.* at 498.

14. *Id.* at 499.

15. *Id.* at 532.

16. *See* Fact Sheet, American FactFinder, http://factfinder.census.gov/home/saff/main.html?_lang=en (select "Nevada" under "Get a Fact Sheet for your community") (last visited Feb. 16, 2007). Note that these numbers are based on the 2000 census because more recent numbers were not available.

17. *Id.* at 500.

18. *Id.* at 502.

19. Governments Division, U.S. Census Bureau, Public Education Finances 2004, at 8 tbl.8 (2006), *available at* http://www2.census.gov/govs/school/04f33pub.pdf.

20. *See id.* at 5 tbl.5.

21. *See id.* at 4 tbl.4.

22. Thomas D. Snyder et al., National Center for Education Statistics, Digest of Education Statistics 2005, at 116 tbl.77 (2006), *available at* http://nces.ed.gov/pubsearch/pubsinfo.asp?pubid=2006030.

23. *Id.* at 98 tbl.65.

In academic performance, Nevada's fourth and eighth grade students scored lower than the national average in mathematics,[24] reading,[25] science,[26] and writing.[27]

Equity Issues

In 2004, revenues spent per student in Nevada's highest poverty districts were determined to be $249 less than the revenues spent in its lowest poverty districts.[28] When adjustments were made for the additional costs of educating students growing up in poverty, however, the funding gap grew to $297.[29] Similarly, Nevada spent $470 less per student in its highest minority districts, and this amount grew to $496 when adjustments for low-income students were made.[30]

Fourth graders eligible for free or reduced-price school lunches had test scores that were 8% lower in mathematics,[31] 12% lower in reading,[32] and 10% lower in writing[33] than those of students who were not eligible. The results were similar for eighth graders eligible for free or reduced-price lunches; their test scores were 8% lower in mathematics,[34] 7% lower in reading,[35] and 16% lower in writing[36] than those of students who were not eligible.

Nevada is one of five states in which no cases have been filed challenging the state education finance system.[37]

---

24. NATIONAL CENTER FOR EDUCATION STATISTICS, U.S. DEPARTMENT OF EDUCATION, THE NATION'S REPORT CARD: MATHEMATICS 2005, at 14 fig.11, 16 fig.12 (2005), *available at* http://nces.ed.gov/nationsreportcard/pdf/ main2005/2006453.pdf [hereinafter MATHEMATICS 2005].

25. NATIONAL CENTER FOR EDUCATION STATISTICS, U.S. DEPARTMENT OF EDUCATION, THE NATION'S REPORT CARD: READING 2005, at 14 fig.11, 16 fig.12 (2005), *available at* http://nces.ed.gov/nationsreportcard/pdf/main2005/2006451.pdf [hereinafter READING 2005].

26. NATIONAL CENTER FOR EDUCATION STATISTICS, U.S. DEPARTMENT OF EDUCATION, THE NATION'S REPORT CARD: SCIENCE 2005, at 16 fig.12, 28 fig.22 (2006), *available at* http://nces.ed.gov/nationsreportcard//pdf/main2005/2006466.pdf [hereinafter SCIENCE 2005].

27. HILARY R. PERSKY ET AL., NATIONAL CENTER FOR EDUCATION STATISTICS, U.S. DEPARTMENT OF EDUCATION, THE NATION'S REPORT CARD: WRITING 2002, at 23 tbl.2.2, 24 tbl.2.3 (2003), *available at* http://nces.ed.gov/nationsreportcard/pdf/main2002/2003529.pdf [hereinafter WRITING 2002].

28. THE EDUCATION TRUST, FUNDING GAPS 2006, at 7 tbl.3 (2006), *available at* http://www2.edtrust.org/NR/rdonlyres/CDEF9403-5A75-437E-93FF-EBF1174181FB/0/FundingGap2006.pdf.

29. *Id.*

30. *Id.* at 7 tbl.4.

31. MATHEMATICS 2005, *supra* note 24, at 20 tbl.5.

32. READING 2005, *supra* note 25, at 20 tbl.5.

33. WRITING 2002, *supra* note 27, at 75 tbl.3.24.

34. MATHEMATICS 2005, *supra* note 24, at 21 tbl.6.

35. READING 2005, *supra* note 25, at 21 tbl.6.

36. WRITING 2002, *supra* note 27, at 76 tbl.3.25.

37. National Access Network, State by State, Nevada, http://www.schoolfunding.info/states/nv/lit_nv.php3 (last visited Mar. 19, 2007).

Availability of Publicly Funded Prekindergarten Programs

The Nevada Early Childhood Education Comprehensive Plan serves children from birth to aged five through grants that are provided to public schools and community-based organizations that tailor eligibility criteria and services to address the needs of their communities, with enrollment priority given always to children from low-income families.[38] Additionally, Nevada funds an initiative called Classroom on Wheels that provides educational opportunities to three- and four-year-olds. Total enrollment in both of these state-funded programs is 973,[39] which represents just 1% of Nevada's 70,055 three- and four-year- old children.[40] The federally funded Head Start program enrolls an additional 2,812 children,[41] which represents 4% of Nevada's three- and four-year-old children.[42]

Where Does Nevada Get Its Revenue?

At the end of fiscal year 2004, Nevada had total revenues of approximately $16.9 billion.[43] Of this amount, 47% was derived from state and local tax revenues and 11% was received from the federal government.[44] The remaining 42% came from other sources, including insurance trust revenue and revenue from government-owned utilities and other commercial or auxiliary enterprises.[45]

Tax Revenue

Nevada collected approximately $8 billion in state and local tax revenue during fiscal year 2004.[46] As a result, Nevada residents paid $3,417 per capita in state and local taxes, an amount which ranked 21st nationally.[47] The different types of tax sources were approximately apportioned as follows:

---

38. W. Steven Barnett et al., National Institute for Early Education Research, The State of Preschool 2006, at 98 (2006), *available at* http://nieer.org/yearbook/pdf/yearbook.pdf.

39. *Id.* at 99.

40. *See id.* at 232.

41. *Id.* at 99.

42. *See id.* at 232.

43. U.S. Census Bureau, State and Local Government Finances 2003–04, http://www.census.gov/govs/www/estimate04.html (last visited Oct. 6, 2006) [hereinafter Government Finances].

44. *Id.*

45. *Id.*

46. The total tax revenues were collected as follows: $4.7 billion by the state and 3.3 billion by local governments. *Id.*

47. *See id.*

Individual income taxes	0.0%
Property taxes	26.9%
General and selective sales taxes	57.3%
Corporate income and other taxes	15.8%
	100.0%[48]

Federal Funding

During fiscal year 2004, 11% of Nevada's total revenues came from the federal government.[49] For every dollar of federal taxes paid, Nevada received $0.73 in federal funding, an amount which ranked 45th nationally and was well below the national average of $1.17.[50]

Lottery Revenues

Nevada does not operate a state lottery.

Legal Structures of Major Tax Sources

Income

Nevada does not impose individual income taxes.

Property

Overview

Nevada has a typical property tax system that taxes the value of property at the local level. Although property taxes are collected at the local level, the state legislature periodically enacts uncodified provisions temporarily levying property taxes for state purposes.[51] Nevada localities collected more than $2 billion in property taxes during fiscal year 2004 and the state collected $132.5 million.[52] As a result, Nevada residents paid $920 per capita in state and local property taxes, an amount which ranked 30th nationally.[53]

---

48. *Id.*
49. *Id.*
50. The Tax Foundation, Federal Spending Received Per Dollar of Taxes Paid by State 2004, http://www.taxfoundation.org/taxdata/show/266.html#ftsbs-20060316 (last visited Oct. 16, 2006).
51. CCH-EXP, NV-TAXRPTR ¶ 20-405, Rates of Tax.
52. Government Finances, *supra* note 43.
53. *See id.*

Defining the Real Property Base

Nevada property is first classified as real property or personal property. The basis for the assessment of real property is "taxable value," which includes two components: 1) the "full cash value" of land and 2) the replacement cost of any improvements less depreciation of the improvements, with the applicable depreciation rate set by statute.[54] Regarding the component "full cash value" of land, all lawful uses to which the property may be put are considered in valuing vacant land, while only the actual use to which the property is put is considered in valuing improved land.[55] Qualifying agricultural and open-space property is granted special use valuation.[56] All taxable property in Nevada is assessed annually at 35% of "taxable value."[57]

Real Property Tax Rates

The average property tax rate during fiscal year 2007 was $3.15 per $100 (31.5 mills or $31.50 per $1,000) of assessed value, with average county-wide rates ranging from $1.94 to $3.66 per $100 of assessed value.[58] The forgoing averages take into account the state property tax rate of $0.17 per $100 of assessed value (1.7 mills or $1.70 per $1,000).[59]

Property tax rates that Nevada localities may impose are constitutionally limited to $5.00 per $100 (50 mills or $50 per $1,000) of assessed value.[60] County tax rates have been further limited by statute to $3.64 per $100 (36.4 mills or $36.40 per $1,000) of assessed value, although the state board of examiners may be directed to fix a lesser or greater amount for any given fiscal year.[61] Cities and unincorporated towns are further limited to tax rates of $3.00 and $1.50 per $100 of assessed value, respectively.[62] Additionally, the rate of growth of each locality's annual property tax revenues is restricted to 6%.[63] Periodic levies of state property taxes are in many instances not included in calculating a locality's rate for purposes of the limitations discussed above.[64]

---

54. *See* Nev. Rev. Stat. § 361.227.

55. *Id.*

56. *Id.* §§ 361A.130, 361A.220.

57. *Id.* § 361.225.

58. Nevada Department of Taxation, Fiscal Year 2006–2007 Property Tax Rates For Nevada Local Governments at III, http://tax.state.nv.us/property_tax.htm (follow "Redbook" link) (last visited Oct. 16, 2006).

59. *Id.*

60. Nev. Const. art. 10, § 2.

61. Nev. Rev. Stat. § 361.453.

62. *Id.* §§ 266.605, 269.115.

63. *See id.* § 354.59811.

64. *See id.* For example, a 2005 addition by the legislature of $0.02 per $100 to the property tax rate is outside of the statutory tax rate cap. *See* S.B. 524, 73rd Leg., Reg. Sess. (Nev. 2005). This state tax is earmarked for the conservation of natural resources and statewide capital improvements. *Id.*

Personal and Intangible Property

Personal intangible property is exempt from taxation in Nevada.[65] All other personal property is taxable unless a specific exemption applies.[66] The value of personal property, except for mobile homes, is determined by subtracting depreciation and obsolescence from the cost of replacement.[67]

Exemptions

Nevada does not provide a homestead exemption. However, senior citizens with qualifying levels of income are eligible for a refund of property taxes paid up to $500.[68] Blind taxpayers in Nevada are entitled to an exemption on all property they own up to assessed value of $3,000 (annually adjusted for inflation).[69] Similar exemptions are available for surviving spouses and orphan children, up to assessed value of $1,000 (inflation adjusted).[70] Qualifying veterans receive an exemption on the first $2,000 (inflation adjusted) of assessed value, while disabled veterans may be eligible for an exemption of $10,000 to $20,000, depending on the total percentage of permanent service-connected disability.[71] Personal property exemptions include household goods, business inventory, consumable business property, boats, certain campers, and certain irrigation equipment.[72]

General and Selective Sales

General Sales

Nevada imposes a general retail sales-and-use tax, which generated 31% of Nevada's total tax revenue during fiscal year 2004.[73] The tax is imposed on the sales and use of tangible personal property.[74] Though services are not taxed, "sale" includes the producing, fabricating, processing, or printing of tangible personal property for consumers who furnish the materials used in the process.[75] Furnishing, preparing, or serving food or drinks is also considered a "sale."[76]

Nevada sales-and-use taxes are imposed on a statewide basis at a rate of 6.5%, which may be increased by local taxes in certain counties.[77] Combined state and local rates

---

65. Nev. Rev. Stat § 361.228.

66. *See id.* § 361.045.

67. *Id.* § 361.227.

68. *See id.* § 427A.515

69. *Id.* § 361.085.

70. *Id.* § 361.080.

71. *Id.* §§ 361.090, 361.091.

72. *Id.* § 361.068.

73. Government Finances, *supra* note 43.

74. Nev. Rev. Stat §§ 372.060, 372.105.

75. *Id.* § 372.060.

76. *Id.*

77. The 6.5% rate is comprised of the following: a 2% state rate under the general Sales and Use Act; a 2.25% state rate under the Local School Support Tax Law, and a 2.25% state-man-

range from 6.5% to 7.38%.[78] Exemptions include, but are not limited to, the following: grocery foods (no exemption for other foods), prescription drugs and medical devices, farm animals, farm animal feed, crop seeds and fertilizer, farm machinery and equipment, mobile homes, motor fuels, and utilities.[79]

Selective Sales

Selective sales taxes made up 26.3% of Nevada's total tax revenue during fiscal year 2004.[80] Of that percentage, motor fuel sales taxes accounted for 5.5%.[81] Nevada residents paid an average of $126 per capita in state motor fuel sales taxes in 2004, an amount which ranked 27th nationally and was above the national average of $115.[82]

Taxes on tobacco products comprised 1.6% of the state's total tax revenue during fiscal year 2004.[83] The Nevada cigarette tax is 40 mills per cigarette.[84] Nevada residents paid an average of $55.32 per capita in state tobacco sales taxes in 2004, an amount which ranked 18th nationally.[85]

In 2004, sales taxes on alcoholic beverages taxes made up 0.4% of Nevada's total tax revenue.[86] Nevada residents paid $14.52 per capita in state alcoholic beverage sales taxes in 2004, an amount which ranked 24th nationally.[87]

The remainder of Nevada's selective sales taxes makes up 18.8% of its total tax revenue. Of this amount, 2.0% represents taxes on utilities and the other 16.8% represents taxes on specific commodities, businesses, or services not reported separately above (e.g., on contractors, lodging, lubricating oil, fuels other than motor fuel, motor vehicles, meals, soft drinks, etc.).[88] Much of the aforementioned 16.8% is likely attributable to taxes on gaming.[89]

Corporate Income and Other

Corporate Income

Nevada does not impose a tax on corporate income.

---

dated local rate under the City-County Relief Law. Nev. Rev. Stat §§ 372.105, 372.185, 374.110, 374.190, 377.040.

78. CCH-EXP, NV-TAXRPTR ¶ 61-735, Local Rates.

79. Nev. Rev. Stat §§ 372.280, 374.286, 372.284, 372.283, 372.316, 372.275.

80. Government Finances, *supra* note 43.

81. *Id.*

82. State Rankings 2006, *supra* note 1, at 327.

83. Government Finances, *supra* note 43.

84. Nev. Rev. Stat § 370.165.

85. State Rankings 2006, *supra* note 1, at 332.

86. Government Finances, *supra* note 43.

87. State Rankings 2006, *supra* note 1, at 335.

88. Government Finances, *supra* note 43. *See also* Governments Division, U.S. Census Bureau, Government Finance and Employment Classification Manual, at ch.7 (2000), *available at* http://ftp2.census.gov/govs/class/classfull.pdf [hereinafter Classification Manual].

89. *See infra* note 94.

Other

During fiscal year 2004, the collection of all other taxes not previously mentioned generated approximately $1.3 billion, which comprised 15.8% of Nevada's total tax revenue.[90] Of that amount, $24.5 million came from estate and gift taxes.[91] Nevada's estate tax is imposed in the amount of the maximum credit allowable against the federal estate tax.[92] Although the Nevada estate tax statutes are still in effect, the repeal of the federal credit for state death taxes[93] has effectively eliminated the Nevada estate tax. Most of the other taxes category is attributable to gambling licenses fees and taxes. During fiscal year 2004, Nevada collected $854.5 million in gaming license fees and taxes.[94] Nevada also imposes a severance tax on mining, which is levied at rates ranging from 2% to 5%.[95] The "other taxes" category is further made up of various license taxes, documentary or stock transfer taxes, severance taxes, and all other taxes not listed separately or provided for in other categories.[96]

Burden Analysis

The overall state and local tax burden on Nevada's taxpayers is extremely regressive. In fact, Nevada has one of the ten most regressive tax systems in the nation.[97] Taxpayers in the lowest quintile—those with incomes of less than $17,000—bear a tax burden of 8.3% of their income, while taxpayers in the top 1%—those with incomes that exceed $297,000—bear a tax burden of just 2% of their income.[98] It is also worth noting that, although Nevada obviously has no control over federal tax policy, federal itemized deductions for state and local personal income and property taxes nonetheless further reduce the burden on taxpayers in the top 1% to 1.8%.[99] Furthermore, between

---

90. Government Finances, *supra* note 43.

91. *Id.*

92. NEV. REV. STAT § 375A.100.

93. *See* Economic Growth and Tax Relief Reconciliation Act of 2001, Pub. L. No. 107-16 (2001).

94. Nevada Gaming Commission and State Gaming Control Board, 2004 Information Sheet, http://gaming.nv.gov/gamefact04.htm (last visited Oct. 16, 2006).

95. *See* NEV. REV. STAT § 362.140.

96. *See* CLASSIFICATION MANUAL, *supra* note 88, at ch.7.

97. *See* ROBERT S. MCINTYRE ET AL., WHO PAYS? A DISTRIBUTIONAL ANALYSIS OF THE TAX SYSTEMS IN ALL 50 STATES 3 (2d ed. 2003), *available at* http://www.itepnet.org/wp2000/text.pdf.

98. *See id.* at 72. Taxpayers in the second quintile bear a 7.5% total tax burden on incomes between $17,000 and $27,000; those in the third quintile bear a 6.3% tax burden on incomes between $27,000 and $42,000; those in the fourth quintile bear a 5.8% tax burden on incomes between $42,000 and $67,000; those in the 80th–95th percentiles bear a 4.9% tax burden on incomes between $67,000 and $125,000; finally, those in the 96th–99th percentiles bear a 3.5% tax burden on incomes between $125,000 and $297,000. *Id.*

99. *Id.* Taxpayers in the lowest quintile did not receive any benefit from these federal offsets, while those in the second quintile were able to reduce their individual tax burdens by 0.1%,

1989 and 2002, the tax burden on the bottom quintile rose by approximately 0.4%, while the burden on the top 1% rose by only 0.1%.[100]

One of the regressive features of Nevada's tax system is that it does not employ an income tax. Moreover, the sales and excises taxes imposed by Nevada are very regressive, with taxpayers in the lowest quintile bearing a tax burden of 6.3% and those in the top 1% bearing a tax burden of just 0.8%.[101] Property taxes in Nevada are slightly regressive, with taxpayers in the lowest quintile bearing a tax burden of 2.0% and those in the top quintile bearing an average tax burden of 1.7%.[102] Note, however, that the most onerous burden is placed on the middle class, who pay an average of 2.2% of their income in property taxes.[103]

---

those in the third quintile by 0.2%, those in the fourth quintile by 0.3%, those in the 80th–95th percentiles by 0.4%, and those in the 96th–99th percentiles by 0.4%. *Id.*

100. *Id.* at 73.

101. *See id.* at 72. Taxpayers in the second quintile bear a 5.2% sales-and-excise tax burden; those in the third quintile bear a 4.3% burden; those in the fourth quintile bear a 3.6% burden; those in the 80th–95th percentiles bear a 2.7% burden; finally, those in the 96th–99th percentiles bear a 1.7% burden. *Id.*

102. *See id.* Taxpayers in the second quintile bear a 2.3% property tax burden; those in the third quintile bear a 2.0% burden; those in the fourth quintile bear a 2.2% burden; those in the 80th–95th percentiles bear a 2.1% burden; those in the 96th–99th percentiles bear a 1.8% burden; finally, those in the top 1% bear a 1.2% burden. *Id.*

103. *See id.*

New Hampshire

General Information

Basic Profile – Geography, Population, and Industry

New Hampshire, "The Granite State," was admitted to the Union in 1788.[1] New Hampshire is located in the northeast region and is bounded on the north by Quebec province in Canada; on the east by Maine and the Atlantic Ocean; on the south by Massachusetts, and on the west by Vermont. New Hampshire is located in the eastern time zone, and its capital is Concord.

New Hampshire ranks 46th in total land and water area (9,350 square miles);[2] in 2005, it ranked 41st in population (1.31 million residents).[3] Its population is approximately 96.1% white and 1.0% black.[4] The state is approximately 35% Catholic; 38% Protestant; and 1.0% Jewish; 26% claim a religion outside the Judeo-Christian tradition or no religion at all.[5] New Hampshire is predominantly urban, with 62.25% of its population living in or around cities.[6] Major industries include agriculture, logging, paper, high-tech computer software, industrial machinery, and winter ski venues in the White Mountains.[7]

Family Income and Poverty Indicators

In 2004, New Hampshire's per capita gross product was $39,926, which was slightly above the national average of $39,725.[8] During this same period, although the median

---

1. State Rankings 2006, vi, 1 (Kathleen O'Leary Morgan & Scott Morgan eds., Morgan Quitno Press 2006).

2. *Id.* at 225

3. *Id.* at 429.

4. New Hampshire Quick Facts from the U.S. Census Bureau, http://quickfacts.census.gov/qfd/states/54000.html (last visited Jan. 30, 2007). The remaining population is made up of 1.7% Asian persons; 0.2% American Indian and Alaska Native persons; and 1.0% persons reporting two or more races. *Id.* Additionally, 2.2% of New Hampshire's total population identify themselves as persons of Hispanic or Latino origin. *Id.* (noting that because Hispanics may be of any race, they are included within the other applicable race categories).

5. Barry A. Kosmin, Egon Mayer & Ariela Keysar, American Religious Identification Survey 2001, at 40, *available at* http://www.gc.cuny.edu/faculty/research_studies/aris.pdf.

6. United States Department of Agriculture, Economic Research Service, New Hampshire Fact Sheet, http://www.ers.usda.gov/StateFacts/NH.htm (last visited Sept. 17, 2006).

7. New Hampshire Business Resource Center, http://www.nheconomy.com/nheconomy/obid/main/index.php?ch_table=link6&ID=1 (last visited on Sept. 20, 2006).

8. State Rankings 2006, *supra* note 1, at 89.

household income in New Hampshire was $57,352,[9] only 5.7% of the state's population was living in poverty, which was substantially below the national average of 12.4% and ranked among the bottom ten states nationally.[10] More specifically, poverty affected 9.4% of New Hampshire's children,[11] 8.3% of its senior citizens,[12] and 5.5% of its families.[13] Of its female-headed households with children, 26.6% lived in poverty,[14] and 16.3% of the state's elementary and secondary school students were eligible for free or reduced-price meals.[15] Of those living in poverty, approximately 2% were black, which represented 18% of New Hampshire's black population and 0.13% of its total population.[16] In an attempt to combat this poverty, New Hampshire spent approximately $1 billion on public welfare programs in 2002,[17] which made up 16.2% of its total government expenditures.[18]

New Hampshire's Public Elementary-Secondary School System

Overall Spending and Performance

For the 2003–2004 school year, New Hampshire spent $8,860 per pupil in its public elementary-secondary school system, which was slightly above the national average of $8,182.[19] Of this amount, 5.6% was provided by the federal government, 45.8% was provided by the state government, and 48.6% was provided by the local governments,[20] with property taxes making up 38.5% of the total funding.[21] Out of these funds, New Hampshire paid its elementary and secondary school teachers an estimated average annual salary of $43,941 during the 2004–2005 school year,[22] and in 2003, it provided a student/teacher ratio of 13.7, which was better than the national average of 15.9.[23]

---

9. *Id.* at 96.

10. *Id.* at 495.

11. *Id.* at 497.

12. *Id.* at 496.

13. *Id.* at 498.

14. *Id.* at 499.

15. *Id.* at 532.

16. *See* Fact Sheet, American FactFinder, http://factfinder.census.gov/home/saff/main.html?_lang=en (select "New Hampshire" under "Get a Fact Sheet for your community") (last visited Feb. 16, 2007). Note that these numbers are based on the 2000 census because more recent numbers were not available.

17. *Id.* at 500.

18. *Id.* at 502.

19. Governments Division, U.S. Census Bureau, Public Education Finances 2004, at 8 tbl.8 (2006), *available at* http://www2.census.gov/govs/school/04f33pub.pdf.

20. *See id.* at 5 tbl.5.

21. *See id.* at 4 tbl.4.

22. Thomas D. Snyder et al., National Center for Education Statistics, Digest of Education Statistics 2005, at 116 tbl.77 (2006) *available at* http://nces.ed.gov/pubsearch/pubsinfo.asp?pubid=2006030.

23. *Id.* at 98 tbl.65.

In academic performance, New Hampshire's fourth and eighth grade students scored higher than the national average in mathematics,[24] reading,[25] and science.[26] New Hampshire's test scores for writing[27] were unavailable.

Equity Issues

In 2004, revenues spent per student in New Hampshire's highest poverty districts were determined to be $1,084 less than the revenues spent in its lowest poverty districts.[28] When adjustments were made for the additional costs of educating students growing up in poverty, however, the funding gap grew to $1,297.[29] Similarly, New Hampshire spent $2,371 less per student in its highest minority districts, and this amount grew to $2,392 when adjustments for low-income students were made.[30]

Fourth graders eligible for free or reduced-price school lunches had test scores that were 7% lower in mathematics[31] and 8% lower in reading[32] than those of students who were not eligible. The results were just slightly better for eighth graders eligible for free or reduced-price lunches; their test scores were 6% lower in mathematics[33] and 7% lower in reading[34] than those of students who were not eligible.

Beginning in 1999, New Hampshire has undergone numerous changes in the school funding system because of challenges against it. Based on rulings of the state supreme court in three cases between the Claremont School System and the governor, New Hampshire first changed its system to include a statewide property tax in its funding.[35]

---

24. NATIONAL CENTER FOR EDUCATION STATISTICS, U.S. DEPARTMENT OF EDUCATION, THE NATION'S REPORT CARD: MATHEMATICS 2005, at 14 fig.11, 16 fig.12 (2005), *available at* http://nces.ed.gov/nationsreportcard/pdf/ main2005/2006453.pdf [hereinafter MATHEMATICS 2005].

25. NATIONAL CENTER FOR EDUCATION STATISTICS, U.S. DEPARTMENT OF EDUCATION, THE NATION'S REPORT CARD: READING 2005, at 14 fig.11, 16 fig.12 (2005), *available at* http://nces.ed.gov/nationsreportcard/pdf/main2005/2006451.pdf [hereinafter READING 2005].

26. *See* NATIONAL CENTER FOR EDUCATION STATISTICS, U.S. DEPARTMENT OF EDUCATION, THE NATION'S REPORT CARD: SCIENCE 2005, at 16 fig.12, 28 fig.22 (2006), *available at* http://nces.ed.gov/nationsreportcard//pdf/main2005/2006466.pdf [hereinafter SCIENCE 2005].

27. HILARY R. PERSKY ET AL., NATIONAL CENTER FOR EDUCATION STATISTICS, U.S. DEPARTMENT OF EDUCATION, THE NATION'S REPORT CARD: WRITING 2002, at 23 tbl.2.2, 24 tbl.2.3 (2003), *available at* http://nces.ed.gov/nationsreportcard/pdf/main2002/2003529.pdf [hereinafter WRITING 2002].

28. THE EDUCATION TRUST, FUNDING GAPS 2006, at 7 tbl.3 (2006), *available at* http://www2.edtrust.org/NR/rdonlyres/CDEF9403-5A75-437E-93FF-EBF1174181FB/0/FundingGap2006.pdf.

29. *Id.*

30. *Id.* at 7 tbl.4.

31. MATHEMATICS 2005, *supra* note 24, at 20 tbl.5.

32. READING 2005, *supra* note 25, at 20 tbl.5.

33. MATHEMATICS 2005, *supra* note 24, at 21 tbl.6.

34. READING 2005, *supra* note 25, at 21 tbl.6.

35. Claremont School District v. Governor, 635 A.2d 1375 (NH 1993); Claremont v. Governor, 703 A.2d 1353 (NH 1997); Claremont v. Governor, 744 A.2d 1107 (NH 1999).

In April 2002, the state supreme court finally held that the state's accountability provisions were inadequate on the basis of the ongoing Claremont lawsuits. In the 2006 case *Londonderry School District v. State*, the court again held that the state's school-funding statutes violated the state constitution and required the state to complete the order to define a "constitutionally adequate system" by June 2007.[36]

Availability of Publicly Funded Prekindergarten Programs

New Hampshire currently offers no public preschool program.[37] The federally funded Head Start program, however, is available and enrolls 1,295 children,[38] which represents just 4% of New Hampshire's 29,967 three- and four-year-old children.[39]

Where Does New Hampshire Gets Its Revenue?

At the end of fiscal year 2004, New Hampshire had total revenues of approximately $8.7 billion.[40] Of this amount, 47% was derived from state and local tax revenues and 18% was received from the federal government.[41] The remaining 35% came from other sources, including the New Hampshire Lottery Commission, insurance trust revenue, and revenue from government-owned utilities and other commercial or auxiliary enterprises.[42]

Tax Revenue

New Hampshire collected approximately $4.1 billion in state and local tax revenue during fiscal year 2004.[43] As a result, New Hampshire residents paid $3,133 per capita in state and local taxes, an amount which ranked 26th nationally.[44] The different types of tax sources were approximately apportioned as follows:

---

36. Londonderry v. State, 2006 WL 563120 (NH 2006).

37. W. STEVEN BARNETT ET AL., NATIONAL INSTITUTE FOR EARLY EDUCATION RESEARCH, THE STATE OF PRESCHOOL 2006, at 101 (2006), *available at* http://nieer.org/yearbook/pdf/yearbook.pdf.

38. *Id.* at 102.

39. BARNETT 2006, *supra* note 37, at 27.

40. U.S. Census Bureau, State and Local Government Finances - 2003–04, http://www.census.gov/govs/www/estimate04.html (last visited Oct. 6, 2006) [hereinafter Government Finances].

41. *Id.*

42. *Id.*

43. The total tax revenues were collected as follows: $2 billion by the state and $2.1 billion by local governments. *Id.*

44. *Id.*

Individual income taxes	1.3%
Property taxes	61.9%
General and selective sales taxes	16.6%
Corporate income and other taxes	20.2%
	100.0%[45]

Federal Funding

During fiscal year 2004, 18% of New Hampshire's total revenues came from the federal government.[46] For every dollar of federal taxes paid, New Hampshire received $0.67 in federal funding, an amount which ranked 48th nationally[47] and was well below the national average of $1.17.[48]

Lottery Revenue

The New Hampshire Lottery Commission, established in 1963, was the first state-run lottery.[49] All profits generated by the Lottery are used for K–12 education.[50] The New Hampshire Lottery Commission had total revenues of $229 million during fiscal year 2005, of which $69.3 million was distributed for educational purposes.[51] New Hampshire is also involved in a Tri-State Lotto under a tristate compact with Maine and Vermont.[52]

Legal Structures of Major Tax Sources

Income

New Hampshire does not tax an individual's earned income.[53] Rather, it taxes income from dividends and interest at a flat rate of 5%.[54] The New Hampshire interest-and-dividends tax is imposed on individuals who are residents or inhabitants of the state for any part of the tax year, whose gross interest and dividend income from all

---

45. *Id.*

46. *Id.*

47. The Tax Foundation, Federal Spending Received Per Dollar of Taxes Paid by State, 2004 http://www.taxfoundation.org/news/show/266.html (last visited Sept. 17,2006).

48. *See id.*

49. North American Association of State and Provincial Lotteries, http://www.naspl.org/Contacts/index.cfm?fuseaction=view&ID=27 (last visited October 20, 2006).

50. *Id.*

51. New Hampshire Lottery, http://www.nhlottery.org/pdf/cafr2005.pdf; http://www.nhlottery.org/supporting-education/yearly.asp (last visited October 20, 2006).

52. N.H. REV. STAT. ANN. § 287-f:1.

53. N.H. REV. STAT. ANN. § 77:3.

54. *Id.* § 77:1.

sources exceeds $2,400 during the taxable period.[55] There is a $1,200 exemption for taxpayers who are either blind or disabled or over the age of 65.[56]

Property

Overview

New Hampshire has a typical property tax system that taxes the value of real property at both the state and local levels.[57] During fiscal year 2004, New Hampshire collected a total of $2.52 billion in property taxes.[58] Of this amount, New Hampshire localities collected $2.03 billion and the state collected $493.6 million.[59] As a result, New Hampshire residents paid $1,940 per capita in property taxes, an amount which ranked 3rd nationally.[60]

Defining the Real Property Tax Base

New Hampshire has only one class of property.[61] Certain types of property, however, qualify for current use valuation, including residences located in industrial or commercial zones; farm, forest, and open-space land; and property that qualifies for a conservation restriction assessment.[62] Methods used by New Hampshire to value all other types of property include the capitalization-of-income approach, the market-data or sales-comparison approach, and the cost approach.[63] Property is reappraised in New Hampshire every five years.[64] The tax rate includes a uniform state tax rate as well as various local tax rates.[65]

Real Property Tax Rates

Beginning on July 1, 2005, the commissioner of the New Hampshire Department of Revenue set property rates at a level that would be able to generate revenue of $363 million when imposed on all persons and property subject to tax.[66] The rates are set after reviewing reports from the municipalities of an annual inventory of properties that are taxed.[67] In 2006, local tax rates per $1,000 of local valuation ranged from 38.93

---

55. *Id.*
56. *Id.* § 77:5.
57. *Id.* § 72:6.
58. Government Finances, *supra* note 40.
59. *Id.*
60. *See id.*
61. CCH-EXP, NH-TAXRPTR ¶ 20-010, Overview.
62. N.H. Rev. Stat. Ann. §§ 79:A-1, 79:A-5, 79-B:3, 79-C:7, 75-11.
63. CCH-EXP, NH-TAXRPTR ¶ 20-615, Valuation Methods in General.
64. N.H. Rev. Stat. Ann. §§ 75-1, 75:8.
65. CCH-EXP, NH-TAXRPTR ¶ 20-405, Rates of Tax.
66. CCH-EXP, PROP-TAX-GUIDE NH , ¶ 71-001, Rates of Tax.
67. *Id.*

in the municipality of Newport to no tax at all in municipalities such as Cambridge and Odell.[68]

Personal and Intangible Property

New Hampshire does not tax personal or intangible property.[69]

Exemptions

Major exemptions include, among other types of property, schools, public property, and residential real estate valued up to $15,000 that is inhabited by legally blind persons, deaf persons, or severely hearing impaired persons.[70] If approved at a regular municipal election, the exemption amount may be increased by a city or town.[71]

General and Selective Sales

General Sales

New Hampshire does not impose a general retail sales or use tax; however, it does impose a meals-and-rooms tax.[72] There is an 8% tax on lodging and restaurant meals,[73] as well as a 7% tax on two-way communications.[74]

Selective Sales

Selective sales taxes make up 16.6% of New Hampshire's total tax revenue.[75] Of that amount, 3.2% comes from motor fuel sales taxes.[76] New Hampshire residents paid an average of $100 per capita in state motor fuel sales taxes in 2004, an amount which ranked 44th nationally and was below the national average of $115.[77]

The tobacco product sales tax makes up 2.5%[78] of New Hampshire's total tax revenue and is imposed at a rate of $0.52 per pack of cigarettes.[79]

In 2004, sales taxes on alcoholic beverages made up 0.3% of New Hampshire's total

---

68. New Hampshire Department of Revenue, http://www.revenue.nh.gov/property_tax/2006/2006tax_rates.rtf (last visited February 21, 2007).

69. CCH-EXP, NH-TAXRPTR ¶ 20-295, Personal Property; CCH-EXP, NH-TAXRPTR ¶ 20-230, Intangible Property.

70. N.H. Rev. Stat. Ann. § 72:37.

71. Id.

72. Id. § 78-A:1.

73. Id. § 78-A:6.

74. Id. § 82-A:3.

75. Government Finances, supra note 40.

76. Id.

77. State Rankings 2006, supra note 1, at 327.

78. State and Local Government Finances, supra note 40.

79. State Rankings 2006, supra note 1, at 333.

tax revenue.[80] New Hampshire residents paid $9.42 per capita in state alcoholic beverage sales taxes in 2004, an amount which ranked 37th nationally.[81]

The remainder of New Hampshire's selective sales taxes makes up 10.6% of its total tax revenue. Of this amount, 1.6% represents taxes on utilities and the other 9.0% represents taxes on other specific commodities, businesses, or services not reported separately above (e.g., on contractors, lodging, lubricating oil, fuels other than motor fuel, motor vehicles, meals, soft drinks, margarine, etc.).[82]

Corporate and Income and Other

Corporate Income

The corporate income tax makes up 10.0% of New Hampshire's total tax revenue[83] and is comprised of both a business profits tax and a business enterprise tax.[84]

Every business in New Hampshire with gross receipts exceeding $50,000 must pay a business profits tax at a rate of 8.5%.[85] This tax is imposed on every business, including corporations, partnerships, limited liability companies, proprietorships, associations, business trusts, real estate trusts, or any other form of organization created for profit and carrying on business in New Hampshire.[86]

In addition, a business enterprise tax must be paid by businesses with an enterprise value tax base exceeding $75,000.[87] The rate of this tax is .75% on the taxable enterprise value tax base, which consists of compensation, interest, and dividends paid by businesses after adjustments.[88]

Other

During fiscal year 2004, the collection of all other taxes not previously mentioned accounted for 10.2% of New Hampshire's total tax revenue.[89] Of this amount, $30.5 million was generated by the estate and gift tax, which is calculated according to the percentage of the decedent's real and tangible personal property located in New Hampshire.[90] If all of the decedent's real and tangible personal property is located in New Hampshire, the tax is equal to the maximum federal estate tax credit allowable for state death taxes.[91] If, however, only a portion of the decedent's real and tangible personal

---

80. Government Finances, *supra* note 40.

81. STATE RANKINGS 2006, *supra* note 1, at 335.

82. *See* GOVERNMENTS DIVISION, U.S. CENSUS BUREAU, GOVERNMENT FINANCE AND EMPLOYMENT CLASSIFICATION MANUAL, at ch.7 (2000), *available at* http://ftp2.census.gov/govs/class/classfull.pdf [hereinafter CLASSIFICATION MANUAL].

83. Government Finances, *supra* note 40.

84. N.H. REV. STAT. ANN. § 77-A:1.

85. *Id.* § 77-A:6; 77-A:2.

86. CCH-EXP, NH-TAXRPTR ¶ 10-005, Overview, Corporate Income Taxes.

87. CCH-EXP, NH-TAXRPTR ¶ 10-535, Non-Income Tax Base Computation.

88. N.H. REV. STAT. ANN. § 77-E:2.

89. Government Finances, *supra* note 40.

90. *Id.*

91. N.H. REV. STAT. ANN. § 88-A:9.

property is located in New Hampshire, the maximum tax credit is determined by multiplying the entire amount of the credit allowable by the percentage that the gross value of the decedent's taxable estate located in New Hampshire bears to the gross value of the entire estate.[92]

The "other taxes" category is further made up of various license taxes, documentary or stock transfer taxes, severance taxes, and all other taxes not listed separately or provided for in other categories.[93]

Burden Analysis

The overall state and local tax burden on New Hampshire taxpayers is extremely regressive. Taxpayers in the lowest quintile—those with incomes of less than $20,000—bear a tax burden of 8.1% of their income, while taxpayers in the top 1%—those with incomes that exceed $474,000—bear a tax burden of just 2.4% of their income.[94] It is also worth noting that, although New Hampshire obviously has no control over federal tax policy, federal itemized deductions for state and local personal income and property taxes nonetheless further reduce the burden on taxpayers in the top 1% to 1.9%.[95] Furthermore, between 1989 and 2002, the tax burden on the bottom quintile rose by approximately 2.5%, while the burden on the top 1% actually fell by 0.7%.[96]

In terms of the income tax, the burden across income groups in New Hampshire is only somewhat progressive, since New Hampshire does not tax an individual's earned income but only dividends and interest. Taxpayers in the lowest quintile bear a tax burden of 0.3%, while those in the top 1% bear a tax burden of 0.6%.[97] In contrast, the sales and excises taxes imposed by New Hampshire are slightly regressive, especially

---

92. *Id.*

93. *See* CLASSIFICATION MANUAL, *supra* note 82, at ch.7.

94. *See* ROBERT S. McINTYRE ET AL., WHO PAYS? A DISTRIBUTIONAL ANALYSIS OF THE TAX SYSTEMS IN ALL 50 STATES 74 (2d ed. 2003), *available at* http://www.itepnet.org/wp2000/text.pdf. Taxpayers in the second quintile bear a 5.7% total tax burden on incomes between $20,000 and $34,000; those in the third quintile bear a 5.8% tax burden on incomes between $34,000 and $55,000; those in the fourth quintile bear a 5.4% tax burden on incomes between $55,000 and $84,000; those in the 80th–95th percentiles bear a 4.9% tax burden on incomes between $84,000 and $159,000; finally, those in the 96th–99th percentiles bear a 3.9% tax burden on incomes between $159,000 and $474,000. *Id.*

95. *Id.* Taxpayers in the lowest quintile did not receive any benefit from these federal offsets, while those in the second lowest quintile were able to reduce their individual tax burdens by 0.1%, those in the third quintile by 0.4%, those in the fourth quintile by 0.6%, those in the 80th–95th percentiles by 0.9%, and those in the 96th–99th percentiles by 0.8%. *Id.*

96. *Id.* at 75.

97. *See id.* at 74. Taxpayers in the second and third quintiles bear no income tax burden; those in the fourth quintile bear a 0.1% burden; those in the 80th–95th percentiles bear a 0.1% burden; finally those in the 96th–99th percentiles bear a 0.4% burden. *Id.* Note, however, that corporate income taxes represent 0.1% of the total income taxes borne by taxpayers in the 96th–99th percentiles and that corporate income taxes represent 0.2% of the total income taxes borne by taxpayers in the top 1%. *Id.*

considering that New Hampshire does not impose a general retail sales or use tax. Taxpayers in the lowest quintile bear a tax burden of 2.8%, while those in the top 1% bear a tax burden of just 0.2%.[98] Property taxes in New Hampshire are also regressive, with taxpayers in the lowest quintile bearing a tax burden of 4.9% and those in the remaining quintiles bearing an average tax burden of 2.7%.[99]

---

98. *See id.* Taxpayers in the second quintile bear a 1.8% sales-and-excise tax burden; those in the third quintile bear a 1.5% burden; those in the fourth quintile bear a 1.2% burden; those in the 80th–95th percentiles bear a 0.9% burden; finally, those in the 96th–99th percentiles bear a 0.5% burden. *Id.*

99. *See id.* Taxpayers in the second quintile bear a 3.8% property tax burden; those in the third quintile bear a 4.3% burden; those in the fourth quintile bear a 4.1% burden; those in the 80th–95th percentiles bear a 3.9% burden; those in the 96th–99th percentiles bear a 2.9% burden; finally, those in the top 1% bear a 1.5% burden. *Id.*

New Jersey

General Information

Basic Profile – Geography, Population, and Industry

Admitted to the Union in 1787, New Jersey is known as the "Garden State."[1] New Jersey is located in the Mid-Atlantic region and is bordered by New York on the north, New York and the Atlantic Ocean on the east, Delaware on the south, and Pennsylvania on the west. The state is located in the eastern time zone, and its capital Trenton.

New Jersey ranks 47th in total area (8,721 square miles);[2] in 2005, it ranked 10th in population (approximately 8.7 million residents).[3] Its population is approximately 76.6% white and 14.5% black.[4] The state is approximately 37% Catholic; 34% Protestant; and 4% Jewish; 25% claim a religion outside the Judeo-Christian tradition or no religion at all.[5] Nearly 100% of New Jersey's population lives in urban areas.[6] Major industries include manufacturing, exports, tourism, finance and banking, and agriculture.[7]

Family Income and Poverty Indicators

In 2004, New Jersey's per capita gross product was $47,904, which ranked 5th nationally and was above the national average of $39,725.[8] During this same period, while

---

1. STATE RANKINGS 2006, vi, 1 (Kathleen O'Leary Morgan & Scott Morgan, eds. Morgan Quitno Press, 2006).

2. *Id.* at 225.

3. *Id.* at 429.

4. New Jersey Quick Facts from the U.S. Census Bureau, http://quickfacts.census.gov/qfd/states/54000.html (last visited Jan. 27, 2007). The remaining population is made up of 0.3% American Indian and Alaskan Native persons; 7.2% Asian persons; 0.1% Native Hawaiian persons and other Pacific Islanders; and 1.3% persons reporting two or more races. *Id.* Additionally, 19.5% of New Jersey's total population identify themselves as persons of Hispanic or Latino origin. *Id.* (noting that because Hispanics may be of any race, they are included within the other applicable race categories).

5. BARRY A. KOSMIN, EGON MAYER & ARIELA KEYSAR, AMERICAN RELIGIOUS IDENTIFICATION SURVEY 2001, at 40, *available at* http://www.gc.cuny.edu/faculty/research_studies/aris.pdf.

6. USDA Economic Research Service, New Jersey Fact Sheet, http://www.ers.usda.gov/StateFacts/NJ.htm (last visited Feb. 17, 2007).

7. NJ Business, http://www.nj.gov/njbusiness/last visited Feb. 17, 2007).

8. STATE RANKINGS 2006, *supra* note 1, at 89.

the median household income in New Jersey was $56,772,[9] 8.2% of the state's population was living in poverty,[10] which was below the national average of 12.4%.[11] More specifically, poverty affected 11.7% of New Jersey's children,[12] 8.2% of its senior citizens,[13] and 6.5% of its families.[14] Of its female-headed households with children, 28.8% lived in poverty,[15] and 26.9% of the state's public elementary and secondary school students were eligible for free or reduced-price meals.[16] Of those living in poverty, approximately 28.6% were black, which represented 17.5% of New Jersey's black population and 2.4% of its total population.[17] In an attempt to combat this poverty, New Jersey spent approximately $6.6 billion on public welfare programs in 2002,[18] which made up 12.2% of its total government expenditures.[19]

New Jersey's Public Elementary-Secondary School System

Overall Spending and Performance

For the 2003–2004 school year, New Jersey spent $12,981 per pupil in its public elementary-secondary school system, which was substantially above the national average of $8,182.[20] Of this amount, 4.3% was provided by the federal government, 42.4% was provided by the state government, and 53.3% was provided by the local governments,[21] with property taxes making up 43.8% of the total funding.[22] Out of these funds, New Jersey paid its elementary and secondary school teachers an estimated average annual salary of $56,600 during the 2004–2005 school year,[23] and it provided a student/teacher ratio of 12.7, which was better than the national average of 15.9.[24]

---

9. *Id.* at 96.

10. *Id.* at 495.

11. *Id.*

12. *Id.* at 497.

13. *Id.* at 496.

14. *Id.* at 498.

15. *Id.* at 499.

16. *Id.* at 532.

17. *See* Fact Sheet, American FactFinder, http://factfinder.census.gov/home/saff/main.html?_lang=en (select "New Jersey" under "Get a Fact Sheet for your community") (last visited Feb. 16, 2007). Note that these numbers are based on the 2000 census because more recent numbers where not available.

18. *Id.* at 500.

19. *Id.* at 502.

20. Governments Division, U.S. Census Bureau, Public Education Finances 2004, at 8 tbl.8 (2006).

21. *See Id.* at 5 tbl.5.

22. *See Id.* at 4 tbl.4.

23. Thomas D. Snyder et al., National Center for Education Statistics, Digest of Education Statistics 2005, at 116 tbl.77 (2006).

24. *Id.* at 98 tbl.65.

In academic performance, New Jersey's fourth grade students scored higher than the national average in mathematics,[25] reading,[26] and science.[27] New Jersey's eighth graders also scored higher than the national average in mathematics,[28] reading,[29] and science.[30]

Equity Issues

In 2004, revenues spent per student in New Jersey's highest poverty districts were determined to be $1,824 less than the revenues spent in its lowest poverty districts.[31] When adjustments were made for the additional costs of educating students growing up in poverty, however, the funding gap decreased to $1,069.[32] On the other hand, New Jersey spent $1,730 more per student in its highest minority districts, although this amount fell to $1,087 when adjustments for low-income students were made.[33]

Fourth graders eligible for free or reduced-price school lunches had test scores that were 9.9% lower in mathematics[34] and 12.5% lower in reading[35] than those of students who were not eligible. The results were generally the same for eighth graders eligible for free or reduced-price lunches; their test scores were 10.3% lower in mathematics[36] and 8.7% lower in reading[37] than those of students who were not eligible.

New Jersey has experienced much litigation related to the equity of school funding, most notably in the *Abbott v. Burke* line of cases.[38] The initial court ruling determined that the plaintiffs met the burden of showing that impoverished urban school districts were receiving inadequate and unequal funding.[39] This hastened a legislative response

---

25. NATIONAL CENTER FOR EDUCATION STATISTICS, U.S. DEPARTMENT OF EDUCATION, THE NATION'S REPORT CARD: MATHEMATICS 2005, at 14 fig.11 (2005), *available at* http://nces.ed.gov/nationsreportcard/pdf/main2005/ 2006453.pdf [hereinafter MATHEMATICS 2005].

26. NATIONAL CENTER FOR EDUCATION STATISTICS, U.S. DEPARTMENT OF EDUCATION, THE NATION'S REPORT CARD: READING 2005, at 14 fig.11 (2005), *available at* http://nces.ed.gov/nationsreportcard/pdf/main2005/2006451.pdf [hereinafter READING 2005].

27. NATIONAL CENTER FOR EDUCATION STATISTICS, U.S. DEPARTMENT OF EDUCATION, THE NATION'S REPORT CARD: SCIENCE 2005, at 16 fig.12 (2006), *available at* http://nces.ed.gov/nationsreportcard//pdf/main2005/2006466.pdf [hereinafter SCIENCE 2005].

28. MATHEMATICS 2005, *supra* note 25, at 16 fig.12.

29. READING 2005, *supra* note 26, at 16 fig.12.

30. SCIENCE 2005, *supra* note 27, at 28 fig.22.

31. THE EDUCATION TRUST, FUNDING GAPS 2006, at 7 tbl.3 (2006), *available at* http://www2.edtrust.org/NR/rdonlyres/CDEF9403-5A75-437E-93FF-EBF1174181FB/0/FundingGap2006.pdf.

32. *Id.*

33. *Id.* at 7 tbl.4.

34. MATHEMATICS 2005, *supra* note 25, at 20 tbl.5.

35. READING 2005, *supra* note 26, at 20 tbl.5.

36. MATHEMATICS 2005, *supra* note 25, at 21 tbl.6.

37. READING 2005, *supra* note 26, at 21 tbl.6.

38. Abbott by Abbott v. Burke, 693 A.2d 417 (N.J. 1997), Abbott by Abbott v. Burke, 710 A.2d 450 (N.J. 1998), and Abbott v. Burke, 798 A.2d 602 (N.J. 2002) (these three cases are the culmination of litigation that began in the early 1980s).

39. Abbott by Abbott v. Burke, 693 A.2d 417 (N.J. 1997).

to increase funding for these newly created "Abbott" districts.[40] In 2004, the New Jersey Supreme Court affirmed an appellate court's ruling that some Abbott districts were not receiving the proper amount of funding from the state to address issues of adequacy.[41]

Availability of Publicly Funded Prekindergarten Programs

The New Jersey's Abbot Program currently serves three- and four-year-old children who are located in the 31 highest poverty districts.[42] Total enrollment in this state-funded program is 46,261,[43] which represents 19.9% of New Jersey's 232,972 three- and four-year-old children.[44] The federally funded Head Start program enrolls an additional 12,463 children,[45] which represents 5.3% of New Jersey's three- and four-year-old children.[46]

Where Does New Jersey Get Its Revenue?

At the end of fiscal year 2004, New Jersey had total revenues of approximately $75.1 billion.[47] Of this amount, 53% was derived from state and local tax revenues and 13% was received from the federal government.[48] The remaining 34% came from other sources, including the New Jersey Lottery, insurance trust revenue, revenue from government-owned utilities, and other commercial or auxiliary enterprises.[49]

Tax Revenue

New Jersey collected approximately $39.6 billion in state and local tax revenue during fiscal year 2004.[50] As a result, New Jersey residents paid $4,555 per capita in state and local taxes, an amount which ranked 3rd nationally.[51] The different types of tax sources were approximately apportioned as follows:

---

40. *Id.*

41. Asbury Park Bd. of Educ. v. N.J. Dep't of Educ., 849 A.2d 158 (N.J. 2004).

42. W. Steven Barnett et al., National Institute for Early Education Research, The State of Preschool 2006, at 102 (2007), *available at* http://nieer.org/yearbook/pdf/yearbook.pdf.

43. *Id.* at 103.

44. *See id.*

45. *Id.*

46. *See id.*

47. U.S. Census Bureau, State and Local Government Finances - 2003–04, http://www.census.gov/govs/www/estimate04.html (last visited Oct. 6, 2006) [hereinafter Government Finances].

48. *Id.*

49. *Id.*

50. The total tax revenues were collected as follows: $14.2 billion by the state and 10.8 billion by local governments. *Id.*

51. *Id.*

Individual income taxes	18.7%
Property taxes	46.1%
General and selective sales taxes	24.7%
Corporate income and other taxes	10.5%
	100.0%[52]

Federal Funding

During fiscal year 2004, 13% of New Jersey's total revenues came from the federal government.[53] For every dollar of federal taxes paid, New Jersey received $0.55 in federal funding, an amount which ranked 50th nationally[54] and was far below the national average of $1.17.[55]

Lottery Revenue

The New Jersey Lottery has been in operation since 1970. Under New Jersey's constitution, all New Jersey Lottery profits are to be used for funding educational programs, promoting school nutrition, funding mental health programs, and assisting programs for veterans.[56] During fiscal year 2006, the Lottery had total revenues of $2.3 billion and net proceeds of $812 million.[57]

Legal Structures of Major Tax Sources

Income

New Jersey employs a broad-based income tax[58] that considers "[s]alaries, wages, tips, fees, commissions, bonuses, and other remuneration received for services rendered whether in cash or in property, and amounts paid or distributed, or deemed paid or distributed, out of a medical savings account that are not excluded from gross income" as a starting point for determining the state's taxable income.[59] However, numerous adjustments may be available to various individuals in calculating this amount.[60] Dur-

---

52. *Id.*
53. *Id.*
54. The Tax Foundation, Federal Spending Received Per Dollar of Taxes Paid by State, 2004 http://www.taxfoundation.org/taxdata/show/266.html (last visited Sept. 17, 2006).
55. *See id.*
56. N.J. STAT. ANN. §§ 5:9-1 to 5:9-22.
57. "New Jersey Lottery 2005 Annual Report," http://www.state.nj.us/lottery/money/annual _report_2005.pdf (last checked Dec. 18, 2006).
58. N.J. STAT. ANN. § 54A:2-1.
59. *Id.* § 54A:5-1.
60. Id. §§ 54A:6-1 − 54A:6-30.

ing fiscal year 2004, New Jersey collected individual income tax of $852 per capita, an amount which ranked 13th nationally.[61]

In New Jersey, a typical family of four (i.e., married taxpayers who file jointly and have two dependent children) are not required to pay any income tax until their combined income exceeds $20,000, an amount which is slightly below the national poverty line of $20,615.[62] New Jersey's income tax structure contains seven tax brackets that impose a minimum marginal rate of 1.4% and a maximum marginal rate of 8.97%.[63] When statutory exemptions are taken into account, the maximum marginal rate applies to every dollar of income exceeding $505,000.[64]

Property

Overview

New Jersey has a property tax system that taxes the value of real estate and tangible personal property at the local level, with only a modest amount of property tax collected at the state level.[65] Personal property not used for business purposes is exempt from taxation.[66] During fiscal year 2004, New Jersey collected approximately $18.2 billion dollars in property tax at the local level and approximately $3.7 million at the state level.[67] As a result, New Jersey residents paid $2,099 per capita in state and local property taxes, an amount which ranked 1st nationally.[68]

Defining the Real Property Tax Base

New Jersey requires that each locality determine the full value of taxable real property and apply an assessment ratio determined by each locality to that full

---

61. STATE RANKINGS 2006, *supra* note 1, at 321 *citing* U.S. Bureau of the Census, Governments Division "2004 State Government Tax Collections," *available at* http://www.census.gov/govs/www/statetax04.html.

62. JASON A. LEVITIS & NICHOLAS JOHNSON, CENTER ON BUDGET AND POLICY PRIORITIES, THE IMPACT OF STATE INCOME TAXES ON LOW-INCOME FAMILIES IN 2006, at 12 (2007). Note that in 2006, New Jersey taxpayers who are married and filing jointly were entitled to personal exemptions of $1,000 for both taxpayer and spouse, and dependent exemptions of $1,500 each. There is no standard deduction offered for New Jersey taxpayers. N.J. STAT. ANN. §§ 54A:2-4, 54A:3-1. Note, however, that the threshold calculation of $20,000 is greater than the sum of these exemptions because it includes additional tax benefits available to low-income families, such as the earned-income tax credit. *See* LEVITIS & JOHNSON, *supra*.

63. N.J. STAT. ANN. § 54A:2-1. New Jersey's middle five tax rates are 1.75%, 2.45%, 3.5%, 5.512%, and 6.37%. *Id.*

64. This total incorporates the exemptions of $5,000, plus the threshold of income of $500,000 for the highest tax bracket. *See supra* notes 62–63.

65. N.J. STAT. ANN. § 54:4-1 (the state imposes a tax only on railway use property) Id. § 54:29A-7.

66. Id. § 54:4-1.

67. Government Finances, *supra* note 47.

68. *See id.*

value.[69] An assessment is taken by each locality on April 1 of each year.[70] If a locality fails to make an assessment valuation, the state requires a default assessment valuation of 50% of the full value.[71] Fair market value is generally determined by the application of standard appraisal methods, including "cost method, the capitalization of income method, and the market or sales comparison method."[72]

Real Property Tax Rates

The New Jersey constitution provides that real property must be taxed at the general tax rate set by the taxing district in which the property is situated.[73] During fiscal year 2006, the tax rates per $1,000 of assessed value ranged from $60.00 in Audubon Park Borough to $4.70 in Avalon Borough.[74] However, these rates must be viewed in the context of the varying valuations used by each locality.

Personal and Intangible Property

Personal property not used for business purposes is exempt from tax.[75] Intangible personal property is not subject to tax at either the state or local level.[76]

Exemptions

New Jersey has an exhaustive list of exemptions based on ownership and use.[77] These exemptions include real estate and personal property owned by and occupied by persons totally disabled; cemeteries; business inventory; life insurance company property; and pollution control facilities.[78]

General and Selective Sales

General Sales

New Jersey imposes a general retail sales-and-use tax, which makes up 15.8% of New Jersey's total tax revenue.[79] This tax is imposed on the sale, distribution, renting, or furnishing of tangible personal property, as well as specified services.[80] These services include (1) installation of tangible materials; (2) tanning and spa services; and (3) trans-

---

69. N.J. Stat. Ann. § 54:4-2.25.

70. Id. § 54:4-2.27.

71. *Id.*

72. CCH-EXP, PROP-TAX-GUIDE NJ ¶ 20-615, Valuation Methods in General. Note that qualifying agricultural property is given special treatment for assessment purposes. Id. §§ 54:4-23.3, 54:4-23.5.

73. N.J. Const. art. VIII, § 1, ¶ 1.

74. CCH-EXP, PROP-TAX-GUIDE NJ ¶ 20-405, Rates of Tax.

75. N.J. Stat. Ann. § 54:4-1.

76. Id. § 54:4-1.

77. Id. §§ 54:4-3 to 54:4-3.161.

78. *Id.*

79. Government Finances, *supra* note 47.

80. N.J. Stat. Ann. § 54:32B-3.

portation services.[81] The state sales tax rate is 7%, and all localities may impose a local rate of up to 2%, for a combined state and local rate of 9%.[82] Exemptions from New Jersey's sales-and-use tax include, among other items, prescription and nonprescription drugs, all food sold in schools, newspapers and other periodicals, and textbooks.[83]

Selective Sales

Selective sales taxes make up 8.9% of New Jersey's total revenue.[84] Of that amount, 1.4%[85] comes from a motor fuel sales tax imposed at a rate of $0.105 per gallon of gasoline.[86] New Jersey residents paid an average of $63 per capita in state motor fuel sales taxes in 2004, an amount which ranked 40th nationally and was below the national average of $115.[87]

In 2004, sales taxes on alcoholic beverages made up 0.2% of New Jersey's total tax revenue.[88] New Jersey residents paid $10.06 per capita in state alcoholic beverage sales taxes in 2004, an amount which ranked 33rd nationally.[89]

The tobacco product sales tax makes up 2.0% of New Jersey's total tax revenue and is imposed at a rate of $2.575 per pack of cigarettes[90] New Jersey residents paid $89.52 per capita in state tobacco sales taxes in 2004, an amount which ranked 4th nationally.[91]

The remainder of New Jersey's selective sales taxes makes up 5.3% of its total tax revenue. Of this amount, 2.4% represents taxes on utilities and the other 2.9% represents taxes on other specific commodities, businesses, or services not reported separately above (e.g., on contractors, lodging, lubricating oil, fuels other than motor fuel, motor vehicles, meals, soft drinks, margarine, etc.).[92]

Corporate Income and Other

Corporate Income

The corporate income tax makes up 4.8% of New Jersey's total tax revenue.[93] New

---

81. *Id.*

82. Id. §§ 54:32B-3, 40:48-8.17.

83. Id. § 54:32B-8 to 54:32B-9.

84. Government Finances, *supra* note 47.

85. *Id.*

86. N.J. STAT. ANN. § 54:39-27.

87. STATE RANKINGS 2006, *supra* note 1, at 327.

88. Government Finances, *supra* note 47.

89. STATE RANKINGS 2006, *supra* note 1, at 335.

90. N.J. STAT. ANN. § 54:40A-8.

91. STATE RANKINGS 2006, *supra* note 1, at 332.

92. *See* GOVERNMENTS DIVISION, U.S. CENSUS BUREAU, GOVERNMENT FINANCE AND EMPLOYMENT CLASSIFICATION MANUAL, at ch.7 (2000), *available at* http://ftp2.census.gov/govs/class/classfull.pdf [hereinafter CLASSIFICATION MANUAL].

93. Government Finances, *supra* note 47.

Jersey has three separate tax brackets for corporate income.[94] New Jersey's broad-based corporate income tax is based on the corporation's federal taxable income.[95]

New Jersey follows the federal income tax treatment of S corporations. Thus, they do not pay corporate income tax; rather income and losses flow through to their shareholders.[96] A similar treatment is afforded to limited partnerships and limited liability partnerships, as well as limited liability companies, assuming they are treated as a partnership for federal tax purposes.[97] However, if a limited liability company is treated as a corporation for federal income tax purposes, the entity is subject to New Jersey's corporate income tax.[98]

Other

During fiscal year 2004, the collection of all other taxes not previously mentioned accounted for 5.7% of New Jersey's total tax revenue. Of this amount, approximately $516 million was generated by the estate and gift tax,[99] which is calculated on the basis of statutory provisions and excludes estate transfers to spouses or children.[100] The "other taxes" category is also made up of motor vehicle license taxes, documentary and stock transfer taxes, severance taxes, and all other taxes not listed separately or provided for in other categories, such as taxes on land based on a specified rate per acre (rather than on assessed value).[101]

Burden Analysis

The overall state and local tax burden on New Jersey taxpayers is very regressive. Taxpayers in the lowest quintile—those with incomes of less than $19,000—bear a tax burden of 12.5% of their income, while taxpayers in the top 1%—those with incomes that exceed $571,000—bear a tax burden of just 8.4% of their income.[102] It is

---

94. N.J. STAT. ANN. § 54:10A-5 (Income less than $50,000 is taxed at 6.5%, income between $50,000 and $100,000 is taxed at 7.5%, and income in excess of $100,000 is taxed at 9%.)

95. *Id.*

96. CCH-EXP, NJ-TAXRPTR ¶ 10-240, Limited Liability Companies (LLCs).

97. *Id.*

98. *Id.*

99. Government Finances, *supra* note 47.

100. N.J. STAT. ANN. § 54:34-2 (Brothers, sisters, and in-laws are taxed as follows: "On any amount in excess of $25,000.00, up to $1,100,000.00, 11%; On any amount in excess of $1,100,000.00, up to $1,400,000.00, 13%; On any amount in excess of $1,400,000.00, up to $1,700,000.00, 14%; On any amount in excess of $ 1,700,000.00, 16%"; and on all other transfers, "On any amount up to $ 700,000.00, 15%; On any amount in excess of $ 700,000.00, 16%"). *Id.*

101. *See* CLASSIFICATION MANUAL, *supra* note 92, at ch.7.

102. *See* ROBERT S. MCINTYRE ET AL., WHO PAYS? A DISTRIBUTIONAL ANALYSIS OF THE TAX SYSTEMS IN ALL 50 STATES 76 (2d ed. 2003), *available at* http://www.itepnet.org/wp2000/text.pdf. Taxpayers in the second quintile bear a 10.2% total tax burden on incomes between $19,000 and $34,000; those in the third quintile bear a 9.9% tax burden on incomes between $34,000 and

also worth noting that, although New Jersey obviously has no control over federal tax policy, federal itemized deductions for state and local personal income and property taxes nonetheless further reduce the burden on taxpayers in the top 1% to 5.0%.[103] Between 1989 and 2002, the tax burden on the bottom quintile rose by approximately 0.6%, while the burden on the top 1% rose by 1.1%.[104]

In terms of the income tax, the burden across income groups in New Jersey is slightly progressive, with taxpayers in the lowest quintile bearing a tax burden of -0.4% and those in the top 1% bearing a tax burden of 6.0%.[105] In contrast, however, the sales and excises taxes imposed by New Jersey are very regressive, with taxpayers in the lowest quintile bearing a tax burden of 7.2%, and those in the top 1% bearing a tax burden of just 0.9%.[106] Property taxes in New Jersey are also regressive, with taxpayers in the lowest quintile bearing a tax burden of 5.6% and those in the remaining quintiles bearing an average tax burden of 3.7%.[107]

$56,000; those in the fourth quintile bear a 9.8% tax burden on incomes between $56,000 and $94,000; those in the 80th–95th percentiles bear a 9.7% tax burden on incomes between $94,000 and $193,000; finally, those in the 96th–99th percentiles bear a 9.5% tax burden on incomes between $193,000 and $571,000. *Id.*

103. *Id.* Taxpayers in the lowest and second lowest quintiles were able to reduce their individual tax burdens by 0.1% and 0.2%, respectively; those in the third quintile by 0.6%; those in the fourth quintile by 1.2%; those in the 80th–95th percentiles by 1.9%; and those in the 96th–99th percentiles by 2.4%. *Id.*

104. *Id.* at 77.

105. *See id.* at 76. Taxpayers in the second quintile bear a 1.0% income tax burden; those in the third quintile bear a 1.6% burden; those in the fourth quintile bear a 2.0% burden; those in the 80th–95th percentiles bear a 3.2% burden; finally, those in the 96th–99th percentiles bear a 4.7% burden. *Id.* Note, however, that of the total income tax burden borne by the top 1% of taxpayers, 5.6% represents individual income taxes and 0.4% represents corporate income taxes. *Id.*

106. *See id.* Taxpayers in the second quintile bear a 5.2% sales-and-excise tax burden; those in the third quintile bear a 3.9% burden; those in the fourth quintile bear a 3.1% burden; those in the 80th–95th percentiles bear a 2.2% burden; finally, those in the 96th–99th percentiles bear a 1.6% burden. *Id.*

107. *See id.* Taxpayers in the second quintile bear a 4.1% property tax burden; those in the third quintile bear a 4.3% burden; those in the fourth quintile bear a 4.6% burden; those in the 80th–95th percentiles bear a 4.2% burden; those in the 96th–99th percentiles bear a 3.2% burden; finally, those in the top 1% bear a 1.5% burden. *Id.*

New Mexico

General Information

Basic Profile – Geography, Population, and Industry

New Mexico was admitted to the Union in 1912. The "Land of Enchantment" is located in the southwest and is bordered by the Arizona on the west; Utah on the northwest; Colorado on the north; Oklahoma on the east; Texas on the east and southeast; and Mexico on the south. New Mexico is located in the mountain time zone, and Santa Fe is the state capital.

New Mexico ranks 36th in population (approximately 1.9 million residents)[1] and 5th in total land and water area (121,590 square miles).[2] Its population is approximately 84.5% white, 2.4% black, and 10.2% American Indian and Alaska Native.[3] Additionally, 43.4% of its population identify themselves as persons of Hispanic or Latino origin.[4] The state is approximately 40% Catholic; 36% Protestant; and less than 0.5% Jewish; 24% claim a religion outside the Judeo-Christian tradition or no religion at all.[5] Roughly 65% of New Mexico's population lives in urban areas.[6] Major industries include mining, durable goods manufacturing, retail trade, real estate, professional and technical services, and health care and social assistance.[7]

---

1. STATE RANKINGS 2006, vi, 429 (Kathleen O'Leary Morgan & Scott Morgan eds., Morgan Quitno Press 2006).

2. *Id.* at 225.

3. New Mexico Quick Facts from the U.S. Census Bureau, http://quickfacts.census.gov/qfd/states/35000.html (last visited Jan. 31, 2007). The remaining population is made up of 1.3% Asian persons; 0.1% Native Hawaiian persons and other Pacific Islanders; and 1.5% persons reporting two or more races. *Id.*

4. *Id.* (noting that because Hispanics and Latinos may be of any race, they are also included within the other applicable race categories). *See id.*

5. *See* BARRY A. KOSMIN, EGON MAYER & ARIELA KEYSAR, AMERICAN RELIGIOUS IDENTIFICATION SURVEY 2001, at 40, *available at* http://www.gc.cuny.edu/faculty/research_studies/aris.pdf.

6. USDA Economic Research Service, New Mexico Fact Sheet, http://www.ers.usda.gov/State-Facts/NM.htm (last visited Oct. 16, 2006).

7. *See* U.S. Department of Commerce Bureau of Economic Analysis, Gross Domestic Product by State, http://www.bea.gov/bea/newsrelarchive/2006/gsp1006.xls (last visited Nov. 10, 2006).

Family Income and Poverty Indicators

In 2004, New Mexico's per capita gross product was $32,061, which ranked among the bottom ten states nationally and was below the national average of $39,725.[8] During this same period, although the median household income in New Mexico was $37,587,[9] 17.5% of New Mexico's population was living in poverty, which was substantially above the national average of 12.4% and ranked third nationally.[10] More specifically, poverty affected 27% of New Mexico's children,[11] 11.9% of its senior citizens,[12] and 15.9% of its families.[13] Of its female-headed households with children, 49.3% lived in poverty,[14] and 58.2% of the state's public elementary and secondary school students were eligible for free or reduced-price meals.[15] Of those living in poverty, approximately 2.2% were black, which represented 21% of New Mexico's black population and 0.4% of its total population.[16] Of those living in poverty, approximately 18.6% were American Indian and Alaska Native, which represented 35.2% of New Mexico's American Indian and Alaska Native population and 3.4% of its total population.[17] In an attempt to combat this poverty, New Mexico spent approximately $2 billion on public welfare programs in 2002,[18] which made up 18.2% of its total government expenditures.[19]

New Mexico's Public Elementary-Secondary School System

Overall Spending and Performance

For the 2003–2004 school year, New Mexico spent $7,331 per pupil in its public elementary-secondary school system, which was substantially below the national average of $8,182.[20] Of this amount, 17.2% was provided by the federal government, 69.7% was provided by the state government, and 13.1% was provided by the local govern-

---

8. STATE RANKINGS 2006, *supra* note 1, at 89.

9. *Id.* at 96.

10. *Id.* at 495.

11. *Id.* at 497.

12. *Id.* at 496.

13. *Id.* at 498.

14. *Id.* at 499.

15. *Id.* at 532.

16. *See* Fact Sheet, American FactFinder, http://factfinder.census.gov/home/saff/main.html?_lang=en (select "New Mexico" under "Get a Fact Sheet for your community") (last visited Feb. 16, 2007). Note that these numbers are based on the 2000 census because more recent numbers were not available.

17. *Id.*

18. *Id.* at 500.

19. *Id.* at 502.

20. GOVERNMENTS DIVISION, U.S. CENSUS BUREAU, PUBLIC EDUCATION FINANCES 2004, at 8 tbl.8 (2006), *available at* http://www2.census.gov/govs/school/04f33pub.pdf.

ments,[21] with property taxes making up 9.9% of the total funding.[22] Out of these funds, New Mexico paid its elementary and secondary school teachers an estimated average annual salary of $39,328 during the 2004–2005 school year,[23] and in 2003, it provided a student/teacher ratio of 15.0, which was slightly better than the national average of 15.9.[24]

In academic performance, New Mexico's fourth and eighth grade students scored lower than the national average in mathematics,[25] reading,[26] science,[27] and writing.[28]

Equity Issues

In 2004, the funding per student in New Mexico's highest poverty districts exceeded that in its lowest poverty districts by $1,106,[29] although when adjustments were made for the additional costs of educating students growing up in poverty, that excess narrowed to $679.[30] Similarly, New Mexico spent $246 more per student in its highest minority districts, although this amount fell to just $18 when adjustments for low-income students were made.[31]

Fourth graders eligible for free or reduced-price school lunches had test scores that were 9% lower in mathematics,[32] 12% lower in reading,[33] and 13% lower in writing[34]

---

21. *See id.* at 5 tbl.5.

22. *See id.* at 4 tbl.4.

23. THOMAS D. SNYDER ET AL., NATIONAL CENTER FOR EDUCATION STATISTICS, DIGEST OF EDUCATION STATISTICS 2005, at 116 tbl.77 (2006) *available at* http://nces.ed.gov/pubsearch/pubs info.asp?pubid=2006030.

24. *Id.* at 98 tbl.65.

25. NATIONAL CENTER FOR EDUCATION STATISTICS, U.S. DEPARTMENT OF EDUCATION, THE NATION'S REPORT CARD: MATHEMATICS 2005, at 14 fig.11, 16 fig.12 (2005), *available at* http://nces.ed.gov/nationsreportcard/pdf/ main2005/2006453.pdf [hereinafter MATHEMATICS 2005].

26. NATIONAL CENTER FOR EDUCATION STATISTICS, U.S. DEPARTMENT OF EDUCATION, THE NATION'S REPORT CARD: READING 2005, at 14 fig.11, 16 fig.12 (2005), *available at* http://nces.ed.gov/nationsreportcard/pdf/main2005/2006451.pdf [hereinafter READING 2005].

27. NATIONAL CENTER FOR EDUCATION STATISTICS, U.S. DEPARTMENT OF EDUCATION, THE NATION'S REPORT CARD: SCIENCE 2005, at 16 fig.12, 28 fig.22 (2006), *available at* http://nces.ed.gov/nationsreportcard//pdf/main2005/2006466.pdf [hereinafter SCIENCE 2005].

28. HILARY R. PERSKY ET AL., NATIONAL CENTER FOR EDUCATION STATISTICS, U.S. DEPARTMENT OF EDUCATION, THE NATION'S REPORT CARD: WRITING 2002, at 23 tbl.2.2, 24 tbl.2.3 (2003), *available at* http://nces.ed.gov/nationsreportcard/pdf/main2002/2003529.pdf [hereinafter WRITING 2002].

29. THE EDUCATION TRUST, FUNDING GAPS 2006, at 7 tbl.3 (2006), *available at* http://www2 .edtrust.org/NR/rdonlyres/CDEF9403-5A75-437E-93FF-EBF1174181FB/0/FundingGap2006.pdf.

30. *Id.*

31. *Id.* at 7 tbl.4.

32. MATHEMATICS 2005, *supra* note 25, at 20 tbl.5.

33. READING 2005, *supra* note 26, at 20 tbl.5.

34. WRITING 2002, *supra* note 28, at 75 tbl.3.24.

than those of students who were not eligible. The results were similar for eighth graders eligible for free or reduced-price lunches; their test scores were 9% lower in mathematics,[35] 8% lower in reading,[36] and 14% lower in writing[37] than those of students who were not eligible.

In response to litigation challenging the equity of New Mexico's school funding system, the legislature passed the 1974 Public School Finance Act,[38] which dramatically increased state funding to education.[39] In *Zuni School District v. State*, a 1999 case in which the plaintiffs challenged the constitutionality of the state's capital funding system for education, a New Mexico trial court ordered the state to "establish and implement a uniform funding system for capital improvements ... and for correcting existing past inequities."[40] The capital funding system instituted by the legislature in response to the order was approved by the court in 2002.[41] However, the *Zuni* plaintiffs challenged the state's compliance with the court order at the state level[42] and took their case to federal court against the U.S. Department of Education.[43] The U.S. Supreme Court granted a writ of certiorari to the *Zuni* plaintiffs, and oral arguments were heard on January 10, 2007.[44]

Availability of Publicly Funded Prekindergarten Programs

The New Mexico Pre-K Program, launched in 2005–2006 and consisting of several programs, serves four-year-olds in families of all income brackets, although two-thirds of the children enrolled in each program must live within the attendance zone of a Title I school and the state gives funding priority to programs in areas with schools that fail to meet math and reading proficiency requirements.[45] The state also funds the Child Development Program, which serves children from birth to aged five who are at risk according to eligibility criteria established by local organizations.[46] Total enroll-

---

35. MATHEMATICS 2005, *supra* note 25, at 21 tbl.6.

36. READING 2005, *supra* note 26, at 21 tbl.6.

37. WRITING 2002, *supra* note 28, at 76 tbl.3.25.

38. *See* N.M. STAT. ANN. § 22-8-1.

39. National Access Network, State by State, New Mexico, http://www.schoolfunding.info/states/nm/lit_nm.php3 (last visited Mar. 19, 2007).

40. *See id.* (quoting *Zuni School District v. State*, CV-98-14-II (Dist. Ct., McKinley County Oct. 14, 1999)).

41. *Id.*

42. National Access Network, State by State, New Mexico, Recent Events, http://www.schoolfunding.info/news/litigation/5-11-06nmfacilitiesreview.php3 (Mar. 19, 2007).

43. *See* Zuni Pub. Sch. Dist. No. 89 v. U.S. Dep't of Educ., 437 F.3d 1289 (10th Cir. 2006).

44. Zuni Pub. Sch. Dist. No. 89 v. U.S. Dep't of Educ., 127 S.Ct. 36 (2006).

45. W. STEVEN BARNETT ET AL., NATIONAL INSTITUTE FOR EARLY EDUCATION RESEARCH, THE STATE OF PRESCHOOL 2006, at 108 (2006), *available at* http://nieer.org/yearbook/pdf/yearbook.pdf.

46. *Id.*

ment in these state-funded programs is 1,959,[47] which represents just 4% of New Mexico's 53,077 three, four, and five-year-old children.[48] Federally funded and state-funded Head Start programs enroll an additional 7,876 and 298 children, respectively,[49] which represents 15% and 1%, respectively, of New Mexico's three- and four-year-old children.[50]

Where Does New Mexico Get Its Revenue?

At the end of fiscal year 2004, New Mexico had total revenues of approximately $14.9 billion.[51] Of this amount, 37% was derived from state and local tax revenues and 25% was received from the federal government.[52] The remaining 38% came from other sources, including the New Mexico Lottery, insurance trust revenue, and revenue from government-owned utilities and other commercial or auxiliary enterprises.[53]

Tax Revenue

New Mexico collected approximately $5.4 billion in state and local tax revenue during fiscal year 2004.[54] As a result, New Mexico residents paid $2,861 per capita in state and local government taxes, an amount which ranked 37th nationally.[55] The different types of tax sources were approximately apportioned as follows:

Individual income taxes	18.5%
Property taxes	15.4%
General and selective sales taxes	48.3%
Corporate income and other taxes	17.8%
	100.0%[56]

Federal Funding

During fiscal year 2004, 25% of New Mexico's total revenues came from the federal government.[57] For every dollar of federal taxes paid, New Mexico received $2.00 in fed-

---

47. *Id.* at 109.

48. *See id.* at 232.

49. *Id.* at 110.

50. *See id.* at 232.

51. U.S. Census Bureau, State and Local Government Finances 2003–04, http://www.census.gov/govs/www/estimate04.html (last visited Oct. 6, 2006) [hereinafter Government Finances].

52. *Id.*

53. *Id.*

54. The total tax revenues were collected as follows: $4 billion by the state and 1.4 billion by local governments. *Id.*

55. *Id.*

56. *Id.*

57. *Id.*

eral funding, an amount which ranked 1st nationally and was far above the national average of $1.17.[58]

Lottery Revenues

New Mexico voters passed a public referendum in 1994 approving the formation of a lottery, and the New Mexico Lottery Act went into effect on July 1, 1995.[59] The stated purpose of the Lottery is to provide tuition assistance to resident undergraduates in New Mexico postsecondary educational institutions.[60] All net income from the Lottery is transferred to the Lottery Tuition Fund.[61] In 2005, the Lottery had gross sales of $139.2 million and a net income of $32.2 million, all of which were earmarked for the Lottery Success Scholarship Program.[62]

Legal Structures of Major Tax Sources

Income

New Mexico employs a broad-based income tax that uses adjusted gross income for federal income tax purposes as a starting point for determining the state's taxable income.[63] However, a fairly large number of adjustments may be available to various individuals in calculating this amount.[64] State law prohibits individual municipalities from imposing income taxes.[65] During fiscal year 2004, New Mexico collected personal income tax of $529 per capita, an amount which ranked 36th nationally.[66]

In New Mexico, a typical family of four (i.e., married taxpayers who file jointly and have two dependent children) are not required to pay any income tax until their combined income exceeds $30,800, an amount which is above the national poverty line of $20,615. [67] New Mexico's income tax structure contains four tax brackets that impose

---

58. *See* The Tax Foundation, Federal Spending Received Per Dollar of Taxes Paid by State 2004, http://www.taxfoundation.org/taxdata/show/266.html (last visited Oct. 16, 2006).

59. The New Mexico Lottery, FAQ, http://www.nmlottery.com/FAQs/faq.htm (last visited Dec. 18, 2006).

60. N.M. Stat. Ann. §6-24-3.

61. New Mexico Lottery Authority, Annual Report FY 2005 (2006), *available at* http://www.nmlottery.com/News/Annual_Reports/NMLA_Annual_Report_2005.pdf (last visited Dec. 18, 2006).

62. *Id.*

63. *See* N.M. Stat. Ann. §7-2-2.

64. *See id.* §7-2-5.

65. *Id.* §3-18-2.

66. State Rankings 2006, *supra* note 1, at 321.

67. Jason A. Levitis, Center On Budget And Policy Priorities, The Impact Of State Income Taxes On Low-Income Families In 2006, at 12 (2007). In 2006, New Mexico taxpayers who were married and filing jointly could claim a standard deduction of $10,300, personal exemptions of $3,300 for each spouse, and dependent exemptions of $3,300 for each child. *See* N.M. Stat. Ann. §§7-2-2(N)(1), 7-2-2(N)(3). Note, however, that the threshold calculation of

a minimum marginal rate of 1.7% and a maximum marginal rate of 5.3%.[68] When statutory exemptions and the standard deduction are taken into account, the maximum marginal rate applies to every dollar of income exceeding $47,500.[69]

Property

Overview

New Mexico has a typical property tax system that taxes the value of real and tangible personal property at the state and local levels. New Mexico localities collected approximately $787 million in property taxes during fiscal year 2004, while the state collected just $53.1 million.[70] As a result, New Mexico residents $441 per capita in property taxes, an amount which ranked 48th nationally.[71]

Defining the Real Property Tax Base

All taxable property in New Mexico is assessed at 33.3% of "value."[72] The relevant measure of "value" is generally fair market value.[73] However, a special valuation method is granted for certain types of property, including agricultural land—a method which is determined on the basis of the land's capacity to produce agricultural products.[74] Property subject to the New Mexico property tax is valued annually.[75]

Real Property Tax Rates

The State of New Mexico generally cannot impose a property tax rate greater than 4 mills ($4 per $1,000), except in some instances to support state educational, penal, and charitable institutions, or to service state debt.[76] The State may not levy a rate in excess of 20 mills ($20 per $1,000) without voter approval, regardless of the purpose of the levy.[77] The rate ceilings for localities are generally as follows: for counties, $11.85

$30,800 is greater than the sum of these deductions and exemptions because it includes additional tax benefits available to low-income families, such as the earned-income tax credit. *See* Levitis, *supra*.

68. N.M. Stat. Ann. §7-2-7. The rates applied to New Mexico's middle two brackets are 3.2% and 4.7%. *Id.*

69. The standard deduction and exemptions of $10,300 and $13,200, respectively, plus the threshold of taxable income for the highest tax bracket of $24,000, equals $47,500. *See supra* notes 67–68.

70. Government Finances, *supra* note 51.

71. *See id.*

72. *See* N.M. Stat. Ann. §§7-35-2(O), 7-37-3.

73. *Id.* §7-36-15.

74. *Id.* §7-36-20.

75. *Id.* §7-38-7.

76. N.M. Const. art. VIII, §2.

77. *Id.*

per $1,000 of net taxable value (11.85 mills); for school districts, $0.50 per $1,000 of net taxable value[78] (.5 mills); for municipalities, $7.65 per $1,000 of net taxable value (7.65 mills); and for learning center districts, $5 per $1,000 of net taxable value (5 mills).[79] Furthermore, annual changes in property tax rates are restricted by a growth rate that is calculated using factors such as inflation and annual increases in property values.[80] The aggregate resident property tax rates for 2004 ranged from 10.7 mills in Floyd to 38.0 mills in Albuquerque.[81] The forgoing rates include the state rate of 1.028 mills.[82]

Personal and Intangible Property

New Mexico does not tax intangible property. Only the following types of tangible personal property are taxable: livestock; manufactured homes; aircraft not registered under the Aircraft Registration Act; private railroad cars not taxed under the Railroad Car Company Tax Act; mineral property; oil and gas pipelines and other property; utilities property; communications system property; railroad property; commercial aircraft; vehicles not registered under the motor vehicle code for which the owner has taken federal depreciation deductions; and other tangible personal property used for business purposes or held for sale or lease for which the owner has taken a federal depreciation deduction.[83]

Personal property that is taxable because the owner claimed federal depreciation deductions is valued on the basis of cost less depreciation and other justifiable factors, provided that the value cannot be less than 12.5% of the cost unless the property ceases to be used and useful in a business activity.[84] Other taxable personal property is generally valued according to special valuation rules.[85]

Exemptions

New Mexico allows a homestead exemption of up to $2,000 of the taxable value.[86] Veterans and their surviving spouses receive a $4,000 exemption on the taxable value

---

78. With voter approval, a local school board may impose an additional property tax of up to $2 per $1,000 for capital improvements. N.M. STAT. ANN. § 22-25-1.

79. *Id.* §§ 7-37-7(B), 21-16A-6.

80. *See id.* § 7-37-7-1. The formula is applied separately to residential and nonresidential property. *Id.*

81. New Mexico Taxation & Revenue Department, 2004 County Rate Certificates, http://www.tax.state.nm.us/pubs/TaxreseStat/countyratecertificates.htm (last visited Mar. 31, 2007).

82. *Id.*

83. N.M. STAT. ANN. § 7-36-8.

84. *Id.* § 7-36-33.

85. For mineral property valuation, see N.M. STAT. ANN. § 7-36-23. For manufactured homes, see § 7-36-26. For railroad property, see § 7-36-31. For utilities property, oil and gas pipelines and equipment, and communications systems, see §§ 7-36-27 to 30. For commercial aircraft, see § 7-36-32.

86. N.M. STAT. ANN. § 7-37-4.

of their property.[87] Pursuant to the Community Development Incentive Act, counties or municipalities may grant exemptions of up to 100% of the taxable value of the commercial personal property of a new business facility for up to 20 years.[88] Other exemptions include cemeteries, charitable organizations, churches, educational organizations, and government and public property.[89]

General and Selective Sales

General Sales

New Mexico imposes a "gross receipts tax," which comprised 35.9% of the state's total tax revenue during fiscal year 2004.[90] This tax is imposed on all gross receipts of a person engaged in business, unless a specific exemption applies.[91] Although the tax is imposed on persons engaged in business, in almost all cases it is passed on to consumers and thus resembles a sales tax.[92] "Gross receipts" encompasses receipts from selling property in New Mexico; leasing property employed in New Mexico; performing services in New Mexico; and selling services performed outside New Mexico, the product of which was initially used in New Mexico.[93] The gross receipts tax generally applies to all services.[94] For purposes of the tax, "property" means real property, tangible personal property, licenses, and franchises.[95]

The gross receipts tax is imposed at a rate of 5% by the state.[96] In addition, municipalities and counties may impose local gross receipts taxes, with statutory limits on the rates that may be imposed for various purposes.[97] The combined state and local rates effective in cities as of December 31, 2006, ranged from 5.56% in Mosquero to 7.86% in Santa Rosa.[98]

Effective January 1, 2005, a deduction was allowed for receipts from the sale of food at retail food stores, effectively eliminating the gross receipts tax on groceries.[99] This deduction does not apply to other food sales, which are taxable.[100] Other exemptions

---

87. *Id.* § 7-37-5.

88. *Id.* § 2-64-3.

89. N.M. CONST. art. VIII, § 3.

90. Government Finances, *supra* note 51.

91. N.M. STAT. ANN. § 7-9-5.

92. New Mexico Taxation and Revenue, Frequently Asked Questions, http://www.tax.state.nm.us/oos/GrossReceiptsTaxFAQ.pdf (last visited Dec. 21, 2006).

93. N.M. ADMIN. CODE tit. 3, § 2.1.14.

94. *See id.* § 2.1.18.

95. N.M. STAT. ANN. § 7-9-3(J). Patents, trademarks, and copyrights were formerly included but were deleted effective July 1, 2006.

96. N.M. STAT. ANN. §§ 7-9-4, 7-9-7.

97. *See id.* §§ 7-19D, 7-19-12, 7-20E, 7-20C, 7-20F.

98. CCH-EXP, NM-TAXRPTR ¶ 61-735, Local Rates.

99. N.M. STAT. ANN. § 7-9-92.

100. *See id.*

include receipts from the sale of prescription drugs, certain medical supplies, gasoline, and vehicles that are subject to a registration fee and an excise tax.[101]

Selective Sales

Selective sales taxes constituted 12.4% of New Mexico's total tax revenue during fiscal year 2004.[102] Of that amount, 3.9% came from motor fuel sales taxes.[103] New Mexico residents paid an average of $111 per capita in state motor fuel sales taxes in 2004, an amount which ranked 40th nationally and was below the national average of $115.[104]

The tobacco product sales tax made up 1.0% of New Mexico's tax revenue during fiscal year 2004.[105] New Mexico residents paid $27.70 per capita in state tobacco sales taxes in 2004, an amount which ranked 35th nationally.[106]

In 2004, sales taxes on alcoholic beverages made up 0.7% of New Mexico's total tax revenue.[107] New Mexico residents paid $19.71 per capita in state alcoholic beverage sales taxes in 2004, an amount which ranked 13th nationally.[108]

The remainder of New Mexico's selective sales taxes constituted 6.8% of its total tax revenue in 2004.[109] Of that percentage, 1.1% represented taxes on utilities and the other 5.7% represented taxes on other specific commodities, businesses, or services not reported separately above (e.g., on contractors, lodging, lubricating oil, fuels other than motor fuel, motor vehicles, meals, soft drinks, margarine, etc.).[110]

Corporate Income and Other

Corporate Income

Corporate income taxes comprised 2.5% of New Mexico's total tax revenue during fiscal year 2004.[111] This broad-based tax is calculated with federal taxable income as the starting point.[112] The corporate income tax applies only to C Corporations. New Mexico follows the federal pass-through treatment of S Corporations, partnerships, and limited liability companies.[113] The corporate income tax structure contains three

---

101. *Id.* §§ 7-9-23, 7-9-26, 7-9-73.

102. Government Finances, *supra* note 51.

103. *Id.*

104. STATE RANKINGS 2006, *supra* note 1, at 327.

105. Government Finances, *supra* note 51.

106. STATE RANKINGS 2006, *supra* note 1, at 332.

107. Government Finances, *supra* note 51.

108. STATE RANKINGS 2006, *supra* note 1, at 335.

109. Government Finances, *supra* note 51.

110. *Id.*; *see* GOVERNMENTS DIVISION, U.S. CENSUS BUREAU, GOVERNMENT FINANCE AND EMPLOYMENT CLASSIFICATION MANUAL, at ch.7 (2000), *available at* http://ftp2.census.gov/govs/class/classfull.pdf [hereinafter CLASSIFICATION MANUAL].

111. Government Finances, *supra* note 51.

112. N.M. STAT. ANN. § 7-2A-2(C).

113. *See id.* §§ 7-2A-2(D), 7-2A-2 (G).

tax brackets that impose a minimum marginal rate of 4.8% and a maximum marginal rate of 7.6%.[114] The maximum marginal rate applies to every dollar of income exceeding $1,000,000.[115]

Other

During fiscal year 2004, the collection of all other taxes not previously mentioned generated $830.8 million, an amount which comprised 15.3% of New Mexico's total tax revenue.[116] Of that amount, $7.4 million came from estate taxes, which are generally imposed in an amount equal to the federal estate tax credit.[117] Although the New Mexico estate tax statutes are still in effect, the repeal of the federal credit for state death taxes[118] has effectively eliminated the New Mexico estate tax.

New Mexico also imposes a corporate franchise tax of $50 per year,[119] an excise tax on the privilege of severing and processing natural resources, and a severance tax on oil and gas.[120]

The "other taxes" category is further made up of various license taxes, documentary or stock transfer taxes, severance taxes, and all other taxes not listed separately or provided for in other categories.[121]

Burden Analysis

The overall state and local tax burden on New Mexico's taxpayers is very regressive. Taxpayers in the lowest quintile—those with incomes of less than $13,000—bear a tax burden of 12.1% of their income, while taxpayers in the top 1%—those with incomes that exceed $243,000—bear a tax burden of just 8.7% of their income.[122] It is also worth noting that, although New Mexico obviously has no control over federal tax

---

114. *Id.* § 7-2A-5.

115. *Id.* Income not over $500,000 is taxed at a rate of 4.8%; thereafter, income between $500,000 and $1,000,000 is taxed at a rate of 6.4%, and income in excess of $1,000,000 is taxed at a rate 7.6%.

116. Government Finances, *supra* note 51.

117. *Id.*; N.M. Stat. Ann. § 7-7-3.

118. *See* Economic Growth and Tax Relief Reconciliation Act of 2001, Pub. L. No. 107-16 (2001).

119. N.M. Stat. Ann. § 7-2A-5.1.

120. *Id.* §§ 7-25-2, 7-26-3, 7-29-4.

121. *See* Classification Manual, *supra* note 110, at ch.7.

122. *See* Robert S. McIntyre et al., Who Pays? A Distributional Analysis of the Tax Systems in All 50 States 78 (2d ed. 2003), *available at* http://www.itepnet.org/wp2000/text.pdf. Taxpayers in the second quintile bear a 11.1% total tax burden on incomes between $13,000 and $23,000; those in the third quintile bear a 10.4% tax burden on incomes between $23,000 and $36,000; those in the fourth quintile bear a 9.7% tax burden on incomes between $36,000 and $60,000; those in the 80th–95th percentiles bear a 9.3% tax burden on incomes between $60,000 and $112,000; finally, those in the 96th–99th percentiles bear a 8.7% tax burden on incomes between $112,000 and $243,000. *Id.*

policy, federal itemized deductions for state and local personal income and property taxes nonetheless further reduce the burden on taxpayers in the top 1% to 6.3%.[123] Furthermore, between 1989 and 2002, the tax burden on the bottom quintile rose by approximately 2.7%, while the burden on the top 1% rose by only 0.1%.[124]

In terms of the income tax, the burden across income groups in New Mexico is slightly progressive, with taxpayers in the lowest quintile bearing a tax burden of -0.3% and those in the top 1% bearing a tax burden of 6.1%.[125] In sharp contrast, however, the sales and excise taxes imposed by New Mexico are extremely regressive, with taxpayers in the lowest quintile bearing a tax burden of 9.7% and those in the top 1% bearing a tax burden of just 1.6%.[126] Property taxes in New Mexico are also regressive, with taxpayers in the lowest quintile bearing a tax burden of 2.7% and those in the top quintile bearing an average tax burden of 1.3%.[127]

---

123. *Id.* Taxpayers in the lowest and second lowest quintile did not receive any benefit from these federal offsets, while those in the third quintile were able to reduce their individual tax burdens by 0.1%, those in the fourth quintile by 0.3%, those in the 80th–95th percentiles by 0.8%, and those in the 96th–99th percentiles by 1.4%. *Id.*

124. *Id.* at 79.

125. *See id.* at 78. Taxpayers in the second quintile bear a 0.7% income tax burden; those in the third quintile bear a 1.5% burden; those in the fourth quintile bear a 2.4% burden; those in the 80th–95th percentiles bear a 3.5% burden; finally, those in the 96th–99th percentiles bear a 4.5% burden. *Id.* Note, however, that these percentages include both individual and corporate income tax burdens; that within the second quintile, corporate income taxes represent 0.1% of this burden; that within the third quintile, corporate income taxes represent less than 0.1% of this burden; that within the fourth quintile, corporate income taxes represent less than 0.1% of this burden; that within the 80th–95th percentiles, corporate income taxes represent 0.1% of this burden; that within the 96th–99th percentiles, corporate income taxes represent 0.1% of this burden; and that in the top 1%, corporate income taxes represent 0.2% of this burden. *Id.*

126. *See id.* Taxpayers in the second quintile bear a 8.8% sales-and-excise tax burden; those in the third quintile bear a 7.2% burden; those in the fourth quintile bear a 5.8% burden; those in the 80th–95th percentiles bear a 4.4% burden; finally, those in the 96th–99th percentiles bear a 2.7% burden. *Id.*

127. *See id.* Taxpayers in the second quintile bear a 1.6% property tax burden; those in the third quintile bear a 1.7% burden; those in the fourth quintile bear a 1.6% burden; those in the 80th–95th percentiles bear a 1.4% burden; those in the 96th–99th percentiles bear a 1.5% burden, finally, those in the top 1% bear a 0.9% burden. *Id.*

New York

General Information

Basic Profile – Geography, Population, and Industry

Admitted to the Union in 1788, New York is known as the "Empire State."[1] It is located in the Mid-Atlantic region and is bordered by Canada on the north; the Atlantic Ocean, Vermont, and Connecticut on the east; New Jersey and Pennsylvania on the south; and Canada, Lake Ontario, and Lake Erie on the west. The state is located in the eastern time zone, and its capital is Albany.

New York ranks 27th in total area (54,556 square miles);[2] in 2005, it ranked 3rd in population (approximately 19.3 million residents).[3] Its population is approximately 73.8% white and 17.4% black.[4] The state is approximately 38% Catholic; 31% Protestant; and 5% Jewish; 26% claim a religion outside the Judeo-Christian tradition or no religion at all.[5] Nearly 91.9% of New York's population lives in urban areas.[6] Major industries include finance and banking, exports, tourism, entertainment, and agriculture.[7]

Family Income and Poverty Indicators

In 2004, New York's per capita gross product was $46,510, which ranked 7th nationally and was above the national average of $39,725.[8] During this same period, while

---

1. STATE RANKINGS 2006, vi, 1 (Kathleen O'Leary Morgan & Scott Morgan, eds. Morgan Quitno Press, 2006).

2. *Id.* at 225.

3. *Id.* at 429.

4. New York Quick Facts from the U.S. Census Bureau, http://quickfacts.census.gov/qfd/states/54000.html (last visited Jan. 27, 2007). The remaining population is made up of 6.7% Asian persons; 0.5% American Indian and/or Alaska Native persons; 0.1% Hawaiian persons or other Pacific Islanders, and 1.5% persons reporting two or more races. *Id.* Additionally, 16.1% of New York's total population identify themselves as persons of Hispanic or Latino origin. *Id.* (noting that because Hispanics may be of any race, they are included within the other applicable race categories).

5. BARRY A. KOSMIN, EGON MAYER & ARIELA KEYSAR, AMERICAN RELIGIOUS IDENTIFICATION SURVEY 2001, at 41, *available at* http://www.gc.cuny.edu/faculty/research_studies/aris.pdf.

6. USDA Economic Research Service, New York Fact Sheet, http://www.ers.usda.gov/StateFacts/NY.htm (last visited Sept. 17, 2006). According to the latest estimates, approximately 1.6 million people live in rural areas, and 17.7 million people live in urban areas. *Id.*

7. New York State / Citizens Guide, http://www.nysegov.com/citGuide.cfm?superCat=28 (last visited Feb. 17, 2007).

8. STATE RANKINGS 2006, *supra* note 1, at 89.

the median household income in New York was $44,228,[9] 14.4% of the state's population was living in poverty, which was just above the national average of 12.4%.[10] More specifically, poverty affected 20.3% of New York's children,[11] 11.3% of its senior citizens,[12] and 11.1% of its families.[13] Of its female-headed households with children, 37.5% lived in poverty.[14] Of those living in poverty ,approximately 26.5% were black, which represented 23.6% of New York's black population and 3.8% of its total population.[15] In an attempt to combat this poverty, New York spent approximately $32.5 billion on public welfare programs in 2002,[16] which made up 20.2% of its total government expenditures.[17]

New York's Public Elementary-Secondary School System

Overall Spending and Performance

For the 2003–2004 school year, New York spent $12,930 per pupil in its public elementary-secondary school system, which was substantially above the national average $8,182.[18] Of this amount, 7.5% was provided by the federal government, 43.6% was provided by the state government, and 48.9% was provided by the local governments,[19] with property taxes making up 28.1% of the total funding.[20] Out of these funds, New York paid its elementary and secondary school teachers an estimated average annual salary of $56,200 during the 2004–2005 school year,[21] and it provided a student/teacher ratio of 13.3, which was better than the national average of 15.9.[22]

---

9. *Id.* at 96.

10. *Id.* at 495.

11. *Id.* at 497.

12. *Id.* at 496.

13. *Id.* at 498.

14. *Id.* at 499.

15. *See* Fact Sheet, American FactFinder, http://factfinder.census.gov/home/saff/main.html?_lang=en (select "New York" under "Get a Fact Sheet for your community") (last visited Feb. 16, 2007). Note that these numbers are based on the 2000 census because more recent numbers were not available.

16. *Id.* at 500.

17. *Id.* at 502.

18. Governments Division, U.S. Census Bureau, Public Education Finances 2004, at 8 tbl.8 (2006).

19. *See Id.* at 5 tbl.5.

20. *See Id.* at 4 tbl.4.

21. Thomas D. Snyder et al., National Center for Education Statistics, Digest of Education Statistics 2005, at 116 tbl.77 (2006).

22. *Id.* at 98 tbl.65.

23. National Center for Education Statistics, U.S. Department of Education, The Nation's Report Card: Mathematics 2005, at 14 fig.11 (2005), *available at* http://nces.ed.gov/nationsreportcard/pdf/main2005/ 2006453.pdf [hereinafter Mathematics 2005].

In academic performance, New York's fourth grade students scored higher than the national average in mathematics,[23] reading,[24] science,[25] and writing.[26] New York's eighth graders also scored higher than the national average in mathematics,[27] reading,[28] science,[29] and writing.[30]

Equity Issues

In 2004, revenues spent per student in New York's highest poverty districts were determined to be $2,319 less than the revenues spent in its lowest poverty districts.[31] When adjustments were made for the additional costs of educating students growing up in poverty, however, the funding gap grew to $2,927.[32] However, New York spent $2,239 more per student in its highest minority districts, and this amount increased to $2,636 when adjustments for low-income students were made.[33]

Fourth graders eligible for free or reduced-price school lunches had test scores that were 8.1% lower in mathematics,[34] 10.3% lower in reading,[35] and 12.8% lower in writing[36] than those of students who were not eligible. The results were generally the same for eighth graders eligible for free or reduced-price lunches; their test scores were 8.2% lower in mathematics,[37] 8.3% lower in reading,[38] and 18.8% lower in writing[39] than those of students who were not eligible.

New York has experienced much litigation related to the equity of school funding, notably in the case *Levittown v. Nyquist*, which held that the state constitution does not

---

24. NATIONAL CENTER FOR EDUCATION STATISTICS, U.S. DEPARTMENT OF EDUCATION, THE NATION'S REPORT CARD: READING 2005, at 14 fig.11 (2005), *available at* http://nces.ed.gov/ nationsreportcard/pdf/main2005/2006451.pdf [hereinafter READING 2005].

25. NATIONAL CENTER FOR EDUCATION STATISTICS, U.S. DEPARTMENT OF EDUCATION, THE NATION'S REPORT CARD: SCIENCE 2005, at 16 fig.12 (2006), *available at* http://nces.ed.gov/ nationsreportcard//pdf/main2005/2006466.pdf [hereinafter SCIENCE 2005].

26. HILARY R. PERSKY ET AL., NATIONAL CENTER FOR EDUCATION STATISTICS, U.S. DEPARTMENT OF EDUCATION, THE NATION'S REPORT CARD: WRITING 2002, at 23 tbl.2.2 (2003), *available at* http://nces.ed.gov/nationsreportcard/pdf/main2002/2003529.pdf [hereinafter WRITING 2002].

27. MATHEMATICS 2005, *supra* note 23, at 16 fig.12.

28. READING 2005, *supra* note 24, at 16 fig.12.

29. SCIENCE 2005, *supra* note 25, at 28 fig.22.

30. WRITING 2002, *supra* note 26, at 24 tbl.2.3.

31. THE EDUCATION TRUST, FUNDING GAPS 2006, at 7 tbl.3 (2006), *available at* http://www2 .edtrust.org/NR/rdonlyres/CDEF9403-5A75-437E-93FF-EBF1174181FB/0/FundingGap2006.pdf.

32. *Id.*

33. *Id.* at 7 tbl.4.

34. MATHEMATICS 2005, *supra* note 23, at 20 tbl.5.

35. READING 2005, *supra* note 24, at 20 tbl.5.

36. WRITING 2002, *supra* note 25, at 75 tbl.3.24.

37. MATHEMATICS 2005, *supra* note 23, at 21 tbl.6.

38. READING 2005, *supra* note 24, at 21 tbl.6.

39. WRITING 2002, *supra* note 25, at 76 tbl.3.25.

require equal funding for education.[40] This determination was successfully challenged by the *Campaign for Fiscal Equity v. State* series of cases which, after having been filed in the early 1990s, were ultimately decided in 2006.[41] The Court of Appeals of New York determined that the adequacy study prepared by the state legislature would be sufficient to provide the necessary funding to at-risk school districts that were in danger of not fulfilling their constitutionally mandated education requirement.[42]

Availability of Publicly Funded Prekindergarten Programs

New York's Targeted Pre-kindergarten Program currently serves four-year-old children who are considered at risk; it extends to three-year-olds in limited situations.[43] Total enrollment in this state-funded program is 72,590,[44] which represents just 14.6% of New York's three- and four-year-old children.[45] The federally funded Head Start program enrolls an additional 43,222 children,[46] which represents 8.0% of New York's three-year-old children and 10% of New York's four-year-old children.[47]

Where Does New York Get Its Revenue?

At the end of fiscal year 2004, New York had total revenues of approximately $224.4 billion.[48] Of this amount, 45.2% was derived from state and local tax revenues and 20.4% was received from the federal government.[49] The remaining 34.4% came from other sources, including the New York Lottery, insurance trust revenue, revenue from government-owned utilities, and other commercial or auxiliary enterprises.[50]

Tax Revenue

New York collected approximately $101.4 billion in state and local tax revenue during fiscal year 2004.[51] As a result, New York residents paid $5,260 per capita in state and

---

40. 439 N.E. 2d 359 (N.Y. 1982).

41. Campaign For Fiscal Equity v. State, 861 N.E.2d 50 (N.Y. 2006).

42. *Id.*

43. W. STEVEN BARNETT ET AL., NATIONAL INSTITUTE FOR EARLY EDUCATION RESEARCH, THE STATE OF PRESCHOOL 2006, at 113 (2007), *available at* http://nieer.org/yearbook/pdf/yearbook.pdf.

44. *Id.* at 114.

45. *See id.* at 222.

46. *Id.* at 114.

47. *See id.*

48. U.S. Census Bureau, State and Local Government Finances 2003–04, http://www.census .gov/govs/www/estimate04.html (last visited Oct. 6, 2006) [hereinafter Government Finances].

49. *Id.*

50. *Id.*

51. *Id.*

local taxes, an amount which ranked 1st nationally.[52] The different types of tax sources were approximately apportioned as follows:

Individual income taxes	30.3%
Property taxes	31.9%
General and selective sales taxes	27.0%
Corporate income and other taxes	10.8%
	100.0%[53]

Federal Funding

During fiscal year 2004, 20.4% of New York's total revenues came from the federal government.[54] For every dollar of federal taxes paid, New York received $0.79 in federal funding, an amount which ranked 42nd nationally[55] and was far below the national average of $1.17.[56]

Lottery Revenue

The New York Lottery has been in operation since 1966. Under New York's constitution, the Lottery's net proceeds, which must be at least 30% of total proceeds, are to be used in a program designed to fund public education.[57] During fiscal year 2006, the Lottery had total revenues of $6.8 billion and net proceeds of $2.2 billion.[58]

Legal Structures of Major Tax Sources

Income

New York employs a broad-based income tax[59] that uses adjusted gross income for federal income tax purposes as a starting point for determining the state's taxable income.[60] However, numerous adjustments may be available to various individuals in calculating this amount.[61] New York also allows the imposition of a local income tax in cities with a population in excess of 1 million residents, which applies only to New York

---

52. *Id.*

53. *Id.*

54. *Id.*

55. The Tax Foundation, Federal Spending Received Per Dollar of Taxes Paid by State 2004, http://www.taxfoundation.org/taxdata/show/266.html (last visited Sept. 17, 2006).

56. *See id.*

57. NY CLS § 1601.

58. "New York Lottery Annual Report," available at: http://www.nylottery.org/ny/nyStore/cgi-bin/ProdSubEV_Cat_333663_NavRoot_304.htm (last checked Dec. 18, 2006).

59. N.Y. TAX LAW § 601.

60. *Id.* § 612.

61. *Id.* §§ 614–616.

City.[62] During fiscal year 2004, New York collected individual income tax of $1,278 per capita, an amount which ranked 2nd nationally.[63]

In New York, a typical family of four (i.e., married taxpayers who file jointly and have two dependent children) are not required to pay any income tax until their combined income exceeds $36,300, an amount which is substantially above the national poverty line of $20,615.[64] New York's income tax structure contains five tax brackets that impose a minimum marginal rate of 4% and a maximum marginal rate of 6.85%.[65] When statutory exemptions and the standard deduction are taken into account, the maximum marginal rate applies to every dollar of income exceeding $37,000.[66]

Property

Overview

New York has a typical property tax system that taxes the value of real property exclusively through local governments.[67] During fiscal year 2004, New York collected approximately $32.3 billion dollars in property taxes at the local level.[68] As a result, New York residents paid $1,677 per capita in state and local property taxes, an amount which ranked 4th nationally.[69]

Defining the Real Property Tax Base

The classification of real property in New York depends on whether or not the property is located in a special assessing unit.[70] Real property located in a special assessing unit is divided into four classes: Class One – residential real property, condominiums of no more than three stories, mobile homes, and vacant land (subject to specific limitations); Class Two – other residential real property not classified as Class One property, except for hotels and motels; Class Three – utility real property; and Class Four –

---

62. *Id.* § 1301.

63. State Rankings 2006, *supra* note 1, at 321.

64. Jason A. Levitis & Nicholas Johnson, Center on Budget and Policy Priorities, The Impact of State Income Taxes on Low-Income Families in 2006, at 12 (2007). Note that New York taxpayers who are married and filing jointly are entitled to a standard deduction of $15,000 and dependent exemptions of $1,000 each. New York no longer offers taxpayers personal exemptions for the taxpayer and/or spouse. N.Y. Tax Law § 614.

65. N.Y. Tax Law § 601. New York's middle three tax rates are 5.25%, 5.5%, and 5.9%. *Id.*

66. This standard deduction and exemptions of $15,000 and $2,000, respectively, plus the threshold of taxable income for the highest tax bracket of $20,000, equals $37,000. *See supra* notes 64–65.

67. N.Y. Real Prop. Tax Law §§ 301 - 302 (personal property excluded by statute). *Id.* § 30.

68. Government Finances, *supra* note 48.

69. *See id.*

70. A special assessing unit is any assessing unit with a population of one million or more; it most notably includes New York City and Nassau County. N.Y. Real Prop. Tax Law § 1801. An assessing unit generally means a city, town, or county with the power to assess real property. *Id.* § 102.

all other real property not included in the aforementioned classes.[71] Real property not located in a special assessing unit is classified as homestead property or nonhomestead property.[72] All real property must be assessed at a "uniform percentage of value"[73] as of March 1 each year for cities and town and as of January 1 for villages.[74] Value is generally determined by the application of standard appraisal methods, including the cost method, the income method, the sales method, and the unit method.[75] In general, cities are required to reassess property values every year.[76]

Real Property Tax Rates

The tax rates imposed on real property vary and are set by each assessing unit.[77] Rates are restricted by the constitution of New York as follows: counties other than New York County, 1.5%; cities and villages, 2%; and New York County, 2.5%.[78]

Personal and Intangible Property

Tangible personal property is exempted by law from taxation in New York.[79] Intangible personal property is prohibited from taxation by the New York constitution.[80]

Exemptions

New York has a list of various exemptions based on use and ownership.[81] This list includes real property owned by charities, firefighters, and the disabled, as well as cemeteries, vineyards, and athletic fields.[82]

General and Selective Sales

General Sales

New York imposes a general retail sales-and-use tax, which makes up 19.1% of its total tax revenue.[83] This tax is imposed on the sale, distribution, renting, or furnishing of tangible personal property, as well as specified services.[84] These services include (1)

---

71. *Id.* § 1802.
72. *Id.* § 1903.
73. *Id.* § 305. Subject to special provisions for certain cities and counties.
74. *Id.* §§ 301–302.
75. CCH-EXP, PROP-TAX-GUIDE NY ¶ 20-615, Valuation Methods in General.
76. N.Y. REAL PROP. TAX LAW §§ 301–302.
77. CCH-EXP, PROP-TAX-GUIDE NY ¶ 20-010. Overview.
78. N.Y. CONST. art, VIII, § 10.
79. N.Y. REAL PROP. TAX LAW § 300.
80. NY CONST. art. XVI, § 3.
81. N.Y. REAL PROP. TAX LAW § 490.
82. *Id.*
83. Government Finances, *supra* note 48.
84. N.Y. TAX. LAW § 1105.

printing and packing materials; (2) installation of personal property; (3) tailoring and dry cleaning; and (4) car service transportation.[85] The state sales tax rate is 4%, and all localities may impose a local rate of up to 3% without permission of the state legislature, for a combined state and local rate of 7%.[86] However, localities may petition the state government to impose an additional sales tax, and 42 of New York's counties have been granted such an addition.[87] The highest composite rate is applied in New York County, which imposes an additional 4.125% on the state rate, for a total of 8.125%.[88] New York offers various exceptions to its sales tax, including unprepared food, drugs, newspapers and other periodicals, and services provided by morticians.[89]

Selective Sales

Selective sales taxes make up 7.9% of New York's total revenue.[90] Of that amount, 0.5%[91] comes from a motor fuel sales tax imposed at a rate of $0.08 per gallon of gasoline outside New York County and a rate of $0.0875 per gallon of gasoline within New York County.[92] New York residents paid an average of $27 per capita in state motor fuel sales taxes in 2004, an mount which ranked 50th nationally and was considerably below the national average of $115.[93]

In 2004, sales taxes on alcoholic beverages made up 0.2% of New York's total tax revenue.[94] New York residents paid $9.91 per capita in state alcoholic beverage sales taxes in 2004, an amount which ranked 34th nationally.[95]

The tobacco product sales tax makes up 1.1% of New York's tax revenues and is imposed at a rate of $1.50 per pack of cigarettes.[96] New York residents paid $52.36 per capita in state tobacco sales taxes in 2004, an amount which ranked 21st nationally.[97]

The remainder of New York's selective sales taxes makes up 6.1% of its total tax revenue. Of this amount, 1.4% represents taxes on utilities and the other 4.7% represents taxes on other specific commodities, businesses, or services not reported separately above (e.g., on contractors, lodging, lubricating oil, fuels other than motor fuel, motor vehicles, meals, soft drinks, margarine, etc.).[98]

---

85. *Id.*

86. N.Y. Tax Law § 1210.

87. *Id.*

88. *Id.*

89. *Id.* § 1115.

90. Government Finances, *supra* note 48.

91. *Id.*

92. N.Y. Tax Law § 284.

93. State Rankings 2006, *supra* note 1, at 327.

94. Government Finances, *supra* note 48.

95. State Rankings 2006, *supra* note 1, at 335.

96. N.Y. Tax Law § 471.

97. State Rankings 2006, *supra* note 1, at 335.

98. *See* Governments Division, U.S. Census Bureau, Government Finance and Employment Classification Manual, at ch.7 (2000), *available at* http://ftp2.census.gov/govs/class/classfull.pdf [hereinafter Classification Manual].

Corporate Income and Other

Corporate Income

The corporate income tax makes up 5.3% of New York's total tax revenue.[99] New York's broad-based corporate income tax is imposed at a flat rate of 7.5% on a corporation's taxable income,[100] which is based on the corporation's federal taxable income.[101]

New York follows the federal income tax treatment of S corporations. Thus, they do not pay New York's corporate income tax; rather, income and losses flow through to their shareholders.[102] A similar treatment is afforded to limited partnerships and limited liability partnerships, as well as limited liability companies, assuming they are treated as a partnership for federal tax purposes.[103] However, if a limited liability company is treated as a corporation for federal income tax purposes, the entity is subject to New York's corporate income tax.[104]

Other

During fiscal year, the collection of all other taxes not previously mentioned accounted for 5.5% of New York's total tax revenue. Of this amount, approximately $736 million was generated by the estate and gift tax,[105] which is calculated on the basis of the federal credit for state death taxes and provides a credit reducing the amount assessed on the basis of the federal tax paid.[106] The "other taxes" category is also made up of motor vehicle license taxes, documentary and stock transfer taxes, severance taxes, and all other taxes not listed separately or provided for in other categories, such as taxes on land based on a specified rate per acre (rather than on assessed value).[107]

Burden Analysis

The overall state and local tax burden on New York taxpayers is very regressive. Taxpayers in the lowest quintile—those with incomes of less than $15,000—bear a tax burden of 12.7% of their income, while taxpayers in the top 1%—those with incomes that exceed $634,000—bear a tax burden of just 9.1% of their income.[108] It is also

---

99. Government Finances, *supra* note 48.

100. N.Y. Tax Law § 210.

101. *Id.*

102. CCH-EXP, NY-TAXRPTR ¶ 10-240, Limited Liability Companies (LLCs).

103. *Id.*

104. *Id.*

105. Government Finances, *supra* note 48.

106. N.Y. Tax Law §§ 951–963.

107. *See* Classification Manual, *supra* note 98, at ch.7.

108. *See* Robert S. McIntyre et al., Who Pays? A Distributional Analysis of the Tax Systems in All 50 States 80 (2d ed. 2003), *available at* http://www.itepnet.org/wp2000/text.pdf. Taxpayers in the second quintile bear a 11.4% total tax burden on incomes between $15,000 and $27,000; those in the third quintile bear a 11.9% tax burden on incomes between $27,000 and

worth noting that, although New York obviously has no control over federal tax policy, federal itemized deductions for state and local personal income and property taxes
nonetheless further reduce the burden on taxpayers in the top 1% to 6.5%.[109] Furthermore, between 1989 and 2002, the tax burden on the bottom quintile declined by
approximately 0.1%, while the burden on the top 1% declined by 1.3%.[110]

In terms of the income tax, the burden across income groups in New York is moderately progressive, with taxpayers in the lowest quintile bearing a tax burden of 1.2%
and those in the top 1% bearing a tax burden of 6.3%.[111] In contrast, however, the sales
and excises taxes imposed by New York are extremely regressive, with taxpayers in the
lowest quintile bearing a tax burden of 9.5% and those in the top 1% bearing a tax
burden of just 1.2%.[112] Property taxes in New York are also regressive, with taxpayers
in the lowest quintile bearing a tax burden of 4.4% and those in the remaining quintiles bearing an average tax burden of 3.2%.[113]

$44,000; those in the fourth quintile bear a 11.9% tax burden on incomes between $44,000 and
$74,000; those in the 80th–95th percentiles bear a 12.0% tax burden on incomes between
$74,000 and $160,000; finally, those in the 96th–99th percentiles bear a 10.6% tax burden on
incomes between $160,000 and $634,000. *Id.*

109. *Id.* Taxpayers in the lowest and second lowest quintiles were able to reduce their individual tax burdens by 0.1%, those in the third quintile by 0.3%, those in the fourth quintile by 0.8%,
those in the 80th–95th percentiles by 1.8%, and those in the 96th–99th percentiles by 2.3%. *Id.*

110. *Id.* at 81.

111. *See id.* at 80. Taxpayers in the second quintile bear a 0.8% income tax burden; those in
the third quintile bear a 2.7% burden; those in the fourth quintile bear a 3.7% burden; those in
the 80th–95th percentiles bear a 4.6% burden; finally, those in the 96th–99th percentiles bear a
5.2% burden. *Id.* Note, however, that of the total income tax burden borne by taxpayers in the top
1%, 6.0% represents individual income taxes and 0.3% represents corporate income taxes. *Id.*

112. *See id.* Taxpayers in the second quintile bear a 7.5% sales-and-excise tax burden; those
in the third quintile bear a 5.7% burden; those in the fourth quintile bear a 4.5% burden; those
in the 80th–95th percentiles bear a 3.4% burden; finally, those in the 96th–99th percentiles bear
a 2.2% burden. *Id.*

113. *See id.* Taxpayers in the second quintile bear a 3.0% property tax burden; those in the
third quintile bear a 3.5% burden; those in the fourth quintile bear a 3.7% burden; those in the
80th–95th percentiles bear a 4.1% burden; those in the 96th–99th percentiles bear a 3.2% burden; finally. those in the top 1% bear a 1.6% burden. *Id.*

North Carolina

General Information

Basic Profile – Geography, Population, and Industry

North Carolina was admitted to the Union in 1789 and is known as the "Tar Heel State."[1] It is located in the South Atlantic region and is bordered by Virginia on the north; the Atlantic Ocean on the east; Tennessee on the west; and Georgia and South Carolina on the south. North Carolina is located in the eastern time zone, and its capital is Raleigh.

In 2005, the state ranked 11th in population (approximately 8.7 million residents);[2] it ranks 28th in total area (53,819 square miles).[3] North Carolina's population is approximately 74.1% white and 21.8% black.[4] The state is 10% Catholic; 69% Protestant (of which 55% are Baptist); and 1% Jewish; 20% claim a religion outside the Judeo-Christian tradition or no religion at all.[5] Roughly 69% of North Carolina's population lives in urban areas.[6] The two major industries in North Carolina are manufacturing and agriculture; in fact, the state leads the nation in the production of bricks, furniture, tobacco, and textiles.[7]

---

1. STATE RANKINGS 2006, vi, 1 (Kathleen O'Leary Morgan & Scott Morgan eds., Morgan Quitno Press 2006).

2. *Id.* at 429.

3. *Id.* at 225.

4. North Carolina Quick Facts from the U.S. Census Bureau, http://quickfacts.census.gov/qfd/states/54000.html (last visited Jan. 27, 2007). The remaining population is made up of 1.8% Asian persons; 1.3% American Indian and/or Alaska Native persons; 0.1% native Hawaiian persons and other Pacific Islanders; and 0.9% persons reporting two or more races. *Id.* Additionally, 6.4% of North Carolina's total population identify themselves as persons of Hispanic or Latino origin. *Id.* (noting that because Hispanics may be of any race, they are included within the other applicable race categories).

5. BARRY A. KOSMIN, EGON MAYER & ARIELA KEYSAR, AMERICAN RELIGIOUS IDENTIFICATION SURVEY 2001, at 40, *available at* http://www.gc.cuny.edu/faculty/research_studies/aris.pdf.

6. USDA Economic Research Service, North Carolina Fact Sheet, http://www.ers.usda.gov/StateFacts/NC.htm (last visited Sept. 17, 2006). According to the latest estimates, approximately 2.7 million people live in rural areas, and 6.0 million people live in urban areas. *Id.*

7. National Geographic, North Carolina, http://www3.nationalgeographic.com/places/states/state_northcarolina.html (last visited Dec. 1, 2006).

Family Income and Poverty Indicators

In 2004, North Carolina's per capita gross product was $39,389, which was just below the national average of $39,725.[8] During this same period, although the median household income in North Carolina was $39,000,[9] 14.8% of North Carolina's population was living in poverty, which was substantially above the national average of 12.4% and the tenth highest poverty rate in the country.[10] More specifically, poverty affected 21.5% of North Carolina's children,[11] 11.6% of its senior citizens,[12] and 12.1% of its families.[13] Of its female-headed households with children, 44% of them lived in poverty,[14] and 44.5% of the state's public elementary and secondary school students were eligible for free or reduced-price meals.[15] Of those living in poverty, approximately 39.6% were black, which represented 21.8% of North Carolina's black population and 4.7% of its total population.[16] In an attempt to combat this poverty, North Carolina spent approximately $7.6 billion on public welfare programs in 2002,[17] which made up 17.2% of its total government expenditures.[18]

North Carolina's Public Elementary-Secondary School System

Overall Spending and Performance

For the 2003–2004 school year, North Carolina spent $6,702 per pupil in its public elementary-secondary school system, which was substantially below the national average of $8,182.[19] Of this amount, 9.7% was provided by the federal government, 57.9% was provided by the state government, and 32.5% was provided by the local governments,[20] with property taxes making up a substantial part of the total fund-

---

8. State Rankings 2006, *supra* note 1, at 89.

9. *Id.* at 96.

10. *Id.* at 495.

11. *Id.* at 497.

12. *Id.* at 496.

13. *Id.* at 498.

14. *Id.* at 499.

15. *Id.* at 532.

16. *See* Fact Sheet, American FactFinder, http://factfinder.census.gov/home/saff/main.html?_lang=en (select "North Carolina" under "Get a Fact Sheet for your community") (last visited Feb. 25, 2007). Note that these numbers are based on the 2000 census because more recent numbers were not available.

17. *Id.* at 500.

18. *Id.* at 502.

19. Governments Division, U.S. Census Bureau, Public Education Finances 2004, at 8 tbl.8 (2006).

20. Although none of the total funding has been specifically designated as provided by property taxes, 28.3% of the total funding comes from "Parent Government Contributions," *see id.* at 4 tbl.4., which is defined as "tax receipts and other amounts appropriated by a parent gov-

ing.[21] Out of these funds, North Carolina paid its elementary and secondary school teachers an estimated average annual salary of $43,313 during the 2004–2005 school year,[22] and it provided a student/teacher ratio of 15.1, which was somewhat better than the national average of 15.9.[23]

In academic performance, North Carolina's fourth grade students scored equal to the national average in reading[24] and science[25] and higher than the national average in mathematics[26] and writing.[27] North Carolina's eighth graders scored higher than the national average in mathematics[28] and writing[29] but lower than the national average in reading[30] and science.[31]

Equity Issues

In 2004, revenues spent per student in North Carolina's highest poverty districts were determined to be $344 less than the revenues spent in its lowest poverty districts.[32] When adjustments were made for the additional costs of educating students growing up in poverty, however, the funding gap grew to $543.[33] Similarly, North Carolina spent $211 less per student in its highest minority districts, and this amount grew to $296 when adjustments for low-income students were made.[34]

---

ernment and transferred to its dependent school system." *Id.* at app. A-1. This amount, however, "[e]xcludes intergovernmental revenue, current charges, and miscellaneous general revenue." *Id.*

21. *See id.* at 4 tbl.4.

22. Thomas D. Snyder et al., National Center for Education Statistics, Digest of Education Statistics 2005, at 116 tbl.77 (2006).

23. *Id.* at 98 tbl.65.

24. National Center for Education Statistics, U.S. Department of Education, The Nation's Report Card: Reading 2005, at 14 fig.11 (2005), *available at* http://nces.ed.gov/nationsreportcard/pdf/main2005/2006451.pdf [hereinafter Reading 2005].

25. National Center for Education Statistics, U.S. Department of Education, The Nation's Report Card: Science 2005, at 16 fig.12 (2006), *available at* http://nces.ed.gov/nationsreportcard//pdf/main2005/2006466.pdf [hereinafter Science 2005].

26. National Center for Education Statistics, U.S. Department of Education, The Nation's Report Card: Mathematics 2005, at 14 fig.11 (2005), *available at* http://nces.ed.gov/nationsreportcard/pdf/main2005/ 2006453.pdf [hereinafter Mathematics 2005].

27. Hilary R. Persky et al., National Center for Education Statistics, U.S. Department of Education, The Nation's Report Card: Writing 2002, at 23 tbl.2.2 (2003), *available at* http://nces.ed.gov/nationsreportcard/pdf/main2002/2003529.pdf [hereinafter Writing 2002].

28. Mathematics 2005, *supra* note 26, at 16 fig.12.

29. Writing 2002, *supra* note 27, at 24 tbl.2.3.

30. Reading 2005, *supra* note 24, at 16 fig.12.

31. Science 2005, *supra* note 25, at 28 fig.22.

32. The Education Trust, Funding Gaps 2006, at 7 tbl.3 (2006), *available at* http://www2 .edtrust.org/NR/rdonlyres/CDEF9403-5A75-437E-93FF-EBF1174181FB/0/FundingGap2006.pdf.

33. *Id.*

34. *Id.* at 7 tbl.4.

Fourth graders eligible for free or reduced-price school lunches had test scores that were 9% lower in mathematics,[35] 12% lower in reading,[36] and 15% lower in writing[37] than those of students who were not eligible. The results were generally the same for eighth graders eligible for free or reduced-price lunches; their test scores were 9% lower in mathematics,[38] 9% lower in reading,[39] and 14% lower in writing[40] than those of students who were not eligible.

The funding of North Carolina's public elementary and secondary school system has been challenged numerous times on both equity and adequacy grounds. In *Leandro v. State*,[41] the Supreme Court of North Carolina concluded that although "the North Carolina Constitution requires that all children have the opportunity for a sound basic education, ... it does not require that equal educational opportunities be afforded students in all of the school districts of the state."[42] On the basis of this decision, in *Hoke County Board of Education v. State*, the Supreme Court of North Carolina agreed with a trial court's decision that the Hoke County School System was not providing the constitutionally required "opportunity for a sound basic education" and that action must be taken by the state to remedy the violation.[43] Consequently, other North Carolina school districts are currently under similar scrutiny.

Availability of Publicly Funded Prekindergarten Programs

North Carolina's "More at Four" prekindergarten program currently serves certain at-risk four-year-old children on the basis of family income and other enumerated risk factors, but it does not serve any three-year-old children.[44] Total enrollment in this state-funded program is 15,227,[45] which represents just 6% of North Carolina's 244,875 three- and four-year-old children.[46] The federally funded Head Start program enrolls an additional 17,175 children,[47] which represents 7% of North Carolina's three- and four-year-old children.[48] Although North Carolina has generally supported its "More at Four" program through general state revenues in the past, beginning in 2006–2007, the program will be funded using revenues generated by the newly established North

35. MATHEMATICS 2005, *supra* note 26, at 20 tbl.5.

36. READING 2005, *supra* note 24, at 20 tbl.5.

37. WRITING 2002, *supra* note 27, at 75 tbl.3.24.

38. MATHEMATICS 2005, *supra* note 26, at 21 tbl.6.

39. READING 2005, *supra* note 24, at 21 tbl.6.

40. WRITING 2002, *supra* note 27, at 76 tbl.3.25.

41. 488 S.E.2d 249 (1997).

42. *Id.* at 257.

43. 599 S.E.2d 365, 381-82 (2004).

44. W. STEVEN BARNETT ET AL., NATIONAL INSTITUTE FOR EARLY EDUCATION RESEARCH, THE STATE OF PRESCHOOL 2006, at 116 (2007), *available at* http://nieer.org/yearbook/pdf/yearbook.pdf.

45. *Id.* at 117.

46. *See id.* at 232.

47. *Id.* at 117.

48. *See id.* at 232.

Carolina Education Lottery, which is expected to increase total funding and allow for an additional 3,200 children.[49]

Where Does North Carolina Get Its Revenue?

At the end of fiscal year 2004, North Carolina had total revenues of approximately $63.5 billion.[50] Of this amount, 39% was derived from state and local tax revenues, while 19% was received from the federal government.[51] The remaining 42% came from other sources, including the North Carolina Educational Lottery, insurance trust revenue, revenue from government-owned utilities, and other commercial or auxiliary enterprises.[52]

Tax Revenue

North Carolina collected approximately $25 billion in state and local tax revenue during fiscal year 2004. As a result, North Carolina residents paid $2,929 per capita in state and local taxes, an amount which ranked 31st nationally. The different types of tax sources were approximately apportioned as follows:

Individual income taxes	30.0%
Property taxes	24.4%
General and selective sales taxes	35.8%
Corporate income and other taxes	9.8%
	100.0%[53]

Federal Funding

During fiscal year 2004, 19% of North Carolina's total revenues came from the federal government.[54] For every dollar of federal taxes paid, North Carolina received $1.10 in federal funding,[55] an amount which ranked 27th nationally and was just below the national average of $1.17.[56]

---

49. *Id.* at 116.

50. U.S. Census Bureau, State and Local Government Finances 2003–04, http://www.census.gov/govs/www/estimate04.html (last visited Dec. 1, 2006) [hereinafter Government Finances].

51. *Id.*

52. *Id.*

53. *Id.*

54. *See id.*

55. The Tax Foundation, Federal Spending Received Per Dollar of Taxes Paid by State 2004, http://www.taxfoundation.org/taxdata/show/266.html (last visited Sept. 17, 2006).

56. *See id.*

Lottery Revenue

The North Carolina Education Lottery was established in August 2005 and began operations in March 2006.[57] One hundred percent of the net proceeds of the North Carolina Education Lottery are used for education programs.[58] Current sales and profit information is not yet available.

Legal Structures of Major Tax Sources

Income

North Carolina employs a broad-based income tax that uses adjusted gross income for federal income tax purposes, with relatively few adjustments, as a starting point for determining the state's taxable income.[59] Cities, towns, townships, and counties are not permitted to levy taxes on income.[60] During fiscal year 2004,, North Carolina collected individual income tax of $849 per capita, an amount which ranked 14th nationally.

In North Carolina, a typical family of four (i.e., married taxpayers who file jointly and have two dependent children) are not required to pay any income tax until their combined income exceeds $19,400, an amount which is below the national poverty line of $20,615.[61] North Carolina's income tax structure contains four tax brackets that impose a minimum marginal rate of 6% and a maximum marginal rate of 8.25%.[62] When statutory exemptions and the standard deduction are taken into account, the maximum marginal rate applies to every dollar of income exceeding $130,200.[63]

---

57. North American Association of State and Provincial Lotteries (NASPL), http://www.naspl.org/Contacts/index.cfm?fuseaction=view&ID=18 (last visited Dec. 28, 2006).

58. North Carolina Education Lottery, Where the Money Goes, http://lottery.nc.gov/where_the_money_goes.aspx (last visited Dec. 28 2006). After assigning 5% of the net revenue to a reserve fund, 50% of the remaining net revenue is used to reduce class-size ratios and to fund prekindergarten programs for at-risk four year olds; 40% is used for school construction; and 10% is used to fund college scholarships for students who qualify for the federal Pell Grant. *Id.*

59. N.C. GEN. STAT. § 105-134.5.

60. N.C. GEN. STAT. § 105-247.

61. JASON A. LEVITIS, CENTER ON BUDGET AND POLICY PRIORITIES, THE IMPACT OF STATE INCOME TAXES ON LOW-INCOME FAMILIES IN 2006, AT 12 (2007). In 2006, North Carolina taxpayers who were married and filing jointly could claim a standard deduction of $6,000, personal exemptions for a total of $2,100, and dependent exemptions of $1,050 each. N.C. GEN. STAT. § 105-134.6. Note, however, that the threshold calculation of $19,400 is greater than the sum of these deductions and exemptions because it includes additional tax benefits available to low-income families, such as the earned-income tax credit. *See* LEVITIS, *supra.*

62. N.C. GEN. STAT. § 105-134.2. Note, however, that for tax years beginning on or after January 1, 2007, the maximum tax rate is reduced to 8%. *Id.* North Carolina's middle two brackets are 7% and 7.75%. *Id.*

63. The standard deduction and four exemptions of $6,000 and $4,200, respectively, plus the threshold of taxable income for the highest tax bracket of $120,000, equals $130,200. *See supra* notes 61–62.

Property

Overview

North Carolina has a typical property tax system that taxes the value of real estate and tangible personal property at the local level.[64] During fiscal year 2004, North Carolina collected approximately $6 billion in property taxes at the local level and none at the state level.[65] As a result, North Carolina residents paid $713 per capita in local property taxes, an amount which ranked 38th nationally.[66]

Defining the Real Property Tax Base

North Carolina has one classification for real property (unless otherwise explicitly exempted or excluded),[67] and both residential and commercial properties are assessed at 100% of the estimated fair market value as of January 1 each year.[68] Fair market value is generally determined by the application of standard appraisal methods, including the cost method, the income method, and the market-data method.[69] However, agricultural and horticultural land that meets certain acreage, income, and ownership requirements may qualify for present-use valuation rather than a valuation based on its highest and best use.[70] In general, counties are required to reassess property values every eight years; however, they are authorized to reassess more frequently if they so desire.[71]

Real Property Tax Rates

The tax rates imposed on real property vary and are set by each locality. In 2005, the tax rates per $1,000 of assessed value ranged from $2.50 (2.5 mills) in Dare County to $19.00 (19 mills) in Scotland County.[72] Each county or city may levy property taxes without restriction as to rate or amount for enumerated purposes.

Personal and Intangible Property

Tangible personal property is subject to local taxation unless specifically exempt,[73] and the tax rates imposed vary among jurisdictions. "Tangible personal property" is defined as all personal property that is not classified as intangible personal property

---

64. N.C. Gen. Stat. § 105-272.

65. Government Finances, *supra* note 50.

66. *See id.*

67. N.C. Gen. Stat. § 105-275.

68. *Id.* § 105-283.

69. CCH-EXP, PROP-TAX-GUIDE NC ¶ 20-615, Valuation Methods in General.

70. N.C. Gen. Stat. § 105-277.4.

71. *Id.* § 105-286.

72. Policy Analysis and Statistics Division, North Carolina Department of Revenue, Property Tax Rates and Latest Year of Revaluation for North Carolina Counties and Municipalities, *available at* http://www.dornc.com/publications/propertyrates.html.

73. N.C. Gen. Stat. § 105-275.

and that is not permanently affixed to real property.[74] Intangible personal property, with the exception of leasehold interests, is not subject to property tax.[75]

Exemptions

North Carolina allows a homestead exemption of $20,000 or 50% of the appraised value of the property (whichever is greater) for homeowners aged 65 and older whose household income is $18,500 or less.[76] Additionally, standing timber, pulpwood, seedlings, saplings, and other forest growth are completely excluded from the property tax, as are household goods, personal effects, and all other nonbusiness personal property.[77]

General and Selective Sales

General Sales

North Carolina imposes a general retail sales-and-use tax that makes up 23.5% of its total tax revenue.[78] This tax is imposed on the sale, lease, and rental of tangible personal property and on a limited number of services.[79] Services taxed include, among others, hotel and motel rentals, dry- cleaning and laundry services, sales of gas and electricity, and telecommunications services.[80] The state sales tax rate is 4.5% until July 1, 2007, at which time the rate will be lowered to 4%.[81] All North Carolina counties are authorized to impose a local sales tax of up to 2.5%,[82] except Mecklenburg County, which is allowed to tax at a rate of up to 3%.[83] Thus, the combined state and local sales-and-use tax rates for most North Carolinians equal 7%, but they can be as high as 7.5%. Exemptions from North Carolina's sales-and-use tax include, among other items, prescription drugs, medical equipment, school lunches, and textbooks, as well as non-prepared food that is not sold from a vending machine.[84] However, food and grocery items are subject to county food taxes at a rate of 2%.[85]

Selective Sales

Selective sales taxes make up 12.3% of North Carolina's total revenue.[86] Of that

---

74. *Id.* § 105-273.
75. *Id.* § 105-275.
76. *Id.* § 105-277.1
77. *Id.* § 105-275.
78. Government Finances, *supra* note 50.
79. N.C. Gen. Stat. § 105-164.4
80. *Id.*
81. *Id.*
82. *Id.* §§ 105-463 to -521
83. CCH-EXP, SALES-TAX-GUIDE NC ¶ 61-710, Local Power to Tax.
84. N.C. Gen. Stat. § 105-164.13.
85. CCH-EXP, SALES-TAX-GUIDE NC ¶ 60-390, Food and Grocery Items.
86. *See* U.S. Census Bureau, Preliminary Estimates of Weighted Average Poverty Thresholds for 2005, http://www.census.gov/hhes/www/poverty/threshld/05prelim.html.

amount, 5.1%[87] comes from a sales tax on the sale of certain motor and aviation fuels.[88] North Carolina residents paid an average of $149 per capita in state motor fuel sales taxes in 2004, an amount which ranked 12th nationally and was well above the national average of $115.[89]

In 2004, sales taxes on alcoholic beverages made up 1.0% of North Carolina's total tax revenue.[90] North Carolina residents paid $24.85 per capita in state alcoholic beverage sales taxes in 2004, an amount which ranked 11th nationally.[91]

The tobacco product sales tax makes up 0.2% of North Carolina's tax revenues and is imposed at a rate of $0.35 per pack of cigarettes.[92]

The remainder of North Carolina's selective sales taxes makes up 6.1% of its total tax revenue. Of this amount, 1.3% represents taxes on utilities and the other 4.8% represents taxes on other specific commodities, businesses, or services not reported separately above (e.g., on contractors, lodging, lubricating oil, fuels other than motor fuel, motor vehicles, meals, soft drinks, margarine, etc.).[93]

Corporate Income and Other

Corporate Income

The corporate income tax makes up 3.3% of North Carolina's total tax revenue.[94] North Carolina's broad-based corporate income tax uses federal taxable income as its starting point[95] and taxes at a flat rate of 6.9% on all C corporations doing business in the state.[96] However, neither S corporations[97] nor other pass-through entities[98] are subject to the North Carolina corporate income tax.

Other

During fiscal year 2004, the collection of all other taxes not previously mentioned accounted for 6.5% of North Carolina's total tax revenue. Of this amount, $145 million was generated by the estate and gift tax, which is calculated on the basis of the maximum credit for state death taxes allowed on the federal estate tax return without

---

87. *Id.*

88. CCH-EXP, SALES-TAX-GUIDE NC ¶ 60-560, Motor Fuels.

89. STATE RANKINGS 2006, *supra* note 1, at 327.

90. Government Finances, *supra* note 50.

91. STATE RANKINGS 2006, *supra* note 1, at 335.

92. NORTH CAROLINA DEPARTMENT OF REVENUE, NORTH CAROLINA 2005 TAX LAW CHANGES, at 4, *at* http://www.dornc.com/practitioner/LawChanges2005.pdf.

93. *See* GOVERNMENTS DIVISION, U.S. CENSUS BUREAU, GOVERNMENT FINANCE AND EMPLOYMENT CLASSIFICATION MANUAL, at ch.7 (2000), *available at* http://ftp2.census.gov/govs/class/classfull.pdf [hereinafter CLASSIFICATION MANUAL].

94. Government Finances, *supra* note 50.

95. *See* N.C. GEN. STAT. § 105-130.5.

96. *Id.* § 105-130.3.

97. *Id.*

98. *Id.* § 59-84.1

regard to the recent termination of that credit for federal estate tax purposes.[99] The "other taxes" category is further made up of various license taxes, documentary or stock transfer taxes, severance taxes, and all other taxes not listed separately or provided for in other categories.[100]

Burden Analysis

The overall state and local tax burden on North Carolina's taxpayers is very regressive. Taxpayers in the lowest quintile—those with incomes of less than $15,000—bear a tax burden of 10.7% of their income, while taxpayers in the top 1%—those with incomes that exceed $333,000—bear a tax burden of 8.9% of their income.[101] It is also worth noting that, although North Carolina obviously has no control over federal tax policy, federal itemized deductions for state and local personal income and property taxes nonetheless further reduce the burden on taxpayers in the top 1% to 6.1%.[102] Furthermore, between 1989 and 2002, the tax burden on the bottom quintile rose by approximately 0.3%, while the burden on the top 1% fell by 1.5%.[103]

In terms of the income tax, the burden across income groups in North Carolina is slightly progressive, with taxpayers in the lowest quintile bearing a tax burden of 1.3% and those in the top 1% bearing a tax burden of 6.6%.[104] In contrast, however, the sales and excises taxes imposed by North Carolina are very regressive, with taxpayers in the

---

99. N.C. GEN. STAT. § 105-32.2.

100. *See* CLASSIFICATION MANUAL, *supra* note 93, at ch. 7.

101. *See* ROBERT S. MCINTYRE ET AL., WHO PAYS? A DISTRIBUTIONAL ANALYSIS OF THE TAX SYSTEMS IN ALL 50 STATES 82 (2d ed. 2003), *available at* http://www.itepnet.org/wp2000/text.pdf. Taxpayers in the second quintile bear a 10.1% total tax burden on incomes between $15,000 and $25,000; those in the third quintile bear a 10.2% tax burden on incomes between $25,000 and $39,000; those in the fourth quintile bear a 9.9% tax burden on incomes between $39,000 and $64,000; those in the 80th–95th percentiles bear a 9.7% tax burden on incomes between $64,000 and $124,000; finally, those in the 96th–99th percentiles bear a 9.1% tax burden on incomes between $124,000 and $333,000. *Id.*

102. *Id.* Taxpayers in the lowest and second lowest quintiles did not receive any benefit from these federal offsets, while those in the third quintile were able to reduce their individual tax burdens by 0.2%, those in the fourth quintile by 0.6%, those in the 80th–95th percentiles by 1.4%, and those in the 96th–99th percentiles by 2.0%. *Id.*

103. *Id.* at 83.

104. *See id.* at 82. Taxpayers in the second quintile bear a 2.5% income tax burden; those in the third quintile bear a 3.4% burden; those in the fourth quintile bear a 4.1% burden; those in the 80th–95th percentiles bear a 4.8% burden; finally, those in the 96th–99th percentiles bear a 5.5% burden. *Id.* Note, however, that these percentages include both individual and corporate income tax burdens; that within the third quintile, corporate income taxes represent 0.1% of this burden; that within the fourth quintile, corporate income taxes represent 0.1% of this burden; that within the 80th–95th percentiles, corporate income taxes represent 0.1% of this burden; that within the 96th–99th percentiles, corporate income taxes represent 0.1% of this burden; and that in the top 1%, corporate income taxes represent 0.3% of this burden. *Id.*

lowest quintile bearing a tax burden of 6.5% and those in the top 1% bearing a tax burden of just 1.1%.[105] Property taxes in North Carolina are also regressive, with taxpayers in the lowest quintile bearing a tax burden of 2.9% and those in the top quintile bearing an average tax burden of 1.6%.[106]

---

105. *See id.* Taxpayers in the second quintile bear a 5.9% sales-and-excise tax burden; those in the third quintile bear a 4.9% burden; those in the fourth quintile bear a 4.0% burden; those in the 80th–95th percentiles bear a 3.0% burden; finally, those in the 96th–99th percentiles bear a 1.9% burden. *Id.*

106. *See id.* Taxpayers in the second quintile bear a 1.6% property tax burden; those in the third quintile bear a 1.9% burden; those in the fourth quintile bear a 1.8% burden; those in the 80th–95th percentiles bear a 1.9% burden; those in the 96th–99th percentiles bear a 1.7% burden; finally, those in the top 1% bear a 1.1% burden. *Id.*

North Dakota

General Information

Basic Profile – Geography, Population, and Industry

Admitted to the Union in 1889, North Dakota is known as the "Peace Garden State."[1] It is located in the northern Great Plains and is considered part of the Midwest. North Dakota is bordered by Canada on the north, Minnesota on the east, South Dakota on the south, and Montana on the west.[2] Most of the state is located in the central time zone, but the southwest portion is located in the mountain time zone.[3] The state capital is Bismarck.[4]

In 2005, North Dakota ranked 48th in population (636,677 residents);[5] it ranks 19th in total area (70,700 square miles).[6] Its population is 92.3% white, 5.3% Native American and Alaska Native persons, and 0.8% black.[7] The state is 30% Catholic; 57% Protestant (of which 61.4% are Lutherans); and less than 0.5% Jewish; 13% claim a religion outside the Judeo-Christian tradition or no religion at all.[8] The population is fairly split, with 46.5% living in cities and towns and 53.5% living in rural areas.[9] Major industries include agriculture, manufacturing, and mining.[10]

---

1. STATE RANKINGS 2006, 1, vi (Kathleen O'Leary Morgan & Scott Morgan, eds., Morgan Quitno Press, 2006).

2. *Id.*

3. Map Maker - Nationalatlas.gov, http://www.nationalatlas.gov/natlas/Natlasstart.asp (last visited January 28, 2007).

4. STATE RANKINGS 2006, *supra* note 1.

5. *Id.* at 429.

6. *Id.* at 225.

7. North Dakota Quick Facts from U.S. Census Bureau, http://quickfacts.census.gov/qfd /states/38000.html (last visited January 28, 2007). The remaining population is made up of 0.7% Asian persons and 0.9% persons reporting two or more races. *Id.* Persons of Hispanic or Latino origin make up 1.6% of the population. *Id.* (noting that because Hispanics may be of any race, they are included within the other applicable race categories).

8. BARRY A. KOSMIN, EGON MAYER & ARIELA KEYSAR, AMERICAN RELIGIOUS IDENTIFICATION SURVEY 2001, at 39, *available at* http://www.gc.cuny.edu/faculty/research_studies/aris.pdf.

9. USDA Economic Research Service, North Dakota Fact Sheet, http://www.ers.usda.gov/ StateFacts/ND.htm (last visited Sept. 17, 2006).

10. North Dakota State Data Center, 14 Economic Briefs 7, *North Dakota Gross State Product (GSP) by Industry* 2, July 2005, *available at* http://www.ndsu.edu/sdc/publications/ ebriefs/EB14_7Press.pdf.

Family Income and Poverty Indicators

In 2004, North Dakota's per capita gross product was $35,654, which was below the national average of $39,725.[11] During this same period, although the median household income in North Dakota was $39,594,[12] 10.3% of the state's population was living in poverty, which was somewhat below the national poverty rate of 12.4%.[13] More specifically, poverty affected 14.8% of North Dakota's children,[14] 10.9% of its senior citizens,[15] and 8.0% of its families.[16] Of its female-headed households with children, 43.5% lived in poverty,[17] and 28.3% of the state's public elementary and secondary school students were eligible for free or reduced-price meals.[18] Of those living in poverty, approximately 0.9% were black, which represented 17.5% of North Dakota's black population and 0.1% of its total population.[19] In an attempt to combat this poverty, North Dakota spent approximately $663.8 million on public welfare programs in 2002,[20] which made up 17.1% of its total government expenditures.[21]

North Dakota's Public Elementary-Secondary School System

Overall Spending and Performance

For the 2003–2004 school year, North Dakota spent $7,727 per pupil in its public elementary-secondary school system, which was slightly below the national average of $8,182.[22] Of this amount, 15.2% was provided by the federal government, 38.1% was provided by the state government, and 46.7% was provided by the local governments,[23] with property taxes making up 37.4% of the total funding.[24] Out of these funds, North Dakota paid its elementary and secondary school teachers an estimated average annual

---

11. STATE RANKINGS 2006, *supra* note 1, at 89.

12. *Id.* at 96.

13. *Id.* at 495.

14. *Id.* at 497.

15. *Id.* at 496.

16. *Id.* at 498.

17. *Id.* at 499.

18. *Id.* at 532.

19. *See* Fact Sheet, American FactFinder, http://factfinder.census.gov/home/saff/main.html?_lang=en (select "North Dakota" under "Get a Fact Sheet for your community") (last visited Feb. 16, 2007). Note that these numbers are based on the 2000 census because more recent numbers where not available.

20. *Id.* at 500.

21. *Id.* at 502.

22. GOVERNMENTS DIVISION, U.S. CENSUS BUREAU, PUBLIC EDUCATION FINANCES 2004, at 8 tbl.8 (2006).

23. *See id.* at 5 tbl.5.

24. *See id.* at 4 tbl.4.

salary of $36,449 during the 2004–2005 school year,[25] and it provided a student/teacher ratio of 12.7, which was better than the national average of 15.9.[26]

In academic performance, North Dakota's fourth grade students scored lower than the national average in writing[27] and higher than the national average in mathematics,[28] reading,[29] and science,[30] while North Dakota's eighth graders scored lower than the national average in writing[31] and higher than the national average in mathematics,[32] reading,[33] and science.[34]

Equity Issues

In 2004, the funding per student in North Dakota's highest poverty districts exceeded that in its lowest poverty districts by $271,[35] although, when adjustments were made for the additional costs of educating students growing up in poverty, that excess narrowed to $17.[36] On the other hand, North Dakota spent $1,259 less per student in its highest minority districts, and this amount grew to $1,290 when adjustments for low-income students were made.[37]

Fourth graders eligible for free or reduced-price school lunches had test scores that were 5.2% lower in mathematics,[38] 7.0% lower in reading,[39] and 7.8% lower in writing[40] than those of students who were not eligible. The results were generally worse for

---

25. Thomas D. Snyder et al., National Center for Education Statistics, Digest of Education Statistics 2005, at 116 tbl.77 (2006).

26. *Id.* at 98 tbl.65.

27. Hilary R. Persky et al., National Center for Education Statistics, U.S. Department of Education, The Nation's Report Card: Writing 2002, at 23 tbl.2.2 (2003), *available at* http://nces.ed.gov/nationsreportcard/pdf/main2002/2003529.pdf [hereinafter Writing 2002].

28. National Center for Education Statistics, U.S. Department of Education, The Nation's Report Card: Mathematics 2005, at 14 fig.11 (2005), *available at* http://nces.ed .gov/nationsreportcard/pdf/main2005/ 2006453.pdf [hereinafter Mathematics 2005].

29. National Center for Education Statistics, U.S. Department of Education, The Nation's Report Card: Reading 2005, at 14 fig.11 (2005), *available at* http://nces.ed.gov/ nationsreportcard/pdf/main2005/2006451.pdf [hereinafter Reading 2005].

30. National Center for Education Statistics, U.S. Department of Education, The Nation's Report Card: Science 2005, at 16 fig.12 (2006), *available at* http://nces.ed.gov/ nationsreportcard//pdf/main2005/2006466.pdf [hereinafter Science 2005].

31. Writing 2002, *supra* note 27, at 24 tbl.2.3.

32. Mathematics 2005, *supra* note 28, at 16 fig.12.

33. Reading 2005, *supra* note 29, at 16 fig.12.

34. Science 2005, *supra* note 30, at 28 fig.22.

35. The Education Trust, Funding Gaps 2006, at 7 tbl.3 (2006), *available at* http://www2 .edtrust.org/NR/rdonlyres/CDEF9403-5A75-437E-93FF-EBF1174181FB/0/FundingGap2006.pdf.

36. *Id.*

37. *Id.* at 7 tbl.4.

38. Mathematics 2005, *supra* note 28, at 20 tbl.5.

39. Reading 2005, *supra* note 29, at 20 tbl.5.

40. Writing 2002, *supra* note 27, at 75 tbl.3.24.

eighth graders eligible for free or reduced-price lunches; their test scores were 6.2% lower in mathematics,[41] 5.1% lower in reading,[42] and 11.3% lower in writing[43] than those of students who were not eligible.

In the case *Bismarck Pub. Sch. Dist. No. 1 v. State*,[44] the North Dakota Supreme Court held that education is a fundamental right under the state constitution,[45] and a majority of three judges held that the state's education finance system was unconstitutional on equal protection grounds.[46] Unfortunately, because a supermajority of four judges is required in North Dakota to declare a statute unconstitutional, the state's funding scheme could not be overturned.[47] The pending case *Williston Pub. Sch. Dist. No. 1 v. State*, which challenges the state's educational funding system on the basis of inadequate and disparate funding, was stayed after a newly proposed plan by the governor that addresses the plaintiffs' claims.[48]

Availability of Publicly Funded Prekindergarten Programs

North Dakota does not have any type of preschool program, but the federally funded Head Start program enrolls 2,822 children,[49] which represents 20.3% of North Dakota's 13,912 three- and four-year-old children.[50]

Where Does North Dakota Get Its Revenue?

At the end of fiscal year 2004, North Dakota had total revenues of approximately $6.5 billion.[51] Of this amount, 29% was derived from state and local tax revenues and 20% was received from the federal government.[52] The remaining 51% came from other sources, including insurance trust revenue and revenue from government-owned utilities and other commercial or auxiliary enterprises.[53]

---

41. MATHEMATICS 2005, *supra* note 28, at 21 tbl.6.

42. READING 2005, *supra* note 29, at 21 tbl.6.

43. WRITING 2002, *supra* note 27, at 76 tbl.3.25.

44. 511 N.W. 2d 247 (N.D. 1994).

45. *Id.* at 256.

46. *Id.* at 262–63.

47. North Dakota, STARTINGAT3.ORG, http://www.startingat3.org/state_laws/statelawsNDdetail.html#toc47.

48. *Id.*

49. W. STEVEN BARNETT ET AL., NATIONAL INSTITUTE FOR EARLY EDUCATION RESEARCH, THE STATE OF PRESCHOOL 2006, at 137–38 (2007), *available at* http://nieer.org/yearbook/pdf/yearbook.pdf.

50. *See id.* at 232.

51. U.S. Census Bureau, State and Local Government Finances - 2003–04, http://www.census.gov/govs/www/estimate04.html (last visited Oct. 10, 2006) [hereinafter Government Finances].

52. *Id.*

53. *Id.*

Tax Revenue

North Dakota collected approximately $1.9 billion in state and local tax revenue during fiscal year 2004.[54] As a result, North Dakota residents paid $2,989 per capita in state and local taxes, an amount which ranked 30th nationally.[55] The different types of tax sources were apportioned as follows:

Individual income taxes	11.3%
Property taxes	30.8%
General and selective sales taxes	39.0%
Corporate income and other taxes	18.9%
	100.0%[56]

Federal Funding

During fiscal year 2004, 20% of North Dakota's total revenues came from the federal government.[57] For every dollar of federal taxes paid, North Dakota received $1.73 in federal funding, an amount which ranked 5th nationally[58] and was well above the national average of $1.17.[59]

Lottery

North Dakota does not have a state lottery.

Legal Structures of Major Tax Sources

Income

North Dakota employs a broad-based income tax that uses adjusted gross income for federal income tax purposes as a starting point for determining the state's taxable income.[60] However, a fairly large number of adjustments may be available to various individuals in calculating this amount.[61] Localities are not provided the power to tax according to either the North Dakota constitution or any state statute.[62] During fiscal

---

54. *Id.*

55. *Id.*

56. *Id.*

57. *Id.*

58. *See* The Tax Foundation, Federal Spending Received Per Dollar of Taxes Paid by State, 2004, http://www.taxfoundation.org/taxdata/show/266.html (last visited Oct. 10, 2006).

59. *See id.*

60. N.D. Cent. Code § 57-38-01(12).

61. *Id.* § 57-38-01.2.

62. CCH-EXP, ND-TAXRPTR ¶ 15-012, Local Power to Tax.

year 2004, North Dakota collected individual income tax of $336 per capita, an amount which ranked 40th nationally.[63]

In North Dakota, a typical family of four (i.e., married taxpayers who file jointly and have two dependent children) are not required to pay any income tax until their combined income exceeds $24,000, an amount which is above the national poverty line of $20,615.[64] North Dakota's income tax structure contains five tax brackets that impose a minimum marginal rate of 2.1% and a maximum marginal rate of 5.54%.[65] When statutory exemptions and the standard deduction are taken into account, the maximum marginal rate applies to every dollar of income exceeding $360,050.[66] It is also noteworthy that North Dakota is one of the very few states that provide for a federal-taxes-owed deduction.[67]

Property

Overview

North Dakota has a typical property tax system that taxes the value of real property at the local level.[68] During fiscal year 2004, North Dakota collected approximately $583 million in property tax at the local level and approximately $1.5 million at the state

---

63. STATE RANKINGS 2006, *supra* note 1, at 321.

64. JASON A. LEVITIS & NICHOLAS JOHNSON, CENTER ON BUDGET AND POLICY PRIORITIES, THE IMPACT OF STATE INCOME TAXES ON LOW-INCOME FAMILIES IN 2006, at 12 (2007). North Dakota does not provide for a standard deduction or personal exemptions because adjusted gross income for federal income tax purposes is the starting point for determining the state's taxable income; therefore the federal standard deduction and personal exemptions are adopted. The federal standard deduction amount is adjusted yearly for inflation. Taxable Income Defined, 26 U.S.C.A. § 63. The 2006 federal standard deduction for married couples filing jointly was $10,300. Internal Revenue Service, Publication 17 (2006), 20. Standard Deduction, http://www.irs .gov/publications/p17/ch20.html#d0e47713 (last visited January 28, 2007). The 2006 federal personal exemption amount was $3,300 each for taxpayer, spouse, and two dependents. Internal Revenue Service, Publication 17 (2006), 3. Personal Exemptions and Dependents, http:// www.irs.gov/publications/p17/ch03.html#d0e10368 (last visited January 28, 2007). Note, however, that the threshold calculation of $24,000 is greater than the sum of these deductions and exemptions because it includes additional tax benefits available to low-income families, such as the earned-income tax credit. *See* LEVITIS, *supra*.

65. N.D. CENT. CODE § 57-38-30.3. The rate schedules are adjusted yearly for inflation. For the 2006 rate schedules, see North Dakota Office of State Tax Commissioner, Form 400-ES Estimated income tax-individuals, *available at* http://www.nd.gov/tax/indincome/forms/2005/400-es.pdf. North Dakota's middle three tax brackets are 3.92%, 4.34%, and 5.04%. *Id.*

66. The standard deduction and exemptions of $10,300 and $13,200 (for four exemptions), respectively, plus the threshold of taxable income for the highest tax bracket of $336,550, equals $360,050. *See supra* notes 64–65.

67. N.D. CENT. CODE § 57-38-01.2(1)(c).

68. *Id.* § 57-02-03. All personal property is exempt from taxation, except for centrally assessed personal property, property subjected to tax which is imposed in lieu of ad valorem taxes, and any kind of personal property that is subject to another type of tax imposed by law. *Id.* § 57-02-08(25).

level.[69] As a result, North Dakota residents paid $919 per capita in state and local property taxes, an amount which ranked 31st nationally.[70]

Defining the Real Property Tax Base

North Dakota has five categories of taxable property: (1) residential property, which is assessed at 9% of its true and full value; (2) agricultural property, which is assessed at 10% of its true and full value; (3) commercial property, which is assessed at 10% of its true and full value; and (4) centrally assessed property (except for wind turbine electric generators), which is assessed at 10% of its true and full value.[71] The true and full value of the property is generally determined by the application of standard appraisal methods, including the cost method, the income method, and the sales method, all of which are commonly used throughout the country.[72] The true and full value of agricultural property is determined by its capitalized average annual gross return, which takes into account the productivity of the property for the previous ten years.[73] North Dakota does not have specific provisions regarding reappraisals.

Real Property Tax Rates

The tax rates imposed on real property vary and are set by each locality. In 2005, the tax rates per $1,000 of assessed value ranged from $61.81 in McKenzie County to $180.75 in Eddy County.[74] Counties are limited to a 23-mill[75] levy for general and special county purposes;[76] however, this limitation does not apply to certain special levies including, among others, a maximum 10-mill levy for regional or county correction centers, a maximum 5-mill levy for emergency medical services, and a maximum 20-mill levy for human services.[77] Cities are limited to a 38-mill levy, unless their population is over 5,000, in which case they may levy a tax of an additional 0.5 mills for each 1,000 in population over 5,000, with a maximum levy of 40 mills.[78] Townships may not levy a tax over 18 mills.[79] Generally, school districts may not increase the aggregate amount levied each year by more than 18%, up to a maximum levy of 185 mills.[80] Park

---

69. Government Finances, *supra* note 51.

70. *Id.*

71. N.D. CENT. CODE § 57-02-27. Wind turbine generators are valued at a different percentage of assessed value. *Id.* § 57-02-27.3.

72. CCH-EXP, PROP-TAX-GUIDE ND ¶ 20-615, Valuation Methods in General.

73. N.D. CENT. CODE § 57-02-27.2.

74. North Dakota Office of State Tax Commissioner, *2005 Property Tax Statistical Report,* available at http://www.nd.gov/tax/property/pubs/stat-rep-05.pdf.

75. 1 mill = $1 per $1,000 of assessed value.

76. N.D. CENT. CODE § 57-15-06.

77. *Id.* § 57-15-06.7. Another interesting levy in this section is a maximum 0.5-mill levy for gopher, rabbit, and crow destruction. *Id.*

78. *Id.* § 57-15-08. Cities may increase the maximum mill levy by up to 10 mills by majority vote. *Id.*

79. *Id.* § 57-15-20.

80. *Id.* § 57-15-14.

districts may levy a tax up to 35 mills.[81] Localities may exceed the maximum rates if their governing bodies vote to do so.[82]

Personal and Intangible Property

Personal property is exempt from the property tax.[83]

Exemptions

There is no general homestead exemption, but the homesteads of disabled veterans and permanently and totally disabled people confined to a wheelchair, as well as up to $5,000 of the value of the homesteads of blind persons, are exempt.[84]

General and Selective Sales

General Sales

North Dakota imposes a general retail sales-and-use tax, which makes up 22.7% of its total tax revenue.[85] The tax is imposed on the sale, lease, or rental of tangible personal property and certain services.[86] These services include the furnishing of communication services; the furnishing of steam, gas or coal; tickets or admissions to places of entertainment or athletic events; the provision of magazines or other periodicals; and hotel or motel rentals.[87] The state sales tax rate is 5%,[88] and certain cities and counties can impose an additional sales tax.[89] Local rates of North Dakota cities range from 1% in most cities to 2.5% in Medora.[90] Cities may also impose a lodging tax of up to 2%; in addition, they may impose a separate lodging and restaurant tax of up to 1%.[91] Exemptions from North Dakota's sales-and-use tax include, among other items, prescription drugs,[92] food, and food ingredients.[93]

---

81. *Id.* § 57-15-12.

82. *Id.* § 57-17-01.

83. *Id.* § 57-02-08(25); *see also supra* note 68.

84. *Id.* § 57-02-08(20)-(22). For a comprehensive list of exceptions, see *Id.* § 57-02-08.

85. Government Finances, *supra* note 51.

86. N.D. Cent. Code § 57-39.2-02.1.

87. *Id.*

88. *Id.*

89. *Id.* § 11-09.1-05 (home-rule counties); *Id.* § 40-05.1-06 (home-rule cities); *Id.* § 57-01-02.1.

90. CCH-EXP, SALES-TAX-GUIDE ND ¶ 61-735, Local Rates.

91. N.D. Cent. Code § 40-57.3-01; *Id.* § 40-57.3-01.1.

92. *Id.* § 57-39.2-04(7).

93. *Id.* § 57-38.2-04.1. Food does not include alcoholic beverages, candy/gum, soft drinks, prepared food, or tobacco. *Id.*

Selective Sales

Selective sales taxes make up 16.4% of North Dakota's total tax revenue.[94] Of that amount, 6.2%[95] comes from a motor fuel sales tax imposed at a rate of $0.23 per gallon of gasoline.[96] North Dakota residents paid an average of $187 per capita in state motor fuel sales taxes in 2004, an amount which ranked 2nd nationally and was well above the national average of $115.[97]

The tobacco product sales tax makes up 1.1%[98] of North Dakota's tax revenues and is imposed at a rate of $0.40 per pack of cigarettes.[99] North Dakota residents paid an average of $33.27 in state tobacco sales taxes in 2004, an amount which ranked 32nd nationally.[100]

In 2004, sales taxes on alcoholic beverages made up 0.3% of North Dakota's total tax revenue.[101] North Dakota residents paid $9.29 per capita in state alcoholic beverage sales taxes in 2004, an amount which ranked 38th nationally.[102]

The remainder of North Dakota's selective sales taxes makes up 8.8% of its total tax revenue.[103] Of this amount, 2.2% represents taxes on utilities and the other 6.6% represents taxes on other specific commodities, businesses, or services not reported separately above(e.g., on contractors, lodging, lubricating oil, fuels other than motor fuel, motor vehicles, meals, soft drinks, margarine, etc.).[104]

Corporate Income and Other

Corporate Income

The corporate income tax makes up 2.6% of North Dakota's total tax revenue.[105] North Dakota's broad-based corporate income tax is imposed on a corporation's North Dakota taxable income, which is based on the corporation's federal taxable income.[106] North Dakota's corporate income tax structure contains five tax brackets that impose a minimum marginal rate of 2.6% and a maximum marginal rate of 6.5%. The maximum marginal rate applies to taxable income over $30,000.[107]

---

94. Government Finances, *supra* note 51.

95. *Id.*

96. N.D. Cent. Code § 57-43.1-02.

97. State Rankings 2006, *supra* note 1, at 327.

98. Government Finances, *supra* note 51.

99. State Rankings 2006, *supra* note 1, at 333.

100. *Id.* at 332.

101. Government Finances, *supra* note 51.

102. State Rankings 2006, *supra* note 1, at 335.

103. Government Finances, *supra* note 51.

104. *See* Governments Division, U.S. Census Bureau, Government Finance and Employment Classification Manual, at ch.7 (2000), *available at* http://ftp2.census.gov/govs/class/classfull.pdf [hereinafter Classification Manual].

105. *Id.*

106. N.D. Cent. Code § 57-38-01.1 (year).

107. *Id.* § 57-38-30. The North Dakota corporate income tax rate structure is as follows: 2.6%

North Dakota follows the federal income tax treatment of S corporations. Thus, they do not pay North Dakota's corporate income tax; rather, income and losses flow through to their shareholders.[108] A similar treatment is afforded to limited partnerships and limited liability partnerships, as well as limited liability companies, assuming they are treated as a partnership for federal tax purposes.[109] However, if a limited liability company is treated as a corporation for federal income tax purposes, the entity is subject to North Dakota's corporate income tax.[110]

Other

During fiscal year 2004, the collection of all other taxes not previously mentioned accounted for 16.3% of North Dakota's total tax revenue.[111] Of this amount, approximately $2.9 million was generated by the estate and gift tax. This tax is calculated on the basis of the maximum tax credit allowable for state death taxes against the federal estate tax.[112] The "other taxes" category is further made up of various license taxes, documentary or stock transfer taxes, severance taxes, and all other taxes not listed separately or provided for in other categories.[113]

Burden Analysis

The overall state and local tax burden on North Dakota's taxpayers is moderately regressive. Taxpayers in the lowest quintile—those with incomes of less than $14,000—bear a tax burden of 10.2% of their income, while taxpayers in the top 1%—those with incomes that exceed $229,000—bear a tax burden of just 6.5% of their income.[114] It is also worth noting that, although North Dakota obviously has no control over federal tax policy, federal itemized deductions for state and local personal income and property taxes nonetheless further reduce the burden on taxpayers in the top 1% to

---

on taxable income up to $3,000; 4.1% on taxable income over $3,000 but not over $8,000; 5.6% on taxable income over $8,000 but not over $20,000; 6.4% on taxable income over $20,000 but not over $30,000; and 6.5% on taxable income over $30,000. *Id.*

108. *Id.* § 57-38-01.4.

109. *Id.* § 57-38-08; *Id.* § 57-38-07.1.

110. *Id.* § 57-38-07.1.

111. Government Finances, *supra* note 51.

112. N.D. Cent. Code § 57-37.1-04.

113. *See* Classification Manual, *supra* note 104, at ch.7.

114. *See* Robert S. McIntyre et al., Who Pays? A Distributional Analysis of the Tax Systems in All 50 States 84 (2d ed. 2003), *available at* http://www.itepnet.org/wp2000/text.pdf. Taxpayers in the second quintile bear a 9.5% total tax burden on incomes between $14,000 and $25,000; those in the third quintile bear a 9.1% tax burden on incomes between $25,000 and $40,000; those in the fourth quintile bear a 8.0% tax burden on incomes between $40,000 and $64,000; those in the 80th–95th percentiles bear a 7.7% tax burden on incomes between $64,000 and $114,000; finally, those in the 96th–99th percentiles bear a 6.4% tax burden on incomes between $114,000 and $229,000. *Id.*

5.1%.[115] However, on a positive note, between 1989 and 2002, the tax burden on the bottom quintile did not change, while the burden on the top 1% rose by 2.1%.[116]

In terms of the income tax, the burden across income groups in North Dakota is moderately progressive, with taxpayers in the lowest quintile bearing a tax burden of 0.3% and those in the top 1% bearing a tax burden of 3.3%.[117] In sharp contrast, however, the sales and excises taxes imposed by North Dakota are very regressive, with taxpayers in the lowest quintile bearing a tax burden of 8.0% and those in the top 1% bearing a tax burden of just 1.3%.[118] The property tax burden in North Dakota, however, is relatively flat across all income levels and averages approximately 2.2%.[119]

---

115. *Id.* Taxpayers in the lowest and second lowest quintile did not receive any benefit from these federal offsets, while those in the third quintile were able to reduce their individual tax burdens by 0.1%, those in the fourth quintile by 0.2%, those in the 80th–95th percentiles by 0.5%, and those in the 96th–99th percentiles by 0.8%. *Id.*

116. *Id.* at 85.

117. *See id.* at 84. Taxpayers in the second quintile bear a 0.8% income tax burden; those in the third quintile bear a 1.2% burden; those in the fourth quintile bear a 1.4% burden; those in the 80th–95th percentiles bear a 1.8% burden; finally, those in the 96th–99th percentiles bear a 2.0% burden. *Id.* Note, however, that these percentages include both individual and corporate income tax burdens and that within the 96th–99th percentiles and the top 1%, corporate income taxes represent 0.1% of the income tax burden. *Id.*

118. *See id.* Taxpayers in the second quintile bear a 6.1% sales-and-excise tax burden; those in the third quintile bear a 5.8% burden; those in the fourth quintile bear a 4.6% burden; those in the 80th–95th percentiles bear a 3.3% burden; finally, those in the 96th–99th percentiles bear a 2.2% burden. *Id.*

119. *See id.* Taxpayers in the bottom quintile bear a 1.9% property tax burden; those in the second quintile bear a 2.5% burden; those in the third quintile bear a 2.2% burden; those in the fourth quintile bear a 2.1% burden; those in the 80th–95th percentiles bear a 2.6% burden; those in the 96th–99th percentiles bear a 2.2% burden; finally, those in the top 1% bear a 1.9% burden. *Id.*

Ohio

General Information

Basic Profile – Geography, Population, and Industry

Admitted to the Union in 1803, Ohio is known as the "Buckeye State."[1] It is located in the Midwest and is bordered by Michigan and Lake Erie on the north, Pennsylvania on the northeast, West Virginia on the southeast, Kentucky on the southwest, and Indiana on the west. Ohio is located in the eastern time zone, and its capital is Columbus.

In 2005, Ohio ranked 7th in population (approximately 11.5 million residents);[2] it ranks 34th in total area (44,825 square miles).[3] Its population is 85.1% white and 11.9% black.[4] The state is 19% Catholic; 55% Protestant; and less than 0.5% Jewish; 26% claim a religion outside the Judeo-Christian tradition or no religion at all.[5] Approximately 80.5% of Ohio's population lives in urban areas.[6] Major industries include advanced electronics, aerospace/defense, food processing, and motor vehicles.[7]

Family Income and Poverty Indicators

In 2004, Ohio's per capita gross product was $36,669, which was below the national average of $39,725.[8] During this same period, although the median household income

---

1. STATE RANKINGS 2006, vi, 1 (Kathleen O'Leary Morgan & Scott Morgan, eds. Morgan Quitno Press, 2006).

2. *Id.* at 429.

3. *Id.* at 225.

4. Ohio QuickFacts from U.S. Census Bureau, http://quickfacts.census.gov/qfd/states/39000.html (last visited January 29, 2007). Other races include 0.2% American Indian and Alaska Native persons; 1.4% Asian persons; and 1.4% persons reporting two or more races. *Id.* Persons of Hispanic or Latino origin make up 2.3% of the population. *Id.* (noting that because Hispanics may be of any race, they are included within the other applicable race categories).

5. BARRY A. KOSMIN, EGON MAYER & ARIELA KEYSAR, AMERICAN RELIGIOUS IDENTIFICATION SURVEY 2001, at 39, *available at* http://www.gc.cuny.edu/faculty/research_studies/aris.pdf.

The all-other-religions category includes other religions not specifically stated, as well as those who claim no religion and those who refused to participate in the survey.

6. USDA Economic Research Service, Ohio Fact Sheet, http://www.ers.usda.gov/StateFacts/OH.htm (last visited December 17, 2006).

7. About Ohio Industries, http://business.ohio.gov/business_cycle/ohio_industries.shtml (last visited December 17, 2006).

8. STATE RANKINGS 2006, *supra* note 1, at 89.

in Ohio was $44,160,[9] 10.8% of the state's population was living in poverty, which was somewhat below the national poverty rate of 12.4%.[10] More specifically, poverty affected 18.0% of Ohio's children,[11] 7.6% of its senior citizens,[12] and 10.0% of its families.[13] Of its female-headed households with children, 40.6% lived in poverty,[14] and 29.5% of the state's public elementary and secondary school students were eligible for free or reduced-price meals.[15] Of those living in poverty, approximately 27.8% were black, which represented 25% of Ohio's black population and 2.9% of its total population.[16] In an attempt to combat this poverty, Ohio spent approximately $12.3 billion on public welfare programs in 2002,[17] which made up 18.3% of its total government expenditures.[18]

Ohio's Public Elementary-Secondary School System

Overall Spending and Performance

For the 2003–2004 school year, Ohio spent $8,963 per pupil in its public elementary-secondary school system, which was slightly above the national average of $8,182.[19] Of this amount, 6.9% was provided by the federal government, 43.9% was provided by the state government, and 49.2% was provided by the local governments,[20] with property taxes making up 40.3% of the total funding.[21] Out of these funds, Ohio paid its elementary and secondary school teachers an estimated average annual salary of $48,612 during the 2004–2005 school year,[22] and it provided a student/teacher ratio of 15.2, which was slightly better than the national average of 15.9.[23]

---

9. *Id.* at 96.

10. *Id.* at 495.

11. *Id.* at 497.

12. *Id.* at 496.

13. *Id.* at 498.

14. *Id.* at 499.

15. *Id.* at 532.

16. *See* Fact Sheet, American FactFinder, http://factfinder.census.gov/home/saff/main.html?_lang=en (select "Ohio" under "Get a Fact Sheet for your community") (last visited Feb. 16, 2007). Note that these numbers are based on the 2000 census because more recent numbers where not available.

17. *Id.* at 500.

18. *Id.* at 502.

19. Governments Division, U.S. Census Bureau, Public Education Finances 2004, at 8 tbl.8 (2006).

20. *See id.* at 5 tbl.5.

21. *See id.* at 4 tbl.4.

22. Thomas D. Snyder et al., National Center for Education Statistics, Digest of Education Statistics 2005, at 116 tbl.77 (2006).

23. *Id.* at 98 tbl.65.

In academic performance, Ohio's fourth grade students scored higher than the national average in mathematics,[24] reading,[25] science,[26] and writing,[27] and Ohio's eighth graders scored higher than the national average in mathematics,[28] reading,[29] science,[30] and writing.[31]

Equity Issues

In 2004, the funding per student in Ohio's highest poverty districts actually exceeded that in its lowest poverty districts by $683,[32] although when adjustments were made for the additional costs of educating students growing up in poverty, that excess narrowed to $113.[33] Similarly, Ohio spent $1,285 more per student in its highest minority districts, although this amount fell to $942 when adjustments for low-income students were made.[34]

Fourth graders eligible for free or reduced-price school lunches had test scores that were 9.9% lower in mathematics,[35] 11.6% lower in reading,[36] and 12.8% lower in writing[37] than those of students who were not eligible. The results were generally better for eighth graders eligible for free or reduced price lunches; their test scores were 8.6% lower in mathematics,[38] 8.4% lower in reading,[39] and 13.8% lower in writing[40] than those of students who were not eligible.

---

24. NATIONAL CENTER FOR EDUCATION STATISTICS, U.S. DEPARTMENT OF EDUCATION, THE NATION'S REPORT CARD: MATHEMATICS 2005, at 14 fig.11 (2005), *available at* http://nces.ed.gov/nationsreportcard/pdf/main2005/ 2006453.pdf [hereinafter MATHEMATICS 2005].

25. NATIONAL CENTER FOR EDUCATION STATISTICS, U.S. DEPARTMENT OF EDUCATION, THE NATION'S REPORT CARD: READING 2005, at 14 fig.11 (2005), *available at* http://nces.ed.gov/nationsreportcard/pdf/main2005/2006451.pdf [hereinafter READING 2005].

26. NATIONAL CENTER FOR EDUCATION STATISTICS, U.S. DEPARTMENT OF EDUCATION, THE NATION'S REPORT CARD: SCIENCE 2005, at 16 fig.12 (2006), *available at* http://nces.ed.gov/nationsreportcard//pdf/main2005/2006466.pdf [hereinafter SCIENCE 2005].

27. HILARY R. PERSKY ET AL., NATIONAL CENTER FOR EDUCATION STATISTICS, U.S. DEPARTMENT OF EDUCATION, THE NATION'S REPORT CARD: WRITING 2002, at 23 tbl.2.2 (2003), *available at* http://nces.ed.gov/nationsreportcard/pdf/main2002/2003529.pdf [hereinafter WRITING 2002].

28. MATHEMATICS 2005, *supra* note 24, at 16 fig.12.

29. READING 2005, *supra* note 25, at 16 fig.12.

30. SCIENCE 2005, *supra* note 26, at 28 fig.22.

31. WRITING 2002, *supra* note 27, at 24 tbl.2.3.

32. THE EDUCATION TRUST, FUNDING GAPS 2006, at 7 tbl.3 (2006), *available at* http://www2.edtrust.org/NR/rdonlyres/CDEF9403-5A75-437E-93FF-EBF1174181FB/0/FundingGap2006.pdf.

33. *Id.*

34. *Id.* at 7 tbl.4.

35. MATHEMATICS 2005, *supra* note 24, at 20 tbl.5.

36. READING 2005, *supra* note 25, at 20 tbl.5.

37. WRITING 2002, *supra* note 27, at 75 tbl.3.24.

38. MATHEMATICS 2005, *supra* note 24, at 21 tbl.6.

39. READING 2005, *supra* note 25, at 21 tbl.6.

40. WRITING 2002, *supra* note 27, at 76 tbl.3.25.

The Ohio Supreme Court has held that "[a] thorough and efficient system of common schools includes facilities in good repair and the supplies, materials, and funds necessary to maintain these facilities in a safe manner, in compliance with all local, state, and federal mandates."[41] Until 2003, the Ohio Supreme Court held in a series of cases[42] that the Ohio education finance system was unconstitutional and in need of "complete systematic overhaul."[43] However, in the 2003 case *State v. Lewis*,[44] the Ohio Supreme Court held that the courts no longer had jurisdiction over the education financing system and that it was up to the general assembly to find a remedy.[45]

Availability of Publicly Funded Prekindergarten Programs

The Public School Preschool Program is available for free to three- and four-year-old children from families at or below 200% of the federal poverty level. [46] Those children from families earning above 100% of the federal poverty level pay on a sliding scale.[47] Total enrollment in this state-funded program is 8,102,[48] which represents just 2.8% of Ohio's 291,480 three- and four-year-old children.[49] The federally funded Head Start program enrolls an additional 32,087 children,[50] which represents 11.0% of Ohio's three- and four-year-old children."[51]

Where Does Ohio Get Its Revenue?

At the end of fiscal year 2004, Ohio had total revenues of approximately $105 billion.[52] Of this amount, 37% was derived from state and local tax revenues and 15% was received from the federal government.[53] The remaining 48% came from other

---

41. DeRolph v. State, 677 N.E.2d 733, 747 (Ohio 1997) [hereinafter DeRolph I].

42. Ohio, STARTINGAT3.ORG, http://www.startingat3.org/state_laws/statelawsOHdetail.html. *See also* DeRolph I, 677 N.E.2d 733; *see also* DeRolph v. State, 780 N.E.2d 529 (Ohio 2002) [herinafter DeRolph II].

43. DeRolph II, 780 N.E.2d at 533.

44. 789 N.E.2d 195 (Ohio 2003).

45. *Id.*

46. W. STEVEN BARNETT ET AL., NATIONAL INSTITUTE FOR EARLY EDUCATION RESEARCH, THE STATE OF PRESCHOOL 2006, at 120 (2007), *available at* http://nieer.org/yearbook/pdf/yearbook.pdf.

47. *Id.*

48. *Id.* at 121.

49. *See id.* at 232.

50. *Id.* at 121.

51. *See id.* at 232.

52. U.S. Census Bureau, State and Local Government Finances - 2003–04, http://www.census.gov/govs/www/estimate04.html (last visited Oct. 17, 2006) [hereinafter Government Finances].

53. *Id.*

sources, including the Ohio Lottery, insurance trust revenue, and revenue from government-owned utilities and other commercial or auxiliary enterprises.[54]

Tax Revenue

Ohio collected approximately $39 billion in state and local tax revenue during fiscal year 2004.[55] As a result, Ohio residents paid $3,419 per capita in state and local taxes, an amount which ranked 20th nationally.[56] The different types of tax sources were apportioned as follows:

Individual income taxes	31.1%
Property taxes	28.7%
General and selective sales taxes	31.5%
Corporate income and other taxes	8.7%
	100.0%[57]

Federal Funding

During fiscal year 2004, 15% of Ohio's total revenues came from the federal government.[58] For every dollar of federal taxes paid, Ohio received $1.01 in federal funding, an amount which ranked 32nd nationally,[59] and was below the national average of $1.17.[60]

Lottery Revenue

The Ohio Lottery has been in operation since August 1974.[61] According to the Ohio constitution, all profits from the Lottery are earmarked for education.[62] During fiscal year 2005, the Lottery had total revenues of approximately $2.16 billion, and approximately $645 million was transferred to the Lottery Profits Education Fund.[63]

---

54. *Id.*

55. *Id.*

56. *Id.*

57. *Id.*

58. *Id.*

59. The Tax Foundation, Federal Spending Received Per Dollar of Taxes Paid by State, 2004 http://www.taxfoundation.org/taxdata/show/266.html (last visited December 17, 2006).

60. *See id.*

61. Ohio Lottery, About the Ohio Lottery, http://www.ohiolottery.com/about/about_us.html (last visited December 17, 2006)

62. Ohio Lottery, A Brief History of the Ohio Lottery, http://www.ohiolottery.com/about/history.html (last visited December 17, 2006).

63. Ohio Lottery Commission, *Comprehensive Annual Financial Report for the Fiscal Years Ended June 30, 2005 and 2004, available at* http://www.ohiolottery.com/pdf/2005_CAFR.pdf.

Legal Structure of Major Tax Sources

Income

Ohio employs a broad-based income tax that uses adjusted gross income for federal income tax purposes as a starting point for determining the state's taxable income.[64] However, a fairly large number of adjustments may be available to various individuals in calculating this amount.[65] Ohio municipal corporations and joint economic development districts have the power to impose an income tax,[66] but they are subject to limitations.[67] During fiscal year 2004, Ohio collected individual income tax of $760 per capita, an amount which ranked 17th nationally.[68]

In Ohio, a typical family of four (i.e., married taxpayers who file jointly and have two dependent children) are not required to pay any income tax until their combined income exceeds $15,600, an amount which is below the national poverty line of $20,615.[69] For the tax year 2006, Ohio's income tax structure contained nine tax brackets that imposed a minimum marginal rate of 0.681% and a maximum marginal rate of 6.870%.[70] When statutory exemptions were taken into account, the maximum marginal rate applied to every dollar of income exceeding $205,600.[71]

---

64. OHIO REV. CODE ANN. § 5747.01(A).

65. *Id.*

66. OHIO REV. CODE ANN. §§ 5747.02, 715.70.

67. *Id.* § 718.01.

68. STATE RANKINGS 2006, *supra* note 1, at 321.

69. JASON A. LEVITIS & NICHOLAS JOHNSON, CENTER ON BUDGET AND POLICY PRIORITIES, THE IMPACT OF STATE INCOME TAXES ON LOW-INCOME FAMILIES IN 2006, at 12 (2007). In 2006, Ohio taxpayers who were married and filing jointly could claim personal exemptions of $1,400 (for each spouse) and dependent exemptions of $1,400. Ohio Department of Taxation, Ohio Income Tax: Individual, http://tax.ohio.gov/divisions/ohio_individual/individual/exemptions .stm (last visited January 29, 2007). Ohio does not provide for either standard or itemized deductions. Note, however, that the threshold calculation of $15,600 is greater than the sum of these exemptions because it includes additional tax benefits available to low-income families, such as the earned-income tax credit. *See* LEVITIS & JOHNSON, *supra*. The personal and dependent exemptions are indexed to the growth in the GDP price deflator yearly. OHIO REV. CODE ANN. § 5747.025.

70. OHIO REV. CODE ANN. § 5747.02(A)(4). Ohio's middle seven tax brackets are 1.361%, 2.722%, 3.403%, 4.083%, 4.546%, 5.444%, and 6.320%. *Id.* The tax rates will be reduced for tax years 2007, 2008, and 2009. After 2009, the rates will stay steady, but beginning in 2010, the income amounts will be adjusted according to the increase in the GDP deflator. *Id.* § 5747.02.

71. The personal and dependent exemptions of $1,400 and $1,400, respectively, plus the threshold of taxable income for the highest tax bracket of $200,000, equals $205,600. *See supra* notes 69–70.

Property

Overview

Ohio has a typical property tax system that taxes the value of real estate, all tangible personal property used in business, and all domestic animals not used in agriculture at both the state and local levels.[72] During fiscal year 2004, Ohio collected approximately $11.2 billion in property tax at the local level and approximately $40.6 million at the state level.[73] As a result, Ohio residents paid $981 per capita in state and local property taxes, an amount which ranked 25th nationally.[74]

Defining the Real Property Tax Base

Under the Ohio constitution, real property is taxed uniformly according to its value.[75] Real property is classified according to its principal and current use for tax reduction purposes.[76] The property is valued at its true value in money, which is determined using the cost approach, the income approach, and the market-data approach of valuation.[77] Agricultural land is valued according to its characteristics and capabilities for use.[78] Real property is assessed at its taxable value, which is calculated as 35% of its true value.[79] Reappraisals must be made at least once every six years.[80]

Real Property Tax Rates

The tax rates imposed on real property vary and are set by each locality. The total tax rate for each locality "includes all levies enacted by a legislative authority or approved by the voters for all taxing jurisdictions in which the property is located."[81] In the 2004 tax year, the statewide average gross millage rate on residential and agricultural real property was 84.19 mills (or $84.19 per $1,000 of value), but the statewide average effective millage rate on all real property was 55.49 mills ($55.49 per $1,000 of value).[82] The difference between these rates arises from tax reduction factors that prevent increases in taxes when the valuation of real property increases.[83] The Ohio constitution limits taxation of property to 1%, or 10 mills, of the property's true value in

---

72. OHIO REV. CODE ANN. § 5709.01. These animals would include pets.

73. Government Finances, *supra* note 52.

74. *Id.*

75. OHIO CONST. ART. XII, § 2.

76. OHIO REV. CODE ANN. § 5713.041. Vacant lots and tracts of real property with no buildings or improvements are classified according to their location and best probable legal use. *Id.*

77. OHIO ADMIN. CODE 5703-25-05.

78. *Id.* 5703-25-11.

79. *Id.* 5703-25-05.

80. OHIO REV. CODE ANN. § 5713.01.

81. Ohio Department of Taxation, *Real Property* 1, *available at* http://tax.ohio.gov/divisions/communications/publications/annual_reports/documents/Real_Property.pdf.

82. *Id.*

83. *Id.*

money, but the levy of taxes may be increased by approval of a majority of voters in a taxing district.[84]

Personal and Intangible Property

Tangible personal property used in business and domestic animals not used in agriculture are subject to taxation.[85] However, the first $10,000 of listed value of taxable personal property owned by a taxpayer is exempt.[86] Intangible personal property is exempt from taxation. Personal property, like real property, is valued according to its true value in money.[87]

Exemptions

Ohio allows for a 10% reduction in a taxpayer's tax bill that applies to all real property that is not intended primarily for use in a business activity and a 2.5% reduction that is permitted for a homestead occupied by a homeowner.[88] Ohio also allows for tax reduction for real property tax which eliminates the effect of increased valuation of existing real property.[89] For tax-reduction purposes, real property is divided into two classes: (1) residential and agricultural property and (2) other real property. Each class has its own tax-reduction factor.[90] There is a further reduction of tax on the homesteads of persons aged 65 and older and on the homesteads of persons permanently and totally disabled.[91]

General and Selective Sales

General Sales

Ohio imposes a general retail sales-and-use tax, which makes up 23.6% of its total tax revenue.[92] The tax is imposed on the retail sale of tangible personal property or taxable services.[93] These services include, among others, the furnishing of lodging by hotels to transient guests; repairing or installing personal property; washing, cleaning, waxing, polishing, or painting motor vehicles; and laundry and dry-cleaning services.[94] The state sales tax rate is 5.5%.[95] In addition, counties can levy an additional sales tax ranging from 1/4% to 1 1/2 %;[96] transit districts can also levy an additional sales tax

---

84. OHIO CONST. Art. XII, §2.
85. OHIO REV. CODE ANN. §5709.01. These animals include pets.
86. *Id.*
87. OHIO ADMIN. CODE 5703-25-05.
88. Ohio Department of Taxation, *supra* note 81; Ohio R.C. §319.301.
89. Ohio Department of Taxation, *supra* note 81.
90. *Id.*
91. OHIO REV. CODE ANN. §323.152.
92. Government Finances, *supra* note 52.
93. OHIO REV. CODE ANN. §5741.02.
94. *Id.* §5739.01.
95. *Id.* §§5739.02(A)(1), 5741.02(A)(1), 5739.025.
96. *Id.* §§5739.021, 5739.026.

ranging from 1/4% to 1 1/2%.[97] Exemptions from Ohio's sales-and-use tax include, among other items, food purchased for home consumption, food stamp purchases, and prescription drugs.[98]

Selective Sales

Selective sales taxes make up 7.8% of Ohio's total tax revenue.[99] Of that amount, 4.0%[100] comes from a motor fuel sales tax imposed at a rate of $0.26 per gallon of gasoline.[101] Ohio residents paid an average of $135 per capita in state motor fuel sales taxes in 2004, an amount which ranked 19th nationally.[102]

The tobacco product sales tax makes up 1.4% of Ohio's total tax revenue[103] and is imposed at a rate of $0.55 per pack of cigarettes.[104] Ohio residents paid an average of $48.70 per capita in state tobacco sales taxes in 2004, an amount which ranked 24th nationally.[105]

In 2004, sales taxes on alcoholic beverages made up 0.3% of Ohio's total tax revenue.[106] Ohio residents paid $7.71 per capita in state alcoholic beverage sales taxes in 2004, an amount which ranked 41st nationally and was well below the national average of $15.74.[107]

The remainder of Ohio's selective sales taxes make up 2.2% of its total tax revenue.[108] Of this amount, 0.8% represents taxes on utilities and the other 1.4% represents taxes on other specific commodities, businesses, or services not reported separately above (e.g., on contractors, lodging, lubricating oil, fuels other than motor fuel, motor vehicles, meals, soft drinks, margarine, etc.).[109]

Corporate Income and Other

Corporate Income

The corporate income tax makes up 2.7% of Ohio's total tax revenue.[110] Ohio has a corporation franchise tax that is imposed on foreign and domestic corporations doing

---

97. *Id.* § 5739.023.

98. *Id.* § 5739.02(B); for a comprehensive list, see Ohio Department of Taxation, *Sales & Use Tax* 4, *available at* http://tax.ohio.gov/divisions/communications/publications/annual_reports/documents/sale_and_use_tax.pdf

99. Government Finances, *supra* note 52.

100. *Id.*

101. STATE RANKINGS 2006, *supra* note 1, at 328.

102. *Id.* at 327.

103. Government Finances, *supra* note 52.

104. STATE RANKINGS 2006, *supra* note 1, at 333.

105. *Id.* at 332.

106. Government Finances, *supra* note 52.

107. STATE RANKINGS 2006, *supra* note 1, at 335.

108. Government Finances, *supra* note 52.

109. *See* GOVERNMENTS DIVISION, U.S. CENSUS BUREAU, GOVERNMENT FINANCE AND EMPLOYMENT CLASSIFICATION MANUAL, at ch.7 (2000), *available at* http://ftp2.census.gov/govs/class/classfull.pdf [hereinafter CLASSIFICATION MANUAL].

110. Government Finances, *supra* note 52.

business in Ohio.[111] This tax is imposed on the value of a corporation's issued and out-standing shares of stock.[112] Two different bases, net income and net worth, are used to determine the value of the stock, and a different tax is imposed on each.[113] The tax imposed on the net-income base is 5.1% on the first $50,000 of taxable income and 8.5% on all taxable income over $50,000.[114] The tax imposed on the net-worth base is 4 mills (or 0.004%), but the maximum tax on the net-worth base is $150,000.[115] The taxpayer pays either the net-income base tax or the net-worth base tax, whichever is larger.[116] S corporations, partnerships, and limited liability companies are not taxed as corporations unless they are classified as such for federal income tax purposes.[117]

Other

During fiscal year 2004, the collection of all other taxes not previously mentioned accounted for 6.0% of Ohio's total tax revenue.[118] Of this amount, approximately $64.2 million was generated by the estate and gift tax,[119] which is based on the value of the decedent's gross estate, less deductions.[120] The "other taxes" category is further made up of various license taxes, documentary or stock transfer taxes, severance taxes, and all other taxes not listed separately or provided for in other categories.[121]

Burden Analysis

The overall state and local tax burden on Ohio's taxpayers is slightly regressive. Taxpayers in the lowest quintile—those with incomes of less than $15,000—bear a tax burden of 11.0% of their income, while taxpayers in the top 1%—those with incomes that exceed $261,000—bear a tax burden of just 9.7% of their income.[122] It is also

---

111. OHIO REV. CODE ANN. §5733.01. This effectively replaces the corporate income tax.

112. Ohio Department of Taxation, *Corporate Franchise Tax* 50-1, *available at* http://tax.ohio.gov/divisions/communications/publications/annual_reports/documents/corporation_franchise_tax.pdf.

113. OHIO REV. CODE ANN. §5733.01; *Id.* §5733.05. For an explanation of how to determine each tax base, see *Corporate Franchise Tax, supra* note 112, at 52.

114. OHIO REV. CODE ANN. §5733.06.

115. *Id.*

116. *Id.* §5733.01.

117. *Id.* §5733.01(E), 5733.09(B), 5701.01.

118. Government Finances, *supra* note 52.

119. *Id.*

120. OHIO REV. CODE ANN. §5731.15 to -.17. For a more in-depth explanation, see Ohio Department of Taxation, *Estate Tax, available at* http://tax.ohio.gov/divisions/communications/publications/annual_reports/documents/estate_tax.pdf.

121. *See* CLASSIFICATION MANUAL, *supra* note 109, at ch.7.

122. *See* ROBERT S. MCINTYRE ET AL., WHO PAYS? A DISTRIBUTIONAL ANALYSIS OF THE TAX SYSTEMS IN ALL 50 STATES 86 (2d ed. 2003), *available at* http://www.itepnet.org/wp2000/text.pdf. Taxpayers in the second quintile bear a 10.7% total tax burden on incomes between $15,000 and $27,000; those in the third quintile bear a 10.7% tax burden on incomes between $27,000 and $41,000; those in the fourth quintile bear a 10.4% tax burden on incomes between $41,000 and

worth noting that, although Ohio obviously has no control over federal tax policy, federal itemized deductions for state and local personal income and property taxes nonetheless further reduce the burden on taxpayers in the top 1% to 6.7%.[123] Furthermore, between 1989 and 2002, the tax burden on the bottom quintile rose by approximately 1.7%, while the burden on the top 1% fell by 0.6%.[124]

In terms of the income tax, the burden across income groups in Ohio is moderately progressive, with taxpayers in the lowest quintile bearing a tax burden of 1.7% and those in the top 1% bearing a tax burden of 7.1%.[125] In sharp contrast, however, the sales and excises taxes imposed by Ohio are very regressive, with taxpayers in the lowest quintile bearing a tax burden of 6.3% and those in the top 1% bearing a tax burden of just 1.0%.[126] Property taxes in Ohio are also regressive, with taxpayers in the lowest quintile bearing a tax burden of 2.9% and those in the top quintile bearing an average tax burden of 1.6%.[127]

$65,000; those in the 80th–95th percentiles bear a 10.4% tax burden on incomes between $65,000 and $117,000; finally, those in the 96th–99th percentiles bear a 10.1% tax burden on incomes between $117,000 and $261,000. *Id.*

123. *Id.* Taxpayers in the lowest quintile did not receive any benefit from these federal offsets, while those in the second quintile were able to reduce their individual tax burdens by 0.1%, those in the third quintile by 0.5%, those in the fourth quintile by 0.7%, those in the 80th–95th percentiles by 1.4%, and those in the 96th–99th percentiles by 2.0%. *Id.*

124. *Id.* at 87.

125. *See id.* at 86. Taxpayers in the second quintile bear a 3.2% income tax burden; those in the third quintile bear a 3.9% burden; those in the fourth quintile bear a 4.6% burden; those in the 80th–95th percentiles bear a 5.2% burden; finally, those in the 96th–99th percentiles bear a 6.0% burden. *Id.* Note, however, that these percentages include both individual and corporate income tax burdens; that within the 96th–99th percentiles, corporate income taxes represent 0.1% of this burden; and that in the top 1%, they represent 0.2% of this burden. *Id.*

126. *See id.* Taxpayers in the second quintile bear a 5.3% sales-and-excise tax burden; those in the third quintile bear a 4.3% burden; those in the fourth quintile bear a 3.6% burden; those in the 80th–95th percentiles bear a 2.8% burden; finally, those in the 96th–99th percentiles bear a 1.8% burden. *Id.*

127. *See id.* Taxpayers in the second quintile bear a 2.2% property tax burden; those in the third quintile bear a 2.5% burden; those in the fourth quintile bear a 2.3% burden; those in the 80th–95th percentiles bear a 2.4% burden; and those in the 96th–99th percentiles bear a 2.3% burden. *Id.*

Oklahoma

General Information

Basic Profile – Geography, Population, and Industry

Admitted to the Union in 1907, Oklahoma is commonly referred to as the "Sooner State".[1] It is located in the south central region and is bordered by Texas and New Mexico on the west, Colorado on the northwest, Kansas on the north, Missouri on the northeast, Arkansas on the east, and Texas on the south. The state is located in the central time zone, and its capital is Oklahoma City.[2]

Oklahoma ranks 20th in total land and water area (approximately 70,000 square miles).[3] In 2005, Oklahoma ranked 28th in population (approximately 3.5 million residents).[4] Its population is approximately 78.5% white, 7.7% black, and 8.1% American Indian and/or Alaska Native.[5] The state is approximately 7% Catholic; 71% Protestant (of which 42% are Baptist); and less than 0.5% Jewish; 22% claim a religion outside the Judeo-Christian tradition or no religion at all.[6] As of 2005, approximately 63% of Oklahoma's residents lived in urban areas.[7] Oklahoma ranks among the leading producers of oil and gas and is also one of the largest suppliers of beef.[8]

---

1. State Rankings 2006, vi, 1 (Kathleen O'Leary Morgan & Scott Morgan eds., Morgan Quitno Press 2006).

2. *Id.*

3. *Id.* at 225.

4. *Id.* at 429.

5. Oklahoma Quick Facts from the U.S. Census Bureau, http://quickfacts.census.gov/qfd/states/40000.html (last visited Jan. 31, 2007). The remaining population is made up of 1.5% Asian persons, 0.1% Native Hawaiian persons and other Pacific Islanders, and 4% persons reporting two or more races. *Id.* Additionally, 6.6% of Oklahoma's total population identify themselves as persons of Hispanic or Latino origin. *Id.* (noting that because Hispanics may be of any race, they are included within the other applicable race categories).

6. Barry A. Kosmin, Egon Mayer & Ariela Keysar, American Religious Identification Survey 2001, at 41, *available at* http://www.gc.cuny.edu/faculty/research_studies/aris.pdf (last visited Jan. 31, 2007).

7. USDA Economic Research Service, Oklahoma Fact Sheet, http://www.ers.usda.gov/StateFacts/OK.htm (last visited Oct. 16, 2006). According to the latest estimates, approximately 1.3 million people live in rural areas, and 2.2 million people live in urban areas. *Id.*

8. Oklahoma, http://www.netstate.com/states/links/ok_links.htm (last visited Oct. 6, 2006).

Family Income and Poverty Indicators

In 2004, Oklahoma's per capita gross product was $30,537, which ranked among the ten lowest states and was below the national average of $39,725.[9] During this same period, while the median household income in Oklahoma was $38,281,[10] 12.6% of Oklahoma's population was living in poverty, which was just above the national average of 12.4%.[11] More specifically, poverty affected 20.5% of Oklahoma's children,[12] 9.1% of its senior citizens,[13] and 12.0% of its families.[14] Of its female-headed households with children, 42.7% lived in poverty,[15] and 53% of the state's public elementary and secondary school students were eligible for free or reduced-price meals.[16] Of those living in poverty, approximately 14% were black, which represented 27% of Oklahoma's black population and 2% of its total population.[17] In an attempt to combat this poverty, Oklahoma spent approximately $3.2 billion on public welfare programs in 2002,[18] which made up 17.6% of its total government expenditures.[19]

Oklahoma's Public Elementary-Secondary School System

Overall Spending and Performance

For the 2003–2004 school year, Oklahoma spent $6,176 per pupil in its public elementary-secondary school system, which was substantially below the national average of $8,182.[20] Of this amount, 12.8% was provided by the federal government, 51.1% was provided by the state government, and 36.1% was provided by the local governments,[21] with property taxes making up 25.9% of the total funding.[22] Out of these funds, Oklahoma paid its elementary and secondary school teachers an estimated av-

---

9. STATE RANKINGS 2006, *supra* note 1, at 89.

10. *Id.* at 96.

11. *Id.* at 495.

12. *Id.* at 497.

13. *Id.* at 496.

14. *Id.* at 498.

15. *Id.* at 499.

16. *Id.* at 532.

17. *See* Fact Sheet, American FactFinder, http://factfinder.census.gov/home/saff/main.html?_lang=en (select Oklahoma under "Get a Fact Sheet for your community") (last visited Feb. 22, 2007). Note that these numbers are based on the 2000 census because more recent numbers were not available.

18. STATE RANKINGS 2006, *supra* note 1, at 500.

19. *Id.* at 502.

20. GOVERNMENTS DIVISION, U.S. CENSUS BUREAU, PUBLIC EDUCATION FINANCES 2004, at 8 tbl.8 (2006).

21. *See id.* at 5 tbl.5.

22. *See id.* at 4 tbl.4.

erage annual salary of $37,141 during the 2004–2005 school year,[23] and in 2003, it provided a student/teacher ratio of 16.0, which was slightly worse than the national average of 15.9.[24]

In academic performance, Oklahoma's fourth grade students scored lower than the national average in mathematics,[25] reading,[26] and writing[27] and higher than the national average in science.[28] Oklahoma's eighth graders, on the other hand, scored lower than the national average in mathematics[29] and writing[30] but equal to the national average in reading[31] and science.[32]

Equity Issues

In 2004, the funding per student in Oklahoma's highest poverty districts exceeded that in its lowest poverty districts by $133.[33] When adjustments were made for the additional costs of educating students growing up in poverty, however, the funding in high poverty districts actually declined by $213.[34] On the other hand, Oklahoma spent $133 less per student in its highest minority districts, and this amount grew to $383 when adjustments for low-income students were made.[35]

Fourth graders eligible for free or reduced-price school lunches had test scores that were 7% lower in mathematics,[36] 9% lower in reading,[37] and 11% lower in writing[38]

23. THOMAS D. SNYDER ET AL., NATIONAL CENTER FOR EDUCATION STATISTICS, DIGEST OF EDUCATION STATISTICS 2005, at 116 tbl.77 (2006).

24. *Id.* at 98 tbl.65.

25. NATIONAL CENTER FOR EDUCATION STATISTICS, U.S. DEPARTMENT OF EDUCATION, THE NATION'S REPORT CARD: MATHEMATICS 2005, at 14 fig.11 (2005), *available at* http://nces.ed.gov/nationsreportcard/pdf/main2005/ 2006453.pdf [hereinafter MATHEMATICS 2005].

26. NATIONAL CENTER FOR EDUCATION STATISTICS, U.S. DEPARTMENT OF EDUCATION, THE NATION'S REPORT CARD: READING 2005, at 14 fig.11 (2005), *available at* http://nces.ed.gov/nationsreportcard/pdf/main2005/2006451.pdf [hereinafter READING 2005].

27. HILARY R. PERSKY ET AL., NATIONAL CENTER FOR EDUCATION STATISTICS, U.S. DEPARTMENT OF EDUCATION, THE NATION'S REPORT CARD: WRITING 2002, at 23 tbl.2.2 (2003), *available at* http://nces.ed.gov/nationsreportcard/pdf/main2002/2003529.pdf [hereinafter WRITING 2002].

28. NATIONAL CENTER FOR EDUCATION STATISTICS, U.S. DEPARTMENT OF EDUCATION, THE NATION'S REPORT CARD: SCIENCE 2005, at 16 fig.12 (2006), *available at* http://nces.ed.gov/nationsreportcard//pdf/main2005/2006466.pdf [hereinafter SCIENCE 2005].

29. MATHEMATICS 2005, *supra* note 25, at 16 fig.12.

30. WRITING 2002, *supra* note 27, at 24 tbl.2.3.

31. READING 2005, *supra* note 26, at 16 fig.12.

32. SCIENCE 2005, *supra* note 28, at 28 fig.22.

33. THE EDUCATION TRUST, FUNDING GAPS 2006, at 7 tbl.3 (2006), *available at* http://www2 .edtrust.org/NR/rdonlyres/CDEF9403-5A75-437E-93FF-EBF1174181FB/0/FundingGap2006.pdf.

34. *Id.*

35. *Id.* at 7 tbl.4.

36. MATHEMATICS 2005, *supra* note 25, at 20 tbl.5.

37. READING 2005, *supra* note 26, at 20 tbl.5.

38. WRITING 2002, *supra* note 27, at 75 tbl.3.24.

than those of students who were not eligible. The results were generally worse for eighth graders eligible for free or reduced price lunches; their test scores were 8% lower in mathematics,[39] 6% lower in reading,[40] and 14% lower in writing[41] than those of students who were not eligible.

In January 2006, the Oklahoma Education Association (OEA), along with three school districts, filed suit against the State of Oklahoma on state constitutional grounds.[42] The plaintiffs contended that the Oklahoma legislature was violating the constitutional mandate that every child "receive a uniform opportunity to a basic, adequate education" by failing to provide adequate levels of education funding.[43] Specifically, the lawsuit challenged the "current levels of education funding for general operating or instructional issues" and the "current levels and method of funding for facilities or capital improvements available to Oklahoma's 540 school districts."[44] In July 2006, the case was dismissed by the trial court on the basis that the lawsuit raised questions that were not appropriate for the judiciary.[45] The plaintiffs appealed the trial court's decision, and the case is currently pending before the Oklahoma Supreme Court.[46]

Availability of Publicly Funded Prekindergarten Programs

Oklahoma's Early Childhood Four-Year-Old program is a free, voluntary program which is available to all four-year-old children in the state; however, it is not available to three-year-old children.[47] Oklahoma is currently in the process of developing an Early Childhood Pilot Program, which, at some point in the future, will provide services to at-risk children and their families.[48] Total enrollment in the state-funded Early Childhood Four-Year-Old program is 33,402,[49] which represents just 35% of Oklahoma's 95,395 three- and four-year-old children.[50] The federally funded Head Start

---

39. MATHEMATICS 2005, *supra* note 25, at 21 tbl.6.

40. READING 2005, *supra* note 26, at 21 tbl.6.

41. WRITING 2002, *supra* note 27, at 76 tbl.3.25.

42. Ok. Education Assoc. v. State of Oklahoma, Case No. CV-2006-2, First Amended Petition for Declaratory & Injunctive Relief at 2 (Dist. Ct. of Oklahoma County, Jan. 24, 2006) *available at* http://www.okea.org/A&E/FirstAmendedA&EPetition.pdf.

43. *Id.*

44. *Id.*

45. National Access Network, Litigation Update: Missouri Plaintiffs Testify; Motions in Kentucky, Indiana, Nebraska, and Oklahoma, http://www.schoolfunding.info/news/litigation/2-20-07litupdate.php3 (last visited Mar. 31, 2007).

46. *Id.*

47. W. STEVEN BARNETT ET AL., NATIONAL INSTITUTE FOR EARLY EDUCATION RESEARCH, THE STATE OF PRESCHOOL 2006, at 122 (2006), *available at* http://nieer.org/yearbook/pdf/yearbook.pdf.

48. *Id.*

49. *Id.* at 123.

50. *See id.* at 232.

program enrolls an additional 14,220 children,[51] which represents 15% of Oklahoma's three- and four-year-old children.[52]

Where Does Oklahoma Get Its Revenue?

At the end of fiscal year 2004, Oklahoma had total revenues of approximately $24 billion.[53] Of this amount, 39% was derived from state and local tax revenues and 20% was received from the federal government.[54] The remaining 41% came from other sources, including the Oklahoma Education Lottery, insurance trust revenue, and revenue from government-owned utilities and other commercial or auxiliary enterprises.

Tax Revenue

Oklahoma collected approximately $9.4 billion in state and local tax revenue during fiscal year 2004.[55] As a result, Oklahoma residents paid $2,677 per capita in state and local government taxes, an amount which ranked 43rd nationally.[56] The different types of tax sources were approximately apportioned as follows:

Individual income taxes	24.6%
Property taxes	17.4%
General and selective sales taxes	38.6%
Corporate income and other taxes	19.4%
	100.0%[57]

Federal Funding

During fiscal year 2004, 20% of Oklahoma's total revenues came from the federal government.[58] For every dollar of federal taxes paid, Oklahoma received $1.48 in federal funding, an amount which ranked 41st nationally[59] and was above the national average of $1.17.[60]

---

51. *Id.* at 123.

52. *See id.* at 232.

53. U.S. Census Bureau, State and Local Government Finances 2003–04, http://www.census.gov/govs/www/estimate04.html (last visited Oct. 16, 2006) [hereinafter Government Finances].

54. *Id.*

55. *Id.* The total tax revenues were collected as follows: $6.4 billion by the state and $3.0 billion by local governments. *Id.*

56. *Id.*

57. *Id.*

58. *Id.*

59. The Tax Foundation, Federal Spending Received per Dollar of Taxes Paid by State 2004, http://www.taxfoundation.org/taxdata/show/266.html (last visited Oct. 16, 2006).

60. *See id.*

Lottery Revenue

In April 2003, the Oklahoma Senate and House passed legislation which created the Oklahoma Education Lottery and the Oklahoma Education Lottery Trust Fund.[61] On November 2, 2004, the citizens of Oklahoma approved the changes to the Oklahoma constitution which officially created the Oklahoma Education Lottery.[62] Sales of instant game tickets began in October 2005. Powerball Lottery sales began in January 2006.[63]

Net proceeds from the Oklahoma Education Lottery are to be transferred to the Oklahoma Education Lottery Trust Fund.[64] This fund is to be used to enhance, but not supplant, funding for education. All funds in the Trust Fund are to be used as follows: 45% for K–12 public education and early childhood development programs; 45% for tuition grants, loans, and scholarships to citizens of Oklahoma to enable such citizens to attend colleges and universities in Oklahoma and for construction of additional educational facilities and technology; 5% for the School Consolidation and Assistance Fund; and 5% for the Teachers' Retirement System Dedicated Revenue Revolving Fund.[65]

Legal Structures of Major Tax Sources

Income

Oklahoma employs a broad-based income tax that uses adjusted gross income for federal income tax purposes as a starting point for determining the state's taxable income.[66] However, a fairly large number of adjustments may be available to various individuals in calculating this amount. During fiscal year 2004, Oklahoma collected individual income tax of $658 per capita, an amount which ranked 25th nationally.[67]

In Oklahoma, a typical family of four (i.e., married taxpayers who file jointly and have two dependent children) are not required to pay any income tax until their combined income exceeds $18,200, an amount which is below the national poverty line of $20,615.[68] Oklahoma's income tax structure contains eight tax brackets that impose a

---

61. Official Home of the Oklahoma Lottery, http://www.lottery.ok.gov/oklahomaeducationlotterytimeline.htm (last visited October 16, 2006).

62. *Id.*

63. *Id.*

64. Okla. Stat. Ann. tit. 3A, § 713.

65. *Id.*

66. Okla. Stat. Ann. tit. 68, § 2358.

67. State Rankings 2006, *supra* note 1, at 321.

68. Jason A. Levitis, Center on Budget and Policy Priorities, The Impact of State Income Taxes on Low-Income Families in 2006, at 12 (2007), *available at* http://www.cbpp .org/2-22-06sfp.pdf. In 2006, Oklahoma taxpayers who were married and filing jointly could claim a standard deduction of $3,000, personal exemptions of $1,000 each, and dependent exemptions of $1,000 each. Okla. Stat. Ann. tit. 68 § 2358. Note, however, that the threshold calculation of $18,200 is greater than the sum of these deductions and exemptions because it includes additional tax benefits available to low-income families, such as the earned-income tax credit. *See*

minimum marginal rate of 0.5% and a maximum marginal rate of 6.25%.[69] When statutory exemptions and the standard deduction are taken into account, the maximum marginal rate applies to every dollar of income exceeding $28,000.[70]

Property

Overview

Oklahoma has a typical property tax system that taxes and collects the value of real and personal property at the local level.[71] Oklahoma localities collected $1.6 billion in property taxes during fiscal year 2004.[72] As a result, Oklahoma residents paid $465 per capita in property taxes, an amount which ranked 47th nationally.[73]

Defining the Real Property Tax Base

Oklahoma has only one classification for real property,[74] and both residential and commercial properties are assessed at between 11 percent and 13.5 percent of the fair cash value as of January 1 of each year.[75] Fair cash value is generally determined using either the cost method, the income method, or the market-data method.[76] The fair cash value of real property used for farming and ranching is calculated on the basis of the income-capitalization approach using cash rent.[77] In general, taxing localities are required to reassess property values at least once every four years.[78]

LEVITIS, *supra.* Note also that for the 2007 tax year, Oklahoma increased the standard deduction for taxpayers who are married and filing jointly to $4,000. OKLA. STAT. ANN. tit. 68 § 2358.

69. OKLA. STAT. ANN. tit. 68 § 2355. Oklahoma's middle six tax brackets are 1%, 2%, 3%, 4%, 5%, and 6%. *Id.*

70. The standard deduction and exemptions of $3,000 and $4,000, respectively, plus the threshold of taxable income for the highest tax bracket of $21,000, equals $28,000. *See supra* note 68.

71. OKLA. STAT. ANN. tit. 68, § 2804.

72. Government Finances, *supra* note 53.

73. *See Id.*

74. OKLA. STAT. ANN. tit. 68, § 2803.

75. OKLA. CONST. art. X, § 8. Fair cash value is the estimated price "the real property would bring at a fair voluntary sale for: 1. The highest and best use for which the property was actually used during the preceding calendar year; or 2. The highest and best use for which the property was last classified for use if not actually used during the preceding calendar year." OKLA. STAT. ANN. tit. 68 § 2817.

76. OKLA. STAT. ANN. tit. 68, § 2817.

77. *Id.* "The rental income shall be calculated using the direct capitalization method based upon factors including, but not limited to: 1. Soil types, as depicted on soil maps published by the Natural Resources Conservation Service of the United States Department of Agriculture; 2. Soil productivity indices approved by the Ad Valorem Division of the Tax Commission; 3. The specific agricultural purpose of the soil based on use categories approved by the Ad Valorem Division of the Tax Commission; and 4. A capitalization rate to be determined annually by the Ad Valorem Division of the Tax Commission based on the sum of the average first mortgage interest rate charged by the Federal Land Bank for the immediately preceding five (5) years, weighted with the prevailing rate or rates for additional loans or equity, and the effective tax rate." *Id.*

78. *Id.*

Real Property Tax Rates

Oklahoma's constitution prohibits the state from assessing and collecting property taxes and limits the assessment by localities to 15 mills on the dollar per taxable year (i.e., 1 mill equals 1 dollar per thousand; therefore, 15 mills equals 15 dollars per thousand).[79] At least 5 mills must be allocated for school district purposes.[80] The board of education of any school district may levy additional county property taxes up to 15 mills for school purposes only.[81] Oklahoma's constitution also prohibits the fair cash value of any parcel of real property from increasing more than 5% in any taxable year.[82] In 2005, the tax rates per $1,000 of assessed value ranged from $98.53 in Oklahoma City (School District 89) to $115.04 in Bethany (School District 88).[83]

Personal and Intangible Property

Tangible personal property is subject to taxation unless specifically exempted.[84] Tangible personal property includes all property not included in the definition of real property.[85] Intangible property is not subject to taxation at either the state or local level.[86] Personal property is assessed for taxation at 10 percent of its fair cash value[87] and is taxed at the same rate as real property, subject to each county's taxing authority.[88]

Exemptions

Household goods, tools, implements, and livestock of heads of household, which do not exceed $100 in value, are exempt from property tax.[89] All growing crops are also exempt from property tax.[90] Citizens of Oklahoma are allowed a homestead exemption which reduces $1,000 from the gross assessed value of the home.[91] In addition, taxpayers with gross household income of $20,000 or less may qualify for an additional $1,000 exemption.[92]

---

79. OKLA. CONST. art. X, § 9.

80. *Id.*

81. *Id.*

82. OKLA. CONST. art. X, § 8B.

83. CCH-EXP, PROP-TAX-GUIDE OK ¶ 71-501, Rates in Cities.

84. OKLA. STAT. ANN. tit. 68, § 2807.

85. *Id.*

86. OKLA. CONST. art. X, § 6A.

87. OKLA. STAT. ANN. tit. 68, § 2817. Fair cash value is estimated at the price the property would bring at a fair, voluntary sale. *Id.*

88. OKLA. CONST. art. X, § 9.

89. OKLA. STAT. ANN. tit. 68, § 2887.

90. *Id.*

91. OKLA. STAT. ANN. tit. 68, § 2889.

92. *Id.* § 2890.

General and Selective Sales

General Sales

Oklahoma imposes a general sales-and-use tax, which makes up 29.5% of Oklahoma's total tax revenue.[93] The tax is imposed on the sale of tangible personal property and on the furnishing of specific services.[94] The tax imposed on the sale of tangible personal property is levied at 4.5 percent of the gross receipts from the sale of such property.[95] Oklahoma law allows incorporated cities and towns to levy sales taxes for general and specific purposes of municipal government.[96] There is presently no maximum local rate that may be levied by cities and towns.[97] However, most cities and towns levy an additional sales tax in the range of 2% to 4.5%.[98] Counties may levy a county sales tax not to exceed 2 percent.[99] The county sales tax is levied in addition to the existing 4.5 percent state and applicable municipal tax.[100]

There are several exemptions from the sales tax, including prescription drugs for human consumption;[101] sales of food or food products for home consumption which are purchased in whole or in part with coupons issued pursuant to the federal food stamp program; fertilizer; and farm machinery, parts, and fuel.[102]

Selective Sales

Selective sales taxes make up 9.1% of Oklahoma's total tax revenue.[103] Of that amount, 4.4%[104] comes from a motor fuel sales tax imposed at a rate of $0.16 per gallon of gasoline and $0.13 per gallon of diesel fuel.[105] Oklahoma residents paid $118 per capita in state motor fuel sales taxes in 2004, an amount which ranked 33rd nationally and was just above the national average of $115.[106]

---

93. Government Finances, *supra* note 53.

94. OKLA. STAT. ANN. tit. 68, § 1354. Specific services include printing and advertising (except for advertising in newspapers and periodicals and on billboards, as well as advertising through the electronic broadcast media, including radio, television, and cable television); transportation and automobile parking; admissions; lodging and meals; telephone service; and the furnishing of other public utilities such as electricity and natural gas, with the exception of water. *Id.*

95. *Id.*

96. OKLA. STAT. ANN. tit. 68, § 2701.

97. *Id.*

98. Oklahoma Tax Commission, Rates and Codes for Sales, Use and Lodging Tax, http://www.tax.ok.gov/publicat/copo4Q06.pdf (last visited Nov. 1, 2006).

99. OKLA. STAT. ANN. tit. 68, § 1370.

100. *Id.*

101. *Id.* § 1357.

102. *Id.* § 1358.

103. Government Finances, *supra* note 53.

104. *Id.*

105. OKLA. STAT. ANN. tit. 68, § 500.4.

106. STATE RANKINGS 2006, *supra* note 1, at 327.

In 2004, sales taxes on alcoholic beverages made up 0.7% of Oklahoma's total tax revenue.[107] Oklahoma residents paid $19.42 per capita in state alcoholic beverage sales taxes in 2004, an amount which ranked 15th nationally.[108]

The tobacco products sales tax makes up 0.7%[109] of Oklahoma's total tax revenue. In 2005, it was imposed at a rate of $1.03 per pack of cigarettes.[110]

The remainder of Oklahoma's selective sales tax makes up 3.3% of its total tax revenue.[111] Of this amount, 1.3% represents taxes on utilities and the other 2% represents taxes on other specific commodities, businesses, or services not reported separately above (e.g. on contractors, lodging, lubricating oil, fuels other than motor fuel, motor vehicles, meals, soft drinks, margarine, etc.).[112]

Corporate Income and Other

Corporate Income

The corporate income tax makes up 1.4% of Oklahoma's tax revenue.[113] Oklahoma has a broad-based corporate income tax which is imposed on domestic and foreign corporations conducting a trade or business in, or deriving income from sources within, the state.[114] The corporate income tax is 6% of taxable income reported to the federal government.[115] Oklahoma follows the federal income tax treatment of S corporations to the extent that income and losses flow through to their shareholders, who pay taxes on the income in Oklahoma.[116] Limited partnerships and limited liability partnerships,[117] as well as limited liability companies, assuming they are treated as a partnership for federal tax purposes,[118] are treated as they are for federal income tax purposes and therefore do not pay Oklahoma's corporate income tax.

Other

During fiscal year 2004, the collection of all other taxes not previously mentioned accounted for 18.0% of Oklahoma's total tax revenue.[119] Of this amount, approximately

---

107. Government Finances, *supra* note 53.

108. STATE RANKINGS 2006, *supra* note 1, at 335.

109. Government Finances, *supra* note 53.

110. STATE RANKINGS 2006, *supra* note 1, at 333.

111. Government Finances, *supra* note 53.

112. *See* GOVERNMENTS DIVISION, U.S. CENSUS BUREAU, GOVERNMENT FINANCE AND EMPLOYMENT CLASSIFICATION MANUAL, at ch. 7 (2000), *available at* http://ftp2.census.gov/govs/class/classfull.pdf [hereinafter CLASSIFICATION MANUAL].

113. U.S. Census Bureau, *supra* note 53.

114. OKLA. STAT. ANN. tit. 68, § 2355.

115. *Id;* OKLA. STAT. ANN. tit. 68, § 2353.

116. *Id.* § 2365.

117. *Id.* § 2363.

118. *Id.* tit. 18, § 2001.

119. Government Finances, *supra* note 53.

$111 million was generated by the estate and gift tax,[120] which is calculated on the basis of the value of the net estate.[121] The "other taxes" category is further made up of various license taxes, franchise taxes,[122] severance taxes and all other taxes not listed separately or provided for in other categories.[123]

Burden Analysis

The overall state and local tax burden on Oklahoma's taxpayers is very regressive. Taxpayers in the lowest quintile—those with incomes of less than $12,000—bear a tax burden of 12.0% of their income, while taxpayers in the top 1%—those with incomes that exceed $252,000—bear a tax burden of just 7.9% of their income.[124] It is also worth noting that, although Oklahoma obviously has no control over federal tax policy, federal itemized deductions for state and local personal income and property taxes nonetheless further reduce the burden on taxpayers in the top 1% to 5.7%.[125] Furthermore, between 1989 and 2002, the tax burden on the bottom quintile rose by approximately 1.1%, while the burden on the top 1% rose by only approximately 0.5%.[126]

---

120. *Id.*

121. OKLA. STAT. ANN. tit. 68, § 803. For the estate of a decedent who dies on or after January 1, 2007, the following rates and brackets are applied to the value of the decedent's net estate: a rate of 0.5% between $0.00 and $10,000; 1% between $10,000 and $20,000; 1.5% between $20,000 and $40,000; 2% between $40,000 and $60,000; 2.5% between $60,000 and $100,000; 3% between $100,000 and $250,000; 6.5% between $250,000 and $500,000; 7% between $500,000 and $750,000; 7.5% between $750,000 and $1,000,000; 8% between $1,000,000 and $3,000,000; 8.5% between $3,000,000 and $5,000,000; 9% between $5,000,000 and $10,000,000; and 10% on the value of the net estate in excess of $10,000,000. *Id.*

122. OKLA. STAT. ANN. tit. 68, § 1203. The franchise tax is levied "upon every corporation, association, joint-stock company and business trust organized under the laws of this state, equal to One Dollar and twenty-five cents ($ 1.25) for each One Thousand Dollars ($ 1,000.00) or fraction thereof of the amount of capital used, invested or employed in the exercise of any power, privilege or right inuring to such organization, within this state."

123. *See* CLASSIFICATION MANUAL, supra note 112, at ch. 7.

124. *See* ROBERT S. MCINTYRE ET AL., WHO PAYS? A DISTRIBUTIONAL ANALYSIS OF THE TAX SYSTEMS IN ALL 50 STATES 88 (2d ed. 2003), *available at* http://www.itepnet.org/wp2000/text.pdf. Taxpayers in the second quintile bear a 11.1% total tax burden on incomes between $12,000 and $22,000; those in the third quintile bear a 11.2% tax burden on incomes between $22,000 and $37,000; those in the fourth quintile bear a 10.6% tax burden on incomes between $37,000 and $60,000; those in the 80th–95th percentiles bear a 9.8% tax burden on incomes between $60,000 and $110,000; finally, those in the 96th–99th percentiles bear a 8.6% tax burden on incomes between $110,000 and $252,000. *Id.*

125. *Id.* Taxpayers in the lowest and second lowest quintiles did not receive any benefit from these federal offsets, while those in the third quintile were able to reduce their individual tax burdens by 0.1%, those in the fourth quintile by 0.4%, those in the 80th–95th percentiles by 1.0%, and those in the 96th–99th percentiles by 1.5%. *Id.*

126. *Id.* at 89.

In terms of the income tax, the burden across income groups in Oklahoma is slightly progressive, with taxpayers in the lowest quintile bearing a tax burden of 0.4% and those in the top 1% bearing a tax burden of 5.3%.[127] In sharp contrast, however, the sales and excise taxes imposed by Oklahoma are extremely regressive, with taxpayers in the lowest quintile bearing a tax burden of 8.8% and those in the top 1% bearing a tax burden of just 1.4%.[128] Property taxes in Oklahoma are also regressive, with taxpayers in the lowest quintile bearing a tax burden of 2.8% and those in the top quintile bearing an average tax burden of 1.5%.[129]

---

127. *See id.* at 88. Taxpayers in the second quintile bear a 1.7% income tax burden; those in the third quintile bear a 2.9% burden; those in the fourth quintile bear a 3.8% burden; those in the 80th–95th percentiles bear a 4.1% burden; finally, those in the 96th–99th percentiles bear a 4.5% burden. *Id.* Note, however, that these percentages include both individual and corporate income tax burdens and that within the top 1%, corporate income taxes represent 0.1% of the income tax burden. *Id.*

128. *See id.* Taxpayers in the second quintile bear a 7.7% sales-and-excise tax burden; those in the third quintile bear a 6.6% burden; those in the fourth quintile bear a 5.1% burden; those in the 80th–95th percentiles bear a 3.9% burden, finally, those in the 96th–99th percentiles bear a 2.6% burden. *Id.*

129. *See id.* Taxpayers in the second quintile bear a 1.7% property tax burden; those in the third quintile bear a 1.7% burden; those in the fourth quintile bear a 1.7% burden; those in the 80th–95th percentiles bear a 1.8% burden; those in the 96th–99th percentiles bear a 1.5% burden; finally, those in the top 1% bear a 1.2% burden. *Id.*

Oregon

General Information

Basic Profile – Geography, Population, and Industry

Oregon was admitted to the Union in 1859. The "Beaver State" is located in the Pacific Northwest and is bordered by the Pacific Ocean on the west, Washington on the north, Idaho on the east, and California and Nevada on the south. Most of Oregon is located in the Pacific time zone, and a small portion along the eastern border is located in the mountain time zone. Salem is the state capital.

Oregon ranks 27th in population (approximately 3.6 million residents)[1] and 9th in total land and water area (98,381 square miles).[2] Its population is approximately 90.8% white and 1.8% black.[3] Additionally, 9.9% of its population identify themselves as persons of Hispanic or Latino origin.[4] The state is approximately 14% Catholic; 51% Protestant; and less than 0.5% Jewish; 35% claim a religion outside the Judeo-Christian tradition or no religion at all.[5] Roughly 77% of Oregon's population lives in urban areas.[6] Major industries include manufacturing, real estate, wholesale trade, retail trade, health care, and social assistance.[7]

Family Income and Poverty Indicators

In 2004, Oregon's per capita gross product was $35,670, which was below the national average of $39,725.[8] During this same period, although the median household

---

1. STATE RANKINGS 2006, vi, 429 (Kathleen O'Leary Morgan & Scott Morgan eds., Morgan Quitno Press 2006).

2. *Id.* at 225.

3. Oregon Quick Facts from the U.S. Census Bureau, http://quickfacts.census.gov/qfd/states/41000.html (last visited Jan. 31, 2007). The remaining population is made up of 1.4% American Indian and Alaska Native persons; 3.4% Asian persons; 0.3% Native Hawaiian persons and other Pacific Islanders; and 2.3% persons reporting two or more races. *Id.*

4. *Id.* (noting that because Hispanics and Latinos may be of any race, they are also included within the other applicable race categories). *See id.*

5. *See* BARRY A. KOSMIN, EGON MAYER & ARIELA KEYSAR, AMERICAN RELIGIOUS IDENTIFICATION SURVEY 2001, at 41, *available at* http://www.gc.cuny.edu/faculty/research_studies/aris.pdf.

6. USDA Economic Research Service, Oregon Fact Sheet, http://www.ers.usda.gov/StateFacts/OR.htm (last visited Oct. 16, 2006).

7. Oregon Economic and Community Development Department, Oregon's Gross State Product, http://www.econ.state.or.us/GSP.pdf (last visited Apr. 1, 2006).

8. STATE RANKINGS 2006, *supra* note 1, at 89.

income in Oregon was $42,617,[9] 11.7% of Oregon's population was living in poverty, which was just below the national average of 12.4%.[10] More specifically, poverty affected 18.3% of Oregon's children,[11] 6.6% of its senior citizens,[12] and 10.4% of its families.[13] Of its female-headed households with children, 41.6% o lived in poverty,[14] and 40.1% of the state's public elementary and secondary school students were eligible for free or reduced-price meals.[15] Of those living in poverty, approximately 3.1% were black, which represented 21.6% of Oregon's black population and 0.4% of its total population.[16] In an attempt to combat this poverty, Oregon spent approximately $4 billion on public welfare programs in 2002,[17] which made up 17.6% of its total government expenditures.[18]

Oregon's Public Elementary-Secondary School System

Overall Spending and Performance

For the 2003–2004 school year, Oregon spent $7,619 per pupil in its public elementary-secondary school system, which was slightly below the national average of $8,182.[19] Of this amount, 9.1% was provided by the federal government, 52.7% was provided by the state government, and 38.2% was provided by the local governments,[20] with property taxes making up 29.2% of the total funding.[21] Out of these funds, Oregon paid its elementary and secondary school teachers an estimated average annual salary of $50,790 during the 2004–2005 school year,[22] but in 2003, it provided a student/teacher ratio of just 20.6, which was far worse than the national average of 15.9.[23]

---

9. *Id.* at 96.

10. *Id.* at 495.

11. *Id.* at 497.

12. *Id.* at 496.

13. *Id.* at 498.

14. *Id.* at 499.

15. *Id.* at 532.

16. *See* Fact Sheet, American FactFinder, http://factfinder.census.gov/home/saff/main.html?_lang=en (select Oregon under "Get a Fact Sheet for your community") (last visited Feb. 16, 2007). Note that these numbers are based on the 2000 census because more recent numbers were not available.

17. *Id.* at 500.

18. *Id.* at 502.

19. Governments Division, U.S. Census Bureau, Public Education Finances 2004, at 8 tbl.8 (2006), *available at* http://www2.census.gov/govs/school/04f33pub.pdf.

20. *See id.* at 5 tbl.5.

21. *See id.* at 4 tbl.4.

22. Thomas D. Snyder et al., National Center for Education Statistics, Digest of Education Statistics 2005, at 116 tbl.77 (2006), *available at* http://nces.ed.gov/pubsearch/pubs info.asp?pubid=2006030.

23. *Id.* at 98 tbl.65.

In academic performance, Oregon's fourth grade students scored lower than the national average in writing,[24] equal to the national average in reading,[25] and higher than the national average in mathematics[26] and science.[27] Oregon's eighth graders, on the other hand, scored higher than the national average in writing,[28] reading,[29] mathematics,[30] and science.[31]

Equity Issues

In 2004, the funding per student in Oregon's highest poverty districts actually exceeded that in its lowest poverty districts by $579,[32] although when adjustments were made for the additional costs of educating students growing up in poverty, that excess narrowed to $302.[33] Similarly, Oregon spent $222 more per student in its highest minority districts, although this amount fell to $127 when adjustments for low-income students were made.[34]

Fourth graders eligible for free or reduced-price school lunches had test scores that were 6% lower in mathematics,[35] 9% lower in reading,[36] and 13% lower in writing[37] than those of students who were not eligible. The results were similar for eighth graders eligible for free or reduced-price lunches; their test scores were 7% lower in mathematics,[38] 6% lower in reading,[39] and 17% lower in writing[40] than those of students who were not eligible.

---

24. HILARY R. PERSKY ET AL., NATIONAL CENTER FOR EDUCATION STATISTICS, U.S. DEPARTMENT OF EDUCATION, THE NATION'S REPORT CARD: WRITING 2002, at 23 tbl.2.2 (2003), *available at* http://nces.ed.gov/nationsreportcard/pdf/main2002/2003529.pdf [hereinafter WRITING 2002].

25. NATIONAL CENTER FOR EDUCATION STATISTICS, U.S. DEPARTMENT OF EDUCATION, THE NATION'S REPORT CARD: READING 2005, at 14 fig.11 (2005), *available at* http://nces.ed.gov/nationsreportcard/pdf/main2005/2006451.pdf [hereinafter READING 2005].

26. NATIONAL CENTER FOR EDUCATION STATISTICS, U.S. DEPARTMENT OF EDUCATION, THE NATION'S REPORT CARD: MATHEMATICS 2005, at 14 fig.11 (2005), *available at* http://nces.ed.gov/nationsreportcard/pdf/main2005/ 2006453.pdf [hereinafter MATHEMATICS 2005].

27. NATIONAL CENTER FOR EDUCATION STATISTICS, U.S. DEPARTMENT OF EDUCATION, THE NATION'S REPORT CARD: SCIENCE 2005, at 16 fig.12 (2006), *available at* http://nces.ed.gov/nationsreportcard//pdf/main2005/2006466.pdf [hereinafter SCIENCE 2005].

28. WRITING 2002, *supra* note 24, at 24 tbl.2.3.

29. READING 2005, *supra* note 25, at 16 fig.12.

30. MATHEMATICS 2005, *supra* note 26, at 16 fig.12.

31. SCIENCE 2005, *supra* note 27, at 28 fig.22.

32. THE EDUCATION TRUST, FUNDING GAPS 2006, at 7 tbl.3 (2006), *available at* http://www2 .edtrust.org/NR/rdonlyres/CDEF9403-5A75-437E-93FF-EBF1174181FB/0/FundingGap2006.pdf.

33. *Id.*

34. *Id.* at 7 tbl.4.

35. MATHEMATICS 2005, *supra* note 26, at 20 tbl.5.

36. READING 2005, *supra* note 25, at 20 tbl.5.

37. WRITING 2002, *supra* note 24, at 75 tbl.3.24.

38. MATHEMATICS 2005, *supra* note 26, at 21 tbl.6.

39. READING 2005, *supra* note 25, at 21 tbl.6.

40. WRITING 2002, *supra* note 24, at 76 tbl.3.25.

In 1976, the Oregon Supreme Court rejected a group of plaintiffs' equal protection challenge of the state's school finance system, holding that the equal protection and education clauses of the Oregon constitution set a minimal standard whereby the state is in compliance "if the state requires and provides for a minimum of educational opportunities in the district and permits the districts to exercise local control over what they desire, and can furnish, over the minimum."[41] Voters used the initiative and referendum process in 1991 to pass a constitutional amendment called Measure 5, which greatly limited local property taxes and required the state to replace the funds lost because of the limitations.[42]

Availability of Publicly Funded Prekindergarten Programs

Oregon's Head Start Prekindergarten program serves three- and four-year-old children whose families have incomes below the federal poverty level or who have identified disabilities.[43] Total enrollment in this state-funded program is 3,486,[44] which represents just 4% of Oregon's 90,733 three- and four-year-old children.[45] Federally funded and state-funded Head Start programs enroll an additional 7,242 and 3,486 children, respectively,[46] which represents 8% and 4%, respectively, of Oregon's three- and four-year-old children.[47]

Where Does Oregon Get Its Revenue?

At the end of fiscal year 2004, Oregon had total revenues of approximately $33.7 billion.[48] Of this amount, 31% was derived from state and local tax revenues and 15% was received from the federal government.[49] The remaining 54% came from other sources, including the Oregon Lottery, insurance trust revenue, and revenue from government-owned utilities and other commercial or auxiliary enterprises.[50]

---

41. Olsen v. State, 554 P.2d 139, 148 (Or. 1976).

42. *See* OR. CONST. art. XI, § 11; National Access Network, State by State, Oregon, http://www.schoolfunding.info/states/or/lit_or.php3 (last visited Mar. 19, 2007).

43. W. STEVEN BARNETT ET AL., NATIONAL INSTITUTE FOR EARLY EDUCATION RESEARCH, THE STATE OF PRESCHOOL 2006, at 124 (2006), *available at* http://nieer.org/yearbook/pdf/yearbook.pdf.

44. *Id.* at 124.

45. *See id.* at 232.

46. *Id.* at 124.

47. *See id.* at 232.

48. U.S. Census Bureau, State and Local Government Finances 2003–04, http://www.census.gov/govs/www/estimate04.html (last visited Oct. 6, 2006) [hereinafter Government Finances].

49. *Id.*

50. *Id.*

Tax Revenue

Oregon collected approximately $10.5 billion in state and local tax revenue during fiscal year 2004.[51] As a result, Oregon residents paid $2,917 per capita in state and local government taxes in 2004, an amount which ranked 32nd nationally.[52] The different types of tax sources were approximately apportioned as follows:

Individual income taxes	41.7%
Property taxes	33.0%
General and selective sales taxes	9.7%
Corporate income and other taxes	15.6%
	100.0%[53]

Federal Funding

During fiscal year 2004, 15% of Oregon's total revenues came from the federal government.[54] For every dollar of federal taxes paid, Oregon received $0.97 in federal funding, an amount which ranked 34th nationally and was below the national average of $1.17.[55]

Lottery Revenues

The Oregon State Lottery was created through the initiative process in 1984, when voters approved an amendment to the Oregon constitution requiring the establishment of a state lottery.[56] The constitution authorizes the appropriation of Lottery revenues for the following purposes: creating jobs; furthering economic development; financing public education; and restoring and protecting Oregon's parks, beaches, watersheds, and critical fish and wildlife habitats.[57] In 2005, the Lottery had gross revenues of $939 million, approximately $401.5 million of which was transferred to the State Economic Development Fund.[58]

---

51. The total tax revenues were collected as follows: $6.1 billion by the state and 4.4 billion by local governments. *Id.*

52. *Id.*

53. *Id.*

54. *Id.*

55. *See* The Tax Foundation, Federal Spending Received Per Dollar of Taxes Paid by State 2004, http://www.taxfoundation.org/taxdata/show/266.html (last visited Oct. 16, 2006).

56. The Oregon Lottery, Laws & Rules, http://www.oregonlottery.org/general/information.shtml#history (last visited Nov. 11, 2006).

57. OR. CONST. art. XV, § 4(d).

58. THE OREGON LOTTERY, 2005 AUDITED FINANCIAL STATEMENTS 6 (2006), *available at* http://www.sos.state.or.us/audits/reports/full/2006/2006-06.pdf (last visited Apr. 1, 2006).

Legal Structures of Major Tax Sources

Income

Oregon employs a broad-based income tax that uses adjusted gross income for federal income tax purposes as a starting point for determining the state's taxable income.[59] However, a fairly large number of adjustments may be available to various individuals in calculating this amount.[60] The Oregon constitution requires the consent of the people or the legislature for any local taxes or duties imposed.[61] Mass transit districts have the authority to levy income taxes within the limits of a district, but such districts currently opt to impose an employer's payroll tax instead of an income tax.[62] During fiscal year 2004, Oregon collected personal income tax of $1,189 per capita, an amount which ranked 4th nationally.[63]

In Oregon, a typical family of four (i.e., married taxpayers who file jointly and have two dependent children) are not required to pay any income tax until their combined income exceeds $17,500, an amount which is below the national poverty line of $20,615.[64] Oregon's income tax structure contains four inflation-indexed tax brackets that impose a minimum marginal rate of 5% and a maximum marginal rate of 9%.[65] When the standard deduction is taken into account, the maximum marginal rate applies to every dollar of income exceeding $17,385.[66]

---

59. OR. REV. STAT. § 316.048.

60. *See* OR. REV. STAT. §§ 316.680 to 316.852.

61. OR. CONST. art. I, § 32.

62. OR. REV. STAT. § 267.370.

63. STATE RANKINGS 2006, *supra* note 1, at 321.

64. JASON A. LEVITIS, CENTER ON BUDGET AND POLICY PRIORITIES, THE IMPACT OF STATE INCOME TAXES ON LOW-INCOME FAMILIES IN 2006, at 12 (2007). In 2006, Oregon taxpayers who were married and filing jointly could claim a standard deduction of $3,685, personal exemption *credits* of $159 for each spouse, and dependent exemption *credits* of $159 for each dependent. *See* OR. REV. STAT. §§ 316.695, 316.085; OREGON DEPARTMENT OF REVENUE, 2006 FORMS 40S AND 40 INSTRUCTIONS 28 (2006), *available at* http://www.oregon.gov/DOR/PERTAX/docs/2006Forms/101-043-06.pdf (last visited Feb. 3, 2006); OREGON DEPARTMENT OF REVENUE, 2006 FORM 40, at line 33, *available at* http://www.oregon.gov/DOR/PERTAX/docs/2006Forms/101-040-06fill.pdf (last visited Feb. 3, 2007). Note, however, that the threshold calculation of $17,500 is greater than the sum of these deductions and exemptions because it includes additional tax benefits available to low-income families, such as the earned-income tax credit. *See* LEVITIS, *supra.*

65. OR. REV. STAT. § 316.037. The rate applied to Oregon's middle tax bracket is 7%. *Id.*; Oregon Department of Revenue, Miscellaneous Oregon Income Tax Information 2002–2006, https://secure.dor.state.or.us/piti/index.cfm?action=topic&id=183 (last visited Mar. 31, 2007).

66. The standard deduction of $3,685, plus the threshold of taxable income for the highest tax bracket of $13,700, equals $17,385. *See supra* notes 64–65.

Property

Overview

Oregon has a typical property tax system that taxes the value of real and tangible personal property at the local level. The state has the authority to impose a property tax to pay bonded indebtedness and interest,[67] but it has not done so since 1940.[68] Though property taxes are generally assessed and collected by localities, the state is responsible for collecting and distributing to the counties taxes on utilities, air transportation property, railroad transportation property, and industrial property with a real market value of $1 million or more.[69] Oregon localities collected more than $3.4 billion in property taxes during fiscal year 2004, and the state collected (and ultimately distributed to counties) $15.9 million.[70] As a result, Oregon residents paid $963 per capita in property taxes, an amount which ranked 28th nationally.[71]

Defining the Real Property Tax Base

Taxable real property in Oregon is generally valued at 100% of real market value,[72] except for farm land and open-space land, which are granted special use valuation.[73] Other types of real property that are granted preferential valuation include certain historic property and rehabilitated residential property.[74] Except for property to which special valuation applies, real property is assessed at the lesser of the property's "maximum assessed value" and real market value.[75] "Maximum assessed value" is the greater of 103% of the property's assessed value from the preceding tax year or 100% of its maximum assessed value from the preceding year.[76] Voters approved this 3% limitation on annual increases in assessed value in 1997 through an initiative called Ballot Measure 50.[77] This limitation does not apply under some circumstances, such as changes in value as a result of improvements, subdivision, and rezoning.[78] Oregon property is assessed annually.[79]

---

67. OR. REV. STAT. §§ 291.445, 311.660.
68. CCH-EXP, OR-TAXRPTR ¶ 20-405, Rates of Tax.
69. *See* OR. REV. STAT. §§ 308.515, 306.126.
70. Government Finances, *supra* note 48.
71. *See id.*
72. *See* OR. REV. STAT. § 308.232.
73. *Id.* §§ 308A.092, 308A.315.
74. *Id.* §§ 358.505, 308.456.
75. *Id.* § 308.146.
76. *Id.*
77. *See* OR. CONST. art. XI, § 11.
78. OR. REV. STAT. § 308.146.
79. OR. REV. STAT. § 308.210.

Real Property Tax Rates

In 1990, Oregon voters approved constitutional limitations on property tax rates of $5 per $1,000 (5 mills) of real market value for funding public schools and $10 per $1,000 (10 mills) of real market value for funding other government operations.[80] Local taxing districts may exceed these caps for limited time periods with voter approval.[81] Additionally, levies to pay principal and interest for bonded debt are exempt from the caps.[82] The average rate imposed statewide during fiscal year 2006 was $15.37 per $1,000 (15.37 mills) of net assessed value, with individual county average rates ranging from 8.85 mills to 16.92 mills.[83] Expressed in terms of real market value instead of assessed value, the average statewide rate was 10.32 mills, with individual county average rates ranging from 5.40 mills to 15.59 mills.[84] The forgoing rates were 100% local, since the state did not collect property taxes for state purposes.[85]

Personal and Intangible Property

Intangible property is not taxed in Oregon.[86] Tangible personal property held for personal use is also exempt.[87] The foregoing exemptions have the effect of limiting taxable personal property to tangible personal property used in a trade or business.[88] Such personal property is valued at 100% of its real market value;[89] like real property, it is assessed at the lesser of real market value and "maximum assessed value."[90] Motor vehicles are exempt from taxes, but registration fees are imposed.[91]

Exemptions

Oregon does not offer a homestead exemption. Real property exemptions include, among others, an exemption for qualifying property owned by businesses in certain low-income areas.[92] Personal property exemptions include farm equipment, logging equipment, and business inventory. [93]

---

80. Or. Const. art. XI, § 11(b); Or. Rev. Stat. § 310.140.

81. Or. Const. art. XI, § 11; Or. Rev. Stat. § 280.060.

82. Or. Const. art. XI, § 11; Or. Rev. Stat. § 310.150.

83. Oregon Department of Revenue, Oregon Property Tax Annual Statistics Fiscal Year 2005–06, at 12, *available at* http://www.oregon.gov/DOR/STATS/docs/303-405-06/303-405-06.pdf (last visited Nov. 13, 2006).

84. *Id.*

85. *See supra* note 68. Note, however, that the state does collect and distribute to the counties taxes on utilities, air transportation property, railroad transportation property, and industrial property with a real market value of $1 million or more. Or. Rev. Stat. §§ 291.445, 311.660.

86. Or. Rev. Stat. § 307.190.

87. *Id.*

88. *See id.*

89. Or. Rev. Stat. § 308.232.

90. *Id.* § 308.146.

91. *Id.* § 803.585.

92. *Id.* § 285C.200.

93. *Id.* §§ 307.394, 307.400, 307.827.

General and Selective Sales

General Sales

Oregon does not impose a general retail sales or use tax.

Selective Sales

Selective sales taxes constituted 9.7% of Oregon's total tax revenue during fiscal year 2004.[94] Of that amount, 4.0% came from motor fuel sales taxes.[95] Oregon residents paid an average of $113 per capita in state motor fuel sales taxes in 2004, an amount which ranked 38th nationally and was below the national average of $115.[96]

The tobacco product sales tax made up 2.5% of Oregon's tax revenue during fiscal year 2004.[97] Oregon residents paid $73.89 per capita in state tobacco sales taxes, an amount which ranked 9th nationally.[98]

Sales taxes on alcoholic beverages made up 0.1% of Oregon's total tax revenue in 2004.[99] Oregon residents paid $3.71 per capita in state alcoholic beverage sales taxes, an amount which ranked 49th nationally.[100]

The remainder of Oregon's selective sales taxes constituted 3.0% of its total tax revenue in 2004.[101] Of that percentage, 1.7% represented taxes on utilities and the other 1.3% represented taxes on other specific commodities, businesses, or services not reported separately above (e.g., on contractors, lodging, lubricating oil, fuels other than motor fuel, motor vehicles, meals, soft drinks, margarine, etc.).[102]

Corporate Income and Other

Corporate Income

The corporate income and corporate excise taxes comprise 3.1% of Oregon's total tax revenue.[103] These broad-based taxes are calculated with federal taxable income as the starting point.[104] The primary difference between the corporate excise and income taxes is that corporations doing business in Oregon pay "excise" taxes, while corporations not doing business in Oregon but earning income from Oregon sources pay "in-

---

94. Government Finances, *supra* note 48.

95. *Id.*

96. STATE RANKINGS 2006, *supra* note 1, at 327.

97. Government Finances, *supra* note 48.

98. STATE RANKINGS 2006, *supra* note 1, at 332.

99. Government Finances, *supra* note 48.

100. STATE RANKINGS 2006, *supra* note 1, at 335.

101. Government Finances, *supra* note 48.

102. *Id.*; *see* GOVERNMENTS DIVISION, U.S. CENSUS BUREAU, GOVERNMENT FINANCE AND EMPLOYMENT CLASSIFICATION MANUAL, at ch.7 (2000), *available at* http://ftp2.census.gov/govs/class/classfull.pdf [hereinafter CLASSIFICATION MANUAL].

103. Government Finances, *supra* note 48.

104. OR. REV. STAT. § 317.010.

come" taxes.[105] The income and excise taxes apply to C corporations, but Oregon generally adopts the federal income tax pass-through treatment of S corporations, partnerships, and limited liability companies.[106] Oregon's corporate excise and income tax is a flat rate of 6%.[107]

Other

During fiscal year 2004, the collection of all other taxes not previously mentioned generated $1.3 billion, an amount which comprised 12.5% of Oregon's total tax revenue.[108] Of that amount, $73.6 million came from inheritance taxes, which are generally equal to 100% of the state death tax credit allowed by the federal estate tax law that was in effect in 2000.[109] The "other taxes" category is further made up of various license taxes, documentary or stock transfer taxes, severance taxes, and all other taxes not listed separately or provided for in other categories.[110]

Burden Analysis

The overall state and local tax burden on Oregon's taxpayers is somewhat regressive. Taxpayers in the lowest quintile — those with incomes of less than $16,000 — bear a tax burden of 9.4% of their income, while taxpayers in the top 1% — those with incomes that exceed $308,000 — bear a tax burden of 8.9% of their income.[111] It is also worth noting that, although Oregon obviously has no control over federal tax policy, federal itemized deductions for state and local personal income and property taxes nonetheless further reduce the burden on taxpayers in the top 1% to 6.1%.[112] Fur-

---

105. Oregon Department of Revenue, Business Taxes, Corporation Excise and Income Tax, http://www.oregon.gov/DOR/BUS/IC-102-401.shtml (last visited Nov. 13, 2006).

106. OR. REV. STAT. §§ 314.732(1), 314.712.

107. *Id.* §§ 317.061, 318.020.

108. Government Finances, *supra* note 48.

109. Oregon Department of Revenue, October 2006 Inheritance Tax Advisory, http://www.oregon.gov/DOR/BUS/inher-adv.shtml (last visited Nov. 13, 2006).

110. *See* CLASSIFICATION MANUAL, *supra* note 102, at ch. 7.

111. *See* ROBERT S. MCINTYRE ET AL., WHO PAYS? A DISTRIBUTIONAL ANALYSIS OF THE TAX SYSTEMS IN ALL 50 STATES 90 (2d ed. 2003), *available at* http://www.itepnet.org/wp2000/text.pdf. Taxpayers in the second quintile bear a 9.1% total tax burden on incomes between $16,000 and $27,000; those in the third quintile bear a 8.5% tax burden on incomes between $27,000 and $44,000; those in the fourth quintile bear a 8.8% tax burden on incomes between $44,000 and $71,000; those in the 80th–95th percentiles bear a 9% tax burden on incomes between $71,000 and $132,000; finally, those in the 96th–99th percentiles bear a 9% tax burden on incomes between $132,000 and $308,000. *Id.*

112. *Id.* Taxpayers in the lowest quintile did not receive any benefit from these federal offsets, while those in the second quintile were able to reduce their individual tax burdens by 0.2%, those in the third quintile by 0.5%, those in the fourth quintile by 0.9%, those in the 80th–95th percentiles by 1.7%, and those in the 96th–99th percentiles by 2.3%. *Id.*

thermore, between 1989 and 2002, the tax burden on the bottom quintile rose by approximately 2.2%, while the burden on the top 1% fell by 0.4%.[113]

In terms of the income tax, the burden across income groups in Oregon is slightly progressive, with taxpayers in the lowest quintile bearing a tax burden of 2.3% and those in the top 1% bearing a tax burden of 7.5%.[114] In contrast, however, the sales and excises taxes imposed by Oregon are slightly regressive, with taxpayers in the lowest quintile bearing a tax burden of 2.9% and those in the top 1% bearing a tax burden of just 0.1%.[115] Property taxes in Oregon are also regressive, with taxpayers in the lowest quintile bearing a tax burden of 4.1% and those in the top quintile bearing an average tax burden of 1.9%.[116]

---

113. *Id.* at 91.

114. *See id.* at 90. Taxpayers in the second quintile bear a 3.8% income tax burden; those in the third quintile bear a 4.7% burden; those in the fourth quintile bear a 5.1% burden; those in the 80th–95th percentiles bear a 6% burden; finally, those in the 96th–99th percentiles bear a 6.6% burden. *Id.* Note, however, that these percentages include both individual and corporate income tax burdens; that within the 96th–99th percentiles, corporate income taxes represent 0.1% of the income tax burden; and that in the top 1%, corporate income taxes represent 0.2% of the burden. *Id.*

115. *See id.* Taxpayers in the second quintile bear a 1.9% sales-and-excise tax burden; those in the third quintile bear a 1.3% burden; those in the fourth quintile bear a 1% burden; those in the 80th–95th percentiles bear a 0.6% burden; finally, those in the 96th–99th percentiles bear a 0.3% burden. *Id.*

116. *See id.* Taxpayers in the second quintile bear a 3.4% property tax burden; those in the third quintile bear a 2.5% burden; those in the fourth quintile bear a 2.7% burden; those in the 80th–95th percentiles bear a 2.4% burden; those in the 96th–99th percentiles bear a 2% burden; finally, those in the top 1% bear a 1.3% burden. *Id.*

Pennsylvania

General Information

Basic Profile – Geography, Population, and Industry

Admitted to the Union in 1787, Pennsylvania is known as the "Keystone State."[1] It is located in the Mid-Atlantic region and is bordered by New York on the north; New Jersey on the east; Delaware, Maryland, and West Virginia on the south; and Ohio on the west. The state is located in the eastern time zone and its capital is Harrisburg.

Pennsylvania ranks 33rd in total area (46,055 square miles).[2] In 2005, it ranked 6th in population (approximately 12.4 million residents).[3] Pennsylvania's population is approximately 86.0% white and 10.6% black.[4] The state is approximately 27% Catholic; 49% Protestant; and 1% Jewish; 23% claim a religion outside the Judeo-Christian tradition or no religion at all.[5] Nearly 84% of Pennsylvania's population lives in urban areas.[6] Major industries include manufacturing, banking and finance, tourism, high technology, and agriculture.[7]

Family Income and Poverty Indicators

In 2004, Pennsylvania's per capita gross product was $37,766, which ranked 25th nationally and was just below the national average of $39,725.[8] During this same pe-

---

1. State Rankings 2006, vi, 1 (Kathleen O'Leary Morgan & Scott Morgan, eds. Morgan Quitno Press, 2006).

2. *Id.* at 225.

3. *Id.* at 429.

4. Pennsylvania Quick Facts from the U.S. Census Bureau, http://quickfacts.census.gov/qfd/states/54000.html (last visited Feb. 17, 2007). The remaining population is made up of 2.2% Asian persons; 0.2% American Indian and/or Alaska Native persons; and 1.0% persons reporting two or more races. *Id.* Additionally, 4.1% of Pennsylvania's total population identify themselves as persons of Hispanic or Latino origin. *Id.* (noting that because Hispanics may be of any race, they are included within the other applicable race categories).

5. Barry A. Kosmin, Egon Mayer & Ariela Keysar, American Religious Identification Survey 2001, at 41, *available at* http://www.gc.cuny.edu/faculty/research_studies/aris.pdf.

6. USDA Economic Research Service, Pennsylvania Fact Sheet, http://www.ers.usda.gov/StateFacts/PA.htm (last visited Sept. 17, 2006). According to the latest estimates, approximately 2 million people live in rural areas, and 10.4 million people live in urban areas. *Id.*

7. PA Powerport, http://www.state.pa.us/papower/taxonomy/taxonomy.asp?DLN=29888 (last visited Feb. 17, 2006).

8. State Rankings 2006, *supra* note 1, at 89.

riod, while the median household income in Pennsylvania was $44,286,[9] 10.4% of the state's population was living in poverty, which was somewhat below the national average of 12.4%.[10] More specifically, poverty affected 16.5% of Pennsylvania's children,[11] 8.1% of its senior citizens,[12] and 8.9% of its families.[13] Of its female-headed households with children, 38.0% lived in poverty,[14] and 28.1% of the state's public elementary and secondary school students were eligible for free or reduced-price meals.[15] Of those living in poverty, approximately 23.4% were black, which represented 25% of Pennsylvania's black population and 2.5% of its total population.[16] In an attempt to combat this poverty, Pennsylvania spent approximately $14.5 billion on public welfare programs in 2002,[17] which made up 19.8% of its total government expenditures.[18]

Pennsylvania's Public Elementary-Secondary School System

Overall Spending and Performance

For the 2003–2004 school year, Pennsylvania spent $9,979 per pupil in its public elementary-secondary school system, which was slightly above the national average of $8,182.[19] Of this amount, 8.0% was provided by the federal government, 35.9% was provided by the state government, and 56.1% was provided by the local governments,[20] with property taxes making up 44.1% of the total funding.[21] Out of these funds, Pennsylvania paid its elementary and secondary school teachers an estimated average annual salary of $52,700 during the 2004–2005 school year,[22] and it provided a student/teacher ratio of 15.2, which was slightly better than the national average of 15.9.[23]

---

9. *Id.* at 96.

10. *Id.* at 495.

11. *Id.* at 497.

12. *Id.* at 496.

13. *Id.* at 498.

14. *Id.* at 499.

15. *Id.* at 532.

16. *See* Fact Sheet, American FactFinder, http://factfinder.census.gov/home/saff/main.html?_lang=en (select "Pennsylvania" under "Get a Fact Sheet for your community") (last visited Feb. 16, 2007). Note that these numbers are based on the 2000 census because more recent numbers where not available.

17. *Id.* at 500.

18. *Id.* at 502.

19. Governments Division, U.S. Census Bureau, Public Education Finances 2004, at 8 tbl.8 (2006).

20. *See id.* at 5 tbl.5.

21. *See id.* at 4 tbl.4.

22. Thomas D. Snyder et al., National Center for Education Statistics, Digest of Education Statistics 2005, at 116 tbl.77 (2006).

23. *Id.* at 98 tbl.65.

In academic performance, Pennsylvania's fourth grade students scored higher than the national average in mathematics,[24] reading,[25] and writing.[26] Pennsylvania's eighth graders also scored higher than the national average in mathematics,[27] reading,[28] and writing.[29]

Equity Issues

In 2004, revenues spent per student in Pennsylvania's highest poverty districts were determined to be $1,001 less than the revenues spent in its lowest poverty districts.[30] When adjustments were made for the additional costs of educating students growing up in poverty, however, the funding gap grew to $1,511.[31] On the other hand, Pennsylvania spent $454 more per student in its highest minority districts, and this amount grew to $709 when adjustments for low-income students were made.[32]

In Pennsylvania, fourth graders eligible for free or reduced-price school lunches had test scores that were 10.0% lower in mathematics,[33] 12.1% lower in reading[34] and 17.5% lower in writing[35] than those of students who were not eligible. The results were generally the same for eighth graders eligible for free or reduced-price lunches; their test scores were 9.3% lower in mathematics,[36] 10.5% lower in reading,[37] and 20.6% lower in writing[38] than those of students who were not eligible.

Pennsylvania has seen some litigation related to issues of equity of school funding from both underfunded rural districts[39] and underfunded urban districts.[40] However,

---

24. NATIONAL CENTER FOR EDUCATION STATISTICS, U.S. DEPARTMENT OF EDUCATION, THE NATION'S REPORT CARD: MATHEMATICS 2005, at 14 fig.11 (2005), *available at* http://nces.ed.gov/nationsreportcard/pdf/main2005/ 2006453.pdf [hereinafter MATHEMATICS 2005].

25. NATIONAL CENTER FOR EDUCATION STATISTICS, U.S. DEPARTMENT OF EDUCATION, THE NATION'S REPORT CARD: READING 2005, at 14 fig.11 (2005), *available at* http://nces.ed.gov/nationsreportcard/pdf/main2005/2006451.pdf [hereinafter READING 2005].

26. HILARY R. PERSKY ET AL., NATIONAL CENTER FOR EDUCATION STATISTICS, U.S. DEPARTMENT OF EDUCATION, THE NATION'S REPORT CARD: WRITING 2002, at 23 tbl.2.2 (2003), *available at* http://nces.ed.gov/nationsreportcard/pdf/main2002/2003529.pdf [hereinafter WRITING 2002].

27. MATHEMATICS 2005, *supra* note 24, at 16 fig.12.

28. READING 2005, *supra* note 25, at 16 fig.12.

29. WRITING 2002, *supra* note 26, at 24 tbl.2.3.

30. THE EDUCATION TRUST, FUNDING GAPS 2006, at 7 tbl.3 (2006), *available at* http://www2.edtrust.org/NR/rdonlyres/CDEF9403-5A75-437E-93FF-EBF1174181FB/0/FundingGap2006.pdf.

31. *Id.*

32. *Id.* at 7 tbl.4.

33. MATHEMATICS 2005, *supra* note 24, at 20 tbl.5.

34. READING 2005, *supra* note 25, at 20 tbl.5.

35. WRITING 2002, *supra* note 26, at 75 tbl.3.24.

36. MATHEMATICS 2005, *supra* note 24, at 21 tbl.6.

37. READING 2005, *supra* note 25, at 21 tbl.6.

38. WRITING 2002, *supra* note 26, at 76 tbl.3.25.

39. Penn. Ass'n of Rural and Small Sch. v. Ridge, 737 A. 2d 246 (Pa. 1999).

40. Powell v. Ridge, 247 F.3d 520 (3rd Cir. 2001).

the Supreme Court of Pennsylvania has determined that school funding issues are outside the court's purview and should be resolved by the state legislature.[41]

Availability of Publicly Funded Prekindergarten Programs

The Pennsylvania's K4 Program currently serves four-year-old children who are considered at risk; it extends to three-year-old children in limited situations.[42] Total enrollment in this state-funded program is 10,995,[43] which represents 3.8% of Pennsylvania's 286,868 three- and four-year-old children.[44] The federally funded Head Start program enrolls an additional 7% of Pennsylvania's three-year-old children and 11% of its four-year-old children.[45]

Where Does Pennsylvania Get Its Revenue?

At the end of fiscal year 2004, Pennsylvania had total revenues of approximately $102.2 billion.[46] Of this amount, 41.8% was derived from state and local tax revenues and 17.7% was received from the federal government.[47] The remaining 40.5% came from other sources, including the Pennsylvania Lottery, insurance trust revenue, revenue from government-owned utilities, and other commercial or auxiliary enterprises.[48]

Tax Revenue

Pennsylvania collected approximately $42.72 billion in state and local tax revenue during fiscal year 2004.[49] As a result, Pennsylvania residents paid $3,447 per capita in state and local taxes, an amount which ranked 19th nationally.[50] The different types of tax sources were approximately apportioned as follows:

---

41. Marrero v. Commonwealth, 739 A.2d 110 (Pa 1999).

42. W. STEVEN BARNETT ET AL., NATIONAL INSTITUTE FOR EARLY EDUCATION RESEARCH, THE STATE OF PRESCHOOL 2006, at 126 (2007), *available at* http://nieer.org/yearbook/pdf/yearbook.pdf.

43. *Id.* at 127.

44. *See id.*

45. *See id.*

46. U.S. Census Bureau, State and Local Government Finances 2003–04, http://www.census.gov/govs/www/estimate04.html (last visited Oct. 6, 2006) [hereinafter Government Finances].

47. *Id.*

48. *Id.*

49. The total tax revenues were collected as follows: $25.3 billion by the state and $17.4 billion by local governments. *Id.*

50. *Id.*

Individual income taxes	24.1%
Property taxes	29.3%
General and selective sales taxes	30.3%
Corporate income and other taxes	16.3%
	100.0%[51]

Federal Funding

During fiscal year 2004, 17.7% of Pennsylvania's total revenues came from the federal government.[52] For every dollar of federal taxes paid, Pennsylvania received $1.06 in federal funding, an amount which ranked 29th nationally[53] and was below the national average of $1.17.[54]

Lottery Revenue

The Pennsylvania Lottery has been in operation since 1971. Under Pennsylvania's constitution, the Lottery's net proceeds, which must be at least 30% of total proceeds, are to be used in a program designed to reduce the burden of property tax for the elderly and the disabled, as well as couples with less than $15,000 in annual income.[55] During fiscal year 2006, the Lottery had total revenues of $3.07 billion and net proceeds of $976 million.[56]

Legal Structures of Major Tax Sources

Income

Pennsylvania employs a broad-based income tax[57] that uses adjusted gross income for federal income tax purposes as a starting point for determining the state's taxable income.[58] However, numerous adjustments may be available to various individuals in calculating this amount.[59] During fiscal year 2004, Pennsylvania collected individual income tax of $591 per capita, an amount which ranked 33rd nationally.[60]

---

51. *Id.*

52. *Id.*

53. The Tax Foundation, Federal Spending Received Per Dollar of Taxes Paid by State, 2004 http://www.taxfoundation.org/taxdata/show/266.html (last visited Sept. 17, 2006).

54. *See id.*

55. 72 P.A. Stat. Ann. §§ 3761-101 to 3761-2103.

56. "Lottery: Annual Report Fiscal Years Ending June 30, 2006," *available at* http://www.palottery.state.pa.us/lottery/cwp/view.asp?A=3&Q=479753 (last checked Dec. 18, 2006).

57. 72 P.A. Stat. Ann. §§ 3402-201 to 3402-802.

58. *Id.*

59. *Id.*

60. State Rankings 2006, *supra* note 1, at 321.

In Pennsylvania, a typical family of four (i.e., married taxpayers who file jointly and have two dependent children) are not required to pay any income tax until their combined income exceeds $32,000, an amount which is substantially above the national poverty line of $20,615.[61] Pennsylvania residents pay a flat tax of 3.07% on all income.[62]

Property

Overview

The State of Pennsylvania imposes a limited tax on personal property;[63] instead, its localities are permitted by state law to assess property taxes at the local level.[64] During fiscal year 2004, Pennsylvania collected approximately $12.4 billion dollars in property taxes at the local level and approximately $68 million at the state level.[65] As a result, Pennsylvania residents paid $1,010 per capita in state and local property taxes, an amount which ranked 24th nationally.[66]

Defining the Real Property Tax Base

Pennsylvania has only one classification for real property, and both residential and commercial properties are assessed at 100% of the estimated fair market value as of January 1 each year.[67] Fair market value is generally determined by considering sale price, comparable sales, rental value, and use.[68]

Real Property Tax Rates

The tax rates imposed on real property vary and are set by each locality.[69] During fiscal year 2006, the tax rates per $1,000 of assessed value ranged from $2.13 in Wayne County to $94.00 in Luzerne County.[70]

Personal and Intangible Property

Tangible personal property is generally exempt from taxation.[71] "Tangible personal property" is defined as all personal property not otherwise classified as intangible per-

---

61. JASON A. LEVITIS & NICHOLAS JOHNSON, CENTER ON BUDGET AND POLICY PRIORITIES, THE IMPACT OF STATE INCOME TAXES ON LOW-INCOME FAMILIES IN 2006, at 12 (2007). Note that Pennsylvania taxpayers who are married and filing jointly are not entitled to a standard deduction or personal and dependent exemptions.

62. Id.

63. 72 P.A. STAT. ANN. §§ 3242-1–3252-15.

64. Id. §§ 5020-1–5020-310.

65. Government Finances, supra note 46.

66. See id.

67. 72 P.A. STAT. ANN. § 5020-201.

68. 53 P.A. STAT. ANN. § 3750-4.

69. 72 P.A. STAT. ANN. §§ 3242-1–3252-15.

70. CCH-EXP, PROP-TAX-GUIDE PA ¶ 20-405, Rates of Tax (while the maximum millage rate is 25, counties can appeal that maximum by showing need).

71. See id.

sonal property or as merchants' capital.[72] Intangible property in Pennsylvania is taxed on mortgages, notes outstanding, and certain types of capital stock at a flat rate of $0.004 per dollar.[73]

Exemptions

Pennsylvania makes exceptions to its property tax provisions for the following purposes: discounts for persons over the age of 65, relief granted for qualified impoverished neighborhoods, discounts for the development of impoverished areas, and abatement for the construction of some new homes.[74]

General and Selective Sales

General Sales

Pennsylvania imposes a general retail sales-and-use tax, which makes up 19.6% of its total tax revenue.[75] This tax is imposed on the sale, distribution, renting, or furnishing of tangible personal property, as well as specified services.[76] The state sales tax rate is 6%, and the only local imposition of sales tax occurs in Philadelphia and Allegheny County at a rate of 1%.[77] Exemptions from Pennsylvania's sales-and-use tax include unprepared food, prescription and nonprescription drugs, firewood, school lunches, and textbooks.[78]

Selective Sales

Selective sales taxes make up 11.6% of Pennsylvania's total revenue.[79] Of that amount, 4.2%[80] comes from a motor fuel sales tax imposed at a rate $0.12 per gallon of gasoline.[81] Pennsylvania residents paid an average of $144 per capita in state motor fuel sales taxes in 2004, an amount which ranked 14th nationally and was above the national average of $115.[82]

In 2004, sales taxes on alcoholic beverages made up 0.5% of Pennsylvania's total tax revenue.[83] Pennsylvania residents paid $17.86 per capita in state alcoholic beverage sales taxes in 2004, an amount which ranked 17th nationally.[84]

---

72. 72 P.A. STAT. ANN. § 4782.
73. *Id.* §§ 3244, 4821.
74. *Id.* §§ 4701 to 4754-6.
75. Government Finances, *supra* note 46.
76. 72 P.A. STAT. ANN. § 7202.
77. 16 P.A. STAT. ANN. § 6152.
78. 72 P.A. STAT. ANN. § 7204.
79. Government Finances, *supra* note 46.
80. *Id.*
81. 75 P.S. § 9004.
82. STATE RANKINGS 2006, *supra* note 1, at 327.
83. Government Finances, *supra* note 46.
84. STATE RANKINGS 2006, *supra* note 1, at 335.

The tobacco product sales tax makes up 2.3% of Pennsylvania's tax revenues and is imposed at a rate of $1.35 per pack of cigarettes.[85] Pennsylvania residents paid $79.17 per capita in state tobacco sales taxes in 2004, an amount which ranked 7th nationally.[86]

The remainder of Pennsylvania's selective sales taxes makes up 4.6% of its total tax revenue. Of this amount, 2.4% represents taxes on utilities and the other 2.2% represents taxes on other specific commodities, businesses, or services not reported separately above (e.g., on contractors, lodging, lubricating oil, fuels other than motor fuel, motor vehicles, meals, soft drinks, margarine, etc.).[87]

Corporate Income and Other

Corporate Income

The corporate income tax makes up 3.9% of Pennsylvania's total tax revenue.[88] Pennsylvania's broad-based corporate income tax is imposed at a flat rate of 9.99% on a corporation's taxable income,[89] which is based on the corporation's federal taxable income.[90]

Pennsylvania follows the federal income tax treatment of S corporations. Thus, they do not pay Pennsylvania's corporate income tax; rather, income and losses flow through to their shareholders.[91] A similar treatment is afforded to limited partnerships and limited liability partnerships, as well as limited liability companies, assuming they are treated as a partnership for federal tax purposes.[92] However, if a limited liability company is treated as a corporation for federal income tax purposes, the entity is subject to Pennsylvania's corporate income tax.[93]

Other

During fiscal year 2004, the collection of all other taxes not previously mentioned accounted for 5.5% of Pennsylvania's total tax revenue. Of this amount, approximately $708 million was generated by the estate and gift tax,[94] which is calculated on the basis of parameters established by statute.[95] The "other taxes" category is also made up of

---

85. 72 P.A. Stat. Ann. § 8208.

86. State Rankings 2006, *supra* note 1, at 332.

87. *See* Governments Division, U.S. Census Bureau, Government Finance and Employment Classification Manual, at ch.7 (2000), *available at* http://ftp2.census.gov/govs/class/classfull.pdf [hereinafter Classification Manual].

88. Government Finances, *supra* note 46.

89. 72 P.A. Stat. Ann. § 7402.

90. *Id.*

91. *Id.* § 7401.

92. *Id.*

93. *Id.*

94. Government Finances, *supra* note 46.

95. 72 P.A. Stat. Ann. § 9116 (4.5% for transfers to parent or grandparent or other lineal descendants; 12% for transfers to siblings; 15% for transfers to all other persons).

motor vehicle license taxes, documentary and stock transfer taxes, severance taxes, and all other taxes not listed separately or provided for in other categories, such as taxes on land based on a specified rate per acre (rather than on assessed value).[96]

Burden Analysis

The overall state and local tax burden on Pennsylvania taxpayers is extremely regressive. Taxpayers in the lowest quintile — those with incomes of less than $16,000 — bear a tax burden of 11.4% of their income, while taxpayers in the top 1% — those with incomes that exceed $301,000 — bear a tax burden of just 4.8% of their income.[97] It is also worth noting that, although Pennsylvania obviously has no control over federal tax policy, federal itemized deductions for state and local personal income and property taxes nonetheless further reduce the burden on taxpayers in the top 1% to 3.5%.[98] Furthermore, between 1989 and 2002, the tax burden on the bottom quintile rose by approximately 2.7%, while the burden on the top 1% rose only marginally by 0.1%.[99]

In terms of the income tax, the burden across income groups in Pennsylvania is almost flat, with taxpayers in the lowest quintile bearing a tax burden of 1.4% and those in the top 1% bearing a tax burden of 2.9%.[100] In contrast, however, the sales and excises taxes imposed by Pennsylvania are very regressive, with taxpayers in the lowest quintile bearing a tax burden of 6% and those in the top 1% bearing a tax burden of just 0.7%.[101]

---

96. *See* CLASSIFICATION MANUAL, *supra* note 87, at ch.7.

97. *See* ROBERT S. MCINTYRE ET AL., WHO PAYS? A DISTRIBUTIONAL ANALYSIS OF THE TAX SYSTEMS IN ALL 50 STATES 92 (2d ed. 2003), *available at* http://www.itepnet.org/wp2000/text.pdf. Taxpayers in the second quintile bear a 9.3% total tax burden on incomes between $16,000 and $28,000; those in the third quintile bear a 9.1% tax burden on incomes between $28,000 and $45,000; those in the fourth quintile bear a 8.7% tax burden on incomes between $45,000 and $71,000; those in the 80th–95th percentiles bear a 7.7% tax burden on incomes between $71,000 and $133,000; finally, those in the 96th–99th percentiles bear a 6.4% tax burden on incomes between $133,000 and $301,000. *Id.*

98. *Id.* Taxpayers in the lowest and second lowest quintiles were able to reduce their individual tax burdens by 0.1%, those in the third quintile by 0.3%, those in the fourth quintile by 0.5%, those in the 80th–95th percentiles by 1.1%, and those in the 96th–99th percentiles by 1.3%. *Id.*

99. *Id.* at 93.

100. *See id.* at 108. Taxpayers in the second quintile bear a 2.1% income tax burden; those in the third quintile bear a 2.4% burden; those in the fourth quintile bear a 2.6% burden; those in the 80th–95th percentiles bear a 2.7% burden; finally, those in the 96th–99th percentiles bear a 2.7% burden. *Id.* Note, however, that of the total income tax burden borne by the top 1% of taxpayers, 2.5% represents individual income taxes and 0.4% represents corporate income taxes. *Id.*

101. *See id.* Taxpayers in the second quintile bear a 4.7% sales-and-excise tax burden; those in the third quintile bear a 3.8 burden; those in the fourth quintile bear a 3.0% burden; those in the 80th–95th percentiles bear a 2.3% burden; finally, those in the 96th–99th percentiles bear a 1.5% burden. *Id.*

Property taxes in Pennsylvania are also regressive, with taxpayers in the lowest quintile bearing a tax burden of 4.0% and those in the top 1% bearing a tax burden of just 1.2%.[102]

---

102. *See id.* Taxpayers in the second quintile bear a 2.5% property tax burden; those in the third quintile bear a 2.9% burden; those in the fourth quintile bear a 3.0% burden; those in the 80th–95th percentiles bear a 2.8% burden; and those in the 96th–99th percentiles bear a 2.3% burden. *Id.*

Rhode Island

General Information

Basic Profile – Geography, Population, and Industry

Admitted to the Union in 1790, Rhode Island is commonly referred to as the "Ocean State."[1] It is located in the northeastern region and is bordered by Massachusetts on the north, the Atlantic Ocean on the southeast, and Connecticut on the west. The state is located in the eastern time zone, and its capital is Providence.[2]

Rhode Island ranks 50th in total area (1,545 square miles) and 43rd in population (approximately 1.08 million residents).[3] Its population is 88.9% white and 6.2% black.[4] Additionally, 10.7% of its population identify themselves as persons of Hispanic or Latino origin.[5] The state is 51% Catholic; 26% Protestant; and less than .5% Jewish; 23% claim a religion outside the Judeo-Christian tradition or no religion at all.[6] Rhode Island is entirely urban, with 100% of its population living in cities and towns.[7] Major industries include tourism, health services, and financial services.[8]

Family Income and Poverty Indicators

In 2004, Rhode Island's per capita gross product was $38,595, which was below the national average of $39,725.[9] During this same period, although the median household

---

1. STATE RANKINGS 2006, vi, 1 (Kathleen O'Leary Morgan & Scott Morgan eds., Morgan Quitno Press 2006).

2. *Id.* at vi.

3. *Id.* at 429.

4. Rhode Island Quick Facts from the U.S. Census Bureau, http://quickfacts.census.gov/qfd/states/44000.html (last visited Jan. 27, 2007). The remaining population is made up of 2.7% Asian persons; 0.6% American Indian and/or Alaska Native persons; 0.1% Native Hawaiian persons and other Pacific Islanders; and 1.5% persons reporting two or more races. *Id.*

5. *Id.* (noting that because Hispanics may be of any race, they are included within the other applicable race categories).

6. BARRY A. KOSMIN, EGON MAYER & ARIELA KEYSAR, AMERICAN RELIGIOUS IDENTIFICATION SURVEY 2001, at 41, *available at* http://www.gc.cuny.edu/faculty/research_studies/aris.pdf.

7. USDA Economic Research Service, Rhode Island Fact Sheet, http://www.ers.usda.gov/StateFacts/RI.htm (last visited Sept. 17, 2006).

8. Know Rhode Island, Rhode Island Office of the Secretary of State, http://www.sec.state.ri.us/library/riinfo/knowrhode/?searchterm=major%20industries (last visited Nov. 12, 2006).

9. STATE RANKINGS 2006, *supra* note 1, at 89.

income in Rhode Island was $46,199,[10] 11.3% of Rhode Island's population was living in poverty, which was below the national average of 12.4%.[11] More specifically, poverty affected 20.7% of Rhode Island's children,[12] 8.5% of its senior citizens,[13] and 10.4% of its families.[14] Of its female-headed households with children, 46.3% lived in poverty,[15] and 35.0% of the state's public elementary and secondary school students were eligible for free or reduced-price meals.[16] Of those living in poverty, approximately 10.4% were black, which represented 26.7% of Rhode Island's black population and 1.2% of its total population.[17] In an attempt to combat this poverty, Rhode Island spent approximately $1.7 billion on public welfare programs in 2002,[18] which made up 24.7% of its total government expenditures.[19]

Rhode Island's Public Elementary-Secondary School System

Overall Spending and Performance

For the 2003–2004 school year, Rhode Island spent $9,903 per pupil in its public elementary-secondary school system, which was slightly above the national average of $8,182.[20] Of this amount, 7.2% was provided by the federal government, 40.5% was provided by the state government, and 52.3% was provided by the local governments,[21] with property taxes making up 4.8% of the total funding.[22] Out of these funds, Rhode Island paid its elementary and secondary school teachers an estimated average annual salary of $53,473 during the 2004–2005 school year,[23] and it provided a student/teacher ratio of 13.4, which was better than the national average of 15.9.[24]

---

10. *Id.* at 96.

11. *Id.* at 495.

12. *Id.* at 497.

13. *Id.* at 496.

14. *Id.* at 498.

15. *Id.* at 499.

16. *Id.* at 532.

17. *See* Fact Sheet, American FactFinder, http://factfinder.census.gov/home/saff/main.html?_lang=en (select "Rhode Island" under "Get a Fact Sheet for your community") (last visited Feb. 16, 2007). Note that these numbers are based on the 2000 census because more recent numbers were not available.

18. STATE RANKINGS 2006, *supra* note 1, at 500.

19. *Id.* at 502.

20. GOVERNMENTS DIVISION, U.S. CENSUS BUREAU, PUBLIC EDUCATION FINANCES 2004, at 8 tbl.8 (2006).

21. *See id.* at 5 tbl.5.

22. *See id.* at 4 tbl.4.

23. THOMAS D. SNYDER ET AL., NATIONAL CENTER FOR EDUCATION STATISTICS, DIGEST OF EDUCATION STATISTICS 2005, at 116 tbl.77 (2006).

24. *Id.* at 98 tbl.65.

In academic performance, Rhode Island's fourth grade students scored lower than the national average in mathematics,[25] reading,[26] and science[27] and higher than the national average in writing,[28] while Rhode Island's eighth graders scored lower than the national average in mathematics,[29] science,[30] and writing[31] and higher than the national average in reading.[32]

Equity Issues

In 2004, the funding per student in Rhode Island's highest poverty districts exceeded that in its lowest poverty districts by $311.[33] When adjustments were made for the additional costs of educating students growing up in poverty, however, the funding in high poverty districts actually declined by $394.[34] On the other hand, Rhode Island spent $21 less per student in its highest minority districts, and this amount grew to $639 when adjustments for low-income students were made.[35]

Fourth graders eligible for free or reduced-price school lunches had test scores that were 10.3% lower in mathematics,[36] 13.6% lower in reading,[37] and 16.6% lower in writing[38] than those of students who were not eligible. The results were generally better for eighth graders eligible for free or reduced-price lunches; their test scores were 10.6% lower in mathematics,[39] 9.7% lower in reading,[40] and 15.5% lower in writing[41] than those of students who were not eligible.

---

25. NATIONAL CENTER FOR EDUCATION STATISTICS, U.S. DEPARTMENT OF EDUCATION, THE NATION'S REPORT CARD: MATHEMATICS 2005, at 14 fig.11 (2005), *available at* http://nces.ed.gov/ nationsreportcard/pdf/main2005/ 2006453.pdf [hereinafter MATHEMATICS 2005].

26. NATIONAL CENTER FOR EDUCATION STATISTICS, U.S. DEPARTMENT OF EDUCATION, THE NATION'S REPORT CARD: READING 2005, at 14 fig.11 (2005), *available at* http://nces.ed.gov/ nationsreportcard/pdf/main2005/2006451.pdf [hereinafter READING 2005].

27. NATIONAL CENTER FOR EDUCATION STATISTICS, U.S. DEPARTMENT OF EDUCATION, THE NATION'S REPORT CARD: SCIENCE 2005, at 16 fig.12 (2006), *available at* http://nces.ed.gov/ nationsreportcard//pdf/main2005/2006466.pdf [hereinafter SCIENCE 2005].

28. HILARY R. PERSKY ET AL., NATIONAL CENTER FOR EDUCATION STATISTICS, U.S. DEPARTMENT OF EDUCATION, THE NATION'S REPORT CARD: WRITING 2002, at 23 tbl.2.2 (2003), *available at* http://nces.ed.gov/nationsreportcard/pdf/main2002/2003529.pdf [hereinafter WRITING 2002].

29. MATHEMATICS 2005, *supra* note 25, at 16 fig.12.

30. SCIENCE 2005, *supra* note 27, at 28 fig.22.

31. WRITING 2002, *supra* note 28, at 24 tbl.2.3.

32. READING 2005, *supra* note 26, at 16 fig.12.

33. THE EDUCATION TRUST, FUNDING GAPS 2006, at 7 tbl.3 (2006), *available at* http://www2 .edtrust.org/NR/rdonlyres/CDEF9403-5A75-437E-93FF-EBF1174181FB/0/FundingGap2006.pdf.

34. *Id.*

35. *Id.* at 7 tbl.4.

36. MATHEMATICS 2005, *supra* note 25, at 20 tbl.5.

37. READING 2005, *supra* note 26, at 20 tbl.5.

38. WRITING 2002, *supra* note 28, at 75 tbl.3.24.

39. MATHEMATICS 2005, *supra* note 25, at 21 tbl.6.

40. READING 2005, *supra* note 26, at 21 tbl.6.

41. WRITING 2002, *supra* note 28, at 76 tbl.3.25.

In 1995, the Rhode Island Supreme Court upheld the state system of school finance in *City of Pawtucket v. Sundlun*.[42] Plaintiffs in this case sued for a declaratory judgment that the state's school funding system "violated the education, equal protection and due process clauses of the state constitution."[43] Although the trial court determined that the plaintiffs would prevail on all three claims, the Supreme Court reversed; however, it did recognize that "funding disparities existed and encouraged additional state funding for public education."[44] A cost study of the Rhode Island School Funding is currently being conducted by R. C. Wood of the University of Florida to evaluate Rhode Island's system.[45]

Availability of Publicly Funded Prekindergarten Programs

Rhode Island has no state-funded prekindergarten programs.[46] The federally funded Head Start program enrolls 1,808 children,[47] which represents 7.2% of Rhode Island's 24,982 three- and four-year-old children.[48]

Where Does Rhode Island Get Its Revenue?

At the end of fiscal year 2004, Rhode Island had total revenues of approximately $9.7 billion.[49] Of this amount, 43% was derived from state and local tax revenues and 22% was received from the federal government.[50] The remaining 35% came from other sources, including the Rhode Island Lottery, insurance trust revenue, and revenue from government-owned utilities and other commercial or auxiliary enterprises.[51]

Tax Revenue

Rhode Island collected approximately $4.2 billion in state and local tax revenue during fiscal year 2004.[52] As a result, Rhode Island residents paid $3,891 per capita in state

---

42. 662 A.2d 40 (R.I. 1995).

43. *Id.*

44. *Id.* at 61.

45. Litigation Update: Rhode Island, *available at* http://www.schoolfunding.info/news/policy/9-14-06CostingOut.php3 (last visited April 4, 2007).

46. W. STEVEN BARNETT ET AL., NATIONAL INSTITUTE FOR EARLY EDUCATION RESEARCH, THE STATE OF PRESCHOOL 2006, at 148 (2007), *available at* http://nieer.org/yearbook/pdf/yearbook.pdf.

47. *Id.* at 133.

48. *See id.* at 232.

49. U.S. Census Bureau, State and Local Government Finances 2003–04, http://www.census.gov/govs/www/estimate04.html (last visited Oct. 6, 2006) [hereinafter Government Finances].

50. *Id.*

51. *Id.*

52. The total tax revenues were collected as follows: $2.4 billion by the state and $1.8 billion by local governments. *Id.*

and local taxes, an amount which ranked 7th nationally.[53] The different types of tax sources were apportioned as follows:

Individual income taxes	21.4%
Property taxes	41.9%
General and selective sales taxes	31.2%
Corporate income and other taxes	5.5%
	100.0%[54]

Federal Funding

During fiscal year 2004, 22% of Rhode Island's total revenues came from the federal government.[55] For every dollar of federal taxes paid, Rhode Island received $1.02 in federal funding, an amount which ranked 31st nationally[56] and was below the national median of $1.17.[57]

Lottery

The Rhode Island Lottery has been in operation since 1974.[58] All proceeds from the Lottery are deposited into Rhode Island's general fund.[59] In 2005, the Rhode Island Lottery had a gross profit of $313 million and operating income of $306 million.[60]

Legal Structure of Major Tax Sources

Income

Rhode Island employs a broad-based income tax[61] that uses adjusted gross income for federal income tax purposes as a starting point for determining the state's taxable income.[62] However, a fairly large number of adjustments may be available to various individuals in calculating this amount.[63] Although Rhode Island has no statutes authorizing or prohibiting a local income tax, no locality has imposed a local income

---

53. *Id.*

54. *Id.*

55. *Id.*

56. The Tax Foundation, Federal Spending Received Per Dollar of Taxes Paid by State 2004, http://www.taxfoundation.org/taxdata/show/266.html (last visited Sept. 17, 2006).

57. *See id.*

58. The Lot About Us, http://www.rilot.com/about.asp#description (last visited Dec.18, 2006).

59. R.I. GEN. LAWS § 42-61-15.

60. Rhode Island Lottery Comprehensive Annual Financial Report for the Fiscal Year ended June 30, 2005, 9, *available at* http://www.rilot.com/docs/financial/CAFR_FYE_June05.pdf (last visited Dec. 13, 2006).

61. R.I. GEN. LAWS § 44-30-1.

62. *Id.* § 44-30-12.

63. *Id.* §§ 44-30-12, 44-30-25.

tax.[64] During fiscal year 2004, Rhode Island collected individual income tax of $833 per capita, an amount which ranked 15th nationally.[65]

Based on the relevant statutory exemptions and standard deductions, a typical family of four (i.e., married taxpayers who file jointly and have two dependent children) are not required to pay any income tax until their combined income exceeds $31,500, an amount which is well above the national poverty line of $20,615.[66]

For tax year 2002 and thereafter, Rhode Island personal income tax is imposed on Rhode Island taxable income at the rate of 25% of the federal income tax rates, including capital gains rates and any other special rates for other types of income that were in effect immediately before the enactment of the Economic Growth and Tax Relief Reconciliation Act of 2001.[67] Starting in 2006, taxpayers may elect to compute income tax liability using either the percentage of federal rate or an alternative flat tax rate.[68] The flat rate gradually decreases from 8% in 2006 to 5.5% in 2011.[69] When statutory exemptions and the standard deduction are taken into account, this flat rate applies to every dollar of income exceeding $21,750.[70]

Property

Overview

Rhode Island has a typical property tax system that taxes the value of real and personal property mostly at the local level. During fiscal year 2004, Rhode Island collected approximately $1.7 billion dollars in property tax at the local level and $1.5 million at the state level.[71] As a result, Rhode Island residents paid $1,629 per capita in state and local property taxes, an amount which ranked 5th nationally.[72]

---

64. CCH-EXP, RI-TAXRPTR ¶ 15-015, Local Power to Tax.

65. STATE RANKINGS 2006, *supra* note 1, at 321.

66. JASON A. LEVITIS, CENTER ON BUDGET AND POLICY PRIORITIES, THE IMPACT OF STATE INCOME TAXES ON LOW-INCOME FAMILIES IN 2006, AT 12 (2007). In 2006, Rhode Island taxpayers who were married and filing jointly could claim a standard deduction of $8,300, personal exemptions of $3,400 each, and dependent exemptions of $3,400 each. R.I. GEN. LAWS § 44-30-2.6, R.I. GEN. LAWS § 44-30-2. Note, however, that the threshold calculation of $31,500 is greater than the sum of these deductions and exemptions because it includes additional tax benefits available to low-income families, such as the earned-income tax credit. *See* LEVITIS, *supra.*

67. R.I. GEN. LAWS § 44-30-2.6.

68. *Id.* § 44-30-2.10.

69. *Id.* For 2006, the flat rate is 8%; for 2007, it is 7.5%; for 2008, it is 7%; for 2009, it is 6.5%; and for 2010, it is 6%. For 2011 and tax years thereafter, the flat rate is 5.5%.

70. The standard deduction and four exemptions of $8,150 and $3,400, respectively, equals $21,750. *See supra* notes 66–68.

71. Government Finances, *supra* note 49.

72. STATE RANKINGS 2006, *supra* note 1, at 294.

Defining the Real Property Tax Base

Rhode Island has five classifications for real property at the state and local levels: farm,[73] forest,[74] commercial, residential, and open space.[75] All real property is assessed at full and fair cash value,[76] except for farm, forest and open-space property, which is either assessed at a lower rate[77] or is exempt from tax altogether.[78] Full and fair cash value is generally determined by the application of standard appraisal methods, including the cost method, the income method, and the market-data method, all of which are commonly used throughout the country.[79] State law requires that all real property be assessed every three years.[80]

Real Property Tax Rates

The real property tax rates, composed of state, town, city, and selected levies, vary and are set by each locality. Taxes are levied in terms of dollars per $1,000 of taxable value and are collected locally.[81] In 2005, the tax rates per $1,000 of assessed value for residential real property ranged from $3.98 in New Shoreham to $30.23 in Providence.[82] In 2005, the tax rates per $1,000 of assessed value for commercial real property ranged from $3.98 in New Shoreham to $38.25 in Woonsocket.[83]

Personal and Intangible Property

Personal property is subject to taxation in Rhode Island unless specifically exempt.[84] All personal property is assessed at full and fair cash value.[85] Full and fair cash value is purchase price for personal property tax purposes.[86] State law requires that all personal property be assessed every nine years.[87] In 2005, the tax rates per $1,000 of assessed value for personal property ranged from $3.98 in New Shoreham to $60.65 in North Providence.[88]

---

73. R.I. Gen. Laws § 44-27-3. Note that several cities and towns in Rhode Island have been authorized by the legislature to establish specified property classifications for assessment purposes, which include residential and commercial classifications. *Id.* § 44-5-11.8.

74. *Id* .§ 44-27-4.

75. *Id.* § 44-27-5.

76. *Id.* § 44-5-12.

77. *Id.* § 44-27-2.

78. *Id.* § 44-3-8.

79. CCH-EXP, RI-TAXRPTR ¶ 20-615, Valuation Methods in General.

80. R.I. Gen. Laws § 44-27-2.

81. CCH-EXP, RI-TAXRPTR ¶ 20-010, Overview.

82. CCH-EXP, RI-TAXRPTR ¶ 20-405, Rates of Tax.

83. *Id.*

84. R.I. Gen. Laws § 44-3-1.

85. *Id.* § 44-5-12.

86. *Id.* § 44-5-12.1.

87. *Id.* § 44-27-2.

88. CCH-EXP, RI-TAXRPTR ¶ 20-405, Rates of Tax.

Exemptions

Some cities and towns have been authorized by Rhode Island to grant a homestead exemption equal to a percentage of the assessed value.[89] Out of the twelve localities authorized, seven have enacted a homestead credit. [90] The highest credit allowed is 45% of the value in Woonsocket.[91] Household goods[92] and intangible personal property are not subject to tax at either the state or local level.[93]

General and Selective Sales

General Sales

Rhode Island imposes a general retail sales-and-use tax, which makes up 19.1% of Rhode Island's total revenue.[94] This tax is imposed on retail sales or rentals of tangible personal property except for sales for resale, hotel and motel stays, and automobile rentals.[95] The state sales tax rate is set at 7%.[96] Major exemptions from Rhode Island sales tax include defined food for home consumption; food stamps purchases; drugs and medicines; certain enumerated farm and agricultural equipment, supplies, and livestock; the sale of tangible personal property to enumerated nonprofit corporations or organizations; and clothing and footwear.[97] Rhode Island has also authorized a 1% local tax on hotels[98] as well as meals and beverages sold at eating establishments.[99]

Selective Sales

Selective sales taxes make up 12.0% of Rhode Island's total tax revenue.[100] Of that amount, 3.2% comes from a motor fuel sales tax, which is imposed at a rate of $0.30 per gallon of gasoline.[101] Rhode Island residents paid an average of $124 per capita in state motor fuel sales taxes in 2004, an amount which ranked 29th nationally and was above the national average of $115.[102]

---

89. CCH-EXP, RI-TAXRPTR ¶ 20-205, Homestead.

90. http://www.muni-info.state.ri.us/documents/TaxRatesFY2007.pdf (last visited Feb. 12, 2007).

91. http://www.ci.woonsocket.ri.us/Woon%20FS%2004.pdf. (last visited Feb. 12, 2007).

92. R.I. Gen. Laws § 44-3-3.

93. *Id.* § 44-3-2.1.

94. Government Finances, *supra* note 49.

95. R.I. Gen. Laws § 44-18-7.

96. *Id.* § 44-18-18.

97. *Id.* § 44-18-30.

98. *Id.* § 44-18-36.1.

99. *Id.* § 44-18-18.1.

100. Government Finances, *supra* note 49.

101. R.I. Gen. Laws § 31-36-7.

102. State Rankings 2006, *supra* note 1, at 327.

In 2004, sales taxes on alcoholic beverages made up 0.3% of Rhode Island's total tax revenue.[103] Rhode Island residents paid $4.30 per capita in state alcoholic beverage sales taxes in 2004, an amount ranked 48th nationally.[104]

The tobacco product sales tax makes up 2.7%[105] of Rhode Island's total tax revenue. This tax is imposed at a rate of 40% of the wholesale price of all tobacco products,[106] except for cigarettes, which are taxed at 123 mills ($2.46) per pack of 20.[107] Rhode Island residents paid $106.96 per capita in state tobacco sales taxes in 2004, an amount which ranked 1st nationally.[108]

The remainder of Rhode Island's selective sales taxes makes up 5.9% of its total tax revenue. Of this amount, 2.1% represents taxes on utilities and the other 3.8% represents taxes on other specific commodities, businesses, or services not reported separately above (e.g., on contractors, lodging, lubricating oil, fuels other than motor fuel, motor vehicles, meals, soft drinks, margarine, etc.). [109]

Corporate Income and Other

Corporate Income

The corporate income tax makes up 1.7% of Rhode Island's total tax revenue.[110] This broad-based corporate income tax is imposed on the Rhode Island net income of corporations doing business within Rhode Island or receiving income from property in the state.[111] The tax is imposed at a flat rate of 9%,[112] but certain reductions are allowed for companies that create new employment opportunities within the state.[113]

Rhode Island follows the federal income tax treatment of S corporations; thus, they are not subject to Rhode Island's corporate income tax.[114] A similar treatment is afforded to limited partnerships, limited liability partnerships,[115] and limited liability companies, assuming they are treated as a partnership for federal tax purposes.[116] If, however, a limited liability company is treated as a corporation for federal income tax purposes, the entity is subject to Rhode Island's corporate income tax.[117]

---

103. Government Finances, *supra* note 49.

104. STATE RANKINGS 2006, *supra* note 1, at 335.

105. Government Finances, *supra* note 49.

106. R.I. GEN. LAWS § 44-20-13.2.

107. *Id.* § 44-20-12.

108. STATE RANKINGS 2006, *supra* note 1, at 332.

109. *See* GOVERNMENTS DIVISION, U.S. CENSUS BUREAU, GOVERNMENT FINANCE AND EMPLOYMENT CLASSIFICATION MANUAL, at ch.7 (2000), *available at* http://ftp2.census.gov/govs/class/classfull.pdf [hereinafter CLASSIFICATION MANUAL].

110. *Id.*

111. R.I. GEN. LAWS § 44-11-2.

112. *Id.*

113. *Id.* § 42-64.5-3.

114. *Id.* § 44-11-2.

115. *Id.* § 44-30-1.

116. *Id.* § 7-16-73.

117. *Id.*

Other

During fiscal year 2004, the collection of all other taxes not previously mentioned accounted for 3.9% of Rhode Island's total tax revenue.[118] Of this amount, $25 million[119] was generated by the estate tax, which is the federal credit for state estate taxes as of January 1, 2001, without incorporating reduction in the federal credit after that date.[120] The "other taxes" category is also made up of motor vehicle license taxes, documentary and stock transfer taxes, severance taxes, and all other taxes not listed separately or provided for in other categories, such as taxes on land based on a specified rate per acre (rather than on assessed value).[121]

Burden Analysis

The overall state and local tax burden on Rhode Island's taxpayers is very regressive. Taxpayers in the lowest quintile—those with incomes of less than $15,000—bear a tax burden of 13% of their income, while taxpayers in the top 1%—those with incomes that exceed $272,000—bear a tax burden of just 8.6% of their income.[122] It is also worth noting that, although Rhode Island obviously has no control over federal tax policy, federal itemized deductions for state and local personal income and property taxes nonetheless further reduce the burden on taxpayers in the top 1% to 6.0%.[123] Furthermore, between 1989 and 2002, the tax burden on the bottom quintile rose by approximately 1.2%, while the burden on the top 1% rose by only 0.3%.[124]

In terms of the income tax, the burden across income groups in Rhode Island is slightly progressive, with taxpayers in the lowest quintile bearing a tax burden of 0.5% and those in the top 1% bearing a tax burden of 5.8%.[125] In sharp contrast, however,

---

118. Government Finances, *supra* note 49.

119. *Id.*

120. R.I. GEN. LAWS § 44-22-1.1.

121. *See* CLASSIFICATION MANUAL, *supra* note 109, at ch.7.

122. *See* ROBERT S. MCINTYRE ET AL., WHO PAYS? A DISTRIBUTIONAL ANALYSIS OF THE TAX SYSTEMS IN ALL 50 STATES 94 (2d ed. 2003), *available at* http://www.itepnet.org/wp2000/text.pdf. Taxpayers in the second quintile bear a 10.8% total tax burden on incomes between $15,000 and $29,000; those in the third quintile bear a 10.7% tax burden on incomes between $29,000 and $47,000; those in the fourth quintile bear a 10.4% tax burden on incomes between $47,000 and $71,000; those in the 80th–95th percentiles bear a 10.2% tax burden on incomes between $71,000 and $144,000; finally, those in the 96th–99th percentiles bear a 9.0% tax burden on incomes between $144,000 and $272,000. *Id.*

123. *Id.* Taxpayers in the lowest quintile did not receive any benefit from these federal offsets, while those in the second quintile were able to reduce their individual tax burdens by 0.1%, those in the third quintile by 0.4%, those in the fourth quintile by 1.0%, those in the 80th–95th percentiles by 1.6%, and those in the 96th–99th percentiles by 1.8%. *Id.*

124. *Id.* at 95.

125. *See id.* at 94. Taxpayers in the second quintile bear a 1.5% income tax burden; those in the third quintile bear a 2.2% burden; those in the fourth quintile bear a 2.6% burden; those in the 80th–95th percentiles bear a 3.4% burden; and those in the 96th–99th percentiles bear a

the sales and excises taxes imposed by Rhode Island are extremely regressive, with tax-payers in the lowest quintile bearing a tax burden of 8.1% and those in the top 1% bearing a tax burden of just 0.8%.[126] Property taxes in Rhode Island are also regressive, with taxpayers in the lowest quintile bearing a tax burden of 4.4% and those in the top quintile bearing an average tax burden of 3.2%.[127]

4.2% burden. *Id.* Note, however, that these percentages include both individual and corporate income tax burdens; that within the within the 96th–99th percentiles. corporate income taxes represent 0.1% of this burden; and that in the top 1%, corporate income taxes represent 0.1% of this burden. *Id.*

126. *See id.* Taxpayers in the second quintile bear a 5.8% sales-and-excise tax burden; those in the third quintile bear a 4.5% burden; those in the fourth quintile bear a 3.4% burden; those in the 80th–95th percentiles bear a 2.6% burden; and those in the 96th–99th percentiles bear a 1.7% burden. *Id.*

127. *See id.* Taxpayers in the second quintile bear a 3.5% property tax burden; those in the third quintile bear a 4.1% burden; those in the fourth quintile bear a 4.4% burden; those in the 80th–95th percentiles bear a 4.3% burden; those in the 96th–99th percentiles bear a 3.2% burden; and those in the top 1% bear a 2.0% burden. *Id.*

South Carolina

General Information

Basic Profile – Geography, Population, and Industry

Admitted to the Union in 1788, South Carolina is commonly referred to as the "Palmetto State."[1] It is located in the southeast region and is bordered by North Carolina on the north, the Atlantic Ocean on the south and east, and Georgia on the south and west. The state located in the eastern time zone, and its capital is Columbia.[2]

South Carolina ranks 40th in total land and water area (approximately 32,000 square miles).[3] In 2005, South Carolina ranked 25th in population (approximately 4.3 million residents).[4] Its population is approximately 68.4% white and 29.2% black.[5] The state is approximately 7% Catholic; 80% Protestant (of which 54% are Baptist); and less than 0.5% Jewish; 13% claim a religion outside the Judeo-Christian tradition or no religion at all.[6] As of 2005, approximately 76% of South Carolina's population lived in urban areas.[7] Major industries include chicken farming, tobacco growing, and textile and chemical manufacturing.[8]

---

1. STATE RANKINGS 2006, vi, 1 (Kathleen O'Leary Morgan & Scott Morgan eds., Morgan Quitno Press 2006).

2. *Id.*

3. *Id.* at 225.

4. *Id.* at 429.

5. South Carolina Quick Facts from the U.S. Census Bureau, http://quickfacts.census.gov/qfd/states/45000.html (last visited Jan. 31, 2007). The remaining population is made up of 1.1% Asian persons, 0.4% American Indian and/or Alaska Native persons, 0.1% Native Hawaiian persons and other Pacific Islanders, and 0.8% persons reporting two or more races. *Id.* Additionally, 3.3% of South Carolina's total population identify themselves as persons of Hispanic or Latino origin. *Id.* (noting that because Hispanics may be of any race, they are included within the other applicable race categories).

6. BARRY A. KOSMIN, EGON MAYER & ARIELA KEYSAR, AMERICAN RELIGIOUS IDENTIFICATION SURVEY 2001, at 41, *available at* http://www.gc.cuny.edu/faculty/research_studies/aris.pdf (last visited Jan. 31, 2007).

7. USDA Economic Research Service, South Carolina Fact Sheet, http://www.ers.usda.gov/StateFacts/SC.htm (last visited Sept. 17, 2006). According to the latest estimates, approximately 3.3 million people live in urban areas, and approximately 1 million people live in rural areas. *Id.*

8. South Carolina, http://www.netstate.com/states/links/sc_links.htm (last visited Nov. 7, 2006).

Family Income and Poverty Indicators

In 2004, South Carolina's per capita gross product was $32,427, which ranked among the bottom ten states nationally and was below the national average of $39,725.[9] During this same period, while the median household income in South Carolina was $39,326,[10] 14.0% of South Carolina's population was living in poverty, which was somewhat above the national average of 12.4%.[11] More specifically, poverty affected 22.5% of South Carolina's children,[12] 13.3% of its senior citizens,[13] and 12.5% of its families.[14] Of its female-headed households with children, 42.3% lived in poverty,[15] and 51% of the state's public elementary and secondary school students were eligible for free or reduced-price meals.[16] Of those living in poverty, approximately 54% were black, which represented 25% of South Carolina's black population and 7% of its total population.[17] In an attempt to combat this poverty, South Carolina spent approximately $4.4 billion on public welfare programs in 2002,[18] which made up 18.4% of its total government expenditures.[19]

South Carolina's Public Elementary-Secondary School System

Overall Spending and Performance

For the 2003–2004 school year, South Carolina spent $7,184 per pupil in its public elementary-secondary school system, which was substantially below the national average of $8,182.[20] Of this amount, 10.4% was provided by the federal government, 46% was provided by the state government, and 43.6% was provided by the local governments,[21] with property taxes making up 34.4% of the total funding.[22] Out of these

---

9. STATE RANKINGS 2006, *supra* note 1, at 89.

10. *Id.* at 96.

11. *Id.* at 495.

12. *Id.* at 497.

13. *Id.* at 496.

14. *Id.* at 498.

15. *Id.* at 499.

16. *Id.* at 532.

17. *See* Fact Sheet, American FactFinder, http://factfinder.census.gov/home/saff/main.html?_lang=en (select "South Carolina" under "Get a Fact Sheet for your community") (last visited Feb. 22, 2007). Note that these numbers are based on the 2000 census because more recent numbers were not available.

18. STATE RANKINGS 2006, *supra* note 1, at 500.

19. *Id.* at 502.

20. GOVERNMENTS DIVISION, U.S. CENSUS BUREAU, PUBLIC EDUCATION FINANCES 2004, at 8 tbl.8 (2006).

21. *See id.* at 5 tbl.5.

22. *See id.* at 4 tbl.4.

funds, South Carolina paid its elementary and secondary school teachers an estimated average annual salary of $42,207 during the 2004–2005 school year,[23] and in 2003, it provided a student/teacher ratio of 15.3, which was slightly better than the national average of 15.9.[24]

In academic performance, South Carolina's fourth and eighth grade students scored lower than the national average in reading,[25] science,[26] and writing[27] but higher than the national average in mathematics.[28]

Equity Issues

In 2004, the funding per student in South Carolina's highest poverty districts exceeded that in its lowest poverty districts by $414,[29] although when adjustments were made for the additional costs of educating students growing up in poverty, that excess narrowed to $127.[30] Similarly, South Carolina spent $392 more per student in its highest minority districts, although this amount fell to $206 when adjustments for low-income students were made.[31]

Fourth graders eligible for free or reduced-price school lunches had test scores that were 9% lower in mathematics,[32] 12% lower in reading,[33] and 12% lower in writing[34] than those of students who were not eligible. The results were similar for eighth graders eligible for free or reduced price lunches; their test scores were 9% lower in mathe-

---

23. THOMAS D. SNYDER ET AL., NATIONAL CENTER FOR EDUCATION STATISTICS, DIGEST OF EDUCATION STATISTICS 2005, at 116 tbl.77 (2006).

24. *Id.* at 98 tbl.65.

25. NATIONAL CENTER FOR EDUCATION STATISTICS, U.S. DEPARTMENT OF EDUCATION, THE NATION'S REPORT CARD: READING 2005, at 14 fig.11, 16 fig.12 (2005), *available at* http://nces.ed.gov/nationsreportcard/pdf/main2005/2006451.pdf [hereinafter READING 2005].

26. NATIONAL CENTER FOR EDUCATION STATISTICS, U.S. DEPARTMENT OF EDUCATION, THE NATION'S REPORT CARD: SCIENCE 2005, at 16 fig.12, 28 fig.22 (2006), *available at* http://nces.ed.gov/nationsreportcard//pdf/main2005/2006466.pdf [hereinafter SCIENCE 2005].

27. HILARY R. PERSKY ET AL., NATIONAL CENTER FOR EDUCATION STATISTICS, U.S. DEPARTMENT OF EDUCATION, THE NATION'S REPORT CARD: WRITING 2002, at 23 tbl.2.2, 24 tbl.2.3 (2003), *available at* http://nces.ed.gov/nationsreportcard/pdf/main2002/2003529.pdf [hereinafter WRITING 2002].

28. NATIONAL CENTER FOR EDUCATION STATISTICS, U.S. DEPARTMENT OF EDUCATION, THE NATION'S REPORT CARD: MATHEMATICS 2005, at 14 fig.11, 16 fig.12 (2005), *available at* http://nces.ed.gov/nationsreportcard/pdf/ main2005/2006453.pdf [hereinafter MATHEMATICS 2005].

29. THE EDUCATION TRUST, FUNDING GAPS 2006, at 7 tbl.3 (2006), *available at* http://www2 .edtrust.org/NR/rdonlyres/CDEF9403-5A75-437E-93FF-EBF1174181FB/0/FundingGap2006.pdf.

30. *Id.*

31. *Id.* at 7 tbl.4.

32. MATHEMATICS 2005, *supra* note 28, at 20 tbl.5.

33. READING 2005, *supra* note 25, at 20 tbl.5.

34. WRITING 2002, *supra* note 27, at 75 tbl.3.24.

matics,[35] 8% lower in reading,[36] and 15% lower in writing[37] than those of students who were not eligible.

In November 1993, the public school students and citizens of forty less-wealthy school districts in South Carolina filed a declaratory judgment action against the state, alleging that South Carolina's school funding system resulted in an inadequate education and therefore violated Article XI, § 3 of the South Carolina constitution.[38] In *Abbeville County School District v. State*, the South Carolina Supreme Court held that the "South Carolina Constitution's education clause requires the General Assembly to provide the opportunity for each child to receive a minimally adequate education."[39] The court found that the plaintiffs did state a claim of "inadequate educational opportunity" and remanded the case back to the trial court for further proceedings.[40] On remand, the Court of Common Pleas of the Third Judicial Circuit of South Carolina concluded that the instructional facilities in the plaintiff's districts were "safe and adequate to provide the opportunity for a minimally adequate education"; however, the plaintiffs did not actually receive a minimally adequate education because of the lack of funding for "early childhood intervention programs designed to address the impact of poverty on their educational abilities and achievements."[41]

Availability of Publicly Funded Prekindergarten Programs

The South Carolina Half-Day Child Development Program is available to four-year-olds who are subject to certain state-specified risk factors; however, the program is not available to three-year-olds.[42] Total enrollment in this state-funded program is 20,117,[43] which represents just 18% of South Carolina's 113,043 three- and four-year-old children.[44] The federally funded Head Start program enrolls an additional 11,723 children,[45] which represents 10% of South Carolina's three- and four-year-old children.[46]

---

35. MATHEMATICS 2005, *supra* note 28, at 21 tbl.6.

36. READING 2005, *supra* note 25, at 21 tbl.6.

37. WRITING 2002, *supra* note 27, at 76 tbl.3.25.

38. Abbeville County Sch. Dist. v. State, 335 S.C. 58, 515 S.E.2d 535 (S.C. 1999).

39. *Id.* at 540. The South Carolina Supreme Court stated that a minimally adequate education required the state to provide students with the "opportunity to acquire: 1) the ability to read, write, and speak the English language, and knowledge of mathematics and physical science; 2) a fundamental knowledge of economic, social, and political systems, and of history and governmental processes; and 3) academic and vocational skills." *Id.*

40. *Id.* at 541.

41. Abbeville County Sch. Dist. v. State, Case No. 93-CP-31-0169, Order at 161-62 (Ct. Common Pleas, 3rd Judicial Cir., Dec. 29. 2005) *available at* http://www.schoolfunding.info/states/sc/Abbeville%20Trial%20Court%20Order%2012-29-05.pdf.

42. W. STEVEN BARNETT ET AL., NATIONAL INSTITUTE FOR EARLY EDUCATION RESEARCH, THE STATE OF PRESCHOOL 2006, at 134 (2006), *available at* http://nieer.org/yearbook/pdf/yearbook.pdf.

43. *Id.* at 135.

44. *See id.* at 232.

45. *Id.* at 135.

46. *See id.* at 232.

Where Does South Carolina Get Its Revenue?

At the end of fiscal year 2004, South Carolina had total revenues of approximately $30.5 billion.[47] Of this amount, 37% was derived from state and local tax revenues and 20% was received from the federal government.[48] The remaining 43% came from other sources, including the South Carolina Education Lottery, insurance trust revenue, and revenue from government-owned utilities and other commercial or auxiliary enterprises.

Tax Revenue

South Carolina collected approximately $11.2 billion in state and local tax revenue during fiscal year 2004.[49] As a result, South Carolina residents paid $2,662 per capita in state and local taxes, an amount which ranked 44th nationally.[50] The different types of tax sources were approximately apportioned as follows:

Individual income taxes	21.8%
Property taxes	33.1%
General and selective sales taxes	35.9%
Corporate income and other taxes	9.2%
	100.0%[51]

Federal Funding

During fiscal year 2004, 20% of South Carolina's total revenues came from the federal government.[52] For every dollar of federal taxes paid, South Carolina received $1.38 in federal funding, an amount which ranked 17th nationally[53] and was far above the national average of $1.17.[54]

Lottery Revenue

The South Carolina Education Lottery was established in 2000 after the citizens of South Carolina voted to amend the constitution to allow for a state-run lottery.[55] The

---

47. U.S. Census Bureau, State and Local Government Finances 2003–04, http://www.census.gov/govs/www/estimate04.html (last visited Oct. 16, 2006) [hereinafter Government Finances].

48. *Id.*

49. *Id.* The total tax revenues were collected as follows: $6.8 billion by the state and $4.4 billion by local governments. *Id.*

50. *Id.*

51. *Id.*

52. *Id.*

53. The Tax Foundation, Federal Spending Received Per Dollar of Taxes Paid by State, 2004 http://www.taxfoundation.org/taxdata/show/266.html (last visited Sept. 17, 2006).

54. *See id.*

55. Official Home of the South Carolina Lottery, Overview, http://www.sceducationlottery.com/educationwins/educationwins.aspx (last visited Dec. 7, 2006).

Lottery has been in operation since 2002.[56] Under South Carolina's constitution, all South Carolina Education Lottery proceeds are to be used only for educational purposes as the General Assembly provides by law.[57] During fiscal year 2005, the Lottery had total revenues of approximately $960 million and net proceeds transferred to the education lottery account of approximately $280 million.[58]

Legal Structures of Major Tax Sources

Income

South Carolina employs a broad-based income tax that uses adjusted gross income for federal income tax purposes as a starting point for determining the state's taxable income.[59] However, a fairly large number of adjustments may be available to various individuals in calculating this amount.[60] During fiscal year 2004, South Carolina collected individual income tax of $581 per person, and amount which ranked 35th nationally.[61]

In South Carolina, a typical family of four (i.e., married taxpayers who file jointly and have two dependent children) are not required to pay any income tax until their combined exceeds $26,800, an amount which is well above the national poverty line of $20,615.[62] South Carolina's income tax structure contains six tax brackets that impose a minimum marginal rate of 2.5% and a maximum marginal rate of 7%.[63] When statu-

---

56. *Id.*

57. S.C. CONST. ANN. art. XVII, § 7. "Proceeds of lottery games must be used to support improvements and enhancements for educational purposes and programs as provided by the General Assembly and that the net proceeds must be used to supplement, not supplant, existing resources for educational purposes and programs." Official Home of the South Carolina Lottery, *supra* note 55.

58. Official Home of the South Carolina Lottery, South Carolina Education Lottery 2005 Annual Financial Report, http://www.sceducationlottery.com/lottery/annual_reports.aspx (last visited Dec. 7, 2006).

59. S.C. CODE ANN. § 12-6-40. "All elections made for federal income tax purposes in connection with Internal Revenue Code sections adopted by this State automatically apply for South Carolina income tax purposes unless otherwise provided." *Id.*

60. *See* S.C. CODE ANN. § 12-6-1110 to -1140.

61. STATE RANKINGS 2006, *supra* note 1, at 321.

62. JASON A. LEVITIS, CENTER ON BUDGET AND POLICY PRIORITIES, THE IMPACT OF STATE INCOME TAXES ON LOW-INCOME FAMILIES IN 2006, at 12 (2007), *available at* http://www.cbpp.org/2-22-06sfp.pdf. Since the starting point for determining South Carolina's taxable income is adjusted gross income for federal income tax purposes, it can be inferred that South Carolina taxpayers are allowed the federal standard deduction and personal and dependent exemptions, which, for 2006, were $10,300 and $3,300, respectively, for married taxpayers filing jointly. 26 C.F.R. § 601.602 (2005). Note, however, that the threshold calculation of $26,800 is greater than the sum of these deductions and exemptions because it includes additional tax benefits available to low-income families, such as the earned-income tax credit. *See* LEVITIS, *supra*.

63. S.C. CODE ANN. § 12-6-510. South Carolina's middle four tax brackets are 3%, 4%, 5% and 6%. *Id.*

tory exemptions and the standard deduction are taken into account, the maximum marginal rate applies to every dollar of income exceeding $36,350.[64]

Property

Overview

South Carolina has a typical property tax system that taxes the value of real estate and personal property almost entirely at the local level.[65] During fiscal year 2004, South Carolina collected approximately $3.69 billion dollars in property taxes at the local level and approximately $11 million at the state level.[66] As a result, South Carolina residents paid $882 per capita in state and local property taxes, an amount which ranked 33rd nationally.[67]

Defining the Real Property Tax Base

The South Carolina constitution requires that all real property be assessed in an equal and uniform manner in one of the following classifications: 1) Primary Residences, 2) Agricultural Property (privately owned), 3) Agricultural Property (corporate owned), 4) Manufacturing, Utility or Mining Property, 5) Transportation Company Property, and 6) Other Real Estate.[68] Both Agricultural Property classifications are valued at their current use value, while the remaining classifications are valued at their fair market value.[69] The aforementioned classifications are assessed at the following rates: 1) Primary Residences – 4% of fair market value, 2) Agricultural Property (privately owned) – 4% of use value, 3) Agricultural Property (corporate owned) – 6% of use value, 4) Manufacturing, Utility or Mining Property – 10.5% of fair market value, 5) Transportation Company Property – 9.5% of fair market value, and 6) Other Real Estate – 6% of fair market value.[70] In general, counties are required to reappraise property values once every five years.[71]

Real Property Tax Rates

The tax rates imposed on real property vary and are set by each taxing authority (county, township, school district, or special district). The millage rate for each taxing authority is determined by the amount of tax revenue needed to meet the general op-

---

64. The standard deduction and exemptions of $10,300 and $13,200, respectively, plus the threshold of taxable income for the highest tax bracket of $12,850, equals $36,350. *See supra* note 62.

65. S.C. CODE ANN. § 12-37-210.

66. Government Finances, *supra* note 47.

67. *See id.*

68. S.C. CONST. ANN. art. X, § 1.

69. *Id.* Fair market value is determined utilizing the income, cost, or sales-comparison approach. South Carolina Department of Revenue, Homeowner's Guide to Property Taxes in South Carolina, http://www.sctax.org/publications/propguid99.html (last visited Jan. 17, 2007).

70. S.C. CONST. ANN. art. X, § 1.

71. S.C. CODE ANN. § 12-43-217.

erating purposes of that taxing authority[72] in addition to any school district taxes approved by the voters of that school district.[73] In 2004, the tax rates per $1,000 of assessed value ranged from $184.80 in Bluffton to $713.60 in Simpsonville.[74]

Personal and Intangible Property

Personal property is subject to local taxation unless specifically exempt,[75] and, like real property, the tax rates imposed vary among jurisdictions. Personal property is defined as "all things, other than real estate, which have any pecuniary value."[76] Intangible personal property is not subject to tax at either the state or local level since it is specifically exempt from taxation.[77] Categories of taxable personal property include inventories of business establishments, farm machinery and equipment, and personal motor vehicles.[78] All other personal property not included in one of the previously mentioned categories is considered other personal property and is assessed at 10.5% of its fair market value.[79]

Exemptions

Household goods and furniture, wearing apparel, livestock, and all inventories are exempt from property taxes.[80] Also exempt is the first $50,000 of the fair market value of the dwelling places of all persons aged 65 and older or persons totally and permanently disabled or legally blind.[81] All other taxpayers are allowed a $100,000 exemption from property taxes levied for school operations on a qualified legal residence.[82]

General and Selective Sales

General Sales

South Carolina imposes a general retail sales-and-use tax, which makes up 25.4% of its total tax revenue.[83] This tax is imposed on the gross proceeds from the sale of tangi-

---

72. S.C. CODE ANN. § 6-1-320.

73. *Id.* § 59-73-30.

74. CCH-EXP, PROP-TAX-GUIDE SC ¶ 400-350, Property Tax Rates by County, Property – Rate of tax – Rates in Cities – 2004 rates., January 2004.

75. S.C. CODE ANN. § 12-37-210.

76. *Id.* § 12-37-10. Personal property also includes "moneys, credits, investments in bonds, stocks, joint-stock companies or otherwise." *Id.*

77. *Id.* § 12-37-220.

78. S.C. CONST. ANN. art. X, § 1. These categories are assessed at the following percentages of their respective fair market values: inventories of business establishments at 6%; farm machinery and equipment at 5%; personal motor vehicles at between 9.75% and 6.00%, depending on the age of the vehicle. *Id.*

79. *Id.*

80. S.C. CODE ANN. § 12-37-220.

81. *Id.* § 12-37-250.

82. *Id.* § 12-37-251.

83. Government Finances, *supra* note 47.

ble personal property and on certain services.[84] These services include laundry services and electricity and communication services.[85] The state sales tax rate is 5%,[86] and all counties may impose an additional tax of 1% each for general property tax relief,[87] transportation facilities,[88] capital projects,[89] and school districts. The total sales tax rate imposed by the state and each county generally ranges from 5% to as high as 7% in certain counties.[90] However, unprepared food that may be purchased with food stamps is taxed at 3%,[91] and accommodations for transients (i.e., hotel and motel rooms and campground spaces) are taxed at 7% (5% state tax and 2% local tax).[92] Exemptions from South Carolina's sales-and-use tax include, among other items, prescription drugs, food purchased with food stamps, school lunches, and feed for poultry and livestock.[93]

Selective Sales

Selective sales taxes make up 10.5% of South Carolina's total revenue.[94] Of that amount, 4.4%[95] comes from a motor fuel sales tax that is imposed at a rate of $0.16 per gallon of gasoline.[96] South Carolina residents paid an average of $117 per capita in state motor fuel sales taxes in 2004, an amount which ranked 35th nationally and was just above the national average of $115.[97]

In 2004, sales taxes on alcoholic beverages made up 1.3% of South Carolina's total tax revenue.[98] South Carolina residents paid $34.94 per capita in state alcoholic beverage sales taxes in 2004, an amount which ranked 2nd nationally.[99]

The tobacco product sales tax makes up 0.3%[100] of South Carolina's tax revenues and is imposed at a rate of $0.7 per pack of cigarettes.[101]

The remainder of South Carolina's selective sales taxes makes up 4.5% of its total tax revenue.[102] Of this amount, 1.1% represents taxes on utilities and the other 3.4% represents taxes on other specific commodities, businesses, or services not reported

---

84. S.C. CODE ANN. § 12-36-910.

85. *Id.*

86. *Id.* On June 1, 2007, the state sales tax will increase by 1% on the sale of all items other than accommodations, items subject to a maximum sales tax, and the sale of unprepared food which may be purchased with food stamps. S.C. CODE ANN. § 12-36-1110.

87. *Id.* § 4-10-20.

88. *Id.* § 4-37-30.

89. *Id.* § 4-10-300.

90. CCH-EXP, SALES-TAX-GUIDE SC ¶ 61-735, Local Rates.

91. S.C. CODE ANN. § 12-36-910.

92. *Id.* § 12-36-920.

93. *Id.* § 12-36-2120.

94. Government Finances, *supra* note 47.

95. *Id.*

96. S.C. CODE ANN. § 12-28-310.

97. STATE RANKINGS 2006, *supra* note 1, at 327.

98. Government Finances, *supra* note 47.

99. STATE RANKINGS 2006, *supra* note 1, at 335.

100. Government Finances, *supra* note 47.

101. STATE RANKINGS 2006, *supra* note 1, at 333.

102. Government Finances, *supra* note 47.

separately above (e.g., on contractors, lodging, lubricating oil, fuels other than motor fuel, motor vehicles, meals, soft drinks, margarine, etc.).[103]

Corporate Income and Other

Corporate Income

The corporate income tax makes up 1.8% of South Carolina's total tax revenue.[104] South Carolina's broad-based corporate income tax is imposed at a rate of 5% on a corporation's South Carolina taxable income,[105] which is based on the corporation's federal taxable income.[106]

South Carolina follows the federal income tax treatment of S corporations. Thus, they do not pay South Carolina's corporate income tax; rather, income and losses flow through to their shareholders.[107] A similar treatment is afforded to all entities treated as partnerships, including limited partnerships, limited liability partnerships, as well as limited liability companies.[108]

Other

During fiscal year 2004, the collection of all other taxes not previously mentioned accounted for 7.4% of South Carolina's total tax revenue.[109] Of this amount, approximately $33 million was generated by the estate and gift tax,[110] which is calculated on the basis of the federal credit for state death taxes allowable by § 2011 of the Internal Revenue Code.[111] The "other taxes" category is also made up of motor vehicle license taxes, documentary and stock transfer taxes, severance taxes, and all other taxes not listed separately or provided for in other categories, such as taxes on land based on a specified rate per acre (rather than on assessed value).[112]

Burden Analysis

The overall state and local tax burden on South Carolina's taxpayers is somewhat regressive. Taxpayers in the lowest quintile — those with incomes of less than $13,000 —

---

103. *See* Governments Division, U.S. Census Bureau, Government Finance And Employment Classification Manual, at ch. 7 (2000), *available at* http://ftp2.census.gov/govs/class/classfull.pdf [hereinafter Classification Manual].

104. Government Finances, *supra* note 47.

105. S.C. Code Ann. § 12-6-530.

106. *Id.* § 12-6-580.

107. *Id.* § 12-6-590.

108. *Id.* § 12-6-600.

109. Government Finances, *supra* note 47.

110. *Id.*

111. S.C. Code Ann. § 12-16-510. Please note, however, that the federal credit for state death taxes was phased out for all deaths occurring after December 31, 2004; thus, South Carolina does not currently have an estate tax.

112. *See* Classification Manual, *supra* note 103, at ch. 7.

bear a tax burden of 7.9% of their income, while taxpayers in the top 1%—those with incomes that exceed $232,000—bear a tax burden of just 7.7% of their income.[113] It is also worth noting that, although South Carolina obviously has no control over federal tax policy, federal itemized deductions for state and local personal income and property taxes nonetheless further reduce the burden on taxpayers in the top 1% to 5.5%.[114] Furthermore, between 1989 and 2002, the tax burden on the bottom quintile fell by approximately 0.1%, while the burden on the top 1% fell by approximately 0.7%.[115]

In terms of the income tax, the burden across income groups in South Carolina is slightly progressive, with taxpayers in the lowest quintile bearing a tax burden of 0.3% and those in the top 1% bearing a tax burden of 5.2%.[116] In sharp contrast, however, the sales and excise taxes imposed by South Carolina are very regressive, with taxpayers in the lowest quintile bearing a tax burden of 5.5% and those in the top 1% bearing a tax burden of just 0.9%.[117] Property taxes in South Carolina are also regressive, with taxpayers in the lowest quintile bearing a tax burden of 2.1% and those in the top quintile bearing an average tax burden of 1.9%.[118]

---

113. *See* ROBERT S. MCINTYRE ET AL., WHO PAYS? A DISTRIBUTIONAL ANALYSIS OF THE TAX SYSTEMS IN ALL 50 STATES 96 (2d ed. 2003), *available at* http://www.itepnet.org/wp2000/text.pdf. Taxpayers in the second quintile bear a 8.3% total tax burden on incomes between $13,000 and $22,000; those in the third quintile bear a 9.0% tax burden on incomes between $22,000 and $35,000; those in the fourth quintile bear a 8.7% tax burden on incomes between $35,000 and $59,000; those in the 80th–95th percentiles bear a 8.8% tax burden on incomes between $59,000 and $110,000; finally, those in the 96th–99th percentiles bear a 8.4% tax burden on incomes between $110,000 and $232,000. *Id.*

114. *Id.* Taxpayers in the lowest two quintiles did not receive any benefit from these federal offsets, while those in the third quintile were able to reduce their individual tax burdens by 0.2%, those in the fourth quintile by 0.3%, those in the 80th–95th percentiles by 1.2%, and those in the 96th–99th percentiles by 1.7%. *Id.*

115. *Id.* at 97. Interestingly, during the same period, the tax burden for the third quintile increased by approximately 0.7%. *Id.*

116. *See Id.* at 96. Taxpayers in the second quintile bear a 1.3% income tax burden; those in the third quintile bear a 2.5% burden; those in the fourth quintile bear a 3.2% burden; those in the 80th–95th percentiles bear a 4.1% burden; finally, those in the 96th–99th percentiles bear a 4.7% burden. *Id.* Note, however, that these percentages include both individual and corporate income tax burdens and that within the top 1%, corporate income taxes represent 0.1% of the income tax burden. *Id.*

117. *See id.* at 96. Taxpayers in the second quintile bear a 5.1% sales-and-excise tax burden; those in the third quintile bear a 4.3% burden; those in the fourth quintile bear a 3.6% burden; those in the 80th–95th percentiles bear a 2.7% burden; finally, those in the 96th–99th percentiles bear a 1.8% burden. *Id.*

118. *See id.* Taxpayers in the second quintile bear a 1.9% property tax burden; those in the third quintile bear a 2.2% burden; those in the fourth quintile bear a 1.9% burden; those in the 80th–95th percentiles bear a 2.0% burden; those in the 96th–99th percentiles bear a 2.0% burden; finally, those in the top 1% bear a 1.6% burden. *Id.*

South Dakota

General Information

Basic Profile – Geography, Population, and Industry

Admitted to the Union in 1889,[1] South Dakota is known as the "Mount Rushmore State."[2] South Dakota is located in the Midwest and is bordered by North Dakota on the north, Iowa and Minnesota on the east, Nebraska on the south, and Wyoming and Montana on the west.[3] The eastern half of the state is located in the central time zone, and the western half is located in the mountain time zone.[4] Pierre is the state capital.[5]

In 2005, South Dakota ranked 46th in population (775,933 residents);[6] it ranks 17th in total area (77,117 square miles).[7] Its population is 88.5% white, 8.8% Native American and Alaska Native, and 0.8% black.[8] The state is 25% Catholic; 62% Protestant; and less than 0.5% Jewish; 13% claim a religion outside the Judeo-Christian tradition or no religion at all.[9] South Dakota's population is fairly split, with 43.8% living in cities and towns and 56.2% in rural areas.[10] Major industries include agriculture, manufacturing, and financial services.[11]

---

1. STATE RANKINGS 2006, 1 (17th ed., Kathleen O'Leary Morgan & Scott Morgan, eds. Morgan Quitno Press, 2006).

2. *Id.* at vi.

3. *Id.*

4. Map Maker - Nationalatlas.gov, http://www.nationalatlas.gov/natlas/Natlasstart.asp (last visited January 28, 2007).

5. STATE RANKINGS 2006, *supra* note 1, at vi.

6. *Id.* at 429.

7. *Id.* at 225.

8. South Dakota QuickFacts from the U.S. Census Bureau, http://quickfacts.census.gov/qfd/states/46000.html (last visited January 29, 2007). The remaining population is made up of 0.7% Asian persons and 1.2% persons reporting two or more races. *Id.* Additionally, persons of Hispanic or Latino origin make up 2.1% of the population. *Id.* (noting that because Hispanics may be of any race, they are included within the other applicable race categories).

9. BARRY A. KOSMIN, EGON MAYER & ARIELA KEYSAR, AMERICAN RELIGIOUS IDENTIFICATION SURVEY 2001, at 39, *available at* http://www.gc.cuny.edu/faculty/research_studies/aris.pdf. In South Dakota, Lutherans make up 27% of the population. They are included in the Protestant category. The all-other-religions category includes other religions not specifically stated as well as those persons who claim no religion and those persons who refused to participate in the survey.

10. USDA Economic Research Service, South Dakota Fact Sheet, http://www.ers.usda.gov/StateFacts/SD.htm (last visited Sept. 17, 2006).

11. South Dakota Governor's Office of Economic Development, South Dakota Profile: At a

Family Income and Poverty Indicators

In 2004, South Dakota's per capita gross product was $38,133, which was below the national average of $39,725.[12] During this same period, although the median household income in South Dakota was $40,518,[13] 12.5% of South Dakota's population was living in poverty, which was just above the national poverty rate of 12.4%.[14] More specifically, poverty affected 14.5% of South Dakota's children,[15] 8.6% of its senior citizens,[16] and 8.4% of its families.[17] Of it female-headed households with children, 38.7% of them lived in poverty, [18] and 31.4% of the state's public elementary and secondary school students were eligible for free or reduced-price meals.[19] Of those living in poverty, approximately 0.9% were black, which represented 19.2% of South Dakota's black population and 0.1% of its total population.[20] In an attempt to combat this poverty, South Dakota spent approximately $604.8 million on public welfare programs in 2002,[21] which made up 15.6% of its total government expenditures.[22]

South Dakota's Public Elementary-Secondary School System

Overall Spending and Performance

For the 2003–2004 school year, South Dakota spent $6,949 per pupil in its public elementary-secondary school system, which was substantially below the national average of $8,182.[23] Of this amount, 15.6% was provided by the federal government, 34.2% was provided by the state government, and 50.3% was provided by the local governments,[24] with property taxes making up 42.6% of the total funding.[25] Out of these

---

Glance Overview, http://www.sdreadytowork.com/facts/demostats/sdprofile/ataglance.asp (October 21, 2006).

12. State Rankings, *supra* note 1, at 89.

13. *Id.* at 96.

14. *Id.* at 495.

15. *Id.* at 497.

16. *Id.* at 496.

17. *Id.* at 498.

18. *Id.* at 499.

19. *Id.* at 532.

20. *See* Fact Sheet, American FactFinder, http://factfinder.census.gov/home/saff/main.html?_lang=en (select South Dakota under "Get a Fact Sheet for your community") (last visited Feb. 16, 2007). Note that these numbers are based on the 2000 census because more recent numbers where not available.

21. *Id.* at 500.

22. *Id.* at 502.

23. GOVERNMENTS DIVISION, U.S. CENSUS BUREAU, PUBLIC EDUCATION FINANCES 2004, at 8 tbl.8 (2006).

24. *See id.* at 5 tbl.5.

25. *See id.* at 4 tbl.4.

funds, South Dakota paid its elementary and secondary school teachers an estimated average annual salary of $34,040 during the 2004–2005 school year,[26] and it provided a student/teacher ratio of 13.6, which was better than the national average of 15.9.[27]

In academic performance, South Dakota's fourth grade students scored higher than the national average in mathematics,[28] reading,[29] and science,[30] and South Dakota's eighth graders scored higher than the national average in mathematics,[31] reading,[32] and science.[33]

Equity Issues

In 2004, revenues spent per student in South Dakota's highest poverty districts were determined to be $147 less than the revenues spent in its lowest poverty districts.[34] When adjustments were made for the additional costs of educating students growing up in poverty, however, the funding gap grew to $438.[35] Similarly, South Dakota spent $962 less per student in its highest minority districts, and this amount grew to $1,140 when adjustments for low-income students were made.[36]

Fourth graders eligible for free or reduced-price school lunches had test scores that were 6.8% lower in mathematics[37] and 9.1% lower in reading[38] than those of students who were not eligible. The results were generally better for eighth graders eligible for free or reduced-price lunches; their test scores were 6.1% lower in mathematics[39] and 5.5% lower in reading[40] than those of students who were not eligible.

---

26. THOMAS D. SNYDER ET AL., NATIONAL CENTER FOR EDUCATION STATISTICS, DIGEST OF EDUCATION STATISTICS 2005, at 116 tbl.77 (2006).

27. *Id.* at 98 tbl.65.

28. NATIONAL CENTER FOR EDUCATION STATISTICS, U.S. DEPARTMENT OF EDUCATION, THE NATION'S REPORT CARD: MATHEMATICS 2005, at 14 fig.11 (2005), *available at* http://nces.ed.gov/nationsreportcard/pdf/main2005/ 2006453.pdf [hereinafter MATHEMATICS 2005].

29. NATIONAL CENTER FOR EDUCATION STATISTICS, U.S. DEPARTMENT OF EDUCATION, THE NATION'S REPORT CARD: READING 2005, at 14 fig.11 (2005), *available at* http://nces.ed.gov/nationsreportcard/pdf/main2005/2006451.pdf [hereinafter READING 2005].

30. NATIONAL CENTER FOR EDUCATION STATISTICS, U.S. DEPARTMENT OF EDUCATION, THE NATION'S REPORT CARD: SCIENCE 2005, at 16 fig.12 (2006) *available at* http://nces.ed.gov/nationsreportcard//pdf/main2005/2006466.pdf [hereinafter SCIENCE 2005].

31. MATHEMATICS 2005, *supra* note 28, at 16 fig.12.

32. READING 2005, *supra* note 29, at 16 fig.12.

33. SCIENCE 2005, *supra* note 30, at 28 fig.22.

34. THE EDUCATION TRUST, FUNDING GAPS 2006, at 7 tbl.3 (2006), *available at* http://www2.edtrust.org/NR/rdonlyres/CDEF9403-5A75-437E-93FF-EBF1174181FB/0/FundingGap2006.pdf.

35. *Id.*

36. *Id.* at 7 tbl.4.

37. MATHEMATICS 2005, *supra* note 28, at 20 tbl.5.

38. READING 2005, *supra* note 29, at 20 tbl.5.

39. MATHEMATICS 2005, *supra* note 28, at 21 tbl.6.

40. READING 2005, *supra* note 29, at 21 tbl.6.

In the unpublished 1994 opinion *Bezdicheck v. State*,[41] a South Dakota circuit court held that the South Dakota education finance system was constitutional because the state constitution merely requires an "adequate education" as opposed to equal levels of per-pupil spending.[42] The case *South Dakota Coalition of Schools v. State*,[43] in which the plaintiffs are challenging the adequacy of education provided to students of the state and the education funding system used to provide students with an adequate education, is currently pending in a South Dakota circuit court.[44]

Availability of Publicly Funded Prekindergarten Programs

South Dakota does not have any type of preschool program, but the federally funded Head Start program enrolls 3,399 children,[45] which represents 17.0% of South Dakota's 20,050 three- and four-year-old children.[46]

Where Does South Dakota Get Its Revenue?

At the end of fiscal year 2004, South Dakota had total revenues of approximately $5.6 billion.[47] Of this amount, 36% was derived from state and local tax revenues and 24% was received from the federal government.[48] The remaining 40% came from other sources, including the South Dakota Lottery, insurance trust revenue, and revenue from government-owned utilities and other commercial or auxiliary enterprises.[49]

Tax Revenue

South Dakota collected approximately $2.0 million in state and local tax revenue during fiscal year 2004.[50] As a result, South Dakota residents paid $2,615 per capita in

---

41. Case No. CIV 91-209 (S.D. Cir. Ct. 1994).

42. *Id.*; *see also* South Dakota, STARTINGAT3.ORG, http://www.startingat3.org/state_laws/state lawsSDdetail.html#toc44.

43. Case No. CIV 06-244 (S.D. Cir. Ct. June 22, 2006).

44. *Id.*

45. W. STEVEN BARNETT ET AL., NATIONAL INSTITUTE FOR EARLY EDUCATION RESEARCH, THE STATE OF PRESCHOOL 2006, at 137–38 (2007), *available at* http://nieer.org/yearbook/pdf/yearbook.pdf.

46. *See id.* at 232.

47. U.S. Census Bureau, State and Local Government Finances - 2003–04, http://www.census.gov/govs/www/estimate04.html (last visited Oct. 10, 2006) [hereinafter Government Finances].

48. *Id.*

49. *Id.*

50. *Id.*

state and local government taxes, an amount which ranked 46th in the nation.[51] The different types of tax sources were apportioned as follows:

Individual income taxes	0.0%
Property taxes	35.0%
General and selective sales taxes	53.1%
Corporate income and other taxes	11.9%
	100.0%[52]

Federal Funding

During fiscal year 2004, 24% of South Dakota's total revenues came from the federal government.[53] For every dollar of federal taxes paid, South Dakota received $1.49 in federal funding, an amount which ranked 10th nationally[54] and was far above the national average of $1.17.[55]

Lottery Revenues

The creation of a state lottery was approved in November 1986 by a 60% vote in a statewide referendum to amend the state constitution.[56] Revenues raised from scratch ticket sales go to the state General Fund.[57] Revenues raised from lottery ticket sales go to the General Fund and the Capital Construction Fund.[58] Revenues from video lottery sales currently go to the Property Tax Reduction Fund.[59]

During fiscal year 2005, South Dakota Lottery scratch ticket sales raised over $3.2 million, all of which was distributed to the state General Fund.[60] Lottery ticket sales raised $3.7 million, the first $1.4 million of which was distributed to the state General Fund by law. The remainder, $2.3 million, was distributed to the Capital Construction fund.[61] Video lottery sales raised over $112 million. Of this amount, $109.1 million was distributed to the Property Tax Reduction Fund.[62]

---

51. *Id.*

52. *Id.*

53. *Id.*

54. The Tax Foundation, Federal Spending Received Per Dollar of Taxes Paid by State, 2004, http://www.taxfoundation.org/taxdata/show/266.html (last visited Oct. 10, 2006).

55. *See id.*

56. South Dakota Lottery, History, http://www.sdlottery.org/history_of_lottery.asp (last visited October 21, 2006).

57. South Dakota Lottery, Where the Money Goes, http://www.sdlottery.org/WhereMoneyGoes.asp (last visited October 21, 2006).

58. *Id.*

59. *Id.*

60. South Dakota Lottery, *FY2005 Annual Report* 3, *available at* http://www.sdlottery.org/pdf%20docs/annual%20report%202005.pdf.

61. *Id.* The Capital Construction Fund "finances ethanol production incentives, water and environment programs and state highway projects." *Id.*

62. *Id.* The other $3 million was distributed as a one-time transfer to the General Fund. *Id.*

Legal Structures of Major Tax Sources

Income

South Dakota does not impose a state income tax.

Property

Overview

The South Dakota property tax system taxes real property and the property of corporations and banks at the local level.[63] Personal property is exempt from taxation unless it is centrally assessed.[64] Property of railroad companies, air flight companies, and public utilities is centrally assessed.[65] During fiscal year 2004, South Dakota localities collected over $705 million in property taxes.[66] As a result, South Dakota residents paid $915 per capita in property taxes, an amount which ranked 32nd nationally.[67]

Defining the Real Property Tax Base

In South Dakota, property is assessed at 100% of its true and full value in money as of November 1 of the year preceding the assessment.[68] In determining the property's true and full value in money, the cost approach, the market approach, and the income approach to appraisal are considered.[69] The true and full value of agricultural land is based on comparable sales of agricultural land which take into account the capacity of the land to produce agricultural products as well as the physical characteristics and use of the land.[70]

Property Tax Reduction Program

South Dakota has a Property Tax Reduction Program which has two essential components: "limiting property taxes at the source, and assessing all property equitably and reflecting market value."[71] In South Dakota, all entities are limited in the amount of property taxes that they can collect.[72] They may only collect the amount that they received the

---

63. S.D. Codified Laws § 10-4-1.

64. *Id.* § 10-4-6.1.

65. South Dakota Department of Revenue & Regulation, Property Tax: Public Utilities, Railroad & Airflight Property Reports, http://www.state.sd.us/drr2/propspectax/assessor/index.htm (last visited October 22, 2006); S.D. Codified Laws § 10-28-1; *Id.* § 10-29-2; *Id.* § 10-33-10; *Id.* § 10-35-2.

66. Government Finances, *supra* note 47. South Dakota does not collect any property taxes at the state level.

67. *Id.*

68. S.D. Codified Laws § 10-6-33.

69. *Id.* § 10-6-33.

70. S.D. Codified Laws § 10-3-33.1.

71. South Dakota Department of Revenue & Regulation, *Your Property Taxes 3, available at* http://www.state.sd.us/drr2/propspectax/booklets/your_property_taxes.pdf. This publication is a very informative guide to South Dakota's property tax system and the Property Tax Reduction Program.

72. *Id.*

previous year plus a small percentage increase to account for inflation, which cannot exceed 3%.[73] Counties may conduct county-wide reappraisals,[74] but because of staff limitations in counties, reappraisal generally occurs within a certain time period, such as three years.[75] By equitably assessing property within a county and limiting the increase in property tax that a county can collect to the previous year's amount plus inflation, a taxpayer's property tax bill cannot increase substantially from year to year regardless of whether property in a county rises in overall value.[76] The property that qualifies for the Property Tax Reduction Program is agricultural or single-family property and owner-occupied property.[77] Commercial properties and rental properties do not qualify.[78]

Real Property Tax Rates

During fiscal year 2004, the property tax rates of South Dakota cities ranged from 1.49% to 3.03% on owner-occupied property.[79] Property tax rates ranged from 1.02% to 1.53% on agricultural property.[80] Property tax rates ranged from 2.03% to 3.81% on all other real property.[81] South Dakota places a 2-mill limit on the amount that the state can levy for property taxes.[82] There is also a 3-mill limitation on the amount that a township may levy, unless the amount is a specified levy.[83] Counties are generally limited to a 12-mill levy, although additional levies are authorized.[84] School district levies are limited to 3.03 mills for agricultural property, 4.76 mills for owner-occupied residences, 4.03 mills for nonagricultural acreage property, and 10.19 mills for all other real property.[85]

Exemptions

Homesteads are exempt from any state tax but not from local property taxes.[86] Motor vehicles are exempt from property tax,[87] as well as all personal property not centrally assessed.[88]

---

73. *Id.*; S.D. CODIFIED LAWS § 10-13-35. This limitation does not apply to school districts.

74. S.D. CODIFIED LAWS § 10-6-51.

75. *Your Property Taxes, supra* note 71, at 3.

76. *Id.* at 2.

77. *Id.* at 4.

78. *Id.*

79. South Dakota Department of Revenue and Regulations, *2004 Annual Report* 27, *available at* http://www.state.sd.us/drr2/publications/annrpt/04_annual_report.pdf.

80. *Id.* at 28.

81. *Id.* at 27.

82. S.D. CODIFIED LAWS § 10-12-2.

83. *Id.* § 10-12-28; *Id.* § 10-12-28.1 (additional 1.2-mill levy for fire protection); *Id.* § 10-12-35; *Id.* § 10-12-36 (may increase levy by 3/4 vote at special election).

84. S.D. CODIFIED LAWS § 10-12-21; *Id.* § 7-27-1 (additional levy for county fairs); *Id.* § 34-31-3 (max .6-mill levy for fire protection).

85. S.D. CODIFIED LAWS § 10-12-42. These are the rates for 2007 and thereafter.

86. S.D. CODIFIED LAWS § 10-4-24.

87. *Id.* § 32-5-78. Separate license fees and taxes are imposed on motor vehicles in lieu of other taxes, including ad valorem property taxes.

88. *Id.* § 10-4-6.1.

General and Selective Sales

General Sales

South Dakota imposes a general retail sales-and-use tax, which makes up 39.1% of the state's total tax revenue.[89] The tax is imposed on "the gross receipts of any business, organization, or person engaged in retail sales, including the selling, leasing, and renting of tangible personal property or the sale of services."[90] Services are subject to taxation unless specifically made exempt by state law.[91] South Dakota has a state sales tax rate of 4%; in addition, a sales tax of up to 2% and a 1% gross receipts tax may be imposed by municipalities.[92] The additional 1% gross receipts tax may be imposed on any combination of alcoholic beverages, eating establishments, lodging, and ticket sales or admissions.[93] Municipal taxes do not apply to the sale or lease of farm machinery.[94] Certain services and products such as health services, food stamp purchases, and prescription drugs and medical supplies are exempt from the South Dakota sales-and-use tax.[95]

Selective Sales

Selective sales taxes make up 14.1% of South Dakota's total tax revenue.[96] Of that amount, 6.9%[97] comes from a motor fuel sales tax imposed at a rate of $0.22 per gallon of gasoline.[98] The tax rate on gasoline of 22% is the highest rate, while the tax rate on jet fuel of 4% is the lowest.[99] South Dakota residents paid $164 per capita in state motor fuel sales taxes in 2004, an amount which ranked 8th nationally.[100]

The sales tax on tobacco products makes up 1.4% of South Dakota's total tax revenue[101] and is imposed at a rate of $0.53 per pack of cigarettes.[102]

---

89. Government Finances, *supra* note 47.

90. South Dakota Department of Revenue & Regulation, *Sales and Use Tax Guide: July 2006* 8, *available at* http://www.state.sd.us/drr2/publications/cetandstguides/salestaxguide.pdf; S.D. CODIFIED LAWS § 10-45-2; *Id.* § 10-45-4.

91. *Sales and Use Tax Guide, supra* note 90; S.D. CODIFIED LAWS § 10-45-4.1.

92. *Sales and Use Tax Guide, supra* note 90, at 8. Municipal sales taxes range from 1% to 2%, and many cities also impose the 1% gross receipt tax. For the rates applied by all South Dakota cities, see South Dakota Department of Revenue and Regulation, *Municipal Tax Bulletin: January 2007* 4-8, *available at* http://www.state.sd.us/drr2/municipaltax/jan07bulletin.pdf.

93. *Sales and Use Tax Guide, supra* note 90, at 12.

94. *Id.* at 8.

95. *Id.* at 23–4. For a comprehensive listing of all services and purchases exempt from the South Dakota sales tax, see *id* at 18–25.

96. Government Finances, *supra* note 47.

97. *Id.*

98. STATE RANKINGS 2006, *supra* note 1, at 328.

99. South Dakota Department of Revenue and Regulation, Motor Vehicle – Motor Fuel, http://www.state.sd.us/drr2/motorvehicle/motorfuel/index.htm (last visited October 26, 2006).

100. STATE RANKINGS 2006, *supra* note 1, at 327.

101. Government Finances, *supra* note 47.

102. STATE RANKINGS 2006, *supra* note 1, at 333.

Sales taxes on alcoholic beverages make up 0.6% of South Dakota's total tax revenue.[103] South Dakota residents paid $16.14 per capita in state alcoholic beverage sales taxes in 2004, an amount which ranked 19th nationally.[104]

The remainder of South Dakota's selective sales taxes makes up 5.8% of its total tax revenue.[105] Of this amount, 0.2% represents taxes on utilities and the other 5.6% represents taxes on other specific commodities, businesses, or services not reported separately above (e.g., on contractors, lodging, lubricating oil, fuels other than motor fuel, motor vehicles, meals, soft drinks, margarine, etc.).[106]

Corporate Income and Other

Corporate Income

South Dakota does not impose a tax on the net income of corporations. Instead, it imposes a franchise tax on the net income of national banks, production credit, and savings and loan associations.[107] It also imposes an annual tax on financial institutions, except for those organized under the laws of the United States, for the privilege of transacting business in the state.[108] The South Dakota franchise tax on national banks and financial institutions brings in over $47 million, which makes up 2.3% of the state's total tax revenue.[109] The franchise tax rates range from 6% on the lowest amount of net income to 0.25% on the highest amount of net income.[110]

---

103. Government Finances, *supra* note 47.

104. STATE RANKINGS 2006, *supra* note 1, at 335.

105. Government Finances, *supra* note 47.

106. *See* GOVERNMENTS DIVISION, U.S. CENSUS BUREAU, GOVERNMENT FINANCE AND EMPLOYMENT CLASSIFICATION MANUAL, at ch.7 (2000), *available at* http://ftp2.census.gov/govs/class/classfull.pdf [hereinafter CLASSIFICATION MANUAL].

107. S.D. CODIFIED LAWS § 10-43-2.1.

108. *Id.* § 10-43-2.

109. Government Finances, *supra* note 47. The franchise tax is classified as a corporate net income tax, even though South Dakota has no tax on the net income of corporations.

110. The rates of this franchise tax are as follows: 6% on South Dakota net income of $400 million or less; 5% on net income greater than $400 million but no more than $425 million; 4% on net income greater than $425 million but no more than $450 million; 3% on net income greater than $450 million but no more than $475 million; 2% on net income greater than $475 million but no more than $500 million; 1% on net income greater than $500 million but no more than $600 million; 0.5% on net income greater than $600 million but no more than $1.2 billion; and 0.25% on income greater than $1.2 billion. S.D. CODIFIED LAWS § 10-43-4. Trust companies must pay either the greater of this franchise tax or $500 if it is a trust company engaging in business for less than one year; $2,000 if it is a trust company engaging in business for one year but less than two; $5,000 if it is a trust company engaging in business for two years but less than three; $10,000 if it is a trust company engaging in business for three years but less than four; or $25,000 if it is a trust company engaging in business for four years or more. S.D. CODIFIED LAWS § 10-43-90.

Other

During fiscal year 2004, the collection of all other taxes not previously mentioned accounted for 9.6% of South Dakota's total tax revenue.[111] Of this amount, over $9.3 million was generated by the estate and gift tax.[112] This tax is calculated on the basis of the amount of the federal death tax credit.[113] The South Dakota inheritance tax was repealed in 2001.[114] The "other taxes" category is further made up of various license taxes, documentary or stock transfer taxes, severance taxes, and all other taxes not listed separately or provided for in other categories.[115]

Burden Analysis

The overall state and local tax burden on South Dakota's taxpayers is very regressive. In fact, South Dakota is one of the ten most regressive states. Taxpayers in the lowest quintile — those with incomes of less than $15,000 — bear a tax burden of 10.0% of their income, while taxpayers in the top 1% — those with incomes that exceed $291,000 — bear a tax burden of just 2.3% of their income.[116] It is also worth noting that, although South Dakota obviously has no control over federal tax policy, federal itemized deductions for state and local personal income and property taxes nonetheless further reduce the burden on taxpayers in the top 1% to 2.1%.[117] Furthermore, between 1989 and 2002, the tax burden on the bottom quintile rose by approximately 0.3%%, while the burden on the top 1% fell by 0.4%.[118]

Since South Dakota does not employ a state income tax, it loses all the progressive benefits that an income tax would bring. The sales and excises taxes imposed by South Dakota are extremely regressive, with taxpayers in the lowest quintile bearing a tax bur-

---

111. *Id.*

112. *Id.*

113. S.D. Codified Laws § 10-40A-3.

114. South Dakota Department of Revenue & Regulation, http://www.state.sd.us/drr2/revenue.html (last visited October 26, 2006).

115. *See* Classification Manual, *supra* note 106, at ch.7.

116. *See* Robert S. McIntyre et al., Who Pays? A Distributional Analysis of the Tax Systems in All 50 States 98 (2d ed. 2003), *available at* http://www.itepnet.org/wp2000/text.pdf. Taxpayers in the second quintile bear a 9.2% total tax burden on incomes between $15,000 and $25,000; those in the third quintile bear a 9.0% tax burden on incomes between $25,000 and $40,000; those in the fourth quintile bear a 7.0% tax burden on incomes between $40,000 and $64,000; those in the 80th–95th percentiles bear a 6.1% tax burden on incomes between $64,000 and $112,000; finally, those in the 96th–99th percentiles bear a 4.5% tax burden on incomes between $112,000 and $291,000. *Id.*

117. *Id.* Taxpayers in the lowest and second lowest quintiles did not receive any benefit from these federal offsets, while those in the third and fourth quintiles were able to reduce their individual tax burdens by 0.1%, those in the 80th–95th percentiles by 0.3%, and those in the 96th–99th percentiles by 0.5%. *Id.*

118. *Id.* at 99.

den of 8.3% and those in the top 1% bearing a tax burden of just 1.0%.[119] Property taxes in South Dakota are slightly regressive, with taxpayers in the lowest quintile bearing a tax burden of 1.7% and those in the top quintile bearing an average tax burden of 1.2%.[120] Note, however, that the most onerous burden is placed on the middle quintile, which pays an average of 2.2% of their income in property taxes.[121]

---

119. *See id.* at 98. Taxpayers in the second quintile bear a 7.6% sales-and-excise tax burden; those in the third quintile bear a 6.1% burden; those in the fourth quintile bear a 4.7% burden; those in the 80th–95th percentiles bear a 3.7% burden; finally, those in the 96th–99th percentiles bear a 2.2% burden. *Id.*

120. *See id.* Taxpayers in the second quintile bear a 1.6% property tax burden; those in the third quintile bear a 2.9% burden; those in the fourth quintile bear a 2.2% burden; those in the 80th–95th percentiles bear a 2.4% burden, and those in the 96th–99th percentiles bear a 2.2% burden. *Id.*

121. *See id.*

Tennessee

General Information

Basic Profile – Geography, Population, and Industry

Admitted to the Union in 1796, Tennessee is commonly referred to as the "Volunteer State."[1] Tennessee is located in the southeast region and is bordered by Kentucky on the north; Virginia on the northeast, North Carolina on the east; Mississippi, Alabama, and Georgia on the south; Arkansas on the west, and Missouri on the northwest. Eastern Tennessee is located in the eastern time zone, and western Tennessee is located in the central time zone. The state capital is Nashville.[2]

Tennessee ranks 36th in total land and water area (approximately 42,000 square miles).[3] In 2005, it ranked 16th in population (approximately 6 million residents).[4] Tennessee's population is approximately 80.7% white and 16.8% black.[5] The state is approximately 6% Catholic; 77% Protestant (of which 51% are Baptist); and less than 0.5% Jewish; 17% claim a religion outside the Judeo-Christian tradition or no religion at all.[6] As of 2005, approximately 73% of Tennessee's population lived in urban areas.[7] Major industries include tobacco growing, processed food manufacturing, automotive manufacturing, and private health care services.[8]

---

1. STATE RANKINGS 2006, vi, 1 (Kathleen O'Leary Morgan & Scott Morgan eds., Morgan Quitno Press 2006).

2. *Id.*

3. *Id.* at 225.

4. *Id.* at 429.

5. Tennessee Quick Facts from the U.S. Census Bureau, http://quickfacts.census.gov/qfd/states/47000.html (last visited Jan. 31, 2007). The remaining population is made up of 1.2% Asian persons, 0.3% American Indian and/or Alaska Native persons, 0.1% Native Hawaiian persons and other Pacific Islanders, and 1% persons reporting two or more races. *Id.* Additionally, 3% of Tennessee's total population identify themselves as persons of Hispanic or Latino origin. *Id.* (noting that because Hispanics may be of any race, they are included within the other applicable race categories).

6. BARRY A. KOSMIN, EGON MAYER & ARIELA KEYSAR, AMERICAN RELIGIOUS IDENTIFICATION SURVEY 2001, at 41, *available at* http://www.gc.cuny.edu/faculty/research_studies/aris.pdf (last visited Jan. 31, 2007).

7. USDA Economic Research Service, Tennessee Fact Sheet, http://www.ers.usda.gov/StateFacts/TN.htm (last visited Sept. 17, 2006). According to the latest estimates, approximately 4.4 people live in urban areas, and approximately 1.6 million people live in rural areas. *Id.*

8. Tennessee, http://www.netstate.com/states/links/tn_links.htm (last visited Dec. 18, 2006).

Family Income and Poverty Indicators

In 2004, Tennessee's per capita gross product was $36,928, which was below the national average of $39,725.[9] During this same period, while the median household income in Tennessee was $38,550,[10] 14.9% of Tennessee's population was living in poverty, which was above the national average of 12.4% and ranked among the bottom ten states nationally.[11] More specifically, poverty affected 20.6% of Tennessee's children,[12] 12.0% of its senior citizens,[13] and 11.6% of its families.[14] Of its female-headed households with children, 42.1% lived in poverty.[15] Of those living in poverty, approximately 30% were black, which represented 24% of Tennessee's black population and 4% of its total population.[16] In an attempt to combat this poverty, Tennessee spent approximately $6.5 billion on public welfare programs in 2002,[17] which made up 22.3% of its total government expenditures.[18]

Tennessee's Public Elementary-Secondary School System

Overall Spending and Performance

For the 2003–2004 school year, Tennessee spent $6,504 per pupil in its public elementary-secondary school system, which was substantially below the national average of $8,182.[19] Of this amount, 11% was provided by the federal government, 43.4% was provided by the state government, and 45.6% was provided by the local governments,[20] with property taxes making up a substantial part of the total funding.[21] Out of these funds, Tennessee paid its elementary and secondary school teachers an estimated av-

---

9. STATE RANKINGS 2006, *supra* note 1, at 89.

10. *Id.* at 96.

11. *Id.* at 495.

12. *Id.* at 497.

13. *Id.* at 496.

14. *Id.* at 498.

15. *Id.* at 499.

16. *See* Fact Sheet, American FactFinder, http://factfinder.census.gov/home/saff/main.html?_lang=en (select Tennessee under "Get a Fact Sheet for your community") (last visited Feb. 22, 2007). Note that these numbers are based on the 2000 census because more recent numbers were not available.

17. STATE RANKINGS 2006, *supra* note 1, at 500.

18. *Id.* at 502.

19. GOVERNMENTS DIVISION, U.S. CENSUS BUREAU, PUBLIC EDUCATION FINANCES 2004, at 8 tbl.8 (2006).

20. *See id.* at 5 tbl.5.

21. Although none of the total funding has been specifically designated as provided by property taxes, 30.3% of the total funding comes from "Parent Government Contributions," *see id.* at 4 tbl.4., which is defined as "tax receipts and other amounts appropriated by a parent government and transferred to its dependent school system." *Id.* at app. A-1. This amount, however, "[e]xcludes intergovernmental revenue, current charges, and miscellaneous general revenue." *Id.*

erage annual salary of $41,527 during the 2004–2005 school year,[22] and in 2003, it provided a student/teacher ratio of 15.7, which was slightly better than the national average of 15.9.[23]

In academic performance, Tennessee's fourth grade students scored lower than the national average in mathematics,[24] reading,[25] and writing[26] but higher than the national average in science.[27] Tennessee's eighth graders scored lower than the national average in mathematics,[28] reading,[29] writing,[30] and science.[31]

Equity Issues

In 2004, the funding per student in Tennessee's highest poverty districts exceeded that in its lowest poverty districts by $591,[32] although when adjustments were made for the additional costs of educating students growing up in poverty, that excess narrowed to $330.[33] Similarly, Tennessee spent $275 more per student in its highest minority districts, although this amount fell to $202 when adjustments for low-income students were made.[34]

Fourth graders eligible for free or reduced-price school lunches had test scores that were 9% lower in mathematics,[35] 12% lower in reading,[36] and 12% lower in writing[37] than those of students who were not eligible. The results were similar for eighth graders eligible for free or reduced price lunches; their test scores were 9% lower in mathe-

---

22. Thomas D. Snyder et al., National Center for Education Statistics, Digest of Education Statistics 2005, at 116 tbl.77 (2006).

23. *Id.* at 98 tbl.65.

24. National Center for Education Statistics, U.S. Department of Education, The Nation's Report Card: Mathematics 2005, at 14 fig.11 (2005), *available at* http://nces.ed.gov/nationsreportcard/pdf/main2005/ 2006453.pdf [hereinafter Mathematics 2005].

25. National Center for Education Statistics, U.S. Department of Education, The Nation's Report Card: Reading 2005, at 14 fig.11 (2005), *available at* http://nces.ed.gov/nationsreportcard/pdf/main2005/2006451.pdf [hereinafter Reading 2005].

26. Hilary R. Persky et al., National Center for Education Statistics, U.S. Department of Education, The Nation's Report Card: Writing 2002, at 23 tbl.2.2 (2003), *available at* http://nces.ed.gov/nationsreportcard/pdf/main2002/2003529.pdf [hereinafter Writing 2002].

27. National Center for Education Statistics, U.S. Department of Education, The Nation's Report Card: Science 2005, at 16 fig.12 (2006) *available at* http://nces.ed.gov/nationsreportcard//pdf/main2005/2006466.pdf [hereinafter Science 2005].

28. Mathematics 2005, *supra* note 24, at 16 fig.12.

29. Reading 2005, *supra* note 25, at 16 fig.12.

30. Writing 2002, *supra* note 26, at 24 tbl.2.3.

31. Science 2005, *supra* note 27, at 28 fig.22.

32. The Education Trust, Funding Gaps 2006, at 7 tbl.3 (2006), *available at* http://www2.edtrust.org/NR/rdonlyres/CDEF9403-5A75-437E-93FF-EBF1174181FB/0/FundingGap2006.pdf.

33. *Id.*

34. *Id.* at 7 tbl.4.

35. Mathematics 2005, *supra* note 24, at 20 tbl.5.

36. Reading 2005, *supra* note 25, at 20 tbl.5.

37. Writing 2002, *supra* note 26, at 75 tbl.3.24.

matics,[38] 8% lower in reading,[39] and 18% lower in writing[40] than those of students who were not eligible.

Over the last 15 years, the funding of Tennessee's public school system has been successfully challenged on grounds that the funding system denied equal educational opportunities to all students and therefore violated Tennessee's constitution.[41] Most recently, in *Small Schools III*, the plaintiffs alleged that the method of funding salaries for teachers was not in accordance with the Basic Education Program (BEP) formula, as mandated in *Small Schools II*, and that therefore it "violate[d] equal protection by denying students substantially equal educational opportunities."[42] The Tennessee Supreme Court held that the "lack of teacher salary equalization according to the BEP formula continues to be a significant constitutional defect in the State's funding scheme."[43] The court further stated that until the salary equalization mandate is met, "the inherent value of education will not be fully realized by all students in the state ... and the students of Tennessee will continue to be unconstitutionally denied substantially equal educational opportunities."[44]

Availability of Publicly Funded Prekindergarten Programs

Tennessee's Early Childhood Education Pilot Program is available to three- and four-year-olds who have certain state-specified risk factors or whose families have an income below 185 percent of the federal poverty level.[45] In 2005, Tennessee began allocating excess lottery funds to the Voluntary Pre-K Initiative, which is available to at-risk four-year-olds.[46] Total enrollment in these state-funded programs is 8,618,[47] which represents just 6% of Tennessee's 152,932 three- and four-year-old children.[48] The federally funded Head Start program enrolls an additional 15,432 children,[49] which represents 10% of Tennessee's three- and four-year-old children.[50]

---

38. MATHEMATICS 2005, *supra* note 24, at 21 tbl.6.

39. READING 2005, *supra* note 25, at 21 tbl.6.

40. WRITING 2002, *supra* note 26, at 76 tbl.3.25.

41. *See* Tennessee Small School Sys. v. McWherter, 851 S.W.2d 139 (Tenn. 1993), Tennessee Small School Sys. v. McWherter, 894 S.W.2d 734 (Tenn. 1995), and Tennessee Small School Sys. v. McWherter, 91 S.W.2d 232 (Tenn. 2002).

42. *Id.*, 91 S.W.2d at 233.

43. *Id.* at 240–41.

44. *Id.*

45. W. STEVEN BARNETT ET AL., NATIONAL INSTITUTE FOR EARLY EDUCATION RESEARCH, THE STATE OF PRESCHOOL 2006, at 138 (2006), *available at* http://nieer.org/yearbook/pdf/yearbook.pdf.

46. *Id.*

47. *Id.* at 139.

48. *See id.* at 232.

49. *Id.* at 139.

50. *See id.* at 232.

Where Does Tennessee Get Its Revenue?

At the end of fiscal year 2004, Tennessee had total revenues of approximately $42 billion.[51] Of this amount, 35% was derived from state and local tax revenues and 23% was received from the federal government.[52] The remaining 42% came from other sources, including the Tennessee Lottery, insurance trust revenue, and revenue from government-owned utilities and other commercial or auxiliary enterprises.

Tax Revenue

Tennessee collected approximately $15 billion in state and local tax revenue during fiscal year 2004.[53] As a result, Tennessee residents paid $2,536 per capita in state and local taxes, an amount which ranked 47th nationally.[54] The different types of tax sources were approximately apportioned as follows:

Individual income taxes	0.9%
Property taxes	24.0%
General and selective sales taxes	59.2%
Corporate income and other taxes	15.9%
	100.0%[55]

Federal Funding

During fiscal year 2004, 23% of Tennessee's total revenues came from the federal government.[56] For every dollar of federal taxes paid, Tennessee received $1.30 in federal expenditures, an amount which ranked 18th nationally[57] and was far above the national average of $1.17.[58]

Lottery Revenue

The Tennessee Lottery was established in 2002 after the citizens of Tennessee voted to amend the constitution to allow for a state-run lottery.[59] The Lottery has been in

---

51. U.S. Census Bureau, State and Local Government Finances 2003–04, http://www.census.gov/govs/www/estimate04.html (last visited Oct. 16, 2006) [hereinafter Government Finances].

52. Id.

53. Id. The total tax revenues were collected as follows: $9.5 billion by the state and $5.5 billion by local governments. Id.

54. Id.

55. Id.

56. Id.

57. The Tax Foundation, Federal Spending Received Per Dollar of Taxes Paid by State 2004, http://www.taxfoundation.org/taxdata/show/266.html (last visited Sept. 17, 2006).

58. See id.

59. Official Home of the Tennessee Lottery, About Us, http://www.tnlottery.com/aboutus/chronology.aspx (last visited Dec. 7, 2006).

operation since 2004.[60] Under Tennessee's constitution, all net proceeds from the Lottery are to be used for capital outlay projects for K–12 educational facilities, early-learning programs, and after-school programs.[61] During fiscal year 2006, the Lottery had total revenues of approximately $790 million and net proceeds transferred to the lottery for education account of $230 million.[62]

Legal Structures of Major Tax Sources

Income

In Tennessee, the individual income tax is limited to income derived from dividends from stocks and interest from bonds.[63] In 2006, Tennessee taxed dividends and interest at a rate of 6%.[64] Tennessee collected individual income tax of $25 per capita, an amount which ranked 43rd nationally.[65]

Property

Overview

Tennessee has a typical property tax system that taxes the value of real and personal property at the local level unless otherwise exempt.[66] During fiscal year 2004, Tennessee collected approximately $3.6 billion dollars in property tax at the local level.[67] As a result Tennessee residents paid $608 per capita in local property taxes, an amount which ranked 41st nationally.[68]

Defining the Real Property Tax Base

Tennessee has only one classification of real property, which is broken into four sub-classifications according to use[69] and assessed at varying percentages of the estimated

---

60. *Id.*

61. TENN. CONST. art. XI, § 5. "The appropriation of funds to support improvements and enhancements for educational programs and purposes and such net proceeds shall be used to supplement, not supplant, non-lottery educational resources for educational programs and purposes." *Id.*

62. Official Home of the Tennessee Lottery, Lottery Reports, Tennessee Lottery 2005 Annual Report, http://www.tnlottery.com/aboutus/chronology.aspx (last visited Dec. 7, 2006).

63. TENN. CODE ANN. § 67-2-102.

64. *Id.* Tennessee exempts taxable income for certain taxpayers as follows: the first $1,250 for individuals; the first $2,500 for taxpayers filing jointly; and all taxable income for taxpayers over the age of 65 with less than $16,200 (individual) or $27,000 (filing jointly) of annual income derived from any source. TENN. CODE ANN. § 67-2-104.

65. STATE RANKINGS 2006, *supra* note 1, at 321.

66. TENN. CODE ANN. § 67-5-101.

67. Government Finances, *supra* note 51.

68. *See id.*

69. TENN. CODE ANN. § 67-5-801.

value as of January 1 each year.[70] The four subclassifications and assessment percentages are as follows: 1) Public Utility Property – 55% of value; 2) Industrial and Commercial Property – 40% of value; 3) Residential Property – 25% of value; and 4) Farm Property – 25% of value.[71] Value is generally determined by the application of standard appraisal methods, including the cost method, the income method, and the market-data method, all of which are commonly used throughout the country.[72] Owners of certain types of land classified as agricultural,[73] forest,[74] or open-space[75] property may request that the county tax assessor value the property at its current use.[76] In general, counties are required to reappraise real property on a continuous six-year cycle.[77]

Real Property Tax Rates

The tax rates imposed on real property vary and are set by each county or municipality on the basis of the certified tax rate.[78] In order to impose any tax above the certified tax rate, the governing body of the county or municipality must advertise the increase and hold a public hearing regarding it.[79] In 2005, the tax rates per $1,000 of assessed value ranged from $28.10 in Morristown to $74.73 in Memphis.[80]

Personal and Intangible Property

Tangible personal property is subject to local taxation unless specifically exempt,[81] and the tax rates imposed vary among jurisdictions. "Tangible personal property" is defined as all property not classified as real property;[82] it is further classified into public utility property, industrial and commercial property, and all other tangible personal property.[83] Public utility property is assessed at 55% of its value; industrial and commercial property is assessed at 30% of its value; and all other tangible personal property is assessed at 5% of its value, which is currently deemed to have no value.[84] While

---

70. *Id.* § 67-5-504.

71. *Id.* § 67-5-801. Property values are determined "from the evidence of its sound, intrinsic and immediate value, for purposes of sale between a willing seller and a willing buyer without consideration of speculative values" and are calculated in accordance with official assessment manuals issued by the state division of property assessments. *Id.* § 67-5-601.

72. CCH-EXP, PROP-TAX-GUIDE TN ¶ 20-615, Valuation Methods in General.

73. TENN. CODE ANN. § 67-5-1005.

74. *Id.* § 67-5-1006.

75. *Id.* § 67-5-1007.

76. *Id.* § 67-5-1008.

77. *Id.* § 67-5-1601.

78. *Id.* § 67-5-1701. The certified tax rate is calculated using the certified assessed value of taxable property within the jurisdiction of the county or municipality and a formula provided by the state board of equalization. *Id.*

79. TENN. CODE ANN. § 67-5-1702.

80. CCH-EXP, PROP-TAX-GUIDE TN ¶ 20-405, Rates of Tax.

81. TENN. CODE ANN. § 67-5-101.

82. *Id.* § 67-5-501.

83. *Id.* § 67-5-901.

84. *Id.*

Tennessee's constitution does allow for the taxing of intangible personal property, the legislature has not enacted any laws taxing such property; therefore, intangible personal property is not currently subject to tax at either the state or local level.[85]

Exemptions

Tennessee exempts the first $7,500 (individual) or $15,000 (filing jointly) of other tangible personal property [86] (currently, all tangible personal property as discussed above) from the property tax. Further, all inventory,[87] growing crops,[88] livestock,[89] and certain low-cost housing for elderly persons is exempt.[90] In addition to these exemptions, elderly low-income homeowners,[91] disabled homeowners,[92] and disabled veterans[93] may be eligible for property tax reimbursements from the state's general funds.

General and Selective Sales

General Sales

Tennessee imposes a general retail sales-and-use tax, which makes up 47.4% of Tennessee's total tax revenue.[94] This tax is imposed on the retail sale, use, rental, furnishing, and storage of tangible personal property, as well as certain services.[95] These services include (1) lodging for less than 90 days; (2) parking garages; (3) laundering or dry-cleaning services; and (4) repair services.[96] The state sales tax rate is 7%,[97] and all localities may impose a local rate of up to 2.75%,[98] for a combined state and local rate of 9.75%. The total sales tax rate imposed by the state and each county generally ranges from 8.5% to 9.75%.[99] However, unprepared food and food ingredients purchased for home consumption are taxed at 6%.[100] Exemptions from Tennessee's sales-and-use tax include, among other items, prescription and over-the-counter drugs,[101] purchases with

---

85. Tenn. Const. art. II, § 28.

86. Tenn. Code Ann. § 67-5-215.

87. *Id.* § 67-5-901.

88. *Id.* § 67-5-216.

89. *Id.*

90. *Id.* § 67-5-207.

91. *Id.* § 67-5-702.

92. *Id.* § 67-5-703.

93. *Id.* § 67-5-704.

94. Government Finances, *supra* note 51.

95. Tenn. Code Ann. § 67-6-201.

96. *Id.* § 67-6-205.

97. *Id.* § 67-6-202. An additional tax of 2.75% is applied to the amount in excess of $1,600.00 but less than $3,200.00 on the sale or use of any single article of personal property. *Id.*

98. Tenn. Code Ann. § 67-6-702. The maximum 2.75% local option base tax rate is applied to the purchase price of any single item less than $1,600.00. *Id.*

99. *See* CCH-EXP, SALES-TAX-GUIDE TN ¶ 61-735, Local Rates.

100. Tenn. Code Ann. § 67-6-228.

101. *Id.* § 67-6-320.

food stamps,[102] industrial machinery and raw materials,[103] farm equipment and machinery,[104] and motor vehicles removed from the state within three days of purchase.[105]

Selective Sales

Selective sales taxes make up 11.8% of Tennessee's total revenue.[106] Of that amount, 5.6%[107] comes from a motor fuel sales tax imposed at a rate of $0.20 per gallon of gasoline[108] and $0.17 per gallon of diesel fuel.[109] Tennessee residents paid an average of $141 in state motor fuel sales taxes in 2004, an amount which ranked 16th nationally and was above the national average of $115.[110]

In 2004, sales taxes on alcoholic beverages made up 1.3% of Tennessee's total tax revenue.[111] Tennessee residents paid $15.62 per capita in state alcoholic beverage sales taxes in 2004, an amount which ranked 21st nationally.[112]

The tobacco product sales tax makes up 0.8%[113] of Tennessee's tax revenues and is imposed at a rate of $0.20 per pack of cigarettes.[114]

The remainder of Tennessee's selective sales taxes makes up 4.2%[115] of its total tax revenue. Of this amount, 0.4%[116] represents taxes on utilities and the other 3.8%[117] represents taxes on other specific commodities, businesses, or services not reported separately above (e.g., on contractors, lodging, lubricating oil, fuels other than motor fuel, motor vehicles, meals, soft drinks, margarine, etc.).[118]

Corporate Income and Other

Corporate Income

The corporate income tax makes up 4.6% of Tennessee's total tax revenue.[119] Tennessee imposes an excise tax on every corporation, subchapter S corporation, limited

---

102. *Id.* § 67-6-337.

103. *Id.* § 67-6-206.

104. Tenn. Code Ann. § 67-6-207.

105. *Id.* § 67-6-343.

106. Government Finances, *supra* note 51.

107. *Id.*

108. Tenn. Code Ann. § 67-3-201.

109. *Id.* § 67-3-202.

110. State Rankings 2006, *supra* note 1, at 327.

111. Government Finances, *supra* note 51.

112. State Rankings 2006, *supra* note 1, at 335.

113. Government Finances, *supra* note 51.

114. State Rankings 2006, *supra* note 1, at 333.

115. Government Finances, *supra* note 51.

116. *Id.*

117. *Id.*

118. *See* Governments Division, U.S. Census Bureau, Government Finance And Employment Classification Manual, at ch. 7 (2000), *available at* http://ftp2.census.gov/govs/class/classfull.pdf [hereinafter Classification Manual].

119. Government Finances, *supra* note 51.

liability company, and limited partnership doing business in Tennessee.[120] General partnerships and sole proprietorships are not subject to the excise tax.[121] The tax is imposed at a rate of 6.5% on the entity's net earnings.[122] For corporations and limited liability companies treated as corporations for federal tax purposes, "net earnings" is defined as federal taxable income or loss before the operating loss deduction.[123] An S corporation's net earnings are calculated as they would have been for federal income tax purposes if the corporation had not elected S status.[124] All entities treated as partnerships for federal tax purposes are required to calculate net earnings as the amount of ordinary income or loss determined under the Internal Revenue Code less self-employment taxes and amounts contributed to the qualified pension or benefit plan of any partner or member.[125]

Other

During fiscal year 2004, the collection of all other taxes not previously mentioned accounted for 11.3% of Tennessee's total tax revenue.[126] Of this amount, approximately $97 million was generated by the estate, inheritance, and gift tax,[127] which is calculated on the basis of the value of the net taxable estate.[128] The "other taxes" category is also made up of motor vehicle license taxes, documentary and stock transfer taxes, severance taxes, and all other taxes not listed separately or provided for in other categories, such as taxes on land based on a specified rate per acre (rather than on assessed value).[129]

Burden Analysis

The overall state and local tax burden on Tennessee's taxpayers is very regressive. In fact, Tennessee is one of the ten most regressive states. Taxpayers in the lowest quintile—those with incomes of less than $14,000—bear a tax burden of 11.7% of their income, while taxpayers in the top 1%—those with incomes that exceed $269,000—bear a tax burden of just 3.4% of their income.[130] It is also worth noting that, although

---

120. Tenn. Code Ann. §67-4-2004.

121. *See id.*

122. Tenn. Code Ann. §67-4-2007.

123. *Id.* §67-4-2006.

124. *Id.*

125. *Id.*

126. Government Finances, *supra* note 51.

127. *Id.*

128. Tenn. Code Ann. §67-8-314. The term estate means the entire estate as determined under the Internal Revenue Code of 1954. *Id.* §67-8-202.

129. *See* Classification Manual, *supra* note 118, at ch. 7.

130. *See* Robert S. McIntyre et al., Who Pays? A Distributional Analysis of the Tax Systems in All 50 States 100 (2d ed. 2003), *available at* http://www.itepnet.org/wp2000/text.pdf. Taxpayers in the second quintile bear a 10.5% total tax burden on incomes between $14,000 and $24,000; those in the third quintile bear a 8.8% tax burden on incomes between

Tennessee obviously has no control over federal tax policy, federal itemized deductions for state and local personal income and property taxes nonetheless further reduce the burden on taxpayers in the top 1% to 3.0%.[131] Furthermore, between 1989 and 2002, the tax burden on the bottom quintile rose by approximately 1.7%, while the burden on the top 1% rose by only approximately 0.4%.[132]

In terms of the income tax, the burden across income groups in Tennessee is slightly progressive, with taxpayers in the lowest quintile bearing a tax burden of 0.1% and those in the top 1% bearing a tax burden of 1.0%.[133] In sharp contrast, however, the sales and excise taxes imposed by Tennessee are extremely regressive, with taxpayers in the lowest quintile bearing a tax burden of 9.6% and those in the top 1% bearing a tax burden of just 1.5%.[134] Property taxes in Tennessee are also regressive, with the taxpayers in the lowest quintile bearing a tax burden of 2.1% and those in the top quintile bearing an average tax burden of 1.3%.[135]

$24,000 and $38,000; those in the fourth quintile bear a 7.4% tax burden on incomes between $38,000 and $61,000; those in the 80th–95th percentiles bear a 6.2% tax burden on incomes between $61,000 and $119,000; finally, those in the 96th–99th percentiles bear a 4.5% tax burden on incomes between $119,000 and $269,000. *Id.*

131. *Id.* Taxpayers in the two lowest quintiles did not receive any benefit from these federal offsets, while those in the third quintile were able to reduce their individual tax burdens by 0.1%, those in the fourth quintile by 0.1%, those in the 80th–95th percentiles by 0.2%, and those in the 96th–99th percentiles by 0.3%. *Id.*

132. *Id.* at 101.

133. *See id.* at 100. Taxpayers in the second quintile bear a 0.1% income tax burden; those in the third quintile bear a 0.1% burden; those in the fourth quintile bear a 0.1% burden; those in the 80th–95th percentiles bear a 0.2% burden; finally, those in the 96th–99th percentiles bear a 0.3% burden. *Id.* Note, however, that these percentages include both individual and corporate income tax burdens; that within the second quintile, corporate income taxes represent 0.1% of this burden; that within the third quintile, corporate income taxes represent 0.1% of this burden; that within the fourth quintile, corporate income taxes represent 0.1% of this burden; that within the 80th–95th percentiles, corporate income taxes represent 0.1% of this burden; that within the 96th–99th percentiles, corporate income taxes represent 0.1% of this burden; and that in the top 1%, corporate income taxes represent 0.5% of this burden. *Id.* Note that Tennessee imposes an income tax only on dividends from stocks and interest from bonds. *Supra* note 31.

134. *See id.* Taxpayers in the second quintile bear a 8.8% sales-and-excise tax burden; those in the third quintile bear a 7.1% burden; those in the fourth quintile bear a 5.9% burden; those in the 80th–95th percentiles bear a 4.5% burden; finally, those in the 96th–99th percentiles bear a 2.8% burden. *Id.*

135. *See id.* Taxpayers in the second quintile bear a 1.6% property tax burden; those in the third quintile bear a 1.6% burden; those in the fourth quintile bear a 1.4% burden; those in the 80th–95th percentiles bear a 1.5% burden; those in the 96th–99th percentiles bear a 1.4% burden; finally, those in the top 1% bear a 0.9% burden. *Id.*

Texas

General Information

Basic Profile – Geography, Population, and Industry

Admitted to the Union in 1845, Texas is commonly referred to as the "Lone Star State."[1] Texas is located in the south central region and is bordered by Oklahoma on the north; Louisiana on the east; the Gulf of Mexico and Mexico on the south; and New Mexico on the west. Most of the state is located in the central time zone; part of western Texas is located in the mountain time zone. The state capital is Austin.[2]

Texas ranks 2nd in total land and water area (approximately 269,000 square miles).[3] In 2005, Texas ranked 2nd in population (approximately 22.9 million residents).[4] Its population is approximately 83.2% white and 11.7% black.[5] Additionally, 35.1% of its total population identify themselves as persons of Hispanic or Latino origin.[6] The state is approximately 28% Catholic; 54% Protestant; and less than 0.5% Jewish; 18% claim a religion outside the Judeo-Christian tradition or no religion at all.[7] As of 2005, approximately 87% of Texas's population lived in urban areas.[8] Major industries include oil and gas, as well as cattle and cotton.[9]

---

1. State Rankings 2006, vi, 1 (Kathleen O'Leary Morgan & Scott Morgan eds., Morgan Quitno Press 2006).

2. *Id.*

3. *Id.* at 225.

4. *Id.* at 429.

5. Texas Quick Facts from the U.S. Census Bureau, http://quickfacts.census.gov/qfd/states/48000.html. (last visited Jan. 31, 2007). The remaining population is made up of 3.3% Asian persons, 0.7% American Indian and/or Alaska Native persons, 0.1% Native Hawaiian persons and other Pacific Islanders, and 1.1% persons reporting two or more races. *Id.*

6. *Id.* Note that because Hispanics and Latinos may be of any race, they are also included within the other applicable race categories. *See id.*

7. Barry A. Kosmin, Egon Mayer & Ariela Keysar, American Religious Identification Survey 2001, at 41, *available at* http://www.gc.cuny.edu/faculty/research_studies/aris.pdf (last visited Jan. 31, 2007).

8. USDA Economic Research Service, Texas Fact Sheet, http://www.ers.usda.gov/State-Facts/TX.htm (last visited Jan. 4, 2007). According to the latest estimates, approximately 19.9 million people live in urban areas, and 3 million people live in rural areas. *Id.*

9. Texas, http://www.netstate.com/states/links/tx_links.htm (last visited Dec. 17, 2006).

Family Income and Poverty Indicators

In 2004, Texas's per capita gross product was $39,345, which was below the national average of $39,725.[10] During this same period, while the median household income in Texas was $41,275,[11] 16.4% of Texas's population was living in poverty, which was substantially above the national average of 12.4% and ranked among the top ten states nationally.[12] More specifically, poverty affected 22.6% of Texas's children,[13] 12.5% of its senior citizens,[14] and 13.5% of its families.[15] Of its female-headed households with children, 39.9% lived in poverty,[16] and 46.7% of the state's public elementary and secondary school students were eligible for free or reduced-price meals.[17] Of those living in poverty, approximately 17% were black, which represented 22% of Texas's black population and 2.5% of its total population.[18] In an attempt to combat this poverty, Texas spent approximately $14.9 billion on public welfare programs in 2002,[19] which made up 13.4% of its total government expenditures.[20]

Texas's Public Elementary-Secondary School System

Overall Spending and Performance

For the 2003–2004 school year, Texas spent $7,104 per pupil in its public elementary-secondary school system, which was substantially below the national average of $8,182.[21] Of this amount, 10.5% was provided by the federal government, 36.8% was provided by the state government, and 52.7% was provided by the local governments,[22] with property taxes making up 48.5% of the total funding.[23] Out of these funds, Texas paid its elementary and secondary school teachers an estimated average annual salary

---

10. STATE RANKINGS 2006, *supra* note 1, at 89.

11. *Id.* at 96.

12. *Id.* at 495.

13. *Id.* at 497.

14. *Id.* at 496.

15. *Id.* at 498.

16. *Id.* at 499.

17. *Id.* at 532.

18. *See* Fact Sheet, American FactFinder, http://factfinder.census.gov/home/saff/main.html?_lang=en (select "Texas" under "Get a Fact Sheet for your community") (last visited Feb. 22, 2007). Note that these numbers are based on the 2000 census because more recent numbers were not available.

19. STATE RANKINGS 2006, *supra* note 1, at 500.

20. *Id.* at 502.

21. GOVERNMENTS DIVISION, U.S. CENSUS BUREAU, PUBLIC EDUCATION FINANCES 2004, at 8 tbl.8 (2006).

22. *See id.* at 5 tbl.5.

23. *See id.* at 4 tbl.4.

of $41,009 during the 2004–2005 school year,[24] and in 2003, it provided a student/teacher ratio of 15.0, which was slightly better than the national average of 15.9.[25]

In academic performance, Texas's fourth grade students scored higher than the national average in mathematics,[26] reading,[27] science,[28] and writing.[29] Texas's eighth graders, on the other hand, scored lower than the national average in reading[30] and science,[31] equal to the national average in writing,[32] and higher than the national average in mathematics.[33]

Equity Issues

In 2004, revenues spent per student in Texas's highest poverty districts were determined to be $249 less than the revenues spent in its lowest poverty districts.[34] When adjustments were made for the additional costs of educating students growing up in poverty, however, the funding gap grew to $757.[35] Similarly, Texas spent $792 less per student in its highest minority districts, and this amount grew to $1,167 when adjustments for low-income students were made.[36]

Fourth graders eligible for free or reduced-price school lunches had test scores that were 8% lower in mathematics,[37] 10% lower in reading,[38] and 10% lower in writing[39]

24. Thomas D. Snyder et al., National Center for Education Statistics, Digest of Education Statistics 2005, at 116 tbl.77 (2006).

25. Id. at 98 tbl.65.

26. National Center for Education Statistics, U.S. Department of Education, The Nation's Report Card: Mathematics 2005, at 14 fig.11 (2005), available at http://nces.ed.gov/nationsreportcard/pdf/main2005/2006453.pdf [hereinafter Mathematics 2005].

27. National Center for Education Statistics, U.S. Department of Education, The Nation's Report Card: Reading 2005, at 14 fig.11 (2005), available at http://nces.ed.gov/nationsreportcard/pdf/main2005/2006451.pdf [hereinafter Reading 2005].

28. National Center for Education Statistics, U.S. Department of Education, The Nation's Report Card: Science 2005, at 16 fig.12 (2006), available at http://nces.ed.gov/nationsreportcard//pdf/main2005/2006466.pdf [hereinafter Science 2005].

29. Hilary R. Persky et al., National Center for Education Statistics, U.S. Department of Education, The Nation's Report Card: Writing 2002, at 23 tbl.2.2 (2003), available at http://nces.ed.gov/nationsreportcard/pdf/main2002/2003529.pdf [hereinafter Writing 2002].

30. Reading 2005, supra note 27, at 16 fig.12.

31. Science 2005, supra note 28, at 28 fig.22.

32. Writing 2002, supra note 29, at 24 tbl.2.3.

33. Mathematics 2005, supra note 26, at 16 fig.12.

34. The Education Trust, Funding Gaps 2006, at 7 tbl.3 (2006), available at http://www2.edtrust.org/NR/rdonlyres/CDEF9403-5A75-437E-93FF-EBF1174181FB/0/FundingGap2006.pdf.

35. Id.

36. Id. at 7 tbl.4.

37. Mathematics 2005, supra note 26, at 20 tbl.5.

38. Reading 2005, supra note 27, at 20 tbl.5.

39. Writing 2002, supra note 29, at 75 tbl.3.24.

than those of students who were not eligible. The results were generally worse for eighth graders eligible for free or reduced-price lunches; their test scores were 9% lower in mathematics,[40] 8% lower in reading,[41] and 17% lower in writing[42] than those of students who were not eligible.

In 2001, the funding of the Texas public school system was challenged on two different fronts, both of which involved violations of the Texas constitution.[43] The first front, consisting of plaintiffs led by West Orange-Cove Consolidated Independent School District, alleged that the local ad valorem tax had become a state property tax, in violation of Tex. Const. art. VIII, § 1-e.[44] The second front, consisting of two groups of intervenors and led by Edgewood Independent School District, alleged that the public school funding system created a situation in which children in property-poor districts did not have equal access to education revenue and that, therefore, the public school funding system was in violation of Tex. Const. art. VII, § 1.[45] The Texas Supreme Court held that the local ad valorem tax had become property tax because state-imposed caps on tax rates had created a situation in which the school districts "lost all meaningful discretion in setting the tax rate."[46] The court further held that while there was "evidence of deficiencies in the public school finance system, … those deficiencies [did] not amount to a violation of article VII, section 1."[47] However, the court stated that the defects in the structure of the public school finance system would continue to expose the funding system to constitutional challenges.[48]

Availability of Publicly Funded Prekindergarten Programs

Texas's Public School Prekindergarten initiative is available to all at-risk four-year-olds and is also available to three-year-olds in a limited number of districts.[49] Total enrollment in this state-funded program is 182,293,[50] which represents just 25% of Texas's 741,968 three- and four-year-old children.[51] The federally funded Head Start program enrolls an additional 62,367 children,[52] which represents 8% of Texas's three- and four-year-old children.[53]

---

40. MATHEMATICS 2005, *supra* note 26, at 21 tbl.6.

41. READING 2005, *supra* note 27, at 21 tbl.6.

42. WRITING 2002, *supra* note 29, at 76 tbl.3.25.

43. Neeley v. W. Orange-Cove Consol. Indep. Sch. Dist., 176 S.W.3d 746 (Tex. 2005).

44. *Id.* at 751.

45. *Id.* at 752.

46. *Id.* at 754.

47. *Id.*

48. *Id.*

49. W. STEVEN BARNETT ET AL., NATIONAL INSTITUTE FOR EARLY EDUCATION RESEARCH, THE STATE OF PRESCHOOL 2006, at 140 (2006), *available at* http://nieer.org/yearbook/pdf/yearbook.pdf.

50. *Id.* at 141.

51. *See id.* at 232.

52. *Id.* at 141.

53. *See id.* at 232.

Where Does Texas Get Its Revenue?

At the end of fiscal year 2004, Texas had total revenues of approximately $153.8 billion.[54] Of this amount, 42% was derived from state and local tax revenues and 18% was received from the federal government.[55] The remaining 40% came from other sources, including the Texas Lottery, insurance trust revenue, and revenue from government-owned utilities and other commercial or auxiliary enterprises.

Tax Revenue

Texas collected approximately $65 billion in state and local tax revenue during fiscal year 2004.[56] As a result, Texas residents paid $2,881 per capita in state and local taxes, an amount which ranked 34th nationally.[57] The different types of tax sources were approximately apportioned as follows:

Individual income taxes	0.0%
Property taxes	43.5%
General and selective sales taxes	45.8%
Other taxes	10.7%
	100.0%[58]

Federal Funding

During fiscal year 2004, 18% of Texas's total revenues came from the federal government.[59] For every dollar of federal taxes paid, Texas received $0.94 in federal funding, which ranked 36th nationally[60] and was below the national average of $1.17.[61]

Lottery Revenue

The Texas Lottery was created in 1991 when the voters of Texas approved a constitutional amendment, and it has been in operation since November 1992.[62] All Texas

---

54. U.S. Census Bureau, State and Local Government Finances 2003–04, http://www.census.gov/govs/www/estimate04.html (last visited Oct. 16, 2006) [hereinafter Government Finances].

55. *Id.*

56. *Id.* The total tax revenues were collected as follows: $31 billion by the state and $34 billion by local governments. *Id.*

57. *Id.*

58. *Id.*

59. *Id.*

60. The Tax Foundation, Federal Spending Received Per Dollar of Taxes Paid by State 2004, http://www.taxfoundation.org/taxdata/show/266.html (last visited Sept. 17, 2006).

61. *See id.*

62. Official Home of the Texas Lottery, Texas Lottery Commission Milestones, http://www.txlottery.org/ export/sites/default/About_Us/Milestones/ (last visited Jan. 5, 2006). The Texas con-

Lottery revenues not used in the administration of the Lottery or paid out as prizes are transferred directly to the foundation school fund for use in education in the state.[63] During fiscal year 2006, the Texas Lottery had total revenues of approximately $3.8 billion and approximately $1 billion in transfers to the foundation school fund.[64]

Legal Structures of Major Tax Sources

Income

Texas does not impose a state income tax.

Property

Overview

Texas has a typical property tax system that taxes the value of real and tangible personal property, unless otherwise exempt, at the local level.[65] During fiscal year 2004, Texas collected approximately $28.2 billion dollars in property tax at the local level.[66] As a result, Texas residents paid $1,254 per capita in state and local property taxes, an amount which ranked 13th nationally.[67]

Defining the Real Property Tax Base

Texas has only one classification for real property, which includes all land, improvements (i.e., building, structure, fixture, fence, and transportable structure), standing timber, mine or quarry and minerals in place.[68] Real property is assessed at 100% of the appraised value[69] (i.e., market value) as of January 1 each year.[70] Market value is generally determined by considering the cost method, the income method, or the market-data method—whichever method is most appropriate for the property.[71] Qualified agricultural land[72] and qualified timberland[73] are valued on the basis of the in-

---

stitution states that the legislature of Texas can authorize, through the passage of general laws, the operation of a state lottery. TEX. CONST. art. III, §47.

63. TEX. GOV'T CODE ANN. §466.355.

64. Official Home of the Texas Lottery, Financial Information, Comprehensive Annual Report For Fiscal Year Ending August, 31, 2006, http://www.txlottery.org/export/sites/default/About_Us/Publications/Financial_Information.html (last visited Jan. 5, 2006).

65. TEX. TAX CODE ANN. §11.01.

66. Government Finances, *supra* note 54.

67. *See id.*

68. TEX. TAX CODE ANN. §1.04.

69. *Id.* §26.02.

70. *Id.* §23.01.

71. TEX. TAX CODE ANN. §23.0101.

72. *Id.*§23.52. Qualified agricultural land refers to "qualified open-space land," which is defined as land that is principally devoted to agricultural use for five of the preceding years. *Id.* §23.51.

73. *Id.* §23.73. "Qualified timberland" is land that is currently and actively used in the pro-

come-capitalization method. In general, each taxing unit is required to reassess property values at least every three years.[74]

Real Property Tax Rates

The tax rates imposed on real property vary and are set by each taxing unit. The
governing body of each taxing unit is allowed to set a rate that will impose the amount
of taxes needed to fund maintenance and operation expenditures for the next year.[75]
In 2005, the tax rates per $1,000 of assessed value ranged from $20.53 in University
Park to $28.44 in Galveston (i.e., 1 dollar per thousand dollars of assessed value equals
1 mill; therefore $20 per thousand equals 20 mills).[76]

Personal and Intangible Property

Tangible personal property is subject to local taxation unless specifically exempt;[77]
like the rates for real property, the tax rates imposed vary among jurisdictions. "Tangible personal property" is defined as all property that is not real property that can be
seen, weighed, measured, felt, or otherwise perceived by the senses.[78] Intangible personal property is not subject to tax at either the state or local level.[79] Tangible personal
property is assessed at 100% of its appraised value, since Texas explicitly prohibits assessment ratios.[80]

Exemptions

Tangible personal property not producing income,[81] income-producing tangible personal property not having a value of more than $500,[82] and farm products[83] are exempt
from the property tax, as is at least $5,000 of the assessed value of real estate and per-
sonal property owned by a disabled veteran.[84] In addition, Texas taxpayers are allowed
a $3,000 county exemption from the assessed value of their residence homestead and
a $15,000 school district exemption.[85]

---

duction of timber or forest products with the intent to produce income for five of the preceding seven years. *Id.* § 23.72.
74. *Id.* § 25.18.
75. *Id.* § 26.05.
76. CCH-EXP, PROP-TAX-GUIDE TX ¶ 20-405, Rates of Tax.
77. Tex. Tax Code Ann. § 11.01.
78. *Id.* § 1.04.
79. *Id.* § 11.02.
80. *Id.* § 26.02.
81. *Id.* § 11.14.
82. *Id.* § 11.145.
83. *Id.* § 11.16.
84. *Id.* § 11.22.
85. *Id.* § 11.13.

General and Selective Sales

General Sales

Texas imposes a general retail sales-and-use tax, which makes up 29.6% of its total tax revenue.[86] This tax is imposed on the sale of every tangible item within the state.[87] Taxable items include tangible personal property[88] and taxable services.[89] The state sales tax rate is 6.25%,[90] and all counties and municipalities may impose an additional rate of up to 1% each for both counties and municipalities, for a maximum combined state and local rate of 8.25%.[91] Combined county and municipal tax rates imposed in addition to the state rate range from 1% to 2%.[92] Exemptions from Texas's sales-and-use tax include food products for human consumption (i.e., groceries),[93] school lunches,[94] food stamp purchases,[95] feed for farm animals,[96] and prescription drugs for humans and animals.[97]

Selective Sales

Selective sales taxes make up 16.2% of Texas's total revenue.[98] Of that amount, 4.5%[99] comes from a motor fuel sales tax imposed at a rate $0.20 per gallon of gasoline.[100] Texas residents paid an average of $130 per capita in state motor fuel sales taxes in 2004, an amount which ranked 23rd nationally and was above the national average of $115.[101]

In 2004, sales taxes on alcoholic beverages made up 0.9% of Texas's total tax revenue.[102] Texas residents paid $26.78 per capita in state alcoholic beverage sales taxes in 2004, an amount which ranked 10th nationally.[103]

---

86. Government Finances, *supra* note 54.

87. Tex. Tax Code Ann. § 151.051.

88. *Id.* § 151.009. Tangible personal property includes all personal property that can be "seen, weighed, measured, felt, or touched or that is perceptible to the senses in any other manner." *Id.*

89. *Id.* § 151.0101. Taxable services include telecommunications services, insurance services, cable television services, security services, information services and real property services, among numerous other services. *Id.*

90. *Id.* § 151.051.

91. *Id.* § 321.103 and Tex. Tax Code Ann. § 323.103.

92. Window on State Government, Local Sales Tax Rate Information Report, http://www.window.state.tx.us/taxinfo/allocsum/taxrates.html (last visited Jan. 5, 2007).

93. Tex. Tax Code Ann. § 151.314.

94. *Id.*

95. *Id.* § 151.3141.

96. *Id.* § 151.316.

97. *Id.* § 151.313.

98. Government Finances, *supra* note 54.

99. *Id.*

100. Tex. Tax Code Ann. § 162.102.

101. State Rankings 2006, *supra* note 1, at 327.

102. Government Finances, *supra* note 54.

103. State Rankings 2006, *supra* note 1, at 335.

The tobacco product sales tax makes up 0.8%[104] of Texas's tax revenues; in 2005, it was imposed at a rate of $0.41 per pack of cigarettes.[105]

The remainder of Texas's selective sales taxes makes up 10% of its total tax revenue. Of this amount, 2.6% represents taxes on utilities and the other 7.4% represents taxes on other specific commodities, businesses, or services not reported separately above (e.g., on contractors, lodging, lubricating oil, fuels other than motor fuel, motor vehicles, meals, soft drinks, margarine, etc.).[106]

Corporate Income and Other

Corporate Income

Texas does not impose any corporate income taxes; however, Texas does impose a corporate franchise tax on each corporation and limited liability company that does business in Texas.[107] General partnerships and sole proprietorships are not subject to the franchise tax.[108] The tax imposed is the greater of 0.25% of the entity's net taxable capital or 4.5% of the entity's net taxable earned surplus.[109]

Other

During fiscal year 2004, the collection of all other taxes not previously mentioned accounted for 10.7% of Texas's total tax revenue. Of this amount, approximately $151 million was generated by the estate and gift tax,[110] which is equal to the amount of the federal credit for state death taxes allowable by the Internal Revenue Code.[111] The "other taxes" category is also made up of motor vehicle license taxes, documentary and stock transfer taxes, franchise taxes[112] , severance taxes, and all other taxes not listed separately or provided for in other categories, such as taxes on land based on a specified rate per acre (rather than on assessed value).[113]

---

104. Government Finances, *supra* note 54.

105. STATE RANKINGS 2006, *supra* note 1, at 333.

106. *See* GOVERNMENTS DIVISION, U.S. CENSUS BUREAU, GOVERNMENT FINANCE AND EMPLOYMENT CLASSIFICATION MANUAL, at ch. 7 (2000), *available at* http://ftp2.census.gov/govs/class/classfull.pdf [hereinafter CLASSIFICATION MANUAL].

107. TEX. TAX CODE ANN. § 171.001.

108. *Id.* § 171.0002.

109. *Id.* § 171.002

110. Government Finances, *supra* note 54.

111. TEX. TAX CODE ANN. § 211.051. Note, however, that the federal credit for state death taxes was phased out for all deaths occurring after December 31, 2004, so Texas does not currently have an estate tax.

112. *See supra* notes 107–109.

113. *See* CLASSIFICATION MANUAL, *supra* note 106, at ch. 7.

Burden Analysis

The overall state and local tax burden on Texas's taxpayers is extremely regressive. In fact, Texas has one of the ten most regressive tax systems in the nation.[114] Taxpayers in the lowest quintile — those with incomes of less than $15,000 — bear a tax burden of 11.4% of their income, while taxpayers in the top 1% — those with incomes that exceed $304,000 — bear a tax burden of just 3.5% of their income.[115] It is also worth noting that, although Texas obviously has no control over federal tax policy, federal itemized deductions for state and local personal income and property taxes nonetheless further reduce the burden on taxpayers in the top 1% to 3.2%.[116] Furthermore, between 1989 and 2002, the tax burden on the bottom quintile rose by approximately 0.1%, while the burden on the top 1% remained unchanged.[117]

One of the regressive features of the tax system in Texas is that it does not employ an income tax. Moreover, the sales and excise taxes imposed by Texas are extremely regressive, with taxpayers in the lowest quintile bearing a tax burden of 8.5% and those in the top 1% bearing a tax burden of just 1.2%.[118] Property taxes in Texas are also regressive, with taxpayers in the lowest quintile bearing a tax burden of 3.0% and those in the top quintile bearing an average tax burden of 2.6%.[119]

---

114. *See* ROBERT S. MCINTYRE ET AL., WHO PAYS? A DISTRIBUTIONAL ANALYSIS OF THE TAX SYSTEMS IN ALL 50 STATES 3 (2d ed. 2003), *available at* http://www.itepnet.org/wp2000/text.pdf.

115. *See id.* at 102. Taxpayers in the second quintile bear a 9.6% total tax burden on incomes between $15,000 and $25,000; those in the third quintile bear a 8.3% tax burden on incomes between $25,000 and $40,000; those in the fourth quintile bear a 7.4% tax burden on incomes between $40,000 and $69,000; those in the 80th–95th percentiles bear a 6.3% tax burden on incomes between $69,000 and $147,000; finally, those in the 96th–99th percentiles bear a 5.1% tax burden on incomes between $147,000 and $304,000. *Id.*

116. *Id.* Taxpayers in the lowest and second lowest quintile did not receive any benefit from these federal offsets, while those in the third quintile were able to reduce their individual tax burdens by 0.1%, those in the fourth quintile by 0.2%, those in the 80th–95th percentiles by 0.5%, and those in the 96th–99th percentiles by 0.6%. *Id.*

117. *Id.* at 103. During the same period, however, the tax burden for the fourth quintile increased by approximately 0.4%, while the tax burden for the 80th–95th percentiles decreased by approximately 0.4%. *Id.*

118. *See id.* at 102. Taxpayers in the second quintile bear a 7.5% sales-and-excise tax burden; those in the third quintile bear a 6.0% burden; those in the fourth quintile bear a 4.7% burden; those in the 80th–95th percentiles bear a 3.4% burden; finally, those in the 96th–99th percentiles bear a 2.2% burden. *Id.*

119. *See id.* at 102. Taxpayers in the second quintile bear a 2.1% property tax burden; those in the third quintile bear a 2.3% burden; those in the fourth quintile bear a 2.7% burden; those in the 80th–95th percentiles bear a 2.9% burden; those in the 96th–99th percentiles bear a 2.8% burden; finally, those in the top 1% bear a 2.1% burden. *Id.*

Utah

General Information

Basic Profile – Geography, Population, and Industry

Admitted to the Union in 1896, Utah is known as the "Beehive State."[1] It is located in the western Rocky Mountains and is bordered by Idaho and Wyoming on the north; Wyoming and Colorado on the east; New Mexico and Arizona on the south; and Nevada on the west. Utah is located in the mountain time zone, and its capital is Salt Lake City.

Utah ranks 13th in total area (84,899 square miles).[2] In 2005, the state ranked 34th in population (approximately 2.5 million residents).[3] Its population is approximately 93.8% white, 1.0% black, 1.3% American Indian and Alaskan Native, and 1.9% Asian.[4] The state is approximately 6% Catholic; 69% Protestant (of which 83% are members of the Church of Jesus Christ of Latter-Day Saints); and less than 0.5% Jewish; 25% claim a religion outside the Judeo-Christian tradition or no religion at all.[5] Nearly 88.7% of Utah's population lives in urban areas.[6] Major industries include agriculture, tourism, and banking and finance.[7]

Family Income and Poverty Indicators

In 2004, Utah's per capita gross product was $34,127, which ranked 38th nationally and was below the national average of $39,725.[8] During this same period, while the

---

1. STATE RANKINGS 2006, vi, 1 (Kathleen O'Leary Morgan & Scott Morgan eds., Morgan Quitno Press, 2006).

2. *Id.* at 225.

3. *Id.* at 429.

4. Utah Quick Facts from the U.S. Census Bureau, http://quickfacts.census.gov/qfd/states/54000.html (last visited Jan. 27, 2007). The remaining population is made up of 0.7% native Hawaiian persons or other Pacific Islanders and 1.3% persons reporting two or more races. *Id.* Additionally, 10.9% of Utah's total population identify themselves as persons of Hispanic or Latino origin. *Id.* (noting that because Hispanics may be of any race, they are included within the other applicable race categories).

5. BARRY A. KOSMIN, EGON MAYER & ARIELA KEYSAR, AMERICAN RELIGIOUS IDENTIFICATION SURVEY 2001, at 41, *available at* http://www.gc.cuny.edu/faculty/research_studies/aris.pdf.

6. USDA Economic Research Service, Utah Fact Sheet, http://www.ers.usda.gov/StateFacts/VA.htm (last visited Feb. 17, 2007). According to the latest estimates, approximately 278,468 people live in rural areas, and 2.2 million people live in urban areas. *Id.*

7. About Utah – Utah.gov, http://www.utah.gov/about/ (last visited Feb. 17, 2007).

8. STATE RANKINGS 2006, *supra* note 1, at 89.

median household income in Utah was $50,614,[9] 9.6% of the state's population was living in poverty, which was somewhat below the national average of 12.4%.[10] More specifically, poverty affected 13.1% of Utah's children,[11] 5.4% of its senior citizens,[12] and 8.2% of its families.[13] Of its female-headed households with children, 35.4% lived in poverty,[14] and 32.1% of the state's public elementary and secondary school students were eligible for free or reduced-price meals.[15] Of those living in poverty approximately 1.5% were black, which represented 17.9% of Utah's black population and 0.1% of its total population.[16] In an attempt to combat this poverty, Utah spent approximately $1.6 billion on public welfare programs in 2002,[17] which made up 12.4% of its total government expenditures.[18]

Utah's Public Elementary-Secondary School System

Overall Spending and Performance

For the 2003–2004 school year, Utah spent $5,008 per pupil in its public elementary-secondary school system, which was substantially below the national average of $8,182.[19] Of this amount, 10.0% was provided by the federal government, 55.3% was provided by the state government, and 34.7% was provided by the local governments,[20] with property taxes making up 29.3% of the total funding.[21] Out of these funds, Utah paid its elementary and secondary school teachers an estimated average annual salary of $39,965 during the 2004–2005 school year,[22] but during the fall of 2003, it provided a student/teacher ratio of only 22.4, which was far worse than the national average of 15.9.[23]

---

9. *Id.* at 96.

10. *Id.* at 495.

11. *Id.* at 497.

12. *Id.* at 496.

13. *Id.* at 498.

14. *Id.* at 499.

15. *Id.* at 532.

16. *See* Fact Sheet, American FactFinder, http://factfinder.census.gov/home/saff/main.html?_lang=en (select "Utah" under "Get a Fact Sheet for your community") (last visited Feb. 16, 2007). Note that these numbers are based on the 2000 census because more recent numbers where not available.

17. *Id.* at 500.

18. *Id.* at 502.

19. Governments Division, U.S. Census Bureau, Public Education Finances 2004, at 8 tbl.8 (2006).

20. *Id.* at 5 tbl.5.

21. *Id.* at 4 tbl.4.

22. Thomas D. Snyder et al., National Center for Education Statistics, Digest of Education Statistics 2005, at 116 tbl.77 (2006).

23. *Id.* at 98 tbl.65.

In academic performance, Utah's fourth grade students scored higher than the national average in mathematics,[24] reading,[25] and science[26] and lower than the national average in writing.[27] Utah's eighth graders also scored higher than the national average in mathematics,[28] reading,[29] and science[30] and lower than the national average in writing.[31]

Equity Issues

In 2004, revenues spent per student in Utah's highest poverty districts were determined to be $860 less than the revenues spent in its lowest poverty districts.[32] When adjustments were made for the additional costs of educating students growing up in poverty, the funding gap decreased to $663.[33] On the other hand, Utah spent $202 more per student in its highest minority districts, and this amount increased to $311 when adjustments for low-income students were made.[34]

Fourth graders eligible for free or reduced-price school lunches had test scores that were 6.1% lower in mathematics,[35] 9.2% lower in reading,[36] and 9.3% lower in writing[37] than those of students who were not eligible. The results were generally the same for eighth graders eligible for free or reduced price lunches; their test scores were 5.6% lower in mathematics,[38] 4.5% lower in reading,[39] and 16.7% lower in writing[40] than those of students who were not eligible.

---

24. NATIONAL CENTER FOR EDUCATION STATISTICS, U.S. DEPARTMENT OF EDUCATION, THE NATION'S REPORT CARD: MATHEMATICS 2005, at 14 fig.11 (2005), *available at* http://nces.ed.gov/ nationsreportcard/pdf/main2005/ 2006453.pdf [hereinafter MATHEMATICS 2005].

25. NATIONAL CENTER FOR EDUCATION STATISTICS, U.S. DEPARTMENT OF EDUCATION, THE NATION'S REPORT CARD: READING 2005, at 14 fig.11 (2005), *available at* http://nces.ed.gov/ nationsreportcard/pdf/main2005/2006451.pdf [hereinafter READING 2005].

26. NATIONAL CENTER FOR EDUCATION STATISTICS, U.S. DEPARTMENT OF EDUCATION, THE NATION'S REPORT CARD: SCIENCE 2005, at 16 fig.12 (2006), *available at* http://nces.ed.gov/ nationsreportcard//pdf/main2005/2006466.pdf [hereinafter SCIENCE 2005].

27. HILARY R. PERSKY ET AL., NATIONAL CENTER FOR EDUCATION STATISTICS, U.S. DEPARTMENT OF EDUCATION, THE NATION'S REPORT CARD: WRITING 2002, at 23 tbl.2.2 (2003), *available at* http://nces.ed.gov/nationsreportcard/pdf/main2002/2003529.pdf [hereinafter WRITING 2002].

28. MATHEMATICS 2005, *supra* note 24, at 16 fig.12.

29. READING 2005, *supra* note 25, at 16 fig.12.

30. SCIENCE 2005, *supra* note 26, at 28 fig.22.

31. WRITING 2002, *supra* note 27, at 24 tbl.2.3.

32. THE EDUCATION TRUST, FUNDING GAPS 2006, at 7 tbl.3 (2006), *available at* http://www2 .edtrust.org/NR/rdonlyres/CDEF9403-5A75-437E-93FF-EBF1174181FB/0/FundingGap2006.pdf.

33. *Id.*

34. *Id.* at 7 tbl.4.

35. MATHEMATICS 2005, *supra* note 24, at 20 tbl.5.

36. READING 2005, *supra* note 25, at 20 tbl.5.

37. WRITING 2002, *supra* note 27, at 75 tbl.3.24.

38. MATHEMATICS 2005, *supra* note 24, at 21 tbl.6.

39. READING 2005, *supra* note 25, at 21 tbl.6.

40. WRITING 2002, *supra* note 27, at 76 tbl.3.25.

Utah has seen virtually no litigation relating to issues of disparate funding among school districts.

Availability of Publicly Funded Prekindergarten Programs

Utah currently has no state prekindergarten program.[41]

Where Does Utah Get Its Revenue?

At the end of fiscal year 2004, Utah had total revenues of approximately $18.9 billion.[42] Of this amount, 35% was derived from state and local tax revenues and 17% was received from the federal government.[43] The remaining 48% came from other sources, including the insurance trust revenue, revenue from government-owned utilities, and other commercial or auxiliary enterprises.[44]

Tax Revenue

Utah collected approximately $6.6 billion in state and local tax revenue during fiscal year 2004.[45] As a result, Utah residents paid $2,735 per capita in state and local taxes, an amount which ranked 41st nationally.[46] The different types of tax sources were approximately apportioned as follows:

Individual income taxes	25.6%
Property taxes	25.2%
General and selective sales taxes	41.8%
Corporate income and other taxes	7.4%
	100.0%[47]

Federal Funding

During fiscal year 2004, 17% of Utah's total revenues came from the federal government.[48] For every dollar of federal taxes paid, Utah received $1.14 in federal fund-

---

41. W. Steven Barnett et al., National Institute for Early Education Research, The State of Preschool 2005, at 142 (2006), *available at* http://nieer.org/yearbook/pdf/yearbook.pdf.

42. U.S. Census Bureau, State and Local Government Finances - 2003–04, http://www.census.gov/govs/www/estimate04.html (last visited Oct. 6, 2006) [hereinafter Government Finances].

43. *Id.*

44. *Id.*

45. *Id.*

46. *Id.*

47. *Id.*

48. *Id.*

ing, an amount which ranked 22nd nationally[49] and was slightly below the national average of $1.17.[50]

Lottery Revenue

Utah does not have a state lottery.

Legal Structures of Major Tax Sources

Income

Utah employs a broad-based income tax[51] that uses adjusted gross income for federal income tax purposes as a starting point for determining taxable income.[52] However, numerous adjustments may be available to various individuals in calculating this amount.[53] The Utah constitution allows the state to give the power to localities to institute a local income tax; however, no localities currently have this power.[54] During fiscal year 2004, Utah collected individual income tax of $699 per capita, which ranked 21st nationally.[55]

In Utah, a typical family of four (i.e., married taxpayers who file jointly and have two dependent children) are not required to pay any income tax until their combined income exceeds $23,500, an amount which is above the national poverty line of $20,615.[56] Utah's income tax structure contains six tax brackets that impose a minimum marginal rate of 2.3% and a maximum marginal rate of 7%.[57] When statutory exemptions and the standard deduction are taken into account, the maximum marginal rate applies to every dollar of income exceeding $26,001.[58]

---

49. The Tax Foundation, Federal Spending Received Per Dollar of Taxes Paid by State, 2004 http://www.taxfoundation.org/taxdata/show/266.html (last visited Sept. 17, 2006).

50. *See id.*

51. UTAH CODE ANN. § 59-10-104.

52. *Id.* § 59-10-114.

53. *Id.*

54. UTAH CONST. art. XIII, § 5,

55. STATE RANKINGS 2006, *supra* note 1, at 321.

56. JASON A. LEVITIS & NICHOLAS JOHNSON, CENTER ON BUDGET AND POLICY PRIORITIES, THE IMPACT OF STATE INCOME TAXES ON LOW-INCOME FAMILIES IN 2006, at 12 (2007). In 2006, Utah taxpayers who were married and filing jointly could claim a standard deduction of $10,300, personal exemptions of $2,550 for both the taxpayer and the spouse, and dependent exemptions of $2,550. UTAH CODE ANN. § 59-10-104.1. Note, however, that the threshold calculation of $23,500 is greater than the sum of these exemptions because it includes additional tax benefits available to low-income families, such as the earned-income tax credit. *See* LEVITIS & JOHNSON, *supra.*

57. UTAH CODE ANN. § 59-10-104. Utah's middle four tax rates are 3.3%, 4.2%, 5.2%, and 6.2%. *Id.*

58. This total is the sum of the standard deduction and exemptions allowable for a family of four, $20,500, plus the threshold of income for the highest taxable bracket, $5,501. *See supra* notes 56–57.

Property

Overview

Utah has a typical property tax system that taxes the value of real estate and tangible personal property at the local level.[59] During fiscal year 2004, Utah collected approximately $1.7 billion dollars in property tax at the local level.[60] As a result, Utah residents paid $689 per capita in local property taxes, an amount which ranked 39th nationally.[61]

Defining the Real Property Tax Base

Utah has only two classifications for real property: residential property is assessed at 55% of fair market value, while all other property is assessed at 100% of the estimated fair market value. Valuations occur on January 1 each year.[62] Fair market value is generally determined by the application of standard appraisal methods, including the cost method, the income method, and the market-data method.[63] In general, cities are required to reassess property values annually.[64]

Real Property Tax Rates

The tax rates imposed on real property vary and are set by each locality.[65] The state sets a maximum range for taxations as follows: localities with a total taxable value above $100 million may impose a rate of $3.20 per $1,000 of assessed value; localities with a total taxable value below $100 million may impose a rate of $3.60 per $1,000 of assessed value.[66] A provision permits a locality to exceed this maximum if it requires financing for any of sixteen enumerated exceptions, including storm or water control, unmet debt obligations, and funding medical and ambulance services.[67] The highest rate is in Box Elder County, with $6.22 per $1,000 of assessed value.[68] The lowest rate is in Deweyville County, with $0.243 per $1,000 of assessed value.[69]

Personal and Intangible Property

Utah reserves the right to tax tangible and intangible property.[70] However, most personal property, tangible or intangible, is listed as an exemption from taxation.[71]

---

59. UTAH CODE ANN. § 59-2-104.

60. Government Finances, *supra* note 42.

61. *See id.*

62. UTAH CODE ANN. § 59-2-103. Note that agricultural use property may be eligible for current use valuation. *Id.* § 59-2-503.

63. CCH-EXP, PROP-TAX-GUIDE UT ¶ 20-615, Valuation Methods in General.

64. UTAH CODE ANN. § 59-2-924.

65. *Id.* § 59-2-104.

66. *Id.* § 59-2-908.

67. *Id.* § 59-2-911.

68. CCH-EXP, PROP-TAX-GUIDE UT ¶ 20-405, Rates of Tax.

69. *Id.*

70. UTAH CONST. art. XIII, § 2(5).

71. UTAH CODE ANN. § 59-2-1101.

Exemptions

Utah has many varied exemptions based on use and ownership. These exemptions include household goods and furnishings, farm machinery, imports and exports, inventories, motor vehicles, livestock, and property owned by nonprofit organizations.[72]

General and Selective Sales

General Sales

Utah imposes a general retail sales-and-use tax, which makes up 30.1% of Utah's total tax revenue.[73] This tax is imposed on the sale, distribution, renting, or furnishing of tangible personal property, as well as specified services.[74] These services include (1) barbers and beauticians; (2) repair and installation; and (3) laundry and dry cleaning.[75] The state sales tax rate is 4.75%, and all localities may impose a local rate of up to 1%, for a combined state and local rate of 5.75%.[76] Counties may exceed this maximum amount by meeting one of the listed exceptions to the maximum.[77] Many localities have exceeded the maximum, the highest being Alta in Salt Lake County, with a rate of 8.1%.[78] Exemptions from Utah's sales-and-use tax include, among other items, prescription and nonprescription drugs, all food purchased with food stamps, school lunches, and agricultural supplies.[79]

Selective Sales

Selective sales taxes make up 11.7% of Utah's total revenue.[80] Of that amount, 5.2%[81] comes from a motor fuel sales tax imposed at a rate of $0.245 per gallon of gasoline.[82] Utah residents paid an average of $142 per capita in state motor fuel sales taxes in 2004, an amount which ranked 15th nationally and was above the national average of $115.[83]

In 2004, sales taxes on alcoholic beverages made up 0.4% of Utah's total tax revenue.[84] Utah residents paid $11.64 per capita in state alcoholic beverage sales taxes in 2004, an amount which ranked 30th nationally.[85]

---

72. *Id.* §§ 59-2-1101 – 59-2-1115.
73. Government Finances, *supra* note 42.
74. Utah Code Ann. § 59-12-103.
75. *Id.*
76. *Id.* §§ 59-12-103, 59-12-204.
77. *Id.* § 59-12-204.
78. CCH-EXP, SALES-TAX-GUIDE UT ¶ 61-735, Rates of Tax.
79. Utah Code Ann. §§ 59-12-104–105.
80. Government Finances, *supra* note 42.
81. *Id.*
82. Utah Code Ann. § 59-13-201.
83. State Rankings 2006, *supra* note 1, at 327.
84. Government Finances, *supra* note 42.
85. State Rankings 2006, *supra* note 1, at 335.

The tobacco product sales tax makes up 0.9% of Utah's tax revenues and is imposed at a rate of $0.695 per pack of cigarettes.[86] Utah residents paid $25.47 per capita in state tobacco sales taxes in 2004, an amount which ranked 38th nationally.[87]

The remainder of Utah's selective sales taxes makes up 5.2% of its total tax revenue. Of this amount, 1.6% represents taxes on utilities and the other 3.6% represents taxes on other specific commodities, businesses, or services not reported separately above (e.g., on contractors, lodging, lubricating oil, fuels other than motor fuel, motor vehicles, meals, soft drinks, margarine, etc.).[88]

Corporate Income and Other

Corporate Income

The corporate income tax makes up 2.2% of Utah's total tax revenue.[89] Utah's broad-based corporate income tax is imposed at a flat rate of 5%, with a minimum payment of $100, on a corporation's taxable income,[90] which is based on the corporation's federal taxable income.[91]

Utah follows the federal income tax treatment of S corporations. Thus, they do not pay Utah's corporate income tax; rather, income and losses flow through to their shareholders.[92] A similar treatment is afforded to limited partnerships and limited liability partnerships, as well as limited liability companies, assuming they are treated as a partnership for federal tax purposes.[93] However, if a limited liability company is treated as a corporation for federal income tax purposes, the entity is subject to Utah's corporate income tax.[94]

Other

During fiscal year 2004, the collection of all other taxes not previously mentioned accounted for 5.2% of Utah's total tax revenue. Of this amount, approximately $9.7 million was generated by the estate and gift tax,[95] which is calculated on the basis of the federal credit for state death taxes allowable by § 2011 of the Internal Revenue Code.[96] The "other taxes" category is also made up of motor vehicle license taxes, documentary and stock transfer taxes, severance taxes, and all other taxes not listed sepa-

---

86. Utah Code Ann. § 59-14-204.

87. State Rankings 2006, *supra* note 1, at 332.

88. *See* Governments Division, U.S. Census Bureau, Government Finance and Employment Classification Manual, at ch.7 (2000), *available at* http://ftp2.census.gov/govs/class/classfull.pdf [hereinafter Classification Manual].

89. Government Finances, *supra* note 42.

90. Utah Code Ann. § 59-7-104.

91. *Id.*

92. CCH-EXP, UT-TAXRPTR ¶ 10-240, Limited Liability Companies (LLCs).

93. *Id.*

94. *Id.*

95. Government Finances, *supra* note 42.

96. Utah Code Ann. § 59-11-203.

rately or provided for in other categories, such as taxes on land based on a specified rate per acre (rather than on assessed value).[97]

Burden Analysis

The overall state and local tax burden on Utah taxpayers is very regressive. Taxpayers in the lowest quintile—those with incomes of less than $16,000—bear a tax burden of 11.5% of their income, while taxpayers in the top 1%—those with incomes that exceed $280,000—bear a tax burden of just 7.6% of their income.[98] It is also worth noting that, although Utah obviously has no control over federal tax policy, federal itemized deductions for state and local personal income and property taxes nonetheless further reduce the burden on taxpayers in the top 1% to 5.5%.[99] Furthermore, between 1989 and 2002, the tax burden on the bottom quintile rose by approximately 0.8%, while the burden on the top 1% actually fell by the same amount.[100]

In terms of the income tax, the burden across income groups in Utah is slightly progressive, with taxpayers in the lowest quintile bearing a tax burden of 1.0% and those in the top 1% bearing a tax burden of 5.2%.[101] In contrast, however, the sales and excises taxes imposed by Utah are extremely regressive, with taxpayers in the lowest quintile bearing a tax burden of 8.3% and those in the top 1% bearing a tax burden of just 1.2%.[102] Property taxes in Utah are also regressive, with taxpayers in the lowest quin-

---

97. *See* CLASSIFICATION MANUAL, *supra* note 88, at ch.7.

98. *See* ROBERT S. MCINTYRE ET AL., WHO PAYS? A DISTRIBUTIONAL ANALYSIS OF THE TAX SYSTEMS IN ALL 50 STATES 104 (2d ed. 2003), *available at* http://www.itepnet.org/wp2000/text.pdf. Taxpayers in the second quintile bear a 12.1% total tax burden on incomes between $16,000 and $27,000; those in the third quintile bear a 11.0% tax burden on incomes between $27,000 and $43,000; those in the fourth quintile bear a 10.5% tax burden on incomes between $43,000 and $67,000; those in the 80th–95th percentiles bear a 9.7% tax burden on incomes between $67,000 and $122,000; finally, those in the 96th–99th percentiles bear a 8.7% tax burden on incomes between $122,000 and $280,000. *Id.*

99. *Id.* Taxpayers in the lowest and second lowest quintiles were able to reduce their individual tax burdens by 0.1%, those in the third quintile by 0.3%, those in the fourth quintile by 0.6%, those in the 80th–95th percentiles by 1.2%, and those in the 96th–99th percentiles by 1.6%. *Id.*

100. *Id.* at 105.

101. *See id.* at 104. Taxpayers in the second quintile bear a 2.4% income tax burden; those in the third quintile bear a 3.1% burden; those in the fourth quintile bear a 3.6% burden; those in the 80th–95th percentiles bear a 4.1% burden; finally, those in the 96th–99th percentiles bear a 4.4% burden. *Id.* Note, however, that of the total income tax burden borne by the top 1%, 5.0% represents individual income taxes and 0.2% represents corporate income taxes. *Id.*

102. *See id.* Taxpayers in the second quintile bear a 7.5% sales-and-excise tax burden; those in the third quintile bear a 5.8% burden; those in the fourth quintile bear a 4.9% burden; those in the 80th–95th percentiles bear a 3.7% burden; finally, those in the 96th–99th percentiles bear a 2.4% burden. *Id.*

tile bearing a tax burden of 2.2% and those in the remaining quintiles bearing an average tax burden of 1.9%.[103]

---

103. *See id.* at 104. Taxpayers in the second quintile bear a 2.2% property tax burden; those in the third quintile bear a 2.1% burden; those in the fourth quintile bear a 2.0% burden; those in the 80th–95th percentiles bear a 2.0% burden; those in the 96th–99th percentiles bear a 1.9% burden; finally, those in the top 1% bear a 1.2% burden. *Id.*

Vermont

General Information

Basic Profile – Geography, Population, and Industry

Vermont, "the Green Mountain State," was admitted to the Union in 1791.[1] Situated in the northeastern United States, Vermont is bordered on the north by the Canadian province of Quebec, on the east by New Hampshire, on the south by Massachusetts, and on the west by New York. It is located in the eastern time zone, and its capital is Montpelier.

Vermont ranks 45th in total land and water area (9,641 square miles).[2] In 2005, the state ranked 49th in population (623,050 residents).[3] Its population is approximately 96.9% white and 0.6% black.[4] The state is approximately 38% Catholic; 30% Protestant; and less than 0.5% Jewish; 32% claim a religion outside the Judeo-Christian tradition or no religion at all.[5] Vermont's population is predominantly rural, with 67.06% of the population living in rural areas.[6] Major industries include dairy farming, maple products, machine and machine tool manufacturing, and tourism.[7]

Family Income and Poverty Indicators

In 2004, Vermont's per capita gross product was $35,286, which was below the national average of $39,725.[8] During this same period, the median household income in

---

1. STATE RANKINGS 2006, vi, 1 (Kathleen O'Leary Morgan & Scott Morgan eds., Morgan Quitno Press 2006).

2. *Id.* at 225.

3. *Id.* at 429.

4. Vermont Quick Facts from the U.S. Census Bureau, http://quickfacts.census.gov/qfd/states/54000.html (last visited Jan. 30, 2007). The remaining population is made up of 1.0% Asian persons; 0.4% American Indian and Alaska Native persons; and 1.1% persons that report two or more races. *Id.* Additionally, 1.1% of Vermont's total population identify themselves as persons of Hispanic or Latino origin. *Id.* (noting that because Hispanics may be of any race, they are included within the other applicable race categories).

5. BARRY A. KOSMIN, EGON MAYER & ARIELA KEYSAR, AMERICAN RELIGIOUS IDENTIFICATION SURVEY 2001, at 41, *available at* http://www.gc.cuny.edu/faculty/research_studies/aris.pdf.

6. United States Department of Agriculture, Economic Research Service, Vermont Fact Sheet, http://www.ers.usda.gov/StateFacts/VT.htm (last visited Sept. 17, 2006).

7. The Official Portal of Vermont, http://www.vermont.gov/find-facts/findindex.html (last visited Sept. 19, 2006).

8. STATE RANKINGS 2006, *supra* note 1, at 89.

Vermont was $45,692,[9] but only 8.8% of the state's population was living in poverty, which was substantially below the national average of 12.4% and ranked among the bottom ten states nationally.[10] More specifically, poverty affected 10.9% of Vermont's children,[11] 7.8% of its senior citizens,[12] and 5.6% of its families.[13] Of its female-headed households with children, 29.1% lived in poverty,[14] and 27.4% of the state's elementary and secondary school students were eligible for free or reduced-price meals.[15] Of those living in poverty, approximately 1.0% were black, which represented 17.6% of Vermont's black population but less than 0.09% of its total population.[16] Vermont spent approximately $757 million on public welfare programs in 2002,[17] which made up 19.9% of its total government expenditures.[18]

Vermont's Public Elementary-Secondary School System

Overall Spending and Performance

For the 2003–2004 school year, Vermont spent $11,128 per pupil in its public elementary-secondary school system, which was substantially above the national average of $8,182.[19] Of this amount, 8.0% was provided by the federal government, 68.0% was provided by the state government, and 23.9% was provided by the local governments,[20] with property taxes making up 18.3% of the total funding.[21] Out of these funds, Vermont paid its elementary and secondary school teachers an estimated average annual salary of $44,535 during the 2004–2005 school year,[22] and in 2003, it provided a student/teacher ratio of 11.3, which was far better than the national average of 15.9.[23]

---

9. *Id.* at 96.

10. *Id.* at 495.

11. *Id.* at 497.

12. *Id.* at 496.

13. *Id.* at 498.

14. *Id.* at 499.

15. *Id.* at 532.

16. *See* Fact Sheet, American FactFinder, http://factfinder.census.gov/home/saff/main.html?_lang=en (select "Vermont" under "Get a Fact Sheet for your community") (last visited Feb. 17, 2007). Note that these numbers are based on the 2000 census because more recent numbers were not available.

17. *Id.* at 500.

18. *Id.* at 502.

19. GOVERNMENTS DIVISION, U.S. CENSUS BUREAU, PUBLIC EDUCATION FINANCES 2004, at 8 tbl.8 (2006), *available at* http://www2.census.gov/govs/school/04f33pub.pdf.

20. *See id.* at 5 tbl.5.

21. *See id.* at 4 tbl.4.

22. THOMAS D. SNYDER ET AL., NATIONAL CENTER FOR EDUCATION STATISTICS, DIGEST OF EDUCATION STATISTICS 2005, at 116 tbl.77 (2006), *available at* http://nces.ed.gov/pubsearch/pubsinfo.asp?pubid=2006030.

23. *Id.* at 98 tbl.65.

In academic performance, Vermont's fourth and eighth grade students scored higher than the national average in mathematics,[24] reading,[25] science,[26] and writing.[27]

Equity Issues

In 2004, revenues spent per student in Vermont's highest poverty districts were determined to be $403 less than the revenues spent in its lowest poverty districts.[28] When adjustments were made for the additional costs of educating students growing up in poverty, however, the funding gap grew to $894.[29] Similarly, Vermont spent $800 less per student in its highest minority districts, although this amount decreased to $613 when adjustments for low-income students were made.[30]

Fourth graders eligible for free or reduced-price school lunches had test scores that were 8% lower in mathematics,[31] 10% lower in reading,[32] and 12% lower in writing[33] than those of students who were not eligible. The results were similar for eighth graders eligible for free or reduced-price lunches; their test scores were 7% lower in mathematics,[34] 7% lower in reading,[35] and 14% lower in writing[36] than those of students who were not eligible.

Funding education in Vermont was revamped under Vermont Act 60: The Equal Educational Opportunity Act (EEOA) in 1997, which created the Education Fund.[37] This legislation was passed in response to *Brigham v. State*, in which plaintiffs sued the state,

24. NATIONAL CENTER FOR EDUCATION STATISTICS, U.S. DEPARTMENT OF EDUCATION, THE NATION'S REPORT CARD: MATHEMATICS 2005, at 14 fig.11, 16 fig.12 (2005), *available at* http://nces.ed.gov/nationsreportcard/pdf/ main2005/2006453.pdf [hereinafter MATHEMATICS 2005].

25. NATIONAL CENTER FOR EDUCATION STATISTICS, U.S. DEPARTMENT OF EDUCATION, THE NATION'S REPORT CARD: READING 2005, at 14 fig.11, 16 fig.12 (2005), *available at* http://nces.ed.gov/nationsreportcard/pdf/main2005/2006451.pdf [hereinafter READING 2005].

26. NATIONAL CENTER FOR EDUCATION STATISTICS, U.S. DEPARTMENT OF EDUCATION, THE NATION'S REPORT CARD: SCIENCE 2005, at 16 fig.12, 28 fig.22 (2006), *available at* http://nces.ed.gov/nationsreportcard//pdf/main2005/2006466.pdf [hereinafter SCIENCE 2005].

27. HILARY R. PERSKY ET AL., NATIONAL CENTER FOR EDUCATION STATISTICS, U.S. DEPARTMENT OF EDUCATION, THE NATION'S REPORT CARD: WRITING 2002, at 23 tbl.2.2, 24 tbl.2.3 (2003), *available at* http://nces.ed.gov/nationsreportcard/pdf/main2002/2003529.pdf [hereinafter WRITING 2002].

28. THE EDUCATION TRUST, FUNDING GAPS 2006, at 7 tbl.3 (2006), *available at* http://www2.edtrust.org/NR/rdonlyres/CDEF9403-5A75-437E-93FF-EBF1174181FB/0/FundingGap2006.pdf.

29. *Id.*

30. *Id.* at 7 tbl.4.

31. MATHEMATICS 2005, *supra* note 24, at 20 tbl.5.

32. READING 2005, *supra* note 25, at 20 tbl.5.

33. WRITING 2002, *supra* note 27, at 75 tbl.3.24.

34. MATHEMATICS 2005, *supra* note 24, at 21 tbl.6.

35. READING 2005, *supra* 25, at 21 tbl.6.

36. WRITING 2002, *supra* note 27, at 76 tbl.3.25.

37. VT. STAT. ANN. tit. 16, § 1 (Publication 60, Added 1997, No. 60, § 2).

claiming the state's education finance system violated the Vermont constitution.[38] Through Act 60, additional funding was provided to cover the higher costs of the state's smallest school districts in the form of an extra $1 million per year to districts with fewer than 100 students.[39] Under Act 60, education tax rates are uniformly tied to local per-pupil spending levels across the state, which narrows the equity disparities between wealthy and poor school districts.[40] Because of a large number of complaints, a compromise was reached in 2003 through Act 68 and then later through Act 130, which revised Act 60 to remove a recapture clause and to codify the state school funding formula.[41]

Availability of Publicly Funded Prekindergarten Programs

Vermont has funds prekindergarten education in two ways: Vermont's Early Education Initiative (EEI) and the Vermont Publicly Funded Prekindergarten.[42] First, EEI awards grants to public schools, Parent-Child Centers, Head Start, and private child care programs for three- and four-year olds who are at risk.[43] At-risk children include those with family incomes below 185% of the federal poverty level or those with "risk factors such as abuse or neglect, social isolation, limited English proficiency, and developmental delays."[44] The Vermont Publicly Funded Prekindergarten program provides for funding for public education for three- and four-year-olds through local public schools on the basis of a formula "allocating 40% of the K–6 education funding level for 10 hours of program per week."[45] Total enrollment in these state-funded programs is 3,934,[46] which represents 31% of Vermont's 12,605 three- and four-year-old children.[47] The federally funded Head Start program enrolls an additional 1,162 children,[48] which represents 9% of Vermont's three- and four-year-old children."[49]

---

38. Brigham v. State, 692 A.2d 384 (Vt. 1997).

39. The Equity Sector, http://www.newrules.org/equity/versmall.html (last visited March 1, 2007).

40. State Board of Education, The Equal Educational Opportunity Act: Measuring Equity, at 4 (2001), *available at* http://www.state.vt.us/educ/new/pdfdoc/pubs/eeo_report_01.pdf.

41. Vermont Department of Education: Overview of Vermont's Education Funding System Under Act 68 & Act 130, at (2006), *available at* http://education.vermont.gov/new/pdfdoc/laws/act68/act68_overview.pdf

42. W. Steven Barnett et al., National Institute for Early Education Research, The State of Preschool 2006, at 144 (2006), *available at* http://nieer.org/yearbook/pdf/yearbook.pdf.

43. *Id.*

44. *Id.*

45. *Id.*

46. *Id.* at 145.

47. *See id.* at 232.

48. *Id.* at 146.

49. *Id.* at 27.

Where Does Vermont Gets Its Revenue?

At the end of fiscal year 2004, Vermont had total revenues of approximately $5.3 billion.[50] Of this amount, 43% was derived from state and local tax revenues and 26% was received from the federal government.[51] The remaining 31% came from other sources, including the Vermont Lottery, insurance trust revenue, and revenue from government-owned utilities and other commercial or auxiliary enterprises.[52]

Tax Revenue

Vermont collected approximately $2.3 billion in state and local tax revenue during fiscal year 2004.[53] As a result, Vermont residents paid $3,681 per capita in state and local taxes, an amount which ranked 13th nationally.[54] The different types of tax sources were apportioned as follows:

Individual income taxes	18.8%
Property taxes	41.6%
General and selective sales taxes	30.3%
Corporate income and other taxes	9.3%
	100.0%[55]

Federal Funding

During fiscal year 2004, 26% of Vermont's total revenues came from the federal government.[56] For every dollar of federal taxes paid, Vermont received $1.12 in federal funding, an amount which ranked 24th nationally[57] and was slightly below the national average of $1.17.[58]

---

50. U.S. Census Bureau, State and Local Government Finances - 2003–04, http://www.census.gov/govs/www/estimate04.html (last visited Oct. 6, 2006) [hereinafter Government Finances].

51. *Id.*

52. *Id.*

53. The total tax revenues were collected as follows: $1.8 billion by the state and $0.5 billion by local governments. *Id.*

54. *See id.*

55. Government Finances, *supra* note 50.

56. *Id.*

57. The Tax Foundation, Federal Spending Received Per Dollar of Taxes Paid by State, 2004 http://www.taxfoundation.org/news/show/266.html (last visited Sept. 17, 2006).

58. *See id.*

Lottery Revenue

The Vermont Lottery has been in operation since 1977.[59] Since 1998, all proceeds from the lottery are required to be used for education.[60] The total gross proceeds from the Vermont Lottery during fiscal year 2005 were $92.82 million, with 22% of the proceeds going to the Vermont Education Fund.[61] Vermont is also involved in a Tri-State Lotto under a tristate compact with Maine and New Hampshire.[62]

Legal Structures of Major Tax Sources

Income

Vermont employs a broad-based income tax that uses adjusted gross income for federal income tax purposes, with very few adjustments, as a starting point for determining state's taxable income.[63] Vermont localities do not have the authority to levy income taxes.[64] During fiscal year 2004, Vermont collected individual income tax of $692 per capita.[65]

In Vermont, a typical family of four (i.e., married taxpayers who file jointly and have two dependent children) are not required to pay any income tax until their combined income exceeds $33,200, an amount which is well above the national poverty line of $20,615.[66] Vermont's income tax structure contains five tax brackets that impose a minimum marginal rate of 3.6% and a maximum marginal rate 9.5%.[67] When statutory

---

59. The Vermont Lottery, http://www.vtlottery.com/about/mission-and-history.asp (last visited October 20, 2006).

60. National Association of State and Provincial Lotteries, http://www.naspl.org/Contacts/index.cfm?fuseaction=view&ID=4 (last visited October 20, 2006).

61. The Vermont Lottery, http://www.vtlottery.com/faqs/faqs.asp#q1 (last visited October 20, 2006).

62. Vt. Stat. Ann. tit. 31, § 673.

63. *Id.* tit. 32, § 5822.

64. All States Guide Portfolio: Vermont 1460. ASTG P vt_1460.

65. State Rankings 2006, *supra* note 1, at 321.

66. Jason A. Levitis, Center on Budget and Policy Priorities, The Impact of State Income Taxes on Low-Income Families in 2006, at 12 (2007). In 2006, Vermont taxpayers who were married and filing jointly could claim personal exemptions of $3,300 for both the taxpayer and his or her spouse and dependent exemptions of $3,300 as defined under the Internal Revenue Code. 26 U.S.C.A. § 151 (2006). Internal Revenue Service, Publication 17 (2006). However, Vermont does not allow for a standard deduction. Note, however, that the threshold calculation of $33,200 is greater than the sum of these exemptions because it includes additional tax benefits available to low-income families, such as the earned-income tax credit. *See* Levitis & Johnson, *supra.*

67. Vt. Stat. Ann. tit. 32, § 5822. Vermont's middle tax brackets are as follows: 7.2%, 8.5%, and 9.0%. *Id.*

exemptions are taken into account, the maximum marginal rate applies to every dollar of income exceeding $349,751.[68]

Vermont is also one of the very few states that provide for a deduction of 40% of adjusted net capital gain income as defined by the IRC under Section 1(h).[69]

Property

Overview

Vermont has a typical property tax system that taxes the value of real property and tangible personal property owned by businesses and utilities at the state and local levels.[70] During fiscal year 2004, Vermont collected a total of $950 million in property taxes.[71] Of this amount, $502 million was collected by Vermont localities and $448 million was collected by the state.[72] As a result, Vermont residents paid $1,531 per capita in property taxes, an amount which ranked 8th nationally.[73]

Defining the Real Property Tax Base

Vermont has two separate tax rates on real property: one for residential property and one for nonresidential property.[74] On April 1 of each year, real property is taxed.[75] In Vermont, the property tax system requires budgeting and then listing.[76] The town first estimates how much it will need to raise for expenses, and then town officials ("listers") determine what properties are taxable and the fair market value of those properties.[77] Property is recorded in a grand list of all the town's property values, and the municipal tax rate is then set on the basis of the amount of expenses needed to be raised.[78]

An education property tax is also imposed statewide at uniform rates on all nonresidential and homestead property.[79] This amount is determined by the state, depending on the necessary level of school funding needed.[80] Dividing the listed value by

---

68. The exemptions of $3,400, plus the threshold of taxable income for the highest tax bracket of $336,551, equals $349,751. *See supra* notes 67–68.

69. VT. STAT. ANN. tit. 32, § 5811(21).

70. *Id.* § 3002.

71. Government Finances, *supra* note 50.

72. *Id.*

73. *See id.*

74. CCH-EXP, VT-TAXRPTR ¶ 20-010, Overview.

75. VT. STAT. ANN. tit. 32, §§ 3002, 3651, 3691.

76. Vermont Property, http://www.vermontproperty.com/newsltr/vtrealestatetaxes.html#Property%20taxes (last visited March 2, 2007).

77. *Id.*

78. VT. STAT. ANN. tit. 32, § 4082.

79. *Id.* § 5402.

80. *Id.*

100 and multiplying the result by the combined school and municipal rate determines the applicable property tax rate on a particular property.[81]

Business personal property, inventory, machinery, and equipment are not subject to the education property tax, but certain business personal property traditionally taxed as real property, such as utility lines, are considered nonresidential property for that tax.[82]

Real Property Tax Rates

The rates of property tax other than the education property tax are set on the basis of necessary expenses annually.[83] For purposes of the education property tax, homesteads, which include a principal residence and land surrounding the principal residence, are taxed at a rate of $1.10 per $100 of assessed value.[84] This rate may, however, be adjusted upwards, depending on the school district's estimated costs.[85] Nonresidential property, on the other hand, is taxed at a rate of $1.59 per $100 of assessed value.[86]

Personal and Intangible Property

Business tangible personal property is also taxed on April 1 of each year at its fair market value and is taxed at a rate determined by the town's listers.[87] Intangibles and personal property owned by individuals are exempt.[88]

Exemptions

Residences located on up to two acres of property may be eligible for tax relief from the state, as determined by comparing the property tax burden with household income.[89] This tax relief comes in the form of a check issued to the homeowner by the state under a program called the "prebate/rebate" program, which was enacted in 1997 in order to "income sensitize" the property tax bills of eligible homeowners.[90] The prebate is calculated on prior-year income and is equalized at a rate of 2%.[91] The equalized homesite value is multiplied by the education tax rate to come up with the home-

---

81. Vermont Property, http://www.vermontproperty.com/newsltr/vtrealestatetaxes.html# Property%20taxes (last visited March 2, 2007).

82. Vt. Stat. Ann. tit. 32, § 5401(10)(D).

83. CCH-EXP, VT-TAXRPTR ¶ 20-405, Rates of Tax.

84. Vt. Stat. Ann. tit. 32, § 5402.

85. Id.

86. Id.

87. Id. § 3618. See also supra note 77 and accompanying text.

88. CCH-EXP, VT-TAXRPTR ¶ 20-505, Exemptions in General.

89. Id.

90. Id.

91. Susan Mesner, Vermont's Property Tax Relief Program: A Study in An Overloaded Circuit Breaker (2005), available at, http://www.taxadmin.org/fta/meet/05rev_est/mesner.pdf.

site school property tax, and the household income for the previous year is multiplied by the household income percentage determined by the state.[92] The latter result is then subtracted from the former to compute the respective prebate check.[93] Several other exemptions are allowed including, among others, air pollution treatment facilities,[94] cemeteries,[95] household goods,[96] and personal apparel.[97]

General and Selective Sales

General Sales

Vermont imposes a general retail sales-and-use tax, which makes up 11.3% of its total tax revenue.[98] This tax applies at a rate of 6% to tangible personal property sold at retail in the state, unless the property is specifically exempt.[99] An additional 1% sales-and-use tax is authorized to be imposed at the local level.[100] Sales tax is also levied on certain services, including public utility services for gas and electricity; providing, fabricating, or printing tangible personal property; amusement charges; and telecommunication.[101] Exemptions from sales tax include, among other items, drugs for human use and "sales of food, food stamps, purchases made with food stamps, food products and beverages sold for human consumption off the premises where sold."[102]

Selective Sales

Selective sales taxes make up about 19% of Vermont's total revenue.[103] Of that amount, 3.8% comes from a motor fuel sales tax.[104] Vermont residents paid an average of $138 per capita in state motor fuel sales taxes in 2004, an amount which ranked 17th nationally and was above the national average of $115.[105]

The tobacco product sales tax made up 2.2%[106] of Vermont's total tax revenue in 2004; it is imposed at a rate of $1.19 per pack of cigarettes.[107]

---

92. *Id.*
93. *Id.*
94. Vt. Stat. Ann. tit. 10, § 570.
95. *Id.* tit. 32, § 3802(7).
96. *Id.* § 3802(8).
97. *Id.*
98. Government Finances, *supra* note 50.
99. Vt. Stat. Ann. tit. 32, § 9771.
100. *Id.* § 5822.
101. *Id.*
102. *Id.* § 9471.
103. Government Finances, *supra* note 50.
104. *Id.*
105. State Rankings 2006, *supra* note 1, at 327.
106. Government Finances, *supra* note 50.
107. State Rankings 2006, *supra* note 1, at 333.

In 2004, the sales tax on alcoholic beverages made up 0.7% of Vermont's tax revenue.[108] Vermont residents paid $27.19 per capita in state alcoholic beverage sales taxes in 2004, an amount which ranked 9th nationally.[109]

The remainder of Vermont's selective sales taxes makes up 12.2% of its total tax revenue. Of this amount, 0.5% represents taxes on utilities and the other 11.7% represents taxes on other specific commodities, businesses, or services not reported separately above (e.g., on contractors, lodging, lubricating oil, fuels other than motor fuel, motor vehicles, meals, soft drinks, etc.).[110]

Corporate and Income and Other

Corporate Income

The corporate income tax makes up 2.7% of Vermont's total tax revenue.[111] "Vermont imposes a broad-based corporate income tax on domestic and foreign corporations carrying on a trade or business in, or deriving income from sources within, the state."[112] C corporations are subject to Vermont's corporate income tax to the extent that they have income taxable by the federal government.[113] As of 2007, Vermont uses three tax brackets in computing the corporate income tax.[114] The minimum tax rate is 6%, and maximum tax rate is 8.5%, which is imposed on taxable incomes in excess of $25,000.[115] S corporations, partnerships, and limited liability companies taxed as partnerships, are subject to a $250 "minimum tax" that is not connected to income.[116] Exempt from the minimum tax are partnerships whose activities are limited to the maintenance and management of their intangible investments, whose annual investment income does not exceed $5,000, and whose total assets do not exceed $20,000.[117]

Other

During fiscal year 2004, the collection of all other taxes not previously mentioned accounted for 6.6% of Vermont's total tax revenue.[118] Of this amount, $14.7 million

---

108. Government Finances, *supra* note 50.

109. STATE RANKINGS 2006, *supra* note 1, at 335.

110. *See* GOVERNMENTS DIVISION, U.S. CENSUS BUREAU, GOVERNMENT FINANCE AND EMPLOYMENT CLASSIFICATION MANUAL, at ch.7 (2000), *available at* http://ftp2.census.gov/govs/class/classfull.pdf [hereinafter CLASSIFICATION MANUAL].

111. Government Finances, *supra* note 50.

112. VT. STAT. ANN. tit. 32, § 5832.

113. *Id.* §§ 5811, 5911.

114. *Id.* § 5832. Corporate income taxes are imposed at a rate of 6% on the first $10,000 of taxable income, 7% on the next $15,000 of taxable income, and 8.5% on taxable income in excess of $25,000.

115. *Id.*

116. *Id.* §§ 5915, 5921.

117. *Id.* § 5921.

118. Government Finances, *supra* note 50.

was generated by the estate and gift tax.[119] Vermont adopted the federal estate and gift tax laws as of 2006 for computing Vermont estate tax.[120] The "other taxes" category is further made up of various license taxes, documentary or stock transfer taxes, severance taxes, and all other taxes not listed separately or provided for in other categories.[121]

Burden Analysis

The overall state and local tax burden on Vermont's taxpayers is somewhat regressive, although Vermont is one of the least regressive states. Taxpayers in the lowest quintile—those with incomes of less than $16,000—bear a tax burden of 10.0% of their income, while taxpayers in the top 1%—those with incomes that exceed $260,000—bear a tax burden of just 9.7% of their income.[122] It is also worth noting that, although Vermont obviously has no control over federal tax policy, federal itemized deductions for state and local personal income and property taxes nonetheless further reduce the burden on taxpayers in the top 1% to 7.1%.[123] Furthermore, between 1989 and 2002, the tax burden on the bottom quintile rose by approximately 2.8%, while the burden on the top 1% rose by only 0.6%.[124]

In terms of the income tax, the burden across income groups in Vermont is moderately progressive, with taxpayers in the lowest quintile bearing a tax burden of 0.5% and those in the top 1% bearing a tax burden of 6.5%.[125] In contrast, however, the sales and excises taxes imposed by Vermont are very regressive, with taxpayers in the lowest quintile bearing a tax burden of 6.5% and those in the top 1% bearing a tax burden of

---

119. *Id.*

120. Vt. Stat. Ann. tit. 32, § 7475.

121. *See* Classification Manual, *supra* note 110, at ch.7.

122. *See* Robert S. McIntyre et al., Who Pays? A Distributional Analysis of the Tax Systems in All 50 States 106 (2d ed. 2003), *available at* http://www.itepnet.org/wp2000/text.pdf. Taxpayers in the second quintile bear a 8.7% total tax burden on incomes between $16,000 and $27,000; those in the third quintile bear a 9.8% tax burden on incomes between $27,000 and $44,000; those in the fourth quintile bear a 10.2% tax burden on incomes between $44,000 and $68,000; those in the 80th–95th percentiles bear a 9.5% tax burden on incomes between $68,000 and $122,000; finally, those in the 96th–99th percentiles bear a 9.6% tax burden on incomes between $122,000 and $260,000. *Id.*

123. *Id.* Taxpayers in the lowest and second lowest quintiles did not receive any benefit from these federal offsets, while those in the third quintile were able to reduce their individual tax burdens by 0.2%, those in the fourth quintile by 0.8%, those in the 80th–95th percentiles by 1.1%, and those in the 96th–99th percentiles by 2.0%. *Id.*

124. *Id.* at 107.

125. *See id.* at 106. Taxpayers in the second quintile bear a 1.0% income tax burden; those in the third quintile bear a 1.8% burden; those in the fourth quintile bear a 2.7% burden; those in the 80th–95th percentiles bear a 3.4% burden; finally, those in the 96th–99th percentiles bear a 4.7% burden. *Id.* Note, however, that of the total income tax burden borne by both the top 1% and those in the 96th–99th percentiles, corporate income taxes make up 0.1% of this burden. *Id.*

just 0.8%.[126] Property taxes in Vermont are also regressive, with taxpayers in the lowest quintile bearing a tax burden of 4.0% and those in the remaining quintiles bearing an average tax burden of 3%.[127]

126. *See id.* Taxpayers in the second quintile bear a 5.2% sales-and-excise tax burden; those in the third quintile bear a 4.6% burden; those in the fourth quintile bear a 3.7% burden; those in the 80th–95th percentiles bear a 2.7% burden; finally, those in the 96th–99th percentiles bear a 1.6% burden. *Id.*

127. *See id.* Taxpayers in the second quintile bear a 2.5% property tax burden; those in the third quintile bear a 3.4% burden; those in the fourth quintile bear a 3.8% burden; those in the 80th–95th percentiles bear a 3.5% burden; those in the 96th–99th percentiles bear a 3.3% burden; finally, those in the top 1% bear a 2.4% burden. *Id.*

Virginia

General Information

Basic Profile – Geography, Population, and Industry

Admitted to the Union in 1788, Virginia is known as the gateway to the south and is commonly referred to as "the Old Dominion State."[1] It is located in the Mid-Atlantic region and is bordered by Washington, D.C., and Maryland on the north; the Atlantic Ocean on the east; North Carolina and Tennessee on the south; and West Virginia and Kentucky on the west. The state is located in the eastern time zone, and its capital is Richmond.

Virginia ranks 35th in total area (42,143 square miles).[2] In 2005, Virginia ranked 12th in population.[3] Its population is 73.6% white and 19.9% black.[4] The state is 14% Catholic; 63% Protestant (of which 48% are Baptist); and 1% Jewish; 22% claim a religion outside the Judeo-Christian tradition or no religion at all.[5] Approximately 85.5% of Virginia's population live in urban areas.[6] Major industries include manufacturing, exports, tourism, high technology, and agriculture.[7]

Family Income and Poverty Indicators

In 2004, Virginia's per capita gross product was $44,021, which ranked among the top ten states nationally and was above the national average of $39,725.[8] During this

---

1. STATE RANKINGS 2006, vi, 1 (Kathleen O'Leary Morgan & Scott Morgan eds., Morgan Quitno Press 2006).

2. *Id.* at 225.

3. *Id.* at 429.

4. Virginia Quick Facts from the U.S. Census Bureau, http://quickfacts.census.gov/qfd/states/54000.html (last visited Jan. 27, 2007). The remaining population is made up of 4.6% Asian persons; 0.3% American Indian and/or Alaska Native persons; and 1.6% persons reporting two or more races. *Id.* Additionally, 6% of Virginia's total population identify themselves as persons of Hispanic or Latino origin. *Id.* (noting that because Hispanics may be of any race, they are included within the other applicable race categories).

5. BARRY A. KOSMIN, EGON MAYER & ARIELA KEYSAR, AMERICAN RELIGIOUS IDENTIFICATION SURVEY 2001, at 41, *available at* http://www.gc.cuny.edu/faculty/research_studies/aris.pdf.

6. USDA Economic Research Service, Virginia Fact Sheet, http://www.ers.usda.gov/StateFacts/VA.htm (last visited Sept. 17, 2006). According to the latest estimates, approximately 1 million people live in rural areas and 6.5 people live in urban areas. *Id.*

7. Fast Facts About Virginia: Virginia is for Lovers, http://www.virginia.org/site/features.asp?FeatureID=139 (last visited Sept. 17, 2006).

8. STATE RANKINGS 2006, *supra* note 1, at 89.

same period, while the median household income in Virginia was $53,275,[9] 9.8% of the state's population was living in poverty, which was below the national average of 12.4%.[10] More specifically, poverty affected 12.6% of Virginia's children,[11] 8.6% of its senior citizens,[12] and 7.2% of its families.[13] Of its female-headed households with children, 30.6% lived in poverty,[14] and 30.2% of the state's elementary and secondary school students were eligible for free or reduced-price meals.[15] Of those living in poverty, approximately 38% were black, which represented 18% of Virginia's black population and 4% of its total population.[16] In an attempt to combat this poverty, Virginia spent approximately $4.7 billion on public welfare programs in 2002,[17] which made up 11.9% of its total government expenditures.[18]

Virginia's Public Elementary-Secondary School System

Overall Spending and Performance

For the 2003–2004 school year, Virginia spent $8,225 per pupil in its public elementary-secondary school system, an amount which hovered around the national average of $8,182.[19] Of this amount, 7% was provided by the federal government, 38.7% was provided by the state government, and 54.3% was provided by the local governments,[20] with property taxes making up a substantial part of the total funding.[21] Out of these funds, Virginia paid its elementary and secondary school teachers an estimated average annual salary of $44,763 during the 2004–2005 school year,[22] and it

---

9. *Id.* at 96.

10. *Id.* at 495.

11. *Id.* at 497.

12. *Id.* at 496.

13. *Id.* at 498.

14. *Id.* at 499.

15. *Id.* at 532.

16. *See* Fact Sheet, American FactFinder, http://factfinder.census.gov/home/saff/main.html?_lang=en (select "Virginia" under "Get a Fact Sheet for your community") (last visited Feb. 16, 2007). Note that these numbers are based on the 2000 census because more recent numbers were not available.

17. *Id.* at 500.

18. *Id.* at 502.

19. Governments Division, U.S. Census Bureau, Public Education Finances 2004, at 8 tbl.8 (2006).

20. *See id.* at 5 tbl.5.

21. Although none of the total funding has been specifically designated as provided by property taxes, 51% of the total funding comes from "Parent Government Contributions," *see id.* at 4 tbl.4., which is defined as "tax receipts and other amounts appropriated by a parent government and transferred to its dependent school system." *Id.* at app. A-1. This amount, however, "[e]xcludes intergovernmental revenue, current charges, and miscellaneous general revenue." *Id.*

22. Thomas D. Snyder et al., National Center for Education Statistics, Digest of Education Statistics 2005, at 116 tbl.77 (2006).

provided a student/teacher ratio of 13.2, which was better than the national average of 15.9.[23]

In academic performance, Virginia's fourth grade students scored higher than the national average in mathematics,[24] reading,[25] science,[26] and writing.[27] Virginia's eighth graders also scored higher than the national average in mathematics,[28] reading,[29] science,[30] and writing.[31]

Equity Issues

In 2004, revenues spent per student in Virginia's highest poverty districts were determined to be $114 less than the revenues spent in its lowest poverty districts.[32] When adjustments were made for the additional costs of educating students growing up in poverty, however, the funding gap grew to $436.[33] On the other hand, Virginia spent $418 more per student in its highest minority districts, although this amount fell to $239 when adjustments for low-income students were made.[34]

Fourth graders eligible for free or reduced-price school lunches had test scores that were 10% lower in mathematics,[35] 11% lower in reading,[36] and 15% lower in writing[37] than those of students who were not eligible. The results were generally the same for eighth graders eligible for free or reduced price lunches; their test scores were 10%

---

23. *Id.* at 98 tbl.65.

24. NATIONAL CENTER FOR EDUCATION STATISTICS, U.S. DEPARTMENT OF EDUCATION, THE NATION'S REPORT CARD: MATHEMATICS 2005, at 14 fig.11 (2005), *available at* http://nces.ed.gov/ nationsreportcard/pdf/main2005/ 2006453.pdf [hereinafter MATHEMATICS 2005].

25. NATIONAL CENTER FOR EDUCATION STATISTICS, U.S. DEPARTMENT OF EDUCATION, THE NATION'S REPORT CARD: READING 2005, at 14 fig.11 (2005), *available at* http://nces.ed.gov/ nationsreportcard/pdf/main2005/2006451.pdf [hereinafter READING 2005].

26. NATIONAL CENTER FOR EDUCATION STATISTICS, U.S. DEPARTMENT OF EDUCATION, THE NATION'S REPORT CARD: SCIENCE 2005, at 16 fig.12 (2006), *available at* http://nces.ed.gov/ nationsreportcard//pdf/main2005/2006466.pdf [hereinafter SCIENCE 2005].

27. HILARY R. PERSKY ET AL., NATIONAL CENTER FOR EDUCATION STATISTICS, U.S. DEPARTMENT OF EDUCATION, THE NATION'S REPORT CARD: WRITING 2002, at 23 tbl.2.2 (2003), *available at* http://nces.ed.gov/nationsreportcard/pdf/main2002/2003529.pdf [hereinafter WRITING 2002].

28. MATHEMATICS 2005, *supra* note 24, at 16 fig.12.

29. READING 2005, *supra* note 25, at 16 fig.12.

30. SCIENCE 2005, *supra* note 26, at 28 fig.22.

31. WRITING 2002, *supra* note 27, at 24 tbl.2.3.

32. THE EDUCATION TRUST, FUNDING GAPS 2006, at 7 tbl.3 (2006), *available at* http://www2 .edtrust.org/NR/rdonlyres/CDEF9403-5A75-437E-93FF-EBF1174181FB/0/FundingGap2006.pdf.

33. *Id.*

34. *Id.* at 7 tbl.4.

35. MATHEMATICS 2005, *supra* note 24, at 20 tbl.5.

36. READING 2005, *supra* note 25, at 20 tbl.5.

37. WRITING 2002, *supra* note 27, at 75 tbl.3.24.

lower in mathematics,[38] 7% lower in reading,[39] and 14% lower in writing[40] than those of students who were not eligible.

The funding of Virginia's public elementary and secondary school systems was challenged on state constitutional grounds on the basis of the substantial disparity between the funding of the wealthiest and poorest school districts.[41] In *Scott v. Commonwealth*, the Supreme Court of Virginia acknowledged the substantial disparities that existed[42] but concluded that "while the elimination of substantial disparity between school divisions may be a worthy goal, it simply is not required by the Constitution" based on the plain meaning of the language contained in the constitution.[43] The court pointed out, however, that the plaintiffs were only challenging the funding disparities between school districts and did not challenge the adequacy of the funding allotted to particular school districts.[44]

Availability of Publicly Funded Prekindergarten Programs

The Virginia Preschool Initiative currently serves four-year-old children who are considered at risk, but it does not serve three-year-old children.[45] Total enrollment in this state-funded program is 11,343,[46] which represents just 5.6% of Virginia's 202,637 three- and four-year-old children.[47] The federally funded Head Start program enrolls an additional 11,505 children,[48] which represents 5.7% of Virginia's three- and four-year-old children.[49]

Where Does Virginia Get Its Revenue?

At the end of fiscal year 2004, Virginia had total revenues of approximately $54 billion.[50] Of this amount, 46% was derived from state and local tax revenues and 13% was received from the federal government. The remaining 41% came from other

---

38. MATHEMATICS 2005, *supra* note 24, at 21 tbl.6.

39. READING 2005, *supra* note 25, at 21 tbl.6.

40. WRITING 2002, *supra* note 27, at 76 tbl.3.25.

41. Scott v. Commonwealth, 443 S.E.2d 138 (Va. 1994).

42. *Id.* at 140.

43. *Id.* at 142–43.

44. *Id.* at 142.

45. W. STEVEN BARNETT ET AL., NATIONAL INSTITUTE FOR EARLY EDUCATION RESEARCH, THE STATE OF PRESCHOOL 2006, at 148 (2007), *available at* http://nieer.org/yearbook/pdf/yearbook.pdf.

46. *Id.* at 149.

47. *See id.* at 232.

48. *Id.* at 149.

49. *See id.* at 232.

50. U.S. Census Bureau, State and Local Government Finances 2003–04, http://www.census.gov/govs/www/estimate04.html (last visited Oct. 6, 2006) [hereinafter Government Finances].

sources, including the Virginia Lottery, insurance trust revenue, revenue from government-owned utilities, and other commercial or auxiliary enterprises.

Tax Revenue

Virginia collected approximately $25 billion in state and local tax revenue during fiscal year 2004.[51] As a result, Virginia residents paid $3,342 per capita in state and local taxes, an amount which ranked 23rd nationally.[52] The different types of tax sources were approximately apportioned as follows:

Individual income taxes	29.7%
Property taxes	30.9%
General and selective sales taxes	29.0%
Corporate income and other taxes	10.4%
	100.0%[53]

Federal Funding

During fiscal year 2004, 13% of Virginia's total revenues came from the federal government.[54] For every dollar of federal taxes paid, Virginia received $1.66 in federal funding, an amount which ranked 43rd nationally[55] and was far above the national average of $1.17.[56]

Lottery Revenue

The Virginia Lottery has been in operation since 1988. Under Virginia's constitution, all Virginia Lottery profits are to be used solely for educational purposes.[57] During fiscal year 2006, the Lottery had total revenues of $1.36 billion and net proceeds of $454.9 million.[58]

---

51. The total tax revenues were collected as follows: $14.2 billion by the state and 10.8 billion by local governments. *Id.*

52. *Id.*

53. *Id.*

54. *Id.*

55. The Tax Foundation, Federal Spending Received Per Dollar of Taxes Paid by State 2004, http://www.taxfoundation.org/taxdata/show/266.html (last visited Sept. 17, 2006).

56. *See id.*

57. Official Home of the Virginia Lottery, Where the Money Goes, http://www.valottery.com/money (last visited Sept. 17, 2006). "In the year 2000, more than 80% of Virginia voters said yes to the creation of the State Lottery Proceeds Fund. The measure, now a permanent part of Virginia's Constitution, directs all Virginia Lottery profits be used solely for educational purposes." *Id.*

58. Virginia Lottery, FY 2006 Distribution of Lottery Proceeds, http://www.valottery.com/money/fy2006_distribution.pdf (last visited Sept. 17, 2006). "In fiscal year 2006, $160.2 million (37%) of Lottery proceeds were distributed to localities to be used for educational priorities as determined by the locality within certain limitations. Another $253.9 million (59%) of the Lot-

Legal Structures of Major Tax Sources

Income

Virginia employs a broad-based income tax[59] that uses adjusted gross income for federal income tax purposes as a starting point for determining state's taxable income.[60] However, numerous adjustments may be available to various individuals in calculating this amount.[61] If approved by local referendum, localities that meet certain population requirements also have the power to levy a local income tax up to 1% for a maximum of five years.[62] During fiscal year 2004, Virginia collected individual income tax of $992 per capita, an amount which ranked 7th nationally.[63]

In Virginia, a typical family of four (i.e., married taxpayers who file jointly and have two dependent children) are not required to pay any income tax until their combined income exceeds $24,200, an amount which is above the national poverty line of $20,615.[64] Virginia's income tax structure contains four tax brackets that impose a minimum marginal rate of 2% and a maximum marginal rate of 5.75%.[65] When statutory exemptions and the standard deduction are taken into account, the maximum marginal rate applies to every dollar of income exceeding $26,600.[66]

Property

Overview

Virginia has a typical property tax system that taxes the value of real estate and tangible personal property at the local level.[67] Certain items, such as the rolling stock of corporations operating railroads, are taxed at the state level,[68] although such taxes make

---

tery proceeds were used to fund a portion of the state's share of the Basic Operation Cost. The other $19.2 million (4%) was used to fund the state's share of the Standards of Quality prevention, intervention, and remediation program." *Id.*

59. VA. CODE ANN. § 58.1-360.

60. *Id.* § 58.1-322.

61. *See, e.g.,* VA. CODE ANN. § 58.1-322.

62. *See id.* §§ 58.1-540, -544, -549.

63. STATE RANKINGS 2006, *supra* note 1, at 321.

64. JASON A. LEVITIS, CENTER ON BUDGET AND POLICY PRIORITIES, THE IMPACT OF STATE INCOME TAXES ON LOW-INCOME FAMILIES IN 2006, AT 12 (2007). In 2006, Virginia taxpayers who were married and filing jointly could claim a standard deduction of $6,000, personal exemptions of $900 each, and dependent exemptions of $900 each. VA. CODE ANN. § 58.1-322. Note, however, that the threshold calculation of $24,200 is greater than the sum of these deductions and exemptions because it includes additional tax benefits available to low-income families, such as the earned-income tax credit. *See* LEVITIS, *supra*.

65. VA. CODE ANN. § 58.1-320. Virginia's middle two brackets are 3% and 5%. *Id.*

66. The standard deduction and four exemptions of $6,000 and $3,600, respectively, plus the threshold of taxable income for the highest tax bracket of $17,000, equals $26,600. *See supra* note 64.

67. VA. CODE ANN. § 58.1-3000.

68. VA. CODE ANN. § 58.1-100.

up an extremely small portion of Virginia's total property tax collections. During fiscal year 2004, Virginia collected approximately $7.7 billion dollars in property tax at the local level and approximately $20 million at the state level.[69] As a result, Virginia residents paid $1,031 per capita in state and local property taxes, an amount which ranked 21st nationally.[70]

Defining the Real Property Tax Base

Virginia has only one classification for real property, and both residential and commercial properties are assessed at 100% of the estimated fair market value as of January 1 each year.[71] Fair market value is generally determined by the application of standard appraisal methods, including the cost method, the income method, and the market-data method.[72] Localities may, at their discretion, employ special use valuation for agricultural, horticultural, forest, and open-space property.[73] In general, cities are required to reassess property values every two years, while counties are required to make reassessments every four years.[74]

Real Property Tax Rates

The tax rates imposed on real property vary and are set by each locality. During fiscal year 2006, the tax rates per $1,000 of assessed value ranged from $1.10 in Marion to $14.50 in Portsmouth.[75] Note, however, that progressive tax rates on residential real estate violate the Virginia constitution and that, therefore, a uniform tax rate for all property within a jurisdiction is constitutionally required.[76]

Personal and Intangible Property

Tangible personal property is subject to local taxation unless specifically exempt;[77] thus, the tax rates imposed vary among jurisdictions.[78] Tangible personal property is defined as all personal property not otherwise classified as intangible personal property or as merchants' capital.[79] Intangible personal property is not subject to tax at either the state or local level.[80] As noted above, however, limited property taxes are levied at the state level on the rolling stock of railroads, freight car companies, and certified

---

69. Government Finances, *supra* note 50.
70. *See id.*
71. VA. CODE ANN. §§ 58.1-3201, 3281.
72. CCH-EXP, PROP-TAX-GUIDE VA ¶ 20-615, Valuation Methods in General.
73. VA. CODE ANN. § 58.1-3236.
74. *Id.* §§ 58.1-3250, 3252.
75. CCH-EXP, PROP-TAX-GUIDE VA ¶ 20-405, Rates of Tax.
76. Va. Op. Att'y Gen. 05-028 (2005).
77. VA. CODE ANN. § 58.1-3500.
78. *See id.*
79. *Id.*
80. *Id.* §§ 58.1-1100, 1101.

motor carriers. These taxes are imposed at the rate of $1 for each $100 of assessed value (which is the equivalent of 10 mills or $10 per $1,000).[81]

Exemptions

Household goods, personal effects, and tangible farm property and products are exempt from the property tax.[82] Real estate and personal property owned by and occupied as the sole dwelling of persons aged 65 and older and of persons permanently and totally disabled who are deemed to be bearing an extraordinary tax burden on that property in relation to their income and financial worth are also exempt.[83]

General and Selective Sales

General Sales

Virginia imposes a general retail sales-and-use tax, which makes up 15.5% of Virginia's total tax revenue.[84] This tax is imposed on the sale, distribution, renting, or furnishing of tangible personal property, as well as specified services.[85] These services include: (1) fabrication of property for consumers who furnish the materials; (2) provision of meals consumed on the premises; and (3) lodging for less than 90 days.[86] The state sales tax rate is 4%, and all localities may impose a local rate of up to 1%, for a combined state and local rate of 5%.[87] However, food purchased for home consumption is taxed at 2.5% (1.5% state tax and 1% local tax).[88] Exemptions from Virginia's sales and use tax include, among other items, prescription and nonprescription drugs, food stamps, school lunches, and textbooks.[89]

Selective Sales

Selective sales taxes make up 13.5% of Virginia's total revenue.[90] Of that amount, 3.6%[91] comes from a motor fuel sales tax imposed at a rate of $0.175 per gallon of gasoline.[92] Virginia residents paid an average of $122 per capita in state motor fuel sales taxes in 2004, an amount which ranked 31st nationally and was just above the national average of $115.[93]

---

81. *Id.* § 58.1-2652.
82. VA. CODE ANN. § 58.1-3504.
83. *Id.* §§ 58.1-3210, 3211.
84. Government Finances, *supra* note 50.
85. VA. CODE ANN. § 58.1-603.
86. 23 VA. ADMIN. CODE 10-210-4040.
87. VA. CODE ANN. §§ 58.1-603, 605.
88. *Id.* § 58.1-611.1.
89. *Id.* § 58.1-609.10.
90. Government Finances, *supra* note 50.
91. *Id.*
92. 23 VA. ADMIN. CODE 10-240-80. *See also* http://www.taxadmin.org/fta/rate/motor_fl.html.
93. STATE RANKINGS 2006, *supra* note 1, at 327.

In 2004, sales taxes on alcoholic beverages made up 0.6% of Virginia's total tax revenue.[94] Virginia residents paid $19.52 per capita in state alcoholic beverage sales taxes in 2004, an amount which ranked 14th nationally.[95]

The tobacco product sales tax makes up 0.3% of Virginia's tax revenues and is imposed at a rate of $0.30 per pack of cigarettes.[96]

The remainder of Virginia's selective sales taxes makes up 9% of its total tax revenue. Of this amount, 2.8% represents taxes on utilities and the other 6.2% represents taxes on other specific commodities, businesses, or services not reported separately above (e.g., on contractors, lodging, lubricating oil, fuels other than motor fuel, motor vehicles, meals, soft drinks, margarine, etc.).[97]

Corporate Income and Other

Corporate Income

The corporate income tax makes up 1.7% of Virginia's total tax revenue.[98] Virginia's broad-based corporate income tax is imposed at a rate of 6% on a corporation's Virginia taxable income,[99] which is based on the corporation's federal taxable income.[100]

Virginia follows the federal income tax treatment of S corporations. Thus, they do not pay Virginia's corporate income tax; rather, income and losses flow through to their shareholders.[101] A similar treatment is afforded to limited partnerships and limited liability partnerships, as well as limited liability companies, assuming they are treated as a partnership for federal tax purposes.[102] However, if a limited liability company is treated as a corporation for federal income tax purposes, the entity is subject to Virginia's corporate income tax.[103]

Other

During fiscal year 2004, the collection of all other taxes not previously mentioned accounted for 8.7% of Virginia's total tax revenue. Of this amount, approximately $149 million was generated by the estate and gift tax,[104] which is calculated on the basis of

94. Government Finances, *supra* note 50.

95. STATE RANKINGS 2006, *supra* note 1, at 335.

96. VA. CODE ANN. § 58.1-1001.

97. *See* GOVERNMENTS DIVISION, U.S. CENSUS BUREAU, GOVERNMENT FINANCE AND EMPLOYMENT CLASSIFICATION MANUAL, at ch.7 (2000), *available at* http://ftp2.census.gov/govs/class/classfull.pdf [hereinafter CLASSIFICATION MANUAL].

98. Government Finances, *supra* note 50.

99. VA. CODE ANN. § 58.1-400.

100. 23 VA. ADMIN. CODE 10-120-100.

101. CCH-EXP, VA-TAXRPTR ¶ 10-240, Limited Liability Companies (LLCs).

102. *Id.*

103. *Id.*

104. Government Finances, *supra* note 50.

the federal credit for state death taxes allowable by § 2011 of the Internal Revenue Code as it existed on January 1, 1978.[105] The "other taxes" category is also made up of motor vehicle license taxes, documentary and stock transfer taxes, severance taxes, and all other taxes not listed separately or provided for in other categories, such as taxes on land based on a specified rate per acre (rather than on assessed value).[106]

Burden Analysis

The overall state and local tax burden on Virginia taxpayers is very regressive. Taxpayers in the lowest quintile — those with incomes of less than $16,000 — bear a tax burden of 9.1% of their income, while taxpayers in the top 1% — those with incomes that exceed $407,000 — bear a tax burden of just 7.0% of their income.[107] It is also worth noting that, although Virginia obviously has no control over federal tax policy, federal itemized deductions for state and local personal income and property taxes nonetheless further reduce the burden on taxpayers in the top 1% to 4.8%.[108] Furthermore, between 1989 and 2002, the tax burden on the bottom quintile rose by approximately 0.4%, while the burden on the top 1% actually fell by the same percentage.[109]

In terms of the income tax, the burden across income groups in Virginia is slightly progressive, with taxpayers in the lowest quintile bearing a tax burden of 1.2% and those in the top 1% bearing a tax burden of 4.9%.[110] In contrast, however, the sales and excises taxes imposed by Virginia are very regressive, with taxpayers in the lowest quintile bearing a tax burden of 5% and those in the top 1% bearing a tax burden of just

---

105. VA. CODE ANN. § 58.1-901. Please note, however, that the Virginia estate tax is repealed for estates of persons who die on or after July 1, 2007.

106. *See* CLASSIFICATION MANUAL, *supra* note 97, at ch.7.

107. *See* ROBERT S. MCINTYRE ET AL., WHO PAYS? A DISTRIBUTIONAL ANALYSIS OF THE TAX SYSTEMS IN ALL 50 STATES 108 (2d ed. 2003), *available at* http://www.itepnet.org/wp2000/ text.pdf. Taxpayers in the second quintile bear a 8.4% total tax burden on incomes between $16,000 and $28,000; those in the third quintile bear a 8.4% tax burden on incomes between $28,000 and $48,000; those in the fourth quintile bear a 8.5% tax burden on incomes between $48,000 and $80,000; those in the 80th–95th percentiles bear a 8.2% tax burden on incomes between $80,000 and $159,000; finally, those in the 96th–99th percentiles bear a 7.7% tax burden on incomes between $159,000 and $407,000. *Id.*

108. *Id.* Taxpayers in the lowest and second lowest quintiles were able to reduce their individual tax burdens by 0.1%, those in the third quintile by 0.3%, those in the fourth quintile by 0.8%, those in the 80th–95th percentiles by 1.5%, and those in the 96th–99th percentiles by 2.0%. *Id.*

109. *Id.* at 109.

110. *See id.* at 108. Taxpayers in the second quintile bear a 2.8% income tax burden; those in the third quintile bear a 3.6% burden; those in the fourth quintile bear a 4.0% burden; those in the 80th–95th percentiles bear a 4.2% burden; finally; those in the 96th–99th percentiles bear a 4.6% burden. *Id.* Note, however, that of the total income tax burden borne by the top 1%, 4.8% represents individual income taxes and 0.1% represents corporate income taxes. *Id.*

0.7%.[111] Property taxes in Virginia are also regressive, with the taxpayers in the lowest quintile bearing a tax burden of 2.8% and those in the remaining quintiles bearing an average tax burden of 1.7%.[112]

---

111. *See id.* Taxpayers in the second quintile bear a 4.0% sales-and-excise tax burden; those in the third quintile bear a 3.3% burden; those in the fourth quintile bear a 2.7% burden; those in the 80th–95th percentiles bear a 2.0% burden; finally, those in the 96th–99th percentiles bear a 1.4% burden. *Id.*

112. *See id.* Taxpayers in the second quintile bear a 1.6% property tax burden; those in the third quintile bear a 1.6% burden; those in the fourth quintile bear a 1.8% burden; those in the 80th–95th percentiles bear a 1.9% burden; those in the 96th–99th percentiles bear a 1.8% burden, finally, those in the top 1% bear a 1.4% burden. *Id.*

Washington

General Information

Basic Profile – Geography, Population, and Industry

Washington was admitted to the Union in 1889. Nicknamed the "Evergreen State," Washington is located in the Pacific Northwest and is bordered by the Pacific Ocean on the west, Oregon on the south, Idaho on the east, and British Columbia, Canada, on the north. It is located in the Pacific time zone, and Olympia is the state capital.

Washington ranks 14th in population (approximately 6.3 million residents)[1] and 18th in total area (71,300 square miles).[2] Its population is approximately 85.0% white, 3.5% black, and 6.4% Asian.[3] Additionally, 8.8% of its population identify themselves as persons of Hispanic or Latino origin.[4] The state is approximately 20% Catholic; 44% Protestant; and 1% Jewish; 35% claim a religion outside the Judeo-Christian tradition or no religion at all.[5] Eighty-seven percent of Washington's population lives in urban areas.[6] Major industries include aerospace, electronics and computers, forest products, life sciences, marine services, software, telecommunications, tourism, and agriculture.[7]

Family Income and Poverty Indicators

In 2004, Washington's per capita gross product was $42,137, which was above the national average of $39,725.[8] During this same period, although the median household

---

1. STATE RANKINGS 2006, vi, 429 (Kathleen O'Leary Morgan & Scott Morgan eds., Morgan Quitno Press 2006).

2. *Id.* at 225.

3. Washington Quick Facts from the U.S. Census Bureau, http://quickfacts.census.gov/qfd/states/53000.html (last visited Jan. 31, 2007). The remaining population is made up of 1.7% American Indian and Alaska Native persons; 0.5% Native Hawaiian persons and other Pacific Islanders; and 3% persons reporting two or more races. *Id.*

4. *Id.* (noting that because Hispanics and Latinos may be of any race, they are also included within the other applicable race categories). *See id.*

5. *See* BARRY A. KOSMIN, EGON MAYER & ARIELA KEYSAR, AMERICAN RELIGIOUS IDENTIFI-CATION SURVEY 2001, at 41, *available at* http://www.gc.cuny.edu/faculty/research_studies/aris.pdf.

6. USDA Economic Research Service, Washington Fact Sheet, http://www.ers.usda.gov/State-Facts/WA.htm (last visited Sept. 17, 2006).

7. *See* Washington State Business and Project Development, Washington Industries, http://www.choosewashington.com/industries (last visited Nov. 10, 2006).

8. STATE RANKINGS 2006, *supra* note 1, at 89.

income in Washington was $48,688,[9] 11.7% of Washington's population was living in poverty, which was just below the national average of 12.4%.[10] More specifically, poverty affected 16.9% of Washington's children,[11] 8.1% of its senior citizens,[12] and 9.4% of its families.[13] Of its female-headed households with children, 34.9% lived in poverty,[14] and 35.5% of the state's public elementary and secondary school students were eligible for free or reduced-price meals.[15] Of those living in poverty, approximately 5.5% were black, which represented 17.7% of Washington's black population and 0.6% of its total population.[16] In an attempt to combat this poverty, Washington spent approximately $6.2 billion on public welfare programs in 2002,[17] which made up 16% of its total government expenditures.[18]

Washington's Public Elementary-Secondary School System

Overall Spending and Performance

For the 2003–2004 school year, Washington spent $7,243 per pupil in its public elementary-secondary school system, which was substantially below the national average of $8,182.[19] Of this amount, 8.5% was provided by the federal government, 61.8% was provided by the state government, and 29.7% was provided by the local governments,[20] with property taxes making up 23.4% of the total funding.[21] Out of these funds, Washington paid its elementary and secondary school teachers an estimated average annual salary of $45,712 during the 2004–2005 school year,[22] but in 2003, it provided a student/teacher ratio of 19.3, which was worse than the national average of 15.9.[23]

---

9. *Id.* at 96.

10. *Id.* at 495.

11. *Id.* at 497.

12. *Id.* at 496.

13. *Id.* at 498.

14. *Id.* at 499.

15. *Id.* at 532.

16. *See* Fact Sheet, American FactFinder, http://factfinder.census.gov/home/saff/main.html?_lang=en (select "Washington" under "Get a Fact Sheet for your community") (last visited Feb. 16, 2007). Note that these numbers are based on the 2000 census because more recent numbers were not available.

17. *Id.* at 500.

18. *Id.* at 502.

19. Governments Division, U.S. Census Bureau, Public Education Finances 2004, at 8 tbl.8 (2006), *available at* http://www2.census.gov/govs/school/04f33pub.pdf.

20. *See id.* at 5 tbl.5.

21. *See id.* at 4 tbl.4.

22. Thomas D. Snyder et al., National Center for Education Statistics, Digest of Education Statistics 2005, at 116 tbl.77 (2006) *available at* http://nces.ed.gov/pubsearch/pubsinfo.asp?pubid=2006030.

23. *Id.* at 98 tbl.65.

In academic performance, Washington's fourth and eighth grade students scored higher than the national average in mathematics,[24] reading,[25] science,[26] and writing.[27]

Equity Issues

In 2004, the funding per student in Washington's highest poverty districts exceeded that in its lowest poverty districts by $196.[28] When adjustments were made for the additional costs of educating students growing up in poverty, however, the funding in high poverty districts actually declined by $110.[29] On the other hand, Washington spent $87 less per student in its highest minority districts, and this amount grew to $225 when adjustments for low-income students were made.[30]

Fourth graders eligible for free or reduced-price school lunches had test scores that were 8% lower in mathematics,[31] 8% lower in reading,[32] and 13% lower in writing[33] than those of students who were not eligible. The results were similar for eighth graders eligible for free or reduced-price lunches; their test scores were 9% lower in mathematics,[34] 8% lower in reading,[35] and 12% lower in writing[36] than those of students who were not eligible.

Only a few years after upholding the constitutionality of Washington's public school funding system,[37] the Supreme Court of Washington held in 1978 that the same system was invalid on the grounds that it did not make ample provision for the education of the state's children as required by Washington's constitution.[38] In response to

24. NATIONAL CENTER FOR EDUCATION STATISTICS, U.S. DEPARTMENT OF EDUCATION, THE NATION'S REPORT CARD: MATHEMATICS 2005, at 14 fig.11, 16 fig.12 (2005), *available at* http://nces.ed.gov/ nationsreportcard/pdf/ main2005/2006453.pdf [hereinafter MATHEMATICS 2005].

25. NATIONAL CENTER FOR EDUCATION STATISTICS, U.S. DEPARTMENT OF EDUCATION, THE NATION'S REPORT CARD: READING 2005, at 14 fig.11, 16 fig.12 (2005), *available at* http://nces.ed.gov/nationsreportcard/pdf/main2005/2006451.pdf [hereinafter READING 2005].

26. NATIONAL CENTER FOR EDUCATION STATISTICS, U.S. DEPARTMENT OF EDUCATION, THE NATION'S REPORT CARD: SCIENCE 2005, at 16 fig.12, 28 fig.22 (2006), *available at* http://nces.ed.gov/nationsreportcard//pdf/main2005/2006466.pdf [hereinafter SCIENCE 2005].

27. HILARY R. PERSKY ET AL., NATIONAL CENTER FOR EDUCATION STATISTICS, U.S. DEPARTMENT OF EDUCATION, THE NATION'S REPORT CARD: WRITING 2002, at 23 tbl.2.2, 24 tbl.2.3 (2003), *available at* http://nces.ed.gov/nationsreportcard/pdf/main2002/2003529.pdf [hereinafter WRITING 2002].

28. THE EDUCATION TRUST, FUNDING GAPS 2006, at 7 tbl.3 (2006), *available at* http://www2 .edtrust.org/NR/rdonlyres/CDEF9403-5A75-437E-93FF-EBF1174181FB/0/FundingGap2006.pdf.

29. *Id.*

30. *Id.* at 7 tbl.4.

31. MATHEMATICS 2005, *supra* note 24, at 20 tbl.5.

32. READING 2005, *supra* note 25, at 20 tbl.5.

33. WRITING 2002, *supra* note 27, at 75 tbl.3.24.

34. MATHEMATICS 2005, *supra* note 24, at 21 tbl.6.

35. READING 2005, *supra* note 25, at 21 tbl.6.

36. WRITING 2002, *supra* note 27, at 76 tbl.3.25.

37. *See* Northshore School District v. Kinnear, 530 P.2d 178 (Wash. 1974).

38. Seattle Sch. Dist. No. 1 of King County v. State, 585 P.2d 71 (Wash. 1978).

the litigation that led to this invalidation, the state legislature enacted the Basic Education Act, which defined the state's basic education obligation and increased state funding to education.[39] Recently, two separate suits have been filed challenging the adequacy of the state's education funding system.[40]

Availability of Publicly Funded Prekindergarten Programs

Washington's Early Childhood Education and Assistance Program serves three- and four-year-old children whose families are at or below 110% of the federal poverty level.[41] Total enrollment in this state-funded program is 5,810,[42] which represents just 4% of Washington's 156,262 three- and four-year-old children.[43] The federally funded Head Start program enrolls an additional 11,020 children,[44] which represents 7% of Washington's three- and four-year-old children.[45]

Where Does Washington Get Its Revenue?

At the end of fiscal year 2004, Washington had total revenues of approximately $54.7 billion.[46] Of this amount, 39% was derived from state and local tax revenues and 14% was received from the federal government.[47] The remaining 47% came from other sources, including the state lottery, insurance trust revenue, and revenue from government-owned utilities and other commercial or auxiliary enterprises.[48]

Tax Revenue

Washington collected approximately $21.4 billion in state and local tax revenue during fiscal year 2004.[49] As a result, Washington residents paid $3,452 per capita in state and local government taxes, an amount which ranked 18th nationally.[50] The different types of tax sources were approximately apportioned as follows:

---

39. The Washington Basic Education Act of 1977, Wash Rev. Code § 28A.150.200 to 310.

40. *See* National Access Network, State by State, Washington, Recent Events, http://www.schoolfunding.info/news/litigation/1-16-07WAmccleary.php3 (last visited Mar. 16, 2007).

41. W. Steven Barnett et al., National Institute for Early Education Research, The State of Preschool 2006, at 150 (2006), *available at* http://nieer.org/yearbook/pdf/yearbook.pdf.

42. *Id.* at 151.

43. *See id.* at 232.

44. *Id.* at 151.

45. *See id.* at 232.

46. U.S. Census Bureau, State and Local Government Finances 2003–04, http://www.census.gov/govs/www/estimate04.html (last visited Oct. 6, 2006) [hereinafter Government Finances].

47. *Id.*

48. *Id.*

49. The total tax revenues were collected as follows: $13.9 billion by the state and 7.5 billion by local governments. *Id.*

50. *Id.*

Individual income taxes	0.0%
Property taxes	29.8%
General and selective sales taxes	60.7%
Corporate income and other taxes	9.5%
	100.0%[51]

Federal Funding

During fiscal year 2004, 14% of Washington's total revenues came from the federal government.[52] For every dollar of federal taxes paid, Washington received $0.88 in federal funding, an amount which ranked 37th nationally and was below the national average of $1.17.[53]

Lottery Revenues

The Washington's Lottery has been operating since 1982.[54] As of July 1, 2005, Lottery proceeds will be used to fund the Education Construction Fund and the Economic Development Strategic Reserve Account, as well as problem gambling prevention and treatment.[55] During fiscal year 2005, Washington's Lottery had $458.1 million of gross revenues and $114.6 million of operating income, $102 million of which was transferred to state education funds.[56]

Legal Structures of Major Tax Sources

Income

Washington does not impose a tax on personal income.

Property

Overview

Washington has a typical property tax system that taxes the value of real and tangible personal property at the state and local levels.[57] During fiscal year 2004, Washing-

---

51. *Id.*

52. Government Finances, *supra* note 46.

53. *See* The Tax Foundation, Federal Spending Received Per Dollar of Taxes Paid by State 2004, http://www.taxfoundation.org/taxdata/show/266.html (last visited Oct. 16, 2006).

54. *See* Wash. Rev. Code § 67.70.

55. Washington's Lottery, A History of Legislation, http://www.walottery.com/sections/AboutUs/Default.aspx?Page=History (last visited Apr. 3, 2007).

56. Washington's Lottery, 2005 Annual Report, *available at* http://www.walottery.com/docs/pdfs/05AnnualReport.pdf (last visited Apr. 3, 2007).

57. *See* Wash. Rev. Code § 84.36.005.

ton localities collected $4.9 billion in property taxes, and the state collected $1.5 billion.[58] As a result, Washington residents paid $1,029 per capita in state and local property taxes, an amount which ranked 22nd nationally.[59]

Defining the Real Property Tax Base

All real property in Washington is generally valued at 100% of its "true and fair value in money" and is assessed on the same basis.[60] "True and fair value" means fair market value.[61] However, open-space land, agricultural land, and timberland are granted current use valuation.[62] In 2006, the total ratio of assessed value to market value for all property in Washington counties ranged from 71.8% in Chelan County to 97.7% in Adams County.[63] Real property is assessed annually[64] and reappraised at least once every four years.[65]

Real Property Tax Rates

The State of Washington is authorized to levy a maximum property tax rate of $3.60 (3.6 mills) per $1,000 of assessed value, while cities and towns are authorized to levy rates of $1.80 (1.8 mills) and $3.375 (3.375 mills) per $1,000, respectively.[66] County road districts are authorized to levy rates of $2.25 (2.25 mills) per $1,000.[67] Further, special purpose taxing districts are authorized to impose regular levies of various rates.[68] The aggregate of all levies may not exceed 1% (10 mills or $10 per $1,000) of "true and fair value,"[69] while the aggregate of all taxing districts other than the state may not exceed $5.90 (5.9 mills) per $1,000 of assessed valuation.[70] Voters may authorize the levy of special rates in excess of the above statutory limitations for periods of no longer than six years.[71] For 2006, the average aggregate rate levied statewide was $11.52 per $1,000 of assessed value, with rates levied in individual counties ranging from $6.89 to $15.42 per $1,000.[72]

---

58. Government Finances, *supra* note 46.

59. *See id.*

60. WASH. REV. CODE § 84.40.030.

61. WASH. ADMIN. CODE § 458-07-030.

62. WASH. REV. CODE § 84.34.060.

63. Washington State Department of Revenue, Table 26: Comparison of Assessment Ratios for Taxes Due in 2005 and 2006 by County, http://dor.wa.gov/content/statistics/2006/Property_Tax_Statistics_2006/default.aspx (last visited Nov. 11, 2006).

64. WASH. REV. CODE § 84.40.020.

65. *Id.* § 84.41.030.

66. *Id.* § 84.52.043.

67. *Id.*

68. *See. id.*

69. WASH. REV. CODE § 84.52.050.

70. *Id.* § 84.52.043.

71. *Id.* § 84.55.050.

72. Washington State Department of Revenue, Table 28: Comparison of Average Levy Rates by Year Due in 1999–2006, http://dor.wa.gov/content/statistics/2006/Property_Tax_Statistics_2006/default.aspx (last visited Nov. 11, 2006).

Personal and Intangible Property

Intangible property is not taxed in Washington.[73] Tangible personal property is generally taxable at "true and fair value,"[74] unless a specific exemption applies.[75]

Exemptions

Washington does not have a general homestead exemption. However, the state offers a homestead exemption to certain senior citizens and disabled veterans, the amount of which depends on the individual's income.[76] Tangible personal property exemptions include business inventory, motor vehicles, household goods and personal effects, certain watercraft, and farming machinery and equipment.[77]

General and Selective Sales

General Sales

Washington imposes a general retail sales-and-use tax, which constituted 45.7% of Washington's total tax revenue during fiscal year 2004.[78] This tax is imposed on tangible personal property and selected services.[79] Examples of taxable services include installing, repairing, cleaning, altering, improving, constructing, or decorating real or personal property of or for consumers; cleaning, fumigating, razing, or moving structures; automobile towing; the furnishing of lodging for less than a month; specified personal business or professional services; renting or leasing tangible personal property; and telephone service.[80] The sales-and-use tax is levied statewide at a rate of 6.5%.[81] An additional 0.3% is added for retail sales of motor vehicles, and an additional tax of 5.9% is levied on retail car rentals.[82] Cities and counties are authorized to levy additional local taxes at a rate of 0.5%.[83] Additional levies may be imposed at the local level for certain special purposes with legislative or voter approval.[84] The actual total rate imposed as of 2006 ranged from 7% to 8.9%.[85] Exemptions from the sales-and-use tax include "food and food ingredients", food purchased with food stamps, drugs,

---

73. WASH. REV. CODE § 84.36.070.
74. *Id.* § 84.40.030.
75. *See id.* § 84.36.005.
76. *Id.* § 84.36.381.
77. *Id.* § 84.36.
78. Government Finances, *supra* note 46.
79. *See* WASH. REV. CODE §§ 82.08.020 and 82.08.010.
80. WASH. REV. CODE § 82.04.050.
81. *Id.* § 82.08.020.
82. *Id.*
83. *Id.* § 82.14.030.
84. *See id.* § 82.14.
85. CCH-EXP, WA-TAXRPTR ¶ 61-735, Local Rates.

and medical supplies.[86] Prepared food, dietary supplements, and soft drinks are not considered "food and food ingredients" and thus do not qualify for the exemption.[87]

Selective Sales

Selective sales taxes constituted 15% of Washington's total tax revenue during fiscal year 2004.[88] Of that amount, 4.3% came from motor fuel sales taxes.[89] Washington residents paid an average of $149 per capita in state motor fuel sales taxes in 2004, an amount which ranked 12th nationally and was well above the national average of $115.[90]

The tobacco product sales tax made up 1.6% of Washington's total tax revenue during fiscal year 2004.[91] The sale of tobacco products is taxed at the same rate as other personal property. As a result, Washington residents paid $56.79 per capita in tobacco product sales taxes in 2004, an amount which ranked 16th nationally.[92]

In 2004, sales taxes on alcoholic beverages made up 0.9% of Washington's total tax revenue.[93] Washington residents paid $31.03 per capita in state alcoholic beverage sales taxes in 2004, an amount which ranked 6th nationally.[94]

The remainder of Washington's selective sales taxes constituted 8.1% of its total tax revenue in 2004.[95] Of that percentage, 3.6% represented taxes on utilities and the other 4.5% represented taxes on other specific commodities, businesses, or services not reported separately above (e.g., on contractors, lodging, lubricating oil, fuels other than motor fuel, motor vehicles, meals, soft drinks, margarine, etc.).[96]

Corporate Income and Other

Corporate Income

Washington does not impose a tax on corporate income.

Other

During fiscal year 2004, the collection of all other taxes not previously mentioned generated over $2 billion, which comprised 9.5% of Washington's total tax revenue.[97]

---

86. See WASH. REV. CODE § 82.08.

87. *Id.*

88. Government Finances, *supra* note 46.

89. *Id.*

90. STATE RANKINGS 2006, *supra* note 1, at 327.

91. Government Finances, *supra* note 46.

92. STATE RANKINGS 2006, *supra* note 1 at 332.

93. Government Finances, *supra* note 46.

94. STATE RANKINGS 2006, *supra* note 1, at 335.

95. Government Finances, *supra* note 46.

96. *Id.; see* GOVERNMENTS DIVISION, U.S. CENSUS BUREAU, GOVERNMENT FINANCE AND EMPLOYMENT CLASSIFICATION MANUAL, at ch.7 (2000), *available at* http://ftp2.census.gov/govs/class/classfull.pdf [hereinafter CLASSIFICATION MANUAL].

97. Government Finances, supra note 46.

Of that amount, $139.9 million came from estate and gift taxes.[98] In 2005, the state supreme court declared Washington's former estate and gift tax invalid on the basis that it was tied to the federal credit for state taxes, which was completely phased out after 2004.[99] Subsequently, the legislature enacted a new stand-alone transfer tax that taxes estates greater than $2 million at rates ranging from 10% to 19%.[100]

The "other taxes" category is further made up of various license taxes, documentary or stock transfer taxes, severance taxes, and all other taxes not listed separately or provided for in other categories.[101]

Burden Analysis

The overall state and local tax burden on the taxpayers of Washington is extremely regressive. In fact, Washington has one of the ten most regressive tax systems in the nation.[102] Taxpayers in the lowest quintile—those with incomes of less than $17,000—bear a tax burden of 17.6% of their income, while taxpayers in the top 1%—those with incomes that exceed $922,000—bear a tax burden of just 3.3% of their income.[103] It is also worth noting that, although Washington obviously has no control over federal tax policy, federal itemized deductions for state and local personal income and property taxes nonetheless further reduce the burden on taxpayers in the top 1% to 3.1%.[104] Furthermore, between 1989 and 2002, the tax burden on the bottom quintile rose by approximately 0.5%, while the burden on the top 1% fell by 0.6%.[105]

One of the regressive features of Washington's tax system is that it does not employ an income tax. Moreover, the sales and excises taxes imposed by Washington are extremely regressive, with taxpayers in the lowest quintile bearing a tax burden of 13.8% and those in the top 1% bearing a tax burden of just 2.4%.[106] Property taxes

---

98. *Id.*

99. Estate of Hemphill v. State Dept. of Revenue, 105 P.3d 391 (Wash. 2005).

100. *See* WASH. REV. CODE § 83.100.

101. *See* CLASSIFICATION MANUAL, supra note 96, at ch. 7.

102. *See* ROBERT S. McINTYRE ET AL., WHO PAYS? A DISTRIBUTIONAL ANALYSIS OF THE TAX SYSTEMS IN ALL 50 STATES 3 (2d ed. 2003), *available at* http://www.itepnet.org/wp2000/text.pdf.

103. *See id.* at 110. Taxpayers in the second quintile bear a 12.9% total tax burden on incomes between $17,000 and $31,000; those in the third quintile bear a 11.3% tax burden on incomes between $31,000 and $48,000; those in the fourth quintile bear a 9.5% tax burden on incomes between $48,000 and $75,000; those in the 80th–95th percentiles bear a 7.9% tax burden on incomes between $75,000 and $143,000; finally those in the 96th–99th percentiles bear a 5.6% tax burden on incomes between $143,000 and $922,000. *Id.*

104. *Id.* Taxpayers in the lowest and second lowest quintiles did not receive any benefit from these federal offsets, while those in the third quintile were able to reduce their individual tax burdens by 0.3%, those in the fourth quintile by 0.4%, those in the 80th–95th percentiles by 0.5%, and those in the 96th–99th percentiles by 0.4%. *Id.*

105. *Id.* at 111.

106. *See id.* at 110. Taxpayers in the second quintile bear a 10.6% sales-and-excise tax burden; those in the third quintile bear a 8.4% burden; those in the fourth quintile bear a 6.9%

in Washington are also regressive, with taxpayers in the lowest quintile bearing a tax burden of 3.8% and those in the top quintile bearing an average tax burden of 1.8%.[107]

burden; those in the 80th–95th percentiles bear a 5.4% burden; finally, those in the 96th–99th percentiles bear a 3.7% burden. *Id.*

107. *See id.* Taxpayers in the second quintile bear a 2.3% property tax burden; those in the third quintile bear a 2.9% burden; those in the fourth quintile bear a 2.6% burden; those in the 80th–95th percentiles bear a 2.5% burden; those in the 96th–99th percentiles bear a 1.9% burden; finally, those in the top 1% bear a 0.9% burden. *Id.*

West Virginia

General Information

Basic Profile – Geography, Population, and Industry

Admitted to the Union in 1863, West Virginia is known as the "Mountain State."[1] It is located in the Mid-Atlantic region, entirely within the Appalachian Mountain range, and is bordered by Pennsylvania on the north, Ohio on the north and west, Kentucky on the west, Maryland on the north and east, and Virginia on the east and south. West Virginia is part of the Eastern time zone, and its capital is Charleston.

West Virginia ranks 41st in total area (24,230 square miles).[2] In 2005, the state ranked 37th in population (approximately 1.8 million residents).[3] Its population is approximately 95.2% white and 3.2% black.[4] The state is 8% Catholic; 67% Protestant; and less than 0.5% Jewish; 24% claim a religion outside the Judeo-Christian tradition or no religion at all.[5] West Virginia's population is fairly split between urban and rural, with 55% of its population living in urban areas and the remaining 45% in rural areas.[6] Major industries include coal production; steel, glass, aluminum, and chemical manufacturing; agriculture, including major commodities such as apples, eggs, poultry, and dairy products; and tourism.[7]

---

1. STATE RANKINGS 2006, vi, 1 (Kathleen O'Leary Morgan & Scott Morgan eds., Morgan Quitno Press 2006).

2. *Id.* at 225.

3. *Id.* at 429.

4. West Virginia Quick Facts from the U.S. Census Bureau, http://quickfacts.census.gov/qfd/states/54000.html (last visited Feb. 27, 2007). The remaining population is made up of 0.6% Asian persons, 0.2% American Indian and/or Alaska Native persons, and 0.8% persons reporting two or more races. *Id.* Additionally, 0.9% of West Virginia's total population identify themselves as persons of Hispanic or Latino origin. *Id.* (noting that because Hispanics may be of any race, they are included within the other applicable race categories).

5. BARRY A. KOSMIN, EGON MAYER & ARIELA KEYSAR, AMERICAN RELIGIOUS IDENTIFICATION SURVEY 2001, at 42, *available at* http://www.gc.cuny.edu/faculty/research_studies/aris.pdf.

6. USDA Economic Research Service, West Virginia Fact Sheet, http://www.ers.usda.gov/StateFacts/WV.htm (last visited Sept. 17, 2006). According to the latest estimates, approximately 816,000 people live in rural areas and 1 million people live in urban areas. *Id.*

7. Infoplease.com, West Virginia State Facts, http://www.infoplease.com/ipa/A0108289.html (last visited Jan. 27 2007).

Family Income and Poverty Indicators

In 2004, West Virginia's per capita gross product was $27,284, which ranked 49th nationally and was well below the national average of $39,725.[8] During this same period, while the median household income in West Virginia was $32,589,[9] 16.1% of the state's population was living in poverty,[10] which was far above the national average of 12.4% and ranked 6th nationally.[11] More specifically, poverty affected 24% of West Virginia's children,[12] 12.1% of its senior citizens,[13] and 14.1% of its families.[14] Of its female-headed households with children, 47.5% lived in poverty,[15] and 49.3% of the state's elementary and secondary school students were eligible for free or reduced-price meals.[16] Of those living in poverty, approximately 5% were black, which represented 29% of West Virginia's black population and 1% of its total population.[17] In an attempt to combat this poverty, West Virginia spent approximately $2.1 billion on public welfare programs in 2002,[18] which made up 21.7% of its total government expenditures.[19]

West Virginia's Elementary-Secondary School System

Overall Spending and Performance

For the 2003–2004 school year, West Virginia spent $8,475 per pupil in its public elementary-secondary school system, an amount which hovered around the national average of $8,182.[20] Of this amount, 11.3% was provided by the federal government, 60% was provided by the state government, and 28.7% was provided by the local governments,[21] with property taxes making up 25.5% of the total funding.[22] Out of these funds, West Virginia paid its elementary and secondary school teachers an estimated

---

8. STATE RANKINGS 2006, *supra* note 1, at 89.

9. *Id.* at 96.

10. *Id.* at 495.

11. *Id.* at 495.

12. *Id.* at 497.

13. *Id.* at 496.

14. *Id.* at 498.

15. *Id.* at 499.

16. *Id.* at 532.

17. *See* Fact Sheet, American FactFinder, http://factfinder.census.gov/home/saff/main.html?_lang=en (select "West Virginia" under "Get a Fact Sheet for your community") (last visited Feb. 27, 2007). Note that these numbers are based on the 2000 census because more recent numbers were not available.

18. *Id.* at 500.

19. *Id.* at 502.

20. GOVERNMENTS DIVISION, U.S. CENSUS BUREAU, PUBLIC EDUCATION FINANCES 2004, at 8 tbl.8 (2006), *available at* http://www2.census.gov/govs/school/04f33pub.pdf.

21. *See id.* at 5 tbl.5.

22. *See id.* at 4 tbl.4.

average annual salary of $38,360 during the 2004–2005 school year,[23] and in 2003, it provided a student/teacher ratio of 14.0, which was better than the national average of 15.9.[24]

In academic performance, West Virginia's fourth grade students scored below the national average in mathematics,[25] reading,[26] and writing[27] but above the national average in science.[28] Its eighth grade students scored below the national average in mathematics,[29] reading,[30] and writing,[31] and equal to the national average in science.[32]

Equity Issues

In 2004, revenues spent per student in West Virginia's highest poverty districts were determined to be $22 less than the revenues spent in its lowest poverty districts.[33] When adjustments were made for the additional costs of educating students growing up in poverty, however, the funding gap grew to $345.[34] On the other hand, West Virginia spent $244 more per student in its highest minority districts, and this amount grew to $290 when adjustments for low-income students were made.[35]

Fourth graders eligible for free or reduced-price school lunches had test scores that were 5% lower in mathematics,[36] 8% lower in reading,[37] and 10% lower in writing[38] than those of students who were not eligible. The results were generally similar for

23. Thomas D. Snyder et al., National Center for Education Statistics, Digest of Education Statistics 2005, at 116 tbl.77 (2006), *available at* http://nces.ed.gov/pubsearch/pubsinfo.asp?pubid=2006030.

24. *Id.* at 98 tbl.65.

25. National Center for Education Statistics, U.S. Department of Education, The Nation's Report Card: Mathematics 2005, at 14 fig.11 (2005), *available at* http://nces.ed.gov/nationsreportcard/pdf/main2005/ 2006453.pdf [hereinafter Mathematics 2005].

26. National Center for Education Statistics, U.S. Department of Education, The Nation's Report Card: Reading 2005, at 14 fig.11 (2005), *available at* http://nces.ed.gov/nationsreportcard/pdf/main2005/2006451.pdf [hereinafter Reading 2005].

27. Hilary R. Persky et al., National Center for Education Statistics, U.S. Department of Education, The Nation's Report Card: Writing 2002, at 23 tbl.2.2 (2003), *available at* http://nces.ed.gov/nationsreportcard/pdf/main2002/2003529.pdf [hereinafter Writing 2002].

28. National Center for Education Statistics, U.S. Department of Education, The Nation's Report Card: Science 2005, at 16 fig.12 (2006) *available at* http://nces.ed.gov/nationsreportcard//pdf/main2005/2006466.pdf [hereinafter Science 2005].

29. Mathematics 2005, *supra*, note 25.

30. Reading 2005, *supra*, note 26.

31. Writing 2002, *supra*, note 27.

32. Science 2005, *supra*, note 28.

33. The Education Trust, Funding Gaps 2006, at 7 tbl.3 (2006), *available at* http://www2.edtrust.org/NR/rdonlyres/CDEF9403-5A75-437E-93FF-EBF1174181FB/0/FundingGap2006.pdf.

34. *Id.*

35. *Id.* at 7 tbl.4.

36. Mathematics 2005, *supra* note 25, at 20 tbl.5.

37. Reading 2005, *supra* note 26, at 20 tbl.5.

38. Writing 2002, *supra* note 27, at 75 tbl.3.24.

eighth graders eligible for free or reduced price lunches; their test scores were 7% lower in mathematics,[39] 7% lower in reading,[40] and 12% lower in writing[41] than those of students who were not eligible.

Recent education financing litigation has aided local boards of education in their efforts to secure equal funding for all school districts. In 2006, the Supreme Court of West Virginia decided on equal protection grounds that school boards that were forced to divert funds to public libraries did not have to count those funds toward the total amount received for public education.[42] The resulting funding measurements are more equitable to school boards which, in the past, had to use education funds to maintain public libraries, to the detriment of their public schools.

Availability of Publicly Funded Prekindergarten Programs

Through the Public School Early Childhood Education initiative, West Virginia's local school boards can create prekindergarten programs to serve all students four years of age and three-year-olds with documented disabilities.[43] The state intends to increase funding in the future to allow more three-year-olds to participate in the program. Current enrollment stands at 8,944,[44] which represents 22% of West Virginia's 40,145 three- and four-year-old children.[45] The federally funded Head Start program enrolls an additional 6,880 children,[46] which represents 17% of West Virginia's three- and four-year-old children.[47]

Where Does West Virginia Get Its Revenue?

At the end of fiscal year 2004, West Virginia had total revenues of approximately $14 billion.[48] Of this amount, 35% was derived from state and local tax revenues and 24% was received from the federal government. The remaining 41% came from other sources, including the West Virginia Lottery, insurance trust revenue, revenue from government-owned utilities and other commercial or auxiliary enterprises.

---

39. MATHEMATICS 2005, *supra* note 25, at 21 tbl.6.

40. READING 2005, *supra* note 26, at 21 tbl.6.

41. WRITING 2002, *supra* note 27, at 76 tbl.3.25.

42. Bd. of Educ. v. W. Va. Bd. of Educ., 639 S.E.2d 893 (W. Va. 2006).

43. W. STEVEN BARNETT ET AL., NATIONAL INSTITUTE FOR EARLY EDUCATION RESEARCH, THE STATE OF PRESCHOOL 2006, at 152 (2006), *available at* http://nieer.org/yearbook/pdf/yearbook.pdf.

44. *Id.* at 153.

45. *See id.* at 232.

46. *Id.* at 153.

47. *See id.* at 232.

48. U.S. Census Bureau, State and Local Government Finances - 2003–04, http://www.census.gov/govs/www/estimate04.html (last visited Oct. 6, 2006). [hereinafter Government Finances].

Tax Revenue

West Virginia collected approximately $5 billion in state and local tax revenue during fiscal year 2004.[49] As a result, West Virginia residents paid $2,740 per capita in state and local taxes, an amount which ranked 40th nationally.[50] The different types of tax sources were approximately apportioned as follows:

Individual income taxes	21.5%
Property taxes	19.7%
General and selective sales taxes	43.3%
Corporate income and other taxes	15.5%
	100.0%[51]

Federal Funding

During fiscal year 2004, 24% of West Virginia's total revenues came from the federal government.[52] For every dollar of federal taxes paid, West Virginia received $1.83 in federal funding, an amount which ranked 48th nationally[53] and was well above the national average of $1.17.[54]

Lottery Revenue

After an amendment to the state constitution in 1984, the West Virginia Lottery began operations in 1986. Profits from the West Virginia Lottery are "transferred to the State Lottery Fund for appropriation by the Legislature to Education, Senior Citizen and Tourism programs."[55] During fiscal year 2006, the Lottery had total revenues of $1.5 billion and net proceeds of $651.7 million.[56]

---

49. The total tax revenues were collected as follows: $3.8 billion by the state and 1.2 billion by local governments. U.S. Census Bureau, State and Local Government Finances - 2003–04, http://www.census.gov/govs/www/estimate04.html (last visited Oct. 6, 2006).

50. *Id.*

51. Government Finances, *supra* note 48.

52. *Id.*

53. The Tax Foundation, Federal Spending Received Per Dollar of Taxes Paid by State, 2004 http://www.taxfoundation.org/taxdata/show/266.html (last visited Sept. 17, 2006).

54. *See id.*

55. West Virginia Lottery, Frequently Asked Questions, http://www.wvlottery.com/aspx/faq.aspx (last visited Jan. 17, 2006). "Since 1989 through 2001, Lottery profits have been dedicated primarily to state programs for education, senior citizens, and tourism. Beginning July 2001, many economic development programs key to prosperity and growth to communities throughout the Mountain State were also funded with Lottery profits." West Virginia Lottery, Comprehensive Annual Financial Report for the fiscal year ended June 30, 2006, *available at* http://www.wvlottery.com/pdf/WVL2006AR.pdf.

56. West Virginia Lottery, Comprehensive Annual Financial Report for the fiscal year ended June 30, 2006, *available at* http://www.wvlottery.com/pdf/WVL2006AR.pdf.

Legal Structures of Major Tax Sources

Income

West Virginia employs a broad-based income tax[57] that uses adjusted gross income for federal income tax purposes, with relatively few adjustments, as a starting point for determining the state's taxable income.[58] Currently, West Virginia localities do not impose an income tax, although the West Virginia constitution does not prohibit them from doing so.[59] During fiscal year 2004, West Virginia collected individual income tax of $589 per capita, an amount which ranked 34th nationally.[60]

In West Virginia, a typical family of four (i.e., married taxpayers who file jointly and have two dependent children) are not required to pay any income tax until their combined income exceeds $10,000, an amount which is far below the national poverty line of $20,615.[61] West Virginia's income tax structure contains five tax brackets that impose a minimum marginal rate of 3% and a maximum marginal rate of 6.5%.[62] When statutory exemptions are taken into account, the maximum marginal rate applies to every dollar of income exceeding $68,000.[63]

Property

Overview

West Virginia has a typical property tax system that taxes the value of real estate and tangible personal property at the local level.[64] During fiscal year 2004, West Virginia collected approximately $9.75 million dollars in property tax at the local level and ap-

---

57. W. VA. CODE § 11-21-3.

58. *Id.* § 11-21-1

59. CCH-EXP, WV-TAXRPTR ¶ 15-030, Local Power to Tax

60. STATE RANKINGS 2006, *supra* note 1, at 321 *citing* U.S. Bureau of the Census, Governments Division "2004 State Government Tax Collections," *available a*t http://www.census.gov/govs/www/statetax04.html.

61. JASON A. LEVITIS, CENTER ON BUDGET AND POLICY PRIORITIES, THE IMPACT OF STATE INCOME TAXES ON LOW-INCOME FAMILIES IN 2006, AT 12 (2007). Note that West Virginia does not allow taxpayers to itemize deductions or claim a standard deduction. CCH-EXP, WV-TAXRPTR ¶¶ 15-508 to -509. Married taxpayers filing jointly are, however, entitled to a personal exemption of $4,000 (both spouses combined) and dependent exemptions of $2,000 each. W. VA. CODE R. § 110-21-16. Note, however, that the threshold calculation of $10,000 is greater than the sum of these exemptions because it includes additional tax benefits available to low-income families, such as the earned-income tax credit. *See* LEVITIS, *supra.*

62. W. VA. CODE § 11-21-4e. West Virginia's middle three tax brackets are 4%, 4.5%, and 6%. *Id.*

63. *See supra* note 61. This amount was calculated using the top tax bracket of $60,000, plus four exemptions at $2,000 each. *Id.*

64. W. VA. CODE § 11-3-1.

proximately $3.3 million at the state level.[65] As a result, West Virginia residents paid $540 per capita in state and local property taxes, an amount which ranked 44th nationally.[66]

Defining the Real Property Tax Base

Property in West Virginia is divided into four classes: Class I property, which includes all tangible personal property employed exclusively in agriculture; Class II property, which includes residential property and farms; Class III property, which includes all real and personal property located outside of municipalities but not in Classes I or II; and Class IV property, which includes all real and personal property located within municipalities but not in Classes I or II.[67] Regardless of classification, however, all property is assessed at only 60% of its current fair market value, except for farms and managed timberland properties, which are assessed on the basis of their current use value.[68] Fair market value is generally determined by the application of standard appraisal methods, including the cost method, the income method, and the market-data method, all of which are commonly used throughout the country.[69] In general, property is required to be reassessed every three years.[70]

Real Property Tax Rates

The tax rates on real property vary and are set by each locality, but state law places a cap on the maximum rates that may be imposed. Currently, "[t]he aggregate of taxes assessed in any one year by all levying bodies ... shall not exceed fifty cents on each one hundred dollars' assessed valuation on Class I property; one dollar on Class II property; one dollar fifty cents on Class III property; and two dollars on Class IV property."[71] During fiscal year 2004, most localities imposed tax rates that equaled or approached the maximum rates allowed by law.[72]

Personal and Intangible Property

West Virginia no longer taxes intangible personal property.[73] Tangible personal property, on the other hand, is taxed the same way as real property. In other words, it is classified on the basis of the same four classifications discussed above; it is valued using the same methods; it is assessed at 60% of the determined value; and it is then taxed at the same rates.[74]

---

65. Government Finances, *supra* note 48.
66. *See id.*
67. W. Va. Code § 11-8-5.
68. *Id.* § 11-1C-1.
69. CCH-EXP, PROP-TAX-GUIDE WV ¶ 20-615, Valuation Methods in General.
70. W. Va. Code § 11-1C-9.
71. *Id.* § 11-8-6.
72. *See* CCH-EXP, PROP-TAX-GUIDE WV ¶ 20-405, Rates of Tax.
73. W. Va. Code § 11-C1-1b.
74. *See* CCH-EXP, PROP-TAX-GUIDE WV ¶ 20-295, Personal Property

Exemptions

Household goods and personal effects not held or used for profit are wholly exempt from the property tax,[75] as is the first $20,000 of value for homesteads that are owned and occupied by persons 65 years of age or older or by persons permanently and totally disabled.[76] Up to $125 in property tax relief is also available to low-income taxpayers who are 65 years of age or older and have a "gross household income" of $5,000 or less.[77] West Virginia does not allow taxpayers a homestead exemption except for the dwellings of senior citizens and permanently disabled people.[78]

General and Selective Sales

General Sales

West Virginia imposes a general retail sales-and-use tax,[79] which makes up 20.6% of its total tax revenue.[80] This tax is imposed on the sale of tangible personal property and all services unless specifically exempt.[81] Exempt services include, among others, personal or professional services,[82] contracting services, and services rendered by employees.[83] The state sales tax rate is 6%.[84] Certain localities may impose up to a 1% sales-and-use tax if they also impose a business-and-occupation tax or up to a 2% sales-and-use tax if they do not.[85] Exemptions from West Virginia's sales-and-use tax include, among other items, prescription drugs, food bought with food stamps, school lunches, textbooks, and day care services.[86] Ordinary sales of food, not including food in a vending machine, are subject to tax rates since January 1, 2006.[87]

Selective Sales

During fiscal year 2004, selective sales taxes made up 22.7% of West Virginia's total revenue.[88] Of that amount, 6.2% came from a motor fuel sales tax.[89] In 2005, the state

---

75. W. Va. Code § 11-3-9.

76. *Id.* § 11-6B-3.

77. *See id.* § 11-25-3.

78. CCH-EXP, PROP-TAX-GUIDE WV ¶ 20-205, Homestead.

79. W. Va. Code §§ 11-15-1, -15A-2.

80. Government Finances, *supra* note 48.

81. W. Va. Code § 11-15-3.

82. *Id.* § 11-15-8.

83. W. Va. Admin. Code R. § 110-15-33.

84. W. Va. Code § 11-15-3.

85. *Id.* § 8-13C-4.

86. CCH-EXP, SALES-TAX-GUIDE WV ¶ 61-010, List of Exemptions, Exceptions, and Exclusions.

87. CCH-EXP, SALES-TAX-GUIDE WV ¶ 60-390, Food and Groceries. Food sales are subject to tax at a reduced rate of 5% from January 1, 2006 through June 30, 2007; a reduced rate of 4% from July 1, 2007 through June 30, 2008; and a reduced rate of 3% effective July 1, 2008. *Id.*

88. Government Finances, *supra* note 48.

89. *Id.*

tax rate on gasoline was $0.27 per gallon.[90] West Virginia residents paid an average of $171 per capita in state motor fuel sales taxes in 2004, an amount which ranked 5th nationally and was far above the national average of $115.[91]

The tobacco product sales tax makes up 2.2%[92] of West Virginia's tax revenues and is imposed at a rate of $0.55 per pack of cigarettes.[93]

In 2004, sales taxes on alcoholic beverages made up 0.2% of West Virginia's total tax revenue.[94] West Virginia residents paid $4.76 per capita in state alcoholic beverage sales taxes in 2004, an amount which ranked 46th nationally.[95]

The remainder of West Virginia's selective sales taxes makes up 14.1% of its total tax revenue. Of this amount, 4.5% represents taxes on utilities and the other 9.6% represents taxes on other specific commodities, businesses, or services not reported separately above (e.g., on contractors, lodging, lubricating oil, fuels other than motor fuel, motor vehicles, meals, soft drinks, margarine, etc.).[96]

Corporate Income and Other

Corporate Income

The corporate income tax makes up 3.7% of West Virginia's total tax revenue.[97] West Virginia's broad-based corporate income tax is imposed at a rate of 9% on a corporation's West Virginia taxable income,[98] which is based on the corporation's federal taxable income.[99]

West Virginia follows the federal income tax treatment of S corporations. Thus, they do not pay West Virginia's corporate income tax; rather, income and losses flow through to their shareholders.[100] A similar treatment is afforded to limited partnerships and limited liability partnerships, as well as limited liability companies, assuming they are treated as a partnership for federal tax purposes.[101]

---

90. STATE RANKINGS 2006, *supra* note 1, at 328.

91. *Id.* at 327.

92. Government Finances, *supra* note 48.

93. STATE RANKINGS 2006, *supra* note 1, at 333.

94. Government Finances, *supra* note 48..

95. STATE RANKINGS 2006, *supra* note 1, at 335.

96. *See* GOVERNMENTS DIVISION, U.S. CENSUS BUREAU, GOVERNMENT FINANCE AND EMPLOYMENT CLASSIFICATION MANUAL, at ch.7 (2000), *available at* http://ftp2.census.gov/govs/class/classfull.pdf [hereinafter CLASSIFICATION MANUAL].

97. U.S. Census Bureau, State and Local Government Finances - 2003–04, http://www.census.gov/govs/www/estimate04.html (last visited Oct. 6, 2006).

98. W. VA. CODE R. § 110-24-4.

99. *Id.* § 110-24-2.

100. CCH-EXP, WV-TAXRPTR ¶ 10-215, S Corporations. Note, however, that S corporations are subject to the West Virginia business franchise tax. *Id.*

101. CCH-EXP, WV-TAXRPTR ¶¶ 10-225, -240. Note, however, that these entities are subject to the West Virginia business franchise tax. *Id.*

Other

During fiscal year 2004, the collection of all other taxes not previously mentioned accounted for 8.7% of West Virginia's total tax revenue. Of this amount, approximately $9 million was generated by the estate and gift tax.[102] Note, however, that beginning on January 1, 2005, the West Virginia estate tax is no longer in effect.[103] The "other taxes" category is also made up of motor vehicle license taxes, documentary and stock transfer taxes, severance taxes, and all other taxes not listed separately or provided for in other categories, such as taxes on land based on a specified rate per acre (rather than on assessed value).[104]

Burden Analysis

The overall state and local tax burden on West Virginia taxpayers is somewhat regressive. Taxpayers in the lowest quintile — those with incomes of less than $12,000 — bear a tax burden of 9.3% of their income, while taxpayers in the top 1% — those with incomes that exceed $207,000 — bear a tax burden of just 8.7% of their income.[105] It is also worth noting that, although West Virginia obviously has no control over federal tax policy, federal itemized deductions for state and local personal income and property taxes nonetheless further reduce the burden on taxpayers in the top 1% to 6.5%.[106] Furthermore, between 1989 and 2002, while the tax burden on the bottom and top quintiles fell by approximately 0.4% and 0.1%, respectively, the burden on the middle class actually rose.[107]

In terms of the income tax, the burden across income groups in West Virginia is slightly progressive, with taxpayers in the lowest quintile bearing a tax burden of 0.6% and those in the top 1% bearing tax burden of 5.7%.[108] In contrast, however, the sales

---

102. Government Finances, *supra* note 48.

103. West Virginia State Tax Department, Publication TSD-393, available at http://www.state.wv.us/taxrev/taxdoc/tsd393.pdf.

104. *See* CLASSIFICATION MANUAL, *supra* note 96, at ch.7.

105. *See* ROBERT S. MCINTYRE ET AL., WHO PAYS? A DISTRIBUTIONAL ANALYSIS OF THE TAX SYSTEMS IN ALL 50 STATES 112 (2d ed. 2003), *available at* http://www.itepnet.org/wp2000/text.pdf. Taxpayers in the second quintile bear a 10.3% total tax burden on incomes between $12,000 and $20,000; those in the third quintile bear a 9.7% tax burden on incomes between $20,000 and $33,000; those in the fourth quintile bear a 9.2% tax burden on incomes between $33,000 and $55,000; those in the 80th–95th percentiles bear a 9.2% tax burden on incomes between $55,000 and $96,000; finally, those in the 96th–99th percentiles bear a 8.8% tax burden on incomes between $96,000 and $207,000. *Id.*

106. *Id.* Taxpayers in the first, second, and third quintiles did not receive any benefit from these federal offsets, while those in the fourth quintile were able to reduce their individual tax burdens by 0.2%, those in the 80th–95th percentiles by 0.6%, and those in the 96th–99th percentiles by 1.3%. *Id.*

107. *Id.* at 113. This resulted in an average tax burden increase of 0.7%. *Id.*

108. *See id.* at 112. Taxpayers in the second quintile bear a 2.1% income tax burden; those in the third quintile bear a 2.6% burden; those in the fourth quintile bear a 3.3% burden; those

and excises taxes imposed by West Virginia are very regressive, with taxpayers in the lowest quintile bearing a tax burden of 7.3% and those in the top 1% bearing a tax burden of just 1.6%.[109] Property taxes in West Virginia are relatively flat, with taxpayers in the lowest quintile bearing a tax burden of 1.4% and those in the top quintile also bearing an average tax burden of 1.4%.[110]

---

in the 80th–95th percentiles bear a 4.2% burden; finally, those in the 96th–99th percentiles bear a 4.9% burden. *Id.* Note, however, that these percentages include both individual and corporate income tax burdens; that within the 96th–99th percentiles, corporate income taxes represent 0.1% of this burden; and that in the top 1%, corporate income taxes represent 0.1% of this burden. *Id.*

109. *See id.* Taxpayers in the second quintile bear a 6.8% sales-and-excise tax burden; those in the third quintile bear a 6% burden; those in the fourth quintile bear a 4.6% burden; those in the 80th–95th percentiles bear a 3.6% burden; finally, those in the 96th–99th percentiles bear a 2.5% burden. *Id.*

110. *See id.* Taxpayers in the second quintile bear a 1.3% property tax burden; those in the third quintile bear a 1.1% burden; those in the fourth quintile bear a 1.3% burden; those in the 80th–95th percentiles bear a 1.4% burden; those in the 96th–99th percentiles bear a 1.4% burden; finally those in the top 1% bear a 1.5% burden. *Id.*

Wisconsin

General Information

Basic Profile – Geography, Population, and Industry

Admitted to the Union in 1848, Wisconsin is known as the "Badger State."[1] It is located in the Great Lakes region and is bordered by Lake Superior on the north, Michigan on the northeast, Lake Michigan on the east, Illinois and Iowa on the south, and Minnesota on the west. The state is located in the central time zone, and its capital is Madison.

In 2005, Wisconsin ranked 20th in population (approximately 5.5 million residents);[2] it ranks 23rd in total land and water area (65,503 square miles).[3] Wisconsin's population is approximately 90.1% white and 6% black.[4] The state is approximately 28% Catholic; 50% Protestant; and less than 1% Jewish; 22% claim a religion outside the Judeo-Christian tradition or no religion at all.[5] Approximately 72.9% of Wisconsin's population lives in urban areas.[6] Major industries include agriculture (dairy products, vegetables, etc.); manufacturing (nonelectrical machinery, food processing); health care; and tourism.[7]

---

1. State Rankings 2006, vi, 1 (Kathleen O'Leary Morgan & Scott Morgan eds., Morgan Quitno Press 2006).

2. *Id.* at 429.

3. *Id.* at 225.

4. Wisconsin Quick Facts from the U.S. Census Bureau, http://quickfacts.census.gov/qfd/states/01000.html (last visited Feb. 21, 2007). The remaining population is made up of 2% Asian persons, 0.9% American Indian or Alaskan Native persons, and 1% persons reporting two or more races. *Id.* Additionally, 4.5% of Wisconsin's population identifies themselves as persons of Hispanic or Latino origin. *Id.*

5. Barry A. Kosmin, Egon Mayer & Ariela Keysar, American Religious Identification Survey 2001, at 40, *available* http://www.gc.cuny.edu/faculty/research_studies/aris.pdf. No other religion represents more than .5% of Wisconsin's population. *Id.* Note that Lutherans are the most heavily represented Protestant denomination, accounting for 22% of Wisconsin's total population. *Id.*

6. USDA Economic Research Service, Wisconsin Fact Sheet, http://www.ers.usda.gov/State-Facts/WI.htm (last visited December 20, 2006).

7. Wisconsin Department of Commerce, Wisconsin Economic Profile, http://www.commerce.state.wi.us/MT/MT-FAX-0703.html (last visited December 20, 2006); Wisconsin, Wikipedia.com, http://en.wikipedia.org/wiki/Wisconsin#Economy (last visited December 20, 2006).

Family Income and Poverty Indicators

In 2004, Wisconsin's per capita gross product was $38,451, which was just below the national average of $39,725.[8] During this same period, although the median household income in Wisconsin was $47,220,[9] 10.2% of Wisconsin's population lived in poverty,[10] which was below the national average of 12.4%.[11] More specifically, poverty affected 13.6% of Wisconsin's children,[12] 7.6% of its senior citizens,[13] and 7.6% of its families.[14] Of its female-headed households with children, 35.5% lived in poverty,[15] and 27.7% of the state's public elementary and secondary school students were eligible for free or re-duced-price meals.[16] Of those living in poverty, approximately 20% were black, which represented 29% of Wisconsin's black population and 2% of its total population.[17] In an attempt to combat this poverty, Wisconsin spent approximately $5.6 billion on pub-lic welfare programs in 2002,[18] which made up 16.4% of its total government expen-ditures.[19]

Wisconsin's Public Elementary-Secondary School System

Overall Spending and Performance

For the 2003–2004 school year, Wisconsin spent $9,226 per pupil in its public ele-mentary-secondary school system, which was slightly above the national average of $8,182.[20] Of this amount, 6.1% was provided by the federal government, 52.2% was provided by the state government, and 41.7% was provided by the local governments,[21] with property taxes composing 37.1% of the total funding.[22] Out of these funds, Wis-consin paid its elementary and secondary school teachers an estimated average annual

---

8. STATE RANKINGS 2006, *supra* note 1, at 89.

9. *Id.* at 96.

10. *Id.* at 495.

11. *Id.* at 495.

12. *Id.* at 497.

13. *Id.* at 496.

14. *Id.* at 498.

15. *Id.* at 499.

16. *Id.* at 532.

17. *See* Fact Sheet, American FactFinder, http://factfinder.census.gov/home/saff/main.html?_lang=en (select "Wisconsin" under "Get a Fact Sheet for your community") (last visited Feb. 16, 2007). Note that these numbers are based on the 2000 census because more recent numbers were not available.

18. *Id.* at 500.

19. *Id.* at 502.

20. GOVERNMENTS DIVISION, U.S. CENSUS BUREAU, PUBLIC EDUCATION FINANCES 2004, at 8 tbl.8 (2006), *available at* http://www2.census.gov/govs/school/04f33pub.pdf.

21. *See id.* at 5 tbl.5.

22. *See id.* at 4 tbl.4.

salary of $43,466 during the 2004–2005 school year,[23] and in 2003, it provided a student/teacher ratio of 15.1, which was slightly better than the national average of 15.9.[24]

In academic performance, Wisconsin's fourth and eighth grade students scored higher than the national average in mathematics,[25] reading,[26] and science.[27] Wisconsin's test scores for writing were unavailable.[28]

Equity Issues

In 2004, revenues spent per student in Wisconsin's highest poverty districts were determined to be $351 less than the revenues spent in its lowest poverty districts.[29] When adjustments were made for the additional costs of educating students growing up in poverty, however, the funding gap grew to $742.[30] Similarly, Wisconsin spent $1,043 less per student in its highest minority districts, and this amount grew to $1,270 when adjustments for low-income students were made.[31]

Fourth graders eligible for free or reduced-price school lunches had test scores that were 10% lower in mathematics[32] and 11% lower in reading[33] than those of students who were not eligible. The results were generally similar for eighth graders eligible for free or reduced-price lunches; their test scores were 10% lower in mathematics[34] and 8% lower in reading[35] than those of students who were not eligible. Wisconsin did not disclose its students' writing scores.

In 2000, the Wisconsin Supreme Court articulated the standard that any future education funding litigation will be based on. In *Vincent v. Voight*, the court held that

---

23. Thomas D. Snyder et al., National Center for Education Statistics, Digest of Education Statistics 2005, at 116 tbl.77 (2006), *available at* http://nces.ed.gov/pubsearch/pubs info.asp?pubid=2006030.

24. *Id.* at 98 tbl.65.

25. National Center for Education Statistics, U.S. Department of Education, The Nation's Report Card: Mathematics 2005, at 14 fig.11, 16 fig.12 (2005), *available at* http://nces.ed.gov/nationsreportcard/pdf/ main2005/2006453.pdf [hereinafter Mathematics 2005].

26. National Center for Education Statistics, U.S. Department of Education, The Nation's Report Card: Reading 2005, at 14 fig.11, 16 fig.12 (2005), *available at* http://nces.ed.gov/nationsreportcard/pdf/main2005/2006451.pdf [hereinafter Reading 2005].

27. National Center for Education Statistics, U.S. Department of Education, The Nation's Report Card: Science 2005, at 16 fig.12, 28 fig.22 (2006), *available at* http://nces.ed.gov/nationsreportcard//pdf/main2005/2006466.pdf [hereinafter Science 2005].

28. *See* Hilary R. Persky et al., National Center for Education Statistics, U.S. Department of Education, The Nation's Report Card: Writing 2002, at 23 tbl.2.2, 24 tbl.2.3 (2003), *available at* http://nces.ed.gov/nationsreportcard/pdf/main2002/2003529.pdf.

29. The Education Trust, Funding Gaps 2006, at 7 tbl.3 (2006), *available at* http://www2 .edtrust.org/NR/rdonlyres/CDEF9403-5A75-437E-93FF-EBF1174181FB/0/FundingGap2006.pdf.

30. *Id.*

31. *Id.* at 7 tbl.4.

32. Mathematics 2005, *supra* note 25, at 20 tbl.5.

33. Reading 2005, *supra* note 26, at 24 tbl.5.

34. Mathematics 2005, *supra* note 25, at 21 tbl.6.

35. Reading 2005, *supra* note 26, at 24 tbl.6.

Wisconsin students have the right to "an equal opportunity for a sound basic education [which] will equip students for their roles as citizens and enable them to succeed
economically and personally."[36] The court found that students were not being denied
this opportunity, and the language of the decision indicates that "adequacy" challenges
have a better chance of success than "equity" challenges.[37]

Availability of Publicly Funded Prekindergarten Programs

Wisconsin's Four-Year-Old Kindergarten (4K) Program is one of the oldest in the
country of its kind and has provided for four-year-old students in about half the state's
school districts since 1873.[38] A separate initiative in Wisconsin provides supplemental
funds to existing federal Head Start grantees in the state, allowing them to provide a
more comprehensive education for three- and four-year-old children. Total enrollment
in the state-funded program is 22,395,[39] which represents 33% of Wisconsin's 134,842
three- and four-year-old children.[40] Federally funded and state-funded Head Start programs enroll an additional 12,644 and 1,196 children, respectively,[41] which represents
9% and 1%, respectively, of Wisconsin's three- and four-year-old children.[42]

Where Does Wisconsin Get Its Revenue?

At the end of fiscal year 2004, Wisconsin had total revenues of approximately $48.7
billion.[43] Of this amount, 42% was derived from state and local tax revenues and 15%
was received from the federal government.[44] The remaining 43% came from other
sources, including the Wisconsin Lottery, insurance trust revenue, and revenue from
government-owned utilities and other commercial or auxiliary enterprises.[45]

Tax Revenues

Wisconsin collected approximately $20.4 billion in state and local tax revenue dur-
ing fiscal year 2004.[46] As a result, Wisconsin residents paid $3,714 per capita in state

---

36. Vincent v. Voight, 614 N.W. 2d 388 (2000).

37. Access: Education Finance Litigation, School Funding Advocacy and Policy, http://www
.schoolfunding.info/states/wi/lit_wi.php3 (last visited March 29, 2007).

38. W. STEVEN BARNETT ET AL., NATIONAL INSTITUTE FOR EARLY EDUCATION RESEARCH, THE
STATE OF PRESCHOOL 2006, at 155 (2006), *available at* http://nieer.org/yearbook/pdf/yearbook.pdf.

39. *Id.*

40. *See id.* at 232.

41. *Id.* at 156.

42. *See id.* at 232.

43. U.S. Census Bureau, State and Local Government Finances - 2003–04, http://www.census
.gov/govs/www/estimate04.html (last visited Oct. 17, 2006) [hereinafter Government Finances].

44. *Id.*

45. *Id.*

46. *Id.*

and local taxes, an amount which ranked 12th nationally.[47] The different types of tax sources were approximately apportioned as follows:

Individual income taxes	25.7%
Property taxes	36.3%
General and selective sales taxes	28.9%
Corporate income and other taxes	9.1%
	100.0%[48]

Federal Funding

During fiscal year ending 2004, 15% of Wisconsin's total revenues came from the federal government.[49] For every dollar of federal taxes paid, Wisconsin received $0.82 in federal funding, an amount which ranked 12th nationally and was below the national average of $1.17.[50]

Lottery Revenues

The Wisconsin Lottery has been in operation since 1988.[51] According to the state constitution, the net proceeds of the Lottery are used only for property tax relief.[52] During fiscal year 2005, the Wisconsin Lottery had total operating revenues of approximately $452.0 million and net proceeds of approximately $130.2 million.[53] Approximately $143.4 million was transferred for property tax relief.[54]

Legal Structure of Major Tax Sources

Income

Wisconsin employs a broad-based income tax that uses adjusted gross income for federal income tax purposes as a starting point for determining the state's taxable income.[55] However, a fairly large number of adjustments may be available to various individuals in calculating this amount.[56] Localities are prohibited from imposing any tax

---

47. *Id.*

48. *Id.*

49. *Id.*

50. The Tax Foundation, Federal Spending Received Per Dollar of Taxes Paid by State, 2004 http://www.taxfoundation.org/taxdata/show/266.html (last visited December 17, 2006).

51. Wisconsin Lottery, Wisconsin wins 95% of the time, http://www.wilottery.com/wiswins.asp (last visited December 20, 2006).

52. W.S.A. Const. art. 4, § 24(6)(a).

53. Wisconsin Department of Revenue, *An Audit: Wisconsin Lottery* 21, *available at* http://www.legis.state.wi.us/LaB/reports/06-8Full.pdf (last visited December 20, 2006).

54. *Id.*

55. WIS. STAT. § 71.01.

56. *Id.* § 71.05(6).

on income.[57] During fiscal year 2004, Wisconsin collected individual income tax of $918 per capita, an amount which ranked 11th nationally.[58]

In Wisconsin, a typical family of four (i.e., married taxpayers who file jointly and have two dependent children) are not required to pay any income tax until their combined income exceeds $25,000, an amount which is above the national poverty line of $20,615.[59] Wisconsin's income tax structure contains four tax brackets that impose a minimum marginal rate of 4.6% and a maximum marginal rate of 6.75%.[60] When statutory exemptions and the standard deduction are taken into account, the maximum marginal rate applies to every dollar of income exceeding $140,210.[61] It is also noteworthy that Wisconsin is one of the very few states that provide for preferential treatment for capital gains.[62]

Property

Overview

Wisconsin has a typical property tax scheme that taxes the value of real property and tangible personal property at the state and local levels.[63] Intangible personal property is exempt from the Wisconsin property tax.[64] During fiscal year 2004, Wisconsin collected approximately $7.3 billion in property tax at the local level and approximately $104 million at the state level.[65] As a result, Wisconsin residents paid $1,350 per capita in state and local property taxes, an amount which ranked 11th nationally.[66]

---

57. *Id.* § 66.0611.

58. STATE RANKINGS 2006, *supra* note 1, at 321 *citing* U.S. Bureau of the Census, Governments Division "2004 State Government Tax Collections" *available at* http://www.census.gov/govs/www/statetax04.html.

59. JASON A. LEVITIS, CENTER ON BUDGET AND POLICY PRIORITIES, THE IMPACT OF STATE INCOME TAXES ON LOW-INCOME FAMILIES IN 2006, AT 12 (2007). In 2006, Wisconsin taxpayers who were married and filing jointly were allowed personal and dependent exemptions of $700 each, as well as a standard deduction of an amount based on their income: $15,420 for taxpayers whose Wisconsin income is between $0 and $17,119; $15,420 minus 19.778% of the amount over $17,120 for taxpayers whose Wisconsin income is over $17,119 but not over $94,175; and $0 for taxpayers whose Wisconsin income is over $94,175. WIS. STAT. § 71.05(23). Note, however, that the threshold calculation of $25,000 is greater than the sum of these deductions and exemptions because it includes additional tax benefits available to low-income families, such as the earned-income tax credit. *See* LEVITIS *supra.*

60. Wisconsin's middle two tax rates are 6.15% and 6.5%. WIS. STATS. § 71.06(2)(g).

61. Since the standard deduction is phased out to zero in the case of taxpayers with income over $94,175, the exemptions, which total $2,800, are added to the threshold of taxable income for the highest tax bracket of $137,410, to equal $140,210. *See supra* note 59.

62. Wisconsin allows for a 60% exclusion from federal adjusted gross income of capital gains on assets held for more than one year. WIS. STAT. § 71.05(6)(b)9.

63. *Id.* § 70.01.

64. *Id.* § 70.112(1).

65. Government Finances, *supra* note 43.

66. *Id.*

Defining the Real Property Tax Base

Wisconsin classifies real property into seven classes on the basis of its use: (1) Residential, (2) Commercial, (3) Manufacturing, (4) Agricultural, (5) Swamp or waste, (6) Productive forest land, and (7) Other.[67] The tax base for real property is its full value, which considers recent arms-length sales of the property and reasonable comparable property[68] and is determined using the comparable-sales method, the income method, and replacement-cost method of valuation.[69] Property must be assessed at full value at least once every five years.[70]

Real Property Tax Rates

The tax rates imposed on real property vary and are set by each taxation district.[71] The state imposes a forestation levy of 0.20 mills (or $0.20 per $1,000).[72] In 2005, average county tax rates range from an effective rate of 0.00994 of the full value in Vilas County to an effective rate of 0.02312 of the full value in Crawford County.[73] Villages are limited from levying more than 1% of the assessed value of all property in the village, unless an increase is voted at a special village election.[74]

Personal and Intangible Property

The Wisconsin property tax applies to all tangible personal property located in the state.[75] Personal property is separated into the following categories: steam and other vessels; machinery, tools, and patterns; furniture, fixtures, and equipment; and all other nonexempt general personal property.[76] Personal property is assessed at its true cash value.[77]

Exemptions

Jewelry, household furnishings, and apparel are exempt from general property taxes.[78] Senior citizens are also eligible for loans to pay property taxes of up to $2,500 on their homes, which are payable upon death.[79] Wisconsin also allows a property tax

---

67. WIS. STAT. § 70.32(2).

68. *Id.* § 70.32. Agricultural forest land and undeveloped land are assessed at 50% of the properties' full value. *id.*

69. CCH-EXP, PROP-TAX-GUIDE WI ¶ 20-615, Valuation Methods in General.

70. WIS. STAT. § 70.05(b).

71. *Id.* § 70.62.

72. *Id.* § 70.58.

73. Wisconsin Department of Revenue, *Town, Village, and City Taxes 2005, available at* http://www.revenue.wi.gov/pubs/slf/tvc05.pdf.

74. WIS. STAT. § 61.45.

75. *Id.* §§ 70.01, 70.04.

76. WIS. STAT. § 70.30.

77. *Id.* § 70.34.

78. *Id.* § 70.111.

79. *Id.* § 234.621.

relief credit and a lottery gaming credit.[80] While there is no homestead exemption, Wisconsin allows taxpayers who own or rent their homestead the use of an income tax credit.[81]

General and Selective Sales

General Sales

Wisconsin imposes a general retail sales-and-use tax, which makes up 20.2% of its total tax revenue.[82] The tax is imposed on the retail sale of tangible personal property or taxable services.[83] Taxable services include, among others, the furnishing of lodging to transient guests; admissions to amusement, athletic or recreational events; cleaning services; parking; and landscaping.[84] The state sales tax rate is 5%.[85] In addition, counties can levy an additional sales tax of 0.5%,[86] a baseball stadium tax rate of 0.1%,[87] a football stadium tax rate of 0.5%,[88] and a premier resort area tax rate of 0.5%.[89] The sales tax rates range from 5% in various counties that do not impose the additional county rates to 5.6% in Milwaukee, Ozaukee, and Washington counties, which impose both the additional 0.5% county tax and the additional 0.1% baseball stadium tax.[90] Exemptions from Wisconsin's sales-and-use tax include, among other items, the sale of food for human consumption off the premises,[91] bottled water,[92] and prescription drugs.[93]

Selective Sales

Selective sales taxes make up 8.7% of Wisconsin's total tax revenue.[94] Of that amount, 4.6%[95] comes from a motor fuel sales tax imposed at a rate of $0.291 per gallon of gasoline.[96] Wisconsin residents paid an average of $187 per capita in state motor fuel sales taxes in 2004, an amount which ranked 2nd nationally.[97]

---

80. *Id.* § 79.10(9)(b); *Id.* § 79.10(9)(bm); *Id.* § 79.10(10).
81. WIS. STAT. § 71.07(04)
82. Government Finances, *supra* note 43.
83. WIS. STAT. § 77.52.
84. *Id.* § 77.52(2).
85. *Id.* § 77.52(1).
86. *Id.* § 77.71(2).
87. *Id.* § 77.705.
88. *Id.* § 77.706.
89. *Id.* § 77.994.
90. Wisconsin Department of Revenue, Tax Rates, http://www.revenue.wi.gov/faqs/pcs/taxrates.html#txrate11 (last visited January 3, 2007).
91. WIS. STAT. § 77.54(20).
92. *Id.*
93. *Id.* § 77.54(14).
94. Government Finances, *supra* note 43.
95. *Id.*
96. STATE RANKINGS 2006, *supra* note 1, at 328.
97. *Id.* at 327.

The sales tax on tobacco products makes up 1.5% of Wisconsin's total tax revenue[98] and is imposed at a rate of $0.77 per pack of cigarettes.[99] Wisconsin residents paid an average of $55.86 per capita in state tobacco sales taxes in 2004, an amount which ranked 17th nationally.[100]

In 2004, sales taxes on alcoholic beverages made up 0.2% of Wisconsin's total tax revenue.[101] Wisconsin residents paid $8.73 per capita in state alcoholic beverage sales taxes in 2004, an amount which ranked 39th nationally and was well below the national average of $15.74.[102]

The remainder of Wisconsin's selective sales taxes makes up 2.4% of its total tax revenue.[103] Of this amount, 1.4% represents taxes on utilities and the other 1.0% represents taxes on other specific commodities, businesses, or services not reported separately above (e.g., on contractors, lodging, lubricating oil, fuels other than motor fuel, motor vehicles, meals, soft drinks, margarine, etc.).[104]

Corporate Income and Other

Corporate Income

The corporate income tax makes up 3.3% of Wisconsin's total tax revenue.[105] Wisconsin has a corporate franchise tax that is imposed on foreign and domestic corporations for the privilege of doing business in Wisconsin.[106] The tax is imposed at a rate of 7.9% on a corporation's Wisconsin taxable income,[107] which is based on the corporation's federal taxable income.[108]

Wisconsin follows the federal income tax treatment of S corporations. Thus, they do not pay Wisconsin's corporate income tax; rather, income and losses flow through to their shareholders.[109] A similar treatment is afforded to limited partnerships and limited liability partnerships, as well as limited liability companies, assuming they are treated as a partnership for federal tax purposes.[110] However, if a limited liability com-

---

98. Government Finances, *supra* note 43.

99. STATE RANKINGS 2006, *supra* note 1, at 333.

100. *Id.* at 332.

101. Government Finances, *supra* note 43.

102. STATE RANKINGS 2006, *supra* note 1, at 335.

103. Government Finances, *supra* note 43.

104. *See* GOVERNMENTS DIVISION, U.S. CENSUS BUREAU, GOVERNMENT FINANCE AND EMPLOYMENT CLASSIFICATION MANUAL, at ch.7 (2000), *available at* http://ftp2.census.gov/govs/class/classfull.pdf [hereinafter CLASSIFICATION MANUAL].

105. Government Finances, *supra* note 43.

106. WIS. STAT. §71.23(2).

107. *Id.* §71.27.

108. *Id.* §71.22.

109. CCH-EXP, MCIT-GUIDE WI ¶ 10-215, S Corporations.

110. CCH-EXP, MCIT-GUIDE WI ¶ 10-220, General Partnerships; CCH-EXP, MCIT-GUIDE WI ¶ 10-225, Limited Partnerships; Limited Liability Partnership; CCH-EXP, MCIT-GUIDE WI ¶ 10-240, Limited Liability Companies (LLCs).

pany is treated as a corporation for federal income tax purposes, the entity is subject to Wisconsin's corporate income tax.[111]

Other

During fiscal year 2004, the collection of all other taxes not previously mentioned accounted for 5.8% of Wisconsin's total tax revenue.[112] Of this amount, approximately $86.4 million was generated by the estate and gift tax, [113] which is based on the value of the federal state death tax credit.[114] The "other taxes" category is further made up of various license taxes, documentary or stock transfer taxes, severance taxes, and all other taxes not listed separately or provided for in other categories.[115]

Burden Analysis

The overall state and local tax burden on Wisconsin's taxpayers is very regressive. Taxpayers in the lowest quintile — those with incomes of less than $18,000 — bear a tax burden of 10.2% of their income, while taxpayers in the top 1% — those with incomes that exceed $263,000 — bear a tax burden of just 8.1% of their income.[116] It is also worth noting that, although Wisconsin obviously has no control over federal tax policy, federal itemized deductions for state and local personal income and property taxes nonetheless further reduce the burden on taxpayers in the top 1% to 5.9%.[117] Furthermore, between 1989 and 2002, the tax burden on the bottom quintile rose by approximately 2.3%, while the burden on the top 1% actually fell by 0.7%.[118]

In terms of the income tax, the burden across income groups in Wisconsin is slightly progressive, with taxpayers in the lowest quintile bearing a tax burden of 0.5%

---

111. *Id.*

112. Government Finances, *supra* note 43.

113. *Id.*

114. Wisconsin Department of Revenue, Estates and Fiduciaries Frequently Asked Questions, http://www.revenue.wi.gov/faqs/ise/estate.html (last visited January 3, 2007).

115. *See* CLASSIFICATION MANUAL, *supra* note 104, at ch.7.

116. *See* ROBERT S. MCINTYRE ET AL., WHO PAYS? A DISTRIBUTIONAL ANALYSIS OF THE TAX SYSTEMS IN ALL 50 STATES 114 (2d ed. 2003), *available at* http://www.itepnet.org/wp2000/text.pdf. Taxpayers in the second quintile bear a 11.7% total tax burden on incomes between $18,000 and $30,000; those in the third quintile bear a 11.9% tax burden on incomes between $30,000 and $48,000; those in the fourth quintile bear a 11.5% tax burden on incomes between $48,000 and $70,000; those in the 80th–95th percentiles bear a 11.2% tax burden on incomes between $70,000 and $121,000; finally, those in the 96th–99th percentiles bear a 10% tax burden on incomes between $121,000 and $263,000. *Id.*

117. *Id.* Taxpayers in the lowest quintile were able to reduce their individual tax burdens by 0.1%, those in the second quintile by 0.2%, those in the third quintile by 0.6%, those in the fourth quintile by 0.9%, those in the 80th–95th percentiles by 1.7%, and those in the 96th–99th percentiles by 1.9%. *Id.*

118. *Id.* at 115.

and those in the top 1% bearing a tax burden of 5.2%.[119] In contrast, however, the sales and excise taxes imposed by Wisconsin are very regressive, with taxpayers in the lowest quintile bearing a tax burden of 6.7% and those in the top 1% bearing a tax burden of just 1.2%.[120] Although not purely regressive, property taxes in Wisconsin place a higher burden on the middle class, who bear an average tax burden of 3.6% compared with taxpayers in the lowest quintile, who bear a burden of 3.1%, and compared with taxpayers in the top quintile, who bear an average burden of 2.7%.[121]

---

119. *See id.* at 114. Taxpayers in the second quintile bear a 2.7% income tax burden; those in the third quintile bear a 3.8% burden; those in the fourth quintile bear a 4.3% burden; those in the 80th–95th percentiles bear a 4.9% burden; finally, those in the 96th–99th percentiles bear a 5.3% burden. *Id.* Note, however, that these percentages include both individual and corporate income tax burdens; that within the 96th–99th percentiles, corporate income taxes represent 0.1% of this burden; and that in the top 1%, corporate income taxes represent 0.2% of this burden. *Id.*

120. *See id.* Taxpayers in the second quintile bear a 5.5% sales-and-excise tax burden; those in the third quintile bear a 4.4% burden; those in the fourth quintile bear a 3.7% burden; those in the 80th–95th percentiles bear a 2.8% burden; finally, those in the 96th–99th percentiles bear a 1.8% burden. *Id.*

121. *Id.* Taxpayers in the second quintile bear a 3.5% property tax burden; those in the third quintile bear a 3.8% burden; those in the fourth quintile bear a 3.5% burden; those in the 80th–95th percentiles bear a 3.4% burden; those in the 96th–99th percentiles bear a 2.9% burden; finally, those in the top 1% bear a 1.7% burden. *Id.*

Wyoming

General Information

Basic Profile – Geography, Population, and Industry

Admitted to the Union in 1890, Wyoming is known as both the "Equality State" and the "Cowboy State."[1] It is located in the eastern Rocky Mountains and is bordered by Montana on the north; South Dakota and Nebraska on the east; Colorado and Utah on the south; and Utah and Idaho on the west. The state is located in the mountain time zone, and its capital is Cheyenne.

Wyoming ranks 10th in total area (97,814 square miles).[2] In 2005, the state ranked 50th in population (approximately 509,924 residents).[3] Its population is approximately 94.8% white, 0.9% black, and 2.4% American Indian.[4] The state is approximately 18% Catholic; 56% Protestant; and 1% Jewish; 25% claim a religion outside the Judeo-Christian tradition or no religion at all.[5] Nearly 69.6% of Wyoming's population lives in rural areas.[6] Major industries include mining, agriculture, and tourism[7]

Family Income and Poverty Indicators

In 2004, Wyoming's per capita gross product was $47,400, which ranked among the top ten states nationally and was above the national average of $39,725.[8] During this

---

1. STATE RANKINGS 2006, vi, 1 (Kathleen O'Leary Morgan & Scott Morgan eds., Morgan Quitno Press, 2006).

2. *Id.* at 225.

3. *Id.* at 429.

4. Wyoming Quick Facts from the U.S. Census Bureau, http://quickfacts.census.gov/qfd/states/54000.html (last visited Jan. 27, 2007). The remaining population is made up of 0.6% Asian persons, 0.1% Native Hawaiian persons or other Pacific Islanders, and 1.2% persons reporting two or more races. *Id.* Additionally, 6.7% of Wyoming's total population identify themselves as persons of Hispanic or Latino origin. *Id.* (noting that because Hispanics may be of any race, they are included within the other applicable race categories).

5. BARRY A. KOSMIN, EGON MAYER & ARIELA KEYSAR, AMERICAN RELIGIOUS IDENTIFICATION SURVEY 2001, at 42, *available at* http://www.gc.cuny.edu/faculty/research_studies/aris.pdf.

6. USDA Economic Research Service, Wyoming Fact Sheet, http://www.ers.usda.gov/StateFacts/WY.htm (last visited Feb. 17, 2006). According to the latest estimates, approximately 354,332 people live in rural areas and 154,962 people live in urban areas. *Id.*

7. Go WYLD! Guide to Wyoming Information, http://gowyld.net/wyoming/index.html (last visited Feb. 17, 2006).

8. STATE RANKINGS 2006, *supra* note 1, at 89.

same period, while the median household income in Wyoming was $43,641,[9] 9.6% of the state's population was living in poverty, which was somewhat below the national average of 12.4%.[10] More specifically, poverty affected 13.6% of Wyoming's children,[11] 6.1% of its senior citizens,[12] and 7.7% of its families.[13] Of its female-headed households with children, 40.6% lived in poverty,[14] and 30.6% of the state's public elementary and secondary school students were eligible for free or reduced-price meals.[15] Of those living in poverty, approximately 0.8% were black, which represented 12.0% of Wyoming's black population and 0.1% of its total population.[16] In an attempt to combat this poverty, Wyoming spent approximately $281 million on public welfare programs in 2002,[17] which made up 9.9% of its total government expenditures.[18]

Wyoming's Public Elementary-Secondary School System

Overall Spending and Performance

For the 2003–2004 school year, Wyoming spent $9,363 per pupil in its public elementary-secondary school system, which was slightly above the national average of $8,182.[19] Of this amount, 9.9% was provided by the federal government, 52.1% was provided by the state government, and 38.0% was provided by the local governments,[20] with property taxes making up 70.6% of the total funding.[21] Out of these funds, Wyoming paid its elementary and secondary school teachers an estimated average annual salary of $40,392 during the 2004–2005 school year,[22] and it provided a student/teacher ratio of 13.3, which was better than the national average of 15.9.[23]

---

9. *Id.* at 96.

10. *Id.* at 495.

11. *Id.* at 497.

12. *Id.* at 496.

13. *Id.* at 498.

14. *Id.* at 499.

15. *Id.* at 532.

16. *See* Fact Sheet, American FactFinder, http://factfinder.census.gov/home/saff/main.html?_lang=en (select "Wyoming" under "Get a Fact Sheet for your community") (last visited Feb. 17, 2007). Note that these numbers are based on the 2000 census because more recent numbers were not available.

17. *Id.* at 500.

18. *Id.* at 502.

19. Governments Division, U.S. Census Bureau, Public Education Finances 2004, at 8 tbl.8 (2006).

20. *See id.* at 5 tbl.5.

21. *See id.* at 4 tbl.4.

22. Thomas D. Snyder et al., National Center for Education Statistics, Digest of Education Statistics 2005, at 116 tbl.77 (2006).

23. *Id.* at 98 tbl.65.

In academic performance, Wyoming's fourth grade students scored higher than the national average in mathematics,[24] reading,[25] and science[26] but lower than the national average in writing.[27] Wyoming's eighth graders also scored higher than the national average in mathematics,[28] reading,[29] and science[30] but lower than the national average in writing.[31]

Equity Issues

In 2004, revenues spent per student in Wyoming's highest poverty districts were determined to be $303 less than the revenues spent in its lowest poverty districts.[32] When adjustments were made for the additional costs of educating students growing up in poverty, however, the funding gap grew to $539.[33] On the other hand, Wyoming spent $1,020 more per student in its highest minority districts, and this amount fell to $655 when adjustments for low-income students were made.[34]

Fourth graders eligible for free or reduced-price school lunches had test scores that were 4.5% lower in mathematics,[35] 5.3% lower in reading,[36] and 7.1% lower in writing[37] than those of students who were not eligible. The results were generally the same for eighth graders eligible for free or reduced-price lunches; their test scores were 5.2% lower in mathematics,[38] 4.8% lower in reading,[39] and 10.8% lower in writing[40] than those of students who were not eligible.

---

24. National Center for Education Statistics, U.S. Department of Education, The Nation's Report Card: Mathematics 2005, at 14 fig.11 (2005), *available at* http://nces.ed.gov/nationsreportcard/pdf/main2005/ 2006453.pdf [hereinafter Mathematics 2005].

25. National Center for Education Statistics, U.S. Department of Education, The Nation's Report Card: Reading 2005, at 14 fig.11 (2005), *available at* http://nces.ed.gov/nationsreportcard/pdf/main2005/2006451.pdf [hereinafter Reading 2005].

26. National Center for Education Statistics, U.S. Department of Education, The Nation's Report Card: Science 2005, at 16 fig.12 (2006), *available at* http://nces.ed.gov/nationsreportcard//pdf/main2005/2006466.pdf [hereinafter Science 2005].

27. Hilary R. Persky et al., National Center for Education Statistics, U.S. Department of Education, The Nation's Report Card: Writing 2002, at 23 tbl.2.2 (2003), *available at* http://nces.ed.gov/nationsreportcard/pdf/main2002/2003529.pdf [hereinafter Writing 2002].

28. Mathematics 2005, *supra* note 24, at 16 fig.12.

29. Reading 2005, *supra* note 25, at 16 fig.12.

30. Science 2005, *supra* note 26, at 28 fig.22.

31. Writing 2002, *supra* note 27, at 24 tbl.2.3.

32. The Education Trust, Funding Gaps 2006, at 7 tbl.3 (2006), *available at* http://www2.edtrust.org/NR/rdonlyres/CDEF9403-5A75-437E-93FF-EBF1174181FB/0/FundingGap2006.pdf.

33. *Id.*

34. *Id.* at 7 tbl.4.

35. Mathematics 2005, *supra* note 24, at 20 tbl.5.

36. Reading 2005, *supra* note 25, at 20 tbl.5.

37. Writing 2002, *supra* note 27, at 75 tbl.3.24.

38. Mathematics 2005, *supra* note 24, at 21 tbl.6.

39. Reading 2005, *supra* note 25, at 21 tbl.6.

40. Writing 2002, *supra* note 27, at 76 tbl.3.25.

The Supreme Court of Wyoming determined in two landmark cases that the state funding system was unconstitutional on equity and adequacy grounds.[41] The *Campbell v. State* decision resulted in subsequent litigation in which the court provided remedial guidelines for legislative review of state funding every five years and recommended inflation adjustments to funding every two years.[42]

Availability of Publicly Funded Prekindergarten Programs

Wyoming currently has no state prekindergarten program.[43]

Where Does Wyoming Get Its Revenue?

At the end of fiscal year 2004, Wyoming had total revenues of approximately $6.82 billion.[44] Of this amount, 33% was derived from state and local tax revenues and 29% was received from the federal government.[45] The remaining 38% came from other sources, including insurance trust revenue, revenue from government-owned utilities and other commercial or auxiliary enterprises.[46]

Tax Revenue

Wyoming collected approximately $2.24 billion in state and local tax revenue during fiscal year 2004.[47] As a result, Wyoming residents paid $4,437 per capita in state and local taxes, an amount which ranked 4th nationally.[48] The different types of tax sources were approximately apportioned as follows:

---

41. Washakie County Sch. Dist. v. Herschler, 606 P. 2d 310 (Wyo. 1980); Campbell County Sch. Dist. v. State, 907 P. 2d 1238 (Wyo. 1995).

42. State v. Campbell County Sch. Dist., 32 P.3d 325 (Wyo. 2001).

43. W. Steven Barnett et al., National Institute for Early Education Research, The State of Preschool 2006, at 151 (2007), *available at* http://nieer.org/yearbook/pdf/yearbook.pdf.

44. U.S. Census Bureau, State and Local Government Finances 2003–04, http://www.census .gov/govs/www/estimate04.html (last visited Oct. 6, 2006) [hereinafter Government Finances].

45. *Id.*

46. *Id.*

47. The total tax revenues were collected as follows: $1.5 billion by the state and $740 million by local governments. *Id.*

48. *Id.*

Individual income taxes	0.0%
Property taxes	30.5%
General and selective sales taxes	32.7%
Corporate income and other taxes	<u>36.8%</u>
	100.0%[49]

Federal Funding

During fiscal year 2004, 29% of Wyoming's total revenues came from the federal government.[50] For every dollar of federal taxes paid, Wyoming received $1.11 in federal funding, an amount which ranked 26th nationally[51] and was just below the national average of $1.17.[52]

Lottery Revenue

Wyoming does not have a state-sponsored lottery system.

Legal Structures of Major Tax Sources

Income

Wyoming does not levy individual income taxes.

Property

Overview

Wyoming has a typical property tax system that taxes the value of real estate at both the state and local levels.[53] During fiscal year 2004, Wyoming collected approximately $544 million dollars in property tax at the local level and approximately $140 million at the state level.[54] As a result, Wyoming residents paid $1,352 per capita in state and local property taxes, an amount which ranked 10th nationally.[55]

---

49. *Id.*

50. *Id.*

51. The Tax Foundation, Federal Spending Received Per Dollar of Taxes Paid by State, 2004 http://www.taxfoundation.org/taxdata/show/266.html (last visited Sept. 17, 2006).

52. *See id.*

53. WYO. STAT. ANN. §§ 39-13-101 - 39-13-111.

54. Government Finances, *supra* note 44.

55. *See id.*

Defining the Real Property Tax Base

Wyoming has two classifications for real property: property used for residential purposes is valued at 9.5% of market value, and property used for industrial purposes is assessed at 11.5% of the estimated fair market value as of January 1 each year.[56] Fair market value is generally determined by the application of "standard appraisal methods" determined by the Wyoming Department of Revenue, and reassessment occurs each year.[57]

Real Property Tax Rates

The tax rates imposed on real property vary and are set by each locality. During fiscal year 2006, the tax rates per $1,000 of assessed value ranged from $59.16 in Teton County to $74.46 in Hot Springs County.[58] These rates are governed by maximum amounts determined by the purpose for the revenue collected.[59]

Personal and Intangible Property

Wyoming exempts all personal intangible property from taxation.[60] However, most personal property, tangible or intangible, is listed as an exemption from taxation.[61]

Exemptions

Wyoming has many varied exemptions based on use and ownership. These exemptions include farm machinery and livestock; imports and exports; inventories; motor vehicles; and property owned by churches and other nonprofit organizations.[62]

General and Selective Sales

General Sales

Wyoming imposes a general retail sales-and-use tax, which makes up 27% of Wyoming's total tax revenue.[63] This tax is imposed on the sale, distribution, renting, or furnishing of tangible personal property, including lodging.[64] The state sales tax rate is 3%, with a special state provision to increase the rate an additional 1% if necessary.[65] All localities may impose a local rate of up to 2%, for a combined state and local rate

---

56. Wyo. Stat. Ann. § 39-13-103.

57. Id.

58. CCH-EXP, PROP-TAX-GUIDE WY ¶ 20-405, Rates of Tax.

59. Wyo. Stat. Ann. § 39-13-104.

60. Id. § 39-13-105.

61. Id.

62. Id.

63. Government Finances, supra note 44.

64. Wyo. Stat. Ann. § 39-15-103.

65. Id. §§ 39-15-103 to 39-15-104.

of 6%.[66] Additionally, localities may impose an additional 4% tax on the sale of lodging.[67] Exemptions from Wyoming's sales-and-use tax include unprepared food, prescription and nonprescription drugs, food stamps, school lunches, and textbooks.[68]

Selective Sales

Selective sales taxes make up 5.7% of Wyoming's total revenue.[69] Of that amount, 3.1%[70] comes from a motor fuel sales tax.[71] Wyoming residents paid an average of $138 per capita in state motor fuel sales taxes in 2004, an amount which ranked 17th nationally and was above the national average of $115.[72]

In 2004, sales taxes on alcoholic beverages made up 0.1% of Wyoming's total tax revenue.[73] Wyoming residents paid $2.63 per capita in state alcoholic beverage sales taxes in 2004, an amount which ranked 50th nationally.[74]

The tobacco product sales tax makes up 0.8% of Wyoming's tax revenues and is imposed at a rate of $0.60 per pack of cigarettes.[75] Wyoming residents paid $36.72 per capita in state tobacco sales taxes in 2004, an amount which ranked 30th nationally.[76]

The remainder of Wyoming's selective sales taxes makes up 1.7% of its total tax revenue. Of this amount, 0.8% represents taxes on utilities and the other 0.9% represents taxes on other specific commodities, businesses, or services not reported separately above (e.g., on contractors, lodging, lubricating oil, fuels other than motor fuel, motor vehicles, meals, soft drinks, margarine, etc.).[77]

Corporate Income and Other

Corporate Income

Wyoming does not assess a corporate income tax.

Other

Most of the remaining 36.8% of Wyoming's annual revenue comes from the imposition of a mineral tax imposed on the excavation of minerals (oil and gas, granite, etc.)

---

66. Wyo. Stat. § 39-15-204.

67. *Id.*

68. *Id.* § 39-15-105.

69. Government Finances, *supra* note 44.

70. *Id.*

71. Wyo. Stat. Ann. § 39-17-103.

72. State Rankings 2006, *supra* note 1, at 327.

73. Government Finances, *supra* note 44.

74. State Rankings 2006, *supra* note 1, at 335.

75. Wyo. Stat. Ann. § 12-3-101.

76. State Rankings 2006, *supra* note 1, at 332.

77. *See* Governments Division, U.S. Census Bureau, Government Finance and Employment Classification Manual, at ch.7 (2000), *available at* http://ftp2.census.gov/govs/class/classfull.pdf [hereinafter Classification Manual].

from the within the state.[78] This tax is assessed on each entity that has received a permit for mining.[79] Each mineral has a separate rate of taxation assessed for its removal. Much of the surplus revenue collected from the mineral tax is placed in a trust fund that allows the government to manage shortcomings that may result from a downturn in mineral prices.[80] As recently as 2002, the interest generated from the trust fund constituted enough income to meet approximately 1/3 of Wyoming's fiscal expenses.[81]

An additional $6 million was generated by the estate and gift tax,[82] which is calculated on the basis of the federal credit for state death taxes allowable by the Internal Revenue Code.[83] The "other taxes" category is also made up of motor vehicle license taxes, documentary and stock transfer taxes, severance taxes, and all other taxes not listed separately or provided for in other categories, such as taxes on land based on a specified rate per acre (rather than on assessed value).[84]

Burden Analysis

The overall state and local tax burden on Wyoming taxpayers is extremely regressive. Taxpayers in the lowest quintile—those with incomes of less than $17,000—bear a tax burden of 7.6% of their income, while taxpayers in the top 1%—those with incomes that exceed $400,000—bear a tax burden of just 1.7% of their income.[85] It is also worth noting that, although Wyoming obviously has no control over federal tax policy, federal itemized deductions for state and local personal income and property taxes nonetheless further reduce the burden on taxpayers in the top 1% to 1.6%.[86] Fur-

---

78. Wyo. Stat. Ann. §§ 39-14-101 to 14-801. (data taken from State of Wyoming Department of Revenue Annual Report 2004, available at: http://revenue.state.wy.us/PortalVBVS/uploads/2004AnnualReport.pdf; last checked Dec. 18, 2006).

79. Wyo. Stat. Ann. §§ 39-14-101 to -14-801.

80. Id..

81. State of Wyoming Department of Revenue Annual Report 2004, available at: http://revenue.state.wy.us/PortalVBVS/uploads/2004AnnualReport.pdf; last checked Dec 18, 2006).

82. Government Finances, supra note 44.

83. Wyo. Stat. Ann. §§ 39-19-103 to 39-19-104.

84. See Classification Manual, supra note 77, at ch.7.

85. See Robert S. McIntyre et al., Who Pays? A Distributional Analysis of the Tax Systems in All 50 States 116 (2d ed. 2003), available at http://www.itepnet.org/wp2000/text.pdf. Taxpayers in the second quintile bear a 6.3% total tax burden on incomes between $17,000 and $27,000; those in the third quintile bear a 5.4% tax burden on incomes between $26,000 and $40,000; those in the fourth quintile bear a 4.4% tax burden on incomes between $40,000 and $66,000; those in the 80th–95th percentiles bear a 4.0% tax burden on incomes between $66,000 and $122,000; finally, those in the 96th–99th percentiles bear a 3.1% tax burden on incomes between $122,000 and $400,000. Id.

86. Id. Taxpayers in the lowest and second lowest quintiles were able to reduce their individual tax burdens by 0.0%, those in the third quintile by 0.1%, those in the fourth quintile by 0.2%, those in the 80th–95th percentiles by 0.3%, and those in the 96th–99th percentiles by 0.1%. Id.

thermore, between 1989 and 2002, the tax burden on the bottom quintile rose by approximately 2.1%, while the burden on the top 1% actually fell by 0.6%.[87]

The sales and excises taxes imposed by Wyoming are very regressive, with taxpayers in the lowest quintile bearing a tax burden of 4.9% and those in the top 1% bearing a tax burden of just 0.5%.[88] Property taxes in Wyoming are also regressive, with taxpayers in the lowest quintile bearing a tax burden of 2.7% and those in the remaining quintiles bearing an average tax burden of 1.7%.[89]

---

87. *Id.* at 117.

88. *See id.* at 116. Taxpayers in the second quintile bear a 4.0% sales-and-excise tax burden; those in the third quintile bear a 3.3% burden; those in the fourth quintile bear a 2.7% burden; those in the 80th–95th percentiles bear a 2.0% burden; finally, those in the 96th–99th percentiles bear a 1.4% burden. *Id.*

89. *See id.* Taxpayers in the second quintile bear a 1.9% property tax burden; those in the third quintile bear a 1.9% burden; those in the fourth quintile bear a 1.5% burden; those in the 80th–95th percentiles bear a 1.7% burden; those in the 96th–99th percentiles bear a 1.7% burden; finally those in the top 1% bear a 1.2% burden. *Id.*

Additional Sources

General Sources

American Bar Association, Section of Taxation, Property Tax Deskbook, 11th Edition 2006 (2006).

BNA Tax Management Portfolios, State Series, Personal Income Taxes, The Bureau of National Affairs, Inc..

BNA Tax Management Portfolios, State Series, Sales and Use Tax, The Bureau of National Affairs, Inc.

Gardner, Robert L., & Dave Stewart, Tax Research Techniques (1993).

Hellerstein, Jerome R., & Walter Hellerstien, State Taxation (3d. ed. 1998) (supplemented semiannually).

Lamb, Margaret Anne, Taxation: An Interdisciplinary Approach to Research (2005).

Multistate Tax Analyst, Corporate Tax Publishers, Inc.

Sales & Use Tax Review, Corporate Tax Publishers, Inc.

Alabama

Alabama Legislative Fiscal Office, Legislator's Guide to Alabama Taxes (2005) (*available at*: www.lfo.state.al.us).

Bryce, James D., *Symposium: Proposed Tax Reform in Alabama*, 43 Ala. L. Rev. 541 (1992).

Chaney, Laura D., *Comment: Alabama's Constitution - A Royal Pain in the Tax: The State's Constitutionally Defective Tax System*, 32 Cumb. L. Rev. 233 (2002).

Ely, Bruce P., and Howard P. Walthall, Sr., *State Constitutional Limitations on Taxing and Spending: How Alabama Compares*, 33 Cumb. L. Rev. 463 (2002).

Hamill, Susan Pace, *An Argument For Tax Reform Based on Judeo-Christian Ethics*, 54 Ala. L. Rev. 1 (2002).

Hamill, Susan Pace, *Constitutional Reform In Alabama: A Necessary Step Towards Achieving a Fair and Efficient Tax Structure*, 33 Cumb. L. Rev. 437 (2003).

Alaska

Sauer, Jennifer H., Tax Reform in Alaska: An AARP Survey of Residents Age 18+ (2004).

Schumacher, Catherine, & Brett Fried, The Impact of the 1997 Tobacco Tax Rate Increase in Alaska: An Update (2000).

Sonneman, Joe, Stealing PFDs: Overspending Income, Refusing to Tax: How Alaska's Political Class Threatens People's Dividends and What You Can Do About It (2004).

van Meurs, Dr. Pedro, Proposal for a Profit Based Production Tax for Alaska (2006) (*available at*: http://www.gov.state.ak.us/oiltax/pdf/PPT_ report.pdf).

Arizona

Busby, James G., Patrick Derdenger & Dawn R. Gabel. Reducing Your Clients' Sales and Use Tax Obligations in Arizona (2005).

Derdenger, Patrick, & Brian W. LaCorte, Property Tax Law in Arizona (2000).

Lipman, Francine J., *Taxing Undocumented Immigrants: Separate, Unequal, and Without Representation*, 59 Tax Law 813 (2006).

Lohman, Judith S., Arizona Kids Tax Credit Program (2006).

Smith, Susan Kimsey, Analysis of Arizona Estate Tax (2006).

Smith, Zachary A., Politics and Public Policy in Arizona: Third Edition (1992).

Tunnell, Tonia A., The Property Tax System in Arizona: A Guide for Legislators (2002).

Arkansas

Brooks, Steven L., *The Venture Capital Investment Act of 2001: Arkansas's Vision for Economic Growth*, 56 Ark. L. Rev. 397 (2003).

Carter, Brian E., *Note, Constitutional Law- Education and Equal Protection—Towards Intelligence and Virtue: Arkansas Embarks on a Court-Mandated Search for an Adequate and Equitable School Funding System. Lake View School District No. 25 v. Huckabee*, 91 S.W.3d 472 (2002), 26 U. Ark. Little Rock L. Rev. 143 (2003).

Carter, Brian E., *Survey of Legislation: Title 26- Taxation*, 26 U. Ark. Little Rock L. Rev. 495 (2004).

Cooper, James H., *Note, The Plain Meaning Rule in Arkansas After Foster v. Jefferson County Quorum Court*, 49 Ark. L. Rev. 559 (1996).

Gitchel, Dent, *The Ben J. Altheimer Symposium- Education Funding at the Crossroads- Introduction: Funding the Education of Arkansas's Children: A Summary of the Problems and Challenges*, 27 U. Ark. Little Rock L. Rev. 1 (2004).

Higle, Patrick F., *Survey of Legislation: Title 26 Tax Law*, 24 U. Ark. Little Rock L. Rev. 613 (2002).

Matthews, David R., *Lessons From Lake View: Some Questions and Answers from Lake View School District No. 25 v. Huckabee*, 56 Ark. L. Rev. 519 (2003).

McDonald, Janet D., Mary F. Hughes, and Gary W. Ritter, *The Ben J. Altheimer Symposium- Education Funding at the Crossroads- Article: School Finance Litigation and Adequacy Studies*, 27 U. Ark. Little Rock L. Rev. 69 (2004).

Pierce, Ray S., *Annual Survey of Caselaw: Tax Law*, 25 U. Ark. Little Rock L. Rev. 1029 (2003).

Pierce, Ray. S., *Tax Law*, 24 U. Ark. Little Rock L. Rev. 1077 (2002).

Polanco, Kimberly, *Annual Survey of Caselaw: Tax Law*, 27 U. Ark. Little Rock L. Rev. 751 (2005).

California

Bone, James S., California Property Tax (2006).

Fox, Joel, The Legend Of Proposition 13: The Great California Tax Revolt (2003).

Gleason, Robert H., *Reevaluation the California Sales Tax: Exemptions, Equity, Effectiveness, and the Need For A Broader Base*, 33 San Diego L. Rev. 1681 (1996).

Kleinrock's California Tax Bulletin, Kleinrock Publishing (*cite as*: Cal. Tax Bull. LEXIS).

Kramer, Liz, *Achieving Equitable Education Through the Courts: A Comparative Analysis of Three States*, 31 J.L. & Educ. 1 (2002).

Pace, Layton L., Charles J. Moll III, & Bruce P. Ely, *Wrestling With Taxes in the Golden State – California's Unconstitutional LLC Fee*, 16 J. Multistate Tax'n 24 (2006).

Sonstelie, Jon, Eric Brunner, & Kenneth Ardon, For Better or For Worse? School Finance Reform in California, Public Policy Institute of California (2000) (*available at*: http://www.ppic.org/content/pubs/report/R_200JSR.pdf.).

Steele, Thomas H., & Charles J. Moll, Property Taxes: California's Property Tax Regime (2004).

Sutton, Giles, *California's New Tax Shelter Rules May Signify a Trend for the Future*, 14 J. Multistate Tax'n 18 (2004).

Wasi, Nada, & Michelle J White, National Bureau of Economic Research, Property Tax Limitations and Mobility: The Lock-In Effect of California's Proposition 13 (2005) (*available at* http://www.nber.org/papers/w11108).

Whittenburg, Gerald E, California Income Tax Fundamentals (2005).

William, Glenn J., & Lawrence O. Picus, *The "Williams" Settlement and the Prospects for Future School Finance Adequacy Litigation in California*, 32 Journal of Education Finance 382 (2007).

Colorado

Beazer, Kenneth L., Ins and Outs of Property Tax in Colorado (2004).

Chase, Adam W., Colorado Sales and Use Tax: A Beginners Basic Course (1999).

Colorado Department of Revenue, Colorado Sales and Use Tax: Reference Guide (2003) (*available at*: http://www.revenue.state.co.us/TPS%5FDir/wrap.asp?incl+salestaxforms).

Colorado Office of State Planning and Budgeting, Colorado Permanent Tax Relief Since 1999 (2005) (*available at*: http://www.state.co.us/gov%5Fdir/govnr%5Fdir/ospb/special.html).

Hildreth, Darby, *Survey Comment: Recent Developments in Tax Law in the Tenth Circuit*, 79 Denv. U. L. Rev. 411 (2002).

Kirk, Ron, & Jason Schrock, Colorado Tax Handbook: Report to the Colorado General Assembly (2005) (*available at*: http://www.state.co.us/gov%5Fdir/leg%5Fdir/lcsstaff/Scrollpages/IFramePages/Interest%5FFrame.htm).

Poling, Matthew W., & Norman H. Wright, Property Tax Law in Colorado (2000).

Connecticut

Farr, J. Steven, and Mark Trachtenberg, *The Edgewood Drama: An Epic Quest for Education Equity*, 17 Yale L. & Pol'y Rev. 607 (1999).

Fox, Kenneth, *The Suspectness of Wealth: Another Look at State Constitutional Adjudication of School Finance Inequalities*, 26 Conn. L. Rev. 1139 (1994).

Ryan, James E., *Schools, Race, and Money*, 109 Yale L.J. 249 (1999).

Stark, Kirk J., *Note, Rethinking Statewide Taxation of Nonresidential Property for Public Schools*, 102 Yale L.J. 805 (1992).

Wetzler, Lauren A., *Symposium: School Finance Litigation: Buying Equality: How School Finance Reform and Desegregation Came to Compete in Connecticut*, 22 Yale L. & Pol'y Rev. 481 (2004).

Delaware

Durante, Charles J., Robert E. Schlusser & Collis O. Townsend, Delaware Non-Profits: Tax and Business Answers (1997).

Fletcher, Michael J., & Michael J. Semes, State Tax Planning Techniques in Delaware (1994).

Forsten, , Richard A., Dennis J. Siebold & Earl Timmons, Real Estate Property Tax in Delaware (1997).

Remington, William M., *Delaware's Tax System in a Digital Age*, 22 Delaware Lawyer 16 (2004).

Florida

Dubov, Pamela M., *Circumventing the Florida Constitution: Property Taxes and Special Assessments, Today's Illusory Distinction*, 30 Stetson L. Rev. 1469 (2001).

Hendrix, Michelle E., & George R. Zodrow, *Sales Taxation of Services: An Economic Perspective*, 30 Fla. St. U.L. Rev. 411 (2003).

Holcombe, Randall G., Principles for Florida's Sales Tax (2000).

Hudson, David M., *Governmental Immunity and Taxation in Florida*, 9 J. Law. & Pub. Pol'y 221 (1998).

Lindquist, Sarah A., *Property Tax Exemptions for the Nontraditional Church: How do we Grant Tax Exemptions to Places of Worship and Not Amusement Parks?*, 33 Fla. St. U.L. Rev. 1149 (2006).

McCabe, B.C., & C. Stream, The Chicken or the Egg: A Recent History Of Public Opinion and Tax Reform in Florida. *Journal of Public Budgeting, Accounting & Financial Management*. 18(2), 167–191 (2006).

Nabors, Robert L., *An Opportunity Lost: Tax Reform and the 1997-1998 Constitution Revision Commission*, 30 Fla. St. U.L. Rev. 477 (2003).

Stark, Kirk J., *The Uneasy Case for Extending the Sales Tax to Services*, 30 Fla. St. U.L. Rev. 435 (2003).

Thomas, Josephine W., *Increasing the Homestead Tax Exemption: "Tax Relief" or Burden on Florida Homeowners and Local Governments?*, 35 Stetson L. Rev. 509 (2006).

Georgia

Bahl, Roy W., & Richard Ross Hawkins, *A Georgia sales tax for the 21st century*. (Atlanta: Georgia Public Policy Foundation (1998)).

Coffey, Sarah Beth, & Alan Essig, *Doing Better: Fair and Adequate Tax Reform in Georgia*, State Tax Notes. Vol. 42, No. 1, October 2, 2006

Morrow, Melissa J., *Twenty-Five Years of Debate: Is Acquisition-value Property Taxation Constitutional? Is it Fair? Is it Good Policy?*, 53 Emory L.J. 587 (2004).

Peaden, Timothy J., & Joel S.Wadsworth, Property Tax Law in Georgia (1998).

Rubenstein, Ross, & Catherine Freeman, *Do Local Sales Taxes for Education Increase Inequities? The Case of Georgia's ESPLOST*, 28(3) Journal of Education Finance 425-42 (2003).

Wheeler, Lauara A., (2000), *The effect of the growth in elderly population on Georgia tax revenues*. Atlanta, Ga: Fiscal Research Program, Andrew Young School of Policy Studies, Georgia State University.

Hawaii

Bay, Maile, & John Bay. Common Ground: Land Stewardship and Tax Planning Options for Land Owners, Farmers, and Rural Communities in Hawaii (1999).

D'Amato, John J., Real Property Tax Law in Hawaii (1995).

Utterdyke, Aileen B., Taxes of Hawaii 2004: A Comprehensive Guide For Taxpayers And Tax Professionals (2004).

Idaho

EchoHawk, Larry, *Balancing State and Tribal Power to Tax in Indian Country*, 40 Idaho L. Rev. 623 (2004).

Huntley, Robert C., *Commentary: Public Education School Funding Litigation in Idaho: A Tale of Legislative Irresponsibility and Delay*, 41 Idaho L. Rev. 247 (2005).

Spinole, Karen L., *Note, The Road Less Traveled—Implications of the Goodman Oil Decision*, 38 Idaho L. Rev. 637 (2002).

Thorpe, Geoffrey L., *Idaho Taxation of Foreign Corporate Income After Kraft v. Iowa*, 39 Idaho L. Rev. 581 (2003).

Illinois

Berek, David A., *Illinois' New Estate-Tax Law*, 91 Ill. B.J. 465 (2003).

Cantlin-Van Wiggeren, Christina M., *Hip-Hip-Hurray for Illinois Taxpayers, or Is It Too Early to Cheer?: An Analysis of In re Consolidated Objections to Tax Levies of School District No. 205, for Years 1991 Through 1996*, 20 N. Ill. U. L. Rev. 711 (2000).

Nepple, James A., *An Illinois Lawyer's Guide to Important Tax Aspects of Limited Liability Companies*, 87 Ill. B.J. 96 (1999).

Ornduff, Jason, *The Illinois Estate Tax – One Year Later*, 18-SEP CBA Rec. 28 (2005).

Oldfield, Kenneth, & Michael Casey, *Why Local Property Taxes are Inappropriate for Financing Illinois Community Colleges: A Strategy for Challenging How the State Funds These Post-Secondary Schools*, 19 S. Ill. U. L.J. 523 (1995).

Tamboro, Nina H., *The Illinois Property Tax System: An Overview*, 10 Loy. Consumer L. Rev. 186 (1998).

Indiana

Jegen, Lawrence A., III & Edward L. Harris, III, *Developments in Indiana Taxation*, 34 Ind. L. Rev. 1003 (2001).

Kaltenmark, Randal J., *Indiana Property Taxes and the Leasing of Property By Tax-Exempt Organizations*, INDIANA BAR ASSOCIATION, pp. 33 (1998).

Michel, Catherine, *Brother, Can You Spare a Dime: Tax Increment Financing in Indiana*, 71 IND. L.J. 457 (1996).

Paganelli, F. Anthony, *Constitutional Analysis of Indiana's Controlled Substance Excise Tax*, 70 IND. L.J. 1301 (1995).

Iowa

Cain, Patricia A., *Dependency, Taxes, and Alternative Families*, 5 J. GENDER RACE & JUST. 267 (2002).

Craft, Matthew M., *LOST and Found: The Unequal Distribution of Local Option Sales Tax Revenue Among Iowa Schools*, 88 IOWA L. REV. 199 (2002).

Lindeen, Jonathan M.,, *BIA Tribal Schools and the No Child Left Behind Act: An Argument for a More Culturally-Sensitive Implementation*, 9 J. GENDER RACE & JUST. 361 (2005).

McEowen, Roger A., & Neil E. Harl, *Selected Farm and Small Business Tax Issues*, 10 DRAKE J. AGRIC. L. 57 (2005).

Schlueter, Hillary, *The Return of Lochnerizing: The Iowa Supreme Court's Invalidation of Gambling Taxes*, 9 J. GENDER RACE & JUST. 713 (2006).

Kansas

Dibello, Diana, *The Changing Sales Tax Regime: Kansas Seeks to Adapt to the Streamlined Sales and Use Tax Project*, 14 J. MULTISTATE TAX'N 28 (2004).

Dickenson, Martin, & Nancy S. Roush, *The New Kansas Estate Tax*, 75 KAN. B.J. 18 (2006).

Hager, Douglas A., *Kansas' Sales and Use Tax Law: Exemptions for Manufacturing Machinery and Equipment and the Integrated Plant Theory*, 37 WASHBURN L.J. 543 (1998).

Lennen, Michael, *The Kansas Retainers' Sales Tax: An Overview*, 62 KAN. B.J. 24 (1993).

Pace, Ryan, A *Review of Kansas Tax Law Governing the Allocation and Apportionment of Income for Multistate Corporations Doing Business in Kansas*, 37 WASHBURN L.J. 703 (1998).

Price, Stephanie, *Equal Protection: The Kansas Supreme Court Upholds Constitutionality of Tax Rate Disparity: Peden v. State, 930 P.2d 1 (Kan. 1996)*, 37 WASHBURN L.J. 203 (1998).

Reitz, Chris, *The Application of Kansas Sales Tax to Transactions Between Affiliated Companies*, 42 U. KAN. L. REV. 461 (1994).

Kentucky

Banoff, Sheldon I., & Richard M. Lipton, *First Court to Validate the Check-The-Box Regulations?*, 103 J. TAX'N 251 (2005).

BUETTNER, FRANK L., PROPERTY TAX LAW IN KENTUCKY (2002).

Edwards, Scott M., *No Kentucky Property Tax on Car Purchased Before But Registered After Assessment Date*, 15 MULTISTATE TAX'N 38 (2005).

Ely, Bruce P., *Noted Trends in the State Taxation of Pass-Through Entities*, 705 PLI/TAX 649 (2006).

HORN, ERICA L., & MARK A. LOYD, KENTUCKY SALES AND USE TAX UPDATE (2005).

Kelly, Erin E., *All Students are Not Created Equal: The Inequitable Combination of Property-Tax-Based School Finance Systems and Local Control*, 45 DUKE L.J. 397 (1995).

Zefi, Jon, Shawn Kane, Andrea Collins & Joseph Carr, *Kentucky Modernization Legislation Has Major Effect on Business*, 16 J. MULTISTATE TAX'N 14 (2006).

Louisiana

CALHOUN, JAYE ANDRAS, & PAULA C. HAYDEL, MULTISTATE TAXATION IN LOUISIANA (2002).

GOULD, NICOLE F., & STEPHEN H. MYERS, LOUISIANA SALES AND USE TAX UPDATE (2004).

Grand, John, *Tax Increment Financing: Louisiana Goes Fishing for New Business*, 66 LA. L. REV. 851 (2006).

McIntyre, Michael J., Paull Mines & Richard D. Pomp, *Designing a Combined Reporting Regime for a State Corporate Income Tax: A Case Study of Louisiana*, 61 LA. L. REV. 699 (2001).

Richardson, James A., & Susan Kalinka, *Louisiana Taxation of Businesses: Two Alternative Proposals*, 61 LA. L. REV. 763 (2001).

RIESS, GEORGE F., & S.T. COHEN, PROPERTY TAX IN LOUISIANA (2000).

Maine

Goodall, Clifford H., & Seth A. Goodall, *Property Tax: A Primer and Modest Proposal For Maine*, 57 ME. L. REV. 585 (2005).

LACHANCE, LAURIE G., TAX REFORM IN MAINE: IS IT NEEDED?: PRESENTATION OF LAURIE G. LACHANCE TO LEGISLATORS' POLICY FORUM ON TAX REFORM (2003).

Murray, Matthew N., *Tax Policy and Development in Maine: A Survey of the Issues*, Maine Policy Review (1992).

Valente, Paul, *Overhauling Maine's Tax System*, Maine Policy Review (1996).

Maryland

BEN, EDWARD H., SALES AND USE TAX IN MARYLAND (2006).

Diamond, Brian T., *Comment: Maryland's Corporate Income Taxation Approach for Multi-Jurisdictional Companies: Moving Toward Uniformity, Yet Still Lacking Ultimate Effectiveness*, 63 MD. L. REV. 1071 (2004).

GEVARTER, STEVEN M., JEFFREY A. MARKOWITZ & DARYL J. SIDLE, REAL ESTATE TAX ISSUES IN MARYLAND (2006).

Leviton, Susan P., *An Adequate Education for All Maryland's Children: Morally Right, Economically Necessary, and Constitutionally Required*, 63 MD. L. REV. 1137 (1993).

MARYLAND BUDGET AND TAX POLICY INSTITUTE. MARYLAND IS A LOW-TAX STATE (SO, WHERE SHOULD WE LOOK TO BALANCE THE BUDGET?) (2002).

SCHAEFER, WILLIAM DONALD U., ASSESSMENT OF MARYLAND'S TAX-FREE WEEK (2001).

Massachusetts

Kingson, Charles I., *How Tax Thinks*, 37 SUFFOLK U. L. REV. 1031 (2004).

Lipman, Francine J., *The Taxation of Undocumented Immigrants: Separate, Unequal, and Without Representation*, 9 HARV. LATINO L. REV. 1 (2006).

Obhof, Larry J., *Rethinking Judicial Activism and Restraint in School Finance Litigation*, 27 HARV. J.L. & PUB. POL'Y 569 (2004).

Papademetriou, Dean, *A Review of Massachusetts Property Tax Abatement Remedies*, 42 B.B.J. 8 (1998).

Rausch, Kate I., Note, *Pay-to-play: A Risky and Largely Unregulated Solution to Save High School Athletic Programs from Elimination*, 39 SUFFOLK U. L. REV. 583 (2006).

Vaughn, Cathryn, *The School Choice Provision of the No Child Left Behind Act and Its Conflict with Desegregation Orders*, 13 B.U. PUB. INT. L.J. 79 (Fall 2003).

Michigan

BISDORF, JEREMY D., PAUL V. McCORD & WAYNE D. ROBERTS. MICHIGAN SALES AND USE TAX UPDATE (2002).

HILPERT, MARK, & ROBERT F. RHOADES, PROPERTY TAX LAW IN MICHIGAN (2005).

JEN, KYLE I., BACKGROUND AND HISTORY: MICHIGAN'S SINGLE BUSINESS TAX (2003).

LOCKWOOD, ANDREW, THE MICHIGAN PROPERTY TAX, REAL AND PERSONAL, 2004 STATISTICAL UPDATE (2006).

McKim, Samuel J., III, *Is Michigan's Ad Valorem Property Tax Becoming Obsolete?*, 77 U. DET. MERCY L. REV. 655 (2000).

Walters, Kelly A., *Sales and Use Taxes - A Goodwill Adjustment Policy Included in the Retail Price of a Vehicle and Subjected to Sales Tax is Exempt From Use Tax Pursuant to the Michigan Use Tax Act. General Motors Corp. v. Dep't of Treasury, Revenue Div., 644 N.W.2d 734 (Mich. 2002)*, 81 U. DET. MERCY L. REV. 141 (2003).
WOLFRAM, GARY, TIME TO TAME THE TAX BEAST IN MICHIGAN (2002).

Minnesota

Foster, Mark M., *Owner's "Checking-the-Box" for Foreign Entity Created Domestic Partnership for Minnesota Tax Purposes*, 16 J. MULTISTATE TAX'N 38 (2007).
Geis, Jerome A., & Barry R. Greller, *The Minnesota Tax Court: The Taxpayer's Choice of Forum, to Litigate a State Tax Liability*, 21 HAMLINE L. REV. 407 (1998).
GSCHLECHT, MIKE, & THOMAS A. ZESSMAN, MINNESOTA SALES & USE TAX: A PRACTICAL APPROACH (2006).
Kakela, Peter, *The Minnesota Taconite Production Tax: An Alternaitve Index*, 16 J. NAT. RESOURCES & ENVTL. L. 43 (1999).
MANZI, NINA, & JOEL MICHAEL, THE FEDERAL EARNED INCOME TAX CREDIT AND THE MINNESOTA WORKING FAMILY CREDIT (2006).
STROM, TIM A., MINNESOTA SCHOOL FINANCE: A GUIDE FOR LEGISLATORS (2006).

Mississippi

BECK, EDDIE, & DAVID W. STEVENS. MISSISSIPPI SALES AND USE TAX FOR MANUFACTURERS (2000).
DICKE, STEPHEN G., FORESTRY INCOME TAX SERIES: BASICS OF BASIS (2003).
STEVENS, DAVID W., & ROBERT B. WHITE, SALES AND USE TAX IN MISSISSIPPI: A BEGINNER'S BASIC COURSE (2006).

Missouri

Department: *The Flag: School District Could Set Property Tax Rate of $2.75 Without a Hancock Vote*, 59 J. MO. B. 285 (2003).
Department: *Taxes in Your Practice: Department of Revenue Defeated in Multi-State Income Tax Case*, 59 J. MO. B. 40 (2003).
Ess, Eric A., *Internet Taxation Without Physical Representation? States Seek Solution to Stope-Commerce Sales Tax Shortfall*, 50 ST. LOUIS L.J. 893 (2006).
Goshorn, Julie A., *In a Tif: Why Missouri Needs Tax Increment Financing Reform*, 77 WASH. U. L. Q. 919 (1999).
Marks, Jason S., *Spackle for the Wall? Pubic Funding for School Vouchers After Locke v. Davey*, 61 J. MO. B. 150 (2005).

McGovern, Bruce A., *The New Provision for Tolling the Limitations Periods for Seeking Tax Refunds: Its History, Operation and Policy, and Suggestions for Reform*, 65 Mo. L. Rev. 797 (2000).

Reinert, Josh, *Tax Increment Financing in Missouri: Is it Time for Blight and But-For to Go*, 45 St. Louis L.J. 1019 (2001).

Simmons, Jennifer A., *The Missouri Use Tax: Matching the Burdens to the Benefits of Ownership*, 70 Mo. L. Rev. 269 (2005).

Van Matre, Craig A., *The Missouri Estate Tax Has Died: Should it be Resurrected, and Was it Constitutional in the First Place*, 61 J. Mo. B. 312 (2005).

Montana

Ellis, Richard J., *Symposium: Signature Gathering in the Initiative Process: How Democratic is it*, 64 Mont. L. Rev. 35 (2003).

Griffith, Alanah, *The Next Chapter in the Taking of Judical Power from the Tribes: Burlington Northern Railroad Company v. Red Wolf*, 62 Mont. L. Rev. 339 (2001).

Harvey, James, Larry Elison, Nancy Sinclair, Chris Tweeten & Orson Swindle, *Symposium: The Taxation of E-Commerce*, 61 Mont. L. Rev. 1 (2000).

Petesch, Gregory J., *Symposium: The State of the Montana Consitution (Turkey Feathers on the Constitutional Eagle)*, 64 Mont. L. Rev. 23 (2003).

Wandler, Hillary A., *Will Montana Breathe Life Into its Positive Constitutional Right to Equal Education Opportunity*, 65 Mont. L. Rev. 343 (2004).

Nebraska

Hurst, Paul H., Toni A. Johnson & Mark S. Katz. Property Tax Law in Nevada (2003).

Kubert, Thomas W., Property Tax In Nebraska, (2001).

LaPuzza, Paul J., *Meet the TERC: Appeals of Property Tax Protests from the Board of Equalization to the Nebraska Tax Equalization and Review Commission*, 32 Creighton L. Rev. 533 (1998).

Nebraska Department of Revenue, Research Division, 1999 Nebraska Tax Burden Study (2002) (*available at* http://www.nlc.state.ne.us/epubs/R5000/B014-1999.pdf).

Volkmer, Ronald R., *Low Income Housing and the Charitable Exemption*, 34 Creighton L. Rev. 47 (2000).

Nevada

Azevedo, Norman J., & David P. Pursell. Sales and Use Tax in Nevada (2004).

Bartlett, John S., *An Argument to Repeal the Sales and Use Tax as a Referendum Law*, 10-APR Nev. Law. 6 (2002).

Hurst, Paul H., Toni A. Johnson, & Mark S. Katz, Property Tax Law in Nevada, (2003).

New Hampshire

Edwards, Scott M., *New Hampshire Still Struggling With School Funding, Property Tax Reform—Latest Effort Found Unconstitutional*, 16-Jul J. Multistate Tax'n 38 (2006).

Ely, Bruce P., *Noted Trends in the State Taxation of Pass-Through Entities*, 705 PLI/Tax 649 (2006).

Minard, Richard A., Shifting the Load: Costs, Effects, and the Potential Impact of Property-Tax Relief for New Hampshire's Seniors (2005).

West, George M., Historical Perspective of Tax Collecting in New Hampshire (2005).

Wolowitz, Mark, *New Hampshire and Oregon Differ on Phase-Ins for Reforming School Funding*, 9-Jan J. Multistate Tax'n 39 (2000).

Wolowitz, Mark, *New Hampshire Reenacts School Funding Package Without Phase-In*, 9-Feb J. Multistate Tax'n 36 (2000).

Wolowitz, Mark, *Latest Version of New Hampshire School Funding Tax Also Unconsitutional*, 11-Jul J. Multistate Tax'n 42 (2001).

Wolowitz, Mark, *New Hampshire High Court, Reversing, Finds Latest Version of School Funding Tax OK*, 11-Aug J. Multistate Tax'n 36 (2001).

New Jersey

Appaluccio, Robert, New Jersey Homeowner's Guide to Property Tax Appeals (2000).

Bogart, T., David F. Bradford & Michael G. Williams, Incidence and Allocation Effects of a State Fiscal Policy Shift: The Florio Initiatives in New Jersey (1992).

Cambria, Judith C., New Jersey's Patchwork Property Tax Relief: Making a Bad System Better (2000).

Crabtree, David E., State and Local Taxation: New Jersey Property Tax (1999).

Forsberg, Mary E., If it Ain't broke … : New Jersey's Income Tax Makes Dollars and Sense (2006)

Hackett, Michael P., *The 2001 Amendment to the New Jersey Property Tax Exemption Statute as It Pertains to Religious Organizations: A Statute that Grants an Overdue Extension of the Complete Exemption but Raises Establishment Clause Concerns with the Partial Exemption*, 4 RUTGERS J. LAW & RELIG. 5 (2003).

INSTITUTE ON TAXATION AND ECONOMIC POLICY (WASHINGTON, D.C.), NEW JERSEY TAXES HIT THE POOR & MIDDLE CLASS HARDER THAN THE WEALTHY (2003).

JONES, CHRISTOPHER, FUNDAMENTAL PROPERTY TAX REFORM: LAND USE IMPLICATIONS OF NEW JERSEY'S TAX DEBATE (2006).

JONES, CHRISTOPHER, & ALEXIS PERROTTA, COMPREHENSIVE PROPERTY TAX REFORM FOR NEW JERSEY (2006).

KRUECKEBERG, DONALD A., FREE NEW JERSEY: THE BURDEN OF PROPERTY TAX EXEMPTIONS (2004).

LYONS, CHARLES R., & ERIC B. SCHNURER, FAIR IMMEDIATE RESPONSIBLE SIMPLIFIED TAX RELIEF: A FIRST FOR NEW JERSEY (2000).

Metzger, John Mackay, *Unitary Taxation in New Jersey*, 28 SETON HALL L. REV. 162 (1997).

OZELLO, JAMES M., UNDERSTANDING NEW JERSEY INDIVIDUAL INCOME TAX LAW: REVISED STATUTES TITLE 54A: NEW JERSEY GROSS INCOME TAX ACT [FOR] 2004 TAX YEAR (2005).

Patel, Ajesh B., *Development in State Constitutional Law 1999: Taxation - Special Assessments—Assessments Imposed by Township on Commercial Properties in a Special Improvement District are Special Assessments Rather than Taxes, and Therefore, Not Subject to the State Constitution's Uniformity Clause. 2nd Roc-Jersey Associates v. Morristown, 158 N.J. 581, 731 A.2d 1 (1999)*, 31 RUTGERS L. J. 1600 (2000).

Pellegrino, Michael G., & Ralph P. Allocca, *Tax Certificates: A Review of the Tax Sale Law*, 26 SETON HALL L. REV. 1607 (1996).

Prebut, David S., *State and Local Taxation of Electronic Commerce: The Forging of Cyberspace Tax Policy*, 24 RUTGERS COMPUTER & TECH. L.J. 345 (1998).

State of New Jersey Property Tax Convention Task Force, *Report to the Governor and Legislature - A Plan to Hold a Property Tax Convention. "Finding A Fairer System"*, 36 RUTGERS L. J. 1295 (2005).

STECKER, SARAH, BURYING INHERITANCE TAX PUTS NEW JERSEY IN THE HOLE (2002).

ZERILLO, JOHN W., NEW JERSEY'S INCOME TAX: HOW PROGRESSIVE? (2003).

New Mexico

Desiderio, Robert J., James La Fata & Maria Siemel McCulley, *New Mexico Taxes: Taking Another Look*, 32 N.M. L. REV. 351 (2002).

VanAmberg, Ronald J., *Separate But Unequal: One School District's Struggle For Fair Educational Facilities Funding In New Mexico*, 83 NEB. L. REV. 882 (2005).

Zimmermann, Anne, *Taxation of Indians: An Analysis and Comparison Of New Mexico And Oklahoma State Tax Laws*, 41 TULSA L. REV. 91 (2005).

New York

Burge, Jason, *Rethinking Fees and Taxes in Light of the New York Coty Health Care Security Act*, 61 N.Y.U. ANN. SURV. AM. L. 679 (2006).

DOYLE, CHRISTOPHER L., ADVANCED SALES AND USE TAX IN NEW YORK (2001).

EOM, TAE HO, & JOHN M. YINGER, EVALUATION OF NEW YORK STATE PROPERTY TAX POLICY (2004).

Inside New York Taxes, Corporate Tax Publishers, Inc.

Kleinrock's New York Tax Bulletin, Kleinrock Publishing (*cite as*: NY. Tax Bull. LEXIS).

LEE, CAROLYN JOY, NEW YORK SALES AND USE TAXES (2003).

Lohman, Judith S., New York's School Tax (2001).

PLATTNER, ROBERT D., 2007 NEW YORK STATE TAX HANDBOOK (2007).

PLATTNER, ROBERT D., NEW YORK PERSONAL INCOME TAX (2001).

PLATTNER, ROBERT D., NEW YORK STATE AND CITY BUDGET LEGISLATION: LAW AND EXPLANATION OF TAX PROVISIONS (2003).

UNITED STATES GENERAL ACCOUNTING OFFICE, REVIEW OF THE ESTIMATES FOR THE IMPACT OF THE SEPTEMBER 11, 2001, TERRORIST ATTACKS ON NEW YORK TAX REVENUES (2002).

North Carolina

CAMERON, AMNA, FOLLOWING THE MONEY: A GUIDE TO NORTH CAROLINA'S TAX SYSTEM AND A BLUEPRINT FOR REFORM AND MODERNIZATION (2004).

CAMPBELL, WILLIAM A., PROPERTY TAX COLLECTION IN NORTH CAROLINA (2000).

Final Report: Governor's Commission to Modernize State Finances (N.C. 2002) (*available at* http://www.osbm.state.nc.us/files/pdf_files/final_rpt_gov_comm.pdf).

Financing the Future Resource Library, Institute for Emerging Issues (*available at*: http://www.ncsu.edu/iei/ 2006EIFlibrary.html (last visited Mar. 31, 2007).

Mejia, Elaine, & Amna Cameron, NC Budget & Tax Center, A 21st Century Revenue Plan: Funding State Government in a Fair and Sustainable Way (2005) (*available at* http://ncjustice.org/media/library/392_21stcentrevplan.pdf#search=%22North %20Carolina%2C%20sources%20of%20revenue%22).

SCHWEKE, WILLIAM, CORPORATION FOR ENTERPRISE DEVELOPMENT, DEVELOPMENT-ENHANCING TAX REFORM IN NORTH CAROLINA: A PATH TO GROWTH WITH EQUITY (2005) (*available at* http://www.cfed.org/imageManager/_documents/NC_ Tax_Reform.pdf).

STEEL, ROBERT PALMER, THE IMPACT OF THE NORTH CAROLINA CIGARETTE EXCISE TAX INCREASE ON CIGARETTE SALES AND TAX REVENUE IN NORTH AND SOUTH CAROLINA (2006).

North Dakota

Fletcher, Matthew L.M., *In Pursuit of Tribal Development as a Substitute for Reservation Tax Revenue*, 80 N. Dak. L. Rev. 759 (2004).

Pearson, Garry A., *The North Dakota Limited Liability Company Act: Formation and Tax Consequences*, 70 N.D. L. Rev. 67 (1994).

Periakaruppan, Muthu, Steven E. Noack, and Kim Sharp, Sales and Use Tax in North Dakota: A Beginner's Basic Course (2000).

Ohio

Baldwin's Ohio Tax Law and Rules, West Publishing.

Conomy, Christopher P., *The Tax Status of Ohio Property Used for Low-Income Housing*, 46 Clev. St. L. Rev. 533 (1998).

Coriell, Karen Bond, *Chaos, Contradiction and Confusion: Ohio's Real Property Tax Exemptions*, 53 Ohio St. L.J. 265 (1992).

Dimengo, Steven A., William G. Nolan & George A. Schueller, Advanced Sales and Use Tax in Ohio (2005).

Engel, Mark A., Alan D. Duffy & Johnathan Brollier. 2006 Ohio Tax Update (2006).

Hill, Edward, Matthew Sattler, Jacob Duritsky, Kevin O'Brien & Claudette Robey, A Review of Tax Expenditure Limitations and Their Impact on State and Local Government in Ohio (2006).

Mottley, J. Donald, & Stephen M. Nechemias, Advanced Sales and Use Tax in Ohio (2006).

Saving, John P., A Historical Assessment of Ohio's Job Creation Tax Credit Program (2005).

Oklahoma

Dauffenbach, Robert, Revenue-Neutral Tax Reform for Oklahoma, Issues and Options Final Report (2001).

Elias, William K., Property Tax in Oklahoma (2000).

Fowler, Rebecca M., Oklahoma Sales and Use Tax (2003).

Healy, John C., Taking Oklahoma's Business Tax Climate into the 21st Century (2001).

Jones, William R., *Increasing State Taxing Power Over Interstate Commerce: Oklahoma Tax Commission v. Jefferson Lines*, 32 Tulsa L.J. 75 (1996).

Kletke, Darrel D., Supplementary Report to the Oklahoma Tax Commission Concerning Recommendations on Oklahoma Rural Land Valuation for Ad Valorem Tax Purposes (2001).

OKLAHOMA BAR ASSOCIATION, LLC FORMATIONS & CONVERSIONS IN OKLAHOMA: AN INTENSIVE INTRODUCTION TO LAW, TAX, AND PRACTICE (2005).

Temple, Judson L., *Recent Developments in Oklahoma Estate Tax: Powers of Appointment, Contingent Remainders, and the Case of Ernst L. Sieber,* 28 OKLA. CITY U.L. REV. 347 (2003).

Oregon

Angeli, David H., *The Oregon Legislature's Constitutional Obligation To Provide An Adequate System of Public Education: Moving From Bold Rhetoric To Effective Action,* 42 WILLAMETTE L. REV. 489 (2006).

CULPEPPER, DAVID A., FIFTH ANNUAL OREGON TAX INSTITUTE (2005).

WILLIAMS, JASON, WHAT TEACHERS THINK, AND WHY THEY LEAVE OREGON SCHOOLS: AN OREGON TAX RESEARCH SPECIAL REPORT OF ANALYSIS AND COMMENTARY (2003).

Pennsylvania

Boak, William, *Annual Survey of Pennsylvania Administrative Law: Taxation: Benedictine Sisters of Pittsburgh: The Continuing Development of a Practical Approach to Property Tax Exemption,* 15 WIDENER L.J. 477 (2006).

BRIDGES, KATHERINE, PROPERTY TAX IN PENNSYLVANIA: FINDINGS FROM A STUDY OF AARP MEMBERS (2006).

FRITZ, , JAMES L., SHARON R. PAXTON & KEITH A. HUNTER, ADVANCED SALES AND USE TAX IN PENNSYLVANIA (2006).

GOODMAN, BERT M., ASSESSMENT LAW & PROCEDURE IN PENNSYLVANIA (2005).

Schulder, Dan A., Alice W. Beck & Kevin J. Moody, Pennsylvania Corporate Taxes (2007 – continuously updated) (*available at*: http://library.bnatax.com/cgi-bin/om%5Fisapi.dll//stl%5Fstatew.nfo/?clientID=162888&infobase=stl%5Fs-tatew.nfo&jump=2300%20da&keep=clientID&softpage=til%5Fdocview%5Ftop).

O'BRIEN, W. TIMOTHY, SALES AND USE TAX IN PENNSYLVANIA (2006).

Oehling, Karen, *Sales Made to Out-of-State Purchasers Picked up at a Pennsylvania Facility are Not Pennsylvania Sales for Purposes of the Pennsylvania Corporate Net Income Tax: Commonwealth of Pennsylvania v. Gilmour Manufacturing Company,* 42 DUQ. L. REV. 921 (2004).

PENNSYLVANIA BAR INSTITUTE, PENNSYLVANIA STATE & LOCAL TAX LAW UPDATE (2006).

Prescott, Loren D., Jr., *Pennsylvania Charities, Tax Exemption, and the Institutions of Purely Public Charity Act,* 73 TEMP. L. REV. 951 (2000).

Viccaro, Marissa P., *The Pennsylvania County Personal Property Tax Is Unconstitutional in Violation of the Commerce Clause: Annenberg v. Commonwealth,* 39 DUQ. L. REV. 681 (2001).

Rhode Island

Abbott, David V., and Stephen M. Robinson, *School Finance Litigation: The Viability of Bringing Suit in the Rhode Island Federal District Court*, 5 ROGER WILLIAMS U. L. REV. 441 (2000).

Barton, Todd, *2003 Survey of Rhode Island Law: Survey Section: Taxation- White v. Clark*, 9 ROGER WILLIAMS U. L. REV. 866 (2004).

Curran, Daniel A., *Property Tax Assessment in the New Era*, 55 RI BAR JNL. 13 (2007).

Dynan, John Timothy, *Tax Law - Domicile for Imposition of Rhode Island Income Tax Is Determined by Taxpayer's Good Faith Intent - DeBlois v. Clark, 764 A.2d 727 (R.I. 2001)*, 35 SUFFOLK U. L. REV. 699 (2001).

Mignanelli, Anthony R., *How Rhode Island Dealt with the Change in the State Death Tax Credit*, 50 RI BAR JNL. 23 (2001).

Salter, Lester H., *Speaking Out: Rhode Island Tax Compromises: The Procedure Could, and Should, Be More User Friendly*, 54 RI BAR JNL. 21 (2006).

South Carolina

Farr, Peter E., *South Carolina's Multimillion Dollar Tax Problem: An Examination of the Manufacturer's Machine Exemption in the South Carolina Sales Tax System*, 55 S.C. L. REV. 665 (2004).

HANDEL, RICK, DEANA WEST & WILLIAM C. WEST, SOUTH CAROLINA CORPORATE INCOME TAXES (2005).

HANDEL, RICK, JOHN C. VON LEHE & JERILYNN VANSTORY, SOUTH CAROLINA PROPERTY TAX (2005).

ULBRICH, HOLLEY H., PUTTING THE PROPERTY TAX IN CONTEXT: REFLECTIONS ON CHANGES IN THE SOUTH CAROLINA CLASSIFIED SYSTEM (2001).

South Dakota

BAATZ,., FRED, THE USE TAX AND THE IMPLICATIONS OF THE USE TAX ON BUSINESS OPERATIONS (2000).

Debelius-Enemark, Barbara, *Recent Education Funding Decisions in the Nation and Their Effect of South Dakota*, 36 S.D. L. REV. 663 (1991).

Tennessee

FLETCHER, GREGORY G., PROPERTY TAX LAW IN TENNESSEE (2001).

Gentle, T.J., *Tennessee Tax Reform: How Does The F & E Tax Affect Your Business?*, 1 Transactions 23 (2000).

GREEN, HARRY A., THE LOCAL PROPERTY TAX IN TENNESSEE (2002).

GREEN, HARRY A., STATE TAX SHARING, FAIRNESS, AND LOCAL GOVERNMENT FINANCE IN TENNESSEE (2004).

JONES, SAMUEL, TENNESSEE SALES AND USE TAX UPDATE (2003).

Parsley, Robert F., *Building a House of Cards: A Policy Evaluation of Tennessee's Tax Reform Act of 2002 With Emphasis on Fairness to the Poor*, 70 TENN. L. REV. 1177 (2003).

Pettigrew, Alice Marie, *The Constitutionality of an Income Tax in Tennessee*, 30 U. MEM. L. REV. 337 (2000).

Texas

GILLILAND, CHARLES E., THE TEXAS PROPERTY TAX SYSTEM (2006).

Kelly, Erin E., *All Students are Not Created Equal: The Inequitable Combination of Property-Tax-Based School Finance Systems and Local Control*, 45 DUKE L.J. 397 (1995).

MARTENS, JIMMY, CHRISTI MONDRIK & THOMAS A. SMITH, SALES AND USE TAX IN TEXAS AND OKLAHOMA (2001).

Ohlenforst, Cynthia M., Jeff W. Dorrill, J. Blake Rice & Sam Megally, *Annual Survey of Texas Law: Taxation*, 59 SMU L. REV. 1565 (2006).

Reinhard, Christine E., *Tangible or Intangible – Is that the Question? Conflict in the Texas Tax Classification System of Computer Software*, 29 ST. MARY'S L. J. 871 (1998).

SCHLOMACH, BYRON, TAX AND EXPENDITURE LIMITATION REFORM: IS IT NEEDED IN TEXAS? (2004).

VEDDER, RICHARD K., & BYRON SCHLOMACH, CHANGING TEXAS' TAX STRUCTURE: A FAIR TAX FOR TEXAS? (2005).

Utah

BUCHI, MARK K., GARY R. THORUP & STEVEN P. YOUNG, THE STREAMLINED SALES TAX PROJECT IN UTAH (2005).

CRAPO, DAVID J., MARC B. JOHNSON & MAXWELL A. MILLER, PROPERTY TAX LAW IN UTAH (2001).

Governor Olene S. Walker's Recommendations on a Tax Structure for Utah's Future (2004) (*available at*: http://www.utah.gov/governor/newsrels/2004/tax%5Freform%5FExecutiveSummary.pdf).

Levi, Deborah Katz, *STuition Tax Credit Proposals in Utah - Their Constitutionality and Feasibility*, 2005 UTAH L. REV. 1047 (2005).

MILLER, MAXWELL A., GARY R. THORUP & STEVEN P. YOUNG, UTAH SALES AND USE TAX UPDATE (2003).

Rashkin, Amy E., *Pollution Control Equipment Sales Tax Refunds: A Review and Discussion of Utah Law*, 21 J. LAND RESOURCES & ENVTL. L. 415 (2001).

Tribe, Stephanie, *Municipalities May Assess Service Fees Against School Districts*, 2005 UTAH L. REV. 315 (2005).

WILLIAMS, THOMAS M., UTAH'S HOUSEHOLD TAX BURDENS (2001).

Vermont

KISSAM, ARIANE CHRISTINE, THE IMPACT OF VERMONT'S TAX SHARING POLICY ON LOCAL DEVELOPMENT EFFORTS (2004).

Porto, Brian L., *Where Do We Go From Here? Vermont Campaign Finance After Randall v. Sorrell*, 32-WTR VT. B.J. 30 (2007).

READY, ELIZABETH M., PAYOFFS AND LAYOFFS: THE HIGH COST OF BUSINESS SUBSIDIES: A COMPLIANCE AUDIT OF THE VERMONT ECONOMIC ADVANCEMENT TAX INCENTIVES PROGRAM ADMINISTERED BY THE VERMONT ECONOMIC PROGRESS COUNCIL AND THE VERMONT TAX DEPARTMENT (2004).

TEACHOUT, SARA, JOINT FISCAL OFFICE, VERMONT ESTATE TAX BRIEF, (2001) (*available at*: http://www.leg.state.vt.us/JFO/Reports/Estate%20Tax%20Brief%2012-2001.pdf).

Vermont Fair Tax Coalition, (2007) (*available at*: http://www.vnrc.org/article/archive/699/).

Vermont's Property Owners Report (2007) (*available at*: http://www.vermontproperty.com/newsltr/vtrealestatetaxes.html).

Vermont Sales Tax Exemption Certificate, (*available at*: http://www.lyndonstate.edu/OfficesServices/StudentServicesCtr/Business/VermontSalesTaxExemptionCertificate/tabid/1162/Default.aspx).

Wolowitz, Mark, *Vermont's School Funding Scheme Ruled Unconstitutional*, 7 J. MULTISTATE TAX'N 93 (1997).

Virginia

BOWMAN, JOHN H., & MICHAEL E. BELL, IMPLICATIONS OF A SPLIT-RATE REAL PROPERTY TAX: AN INITIAL LOOK AT THREE VIRGINIA LOCAL GOVERNMENT AREAS (2004).

CUMMINS, RACHELLE, INTO THE BLACK: A SURVEY OF VIRGINIA VOTERS ON STATE SERVICE CUTS AND TAX CHANGES (2004).

Hampton Roads Planning District Commission, *It's Time to Talk About Tax Reform in Virginia*, 30 ST. TAX NOTES 1009 (2003).

KNAPP, JOHN L., WILLIAM M. SHOBE & STEPHEN C. KULP. VIRGINIA LOCAL TAX RATES ... : INFORMATION FOR ALL CITIES AND COUNTIES AND SELECTED INCORPORATED TOWNS (2006).

REPORT OF THE COMMISSION ON VIRGINIA'S STATE AND LOCAL TAX STRUCTURE FOR THE 21ST CENTURY, HD-22 (2001).

Robinson, Mildred Wigfall, *Tax Reform: Saving Virginia's Economy and Easing Regressiveness*, VA. ISSUES & ANSWERS, Fall 2002 Vol. 9 No. 1.

SLIVINSKI, STEPHEN A., & J. SCOTT MOODY, TAX FOUNDATION, THE PATH TO RE-
FORMING VIRGINIA'S TAX CODE (2004).

VIRGINIA DEPARTMENT OF TAXATION, VIRGINIA TAX FACTS (2006) (*available at*
http://www.tax.virginia.gov/web_PDFs/taxfacts.pdf).

VIRGINIA DIVISION OF LEGISLATIVE SERVICES, A LEGISLATOR'S GUIDE TO TAXATION
IN VIRGINIA (2001) (*available at* http://www.virginia-organizing.org/campaign/
legistlator_guide.pdf).

The Virginia Organizing Project, Tax Reform Campaign, www.virginia-organizing
.org/tax_reform.php (2006).

Washington

CHAPMAN, JEFF, WASHINGTON STATE BUDGET AND POLICY CENTER, BALANCING ADE-
QUACY AND EQUITY IN WASHINGTON STATE'S PROPERTY TAX (2007) (*available at*:
http://www.budgetandpolicy.org/documents/propertytax.pdf.).

GARDNER, MARK, ECONOMIC OPPORTUNITY INSTITUTE, AN INCREMENTAL APPROACH
TO IMPROVE WASHINGTON STATE'S TAX SYSTEM – A PROPOSAL FOR A TAX ON
HIGH INCOME HOUSEHOLDS (2004) (*available at*: http://www.eoionline.org/
Taxes/HighIncomeHouseholds.pdf.).

SMITH, JASON, ECONOMIC OPPORTUNITY INSTITUTE, A CONCISE HISTORY OF WASH-
INGTON'S TAX STRUCTURE (2002) (*available at*: http://www.eoionline.org/
Taxes/WATaxHistory.pdf.).

WATKINS, MARILYN P., ECONOMIC OPPORTUNITY INSTITUTE, NEW TAX BREAKS IN
WASHINGTON 2004-2006 (2006) (*available at*: http://www.eoionline.org/Taxes/
WATaxPolicy-NewTaxBreaks20042006.pdf.).

West Virginia

CAPEHART, ROBIN C., MICHAEL E. CARYL, DEAN CALVIN A. KENT, AND DALE W.
STEAGER, RECOMMENDATIONS TO THE GOVERNOR: PRESENTED TO GOVERNOR
CECIL H. UNDERWOOD, DECEMBER 1999 (2000).

DANIELS, N.T., & C.P. HAMRICK, III, WEST VIRGINIA SALES AND USE TAX UPDATE
(1997).

WEST VIRGINIA DEPARTMENT OF REVENUE, WEST VIRGINIA TAX EXPENDITURE
STUDY: EXPENDITURES FOR CONSUMERS SALES TAX AND USE TAX (2001).

WEST VIRGINIA DEPARTMENT OF REVENUE, WEST VIRGINIA TAX EXPENDITURE
STUDY: EXPENDITURES FOR SPECIAL BUSINESS TAXES, BUSINESS LICENCE TAXES,
EXCISE TAXES AND PROPERTY TAXES (2003).

Wisconsin

Knavel, Kathleen, *Wisconsin's Tax Incremental Finance Law: How Wisconsin's Cities Subsidize Sprawl*, 8 WIS. ENVTL. L.J. 115 (2002).

Lindsey, Vada Waters, *Tax Incentive: The Vulnerability of Using Tax Incentives in Wisconsin*, 88 MARQ. L. REV. 107 (2004).

McChrystal, Michael, *Wisconsin Tax Policy: Serious Flaws, Compelling, Solutions*, 88 MARQ. L. REV. 1 (2004).

Stark, Jack, *The Authority To Tax In Wisconsin*, 77 MARQ. L. REV. 457 (1994).

Wyoming

BRIDGES, KATHERINE, INCREASING THE CIGARETTE TAX RATE IN WYOMING TO MAINTAIN STATE PROGRAMS: AN AARP SURVEY (2003).

Roberts, Phil, *A History of the Wyoming Sales Tax and How Lawmakers Chose it From Among Severance Taxes, an Income Tax, Gambling, and a Lottery*, 4 WYO. L. REV. 157 (2004).

Tangeman, Jason M., *Mineral Taxation – When is a Refund of Ad Valorem Mineral Taxes Appropriate? The Wyoming Supreme Court Answers the Question, But Invites a Storm of Controversy. Amoco Production Company v. Board of Commissioners of Carbon County and Amoco Production Company v. Board of Commissioners of Sweetwater County, 876 P.2d 989 (Wyo. 1994)*, 30 LAND & WATER L. REV. 129 (1995).

WYOMING TAX REFORM 2000 COMMITTEE, BUILDING WYOMING'S TAX STRUCTURE FOR THE 21ST CENTURY: REPORT OF THE STATE OF WYOMING TAX REFORM 2000 COMMITTEE (1999).